# Library

## EDUCATIONAL TESTING
## SERVICE

# BIOMETRIKA TABLES FOR STATISTICIANS

## VOLUME I

*To all those who have helped to compute numerical tables*
*which reduce the labour of statistical arithmetic*

# BIOMETRIKA TABLES FOR STATISTICIANS

## VOLUME I

EDITED BY

**E. S. PEARSON**

AND

**H. O. HARTLEY**

BIOMETRIKA TRUST

1976

PUBLISHED BY
BIOMETRIKA TRUST
UNIVERSITY COLLEGE LONDON
GOWER STREET WC1E 6BT
ENGLAND

ISBN 0 904653 10 2

*First Edition* 1954
*Reprinted* 1956
*Second Edition* 1958
*Reprinted* 1962
*Third Edition* 1966
*Reprinted with additions* 1970
*Reprinted with corrections* 1976

*First printed in Great Britain at the University Printing House, Cambridge*
*Reprinted in Great Britain by Lowe and Brydone (Printers) Ltd, Thetford, Norfolk*

# LIST OF CONTENTS

References under each table heading to page numbers in the Introduction are given in three groups, (i) mathematical definition of function; (ii) method of interpolation in table; (iii) description of uses and relation to other tables.

## I. TABLES OF THE NORMAL PROBABILITY FUNCTION

## II. BASIC TABLES DERIVED FROM THE NORMAL FUNCTION

## III. FURTHER TABLES OF PROBABILITY INTEGRALS, PERCENTAGE POINTS, ETC., OF DISTRIBUTIONS DERIVED FROM THE NORMAL FUNCTION

## VI. AUXILIARY TABLES

## VII. ADDENDUM TO SECOND IMPRESSION OF THIRD EDITION

# PREFACE

The Founders of *Biometrika* in 1901 put forward as one of their objectives the provision of a series of numerical tables which would 'reduce the labour of statistical arithmetic'. During the next twelve years there appeared in the current volumes of the journal a considerable number of these tables, computed by many different workers associated in various ways with Karl Pearson's Biometric Laboratory. In 1914 these tables and a number of others hitherto unpublished were put together to form the first volume of *Tables for Statisticians and Biometricians*. This volume was reissued four times, between 1924 and 1948, but no alteration in its form was made.

In 1931 Karl Pearson issued a second volume of tables with the same title, again making use of many tables which had been published in *Biometrika* during the years 1914–30 and for which the type had been moulded. This volume, which ran out of print in 1945, was not reissued.

The rapid expansion of statistical theory in the decade 1925–35 with the development of new techniques made many of the older tables obsolete and called for the introduction of fresh ones. When, therefore, one of us became responsible for the management of *Biometrika* in 1936, it was soon clear that only a complete recasting of the two volumes would provide a series of tables meeting current needs. The prospect of a new issue of tables commonly inspires the table-maker to break fresh ground, and it was over this work, under the encouraging guidance of L. J. Comrie, that the present compilers were brought together.

The plan for computation of tables of the percentage points of the Beta distribution and of more extensive tables than then existed of percentage points of Student's $t$, of $\chi^2$ and of the variance ratio, $F$, had been sketched out before *Statistical Tables for Biological, Agricultural and Medical Research* by Professor Fisher and Dr Yates appeared in 1938. But it is evident in these and other tables how much we have owed to the scheme of tabular presentation first used by Fisher in his *Statistical Methods for Research Workers*.

The onset of war in 1939 modified our plans. The issue of a new book of tables had to be postponed indefinitely, but it was decided to continue with the programme of computation as circumstances allowed and to publish each new table, when completed, in *Biometrika*, making it readily available in 'separate' form. This procedure, forced on us by war and post-war conditions, with its temptation to complete 'just one more table', has already continued too long, and we realize that the present publication of the tables in a collected series with a comprehensive Introduction is already overdue.

In compiling the tables, several considerations have determined the form adopted. In the first place it was clear, even after a fairly drastic process of weeding out, that more tables needing reissue had been published in *Biometrika* than could be contained in a single handy volume. Within the complete series, many of the tables fall into natural groupings, each dealing with a single function or set of allied functions. Within a group there may be one table in frequent use and another only required on rare occasions. One course would be to publish all tables of a group in the same volume; another, to put together in a first volume all the more commonly used tables and leave their more specialized companions to a second volume. We have adopted the latter plan, as more generally acceptable to the common user. It is for this reason that tables of percentage points of certain functions appear in the present volume while the issue of tables of the probability integral is deferred, e.g. for the mean deviation in samples from a normal population. In selecting the tables to be included, we have had valuable advice from our colleagues, in particular from Dr John Wishart and Professor M. G. Kendall. The final choice, however, has been ours, and the selection made will inevitably have been biased by our personal idiosyncrasies.

To keep the cost of production within bounds we have had to use a considerable number of stereos moulded from type of earlier tables. Thus the existing material from which we were able to draw has been largely conditioned by the scope of *Biometrika* and the work of those who have contributed to it in past years. Again, because of the need to use old material, we have felt unable in several places to introduce small improvements in lay-out and typographical detail which the specialist table-maker might expect of us. This requirement, for example, explains the retention of Sheppard's original format in Table 1 with its first and second difference columns. Partly for this reason also, we have reissued tables of several fundamental functions to the full number of decimal places originally published, although for most purposes a simpler form of table would be adequate. On the whole, we think that the majority of statisticians will be prepared to accept the slight inconvenience of additional page-turning for the sake of those few occasions when rather greater accuracy is required.

The compiler of a book of mathematical tables has always to face a somewhat difficult problem in deciding the character and scope of his Introduction. Broadly, we have tried to write our account so that within each of several connected sections the definitions and descriptions are developed in a rough logical sequence. The table-user will often only need to refer to a paged list of contents to locate the table which he knows he wants, but in so far as he does wish to see as a whole the range of tables we are providing, we have tried to write so that he can get a connected and orderly picture by consecutive reading of the Introduction.

In settling the further question of the amount of introductory matter to devote to each table, we have kept in mind a number of points: that a clear definition of the mathematical functions involved and of the links between them is essential; that, in presenting tables to be used in drawing conclusions from observational data in terms of probability, some comment on the processes of inference can hardly be avoided; that tables provided to assist in the several stages of a lengthy computational procedure, should be accompanied by rather detailed illustrative examples; that, while the uses of many of the fundamental tables are too well known to call for much comment, there are other tables concerned with methods of analysis recently introduced which require fuller explanation. On the whole, therefore, it will be found that the more special and possibly lesser known tables have been rather fully explained and illustrated, whilst essentials only are given for the well-known standard tables. Thus the allotment of introductory space is not closely related to the importance or expected usefulness of a table.

We have tried to use terminology which is generally familiar to statisticians. With notation, we have not allowed rigorous consistency to interfere with common usage, except perhaps in one point. The letter $P$ has been used in statistical literature and tables indiscriminately to represent the integrals from the lower and upper terminals of a probability density function. We have used it solely as the integral from the lower terminal, i.e. to describe what is usually defined as the probability integral of the distribution; we have introduced $Q = 1 - P$ for the upper tail integral. Some account of the general principles we have adopted in our use of notation is given in a preliminary note (pp. xiii–xiv).

There is one general matter to which it is well to draw attention here. A large part of the techniques of modern statistical theory is based on the assumption that the underlying random variable is 'normally' distributed. The limitation may not hold rigorously in practice in the sense that the technique becomes invalid if the distribution law is different. Nevertheless, mathematically the assumption is present. Of the fifty-four tables in this volume, the main purpose of perhaps thirty lies in the analysis of data involving normally distributed variables. It would have been beyond the scope of our Introduction to attempt to indicate the extent to which different tests or methods of estimation are affected by departure from normality. Some of them are reasonably safe, others are very sensitive even in large samples. The price to be paid for the immense scope of 'normal theory' and the convenience of its derived tables is constant vigilance.

Many computers of all ranks have contributed to the construction of these tables. As workers in the early years we may mention W. F. Sheppard, W. P. Elderton, Alice Lee and H. E. Soper; in the later period, Catherine Thompson, Maxine Merrington and Joyce May. Recently some valuable help was obtained from the Mathematics Division of the National Physical Laboratory. In Appendix II, p. 101, we have indicated the origin of individual tables and the name or names of the computers. In the last stages of preparation we are indebted to Dr John Wishart, Mr P. G. Moore and Miss Joyce May for careful proof-reading which has enabled us to remove a number of obscurities and errors.

Special acknowledgement must be made for help received from other publications: to Sir Ronald Fisher, Dr Frank Yates and Messrs Oliver and Boyd Ltd.; to Dr D. van der Reyden and the Editors of the *Onderstepoort Journal of Veterinary Science and Animal Industry*; to Professor M. G. Kendall and Messrs Charles Griffin and Co. Ltd.; to Professor Truman Kelley and the Harvard University Press; to Messrs W. & R. Chambers Ltd. Details are given in Appendix II against the tables concerned.

Throughout our work we have been very conscious of how much the user of the statistical table owes to Karl Pearson. Many of the tables whose computation he planned have now been outdated or have required considerable remodelling; but much of his work remains, and we believe that this new series of revised tables is conceived in the tradition which he set. It should be recalled also that we have made use in many places of those two fundamental tables of the incomplete gamma- and beta-functions whose importance he had the foresight to realize and whose computation and publication he carried through against many odds.

Finally, we can repeat what Pearson wrote in 1914, in the Preface to his first volume of *Tables for Statisticians and Biometricians*: 'To those who have had experience of numerical tables prepared elsewhere, the excellence of the Cambridge first proof of columns of figures is a joy, which deserves the fullest acknowledgement.' We have indeed been fortunate in having still at hand the services of the Cambridge University Press.

*Department of Statistics*            E. S. PEARSON
  *University College, London*            H. O. HARTLEY
*October* 1953

# PREFACE TO SECOND EDITION

The opportunity of this re-issue has been taken to make a few minor alterations in the text of the Introduction and in the Tables. Any more extensive recasting must await the production of Volume II.

In one or two places the statements regarding accuracy of interpolation have been found to be too optimistic. Thus alterations have been made on pp. 14–15 where the $\frac{1}{2}\phi^2\delta^2$ term has now been included in equations (24)–(27). Again, the statement in paragraph (*a*) on p. 23 regarding interpolation in the tables of the *t*-distribution has needed modification. At the top of p. 27, there has been some rewording of § 6·1 which it is hoped will reduce the risk of misinterpretation of the meaning of Table 11. H. A. David's corrected values for the upper percentage points of the extreme studentized deviate from the sample mean have been inserted in Table 26, to which his columns for $n = 12$ have been added.

Finally, an index to the Tables (but not to the Introduction) has been added on pp. 239–40. We are indebted to Mrs Maxine Merrington for help in preparing this index. When the reader has identified the Table he wishes to use, the relevant pages in the Introduction can be found from the List of Contents on pp. v–vii.

E.S.P.
H.O.H.

*April 1958*

# PREFACE TO THIRD EDITION

This new edition contains a number of alterations and additions which fall under the following main headings: (a) removal of errors detected in certain of the original tables; (b) extension of some of these tables; (c) inclusion of seven new tables. It is desirable to enlarge on these changes in a little detail.

(a) *Removal of errors.* The original volume contained a number of tables computed during the 1940s and first published in *Biometrika*. With the computation by hand-machine then used, we did not consider it justifiable to proceed to the large number of decimal places needed to ensure that there were no cut-off errors in the last figure tabled. It was therefore realized that our results would contain a number of entries out by one unit in the last place. With the aid of some extensive calculations on electronic computers recently carried out in the United States, we hope that we have been able to remove the majority of errors, particularly in Tables 8, 16, 20, 22 and 23. We are most grateful to Dr H. L. Harter and his colleagues, to Dr D. E. Amos and to Professor D. B. Owen for help in this connexion.

(b) *Extension of existing tables.* We have added to Table 11 two pages giving 2·5 % and 0·5 % critical levels of $v = (y - \eta)/\sqrt{(\lambda_1 s_1^2 + \lambda_2 s_2^2)}$ already published by W. H. Trickett, B. L. Welch & G. S. James. The table of the percentage points of the B-distribution (Table 16) has been extended to include the 0·25 % and 0·1 % points calculated by D. E. Amos. Table 26 for the percentage points of the extreme studentized deviate, $(x_n - \bar{x})/s_\nu$, has been recast; it now includes additional upper percentage points computed by H. A. David and a few values for degrees of freedom $\nu < 10$ computed by K. C. S. Pillai. The very slowly changing values of the lower percentage points have been omitted, but some remarks on how to determine these are included in §13 of the Introduction.

Table 29, giving percentage points of the studentized range $(x_n - x_1)/s_\nu$, has also been recast, now giving 10 % as well as more accurate 5 % and 1 % values; here again the less important lower percentage points have had to be omitted for reasons of space. The new table is based on tables published by J. Pachares and by H. L. Harter, D. S. Clemm & E. H. Guthrie.

Finally, it has been possible to add some new values for $50 \leqslant n < 200$ to Table 34C, giving percentage points of the distribution of $b_2 = m_4/m_2^2$ used in tests of normality.

(c) *New tables.* We have decided to take this opportunity of incorporating some additional tables in the present Volume I. All of these have already been published wholly or in part elsewhere. We hope that they will be of value to the working statistician in carrying out a variety of 'quick' tests which are often useful in a preliminary survey of data. As such, they seemed to us more appropriately included here than in the long promised Volume II of these *Tables.*

To avoid altering the present series of table numbers, the new tables have been given letters a, b, etc. attached to the number of the existing table which they seem to follow most appropriately.

Two of these new tables, *Tables 26a and b*, computed by C. P. Quesenberry & H. A. David, extend the use of the table of percentage points of the extreme studentized deviate $(x_n - \bar{x})/s_\nu$ by enabling the 'within sample of $n$' sum of squares to be added to the independent sum of squares $\nu s_\nu^2$ in estimating the denominator standard deviation. As a special case, putting $\nu = 0$, the table provides percentage points of the ratio of the extreme deviate from the sample mean to the standard deviation in the same sample.

The next group of three tables are for use with some further tests involving the sample range. Table 29$a$, due to P. G. Moore, gives percentage points of the two-sample ratio $|\bar{x}_1 - \bar{x}_2|/(w_1 + w_2)$ and provides a test based on range analogous to Student's two-sample $t$-test. Table 29$b$, first published by H. L. Harter, contains percentage points of the ratio of two independent ranges, $w_1/w_2$, providing an analogue to the variance-ratio $F$-test. Table 29$c$ gives percentage points of the ratio of range to standard deviation calculated from the same sample; this ratio provides a quick test which can be useful in detecting abnormality in sample pattern and, possibly, errors in computation.

Finally Tables 31$a$ and $b$ fit naturally after Table 31, which gives percentage points of the ratio of the maximum to the minimum variance in a set of $k$ independent variance estimates $s_t^2$ $(t = 1, ..., k)$ each based on $\nu$ degrees of freedom. Table 31$a$ gives corresponding points for the ratio $s_{\text{max.}}^2/\sum s_t^2$; the test involved was first put forward by W. G. Cochran and more fully tabled by C. Eisenhart, M. W. Hastay & W. A. Wallis. Table 31$b$ is concerned with an analogous test using sample ranges, viz. involving the ratio $w_{\text{max.}}/\sum w_t$. The upper 5 % points tabled here are due to C. I. Bliss, W. G. Cochran & J. W. Tukey.

The incorporation of these new tables has inevitably involved some modification to our Introduction. This has been met by the enlargement of §§13 and 14 by the addition of six new pages.

We should like to thank most warmly the many statisticians who have made possible this expansion and we hope improvement in the present volume. If we have failed to mention any by name, we must ask their forgiveness. Full references to sources of the new material are included in Appendices I and II. Finally, we are grateful to Miss S. M. Burrough of the Mathematics Department, University College London for her careful work in computing and checking some of our figures.

E.S.P.

*April 1965*
H.O.H.

# PREFACE TO 1976 REPRINT OF THIRD EDITION

We have taken the opportunity of a reprint to introduce some new results in connection with tests for departure from normality, based on a paper by R. B. D'Agostino and E. S. Pearson (*Biometrika*, 1973, **60,** 613–22). This has involved a complete re-arrangement of Tables 34B and C which give percentage points for $\sqrt{b_1}$ and $b_2$. For lower values of the sample size, $n$, 2·5 and 0·5 % points are now included, making it possible to apply 5 and 1 % two-tail tests as well as single-tail tests. The additions based on extensive computer simulation combined with curve fitting must be described as empirical, not exact, particularly in the case of $b_2$. It has been possible to include this new information in the space available by excluding the previous results for $n > 1000$. For such large samples, the hypothesis of normality will nearly always be rejected on the basis of a significance test although in many cases the common normal theory procedures may be used without any serious risk of error. Again, a sample of 1000 or more observations will often provide enough evidence to carry out an appropriate transformation, e.g. by taking as variable $x' = \log (x-a)$.

A few minor misprints have also been corrected.

Note also the Addendum to 1st reprint (1970) of Table 31c, pp. 264–5 (reference on p. 202 footnote) and of Table 32a, pp. 266–7 (reference on p. 205).

E.S.P.

*November, 1975*
H.O.H.

# COMMENTS ON NOTATION

1. The following notes indicate certain general forms of notation we have used in connexion with measures of probability and the broad principles adopted in assigning letters and symbols to statistical quantities.

2. If $x$ is a random variable distributed continuously in the interval $(a_1, a_2)$, $f(x)$ has been written for its *probability density function*, often described as its *frequency function*. We have written* what is commonly known as the *probability integral* in the form

$$P(x) = \int_{a_1}^{x} f(u)\, du.$$

Further, we define
$$Q(x) = 1 - P(x) = \int_{x}^{a_2} f(u)\, du.$$

Where there is little chance of confusion and particularly as a column heading in a table, $P$ or $Q$ have been put in place of $P(x)$ or $Q(x)$.

3. When it is desirable to indicate that a frequency function or probability integral depends on the values of one or more *parameters*, say on $\theta_1, \theta_2$, whose values are changing throughout a table, we write $f(x \mid \theta_1, \theta_2)$, $P(x \mid \theta_1, \theta_2)$ or $Q(x \mid \theta_1, \theta_2)$. For example, in the case of a single parameter, the probability integral of Student's $t$ based on $\nu$ degrees of freedom is written

$$P(t \mid \nu) = \int_{-\infty}^{t} f(u \mid \nu)\, du = \Gamma(\tfrac{1}{2}(\nu + 1))\, (\Gamma(\tfrac{1}{2}\nu))^{-1}\, (\nu\pi)^{-\frac{1}{2}} \int_{-\infty}^{t} \left(1 + \frac{u^2}{\nu}\right)^{-\frac{1}{2}(\nu+1)} du.$$

4. Sometimes it has been convenient to express certain probability statements involving inequalities in a shortened form; for example, on p. 20 the expression

$$\Pr\{\,|t| > 1{\cdot}97 \mid \nu = 11\} = 0{\cdot}074$$

is written in place of the long sentence: the probability that the numerical value of $t$ is greater than 1·97 (when the degrees of freedom of the variance estimate are 11) equals 0·074.

5. If a random variable can assume only *integral values*, e.g. $i = 0, 1, 2, \ldots$, $f(c)$ has been used to denote the probability that $i = c$. The dependence of this probability on the values of one or more parameters has been again indicated by writing $f(i \mid \theta)$, $f(i \mid \theta_1, \theta_2)$, etc. The *cumulative sum* of the terms of such a distribution has been indicated by a summation sign; for example, the sum of the first $c + 1$ terms of the binomial series $(q + p)^n$, may be written

$$\sum_{i=0}^{c} f(i \mid n, p) = \sum_{i=0}^{c} \binom{n}{i} p^i (1 - p)^{n-i}.$$

6. In dealing with tests of significance, according to the problem considered, the risk of rejecting the hypothesis tested when it is true† may be obtained from an integral calculated from the lower tail of a sampling distribution ($P$), from the upper tail ($Q$), or by summing integrals from both tails. To avoid confusion, a separate notation is required to denote this risk or *level of significance*; we have used the letter $\alpha$, which in practice will assume values such as

---

* With the exception of the incomplete B-function integral $I_x(a, b)$; see p. 32.
† I.e. Neyman and Pearson's 'first kind of error'.

0·05, 0·01, etc. (or 100$\alpha$, such values as 5%, 1%, etc.). Thus the term *significance level* is reserved for a probability whilst we denote by a *percentage point* the critical value of the statistic associated with this level. Moreover, $\alpha$ has also been used in connexion with the determination of *confidence intervals* in the problem of estimation.

7. The symbol $\mathscr{E}$ has been used to indicate the *expectation* of a random variable. Thus if $x$ has a continuous frequency function $f(x)$ in the interval $(a_1, a_2)$,

$$\mathscr{E}(x) = \int_{a_1}^{a_2} xf(x)\,dx.$$

8. Complete consistency in the use of statistical notation seems unattainable unless certain long-established usages are discarded. In general, Greek letters have been used for population parameters for which the corresponding Roman letters denote the sample estimators; thus we have $\rho$ and $r$, $\sigma^2$ and $s^2$, $\beta$ and $b$, etc. However, we have not hesitated to use $\chi^2$ as a random variable nor $p = 1 - q$ for the probability of an event in binomial sampling. In this respect we have had to regard the Introduction and tables as a whole, which means that in some sections an obvious lettering cannot be used, since confusion would arise in following the same notation elsewhere. For example, having adopted $p$ and $q$ in connexion with the binomial, we cannot use the standard notation $I_x(p, q)$ for the incomplete B-function, as this provides the cumulative sum of binomial terms in a form in which the two $p$'s would have different meanings. The function has therefore been taken as $I_x(a, b)$. On the other hand, commonly adopted notation has been retained where the same symbol is used to denote quantities unlikely to be confused. For example, $w$ denotes the range in normal samples as well as the weight, $Z^2/(PQ)$, in probit analysis, while $W$ is used both for the standardized range and the concordance coefficient.

9. The main details of notation are given most appropriately as they arise in the Introduction. It is sufficient to note here that with $n$, $n_1$, $n_2$, etc., reserved for sample sizes, group frequencies, etc., we have adopted the common practice of using $\nu$, $\nu_1$, $\nu_2$, etc., for degrees of freedom; that $s^2$ is always used as an unbiased mean-square estimator of a variance $\sigma^2$, i.e. $\mathscr{E}(s^2) = \sigma^2$; and that we have retained Karl Pearson's $\beta_1, \beta_2$ notation for the well-known moment ratios, rather than introduce $\gamma_1 = \sqrt{\beta_1}$ and $\gamma_2 = \beta_2 - 3$, because we wish to make use of his classification of distributions into frequency curve types.

# INTRODUCTION

## I. TABLES OF THE NORMAL PROBABILITY FUNCTION

### 1. THE STANDARD NORMAL TABLES (TABLES 1–5)

#### 1·1   Definitions and notation

The equation of the normal or Gaussian frequency function may be written in the standardized form

$$Z(X) = f(X) = \frac{1}{\sqrt{(2\pi)}} e^{-\frac{1}{2}X^2} \tag{1}$$

Regarded as a random variable, $X$ has a mean or expectation of zero and a unit standard deviation. The probability integral is then

$$P(X) = \int_{-\infty}^{X} \frac{1}{\sqrt{(2\pi)}} e^{-\frac{1}{2}u^2} du \quad \text{while} \quad Q(X) = 1 - P(X). \tag{2}$$

If $x$ is a random variable, normally distributed about a mean $\mu$ and with standard deviation $\sigma$ (variance $\sigma^2$), the standard tables may be used by setting

$$X = (x - \mu)/\sigma \tag{3}$$

and remembering that the ordinate of the distribution curve for $x$ is $Z/\sigma$. Fig. 1 presents the relationship between $X$, $Z$, $P(X)$ and $Q(X)$. The change in notation from W. F. Sheppard's (1902) original $x$, $z$ and $\frac{1}{2}(1 + \alpha)$, respectively, will be noted. From the symmetry we see that

$$Z(-X) = Z(X), \quad P(-X) = 1 - P(X) = Q(X).$$

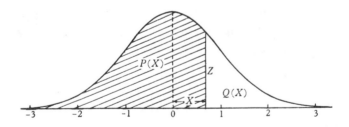

Fig. 1.

Table 1 is the fundamental table of the normal integral $P(X)$ and the ordinate $Z(X)$ due to W. F. Sheppard. Table 2 provides an extension for the tail area of the distribution in logarithmic form, i.e. it gives $-\log_{10}\{1 - P(X)\}$. Tables 3 and 4 give the normal deviates $X(P)$, and Table 5 the ordinates $Z(P)$ in terms of $P$ and $Q$. Table 6, which introduces the additional notation, $Y = X + 5$, is primarily designed to facilitate probit analysis; its use is described in §§ 2·1 and 2·2 below.

The applications are so numerous and well known that we shall confine attention to illustration on a single series of data.

*Example* 1. The following results were given by Latter (1906) for the distribution of the length of 717 eggs of the cuckoo (*Cuculus canorus*) found in nests in the British Isles:

| Length (central values in mm.) | 19·25 | 20·25 | 21·25 | 22·25 | 23·25 | 24·25 | 25·25 | 26·25 |
|---|---|---|---|---|---|---|---|---|
| Frequency | 3 | 22 | 123 | 300 | 201 | 61 | 6 | 1 |

Graduate this distribution by a normal curve.

The values of the mean and standard deviation, using Sheppard's correction for grouping in calculating the latter, are found to be:

$$\text{mean} = 22\cdot48570 \text{ mm.}, \quad \text{standard deviation} = 0\cdot954631 \text{ mm.*}$$

Taking these as estimates of $\mu$ and $\sigma$, the work required is set out in the following table:

| Group boundary $x$-values (1) | $x - \mu$ (2) | $X = (x-\mu)/\sigma$ (3) | $P(X)$ (4) | $\Delta P(X)$ (5) | $717 \times \Delta P(X)$ (6) | Observed frequencies (7) |
|---|---|---|---|---|---|---|
| 18·75 | − 3·73570 | − 3·91324 | 0·00005 | | | |
| 19·75 | − 2·73570 | − 2·86571 | ·00208 | 0·00203 | 1·5 | 3 |
| 20·75 | − 1·73570 | − 1·81819 | ·03452 | ·03244 | 23·3 | 22 |
| 21·75 | − 0·73570 | − 0·77066 | ·22045 | ·18593 | 133·3 | 123 |
| 22·75 | 0·26430 | 0·27686 | ·60906 | ·38861 | 278·6 | 300 |
| 23·75 | 1·26430 | 1·32439 | ·90731 | ·29825 | 213·8 | 201 |
| 24·75 | 2·26430 | 2·37191 | ·99115 | ·08384 | 60·1 | 61 |
| 25·75 | 3·26430 | 3·41944 | ·99969 | ·00854 | 6·1 | 6 |
| 26·75 | 4·26430 | 4·46696 | 1·00000 | ·00031 | 0·2 | 1 |
| | | | | Total | 716·9 | 717 |

The values of $P(X)$ in col. 4 are obtained from Table 1, using linear interpolation. Col. 6 shows the graduated frequencies which may be compared with the observed frequencies in col. 7. The agreement is satisfactory,† although there is a suggestion that the egg-length distribution has a rather more peaked top than the normal curve.

Two further questions might be asked which will illustrate the use of additional tables in this series.‡ Suppose that it was wished to classify cuckoos' eggs by length into three groups described as long, medium and short, in such a way that roughly $\frac{1}{6}$ of the eggs might be expected to fall into each of the extreme groups and $\frac{2}{3}$ into the medium group:

(a) Where should the divisions on the length scale be made?

(b) What would be the average lengths of the eggs in the extreme categories? (The expected value of the average of the medium group would clearly be $\mu$.)

* In order to provide a detailed numerical illustration of the use of Table 1, rather more figures have been given in the values of mean and standard deviation than would ordinarily be retained. Thus to ensure that the figures in col. 6 of the table above were not in error by more than one unit in the last place, 4-decimal accuracy in mean and standard deviation would probably have been sufficient.

† Pooling together two groups at each tail and applying the usual test for goodness of fit (§§ 3·2 and 3·4 below), it is found that $\chi^2 = 3\cdot30$ with $6 - 3 = 3$ degrees of freedom, so that departure from normality cannot be established as significant by this test.

‡ We shall assume that egg-length in the population is normally distributed with the observed values of mean and standard deviation.

To answer (a) we require the values of $x = \mu + \sigma X$ for which $P(X) = 0 \cdot 16\dot{6}$ and $0 \cdot 83\dot{3}$. Turning to Table 4 and using linear interpolation we find that these values of $X$ are

$$\mp (0 \cdot 9701 - \tfrac{2}{3} 0 \cdot 0040) = \mp 0 \cdot 9674.$$

Hence, using the sample estimates of $\mu$ and $\sigma$ given above, the divisions for $x$ will lie at

$$22 \cdot 4857 \mp 0 \cdot 9674 \times 0 \cdot 9546 = 21 \cdot 56 \text{ and } 23 \cdot 41 \text{ mm}.$$

To answer (b), we make use of the following result. If a truncated section of the standardized normal distribution is taken, bounded by ordinates at $X_i$ and $X_j$, then the distance of the mean of this section from the origin, $X = 0$, is

$$\{Z(X_i) - Z(X_j)\} / \{P(X_j) - P(X_i)\}.$$

For the category of 'short' eggs, $X_i = -\infty$, $Z(X_i) = 0$, $P(X_i) = 0$ and $P(X_j) = \tfrac{1}{6}$. The value of $Z(X_j)$ may be found by entering Table 5 with $P(X_j) = 0 \cdot 1667$. Thus, using linear interpolation, we find $Z = (0 \cdot 24921 + \tfrac{2}{3} 0 \cdot 00096) = 0 \cdot 24985$ and, from the expression given above, the average value of $X$ for the lower $\tfrac{1}{6}$ tail area of the normal distribution is

$$-0 \cdot 24985 \div \tfrac{1}{6} = -1 \cdot 4991.$$

Hence, in terms of $x$, the average lengths of eggs in the 'short' and 'long' categories may be expected to be
$$22 \cdot 4857 \mp 1 \cdot 4991 \times 0 \cdot 9546 = 21 \cdot 05 \text{ and } 23 \cdot 92 \text{ mm}.$$

### 1·3  *Note on the use of significance points*

Table 4 may be used to determine specified *significance points* for a normally distributed variable, i.e. to find the values of $X = (x - \mu)/\sigma$, the probability of exceeding which has certain conventional values, such as $0 \cdot 10$, $0 \cdot 05$, $0 \cdot 01$ or $0 \cdot 001$. It should be noted that according to the nature of his problem the statistician may be concerned with

(a) a *single-tail* test, e.g. he asks whether an observed value of $x$ exceeds $\mu$ by an exceptional amount;

(b) a *double-tail* test, e.g. he asks whether the magnitude of the difference $|x - \mu|$ is exceptional.

This distinction is discussed more fully in connexion with Student's $t$-distribution in §5·2 below.

### 1·4  *Interpolation in Tables 1–5*

To an accuracy of 5 decimals, which is usually adequate, linear interpolation can be used in Table 1 for both $P(X)$ and $Z(X)$. For example, to find the value of $P(X)$ for $X = 0 \cdot 41667$ we have (to 5-decimal accuracy)

$$P(0 \cdot 41667) = 0 \cdot 659097 + 0 \cdot 003660 \, (0 \cdot 667)$$
$$= 0 \cdot 66154.$$

In general, if $X_0$ is the tabular argument next to and below the given $X$, $\theta = 100(X - X_0)$, the fraction of interpolation (since the tabular interval is $0 \cdot 01$), and $\delta_{\frac{1}{2}} = P(X_0 + 0 \cdot 01) - P(X_0)$, then

$$P(X) \cong P(X_0) + \theta \times \delta_{\frac{1}{2}}.$$

Alternatively, we may use the Lagrangian formula

$$P(X) = (1 - \theta) P(X_0) + \theta P(X_0 + 0 \cdot 01).$$

The first equation is usually preferable when working with a machine, as the settings of $P(X_0)$ and $\delta_{\frac{1}{2}}$ can first be checked by forming $P(X_0) + \delta_{\frac{1}{2}}$ and comparing with the tabled $P(X_0 + 0 \cdot 01)$.

In this connexion it should be noted that the values of $\delta$ and $\delta^2$ do not always agree in the last figure with the differences of the corresponding tabulated values of $P$ (or $Z$). These discrepancies have arisen because W. F. Sheppard's original calculations were made to two or three more places; the figures were then cut down to 7 decimals, the differences as well as the values of the function being rounded off separately so as to be as near their true values as possible (see Sheppard (1902), pp. 177, 180).

If 7-decimal accuracy is required, the further correction term $\frac{1}{4}\theta(\theta-1)(\delta_0^2+\delta_1^2)$ should be added, where $\delta_0^2$ and $\delta_1^2$ are the central second differences tabulated in line with $P(X_0)$ and $P(X_0+0\cdot01)$ and $\frac{1}{4}\theta(\theta-1)=B''(\theta)$ is the second Bessel coefficient for which tables are available (see, for example, Comrie, 1936). The signs of the $\delta^2$ at the top of each column should be noted. Since $B''(\theta)<0$, the correction term will be of opposite sign to that of the $\delta^2$. If $|\delta^2|<4$, no correction term is needed, and if $|\delta^2|<40$ no correction is needed to 6-decimal accuracy.

The rules for interpolating $Z$ are identical.

Interpolation in Table 2 will not normally be required, since usually only the order of magnitude of the extreme tail area is needed, but interpolates accurate to about 4 decimals can be obtained up to $X=90$ with the 4-point Lagrangian formula

$$f_\theta = L_{-1}(\theta)f_{-1}+L_0(\theta)f_0+L_1(\theta)f_1+L_2(\theta)f_2,$$

where the Lagrangian multipliers $L(\theta)$ are tabulated, for example, by Comrie (1936).

The same type of formula may be used in Tables 3, 4 and 5, although here linear interpolation is adequate over most of the range; it is certainly sufficient for 3-decimal accuracy except in the top left-hand corner of each table where any interpolation will break down. In these latter cases, inverse interpolation in Tables 1 and 2 must be used.

*Illustration.* Find $X(0\cdot999356)$.

By linear interpolation in Table 3

$$0\cdot44(3\cdot1947)+0\cdot56(3\cdot2389)=3\cdot2195.$$

By four-point Lagrangian interpolation

$$-0\cdot0591(3\cdot1559)+0\cdot4942(3\cdot1947)+0\cdot6290(3\cdot2389)-0\cdot0641(3\cdot2905)=3\cdot2187.$$

The correct value is $3\cdot21864$.

## 2. PROBIT ANALYSIS (TABLE 6)*

### 2·1 *Theory and definitions*

The method of probit analysis is applied in situations where the individuals in a population require a varying 'stimulus' to produce a characteristic quantal 'response' and where our objective is to estimate the parameters of this distribution of critical stimuli. Such problems arise, for example, in dosage-mortality studies, in biological assay and in tests on the detonation of explosives. An ample description of the theory and its uses has been given in a number of publications (see, for example, Bliss, 1952; Finney, 1952), but the following summary may be helpful to users of the present table.

It is assumed that the stimulus, $x$, is measured on a scale for which individual tolerances are normally distributed; often, for example, the logarithm of the stimulating dose rather than

* This table was computed by D. J. Finney & W. L. Stevens (1948), and we are indebted to these authors for permission to reproduce. For convenience in use, abbreviated values of $P$ have been added as a first column to their original table. These $P$-values are only given for $Y\geqslant5\cdot00$. For the values of $Y<5\cdot00$ given in the last column, $P$ must be obtained by subtracting from unity the corresponding figure in the first column. E.g. for $Y=4\cdot86$, $P=1-0\cdot556=0\cdot444$. For higher accuracy, Tables 1, 3 and 4 may be consulted.

the dose itself is used as a variable in order to satisfy this condition more closely. The relation between the stimulus $x$ and the probability $P$ that an individual selected at random will respond to it, is then given by equation (2), where $X = (x - \mu)/\sigma$. In order to avoid the necessity of computing with negative numbers it is customary to use the *probit*

$$Y = X + 5 \tag{4}$$

in place of the so-called *normal equivalent deviate* $X$. Thus

$$P = \frac{1}{\sqrt{(2\pi)}} \int_{-\infty}^{Y-5} e^{-\frac{1}{2}u^2} du, \tag{5}$$

$$Q = 1 - P = \frac{1}{\sqrt{(2\pi)}} \int_{Y-5}^{\infty} e^{-\frac{1}{2}u^2} du. \tag{6}$$

If now out of $n_t$ individuals who are given the stimulus $x_t$ $(t = 1, 2, \ldots, k)$, $r_t$ respond, we may write

$$p_t = 1 - q_t = r_t/n_t, \tag{7}$$

and the corresponding probits $y_t$ will be the values of $Y$ obtained by inserting $p_t$ for $P$ in the relation (5). The values $y_t$, when plotted as ordinates against the abscissae $x_t$, should then only differ through sampling fluctuations in the observed $r_t$ from corresponding points on the population line

$$Y = 5 + (x - \mu)/\sigma. \tag{8}$$

The statistical problem is essentially that of estimating the parameters $\mu$ and $\sigma$ in (8), where the observed $y_t$ have unequal weights. This we do by fitting the regression line

$$y = a + bx.$$

Writing $n_t w_t$ for the weight of $y_t$ and omitting the subscript $t$ for convenience, standard regression theory provides the solution

$$\left. \begin{aligned} b &= \text{estimate of } \frac{1}{\sigma} = \frac{\Sigma nw(x - \bar{x})(y - \bar{y})}{\Sigma nw(x - \bar{x})^2} = \frac{\Sigma nw \Sigma nwxy - \Sigma nwx \Sigma nwy}{\Sigma nw \Sigma nwx^2 - (\Sigma nwx)^2}, \\ a &= \text{estimate of } (5 - \mu/\sigma) = \bar{y} - b\bar{x}, \end{aligned} \right\} \tag{9}$$

where $\bar{x}$ and $\bar{y}$ are the weighted means, or

$$\bar{x} = \Sigma nwx/\Sigma nw, \quad \bar{y} = \Sigma nwy/\Sigma nw. \tag{10}$$

The maximum-likelihood method of estimation leads to equations (9) and (10) in which the probits $y_t$ are replaced by the *working probits* defined below, and these are used in conjunction with weights $w_t$, given by*

$$w_t = Z_t^2/(P_t Q_t), \tag{11}$$

$P$, $Q$ and $Z$ being as defined in equations (1) and (2) above. Since the working probits and weights can only be estimated from the data, the solution must follow an iterative process; this may be carried out as follows:

(a) From the observed $p_t$, defined in (7) above, find $y_t$, using the first two columns of Table 6, and make a rough plot of $y_t$ against $x_t$.

(b) As a first approximation, a straight line fitted by eye to the points $(x_t, y_t)$ may be used to obtain a set of provisional or *expected probits* $Y'_t$ corresponding to $x_t$.

(c) The next step is to obtain a series of *working probits*, $y'_t$, and their weighting coefficients $w'_t$ to use in relations (9) and so obtain a second approximation to the regression line. These working probits are obtained from either

$$y = Y + Q/Z - q/Z \tag{12}$$

or
$$y = Y - P/Z + p/Z, \tag{13}$$

* It may be noted that the sampling variance of $y_t$ is approximately $P_t Q_t/(n_t Z_t^2)$.

5

as most convenient, where we find

$$\text{the } range = 1/Z$$
$$\text{and} \quad \text{the } maximum\ working\ probit,\ Y_{\max} = Y + Q/Z$$
$$\text{or} \quad \text{the } minimum\ working\ probit,\ Y_{\min} = Y - P/Z,$$

by entering Table 6 with the expected probits $Y'_t$, $q$ or $p$ being as before the observed proportion of individuals failing to respond ($q$) or responding ($p$). It will be noticed that under this procedure, if there is a zero or 100 % response ($p = 0$ or 1), the solution allows us to use this result in the form of working probits of $Y - P/Z$ and $Y + Q/Z$.

(d) The appropriate weights $n_t w'_t$ based on (11) are also found, again entering Table 6 with $Y'_t$.

(e) We then use these weights and the working probits $y'_t$ to compute the coefficients $a$ and $b$ of equations (9).

(f) The values of the probits $Y''_t$ obtained from this second approximation to the regression line may be used to repeat the cycle of the iterative process, Table 6 being entered to obtain fresh working probits $y''_t$ and weights $n_t w''_t$. The iteration is continued until the process has 'settled down'.

It will be noticed that the table gives

$$Y_{\max} \text{ for } \quad Y = 3 \cdot 58\,(0 \cdot 01)\,9 \cdot 00, \qquad Y_{\min} \text{ for } \quad Y = 1 \cdot 00\,(0 \cdot 01)\,6 \cdot 42,$$
$$1/Z \text{ and } w \text{ for } \quad Y = 1 \cdot 00\,(0 \cdot 01)\,9 \cdot 00.$$

Below $Y = 3 \cdot 58$, $Y_{\max}$ exceeds $10 \cdot 00$, and above $Y = 6 \cdot 42$, $Y_{\min}$ is negative; it is then almost always more convenient to calculate the working probits from the other function, but the function not tabulated can easily be obtained from the relationship

$$Y_{\max} - Y_{\min} = 1/Z.$$

### 2·2  Illustration of application of Table 6

*Example* 2. As part of a large investigation into the nature of the fall-off with distance in the blast effect of explosive charges, an experiment was conducted as follows. A given weight of charge was detonated at a distance $x$ from a standard disk of cardboard, and a record made of whether the disk was perforated or not. This was done 16 times at each of the five distances shown in the first column of the table on p. 8 below. This table shows in the second column the working-scale values, $x_t = \frac{1}{4}(53 - \text{distance})$, and in the third column the corresponding number of perforations, $r_t$. Throughout, $n_t = 16$.

Clearly there is no unique critical distance, such that no cards are perforated beyond this distance and all within it. If, however, we make the assumption that for a given weight of charge the critical distance in successive experiments is approximately normally distributed about a mean $\mu$ with standard deviation $\sigma$, we may use the technique described in the preceding section to estimate the values of these parameters. The investigation could then be extended to examine the effect on $\mu$ and $\sigma$ of changes in the charge-weight or type of explosive.

The first section of the table on p. 8 gives, besides $x_t$ and $r_t$, $p_t = \frac{1}{16}r_t$ and $y_t$, the last values obtained following the procedure described in para. (a) of p. 5. The three available values of $y_t$ were then plotted against $x_t$ and a rough line fitted to the points by eye as shown in Fig. 2;*

---

* It is known from experience that when the data include a 'no response' and/or an 'all response' record, one will usually do well to start with a line which is somewhat steeper than the 'eye estimate' based on the remaining points. This practice was not followed here so that the convergence is rather slow.

6

from this line the five values of the *expected probits* $Y'_t$ corresponding to $x_t = 0, 1, 2, 3, 4$ were read off (para. (*b*) of p. 5).

We are now ready to obtain from Table 6 the quantities required for fitting the second approximation to the regression line (regarding the line fitted by eye as the first approximation). The number of decimals given in Table 6 makes provision for the rare occasions when high precision is required. In the present example, as in most practical situations, one decimal in $Y_t$ and two in $y_t$ would be adequate. The calculations, however, are here carried to a higher accuracy to illustrate both the interpolation in the table and the convergence of the process, which is taken beyond the accuracy warranted by the standard errors of the estimates.

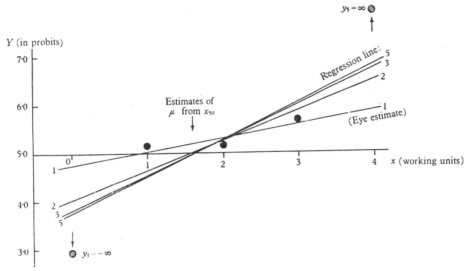

Fig. 2. Successive approximations to probit regression line (Example 2).

Entering Table 6 with $Y'_t$, we obtain the corresponding values of the minimum working probit ($Y'_{\min.}$), the range ($1/Z'$) and then computing values of $y'_t$ (see equation (13)) from

$$y'_t = Y'_{\min.} + p_t \times 1/Z'$$

directly on a machine, we enter the answers in the next column of the table, as shown. Next, re-entering Table 6 at argument $Y'_t$, we obtain the weighting coefficients $w'_t$; these are copied down, as well as set on the machine to compute the products $w'_t x_t$ shown in the next column.*

We now calculate the constants in the second approximation to the regression line, noting that a constant multiplier, $n_t = 16$, may be omitted from all numerators and denominators. Equations (10) and (9) for purposes of computing become

$$\bar{x} = \Sigma w'_t x_t / \Sigma w'_t, \quad \bar{y} = \Sigma (w'_t)(y'_t) / \Sigma w'_t,$$

$$b = \frac{[\Sigma w'_t][\Sigma(w'_t x_t)(y'_t)] - [\Sigma w'_t x_t][\Sigma(w'_t)(y'_t)]}{[\Sigma w'_t][\Sigma(w'_t x_t)(x_t)] - [\Sigma w'_t x_t]^2}.$$

These formulae are arranged to show that the following operations must be performed on the appropriate columns of the table below:

| | | |
|---|---|---|
| Totals for | $w'_t x_t$, | $w'_t$ |
| Sums of products for | $w'_t$ by $y'_t$, | $w'_t x_t$ by $y'_t$ and $x_t$ |

* If the $n_t$ are not constant (as they are in the present example), the products $n_t w'_t$ and $n_t w'_t x_t$ must be entered instead.

The resulting values of the coefficients, $b = 0.619$ and $a = \bar{y} - b\bar{x} = 4.017$, are shown at the bottom of the table.

We have now to continue the iterative process. From the equation

$$y = 4.017 + 0.619x,$$

we obtain the five probit values $Y_t''$ (at $x_t = 0, 1, 2, 3, 4$) shown in the last column of the upper section of the table. These in turn, when used in Table 6, provide fresh values of working probits $y_t$ and fresh weights, leading to the calculation of new values for $a$ and $b$.

This process was carried out four times; we have recorded only the values of $a$ and $b$, and of the final probits $Y_t^{\text{v}}$ calculated from the fifth approximation to the probit line

$$y = 3.7747 + 0.7568x.$$

The sixth approximation is shown merely to confirm the convergence.

To avoid accumulation of rounding-off errors more figures have sometimes been retained than are warranted by the accuracy of the quantities on which they are based. $Y_t'$ and $Y_t''$ have been used to 2 decimals, $Y_t'''$ to $Y_t^{\text{v}}$ to 3 decimals, and the resulting values of $y_t$, $w_t x_t$, $b$ and $a$ have been taken to one more decimal.

| $x_t$ | | $r_t$ | $p_t$ | $y_t$ | $Y_t'$ | $y'$ | $w_t'$ | $w_t' x_t$ | $Y_t''$ |
|---|---|---|---|---|---|---|---|---|---|
| ft. | Working scale | | | | | | | | |
| 53 | 0 | 0 | 0 | $-\infty$ | 4.75 | 3.712 | 0.6223 | 0 | 4.02 |
| 49 | 1 | 9 | 0.5625 | 5.16 | 5.02 | 5.157 | 0.6365 | 0.636 | 4.64 |
| 45 | 2 | 9 | 0.5625 | 5.16 | 5.30 | 5.155 | 0.6161 | 1.232 | 5.26 |
| 41 | 3 | 12 | 0.7500 | 5.67 | 5.57 | 5.671 | 0.5652 | 1.696 | 5.87 |
| 37 | 4 | 16 | 1 | $\infty$ | 5.85 | 6.561 | 0.4873 | 1.949 | 6.49 |

| $x_t$ | $Y_t^{\text{v}}$ | $y_t^{\text{v}}$ | $w_t^{\text{v}}$ | $w_t^{\text{v}} x_t$ | $P_t$ | $16P_t$ | $r_t$ |
|---|---|---|---|---|---|---|---|
| 0 | 3.775 | 3.1896 | 0.3617 | 0 | 0.1103 | 1.76 | 0 |
| 1 | 4.532 | 5.2105 | 0.5876 | 0.5876 | 0.3199 | 5.12 | 9 |
| 2 | 5.288 | 5.1552 | 0.6177 | 1.2354 | 0.6133 | 9.81 | 9 |
| 3 | 6.045 | 5.6036 | 0.4235 | 1.2705 | 0.8520 | 13.63 | 12 |
| 4 | 6.802 | 7.2567 | 0.1794 | 0.7176 | 0.9642 | 15.43 | 16 |

Successive approximations:

| | $a$ | $b$ | $x_{50} = (5-a)/b$ | |
|---|---|---|---|---|
| | | | Working scale | ft. |
| Second | 4.017 | 0.619 | 1.59 | 46.6 |
| Third | 3.820 | 0.731 | 1.61 | 46.6 |
| Fourth | 3.7791 | 0.7546 | 1.618 | 46.53 |
| Fifth | 3.7747 | 0.7568 | 1.619 | 46.52 |
| [Sixth | 3.7744 | 0.7569 | 1.619 | 46.52] |

Est. s.e. = 0.90.

We may also use the solution to obtain expected frequencies of perforations at the five distances. Either from the first two columns of Table 6 or through equation (5) and Table 1, the final approximations $Y_t^{\gamma}$ provide estimates of $P_t$ and hence of the expectations $16P_t$. These are given in the second section of the table, where they are compared with the observed $r_t$.

If none of the expected frequencies $n_t P_t$ or $n_t Q_t$ is very small, we may calculate

$$\chi^2 = \sum_t (r_t - n_t P_t)^2 / (n_t P_t Q_t),$$

and so obtain a test of the significance of discrepancies between observation and theory. The degrees of freedom will be two less than the number of levels of $x$ used in the experiment, since the two parameters, $\mu$ and $\sigma$, have been estimated from the data.* Finney (1952, pp. 52–4) describes an alternative method of computing $\chi^2$ as the weighted sum of squares of deviations of the working probits from the regression line. The two values of $\chi^2$ are not identical until the maximum-likelihood solution is reached.

In the present example, both methods give a value, $\chi^2 = 8 \cdot 4$, with degrees of freedom $5 - 2 = 3$, which is just significant at the 5 % level (Table 8). Since, however, some of the expectations are very small ($16Q_5 = 0 \cdot 57$ and $16P_1 = 1 \cdot 76$), it is a little doubtful whether reference to the $\chi^2$ distribution is appropriate.

It will be noted that the estimate of $\mu$ is $(5 - a)/b$. This is the estimate of the value of $x$ at which there is a 50:50 chance of a 'response'; in dosage-mortality work it is often described as the *median lethal dose* (L.D. 50) or *median effective dose* (E.D. 50). In the table we have given the successive estimates of E.D. 50 under the heading $x_{50}$. It is seen that to 2-decimal accuracy (in ft.) these have settled to a constant value at the fourth approximation. Using the large-sample formula for the standard error of $x_{50}$ (see, for example, Finney, 1952, equation (3·6)), namely,

$$\sigma(x_{50}) = \{1/\Sigma nw + (x_{50} - \bar{x})^2/\Sigma nw(x - \bar{x})^2\}^{\frac{1}{2}}/b, \tag{14}$$

we obtain, for the final estimate, a standard error of $0 \cdot 225$ in working units or $0 \cdot 90$ in ft. For a description of a small-sample technique for obtaining an interval estimate for E.D. 50, Finney (1952, § 19) may be consulted. The final estimate of $\sigma$ is the reciprocal of $b$, i.e. $1 \cdot 321$ (4) or $5 \cdot 29$ ft.

## II. BASIC TABLES DERIVED FROM THE NORMAL FUNCTION

### 3. THE $\chi^2$-INTEGRAL (TABLES 7 AND 8)

#### 3·1 *Definition*

As is well known, the $\chi^2$-integral, the incomplete $\Gamma$-function, the integral of Karl Pearson's Type III distribution and the cumulative sum of terms of the Poisson distribution are all different forms of the same mathematical function. We shall first define this function in terms of the $\chi^2$-integral. If $X_1, X_2, ..., X_\nu$ are $\nu$ independent normal variates each with expectation zero and unit standard deviation, then

$$\chi^2 = \sum_{i=1}^{\nu} X_i^2$$

has for its probability integral

$$P(\chi^2 \mid \nu) = 2^{-\frac{1}{2}\nu} \{\Gamma(\tfrac{1}{2}\nu)\}^{-1} \int_0^{\chi^2} e^{-\frac{1}{2}x} x^{\frac{1}{2}\nu - 1} dx. \tag{15}$$

The quantity $\nu$ is generally called the *degrees of freedom* of $\chi^2$.

* This is a particular application of the $\chi^2$ test for goodness of fit described in §3·2 below.

Because of its use in tests of significance, Table 7 gives the complement of the probability integral, i.e.
$$Q(\chi^2 \mid \nu) = 1 - P(\chi^2 \mid \nu),$$
that is to say, the chance that $\Sigma X_i^2$ exceeds a given value, $\chi^2$. Table 8 gives certain percentage points of the distribution, i.e. the values of $\chi^2$ for which $Q(\chi^2 \mid \nu) = 0.995, 0.99, \dots, 0.01, 0.005$ and $0.001$.

It will be useful to put on record here, for later reference, the values of certain of the moment coefficients of the frequency function $f(\chi^2)$ of $\chi^2$, for which equation (15) gives the probability integral. Writing $\kappa_r$ for the $r$th cumulant and $\mu_r$ for the $r$th moment about the mean, then

$$\kappa_r = \nu 2^{r-1}(r-1)! \tag{16}$$

Hence
$$\kappa_1 = \mathscr{E}(\chi^2) = \nu,$$

$$\mu_2 = 2\nu, \quad \mu_3 = 8\nu, \quad \mu_4 = 48\nu + 12\nu^2,$$

$$\beta_1 = \mu_3^2/\mu_2^3 = 8/\nu, \quad \beta_2 = \mu_4/\mu_2^2 = 3 + 12/\nu.$$

### 3·2   Applications; analysis of variance and goodness of fit

The integral and its associated frequency function occur in numerous ways in the theory of statistical tests. In the analysis of variance, for example, the fundamental sum of squares of standardized deviates, which may be broken up into component parts each following a $\chi^2$-distribution, is obtained by an appropriate orthogonal transformation of the observable variables.

In other problems the $\chi^2$-distribution may be used as a mathematical approximation. An illustration of this type of application is provided in Example 4, but the best known case in point concerns the test of goodness of fit where the observations are the frequencies of occurrence of events in a number of alternative categories. Here, if an observation must fall into one or other of $k$ alternative groups, if $n_t$ are found in the $t$th group ($t = 1, 2, \dots, k$), if $N = \sum_t n_t$, and if the probability, on the hypothesis tested, of an observation falling in this group is $p_t$, then

$$\chi^2 = \sum_{t=1}^{k} \frac{(n_t - N p_t)^2}{N p_t} = \sum_{t=1}^{k} \frac{n_t^2}{N p_t} - N \tag{17}$$

will have a sampling distribution whose probability integral is represented approximately by equation (15), if the hypothesis tested is true. The degrees of freedom, $\nu$, will equal the number of categories, $k$, less the number of linear or approximately linear independent relations holding among the $k$ differences $n_t - N p_t$ (see Example 3, p. 11).* To avoid stretching the approximation too far, none of the expected frequencies $N p_t$ used in the test should be less than about 4 or 5.

### 3·3   Relation to the Poisson distribution

For even values of $\nu$ (for which the entries are given in bold type in Table 7) the integral (15) can be written as

$$Q(\chi^2 \mid \nu) = 1 - P(\chi^2 \mid \nu) = \sum_{j=0}^{c-1} \frac{e^{-m} m^j}{j!}, \tag{18}$$

with $m = \tfrac{1}{2}\chi^2$ and $c = \tfrac{1}{2}\nu$. Thus Table 7 gives the cumulative sum of the terms of the Poisson series with mean $m = \tfrac{1}{2}\chi^2$, up to but excluding the term for which $c = \tfrac{1}{2}\nu$. The table, therefore, supplements the later table of individual Poisson terms (Table 39) which does not adequately cover values of $m$ less than unity.

* If the hypothetical $p_t$ are functions of certain parameters whose values are determined by fitting a theoretical law to the observations, certain conditions must, of course, hold concerning the method of fitting employed.

10

*Example* 3. Snedecor (1946, p. 441) quotes data of Leggatt (1935) on the pollution of seeds of *Phleum pratense* by the presence of a few noxious weed seeds. The table below shows the frequency with which 0, 1, 2, ... of these weed seeds were found in 98 quarter-ounce subsamples of *Ph. pratense*. We shall now use Table 7* to graduate the observed frequencies $n_t$ by a Poisson distribution and afterwards to test for goodness of fit.

| No. of noxious seeds $x_t$ | Observed frequency of occurrence $n_t$ | Poisson frequency $Np_t$ | $n_t - Np_t$ | $\dfrac{(n_t - Np_t)^2}{Np_t}$ |
|:---:|:---:|:---:|:---:|:---:|
| 0 | 3 | 4·8 | −1·8 | 0·67 |
| 1 | 17 | 14·4 | 2·6 | 0·47 |
| 2 | 26 | 21·8 | 4·2 | 0·81 |
| 3 | 16 | 22·0 | −6·0 | 1·64 |
| 4 | 18 | 16·6 | 1·4 | 0·12 |
| 5 | 9 | 10·0 | −1·0 | 0·10 |
| 6 | 3 ⎫ | 5·0 ⎫ | | |
| 7 | 5 ⎪ | 2·2 ⎪ | | |
| 8 | 0 ⎬ 9 | 0·8 ⎬ 8·4 | 0·6 | 0·04 |
| 9 | 1 ⎭ | 0·3 ⎪ | | |
| 10 | — | 0·1 ⎭ | | |
| Total | 98 | 98·0 | 0·0 | 3·85 |

The mean of the observed frequencies in col. 2, $\bar{x} = 3\cdot020$, provides the estimate of $m$ with which to enter Table 7. The nearest tabular column is $m = 3\cdot0$, from which our value differs by $\phi = 3\cdot020 - 3\cdot0 = 0\cdot020$. The cumulative Poisson distribution for $m = 3\cdot020$ is now obtained† by multiplying, for each $c$, the entry in the column $m = 3\cdot0$ by $1 - \phi = 0\cdot98$ and adding the bold-type entry above it (i.e. the entry for $c - 1$) multiplied by $\phi = 0\cdot020$. Thus we find:

Cumulative Poisson sum for $c = 1$:    $(0\cdot04979)(0\cdot98) + (0)(0\cdot02)$        $= 0\cdot0488$.

Cumulative Poisson sum for $c = 2$:    $(0\cdot19915)(0\cdot98) + (0\cdot04979)(0\cdot02) = 0\cdot1962$.

The differences between these cumulative entries multiplied by $N = 98$ give the expected values $Np_t$ shown in the third column of the table.

We may now test the goodness of fit of the Poisson distribution. In order to compute the $\chi^2$ of equation (17) we note that the last five expected frequencies do not exceed 5 and hence club these together as shown, so that the total number of differences, $n_t - Np_t$, is $k = 7$. The seven values of $(n_t - Np_t)^2/(Np_t)$ are shown in the last column together with their total, $\chi^2 = 3\cdot85$. Since the seven differences $n_t - Np_t$ must satisfy the two conditions

$$\sum_t (n_t - Np_t) = 0 \quad \text{and} \quad \sum_t (n_t - Np_t)\, x_t = 0,$$

the degrees of freedom, $\nu$, for $\chi^2$ are $\nu = 7 - 2 = 5$. Entering Table 7 for $\nu = 5$ and $\chi^2 = 3\cdot85$ we find that $Q(3\cdot8 \mid 5) = 0\cdot58$, so that a value of $\chi^2$, as large or larger than this, might have arisen through chance sampling fluctuations on nearly six occasions out of ten; on the evidence available, therefore, we have no reason to question the appropriateness of the Poisson law, i.e. the random distribution of weed seeds among the others.

* For conditions under which the use of Table 39 may be preferable, see §21.

† This method of interpolation is described in §3·8*b*, except that in this example the $\phi^2$ terms may be omitted.

Instead of obtaining the exact value of $Q(\chi^2 \mid \nu)$ from Table 7 we may be content to know whether the observed value of $\chi^2$ does or does not exceed some specified percentage point, e.g. the 5 % point. Table 8 shows that for $\nu = 5$ the 5 % point for $\chi^2$ is 11·070. Since the observed value of 3·85 is well within this limit we can say that the departure from the Poisson law is not significant at the 5 % level, thereby reaching a similar conclusion to that found above.

### 3·5 *Relation to the incomplete Γ-function, and to the Pearson Type III curve; other applications*

If in the integral (15) we regard $\tfrac{1}{2}x$ as the variable of integration, we recognize the expression as the incomplete Γ-integral or incomplete Γ-function for Γ-argument $\tfrac{1}{2}\nu$, normalized by division by $\Gamma(\tfrac{1}{2}\nu)$ to make the complete integral equal unity. The most extensive table of this integral is Karl Pearson's (1922) 7-decimal table; his notation is related to the present notation as follows:

| | | | |
|---|---|---|---|
| Pearson | $I(u, p)$ | $p$ | $u$ |
| Present table | $P(\chi^2 \mid \nu)$ | $\tfrac{1}{2}\nu - 1$ | $\tfrac{1}{2}\chi^2 / \surd(p+1) = \chi^2 / \surd(2\nu)$ |

Pearson's argument $u$ was chosen to standardize the variable by division by its standard deviation which, for $\chi^2$, is $\surd(2\nu)$. Whilst this device has the advantage of providing a uniform tabular range and interval for all $\nu$, the transformation to argument $u$ necessitates extra labour and often additional interpolation which is here avoided.

By changing the scale and origin of the Γ-integral we obtain the general form of the probability integral of the Pearson Type III distribution (see § 23·1 below), namely,

$$P(x \mid \gamma, a) = y_0 \int_{-a}^{x} \left(1 + \frac{v}{a}\right)^{\gamma a} e^{-\gamma v} \, dv.$$

This can clearly be related to the $\chi^2$-integral by setting

$$\nu = 2\gamma a + 2, \quad \chi^2 = 2\gamma(x + a).$$

Hence Table 7 could be used to compute values of the probability integral of Type III frequency curves, the interpolation to fractional degrees of freedom, $\nu$, being discussed in § 3·8 (c). In so far as these curves have been found useful in approximating to a number of the less tractable distributions of statistical theory, Tables 7 and 8 provide approximate solutions to tests involving such statistics. The $\chi^2$-approximation used in testing for heterogeneity of variances is a case in point (see § 16·1); so are numerous likelihood criteria in multivariate analysis (see, for example, Box, 1949).

As an illustration of this type of application we shall take the case of obtaining an approximation to the distribution of a special form of *non-central* $\chi^2$, namely,

$$\chi'^2 = \sum_{i=1}^{n} \frac{(x_i + \alpha_i - \bar{x} - \bar{\alpha})^2}{\sigma^2},$$

where the $x_i$ are $n$ independent normal deviates (i.e. have expectation zero) with a common variance $\sigma^2$ and the $\alpha_i$ are $n$ constant parameters with a mean of $\bar{\alpha}$. It can be shown (Patnaik, 1949) that $\chi'^2/C$ has approximately the probability integral (15) of $\chi^2$ with $\nu'$ degrees of freedom, where

$$C = (\nu + 2\lambda)/(\nu + \lambda), \quad \nu' = (\nu + \lambda)^2/(\nu + 2\lambda), \quad \nu = n - 1, \tag{19}$$

these relations being expressed in terms of a single 'non-centrality' parameter defined by

$$\lambda = \sum_{i=1}^{n} \frac{(\alpha_i - \bar{\alpha})^2}{\sigma^2}. \tag{20}$$

It will be noted that $\nu'$ will in general be fractional.

### 3·6  *Applications. Approximation to the non-central $\chi^2$-distribution*

*Example* 4.  A sample of twenty observations $x_i$ $(i = 1, 2, \ldots, 20)$ was to have been drawn from a normal population with a known variance of 4. It is, however, suspected that accidentally an unspecified subsample of ten of the $x_i$ may all have been increased by the same amount of $\Delta = 4$. The sum of squares of deviations $\Sigma(x_i - \bar{x})^2$ is found to be 148. Does this result indicate that the suspected increase has taken place?

If no increase has occurred, the sum $\frac{1}{4}\Sigma(x_i - \bar{x})^2 = 37$ would be a random sample value of $\chi^2$ for $\nu = 19$ degrees of freedom; Table 8 shows that it exceeds the 1 % value of $\chi^2$ (36·2), throwing doubt on the hypothesis of no increase.

On the other hand, if the increase of $\Delta$ *has* in fact occurred, ten of the $x_i$ would have come from a population with mean $\mu + \Delta$ and ten from a population with mean $\mu$. Hence we are dealing with a non-central $\chi^2$ for which from (20)

$$\lambda = 20(\tfrac{1}{2}\Delta)^2/4 = 20.$$

Further, from the relations (19),

$$C = (19 + 40)/(19 + 20) = 1\cdot51, \quad \nu' = (19 + 20)^2/(19 + 40) = 25\cdot8.$$

Accordingly

$$\chi'^2/C = \tfrac{1}{4}\sum_i (x_i - \bar{x})^2/1\cdot51$$

would be distributed approximately as $\chi^2$ with 26 degrees of freedom. The observed numerical value is $\frac{1}{4}\,148/1\cdot51 = 24\cdot5$ and is now slightly less than the expected value, $\nu' = 25\cdot8$. The observations are therefore clearly consistent with the hypothesis that for ten of the observations an increase in mean of $\Delta = 4$ has occurred.

### 3·7  *Applications to expansions in series*

The tables also can be used as a basis for the expansion of distribution functions in Gram-Charlier or Laguerre series, which may be shown to be equivalent to series of $\chi^2$ distributions progressing in integral steps of degrees of freedom.

### 3·8  *Interpolation in Table* 7

(*a*)  *Single-entry interpolation $\chi^2$-wise*

With no differences tabulated, Lagrangian interpolation or Aitken's iterative method may be used. We describe here a somewhat simpler method based on a Taylor expansion which utilizes the relations

$$\left. \begin{aligned} \frac{\partial Q}{\partial \chi^2} &= \tfrac{1}{2}\{Q(\chi^2 \mid \nu - 2) - Q(\chi^2 \mid \nu)\}, \\[1mm] \frac{\partial^2 Q}{\partial \chi^{2\,2}} &= \tfrac{1}{4}\{Q(\chi^2 \mid \nu - 4) - 2Q(\chi^2 \mid \nu - 2) + Q(\chi^2 \mid \nu)\}. \end{aligned} \right\} \tag{21}$$

Let $\chi_0^2$ denote the tabular argument nearest to the given value of $\chi^2$ for which the answer is required and let $\theta = \chi^2 - \chi_0^2$.* Then from the second-order Taylor expansion we obtain

$$\begin{aligned} 2Q(\chi^2 \mid \nu) = \;& Q(\chi_0^2 \mid \nu - 4)\,(\tfrac{1}{2}\theta)^2 + \\ & Q(\chi_0^2 \mid \nu - 2)\,\{\theta - 2(\tfrac{1}{2}\theta)^2\} + \\ & Q(\chi_0^2 \mid \nu)\,\{2 - \theta + (\tfrac{1}{2}\theta)^2\}. \end{aligned} \tag{22}$$

---

\* Note that $\theta$ is here the argument increment and not the fraction of interpolation as used elsewhere, e.g. in §1·4.

*Illustration.* To find $Q(3\cdot64132\,|\,12)$ the following method is suggested:

Copy down $\theta = 0\cdot04132$, form and copy $(\tfrac{1}{2}\theta)^2 = 0\cdot00043$,

and finally compute the sum of products

$$Q(3\cdot64132\,|\,12) = \tfrac{1}{2}\{0\cdot89129\,(0\cdot00043) +$$
$$0\cdot96359\,(0\cdot04132 - 0\cdot00086) +$$
$$0\cdot98962\,(2 - 0\cdot04132 + 0\cdot00043)\}$$
$$= 0\cdot98907.$$

On a calculating machine the $Q$ entries would be set as multiplicands and the terms inside the parentheses ( ) applied in turn as multipliers; the sum of products so formed is then immediately divided by 2.

The fifth decimal computed from (22) may be a few units of error. Where 3-decimal accuracy is adequate, linear interpolation is usually sufficient and the $(\tfrac{1}{2}\theta)^2$ terms of (22) may be omitted.

### (b) Single-entry interpolation m-wise

The method is almost identical with that described above. Let $m_0$ denote the tabular argument nearest to $m$ and $\phi = m - m_0$; then

$$Q(m\,|\,c) = Q(m_0\,|\,c-2)\,\tfrac{1}{2}\phi^2 +$$
$$Q(m_0\,|\,c-1)\,(\phi - \phi^2) +$$
$$Q(m_0\,|\,c)\,(1 - \phi + \tfrac{1}{2}\phi^2). \tag{23}$$

For details of computation see the illustration given in § 3·4 above.

### (c) Double-entry interpolation

When it is intended to use the present table for the evaluation of the $\chi^2$-integral for fractional degrees of freedom (or odd degrees of freedom, $\nu > 30$), double-entry interpolation for both intermediate $\nu$ and $\chi^2$ is necessary. Similarly, when using the present tables for computing the general Type III probability integral quoted on p. 12 above, fractional $\nu$ and $\chi^2$ will usually arise. In this case the relations (21) are particularly useful, as they allow the differential with regard to $\chi^2$ to be expressed in terms of the very entries $Q(\chi_0^2\,|\,\nu)$ which are required for the Lagrangian interpolation $\nu$-wise.

Let $\chi_0^2$ denote the tabular argument nearest to the given $\chi^2$ and $\nu_0$ the tabular line heading nearest to, but smaller than the given $\nu$; then the following formulae and methods are suggested in which we must distinguish two cases:

(i) $\nu > 30$

Let $\omega = \tfrac{1}{2}(\nu - \nu_0)$, $\phi = \tfrac{1}{2}(\chi^2 - \chi_0^2)$. Compute and copy $\omega\phi$, $\phi^2$ and $\omega^2$ and finally obtain the interpolate as the sum of products:

$$Q(\chi^2\,|\,\nu) = Q(\chi^2\,|\,\nu_0 - 4)\,(\tfrac{1}{2}\phi^2) + Q(\chi_0^2\,|\,\nu_0 - 2)\,(\tfrac{1}{2}\omega^2 - \tfrac{1}{2}\omega + \phi - \phi^2 - \omega\phi) +$$
$$Q(\chi_0^2\,|\,\nu_0)\,(1 - \omega^2 - \phi + \tfrac{1}{2}\phi^2 + 2\omega\phi) +$$
$$Q(\chi_0^2\,|\,\nu_0 + 2)\,(\tfrac{1}{2}\omega^2 + \tfrac{1}{2}\omega - \omega\phi). \tag{24}$$

On a calculating machine, the multiplicands $Q$ are set and the terms within the parentheses applied in turn as multipliers.

*Illustration.* Find $Q(25 \cdot 2154 \mid 39)$.

We have $\omega = 0 \cdot 5$, $\phi = 0 \cdot 1077$, whence $\omega^2 = 0 \cdot 25$, $\phi^2 = 0 \cdot 0116$, $\phi\omega = 0 \cdot 0538$. Hence we obtain

$$Q(25 \cdot 2154 \mid 39) = 0 \cdot 86931 \, (0 \cdot 0058) + 0 \cdot 91584 \, (0 \cdot 125 - 0 \cdot 25 + 0 \cdot 1077 - 0 \cdot 0116 - 0 \cdot 0538) +$$
$$0 \cdot 94815 \, (1 - 0 \cdot 25 - 0 \cdot 1077 + 0 \cdot 0058 + 0 \cdot 1077) +$$
$$0 \cdot 96941 \, (0 \cdot 125 + 0 \cdot 25 - 0 \cdot 0538)$$
$$= 0 \cdot 95729.$$

The exact interpolate is $0 \cdot 95706$.

The main terms neglected in equation (24) are $B'' \delta^3$ and $-2B'' \phi \delta^3$, where $B'' = \frac{1}{4}\omega(\omega - 1)$ and all differences $\delta$ are taken with regard to $\nu$. Of these terms, the first is usually the largest and may result in an error of a few units in the fourth decimal. If higher, accuracy is needed, a table of Lagrangian interpolation coefficients $L_{-1}$, $L_0$, $L_1$ and $L_2$ may be used in conjunction with the following formula:

$$Q(\chi^2 \mid \nu) = Q(\chi_0^2 \mid \nu_0 - 4) \, (\tfrac{1}{2}\phi^2) +$$
$$Q(\chi_0^2 \mid \nu_0 - 2) \, (L_{-1}(\omega) + \phi - \phi^2 - \omega\phi) +$$
$$Q(\chi_0^2 \mid \nu_0) \, (L_0(\omega) - \phi + \tfrac{1}{2}\phi^2 + 2\omega\phi) +$$
$$Q(\chi_0^2 \mid \nu_0 + 2) \, (L_1(\omega) - \omega\phi) +$$
$$Q(\chi_0^2 \mid \nu_0 + 4) \, L_2(\omega). \tag{25}$$

With this formula, the first of the above error terms is eliminated and the remaining error may sometimes amount to a few units in the fifth decimal, but is often smaller than $5 \times 10^{-6}$. In the present example equation (25) yields $0 \cdot 95710$.

(ii) $\nu < 30$

Let $\omega = \nu - \nu_0$ and again $\phi = \frac{1}{2}(\chi^2 - \chi_0^2)$. Compute and copy $\omega\phi$ and $\omega^2$, and hence find the interpolate as the sum of products

$$Q(\chi^2 \mid \nu) = Q(\chi_0^2 \mid \nu_0 - 4) \, \tfrac{1}{2}\phi^2 +$$
$$Q(\chi_0^2 \mid \nu_0 - 2) \, (\phi - \phi^2 - \omega\phi) +$$
$$Q(\chi_0^2 \mid \nu_0 - 1) \, (\tfrac{1}{2}\omega^2 - \tfrac{1}{2}\omega + \omega\phi) +$$
$$Q(\chi_0^2 \mid \nu_0) \, (1 - \omega^2 - \phi + \tfrac{1}{2}\phi^2 + \omega\phi) +$$
$$Q(\chi_0^2 \mid \nu_0 + 1) \, (\tfrac{1}{2}\omega^2 + \tfrac{1}{2}\omega - \omega\phi). \tag{26}$$

For operation on a calculating machine proceed as when using equation (24).

*Illustration.* Find $Q(5 \cdot 8764 \mid 10 \cdot 3148)$.

We have $\omega = 0 \cdot 3148$, $\phi = 0 \cdot 0382$, whence $\omega^2 = 0 \cdot 09910$, $\omega\phi = 0 \cdot 01203$, $\phi^2 = 0 \cdot 00146$, so that

$$Q(5 \cdot 8764 \mid 10 \cdot 3148) = 0 \cdot 44596 \, (0 \cdot 00073) + 0 \cdot 66962 \, (0 \cdot 0382 - 0 \cdot 00146 - 0 \cdot 01203) +$$
$$0 \cdot 75976 \, (0 \cdot 04955 - 0 \cdot 1574 + 0 \cdot 01203) +$$
$$0 \cdot 83178 \, (1 - 0 \cdot 09910 - 0 \cdot 0382 + 0 \cdot 00073 + 0 \cdot 01203) +$$
$$0 \cdot 88637 \, (0 \cdot 04955 + 0 \cdot 1574 - 0 \cdot 01203)$$
$$= 0 \cdot 84503.$$

The main terms neglected in equation (26) are $B'' \delta^3$ and $-4B'' \phi \delta^3$, where $B'' = \frac{1}{4}\omega(\omega - 1)$ and all differences $\delta$ are taken with regard to $\nu$. The error may be a few units in the fourth decimal except near the singularity $\nu = 0$, $\chi^2 = 0$, where interpolation $\nu$-wise by this method is

15

not possible.* If higher accuracy is required, a table of the four-point Lagrangian coefficients may be used in conjunction with the following formula:

$$Q(\chi^2 \mid \nu) = Q(\chi_0^2 \mid \nu_0 - 4)\, \tfrac{1}{2}\phi^2 + Q(\chi_0^2 \mid \nu_0 - 2)\,(L_{-1}(1+\omega) + \phi - \phi^2 - \omega\phi) +$$
$$Q(\chi_0^2 \mid \nu - 1)\,(L_0(1+\omega) + \omega\phi) + Q(\chi_0^2 \mid \nu_0)\,(L_1(1+\omega) - \phi + \tfrac{1}{2}\phi^2 + \omega\phi) +$$
$$Q(\chi_0^2 \mid \nu_0 + 1)\,(L_2(1+\omega) - \omega\phi). \tag{27}$$

### (d) Single-entry interpolation $\nu$-wise

The necessity for this type of interpolation does not arise very often, as interpolation $\nu$-wise usually occurs in conjunction with interpolation $\chi^2$-wise, thereby leading to double-entry interpolation. The formulae (25), (26) and (27) may be used with $\phi = 0$. For higher accuracy, a six-point Lagrangian formula may be employed.

### 3·9  Interpolation in Table 8

Although values of $\chi^2$ for intermediate probability levels are obtainable by Lagrangian formulae or by special methods† (Simaika, 1942), we recommend in such cases inverse interpolation in Table 7, and shall confine ourselves here to interpolation to intermediate values of $\nu$, whether integral or fractional. For $\nu < 30$, Lagrangian interpolation at unit interval is convenient. Except for the top left-hand corner of the table, the four-point formula will be found to yield sufficient accuracy, and often simple linear interpolation will be adequate. For small $\nu$ and large $Q = 1 - P$ (top left-hand corner) approximate values $\chi_0^2$ can be directly computed from

$$\tfrac{1}{2}\chi_0^2 = \{P\,\Gamma(\tfrac{1}{2}\nu + 1)\}^{2/\nu},$$

and their accuracy improved by the next iterate

$$\tfrac{1}{2}\chi_1^2 = \tfrac{1}{2}\chi_0^2\{1 + \tfrac{1}{2}\chi_0^2/(\tfrac{1}{2}\nu + 1)\},$$

These formulae are readily obtained from an approximate expansion of (15) for small $\chi^2$.

For $30 < \nu < 100$ Lagrangian interpolation at interval 10 is needed, and we give below the four-point Lagrangian coefficients required for integer $\nu$. The accuracy, to 4 or 5 figures, increases with $\nu$.

| Unit figure of $\nu$ | $L_{-10}$ | $L_0$ | $L_{10}$ | $L_{20}$ | Unit figure of $\nu$ |
|---|---|---|---|---|---|
| | $-$ | $+$ | $+$ | $-$ | |
| 0 | 0·0000 | 1·0000 | 0·0000 | 0·0000 | |
| 1 | 0·0285 | 0·9405 | 0·1045 | 0·0165 | 9 |
| 2 | 0·0480 | 0·8640 | 0·2160 | 0·0320 | 8 |
| 3 | 0·0595 | 0·7735 | 0·3315 | 0·0455 | 7 |
| 4 | 0·0640 | 0·6720 | 0·4480 | 0·0560 | 6 |
| 5 | 0·0625 | 0·5625 | 0·5625 | 0·0625 | 5 |
| | $-$ | $+$ | $+$ | $-$ | |
| | $L_{20}$ | $L_{10}$ | $L_0$ | $L_{-10}$ | |

\* For $\chi^2 \leqslant 1$, instead of interpolating $\nu$-wise in the table we may compute any required value of $Q(\chi^2 \mid \nu)$ directly from the series

$$Q(\chi^2 \mid \nu) = 1 - e^{-m} \sum_{j=0}^{\infty} \frac{m^{c+j}}{\Gamma(c + j + 1)},$$

where $c = \tfrac{1}{2}\nu$; this converges rapidly. A few values of the $\Gamma$-function for fractional arguments are required for its evaluation.

† As a rough approximation, we may use linear interpolation for $\chi^2$ with argument $\log Q$ or $\log(1 - Q) = \log P$, whichever is the smaller.

16

For $\nu > 100$ the percentage points of $\chi^2$ can be computed from either the Fisher or, for higher accuracy, from the cubic Wilson-Hilferty formula shown at the bottom of the table, the required normal percentage points $X$ being shown in the last tabular line.

## 4. MOMENTS OF THE DISTRIBUTION OF $s/\sigma = \chi/\sqrt{\nu}$ AND CONFIDENCE LIMITS FOR $\sigma$ (TABLE 35)*

### 4·1 *Definitions: the distribution of $s^2$ and $s$*

Since the sum of squares of $\nu$ independent unit normal deviates is distributed as $\chi^2$ (see § 3·1), it follows that if the sum of squares of $\nu$ independent normal deviates, each having a variance $\sigma^2$, is divided by $\nu$, a statistic is obtained which is distributed as $\chi^2\sigma^2/\nu$. Further, since the expectation of $\chi^2$ is $\nu$, the expectation of this statistic will be $\sigma^2$. This result, taken when necessary in conjunction with an orthogonal transformation of the variates, is used again and again in statistical theory to obtain estimates of unknown variances and to use these estimates in a variety of statistical tests. We shall here denote a statistic of this character by $s^2$ and shall speak of it as a mean square estimate† of $\sigma^2$, based on $\nu$ degrees of freedom.

As $s^2 = \chi^2\sigma^2/\nu$ and in view of the equation (15) giving the probability integral of $\chi^2$, it follows that the frequency function of $s^2$ has the form

$$f(s^2) = (\tfrac{1}{2}\nu)^{\frac{1}{2}\nu} \{\Gamma(\tfrac{1}{2}\nu)\}^{-1} \sigma^{-\nu}(s^2)^{\frac{1}{2}\nu-1} e^{-\frac{1}{2}\nu s^2/\sigma^2}. \tag{28}$$

While it is generally simpler, both from the mathematical and computational points of view, to work in terms of $s^2$, and therefore of $\chi^2$, there are certain problems, e.g. in connexion with Student's ratio, $t$, discussed below, in which it is more convenient to work with $s$ (or $\chi$). The frequency function of $s$ may be derived at once from (28), namely,

$$f(s) = 2(\tfrac{1}{2}\nu)^{\frac{1}{2}\nu} \{\Gamma(\tfrac{1}{2}\nu)\}^{-1} \sigma^{-\nu}s^{\nu-1} e^{-\frac{1}{2}\nu s^2/\sigma^2}. \tag{29}$$

Table 35 contains values of the expectation, the standard deviation and of the moment ratios $\beta_1 = \mu_3^2/\mu_2^3$ and $\beta_2 = \mu_4/\mu_2^2$ of $s/\sigma$. The moments about the mean cannot be expressed in any simple form, but have been calculated from the moments about zero, which are given by

$$\mu_r' = (2/\nu)^{\frac{1}{2}r} \frac{\Gamma\{\tfrac{1}{2}(\nu+r)\}}{\Gamma(\tfrac{1}{2}\nu)}. \tag{30}$$

The figures in cols. 7–10 of the table, used in the determination of confidence limits for $\sigma$, are defined in § 4·3.

### 4·2 *Applications of moments*

The expectation of $s$ is not, of course, equal to $\sigma$; col. 2 of Table 35 indicates the rate of approach of $\mathscr{E}(s/\sigma)$ to unity. If $s$ is divided by the appropriate factor taken from this column, then we have an unbiased estimator of $\sigma$, as distinct from $s^2$ which is an unbiased estimator of $\sigma^2$. Col. 4 of the table gives the ratio of col. 3, the standard deviation of $s/\sigma$, to $1/\sqrt{(2\nu)}$, and therefore shows the approach of the true standard error of $s$ to its large sample limit $\sigma/\sqrt{(2\nu)}$.

It should be noted that since s.d. of $\chi = \sqrt{\nu} \times$ s.d. of $(s/\sigma)$, the standard deviation of $\chi$ (with $\nu$ degrees of freedom) is obtained by multiplying the figures in col. 4 by $1/\sqrt{2} = 0·7071$. The figures in cols. 5 and 6 give an indication of the approach of the distributions of $s$ and $\chi$ to the normal.

A practical use of these results is illustrated below in §§ 12·6 and 12·7.

---

* In planning the arrangement of pages, it was found convenient to place this table as no. 35, rather late in the sequence of tables.

† To make its character quite clear it might alternatively be termed an unbiased $\chi^2$-estimate of $\sigma^2$.

## 4·3  *Confidence limits for a standard deviation*

The distribution of $\chi^2$ may be used to obtain what is termed an *interval estimate* for the unknown value of a population variance (or standard deviation). A rather fuller description of the principles underlying the theory of confidence intervals is given in § 22 below; a brief description of the derivation and use of the factors given in cols. 7–10 of Table 35 will be here sufficient.

Suppose that a random set of observations provides a mean square estimate, $s^2$, having $\nu$ degrees of freedom, of a population variance $\sigma^2$. Then $s^2$ is distributed as $\chi^2 \sigma^2 / \nu$. It follows that there is a probability, $\alpha$, that $s^2 > \chi_\alpha^2 \sigma^2 / \nu$ and a probability, $\alpha$, that $s^2 < \chi_{1-\alpha}^2 \sigma^2 / \nu$, where $\chi_\alpha^2$ and $\chi_{1-\alpha}^2$ are, respectively, the upper and lower $100\alpha \%$ points of the $\chi^2$ distribution for $\nu$ degrees of freedom, i.e. (using the notation of § 3·1*) where

$$1 - P(\chi_\alpha^2 \mid \nu) = \alpha = P(\chi_{1-\alpha}^2 \mid \nu).$$

These two probability statements are clearly equivalent to the following: there is a probability of $\alpha$ that $s \sqrt{\nu}/\chi_\alpha > \sigma$ and a probability of $\alpha$ that $s \sqrt{\nu}/\chi_{1-\alpha} < \sigma$. Since, for $\alpha < 0·5$, $\sqrt{\nu}/\chi_\alpha < \sqrt{\nu}/\chi_{1-\alpha}$, it follows that the probability is $1 - 2\alpha$ that the unknown $\sigma$ is included between the limits $s \sqrt{\nu}/\chi_\alpha$ and $s \sqrt{\nu}/\chi_{1-\alpha}$, or

$$\Pr \left\{ \frac{s \sqrt{\nu}}{\chi_\alpha} \leqslant \sigma \leqslant \frac{s \sqrt{\nu}}{\chi_{1-\alpha}} \right\} = 1 - 2\alpha. \tag{31}$$

It will be seen that the two limits are random variables whose values depend only on the observations; their position and distance apart will vary from one sampling to another. The probability statement must be interpreted in the sense that if we determine the limits for $\sigma$ from the observations by the formulae given above, we are following a procedure which will give in the long run an interval estimate including the true $\sigma$ in a proportion of about $1 - 2\alpha$ cases. Further, this statement is true even if the successive samples are drawn from populations having different standard deviations. The limits are termed *confidence limits* and $1 - 2\alpha$, often expressed as a percentage, is termed the *confidence coefficient*.

Table 35 gives in cols. 7–10 the factors $\sqrt{\nu}/\chi_\alpha$ and $\sqrt{\nu}/\chi_{1-\alpha}$, by which $s$ must be multiplied to obtain 'central' intervals, with $\alpha = 0·025$ and $0·005$ or $1 - 2\alpha = 0·95$ and $0·99$. These factors were computed from the appropriate percentage points of the $\chi^2$-distribution given in Table 8. Clearly considerable variety in the form of interval is possible; for example, we might use Table 8 to derive 'non-central' intervals based on $\chi_{\alpha_1}^2$, and $\chi_{1-\alpha_2}^2$, where $\alpha_1 \neq \alpha_2$, giving a confidence coefficient $1 - \alpha_1 - \alpha_2$.

In making use of these results it is essential to bear in mind two underlying assumptions; the probability statement associated with the interval is only valid if (*a*) the observed variables are approximately normally distributed and (*b*) the sampling is random, so that the frequency law for $s^2$ of equation (28) holds good.

## 4·4  *Application of confidence interval theory*

*Example* 5. The following (taken from E. S. Pearson, 1935*b*, p. 22) are breaking strengths in lb. of twelve strips of a certain cotton fabric:

$$
\begin{array}{cccccc}
163 & 175 & 161 & 154 & 166 & 174 \\
166 & 173 & 164 & 181 & 170 & 158
\end{array}
$$

---

\* Clearly in the notation of Table 8, $\chi_\alpha^2 = \chi^2(Q \mid \nu)$ for $Q = \alpha$.

Assuming that the figures represent random and independent observations of a normally distributed variable, determine the 95 and 99 % central confidence intervals for the population standard deviation.

It is found that

$$\Sigma x = 2005 \qquad \Sigma x^2 = 335669 \qquad \bar{x} = 167{\cdot}08\,\text{lb.}$$

$$\Sigma (x - \bar{x})^2 = 666{\cdot}92 \qquad s^2 = 60{\cdot}63 \qquad s = 7{\cdot}786\,\text{lb.}$$

Hence entering Table 35 with $\nu = 11$, we obtain

95 % confidence limits: $0{\cdot}708 \times 7{\cdot}79 = 5{\cdot}52$ lb. and

$1{\cdot}70 \ \times 7{\cdot}79 = 13{\cdot}2$ lb.

99 % confidence limits: $0{\cdot}641 \times 7{\cdot}79 = 4{\cdot}99$ lb. and

$2{\cdot}06 \ \times 7{\cdot}79 = 16{\cdot}0$ lb.

Thus in adopting this procedure, which in the present instance leads to the assertion that $5{\cdot}5 \leqslant \sigma \leqslant 13{\cdot}2$, we shall be correct in the long run in 95 % of cases. If we wish to reduce the risk of error, we must at the same time widen the interval; thus the statement $5{\cdot}0 \leqslant \sigma \leqslant 16{\cdot}0$ can be associated with a 99 % confidence coefficient.

## 5. The $t$-distribution (Tables 9, 10 and 12)

### 5·1 Definition

If (a) $y$ is a normally distributed variable with expectation zero and standard deviation $\sigma_y$, and (b) $s_y^2$ is a mean square estimate of $\sigma_y^2$ based on $\nu$ degrees of freedom* and independent of $y$, then the probability integral of the ratio

$$t = \frac{y}{s_y}$$

assumes the Student form

$$P(t \mid \nu) = \Gamma\{\tfrac{1}{2}(\nu + 1)\} \{\Gamma(\tfrac{1}{2}\nu)\}^{-1} (\nu\pi)^{-\frac{1}{2}} \int_{-\infty}^{t} \left(1 + \frac{u^2}{\nu}\right)^{-\frac{1}{2}(\nu+1)} du. \tag{32}$$

Clearly the $t$-distribution is symmetrical, so that if

$$Q(t \mid \nu) = 1 - P(t \mid \nu), \quad \text{then} \quad P(-t \mid \nu) = Q(t \mid \nu).$$

It will be noted that this integral depends only on $\nu$, the number of *degrees of freedom* of the estimate of $\sigma_y^2$.

Table 9 gives values of $P(t \mid \nu)$ for argument $t$ and $\nu$, while Table 12 is the corresponding table of percentage points, i.e. it gives the values of $t$ for certain conventional 'levels' of the integral.

### 5·2 Applications. The significance of a mean of a single sample

The $t$-distribution, with slightly different notation, was first derived by W. S. Gosset (Student) in 1908 to deal with the simple problem in which $y$ is the deviation of the mean, $\bar{x}$, of a random sample of $n$ normally distributed observations $x_1, x_2, \ldots, x_n$ from a population value $\mu$, and $s_y^2$ is the mean-square estimate of the variance of $\bar{x}$ obtained from the same sample. Thus

$$\left. \begin{array}{l} \bar{x} = \sum_i x_i/n, \quad s^2 = \sum_i (x_i - \bar{x})^2/(n - 1), \quad s_y^2 = s^2/n, \\[2mm] t = (\bar{x} - \mu)\sqrt{n}/s, \quad \nu = n - 1. \end{array} \right\} \tag{33}$$

* For a definition of such an estimate, see §4·1; $s_y^2$ will have the probability distribution of equation (28).

*Example* 6. Consider the twelve observations of breaking strength of cotton fabric used in Example 5, p. 18. We may ask whether these results are consistent with the hypothesis that the fabric sampled is one for which the average strength of strips tested in this way is $\mu = 171 \cdot 5$ lb. We have

$$\bar{x} = 167 \cdot 08 \text{ lb.}, \quad s = 7 \cdot 786 \text{ lb.}, \quad s/\sqrt{n} = 2 \cdot 248,$$

$$t = (167 \cdot 08 - 171 \cdot 5)/2 \cdot 248 = -1 \cdot 97, \quad \nu = 11.$$

Turning to Table 9, visual inspection shows that to 3-decimal accuracy $P(1 \cdot 97 \mid 11) = 0 \cdot 963$. The interpretation of this result depends to some extent on the nature of the problem investigated.

In carrying out the test of a given statistical hypothesis* we have in general two considerations to bear in mind. In the first place we do not want to run an undue risk of rejecting the hypothesis tested when it is true; in the second place we wish to use a form of test which provides as large a chance as possible of establishing the existence of that type of effect or change we think most likely to occur or regard it as most important not to overlook, if it is present. If, then, in the present illustration, we were on the look-out for a change in mean $\mu$, in either direction from $171 \cdot 5$ lb., we should regard large positive and negative values of $t$ as significant, and it would be appropriate to use the $t$-test in its symmetrical or double-tail form. Thus we should note that

$$\Pr\{|t| > 1 \cdot 97 \mid \nu = 11\} = 2 \times 0 \cdot 037 = 0 \cdot 074.\dagger$$

Thus as large a departure ($+$ or $-$) in $\bar{x}$ from $\mu = 171 \cdot 5$ (expressed in terms of the estimated standard error derived from the data) would occur through chance about once in every thirteen or fourteen samples. The discrepancy is therefore hardly significant.

If, however, as seems likely in the present illustration, we are only concerned with a change in mean in one direction, i.e. here, in a fall in average strength, we should only want to know whether a large negative value of $t$ was statistically significant. We should therefore use the asymmetrical or single-tail form of the test and note that

$$\Pr\{t < -1 \cdot 97 \mid \nu = 11\} = 0 \cdot 037.$$

Thus we should regard the difference between $\bar{x} = 167 \cdot 08$ and $\mu = 171 \cdot 5$ as of greater significance than in the first situation.

It is common practice not to determine a precise value for $P(t \mid \nu)$, but to base conclusions on whether $|t|$ or $t$ falls beyond a pre-selected *significance point*, chosen according to the risk the statistician is prepared to accept of rejecting the hypothesis tested when it is in fact true. Thus if his practice is to note for further investigation any result for which the appropriate test statistic falls beyond its 5 % significance point, he will refer the value $t = 1 \cdot 97$ to Table 12. Here he will find that, when $\nu = 11$, for the double-tail test the 5 % point for $t$ is $2 \cdot 201$ and for the single-tail test it is $1 \cdot 796$. Thus if he is looking for a change in mean in either direction, he will find that $t$ is not significant at the 5 % level; but if he is interested in a decrease in mean only, the result is significant at this level.

---

\* In this case where we ask whether $\mu - 171 \cdot 5 = 0$, it may appropriately be termed a *null hypothesis*.

† It is convenient to use this form of summary statement in place of the longer sentence: the probability that the numerical value of $t$ is greater than $1 \cdot 97$ (when the degrees of freedom of the variance estimate is 11) equals $0 \cdot 074$.

### 5·3   *The difference in the means of two samples*

Probably the most common application of the $t$-test occurs when two independent samples are available and, while we believe that the observations are subject to a common variance $\sigma^2$ and are approximately normally distributed, we are on the look-out for a possible difference in the means. Thus if we have:

| | No. of observations | Mean | Sum of squares |
|---|---|---|---|
| 1st sample, $x_{11}, x_{12}, \ldots, x_{1n_1}$. | $n_1$ | $\bar{x}_1$ | $\sum\limits_{i=1}^{n_1} (x_{1i} - \bar{x}_1)^2$ |
| 2nd sample, $x_{21}, x_{22}, \ldots, x_{2n_2}$. | $n_2$ | $\bar{x}_2$ | $\sum\limits_{i=1}^{n_2} (x_{2i} - \bar{x}_2)^2$ |

the parts of $y$ and $\sigma_y^2$ of § 5·1 will be played by $\bar{x}_1 - \bar{x}_2$ and $\sigma^2(1/n_1 + 1/n_2)$, where $\sigma^2$ is the assumed common variance of $x$ in the two populations. $\sigma^2$ will now be estimated from the pooled sum of squares, i.e. by

$$s^2 = \left\{ \sum_{i=1}^{n_1} (x_{1i} - \bar{x}_1)^2 + \sum_{i=1}^{n_2} (x_{2i} - \bar{x}_2)^2 \right\} \bigg/ (n_1 + n_2 - 2), \tag{34}$$

which is a mean-square estimate of the common variance based on $n_1 + n_2 - 2$ degrees of freedom. It follows that

$$t = (\bar{x}_1 - \bar{x}_2) \bigg/ \left\{ s \sqrt{\left( \frac{1}{n_1} + \frac{1}{n_2} \right)} \right\} \tag{35}$$

will be distributed as Student's $t$, i.e. will have $P(t \mid \nu)$, with $\nu = n_1 + n_2 - 2$, for its probability integral, if the populations sampled have a common mean. The test may again be used in double- or single-tail form according to the problem investigated.

### 5·4   *Application of the t-distribution in regression problems*

The distribution is also applied in a number of regression problems. Suppose, for example, that we have a sample of $n$ paired observations $(x_i, y_i)$ and may assume that $y_i$ is distributed normally about a mean of $\alpha + \beta x_i$ with variance $\sigma^2$, independent of $x_i$. Then an estimate of $\beta$ is obtained from the sample regression coefficient

$$b = \sum_{i=1}^{n} (y_i - \bar{y})(x_i - \bar{x}) \bigg/ \sum_{i=1}^{n} (x_i - \bar{x})^2.$$

If the $x_i$ are regarded as fixed, the $y_i$ alone varying from sample to sample, $b$ is then a weighted linear function of the normal $y_i$ and is itself normally distributed about a mean of $\beta$ with variance $\sigma^2 / \sum\limits_{i} (x_i - \bar{x})^2$. $\sigma^2$ may be independently estimated from the residual sum of squares about the sample regression line, i.e. by

$$s^2 = \frac{\sum\limits_{i} (y_i - \bar{y})^2 - b^2 \sum\limits_{i} (x_i - \bar{x})^2}{n - 2},$$

where $s^2$ has the frequency function $f(s^2)$ of equation (28) with $\nu = n - 2$. It follows that

$$t = (b - \beta) \sqrt{\{ \sum_{i} (x_i - \bar{x})^2 \}} / s$$

is distributed as the Student ratio with $\nu = n - 2$. The application to a test of significance or to an interval estimate for $\beta$ follows at once.

Since the distribution of $t$ is a function of $\nu$ only, being independent of the particular values of $x_i$, the restriction of fixed $x$-values can be removed.

A natural extension of the theory is made in the case of two independent samples of $n_1$ and $n_2$ paired observations, which provide estimates of regression, $b_1$ and $b_2$. The estimate of the assumed common array variance of the $y$'s is now obtained from the pooled sums of squares of the residuals from the two fitted regression lines, the degrees of freedom of this estimate, $s^2$, being now $\nu = n_1 + n_2 - 4$. If the regression coefficient $\beta$ is the same in both populations sampled, then

$$t = \frac{b_1 - b_2}{s\sqrt{\left(1 \bigg/ \sum\limits_{i=1}^{n_1}(x_{1i} - \bar{x}_1)^2 + 1 \bigg/ \sum\limits_{i=1}^{n_2}(x_{2i} - \bar{x}_2)^2\right)}}$$

will follow Student's distribution.

Numerous other applications of the $t$-test follow from the simple basis of the fundamental distribution, namely, that it is the distribution of the ratio of a normal deviate to an independent root-mean-square estimate of its standard deviation.

## 5·5   Confidence limits for a mean

Apart from its use in tests of significance, the $t$-distribution may be used to obtain an *interval estimate* for an unknown population mean $\mu$, for the difference between two means $\mu_1 - \mu_2$, for the difference between two regression coefficients, etc.

The argument is similar to that used in deriving confidence limits for $\sigma$ (see §4·3), this time inverting the probability statement regarding Student's ratio $t$. Thus if a random sample of $n$ observations $x_1, x_2, \ldots, x_n$ is drawn from a normal population with mean $\mu$, if $\bar{x}$ is the sample mean and if $s^2 = \sum\limits_i (x_i - \bar{x})^2/(n-1)$, then the probability is $\alpha$ that

$$\mu_A = \bar{x} - t_\alpha s/\sqrt{n} \geqslant \mu.$$

Similarly, it is $\alpha$ that     $\mu_B = \bar{x} + t_\alpha s/\sqrt{n} \leqslant \mu,$
where $t_\alpha$ is the value of $t$ satisfying

$$Q(t_\alpha \mid n-1) = 1 - P(t_\alpha \mid n-1) = \alpha,$$

i.e. $t_\alpha$ is the $100\alpha\%$ point of $t$ for $\nu = n-1$ degrees of freedom. Further, it follows that there is a probability of $1 - 2\alpha$ that the population mean $\mu$ is included between the limits $\mu_A$ and $\mu_B$ which are random variables, depending on the sample $x$-values above. $\mu_A$ and $\mu_B$ are the *confidence limits* and $1 - 2\alpha$ the *confidence coefficient*.

*Example* 7. Let us suppose we have the sample of twelve observations used in Examples 5 and 6, pp. 18, 20. Take $\alpha = 0\cdot025$; Table 12 shows that if $Q(t_\alpha \mid 11) = 0\cdot025$, $t_\alpha = 2\cdot201$. Then

$$\mu_A = 167\cdot08 - 2\cdot201 \times 2\cdot248 = 162\cdot1,$$

$$\mu_B = 167\cdot08 + 2\cdot201 \times 2\cdot248 = 172\cdot0.$$

Thus we say that there is a probability of $1 - 2\alpha = 0\cdot95$ that the limits $162\cdot1$ and $172\cdot0$ lb. include the unknown population mean. The interval will of course vary in length and position from sample to sample, and the probability statement must be interpreted as meaning that if we determine $\mu_A$ and $\mu_B$ from a sample as indicated, we are following a procedure which will give an interval including the true mean in the long run in about nineteen cases out of twenty.

## (a) *Single-entry interpolation for t*

Since no differences are provided in the table, a brief discussion of Lagrangian interpolation formulae is appropriate. Let $t_{-1}$, $t_0$, $t_1$ denote three consecutive tabular arguments such that $t_0 \leqslant t \leqslant t_1$, and let
$$P_i = P(t_i \mid \nu), \quad \theta = (t - t_0)/(t_1 - t_0).$$

Then we have the following formulae:

$$
\begin{aligned}
\text{(linear)} \quad & P(t \mid \nu) \sim P_0(1 - \theta) + P_1\theta, \\
\text{(three-point)} \quad & P(t \mid \nu) = P_{-1}(\tfrac{1}{2}\theta^2 - \tfrac{1}{2}\theta) + P_0(1 - \theta^2) + P_1(\tfrac{1}{2}\theta^2 + \tfrac{1}{2}\theta).
\end{aligned}
\tag{36}
$$

The three-point formula (36) gives 5-decimal accuracy for $\nu \geqslant 20$. For $\nu \leqslant 20$ the maximum error is about (a) $10^{-5}$ for $t \geqslant 0\cdot7$ and (b) $4 \times 10^{-5}$ for $0 \leqslant t \leqslant 0\cdot7$. To obtain 5-decimal accuracy throughout, use (36) and repeat the computation with $\theta$ replaced by $(1 - \theta)$ and $P_2$, $P_1$ and $P_0$ substituted for $P_{-1}$, $P_0$ and $P_1$, respectively. Compare the two answers as a check on the calculations: if they agree to 4 decimals, their average should yield an interpolate accurate to 5 and checked to 4 decimals.

The accuracy of the linear formula depends on the argument range as follows: For $1 \leqslant \nu \leqslant 20$, $0 < t < 4$, the maximum error is three units in the fourth decimal; for $1 \leqslant \nu \leqslant 20$, $4 < t$, it is four units in the fifth decimal; for $20 \leqslant \nu < \infty$, $0 < t < 2$, it is eight units in the fifth decimal and for $20 \leqslant \nu \leqslant \infty$, $2 < t$, it is twelve units in the fifth decimal.

## (b) *Single-entry interpolation for integer ν*

For intermediate integers, $\nu > 20$, linear harmonic interpolation with argument $120/\nu$ will yield interpolates accurate to one unit in the fifth decimal.

## (c) *Double-entry interpolation*

Interpolation to fractional $\nu$ may sometimes be required, as, for instance, when using the table to compute the probability integral of the general Pearson Type VII frequency curve

$$f(x) = \frac{\Gamma(m)}{a \sqrt{\pi}\, \Gamma(m - \tfrac{1}{2})} \left(1 + \frac{x^2}{a^2}\right)^{-m}$$

Here we can obtain $\int_{-\infty}^{x} f(x)\, dx$ by entering the present table with $\nu = 2m - 1$, $t = x \sqrt{\nu}/a$, and double-entry interpolation becomes necessary. For most practical purposes double-linear interpolation will be adequate.

Let $4 \leqslant \nu = 2m - 1 \leqslant 24$, and let $\nu_0$ and $\nu_1$ denote two consecutive tabular $\nu$ such that $\nu_0 \leqslant \nu \leqslant \nu_1$. Then compute $\phi = \nu - \nu_0$, $\theta$ as defined above and $\theta\phi$. The interpolate is

$$P(t \mid \nu) = P_{00}(1 - \theta - \phi + \theta\phi) + P_{10}(\theta - \theta\phi) + P_{01}(\phi - \theta\phi) + P_{11}\theta\phi, \tag{37}$$

where $P_{ij} = P(t_i \mid \nu_j)$. If $\nu > 24$ the same formula may be used, defining $\phi$ harmonically by $\phi = 120(\nu_1 - \nu)/(\nu_1\nu)$ and interchanging $\nu_0$ and $\nu_1$ in (37). If $\nu < 4$ it may be preferable to obtain $P(t \mid \nu)$ directly by numerical quadrature.

## (d) *Values outside range of Table 9*

In Table 9 the slowly convergent tail of the $t$-distribution for small $\nu$ has been sacrificed in order to keep the tabular $t$-interval uniform for all $\nu$ below 20. To cover the tail region, a few

---

\* Linear interpolation in Table 12, using $\log Q$ as argument, will give approximate values for $t$ at intermediate probability levels (see Simaika, 1942, p. 271).

landmarks are provided at the bottom of the second page of Table 9 in the form of percentage points. Other values may be readily obtained from the approximate formula

$$1 - P(t \mid \nu) = c_\nu t^{-\nu}, \tag{38}$$

with the $c_\nu$ given below:

| $\nu$ | 1 | 2 | 3 | 4 | 5 | 6 | 7 |
|---|---|---|---|---|---|---|---|
| $c_\nu$ | 0·317 | 0·488 | 1·04 | 2·7 | 8·2 | 26 | 84 |

For $\nu = 1$, only four accurate decimals are given by (38), but since

$$P(t \mid 1) = \tfrac{1}{2} + (\tan^{-1} t)/\pi,$$

more accurate values can be obtained from tables of the inverse tangent if required. Where the table terminates before the bottom of a column is reached, the entry in the first blank space is 1·00000 to 5-decimal accuracy.

### 5·7   *The power of the t-test; definition of the concept (Table 10)*

The chart of Table 10 is arranged to answer questions of the following type. If the $t$-test is applied at a specified level of significance, say at the 5 % level,

(a) for a fixed size of sample, what is the probability that the test will establish a given effect as significant, or

(b) how large a sample is required in order that the odds may be, say, 99 to 1 on establishing the significance of this effect?

The solution depends on the distribution of a *non-central* Student ratio,

$$t' = (y + \Delta)/s_y = y'/s_y,$$

where $y$ and $s_y$ are defined as before and $\Delta$ is a parameter representing the degree of non-centrality. For example, in the application discussed in §5·3, $\Delta$ would be the difference between the true means of the populations from which the two samples have been drawn. It may be shown that the distribution of $t'$ depends only on $\nu$, the degrees of freedom of the variance estimate $s_y^2$ and on the ratio $\Delta/\sigma_y$. For discussion of the distribution of $t'$ and for references to other available tables see Johnson & Welch (1940), Greenwood & Hartley (1962).

If we write $f(t' \mid \nu, \Delta/\sigma_y)$ as the frequency function of $t'$, then answers to the questions raised above require a knowledge of the following integrals:

(i) For the double-tail $t$-test,

$$\int_{-\infty}^{-t_{\frac{1}{2}\alpha}} f(t' \mid \nu, \Delta/\sigma_y)\, dt' + \int_{t_{\frac{1}{2}\alpha}}^{\infty} f(t' \mid \nu, \Delta/\sigma_y)\, dt'. \tag{39}$$

(ii) For the single-tail $t$-test (with $\Delta \geqslant 0$)

$$\int_{t_\alpha}^{\infty} f(t' \mid \nu, \Delta/\sigma_y)\, dt', \tag{40}$$

where $Q(t_\alpha \mid \nu) = \alpha$ defines the significance point for $t$ used in the test. The value of the integral, (39) or (40), considered as a function of $\Delta/\sigma_y$ provides the *power function* of the corresponding test.

The chart shows on a logarithmic scale the integral (39) for $\alpha = 0·05$ and $0·01$. The horizontal scale is in terms of $\phi = \Delta/\sigma_y \times 1/\sqrt{2}$.* The degrees of freedom associated with $s_y$ are denoted by $\nu$, and separate curves are shown for $\nu = 6\,(1)\,10$ and afterwards for values at the harmonic

---

* This chart forms one of a series of 8 charts, already published, constructed for the more general problem of analysis of variance tests, where the $\phi$-notation was more appropriate (see Pearson & Hartley, 1951).

intervals 12, 15, 20, 30, 60 and $\infty$. The limiting case with $\nu = \infty$ corresponds to the situation where the value of $\sigma_y$ is known and the distributions of both $t$ and of $t'$ are normal curves.

Since the first of the two integrals in (39) becomes rapidly negligible as $\Delta/\sigma_y$ increases above zero (and similarly for the second term as $\Delta/\sigma_y$ decreases below zero), it follows that the chart can also be used to give the integral (40) associated with the single-tail $t$-test for significance levels $\alpha = 0.025$ and $0.005$.

### 5·8   *Illustration of the use of the power chart*

*Example* 8. Consideration is being given to an experiment in which the effect of two treatments $A$ and $B$ on a variable characteristic $x$ are to be compared. It is believed that $x$ is roughly normally distributed and that the variance $\sigma^2$ among the individuals will be the same for either treatment, but it is possible that the mean values of the character, $\mu_A$ and $\mu_B$, will differ in the two cases. It is further held that the experiment should be planned on a sufficient scale to detect any real difference $|\mu_A - \mu_B|$ which exceeds $2\sigma$. Supposing each treatment is applied to an equal number of individuals, $n$, how large should $n$ be? In putting the question in this way, it is realized that the precise value of $\sigma$ is not known, so that the variance must be estimated from the experimental results and the $t$-test used. However, it will generally be the case that experience has given a rough lead on the value of $\sigma$, so that the experimenter can specify broadly at what multiple of $\sigma$ the difference $|\mu_A - \mu_B|$ would become of practical significance.

To come to grips with the problem, the statistician must be prepared to assign to the risks involved some numerical values which, though somewhat arbitrary, will help him to explore the position. Suppose, then, that he asks how large the sample sizes $n$ must be so that, using the 5 % level to judge significance of $t$ (double-tail test, $\alpha = 0.05$), the chance of establishing significance if $|\mu_A - \mu_B|/\sigma \geqslant 2$ is at least $0.98$. The test will be based on the expression for $t$ of equations (34) and (35) with $n_1 = n_2 = n$ and $\nu = 2(n-1)$.

We must first consider the form assumed by $\Delta/\sigma_y$. In this case $\sigma_y$ is the standard error of the difference in sample means $\bar{x}_1 - \bar{x}_2$, i.e. $\sigma_y = \sigma \sqrt{(2/n)}$, so that

$$\phi = \frac{\Delta}{\sigma_y} \frac{1}{\sqrt{2}} = \tfrac{1}{2} \sqrt{n} \frac{\mu_A - \mu_B}{\sigma}.$$

We have therefore to find the value of $n$ just large enough to make $\phi = \sqrt{n}$ exceed the value needed to give a $0.98$ chance of establishing significance when $\nu = 2(n-1)$. The table below gives the relevant information, where the critical values of $\phi$ are the abscissae of the points on the chart where the members of the family of curves with $\nu = 10, 12, 15$ and $20$ and $\alpha = 0.05$ cut the horizontal grid drawn at $\beta = 0.98$:

| $\nu = 2(n-1)$ | 10 | 12 | 15 | 20 |
|---|---|---|---|---|
| $n = \tfrac{1}{2}\nu + 1$ | 6 | 7 | 8·5 | 11 |
| $\sqrt{n}$ | 2·45 | 2·65 | 2·92 | 3·32 |
| Critical $\phi$ | 3·16 | 3·10 | 3·04 | 2·98 |

From a rough plot, it will be seen that the cross-over occurs very nearly at $n = 9$, so that we may conclude that with two samples of nine observations the chance would be at least $0.98$ of establishing a difference of $|\mu_A - \mu_B| \geqslant 2\sigma$ as significant at the 5 % level.

## 6. TEST FOR COMPARISONS INVOLVING TWO VARIANCES, WHICH MUST BE SEPARATELY ESTIMATED (TABLE 11)

### 6·1 *Definition*

In order that $s_y^2$, the estimate of the variance of $y$ used in the Student ratio, should have the frequency function of equation (28), it is essential that it should be based on the sum of squares of $\nu$ independent normal deviates, all having a common variance. Thus in the two sample comparisons discussed in § 5·3, it was necessary that the variance of $x$ should be the same, or approximately so, in both populations sampled.

It will sometimes happen, however, that the variance of $y$ cannot be simply estimated in this way. Thus two samples may have been drawn from normal populations with standard deviations $\sigma_1$ and $\sigma_2$, where the ratio $\sigma_1/\sigma_2$ is unknown and thought likely to differ considerably from unity. In this case the sampling variance of $\bar{x}_1 - \bar{x}_2$ is $\sigma_1^2/n_1 + \sigma_2^2/n_2$ and not $\sigma^2(1/n_1 + 1/n_2)$. This variance may be estimated from $s_1^2/n_1 + s_2^2/n_2$, where

$$s_j^2 = \sum_{i=1}^{n_j} \frac{(x_{ji} - \bar{x}_j)^2}{n_j - 1} \quad (j = 1, 2),$$

but this estimator no longer has the sampling distribution of equation (28), although $s_1^2$ and $s_2^2$, separately, will still follow this law.

R. A. Fisher (following Behrens) has proposed a test for the equality of the population means for use in this situation and tables have been computed by P. V. Sukhatme (see Fisher & Yates, 1963, Tables VI and VI 1). This work, however, involves the use of an argument which is not universally accepted by statisticians. One of the consequences of the use of the Fisher-Behrens test is that, if the null hypothesis is true, the probability (in the usual direct sense) of rejecting it will not equal the figure specified as the level of significance. Fisher, indeed, does not consider this to be a drawback. It should be noted, however, that the table given in the present volume is not related to the Fisher-Behrens test in any way. It is the result of an attempt to produce a test which *does* satisfy the condition that the probability of rejection of the hypothesis tested (or of the truth of a confidence statement) will be equal to a specified figure. The theory of this test is due to B. L. Welch (1947) and the table is computed by A. A. Aspin, W. H. Trickett, B. L. Welch and G. S. James.

The test is applicable to a more general situation than the comparison of two sample means. Let $y$ be a normally distributed variable with expectation $\eta$, and suppose that the sampling variance of $y$ is of the form $\lambda_1 \sigma_1^2 + \lambda_2 \sigma_2^2$, where

(*a*) $\lambda_1$ and $\lambda_2$ are known positive constants,

(*b*) $\sigma_1^2$ and $\sigma_2^2$ can be estimated independently by statistics $s_1^2$ and $s_2^2$, with degrees of freedom $\nu_1$ and $\nu_2$, which have frequency functions given by equation (28), and are independent of each other and of $y$.

Then the table gives, for four probability levels, critical values of the ratio

$$v = (y - \eta)/(\lambda_1 s_1^2 + \lambda_2 s_2^2)^{\frac{1}{2}}. \tag{41}$$

The nature of the problem and its solution is such that the critical levels for $v$ cannot be fixed independently of all sample statistics. They are in fact functions of (i) $\nu_1$ and $\nu_2$, (ii) the significance level $\alpha$ and (iii) the ratio of the observed sample variances, which may be conveniently expressed in the form

$$c = \lambda_1 s_1^2/(\lambda_1 s_1^2 + \lambda_2 s_2^2). \tag{42}$$

26

The quantity tabled may therefore be written as $V(c; \nu_1, \nu_2, \alpha)$ and has the property that

$$\Pr\{v \geqslant V(c; \nu_1, \nu_2, \alpha)\} = \alpha,$$

whatever may be the value of the unknown population variances $\sigma_1^2$ and $\sigma_2^2$. The reference set in which probabilities are calculated is that of the totality of possible samples with $y$, $s_1^2$ and $s_2^2$ all free to vary. The numerical values in the table are not therefore comparable with any which may be derived from other probability interpretations.

Four probability levels are given for the single-tail test, namely for $\alpha = 0.05$, $0.025$, $0.01$ and $0.005$. For the double-tail test, $\Pr\{|v| \geqslant V(c; \nu_1, \nu_2, \alpha)\} = 2\alpha$. Although the values of $V$ have been rounded off to 2 decimal places, the probability of $v$ exceeding the tabled value will practically always equal $\alpha$ to 3 decimal places for $\alpha = 0.05$ and $0.025$ and to 4 decimal places for $\alpha = 0.01$ and $0.005$.

Linear interpolation is adequate everywhere except, for each $\nu$, in the panel which includes $\nu = \infty$; here harmonic linear interpolation with $20/\nu$ or $30/\nu$ as argument will be required.

The method of computation described by Welch does not, in general, provide two decimal place accuracy in $V(c; \nu_1, \nu_2, \alpha)$ for degrees of freedom smaller than those shown in the table. As is seen, this limitation is more severe the smaller $\alpha$.

### 6·2  Application of Table 11

*Example* 9. A useful application occurs in the case already discussed of the test of significance of the difference between two means, when the population variances cannot be assumed equal. If the population means are $\mu_1$ and $\mu_2$, set $\eta = \mu_1 - \mu_2$ while $y = \bar{x}_1 - \bar{x}_2$. Then

$$\lambda = 1/n_1, \quad \lambda_2 = 1/n_2,$$

$$v = \frac{(\bar{x}_1 - \bar{x}_2) - (\mu_1 - \mu_2)}{(s_1^2/n_1 + s_2^2/n_2)^{\frac{1}{2}}}, \qquad c = \frac{s_1^2/n_1}{s_1^2/n_1 + s_2^2/n_2}, \quad \nu_1 = n_1 - 1, \quad \nu_2 = n_2 - 1.$$

The tables may then be used to make inferences regarding $\mu_1 - \mu_2$. Thus if $n_1 = 10$, $n_2 = 15$, $\bar{x}_1 = 73.4$, $\bar{x}_2 = 47.1$, $s_1^2 = 51$, $s_2^2 = 141$, we shall have

$$v = \frac{26.3 - (\mu_1 - \mu_2)}{3.81}, \qquad c = 0.352, \quad \nu_1 = 9, \quad \nu_2 = 14.$$

From the tables $\qquad V(c; \nu_1, \nu_2, \alpha) = V(0.352; 9, 14, 0.05) = 1.71.$

If it were a matter of testing the consistency of the data with the hypothesis that $\mu_1 = \mu_2$, we should have $v = 26.3/3.81 = 6.90$, which is clearly far beyond the tabled 5 % point.

In obtaining an *interval estimate* for $\mu_1 - \mu_2$ we should note that in the above description of the tables we have been dealing explicitly with single-tail probabilities. The chance that $v$ exceeds the tabled value *numerically*, either in the positive or negative direction, is $2\alpha$. Thus in the sense of confidence interval theory, (see §§ 4·3, 5·5)

$$\Pr\{-1.71 \leqslant [26.3 - (\mu_1 - \mu_2)]/3.81 \leqslant 1.71\} = 1 - 2\alpha = 0.90,$$

i.e. $\qquad\qquad\qquad \Pr\{19.8 \leqslant \mu_1 - \mu_2 \leqslant 32.8\} = 0.90,$

so that the 90 % confidence limits for $\mu_1 - \mu_2$ are 19·8 and 32·8.

The tables may also be used for the comparison of two regression coefficients, where the array distributions in the two populations are normal and homoscedastic, but the two within-array variances are thought likely to be unequal.

## 7. THE CORRELATION COEFFICIENT IN NORMAL SAMPLES
### (TABLES 13, 14 AND 15)

#### 7·1  *Definitions and tables*

The bivariate normal distribution law has the form

$$f(x,y) = [2\pi\sigma_x\sigma_y \sqrt{(1-\rho^2)}]^{-1} \exp\left\{-\frac{1}{2(1-\rho^2)}\left[\left(\frac{x-\mu_x}{\sigma_x}\right)^2 - 2\rho\left(\frac{x-\mu_x}{\sigma_x}\right)\left(\frac{y-\mu_y}{\sigma_y}\right) + \left(\frac{y-\mu_y}{\sigma_y}\right)^2\right]\right\}.$$

(43)

It depends on five parameters: the means of $x$ and $y$, $\mu_x$ and $\mu_y$; the standard deviations of $x$ and $y$, $\sigma_x$ and $\sigma_y$; the coefficient of correlation, $\rho$. Given that this law holds, the intensity of the relationship between $x$ and $y$ is thus completely specified by the single parameter $\rho$.

If $x_i$, $y_i$ $(i = 1, 2, ..., n)$ denote a random sample of $n$ paired observations from (43), then $\rho$ may be estimated from the sample product-moment correlation coefficient $r$, defined by

$$r = \frac{\sum_i (x_i - \bar{x})(y_i - \bar{y})}{\{\sum_i (x_i - \bar{x})^2 \cdot \sum_i (y_i - \bar{y})^2\}^{\frac{1}{2}}},$$

where $\bar{x}$ and $\bar{y}$ are the mean values of $x$ and $y$ in the sample.

The frequency function of $r$, which clearly depends on $\rho$ and $n$ only, was first derived by R. A. Fisher (1915) and is given by

$$f(r \mid n, \rho) = \frac{(1-\rho^2)^{\frac{1}{2}(n-1)}}{\pi(n-3)!} (1-r^2)^{\frac{1}{2}(n-4)} \frac{d^{n-2}}{d(r\rho)^{n-2}} \left(\frac{\cos^{-1}(-r\rho)}{\sqrt{(1-r^2\rho^2)}}\right).$$

(44)

Tables of this function and of its probability integral were computed by F. N. David (1938), for $\rho = 0 \cdot 0\,(0 \cdot 1)\,0 \cdot 9$ and $n = 3\,(1)\,25, 50, 100, 200, 400$. The present volume contains three tables which will be found useful in handling some, if not all, aspects of the correlation problem.

#### (a) *Charts of Table* 15

If we write
$$P(r \mid n, \rho) = \int_{-1}^{r} f(u \mid n, \rho)\, du$$

for the probability integral of the distribution (44), Table 15 shows in graphical form the roots $\rho_A$ and $\rho_B$ $(> \rho_A)$ of

$$\alpha = P(r \mid n, \rho_B) \quad \text{and} \quad 1 - \alpha = P(r \mid n, \rho_A),$$

plotted against $r$ for a number of selected sample sizes $n$. These graphs are assembled in two charts, taken from David's 1938 Tables, corresponding to $\alpha = 0 \cdot 025$ and $0 \cdot 005$.

#### (b) *Percentage points of the distribution* $f(r \mid n, \rho = 0)$ *(Table* 13)

In the special case, $\rho = 0$, we have from (44)

$$f(r \mid n, 0) = \frac{\Gamma(\frac{1}{2}n - \frac{1}{2})}{\sqrt{\pi}\,\Gamma(\frac{1}{2}n - 1)} (1-r^2)^{\frac{1}{2}(n-4)},$$

(45)

which can be transformed into the distribution of $t$ (§ 5·1) for $\nu = n - 2$ degrees of freedom, through the relation
$$r^2 = t^2/(\nu + t^2).$$

(46)

Table 13 gives the percentage points of the distribution (45); alternatively, these could be calculated from the percentage points of $t$ (Table 12) by means of (46).

The distribution (45) has a variance of $1/(n-1)$, and it tends fairly rapidly to the normal form as $n$ increases.

*(c)  Table to assist the application of Fisher's z-transformation (Table* 14)

In order to deal with the general distribution (44), Fisher (1921*a*) introduced the transformation

$$z = \tfrac{1}{2}\log_e \frac{1+r}{1-r} = \tanh^{-1} r, \quad \zeta = \tanh^{-1}\rho, \tag{47}$$

and showed that the moments of $z$ could be expanded in series of inverse powers of $n-1$. These expressions are as follows:*

$$
\left.
\begin{aligned}
\text{Mean } z &= \zeta + \frac{\rho}{2(n-1)}\left\{1 + \frac{5+\rho^2}{4(n-1)} + \cdots\right\}, \\
\mu_2(z) &= \frac{1}{n-1}\left\{1 + \frac{4-\rho^2}{2(n-1)} + \frac{22-6\rho^2-3\rho^4}{6(n-1)^2} + \cdots\right\}, \\
\beta_1(z) &= \frac{\mu_3^2}{\mu_2^3} = \frac{\rho^6}{(n-1)^3} + \cdots, \\
\beta_2(z) &= \frac{\mu_4}{\mu_2^2} = 3 + \frac{2}{n-1} + \frac{4+2\rho^2-3\rho^4}{(n-1)^2} + \cdots.
\end{aligned}
\right\} \tag{48}
$$

From these results he concluded that $z$ could be regarded as approximately normally distributed about a mean of $\zeta = \tanh^{-1}\rho$, with variance $1/(n-3)$. This approximation has been shown to be remarkably effective, the greatest error, which can in some situations be allowed for, arising from the neglect of the term $\tfrac{1}{2}\rho/(n-1)$ in the expression for mean $z$.

The function $z = \tanh^{-1} r$ is given in Table 14; with its help certain tests regarding correlation coefficients can be reduced to familiar tests based on the normal distribution. Methods for interpolation in the table are given at the foot. These may result in errors of a unit in the last figure.

### 7·2    *Applications. Tests regarding the correlation in a single sample*

*Example* 10*a*. In a sample of twenty-five pairs of normally correlated observations, $(x, y)$, a correlation of $r = 0.65$ was found. Is this result consistent with a population correlation coefficient of $\rho = 0.5$?

We find from Table 14 that $z = 0.775$, $\zeta = 0.549$, and therefore the question asked is equivalent to the following: can

$$X = (z-\zeta)\sqrt{(n-3)} = (0.775 - 0.549)\sqrt{22} = 1.06$$

be reasonably regarded as a random normal deviate, having unit standard deviation? Clearly this is so, and the observed result is consistent with the hypothesis. It will be noted that if we introduced the second term in the series for mean $z$ (see equations (48)), namely,

$$\tfrac{1}{2}\rho/(n-1) = \tfrac{1}{2}\,0.50/24 = 0.010,$$

the conclusion would not be altered.

We may also deal with this question by reference to the charts of Table 15. The first of these shows that for $n = 25$ and $\rho = 0.5$ the upper $2.5\%$ level for $r$ lies at about $0.75$, well beyond the observed $r = 0.65$.

The significance points for the special case $\rho = 0$, given in Table 13, are of particular importance, as they enable us to judge whether an observed sample correlation is or is not indicative of any real correlation in the population. For medium and large samples we may test this result

---

* The equations (48) are those given by Gayen (1951), who found that an error in one of Fisher's original formulae (1921*a*, first equation on p. 13) made certain corrections to the moment expansions necessary.

by dividing the observed $r$ by $1/\sqrt{(n-1)}$, its standard error on the assumption that $\rho = 0$ and referring to the normal probability scale, i.e. by asking whether $r\sqrt{(n-1)}$ can be regarded as a unit normal deviate. For small samples, Table 13 provides an immediate and more precise answer.

*Example* 10*b*. We may ask whether the correlation of $r = 0.65$ referred to above is clearly indicative of a real correlation in the population sampled, when the sample consists of only twenty-five observations. We see at once from Table 13, using the double-tail test for $\nu = n - 2 = 23$, that the observed $r$ falls beyond even the $0.1\%$ point which lies at $0.62$. The correlation is, therefore, clearly significant.

### 7·3   *Confidence limits for $\rho$*

The charts of Table 15 may be used to derive an *interval estimate* for $\rho$ from a sample value of $r$. The probability argument will follow the lines already used in §§ 4·3 and 5·5. The *confidence coefficients*, using the central interval, are $1 - 2\alpha = 0.95$ for the first chart and $1 - 2\alpha = 0.99$ for the second.

*Example* 10*c*. Take the case of a sample of twenty-five pairs of observations, giving a correlation $r = 0.65$. Assuming that this sample has been randomly drawn from a bivariate normal population, what limits may be assigned to $\rho$? Turning to the first chart, we note that the ordinate at $r = 0.65$ cuts the curves for $n = 25$ at $\rho_A = 0.34$ and $\rho_B = 0.82$. Hence we may say that

$$0.34 \leqslant \rho \leqslant 0.82,$$

with a probability $0.95$ (in the sense defined) of being correct. If we do not wish to accept so large a risk of error, we may turn to the second chart and, again, reading off the $\rho$-values of the points where the ordinate at $r = 0.65$ cuts the pair of curves for $n = 25$, obtain the inequality

$$0.21 \leqslant \rho \leqslant 0.87$$

for a confidence coefficient $0.99$ (see §§ 4·3, 5·5)

### 7·4   *The significance of the difference between two sample correlations*

If two independent samples of $n_1$ and $n_2$ paired observations give correlation coefficients $r_1$ and $r_2$, respectively, we may ask whether these values are consistent with the hypothesis that the population correlations $\rho_1$ and $\rho_2$ are the same. Using the $z$-transformation, it is only necessary to refer the ratio

$$X = (z_1 - z_2)/\{1/(n_1 - 3) + 1/(n_2 - 3)\}^{\frac{1}{2}}$$

to the normal probability scale.*

*Example* 11. Suppose that

$$n_1 = 30, \quad r_1 = 0.612; \qquad n_2 = 40, \quad r_2 = 0.423.$$

Is the difference between $r_1$ and $r_2$ significant? We find from Table 14 that

$$z_1 = 0.712, \quad z_2 = 0.451.$$

Hence
$$X = (0.712 - 0.451)/\{\tfrac{1}{27} + \tfrac{1}{37}\}^{\frac{1}{2}} = 1.03.$$

Clearly the result is not significant.

---

* The error involved in omitting the corrective terms $\tfrac{1}{2}\rho/(n-1)$ and assuming that if $\rho_1 = \rho_2$ then $\zeta_1 = \zeta_2$, can always be assessed roughly, e.g. by inserting $\tfrac{1}{2}(r_1 + r_2)$ as an assumed common value of $\rho$.

The property that $(z - \zeta) \sqrt{(n-3)}$ is approximately a unit normal deviate makes available a variety of tests based on the distribution of $\chi^2$.

*Example* 12. The following results from a paper by Tschepourkowsky (1905) have been used by Tippett (1952, §9·23) and F. N. David (1938, p. xxiv) to illustrate tests for heterogeneity among correlation coefficients. Col. 3 of the table gives the values of the correlation, $r_t$, between cephalic index and upper face form, for samples of $n_t$ (col. 2) skulls from each of the $k = 13$ different races shown in col. 1. The form of analysis will depend on what are the alternatives to the hypothesis which it is wished to test. Thus, assuming that the two characters are normally correlated:

(a) We may ask whether the data are consistent with the hypothesis that there is a common, but unknown, value of $\rho$ for all thirteen races. The alternative is, here, that there are different correlations $\rho_t$ for the races.

(b) Or, again, we may ask whether the assumed common correlation $\rho$ has a specified value $\rho_0$, the alternative being that $\rho \neq \rho_0$.

(c) In certain situations we may wish to test directly whether a set of correlation coefficients $r_t$ are consistent with a specified population correlation $\rho_0$, the alternative being different correlations $\rho_t$.

| Race (1) | No. of skulls $n_t$ (2) | Correlation $r_t$ (3) | $z_t$ (4) | $n_t - 3$ (5) |
|---|---|---|---|---|
| Australians | 66 | $+0·089$ | $+0·089$ | 63 |
| Negroes | 77 | $+0·182$ | $+0·184$ | 74 |
| Duke of York Islanders | 53 | $-0·093$ | $-0·093$ | 50 |
| Malays | 60 | $-0·185$ | $-0·187$ | 57 |
| Fijians | 32 | $+0·217$ | $+0·221$ | 29 |
| Papuans | 39 | $-0·255$ | $-0·261$ | 36 |
| Polynesians | 44 | $+0·002$ | $+0·002$ | 41 |
| Alfourous | 19 | $-0·302$ | $-0·312$ | 16 |
| Micronesians | 32 | $-0·251$ | $-0·256$ | 29 |
| Copts | 34 | $-0·147$ | $-0·148$ | 31 |
| Etruscans | 47 | $-0·021$ | $-0·021$ | 44 |
| Europeans | 80 | $-0·198$ | $-0·201$ | 77 |
| Ancient Thebans | 152 | $-0·067$ | $-0·067$ | 149 |
| Total | 735 | | | 696 |

*Case* (a). Col. 4 of the table shows the value of $z_t$ obtained from Table 14, while col. 5 shows $n_t - 3$, the reciprocal of the approximate sampling variance of $z_t$. We now calculate

$$\chi^2 = \sum_t (n_t - 3)(z_t - \bar{z})^2, \tag{49}$$

where

$$\bar{z} = \sum_t (n_t - 3) z_t / \sum_t (n_t - 3), \quad k = 13. \tag{50}$$

We find $\bar{z} = -0·0609$, $\chi^2 = 14·65$. The appropriate degrees of freedom will be $\nu = k - 1 = 12$. Referring to Table 8, we find that the observed $\chi^2$ falls well below the 5% point (21·03), so that there appears no reason to reject the assumption of a common correlation coefficient. A good estimate of this common value is given by $\hat{\rho} = \tanh \bar{z} = -0·061$.

31

*Case* (*b*). In view of (50), the sampling variance of $\bar{z}$ is $1/\{\sum_t (n_t - 3)\}$. We therefore deal with this case by calculating the ratio

$$X = (\bar{z} - \zeta_0)\sqrt{(\sum_t (n_t - 3))},\tag{51}$$

where $\zeta_0 = \tanh^{-1}\rho_0$, and referring to the normal probability scale. If, for the data of the example, we wish to test whether $\rho_0 = 0$, i.e. whether $\zeta_0 = 0$, we find

$$X = -0.0609\sqrt{696} = -1.607,$$

a figure which is not significant at the 5 % level (Table 4).

*Case* (*c*). This may be regarded as a fusion of tests (*a*) and (*b*). Indeed, on adding $X^2$ from (51) to the $\chi^2$ of (49) we obtain $\sum_t (n_t - 3)(z_t - \zeta_0)^2$, a $\chi^2$ for $k = 13$ degrees of freedom which, in our example, is $17.23$, confirming the insignificant results of (*a*) and (*b*). Normally, however, we would compute the separate components (49) and (51) in order not to confuse the issues, (*a*) and (*b*).

*Other cases.* It is clear that certain more complex problems, with samples falling into different groups, will lead to tests on the transformed variables $z$ following the appropriate analysis of variance patterns.

## 8. The incomplete B-function (Tables 16 and 17)

### 8·1  *Definitions*

The incomplete B-function ratio is defined as

$$I_x(a, b) = \frac{B_x(a, b)}{B(a, b)}$$
$$= \frac{\Gamma(a+b)}{\Gamma(a)\,\Gamma(b)}\int_0^x u^{a-1}(1-u)^{b-1}\,du.\tag{52}$$

In the notation which we have used hitherto for a probability integral, we should write

$$P(x\,|\,a, b) = I_x(a, b).$$

It appears, however, preferable to retain the traditional notation for this integral.*

When the fundamental 7-decimal-place tables of this function were published by Karl Pearson (1934) it was realized that they might form a basis for shorter tables suited for use in special problems. The present Table 16 satisfies a requirement of this kind; it gives lower percentage points of the distribution of $x$, i.e. the roots $x(I\,|\,a, b)$ of $I_x(a, b) = P$ for $P = 0.001$, $0.0025, 0.005, 0.01, 0.025, 0.05, 0.10, 0.25$ and $0.50$. The corresponding upper percentage points can be obtained from the relation

$$I_x(a, b) = 1 - I_{1-x}(b, a),\tag{53}$$

i.e. by interchanging $a$ and $b$ and taking $1 - x$ as the percentage point.

The chart of Table 17, whose use is explained in § 8·2 below, gives $I_x(a, b)$ directly to graphical accuracy, but for ranges of argument slightly exceeding those of Pearson's tables. It is believed that it will be of value in a number of applications where the percentage point Tables 16 and 18 are not appropriate, and where Karl Pearson's (1934) tables are not available.

---

\* Because of the importance of the application to the binomial, where $x$ corresponds to the $p$ in the expansion of $(q+p)^n$, we have altered the traditional notation from $I_x(p, q)$ to $I_x(a, b)$ to avoid confusion.

Probably the most important applications of the incomplete B-function follow from:

(a) *Its relation to the distribution of the variance ratio, F* (see §§ 9·1, 9·2 below)

If $\chi_1^2$ and $\chi_2^2$ are two independent statistics, each distributed as $\chi^2$ (i.e. with the probability integral of equation (15)) and having $\nu_1$ and $\nu_2$ degrees of freedom, respectively, then the frequency function of

$$x = \chi_1^2/(\chi_1^2 + \chi_2^2)$$

is
$$f(x \mid \nu_1, \nu_2) = \frac{\Gamma(\tfrac{1}{2}\nu_1 + \tfrac{1}{2}\nu_2)}{\Gamma(\tfrac{1}{2}\nu_1)\,\Gamma(\tfrac{1}{2}\nu_2)}\, x^{\frac{1}{2}\nu_1 - 1}(1 - x)^{\frac{1}{2}\nu_2 - 1}. \tag{54}$$

If we now divide each $\chi^2$ by its degrees of freedom and take the ratio of the quotients

$$F = \nu_2 \chi_1^2/(\nu_1 \chi_2^2),$$

it will follow that the probability that $F$ exceeds a specified value, $F_0$, is

$$\int_{F_0}^{\infty} f(F \mid \nu_1, \nu_2)\, dF = I_{x_0}(\tfrac{1}{2}\nu_2, \tfrac{1}{2}\nu_1), \tag{55}$$

where
$$x_0 = \nu_2/(\nu_2 + \nu_1 F_0). \tag{56}$$

Table 18 was, in fact, derived in this way from Table 16.

(b) *Its relation to the cumulative sum of the terms of the binomial expansion* $(q + p)^n$

Here
$$\sum_{i=a}^{n} \binom{n}{i} p^i (1 - p)^{n-i} = I_p(a, n - a + 1). \tag{57}$$

For a few selected values of $n$, individual terms of the binomial distribution $\binom{n}{i} p^i (1 - p)^{n-i}$ are given in Table 37 which is mainly intended for illustrative purposes. This table is discussed in § 18 below. More comprehensive tables of the binomial distribution are now available elsewhere (see, for example, National Bureau of Standards, Applied Mathematics Series, no. 6, 1950).

The charts of Table 41, discussed in § 22·3 give a method of obtaining confidence intervals for the binomial probability $p$, based on an observed proportion of successes $i/n$, for selected values of sample sizes $n$.

(c) *Its relation to the Pearson Type I curve*

The probability integral of this curve (see § 23·1 below) namely, of

$$y = y_0 \left(1 + \frac{x'}{a_1}\right)^{m_1} \left(1 - \frac{x'}{a_2}\right)^{m_2}, \quad (-a_1 \leqslant x' \leqslant a_2), \tag{58}$$

can be obtained from the integral (52) by setting

$$x = (a_1 + x')/(a_1 + a_2), \quad a = m_1 + 1, \quad b = m_2 + 1.$$

The Type I curve has been found to play a part similar to that of the Type III curve in approximating to some of the less tractable distributions of statistical theory (see §§ 3·5 and 8·4).

Numerous other applications of the integral are given by Karl Pearson (1934), and some of these are discussed below.

### 8·2    *Description and use of the chart in Table* 17

On the top edge of the chart a scale of $b \ (= \tfrac{1}{2}\nu_1)$ is provided which is split into three sections:

$$\text{A, } 1 \leqslant b \leqslant 4; \quad \text{B, } 4 \leqslant b \leqslant 15; \quad \text{C, } 15 \leqslant b \leqslant 60.$$

These scales form the upper margins of the three corresponding chart sections A, B and C.

Each section is further divided into upper and lower parts. The lower part contains a family of curves corresponding to the values of the parameter $a$ ($= \frac{1}{2}\nu_2$) shown at the right-hand end of the curves, while the top part contains a family of curves corresponding to selected values of the probability $I_x(a, b)$. Both families are referred to the same abscissa scale $b$ at the top edge. The two families are linked by the aid of $x$-scales provided on the ruler enclosed in the pocket inside the back cover of the volume. Each $x$-scale is marked with an arrow ($\rightarrow$) at the 'pivot point', whose significance is explained below.

To find $P = I_x(a, b)$ for given $a$, $b$ and $x$, with $a \geqslant b$, we proceed as follows. Choosing the appropriate scale (A, B or C), place the ruler vertically on the chart so that its $x$-scale intersects the abscissa scale (at top of chart) at the given value of $b$. Slide the rule up or down this vertical until its pivot mark ($\rightarrow$) is at the intersection of the vertical with the curve corresponding to the given value of $a$ in the bottom part. With the $x$-scale in this position the required value of $P = I_x(a, b)$ can be read off in the top part opposite the given $x$.

When $a < b$ find $I_{1-x}(b, a)$ and use relation (53).

### 8·3    Illustration of applications of the chart

*Example* 13*a*. Given $a = 30$, $b = 5$, it is required to find $I_x(a, b)$ for $x = 0.70$, $0.94$ and $0.96$. Following the above procedure we find from section B of the chart:

$$I_{0.70}(30, 5) = 0.012, \quad I_{0.94}(30, 5) = 0.95\,(2), \quad I_{0.96}(30, 5) = 0.99\,(0).$$

*Example* 13*b*. In binomial theory, given that $p = 0.2$ and $n = 25$, it is required to find the chance of obtaining at least $a = 10$ successes. Reference to equation (57) shows that this chance is given by $I_{0.2}(10, 16)$ or $1 - I_{0.8}(16, 10)$, so that, using section B, we find it to be equal to $1 - 0.985 = 0.015$.

*Example* 13*c*. Given $\nu_1 = 40$ and $\nu_2 = 120$ degrees of freedom, find the chance that $F \geqslant 1.5$. We have from (56),    $$x_0 = 120/(120 + 1.5 \times 40) = 120/180 = 0.667,$$

and using section C we find this chance to be a little over $0.05$, a result confirmed by the $5\%$ value of $F$, given in Table 18 as $1.50$.

*Example* 14.\* A choice between two manufactured products, I and II, is to be made. The relative variability, $\sigma_1^2/\sigma_2^2$, of a characteristic of the two products is relevant, but of secondary importance in the sense that: (*a*) it is immaterial which is chosen if $\sigma_1^2/\sigma_2^2 = 2$, (*b*) product I will be preferred if $\sigma_1^2/\sigma_2^2 < 2$, and (*c*) product II if $\sigma_1^2/\sigma_2^2 > 2$. The characteristic is to be measured for samples of 41 items from each of the products, the two sample mean-square estimates of variance $s_1^2$ and $s_2^2$ are to be computed, and it is decided to accept product I if $s_1^2/s_2^2 < 2$ and product II if $s_1^2/s_2^2 > 2$. What is the chance that product I will be accepted if, in fact, $\sigma_1^2/\sigma_2^2 = 1.2$?

If $\sigma_1^2/\sigma_2^2 = 1.2$, the ratio $s_1^2/s_2^2$ is distributed as $1.2F$ for $\nu_1 = 40$, $\nu_2 = 40$ degrees of freedom, so that we must find

$$\Pr\{1.2F < 2\} = \Pr\{F < 1.67\}.$$

From (56) we compute the equivalent $x_0$ value as

$$x_0 = 40/(40 + 1.67 \times 40) = 1/2.67 = 0.375.$$

Placing the ruler $x$-scale for section C on the vertical marked $b = \frac{1}{2}\nu_1 = 20$ and pivoting it to $a = \frac{1}{2}\nu_2 = 20$, we read opposite $x = 0.375$ that $I_{0.375}(20, 20) = 0.05$ so that our chance is $0.95$ or $95\%$.

\* A similar example is discussed by Eisenhart *et al.* (1947).

In a number of problems there is a direct requirement for the percentage levels of $x$ rather than those of the transformed variables $F$ or Fisher's $z = \frac{1}{2}\log_e F$. A case in point concerns the multiple correlation coefficient $R$ in samples from uncorrelated normally distributed material. Thus if for each of $n$ 'subjects', $k+1$ variables have been measured and it is desired to assess the dependence of one of these (say $y$) on the $k$ remaining variables $(x_1, \ldots, x_k)$, then $R^2$ is given by

$$R^2 = S_1/(S_1 + S_2),$$

where $S_1$ is the sums of squares component of $y$ due to its multilinear regression on the $x_i$ and $S_2$ is the residual sum of squares about this regression. A comparison with (54) shows that, in the case of independence, $R^2$ is directly distributed as a B-variable with $a = \frac{1}{2}k$, $b = \frac{1}{2}(n-k-1)$.

Again, if a random variable can assume only values between 0 and 1, if it has a mean value of $\mu_1'$ and a second moment about 0 of $\mu_2'$, then $I_x(a, b)$ with

$$\left.\begin{aligned} a &= \mu_1'(\mu_1' - \mu_2')/(\mu_2' - \mu_1'^2), \\ b &= (1-\mu_1')\,(\mu_1' - \mu_2')/(\mu_2' - \mu_1'^2), \end{aligned}\right\} \tag{59}$$

will often give a very close approximation to the true probability integral. The assumption here made is that the distribution may be represented by a Type I curve having the correct terminal points and first two moments. Use has been made of this approximation by Neyman & Pearson (1931), Bishop (1939) and others in determining probability levels for test statistics derived by application of the likelihood-ratio principle. Earlier, Karl Pearson had used a four-moment fit of a Type I curve to graduate the hypergeometric distribution (see Karl Pearson, 1934, p. xxxvi).

8·5   *Interpolation in Table* 16

The methods of Lagrangian interpolation which may be used have been discussed in detail by Hartley (1941) and are partly based on a special table of Lagrangian coefficients for harmonic interpolation (Comrie & Hartley, 1941). Here we confine ourselves to interpolation in the neighbourhood of the singular point $a = b = \infty$. If $x$ is required for values $2a = \nu_2 > 60$, $2b = \nu_1 > 40$, interpolation between the tabular values is not possible and $x$ has to be computed *ab initio*.

Numerous approximate formulae for the incomplete B-function are valid in this range (Soper, 1921; Wishart, 1927); others give the percentage points $x(I \mid a, b)$ directly (Halton Thomson, 1947; Carter, 1947; Wise, 1950; and also Cochran, 1940, who deals with Fisher's $z$-transformation of $x(I \mid a, b)$). When $a$ and $b$ are both moderately large, Carter's formula appears to be convenient and may be used as follows:

If $X$ denotes the standardized normal deviate corresponding to $P = 1 - I$, and if $\lambda = \frac{1}{6}(X^2 - 3)$, $\tau = \frac{1}{2}\lambda + \frac{5}{12}$ (all tabled below), we compute in turn

$$A = \frac{1}{12}\left(\frac{1}{a-\frac{1}{2}} + \frac{1}{b-\frac{1}{2}}\right), \quad h = \frac{1}{3A},$$

$$z = X\,\sqrt{(h+\lambda)/h} - \left(\frac{1}{b-\frac{1}{2}} - \frac{1}{a-\frac{1}{2}}\right)(\tau - A),$$

$$x(I \mid a, b) = a/(a + be^{2z}).$$

| $P$ | 0·50 | 0·25 | 0·10 | 0·05 | 0·025 | 0·01 | 0·005 |
|---|---|---|---|---|---|---|---|
| $X$ | 0 | 0·6745 | 1·2816 | 1·6449 | 1·9600 | 2·3263 | 2·5758 |
| $\lambda$ | $-0\cdot5000$ | $-0\cdot4242$ | $-0\cdot2263$ | $-0\cdot0491$ | 0·1402 | 0·4020 | 0·6058 |
| $\tau$ | 0·1667 | 0·2046 | 0·3035 | 0·3921 | 0·4868 | 0·6177 | 0·7196 |

As an illustration we may recompute the tabular value $x(0.01 \mid 60, 20)$, i.e. the entry for $2a = 120$ and $2b = 40$ in the section of Table 16 for $I = 0.01$.

We obtain
$$1/(a - \tfrac{1}{2}) = 0.0168067, \quad 1/(b - \tfrac{1}{2}) = 0.0512821,$$

$$A = 0.00567407, \quad h = 58.747,$$

$$z = \frac{2.3263 \sqrt{59.149}}{58.747} - 0.0344754 \times 0.6120 = 0.28345.$$

Hence $x = 0.62988$, which agrees with the tabular entry.

## 9. The $F$-distribution (Tables 18 and 19)

### 9·1  Definition and relation to other tables

Consider two independent $\chi^2$-values, $\chi_1^2$ and $\chi_2^2$, based respectively on $\nu_1$ and $\nu_2$ degrees of freedom; the variance ratio $F$ is defined by

$$F = \frac{\chi_1^2}{\nu_1} \bigg/ \frac{\chi_2^2}{\nu_2}, \tag{60}$$

and has for its frequency function

$$f(F) = \frac{\Gamma(\tfrac{1}{2}\nu_1 + \tfrac{1}{2}\nu_2)}{\Gamma(\tfrac{1}{2}\nu_1)\,\Gamma(\tfrac{1}{2}\nu_2)} \nu_1^{\frac{1}{2}\nu_1} \nu_2^{\frac{1}{2}\nu_2} F^{\frac{1}{2}\nu_1 - 1} (\nu_2 + \nu_1 F)^{-\frac{1}{2}(\nu_1 + \nu_2)}. \tag{61}$$

It is useful to note that

$$\text{Mean } F = \nu_2/(\nu_2 - 2) \quad \text{for} \quad \nu_2 > 2,$$

$$\sigma_F = \frac{\nu_2}{\nu_2 - 2} \left\{ \frac{2(\nu_1 + \nu_2 - 2)}{\nu_1(\nu_2 - 4)} \right\}^{\frac{1}{2}} \quad \text{for} \quad \nu_2 > 4.$$

For large $\nu_2$, $F$ tends to be distributed as $\chi^2/\nu_1$ with a mean of unity and standard deviation $\sqrt{(2/\nu_1)}$. Table 18 gives seven upper percentage points of $F$, that is to say, it gives the roots, $F(Q \mid \nu_1, \nu_2)$, of the equation

$$Q = \int_{F(Q \mid \nu_1, \nu_2)}^{\infty} f(F)\, dF$$

for $Q = 1 - P = 0.25, 0.10, 0.05, 0.025, 0.01, 0.005$ and $0.001$. Except in the case of the 0·1 % points, all the results were obtained by rounding off the values in Merrington & Thompson's (1943) table of percentage points of $F$. Where the rounding-off was uncertain, values were recomputed from Karl Pearson's *Tables of the Incomplete B-function* or *ab initio*. A table of 0·1 % points of $z = \tfrac{1}{2}\log_e F$ was originally computed by Colcord & Deming (1935); the 0·1 % tables of $F$ and $z$ given by Fisher & Yates (1938) were based on this table. Norton (1952) has recently checked the Fisher & Yates tables and given a list of corrections. The present 0·1 % table for $F$ utilizes all this information. In addition, a recalculation has been made of all entries given by Colcord & Deming but not by Fisher & Yates, i.e. entries with $\nu_1 = 7, 9, 10, 11$. 15, 20, 30, 40, 60 and 120.

For consistency throughout the volume the symbol $P$ is retained to denote the conventional probability integral; it follows that, as in the case of the $\chi^2$-test, $Q = 1 - P$ is used to denote the upper-tail area of the distribution usually required in tests of significance. To obtain lower percentage points it is only necessary to interchange the values of $\nu_1$ and $\nu_2$ in entering the table and to take for $F$ the reciprocal of the value so obtained. For example, if $\nu_1 = 12$, $\nu_2 = 40$ the upper 0·5 % point is seen to be $F(0.005 \mid 12, 40) = 2.95$ whilst the lower 0·5 % point is

$$F(0.995 \mid 12, 40) = 1/F(0.005 \mid 40, 12) = 1/(4.23) = 0.236.$$

The marginal row of each table under the heading $\nu_2 = \infty$ provides the corresponding upper percentage point of the distribution of $\chi^2/\nu$ with $\nu = \nu_1$ degrees of freedom. The marginal column of each table for $\nu_1 = \infty$ gives the upper percentage points of $\nu/\chi^2$ or its reciprocal gives the lower percentage point of $\chi^2/\nu$ with $\nu = \nu_2$ degrees of freedom. The percentage points of the $t$-distribution for $\nu = \nu_2$ degrees of freedom may be obtained from the columns of the tables headed $\nu_1 = 1$, since in this case $t = \sqrt{F}$.

The link between the distribution of $F$ and the B-variable, $x$, has already been referred to (§ 8·1). This well-known relation enables us:

(a) To compute percentage points of $F$ from those of $x$, utilizing the greater accuracy of $x$ in Table 16.

(b) To obtain values of the probability integral of $F$, either from Karl Pearson's (1934) tables or, more approximately, from the chart of Table 17 for $I_x(a, b)$.

In both these cases we use the relation

$$\int_{F_0}^{\infty} f(F \mid \nu_1, \nu_2)\, dF = I_{x_0}(a, b),$$

where

$$F_0 = a(1-x_0)/(bx_0), \quad a = \tfrac{1}{2}\nu_2, \quad b = \tfrac{1}{2}\nu_1. \tag{62}$$

### 9·2    *Application to the analysis of variance*

In the terminology of the analysis of variance, let $S_1$ and $S_2$ be two component sums of squares having, respectively, $\nu_1$ and $\nu_2$ degrees of freedom, which have arisen in the analysis of a system of normal variates. If all the variates have a common standard deviation $\sigma$ and if $S_1$ and $S_2$ are independent, then $S_1/\sigma^2$ and $S_2/\sigma^2$ are distributed independently as $\chi^2$ with $\nu_1$ and $\nu_2$ degrees of freedom respectively. Introducing the mean squares, $s_1^2 = S_1/\nu_1$ and $s_2^2 = S_2/\nu_2$, as two independent estimates of $\sigma^2$, the variance ratio

$$F = \frac{s_1^2}{s_2^2} = \frac{S_1}{\nu_1 \sigma^2} \bigg/ \frac{S_2}{\nu_2 \sigma^2}$$

is clearly of the form (60) and is accordingly distributed in the standard $F$-distribution (61), which is independent of the unknown value of $\sigma^2$. This ratio may therefore be used for the comparison of any two independent variance estimates obtained in an analysis of variance decomposition. We confine ourselves here to illustrating the use of Table 18 in terms of one simple example.

*Example* 15. The table on p. 38 shows measurements of tensile strength $x_{ti}$ $(i = 1, \ldots, n;$ $t = 1, \ldots, k)$ made on $n = 6$ specimens of rubber randomly selected from each of $k = 5$ different batches.

If all the $x_{ti}$ were random observations from the same normal population, having a variance $\sigma^2$, we could obtain two different estimates of $\sigma^2$ by computing the mean squares:

(i)
$$s_1^2 = \frac{S_1}{\nu_1} = n \sum_{t=1}^{k} \frac{(\bar{x}_{t.} - \bar{x}_{..})^2}{k-1},$$

described as the *between-batch* mean square, based on $\nu_1 = k-1$ degrees of freedom, and

(ii)
$$s_2^2 = \frac{S_2}{\nu_2} = \sum_{t=1}^{k} \sum_{i=1}^{n} \frac{(x_{ti} - \bar{x}_{t.})^2}{nk-k},$$

described as the *within-batch* mean square, based on $\nu_2 = k(n-1)$ degrees of freedom.

37

*Measurements of tensile strength (in kg./cm.²) of specimens of rubber*

| Specimen no. | Batch no. | | | | |
|---|---|---|---|---|---|
| | $t = 1$ | $t = 2$ | $t = 3$ | $t = 4$ | $t = 5$ |
| $i = 1$ | 177 | 116 | 170 | 181 | 177 |
| 2 | 172 | 179 | 156 | 190 | 186 |
| 3 | 137 | 182 | 188 | 210 | 199 |
| 4 | 196 | 143 | 212 | 173 | 202 |
| 5 | 145 | 156 | 164 | 172 | 204 |
| 6 | 168 | 174 | 184 | 187 | 198 |
| Mean, $\bar{x}_t.$ | 165·8 | 158·3 | 179·0 | 185·5 | 194·3 |
| Mean square | 468·6 | 653·1 | 406·0 | 196·3 | 111·5 |
| Range | 59 | 66 | 56 | 38 | 27 |
| Grand mean, $\bar{x}.. = 176·6$ | | | | | |

It can be shown that under these conditions $S_1/\sigma^2$ and $S_2/\sigma^2$ are independent $\chi^2$-values, so that the ratio $F = s_1^2/s_2^2$ would follow the distribution (61). Suppose, however, that while the batch variances are the same, their means differ. Then while $s_2^2$ will still remain an unbiased estimator of $\sigma^2$, the expectation of $s_1^2$ will now be greater than $\sigma^2$. We investigate this possibility of departure from the null hypothesis of equal means by finding whether the observed value of $F$ is displaced exceptionally towards the upper tail of the $F$-distribution.

In our example $\qquad s_1^2 = 1273·5, \quad \nu_1 = 4; \qquad s_2^2 = 367·1, \quad \nu_2 = 25.$

Hence $F = 3·47$, a value considerably larger than 1. Turning to Table 18, we find that the observed $F$ falls between the 2·5 % point at 3·35 and the 1 % point at 4·18. It is thus significant at the 2·5 % level (and *a fortiori* at the 5 % level), though not at the 1 % level. On the hypothesis tested it is, therefore, unusually large, and we should suspect the presence of real differences in batch means.

### 9·3 *Tests using both upper and lower tails of the F-distribution*

In the majority of applications in the analysis of variance we are concerned with comparing (i) a 'treatment' mean square which possible systematic effects or other disturbing causes may have enhanced, with (ii) an 'error' mean square, which will be an unbiased estimate of the error variance whether the treatment effects are present or not. Hence, as in the preceding example, we set out to detect effects causing large values of $F$ and are therefore concerned with a single-tail test based on the *upper* percentage points of the distribution. Sometimes, however, we may need to use a double-tail test, because large excesses of $s_2^2$ over $s_1^2$ *or* of $s_1^2$ over $s_2^2$ are of equal importance.

This is the case, for example, if we have two samples of size $n_1$ and $n_2$, one from each of two normal populations, and wish to use the variance estimates, $s_1^2$ and $s_2^2$, to judge whether the population variances, $\sigma_1^2$ and $\sigma_2^2$, differ. Suppose that we wish to arrange the test so that the probability is 0·05 of rejecting the hypothesis that $\sigma_1^2 = \sigma_2^2$ when, in fact, it is true. Then, if the labels '1' and '2' were randomly assigned to the two samples it would seem reasonable to regard the difference as significant if $F = s_1^2/s_2^2$ is either (a) below the lower $2 \cdot 5\%$ point or (b) above the upper $2 \cdot 5\%$ point of the appropriate $F$-distribution, i.e. of

$$f(F \mid \nu_1 = n_1 - 1, \nu_2 = n_2 - 1).$$

Since, if $\sigma_1^2 = \sigma_2^2$, the probability of (a) equals the probability that $F = s_2^2/s_1^2$ is above the upper $2 \cdot 5\%$ point of $f(F \mid \nu_1 = n_2 - 1, \nu_2 = n_1 - 1)$, it follows that a double-tail test at the $5\%$ level will be achieved by taking *whichever of the two variance estimates is the larger as the numerator*, and comparing the ratio with the $2 \cdot 5\%$ $F$-value.

*Example* 16. Let us examine whether the variance estimates from two (randomly selected) batches from the data of Example 15, say batches 2 and 4, differ significantly. We calculate $F = 653/196 = 3 \cdot 33$, and note that it does not exceed the $2 \cdot 5\%$ point for $F$ with $\nu_1 = \nu_2 = 5$ degrees of freedom, which Table 18 shows to fall at $7 \cdot 15$. Clearly no significant difference between the variances in batches 2 and 4 is indicated.

A test of whether there is evidence of heterogeneity among the $k = 5$ variances, taken as a whole, is discussed and applied in §16 below.

### 9·4    *Relation to the Pearson Type VI curve*

The $F$-distribution is related to the Pearson Type VI curve (see § 23·1 below)

$$y = y_0 (x' - a)^{q_2} x'^{-q_1} \quad (a \leqslant x' \leqslant \infty), \tag{63}$$

through the transformation $x' = a(1 + \nu_1 F/\nu_2)$, where

$$\nu_1 = 2(q_2 + 1), \quad \nu_2 = 2(q_1 - q_2 - 1).$$

Table 18, therefore, provides percentage points for these distributions, but if the reciprocal transformation (62) is employed as well, the percentage points can be obtained to a higher accuracy from those for the incomplete B-variable, $x$, given in Table 16. In so far as the Type VI distribution has been found useful as an approximation to less tractable distributions in statistical theory (see, for example, Box, 1949), the present tables provide approximate percentage points for such statistics.

### 9·5    *Tests of significance for the largest F-ratio (Table 19)*

In the analysis of variance it frequently occurs that a number, $k$, of independent 'treatment' mean squares $s_1^2, \ldots, s_k^2$, each based on $m$ degrees of freedom and measuring different 'effects', must all be gauged against an independent 'error' mean square $s_0^2$, based on $\nu$ degrees of freedom. It is clear that if we were to form for each of the $k$ mean squares, $s_i^2$, the $F$-ratio $s_i^2/s_0^2$ and refer these to the ordinary $F$-tables, the largest of these $F$-ratios, say $s_{\max}^2/s_0^2$, would have a greater chance of being declared significant than one *randomly* selected from the set (to which the $F$-tables would be applicable). This source of bias can be avoided if the percentage points (in random sampling) of the largest $F$-ratio, $s_{\max}^2/s_0^2$, in a set of $k$ ratios are used, as shown below. Such tables would depend on $k$, the number of independent random mean squares $s_i^2$, on $m$, their degrees of freedom and on $\nu$, the degrees of freedom of the error mean square $s_0^2$.

Table 19 (taken from K. R. Nair, 1948$a$) gives such upper 5 and 1 % points for the special case $m = 1$, which arises in the important class of factorial experiments of the $2^l$ type (such as that analysed in Example 17 below).

In other cases, an approximation suggested by Hartley (1938) and examined in detail by Finney (1941) for $m = 2$, regards the $F$-ratios as independent, so that the probability that $s^2_{max.}/s^2_0$ exceeds $F^*$ (say) is approximately evaluated from

$$1 - \left\{ \int_0^{F^*} f(F \mid m, \nu)\, dF \right\}^k \sim k \int_{F^*}^{\infty} f(F \mid m, \nu)\, dF.$$

From the form of this expression we note that the upper $100\alpha/k\%$ point of $F$ for $m$ and $\nu$ degrees of freedom is approximately equal to the $100\alpha\%$ point of the distribution of $s^2_{max.}/s^2_0$. Thus we may be able to utilize the extreme percentage points of $F$ for this test, provided $k$ is not too great.

*Example* 17. Wishart (1938) gives an example of a uniformity trial on asparagus with dummy treatments $(N, P, K)$ superimposed. The analysis of variance table (with NPK confounded), is shown below:

| Source of variation | Degrees of freedom | Mean square | $F$-ratio |
|---|---|---|---|
| Blocks | 7 | 6543·2 | — |
| N | 1 | 488·3 | 0·35 |
| P | 1 | 69·0 | 0·05 |
| K | 1 | 34·0 | 0·02 |
| NP | 1 | 830·3 | 0·60 |
| NK | 1 | 57·8 | 0·04 |
| PK | 1 | 9765·0 | 7·02 |
| Error | 18 | 1391·2 | — |

The largest mean square is that for PK, and the variance ratio $s^2_{max.}/s^2_0 = 7·02$ would be returned as significant if compared with the 5% point of $F$ for $\nu_1 = 1$, $\nu_2 = 18$, namely, 4·41. However, using the appropriate test and entering Table 19 for $k = 6$, $\nu = 18$, we find by interpolation a 5% point of 8·59 which is not exceeded; thus the dummy PK effect should be returned as insignificant. If we were to use the approximate test mentioned above at the 5% level, we would compare an observed value of 7·02 with the $\frac{5}{6}\%$ point of $F$ for $\nu_1 = 1$, $\nu_2 = 18$. Interpolating for a 0·833% point between the 2·5, 1 and 0·5% points for $\nu_1 = 1$, $\nu_2 = 18$, using a 3-point Lagrangian, we obtain a value of 8·87, which is slightly in excess of the exact value (8·59) and again returns the observed ratio of 7·02 as insignificant.

No exact tests are available

(a) for the second largest, third largest, etc., mean square,

(b) for the ordered mean squares based on different degrees of freedom.


## III. FURTHER TABLES OF PROBABILITY INTEGRALS, PERCENTAGE POINTS, ETC., OF DISTRIBUTIONS DERIVED FROM THE NORMAL FUNCTION (TABLES 20–35)

The tables collected together in this group, while of less importance than those of the preceding group, will be found of considerable use in a number of directions. Contained in the section are tables dealing with the distribution of statistics based on ordered observations, e.g. on the extreme values in a sample. These distributions are of importance both in quick assessments of significance in connexion with outlying observations or groups of observations and, in the case of range, in providing alternative means of estimating variance. The section also contains tables which can be used to investigate the validity of the assumptions, in general necessary in the application of analysis of variance technique, regarding (a) homogeneity of variance and (b) normality of distribution. In so far as is possible the tables will be described and illustrated in a logical sequence. For obvious reasons of economy in printing, the arrangement of the tables in the book does not always follow in quite this order.

### 10. The mean deviation: moments and percentage points
### (Tables 20 and 21)
#### 10·1 Definitions

If $x_1, x_2, \ldots, x_n$ is a random sample of $n$ observations, the mean deviation (from the mean) is defined by

$$m = \sum_{i=1}^{n} |x_i - \bar{x}|/n,$$

where $\bar{x}$ is the arithmetic mean of the observations. If the population sampled is normal with standard deviation $\sigma$, no simple expression exists for the frequency function $f(m)$ of the distribution of $m$, except in the cases $n = 2, 3$. Computations have, however, been made of the probability integral of $m/\sigma$ for $n = 2\,(1)\,10$, from the formula for the distribution of $m$ derived by H. J. Godwin (1945), who showed that (for $\sigma = 1$)

$$f(m) = n^{\frac{3}{2}}\, 2^{-\frac{1}{2}(n+1)}\, \pi^{-\frac{1}{2}(n-1)} \sum_{i=1}^{n-1} \binom{n}{i} \exp\left\{-\frac{m^2 n^3}{8i(n-i)}\right\} G_{i-1}(\tfrac{1}{2}mn)\, G_{n-i-1}(\tfrac{1}{2}mn),$$

where $G_r(x)$ is defined by the recurrence formula (70), p. 49. For a description of the method of computation, see Hartley (1945). This table has not been reproduced in the present volume, but Table 21 gives certain lower and upper percentage points of the standardized mean deviation $m/\sigma$ calculated from the probability integral table.

The expectation and variance of $m$ for a normal population, derived first by Helmert (1876), and later by Fisher (1920), are as follows:

$$\mathscr{E}(m) = \sigma\left\{\frac{2(n-1)}{n\pi}\right\}^{\frac{1}{2}}, \tag{64}$$

$$\operatorname{var}(m) = \sigma^2\, \frac{2(n-1)}{n^2\pi} \left\{\tfrac{1}{2}\pi + [n(n-2)]^{\frac{1}{2}} - n + \sin^{-1}\frac{1}{n-1}\right\}. \tag{65}$$

Geary (1936)* has provided expansions in inverse powers of $n-1$ from which the third and fourth moments, $\mu_3$ and $\mu_4$ of $m$ can be calculated. Table 20 gives the expectation, variance and standard deviation calculated from equations (64) and (65), as well as the moment ratios $\beta_1 = \mu_3^2/\mu_2^3$, $\beta_2 = \mu_4/\mu_2^2$ calculated from Geary's formulae. For $n \leqslant 6$, exact values for $\beta_1$ were obtained from Geary's work. For $n = 3$, Mr A. R. Kamat has provided us with an exact value for $\beta_2$ while he and Mr J. H. Cadwell (1953) have pointed out a correction needed to Fisher's (1920) value for $n = 4$. All values of $\beta_1$ and $\beta_2$ for $n \leqslant 6$ were checked by applying numerical integration to Godwin and Hartley's table of the probability integral of $m$.† When $n = 2$, $m$ is distributed as the modulus of a normal deviate. The extent of error involved when $n = 10$ by assuming that $m$ is normally distributed with an expectation and variance given by equations (64) and (65) is shown by the values of the percentage points, under the heading 'normal approximation' in Table 21. For the more extreme points, the

---

* See also E. S. Pearson (1945, 1948).  † *Biometrika*, **33**, 259.

error is still appreciable. A considerably more accurate approximation, by which the lower and upper 5, 2·5, 1 and 0·5 % points may be obtained using Table 42, is described below in Example 49, p. 83.

### 10·2  *Applications*

*Example* 18. The probability integral and percentage points of $m/\sigma$ were originally calculated in connexion with quality control, because in certain fields of production it was customary to estimate within-lot variation from the mean deviation rather than the standard deviation or range. For example, if (*a*) it is desired to control the variability in running time of certain fuses so that the standard deviation for the fuses in a large lot does not exceed 0·5 sec. under specified firing conditions, and (*b*) standard proof routine involves firing eight fuses per lot under these conditions, then inner and outer *control limits* for the mean deviation may be obtained as follows from the 2·5 and 0·1 % points of the table:

Inner control limits at

$$0\cdot5 \times 0\cdot372 = 0\cdot19 \text{ sec.} \quad \text{and} \quad 0\cdot5 \times 1\cdot196 = 0\cdot60 \text{ sec.}$$

Outer control limits at

$$0\cdot5 \times 0\cdot220 = 0\cdot11 \text{ sec.} \quad \text{and} \quad 0\cdot5 \times 1\cdot499 = 0\cdot75 \text{ sec.}$$

While the upper control limits will naturally be of most value in detecting first signs of trouble in the shape of increasing variability, the lower limits may also be useful, since factors leading to greater consistency in production may be worth while following up.

The figures for the expected value and the standard deviation of $m/\sigma$ given in Table 20 may also be used to obtain an estimate of $\sigma$, and of the standard error of this estimate, based on the mean deviation found from one or a number of small samples. This procedure is illustrated in Example 22, p. 47 below.

## 11.  Percentage points of the extreme standardized deviate, $X_n = (x_n - \mu)/\sigma$ (Table 24)

### 11·1  *Definitions*

If the observations in a sample of $n$ are arranged in ascending order of magnitude $x_1, x_2, \ldots, x_n$, the extreme values will be denoted by $x_1$ and $x_n$, while their values standardized with regard to the population mean and standard deviation may be written

$$X_1 = (x_1 - \mu)/\sigma, \quad X_n = (x_n - \mu)/\sigma.$$

If the sample is drawn from a normal population the probability integral of $X_n$ is given by

$$P(X_n) = \left\{ \int_{-\infty}^{X_n} \frac{1}{\sqrt{(2\pi)}} e^{-\frac{1}{2}u^2} du \right\}^n. \tag{66}$$

Tables giving values of this probability integral for certain sample sizes were first computed by Tippett (1925); these were reproduced in *Tables for Statisticians and Biometricians*, vol. II (1931), together with a table giving certain percentage points of $X_n$ (Tables XXI and XXI *bis*). The first table is not reproduced here; the second appears in a modified form as Table 24.

As given, the table relates to $X_n$; the percentage points for $X_1$ will be obtained by changing the sign of the figures and reversing the headings 'lower' and 'upper'. Thus while the probability is 0·05 that the *highest* value of $x$ in a sample of $n = 4$ will have a value *below* $\mu - 0\cdot068\sigma$, it is also clearly 0·05 that the *lowest* value of $x$ will exceed $\mu + 0\cdot068\sigma$.

The upper percentage points of $X_n$ are helpful in determining whether outlying observations belong to a specified normal distribution. The lower percentage points are perhaps less useful, but they may be of value as rough exploratory yardsticks, and they are instructive in showing the vagaries to which random samples are sometimes subject. For example, since the lower 2·5 % point of $X_n$ is just negative, and hence the upper 2·5 % point of $X_1$ is just positive, it is seen that in 1 out of 20 samples of $n = 5$, all the observations will fall either above or below the population mean. The table may also be useful in certain quality control problems, of which the following is an illustration.

*Example* 19. In the mass production of a certain article a firm aims at an average breaking strength of 176 lb., and a variability in strength which should not exceed a value measured by a standard deviation of 12 lb. In order to ensure that the production is kept under control, tests of breaking strength are applied at intervals to samples of 20 articles, and a simple check rule is required to be given to the foreman in charge of these tests. There is reason to believe that the distribution of breaking strength of this product when the manufacture is properly controlled is approximately normal.

The following rule is suggested:

The foreman should report when

(a) the sum of the breaking strength of the 20 articles in the sample is less than 3395 lb.; or when

(b) the lowest breaking strength is less than 136 lb.

This rule has the following basis:

The standard error of the mean of samples of 20 is $12/\sqrt{20} = 2\cdot683$ lb. Table 24 shows that the deviation corresponding to the lower 1 % point of $X_1$ is $-2\cdot326$ in samples of 1 and $-3\cdot289$ in samples of 20. Hence the mean in a random sample of 20 should only once in a hundred times be less than $176 - 2\cdot326 \times 2\cdot683 = 169\cdot76$ lb., and the sum of the 20 breaking strengths should not be less than $20 \times 169\cdot76 = 3395\cdot2$ lb. Again, the lowest value in the sample should only be less than $176 - 3\cdot289 \times 12 = 136\cdot53$ lb. in 1 % of samples. Of course the strengths of the mean and of the weakest individuals are correlated, and a more exhaustive test might be applied, based on the mean and standard deviation of the sample. But if one of the main purposes in controlling variability is to prevent articles appearing below a certain level of strength, the use of the lower limit seems to be suitable. The test is also much simpler in application than one involving the calculation of the standard deviation of the sample.

## 12. The distribution of the range (Tables 20, 22, 23 and 27)

### 12·1 *Definitions*

If $x_1$ and $x_n$ are the lowest and highest values of the variate in a sample of $n$ observations,

$$w = x_n - x_1$$

is the *range* of the sample.

In standardized form $\qquad W = X_n - X_1 = (x_n - x_1)/\sigma.$

Where it is necessary to make clear the size of the sample involved, we shall write $w_n$ or $W_n$.

In general, if $f(X)$ is the frequency function of a standardized variable $X$, then the probability integral of $W$ for a sample of $n$ may be expressed in the form

$$P(W \mid n) = n \int_{-\infty}^{\infty} f(X) \left\{ \int_{X}^{X+W} f(u)\, du \right\}^{n-1} dX. \qquad (67)$$

43

Table 23 gives values of $P(W \mid n)$ for the normal frequency function $f(X) = (2\pi)^{-\frac{1}{2}} e^{-\frac{1}{2}X^2}$, and for $n = 2$ (1) 20, $W = 0{\cdot}00$ (0·05) 7·25. The method of computation has been described by Hartley (1942). The table is perhaps mainly of value as a fundamental table which has formed the starting point for certain theoretical investigations into the properties of range distribution and for several derived tables of considerable practical utility described below. Small errors in the original table have been corrected by reference to Harter *et al.* (1959).

## 12·2 *Application*

We give below a rather special example of the direct application of Table 23 to a problem in machine-part assembly.

*Example* 20. Electromagnetic relays are manufactured to a specified-setting-up time. This is the time elapsing between the primary impulse in the coil and the complete contact in the secondary circuit of the relay. For each individual relay the actual setting-up time may differ from specification but will stay practically constant in time. Sets of, say, 15 relays are now assembled in a machine. To prevent 'arcing', a cam must keep the secondary circuit broken from before the first relay has set up until after the last relay has set up. The length of the break interval is a fixed characteristic of the cam and samples of 15 relays whose range in setting-up time exceeds this interval cannot, therefore, be fitted. Thus, on testing, the slowest or the fastest relay will have to be replaced, and it is necessary to keep the frequency of such replacements below a reasonably low percentage. Table 23 gives this frequency if we have adequate information on the standard deviation $\sigma$ of the setting up times. Suppose, for example, that $\sigma = \frac{1}{25}$ sec. and that the cam has a break interval of $\frac{1}{5}$ sec., then $W = 0{\cdot}20/0{\cdot}04 = 5$, so that entering Table 23 for $n = 15$, $W = 5$ we find $P(5 \mid 15) = 0{\cdot}9688$; thus the expected percentage frequency of replacements is $100 \, (1 - P(5 \mid 15)) = 3{\cdot}12$.

In general, the formulae

$$W = \frac{\text{Cam break interval}}{\text{Standard deviation of setting-up times}},$$

$$100 \, (1 - P(W \mid n)) = \text{percentage frequency of necessary replacements},$$

where $n$ is the number of relays assembled in the machine, relate the variation of the relays to the cam-break interval. The table may therefore be used as a guide when deciding on tolerance limits in the manufacture of relays or in designing a cam to make it fit the relays.

## 12·3 *Interpolation in Table* 23

If $W = W_0 + 0{\cdot}05\theta$ (where $W_0$ is the tabular argument nearest to and smaller than $W$), interpolates from the linear formula

$$P(W \mid n) = (1 - \theta) \, P(W_0 \mid n) + \theta P(W_0 + 0{\cdot}05 \mid n)$$

should be (*a*) decreased by a unit in the fourth decimal if $0{\cdot}005 \leqslant P \leqslant 0{\cdot}40$ and $0{\cdot}1 \leqslant \theta \leqslant 0{\cdot}9$ and (*b*) increased by a unit in the fourth decimal if $0{\cdot}5 \leqslant P \leqslant 0{\cdot}97$ and $0{\cdot}1 \leqslant \theta \leqslant 0{\cdot}9$. When $n = 2$, instead of (*a*) and (*b*), add a unit in the fourth decimal if $0{\cdot}40 \leqslant P \leqslant 0{\cdot}92$ and $0{\cdot}1 \leqslant \theta \leqslant 0{\cdot}9$. This procedure will normally give results to within a unit in the fourth decimal.

## 12·4 *The percentage points of the range (Table* 22)

Inverse interpolation in Table 23 provides the percentage points of the range given in Table 22 for $n = 2$ (1) 20. This table is clearly useful in problems of industrial quality control where a check is being kept on the variability of the product.

*Example* 21. The same example may be taken as was used in § 10·2 to illustrate the table of the percentage points for the mean deviation. The critical standard deviation in time of fuse-running being fixed at 0·5 sec., inner and outer control limits for the range of observed times, in a sample of eight fuses, may be obtained as follows from the columns headed 2·5 % and 0·1 %.

Inner control limits at

$$0·5 \times 1·41 = 0·70 \, \text{sec.} \quad \text{and} \quad 0·5 \times 4·61 = 2·30 \, \text{sec.}$$

Outer control limits at

$$0·5 \times 0·83 = 0·41 \, \text{sec.} \quad \text{and} \quad 0·5 \times 5·82 = 2·91 \, \text{sec.}$$

### 12·5   *The moments of the distribution of the range* (*Tables* 20 *and* 27)

If $P(X) = 1 - Q(X)$ is the probability integral of a standardized random variable $X$, where $-\infty \leqslant X \leqslant \infty$, then it is known (see Karl Pearson, 1902; and Tippett, 1925) that the expectation and variance of the distribution of the range, $W$, in samples of size $n$ may be written in the form

$$
\left.
\begin{aligned}
\mathscr{E}(W) &= \int_{-\infty}^{\infty} \{1 - [Q(u)]^n - [P(u)]^n\} \, du, \\
\text{var}(W) &= 2 \int_{-\infty}^{\infty} du \int_{-\infty}^{u} \{1 - [P(u)]^n - [Q(v)]^n + [P(u) - P(v)]^n\} \, dv - \{\mathscr{E}(W)\}^2.
\end{aligned}
\right\}
\tag{68}
$$

Expressions of increasing complexity, which must be evaluated by quadrature, may be obtained for the higher moments. If the population sampled is normal, the probability integral of equation (2) will be substituted for $P(X)$.

Simpler formulae for the moments $\mu_r^*(n)$ of range about a working origin $W^*$ can, of course, be based on its probability integral $P(W \mid n)$ in the form

$$
\mu_r^*(n) = (-W^*)^r + r \int_0^{\infty} (1 - P(W \mid n))(W - W^*)^{r-1} \, dW,
\tag{69}
$$

but the accuracy obtainable from these is restricted by that available for $P(W \mid n)$.

Tippett (1925) used the first relation (68) to compute the expectation of $W_n = w_n/\sigma$ in samples from a normal population, for $n = 2\,(1)\,1000$. This table, given in his paper, was reproduced in *Tables for Statisticians and Biometricians*, vol. II, Table XXII. In the present reissue we have included as Table 27 only the first half of this table, for $n = 2\,(1)\,499$.† Tippett also calculated a few values of $\sigma(W)$ and of the moment ratios $\beta_1(W)$ and $\beta_2(W)$ using an approximate process, and on the basis of these provided charts for these statistics for sample sizes up to 1000. Much more accurate values of the moments for $n \leqslant 100$ have since been obtained by Harter *et al.* (1959) and also, for the single case of $n = 200$, by Harley & Pearson (1957). The following figures have been taken from these publications.

| $n$ | $\mathscr{E}(W)$ | $\sigma(W)$ | $\beta_1(W)$ | $\beta_2(W)$ |
|------|------|------|------|------|
| 60 | 4·63856 | 0·639 | 0·201 | 3·35 |
| 100 | 5·01519 | 0·605 | 0·223 | 3·39 |
| 200 | 5·49209 | 0·566 | 0·252 | 3·44 |
| 500 | 6·07340 | 0·524 | 0·285 | 3·50 |
| 1000 | 6·48287 | 0·497 | 0·309 | 3·54 |

† Additional values for $n = 500\,(10)\,1000$ have been printed below the main table.

Table 20 of the present volume contains for $n = 2\,(1)\,20$ values of $\mathscr{E}(W)$ or in common notation $d_n$, var $(W)$ and its square root $\sigma(W)$, $\beta_1(W)$ and $\beta_2(W)$, as well as certain special quantities derived from $d_n$ and var $(W)$, whose use is described on p. 54 below. The values have been checked against Harter's table and a considerable number of last figure errors in the original table were found and corrected.

## 12·6  Applications

### (a)  Estimation of the standard deviation

Using again the common notation, we may write

$$\mathscr{E}(W_n) = \mathscr{E}(w_n/\sigma) = d_n;$$

it follows that the range between the extreme observations in a sample, divided by the appropriate numerical factor $d_n$, has an expectation of $\sigma$, i.e. $w_n/d_n$ is an unbiased estimate of $\sigma$. Further, the standard error of this estimate will be $\sigma(W_n) \times \sigma/d_n$, i.e. is obtained by multiplying $\sigma$ by the coefficient of variation of the range. To assist in the computation of the range estimate in small samples the reciprocal of $d_n$ is given in the second column of Table 22. It is now possible to compare the reliability, measured by the standard error, of three alternative estimators of the standard deviation, $\sigma$, in a normal population, namely, those obtained from the sample standard deviation, the mean deviation and the range. As in the case of the range, the first and second estimators can be adjusted so that their expectations are $\sigma$, by division by factors (depending on the sample size $n$) obtainable from equations (30) and (64). Thus using Tables 35 (for $s$) and 20 (for $m$ and for $w$), we reach the comparison shown in the following table, where figures in columns 2, 3 and 4 are the coefficients of variation of $s$, $m$ and $w$, respectively.

*Standard errors of alternative unbiased estimators of $\sigma$ (expressed in terms of $\sigma$ as unit)*

| Sample size $n$ | S.D. estimate | M.D. estimate | Range estimate | Range estimate ÷ S.D. estimate |
|---|---|---|---|---|
| 2  | 0·756 | 0·756 | 0·756 | 1·00 |
| 3  | ·523  | ·525  | ·525  | 1·00 |
| 4  | ·422  | ·430  | ·427  | 1·01 |
| 5  | ·363  | ·373  | ·372  | 1·02 |
| 6  | 0·323 | 0·334 | 0·335 | 1·04 |
| 7  | ·294  | ·306  | ·308  | 1·05 |
| 8  | ·272  | ·283  | ·288  | 1·06 |
| 9  | ·254  | ·265  | ·272  | 1·07 |
| 10 | 0·239 | 0·250 | 0·259 | 1·08 |
| 12 | ·215  | ·227  | ·239  | 1·11 |
| 15 | ·191  | ·201  | ·218  | 1·14 |
| 20 | ·163  | ·173  | ·195  | 1·20 |

It is seen that, up to samples of 6, the range estimator is as reliable as that based on the mean deviation and up to $n = 10$ there is very little to choose between them. Beyond this, the relative accuracy of the range estimator falls off progressively. It will be seen from Table 20 that the distribution of mean deviation tends to normality with increasing $n$, its $\beta_1$ and $\beta_2$ coefficients tending to 0 and 3; on the other hand, the distribution of range approaches the normal most closely in the neighbourhood of $n = 8 - 10$, and afterwards diverges, $\beta_1$ and $\beta_2$ tending to limiting values of 0·6493 and 4·2000 (Gumbel, 1949).

*(b)* *The use of mean range*

As the sample size increases, the distribution of the extreme observations in a sample, and therefore that of the range, will depend more and more on the form of the tails of the population frequency curve. The distribution of range will therefore be rather sensitive to departure from normality of a kind which it is very difficult to detect in practice. For this reason and because the ratio of the coefficient of variation of $w$ to that of $s$ increases without limit as $n \to \infty$, it is common to estimate $\sigma$ from the mean range of the observations in a number of small groups. If $k$ samples of $n$ observations are available, and we write the mean value of their ranges as $\overline{w}_n$, we may use $\overline{w}_n/d_n$ as an estimator of $\sigma$. This will have a standard error of $\sigma(W_n) \times \sigma/(\sqrt{k}\, d_n)$. Further, the sampling distribution of this estimator will have moment ratios

$$\beta_1(\overline{w}_n) = \beta_1(W_n)/k, \quad \beta_2(\overline{w}_n) = 3 + \{\beta_2(W_n) - 3\}/k,$$

and its approach to the normal form may be examined with the help of Table 20.

### 12·7   *Illustrative examples*

*Example* 22 (use of Tables 20 and 35). Example 15 (p. 37) contains measurements of tensile strength of six specimens of rubber drawn from each of five batches. These data may be used to obtain a range estimate of the within-batch standard deviation, $\sigma$, and also to make comparisons of alternative estimators of $\sigma$. It is necessary to assume that the within-batch variation is approximately normal and has a variance which is common from batch to batch. The following table shows the five sample variance estimates $s^2$ (and their square roots, $s$), the mean deviations ($m$) and the ranges ($w$). While $s^2$ is an unbiased estimator of $\sigma^2$, the expectation of $s$ is less than $\sigma$. All three statistics therefore need adjustment before they give unbiased estimates of $\sigma$:

(i) Since $n = 6$, $\nu = 5$, $s$ must be divided by $(\tfrac{2}{5})^{\frac{1}{2}} \Gamma(3)/\Gamma(2\cdot5)$ (putting $r = 1$ in equation (30)), whose numerical value col. 2 of Table 35 shows to be 0·9515.

(ii) The value of $m$ must be divided by $\{2 \times 5/(6\pi)\}^{\frac{1}{2}}$ (see equation (64)); Table 20, col. 2, gives the value 0·7284.

(iii) The value of $w$ must be divided by $d_6$ given as 2·5344 in Table 20, col. 7.

| Estimator | Sample no. | | | | | Mean value |
|---|---|---|---|---|---|---|
| | 1 | 2 | 3 | 4 | 5 | |
| Variance, $s^2$ | 468·6 | 653·1 | 406·0 | 196·3 | 111·5 | 367·1 |
| Standard deviation, $s$ | 21·6 | 25·6 | 20·1 | 14·0 | 10·6 | |
| Unbiased estimate | **22·7** | **26·9** | **21·1** | **14·7** | **11·1** | **19·3** |
| Mean deviation, $m$ | 16·6 | 20·0 | 15·7 | 10·2 | 8·6 | |
| Unbiased estimate | **22·8** | **27·5** | **21·6** | **14·0** | **11·8** | **19·5** |
| Range, $w$ | 59 | 66 | 56 | 38 | 27 | |
| Unbiased estimate | **23·3** | **26·0** | **22·1** | **15·0** | **10·7** | **19·4** |

N.B. The unit of measurement for the estimates of $\sigma$ is kg./cm.²

The high correlation between the corresponding sample values of the three estimators is particularly noticeable. If common estimates are calculated by taking the mean of the five sample values, we obtain the figures in the last column of the table, namely, 19·34, 19·54 and 19·42, in close agreement.

(iv) If the five variance estimates are summed and averaged, we obtain 367·1, with square root 19·16. The latter will be a slightly biased estimate of $\sigma$; as the total degrees of freedom are $\nu = 25$, the appropriate corrective factor taken from Table 35, col. 2, is 0·9901, giving as an unbiased estimate $19·16/0·9901 = 19·3$ (5).

The standard errors of these four alternative pooled estimates of $\sigma$ may be obtained as follows:

(i) For estimate based on mean $s$,

$$\sigma \times \text{s.d.}(s/\sigma)/\{\mathscr{E}(s/\sigma) \times \sqrt{5}\} = 0·145\sigma \quad \text{(Table 35)}.$$

(ii) For estimate based on mean $m$,

$$\sigma \times \text{s.d.}(m/\sigma)/\{\mathscr{E}(m/\sigma) \times \sqrt{5}\} = 0·150\sigma \quad \text{(Table 20)}.$$

(iii) For estimate based on mean $w$,

$$\sigma \times \text{s.d.}(w/\sigma)/\{\mathscr{E}(w/\sigma) \times \sqrt{5}\} = 0·150\sigma \quad \text{(Table 20)}.$$

(iv) For estimate based on the total within-sample sum of squares ($\nu = 25$), Table 35 shows that the standard error when corrected for bias will be

$$\sigma \times 0·1407/0·9901 = 0·142\sigma.$$

If we substitute for the unknown $\sigma$ a value of, say, 19·4 based on the sample estimates, it is seen that these standard errors lie between 2·7 and 2·9 kg./cm.² While, therefore, the fourth method, based on the usual analysis of variance procedure of averaging the individual sample sums of squared deviations before taking the square root, provides the unbiased estimate of $\sigma$ with the smallest standard error, it is clear that the differences between the four estimates are very much smaller than the standard error of any one of them. This is due to the very high correlation which exists between the alternative estimators.

*Example* 23 (use of Table 27). Tippett's table of the expectation of $w/\sigma$, i.e. $d_n$, in medium or large samples from a normal population may be of value in certain theoretical investigations, but is more likely to be useful in rough assessments of the homogeneity or accuracy of data. For example, it has been suggested that a useful check against major arithmetical errors in calculating a standard deviation is provided by comparing the figure obtained for $s$ with the range of the observations, divided by the appropriate $d_n$ factor. The following discussion illustrates this suggestion.

Hooke (1926) gives tables of the individual measurements of a large number of cranial characters, made on a series of skulls (probably of the seventeenth century) dug up during excavations in Farringdon Street, London, in 1924–5. The table on p. 49 gives information regarding four only of the cranial characters:

$L$ = glabellar-occipital length,   $B$ = maximum parietal breadth,
$LB$ = length from basion to nasion,   $S$ = arc from nasion to opisthion.

The values of $d_n$ in col. 4 are taken from Table 27. The standard errors of $s$, in col. 6, are estimated from $s/\sqrt{(2n)}$, and those in col. 5 from $\text{s.d.}(w/\sigma) \times s/d_n$. The four values of $\text{s.d.}(w/\sigma)$ were read from Diagram VI of Tippett's (1925) paper.

A comparison of the standard errors of the two estimates of $\sigma$ shows at once the inefficiency of the range estimator computed in this way from a single large sample. As the two estimates

48

are correlated,* care is needed in testing whether the differences between them are significant. A more satisfactory check is obtained by calculating the ratios of range to standard deviation $w_n/s_n$ and referring these values to Table 29$c$, discussed more fully on p. 59. It is seen that all the four values of the ratio given in the last column of the table below lie between the lower and upper 10 % significance levels obtainable from Table 29$c$. No abnormalities of the distributions of the four cranial characters are therefore indicated by the $w/s$ criterion.

| Character | $n$ | Range | $d_n$ | Estimates of $\sigma$ and their s.e.'s | | $\dfrac{w}{s}$ |
| | | | | From range | From sample s.d. | |
|---|---|---|---|---|---|---|
| (1) | (2) | (3) | (4) | (5) | (6) | (7) |
| $L$ | 141 | 30·5 | 5·256 | 5·80 ± 0·72 | 6·46 ± 0·38 | 4·72 |
| $B$ | 142 | 28·0 | 5·261 | 5·32 ± 0·65 | 5·90 ± 0·35 | 4·75 |
| $LB$ | 119 | 23·0 | 5·138 | 4·48 ± 0·52 | 4·47 ± 0·29 | 5·15 |
| $S$ | 129 | 75·5 | 5·195 | 14·53 ± 1·61 | 14·20 ± 0·88 | 5·32 |

N.B. The unit is 1 mm.

### 13. The extreme normal deviate measured from the sample mean and its studentized form† (Tables 25, 26, 26$a$ and 26$b$)

The determination of the extreme standardized deviate $X_n = (x_n - \mu)/\sigma$ from the observed extreme variate $x_n$, depends on a knowledge of both $\mu$ and $\sigma$ and the computation of the standardized mean deviation $m/\sigma$ and range $W = w/\sigma$, on a knowledge of $\sigma$. Indeed, it is this relation to $\sigma$ which make these latter statistics suitable estimators of $\sigma$. However, in the applications (such as Examples 19 (p. 43), 21 (p. 45) and 24 (p. 50)), where $X_n$ and $W$ are used as indicators of departures from a basic normal distribution, we require, for the computation of the standardized statistics $X$ and $W$, a knowledge of $\mu$ and/or $\sigma$. Since these will often not be known, it is desirable to have statistics in which $\mu$ only, $\mu$ and $\sigma$, or $\sigma$ only, are replaced by appropriate estimates, and Tables 25 and 26 are concerned with such statistics.

Table 25 gives percentage points of $u = (x_n - \bar{x})/\sigma$ or $u = -(x_1 - \bar{x})/\sigma$, i.e. of the deviation of the largest (smallest) observation in a sample of $n$ from the sample mean $\bar{x}$, divided by the standard deviation of the sampled normal population. This statistic, although independent of $\mu$, still depends on $\sigma$. The probability integral, originally derived by McKay (1935) and tabulated by K. R. Nair (1948$b$), is given by

$$P(u \mid n) = \sqrt{n}\,(2\pi)^{-\frac{1}{2}(n-1)} G_{n-1}(nu),$$

where the $r$th $G$-function is defined by the recurrence relation

$$G_r(x) = \int_0^x \exp\left\{-\frac{\iota^2}{2r(r+1)}\right\} G_{r-1}(t)\,dt, \quad G_0(x) = 1. \tag{70}$$

The criterion will be useful in deciding whether to reject an outlying observation as anomalous when no knowledge about the population mean $\mu$ is available, but $\sigma$ is known from previous experience.

---

* It can be shown that this correlation is given by [s.d. $(s)/\mathscr{E}(s)$]/[s.d. $(w)/\mathscr{E}(w)$].
† For use of the term 'studentized', see p. 52, footnote.

*Example* 24. The following illustration has been given by McKay (1935). In the course of routine testing of a standard leather product from a tannery, five parallel tests yielded the following values for the hide substance content of the leather specimens: 32·44, 36·45, 39·64, 40·13, 41·09. The first observation appears rather low. Long experience with the product in question has established a value of 2·2 for the standard deviation $\sigma$. We find

$$u = (37 \cdot 95 - 32 \cdot 44)/2 \cdot 2 = 2 \cdot 5;$$

this exceeds the 5 % value of Table 25, and we conclude that the first observation may well be anomalous.

More often than not, however, $\sigma$ will also be unknown. Suppose first that there is available a root-mean-square estimate $s$ of $\sigma$ based on $\nu$ degrees of freedom and independent of the sample under consideration.

Table 26 gives six upper percentage points of the studentized extreme deviate

$$t_n = (x_n - \bar{x})/s \quad \text{or} \quad t_1 = (\bar{x} - x_1)/s.$$

It is based on the original tabulations by K. R. Nair (1948$b$, 1952), later revised and slightly extended by H. A. David (1956). For the upper 5 and 1 % points values for $\nu = 5$ (1) 9 have been added from K. C. S. Pillai (1959).

Lower 5 % and 1 % points were also computed by Nair for $\nu = 10$, 15 and 30 but are not reproduced here. For $\nu \geqslant 10$ these lower percentage points only change slightly with increasing $\nu$. The values for $\nu = \infty$ are those given in the 4th and 6th columns, respectively, of Table 25 while for $\nu = 10$ we have:

| $n$ | | 3 | 4 | 5 | 6 | 7 | 8 | 9 |
|---|---|---|---|---|---|---|---|---|
| Lower $\{$ | 1 % point | 0·09 | 0·19 | 0·29 | 0·37 | 0·43 | 0·49 | 0·54 |
| | 5 % point | ·20 | ·35 | ·46 | ·55 | ·62 | ·69 | ·74 |

In the application of this statistic to an analysis of variance of, say, variety trials, the sample would be represented by the $n$ varietal means $\bar{x}_t$, of which $\bar{x}_n$, 'the best yielder', would be tested against the general mean $\bar{x}$, whilst the independent estimate of standard deviation would be provided by $s_\nu = s/\sqrt{k}$, where $k$ is the number of replicates and $s^2$ is the error mean square.

*Example* 25. Snedecor (1946, p. 266) gives the results of a randomized block experiment for four strains of wheat, replicated in five blocks, with data and analysis of variance set out below:

| Block | Strain | | | |
|---|---|---|---|---|
| | A | B | C | D |
| 1 | 32·3 | 33·3 | 30·8 | 29·3 |
| 2 | 34·0 | 33·0 | 34·3 | 26·0 |
| 3 | 34·3 | 36·3 | 35·3 | 29·8 |
| 4 | 35·0 | 36·8 | 32·3 | 28·0 |
| 5 | 36·5 | 34·5 | 35·8 | 28·8 |
| Mean | 34·4 | 34·8 | 33·7 | 28·4 |

Grand mean 32·8

**50**

|  | Sum of squares | D.F. | Mean square |
|---|---|---|---|
| Blocks | 21·46 | 4 | 5·36 |
| Strains | 134·45 | 3 | 44·82 |
| Error | 26·26 | 12 | 2·19 |
| Total | 182·17 | 19 | |

In testing for the significance of a strain effect, we find $F = 44\!\cdot\!82/2\!\cdot\!19 = 20\!\cdot\!5$, $\nu_1 = 3$ and $\nu_2 = 12$ degrees of freedom. To quote Snedecor: 'one suspects that the highly significant $F$ is attributable largely to the small yield of strain $D$.' To test this we compute

$$t_n = (32\!\cdot\!8 - 28\!\cdot\!4)/\sqrt{(\tfrac{1}{5} \times 2\!\cdot\!19)} = 6\!\cdot\!6,$$

which is well beyond the 0·1 % significance level given in Table 26.

Had the error mean square been 13 instead of 2·19 (an error of 11 % per plot which is frequently encountered), the $F$-ratio would become insignificant, but on testing the difference between $D$ and the general mean we obtain $t_n = 2\!\cdot\!7$. Entering Table 26 with $n = 4$ and $\nu = 12$, we find that this value is significant at the 2·5 % level, so that this test would have been able to detect the low-yielding strain, $D$, in spite of the $F$-test failing to detect any difference between strains in general.

Under the foregoing conditions one may wish to base the estimation of $\sigma$ not only on the 'external' estimate $s_\nu$ but also on the 'internal' sum of squares $\Sigma(x_i - \bar{x})^2$, i.e. the sum of squares of the sample for which $x_n$ is the largest and $x_1$ the smallest item. Table 26$a$ (Quesenberry & David, 1961) provides upper 5 % and 1 % points of

$$b_n = (x_n - \bar{x})/S \quad \text{or} \quad b_1 = (\bar{x} - x_1)/S,$$

where

$$S^2 = \sum_{i=1}^{n} (x_i - \bar{x})^2 + \nu s_\nu^2.$$

Percentage points of the corresponding two-sided statistic

$$b^* = \max |x_i - \bar{x}|/S$$

are given in Table 26$b$, a condensed version of that in Quesenberry & David (1961). These $b$-statistics are known to have desirable optimal properties for the detection of a *single* outlier or, in the analysis of variance situation, of a single outlying population (the latter being the so-called slippage problem).

It is believed that Tables 26$a$ and $b$ will rarely be in error by more than a unit in the third decimal place.

In *Example* 25 we have

$$b_1 = (32\!\cdot\!8 - 28\!\cdot\!4)/\sqrt{[(134\!\cdot\!45 + 26\!\cdot\!26)/5]} = 0\!\cdot\!78.$$

Entering Table 26$a$ with $n = 4$, $\nu = 15$ we see that $b_1$ is highly significant. With error mean square 13 instead of 2·19 we find $b_1 = 0\!\cdot\!58$ which is still significant at the 1 % level. In the absence of outside knowledge a two-sided test is perhaps more appropriate in the present example. Table 26$b$ shows that our value of $b^*$ (which here equals $b_1 = 0\!\cdot\!58$) is just significant at the 1 % level.

So far we have supposed that an independent estimate $s_\nu$ of $\sigma$ is available. In the absence of such external information one has to base the estimation of $\sigma$ purely on the internal component computed from the sample under consideration. This case was originally investigated by Thompson (1935) and later in more detail and in amended form by Pearson & Chandra Sekar (1936). It is covered by Tables 26a and b as the special case $\nu = 0$. Thus in *Example* 24, in the absence of knowledge on $\sigma$, we compute the sum of squares about their mean for the five observations, $S^2 = 50 \cdot 08$, and hence have

$$b_1 = (37 \cdot 95 - 32 \cdot 44)/7 \cdot 08 = 0 \cdot 78.$$

Here $n = 5$, $\nu = 0$, and this value of $b_1$ is not significant according to Table 26a.

The different conclusion reached lies in the fact that we are now estimating the standard deviation from the five observations in the sample, which include possible abnormal values, i.e. we take as our estimate of $\sigma$, $s = \sqrt{(\frac{1}{4} \times 50 \cdot 08)} = 3 \cdot 54$. Before, under the conditions of *Example* 24, we supposed a reliable value of $\sigma = 2 \cdot 2$ was available from past experience.

## 14. Further tables based on range (Tables 29, 29a, b, c, 30, 31b and c)

In this section we shall discuss a number of tables, several of which were not included in the original edition of this volume. All are dependent on the distribution of the range in samples from a normal population. In a variety of situations they will provide the statistician with quick answers which can later be confirmed if necessary by a more orthodox technique.

*Table* 29. Upper percentage points of the studentized range, $q = w_n/s_\nu$.

*Table* 29a. Upper percentage points of the ratio $u = |\bar{x}_1 - \bar{x}_2|/(w_1 + w_2)$.

*Table* 29b. Upper percentage points of the ratio of two independent ranges, $F' = w_1/w_2$.

*Table* 29c. Percentage points of the ratio of the range to the standard deviation, $w/s$, where $w$ and $s$ are derived from the same sample of $n$ observations.

*Tables* 30 (A *and* B). Tables for the analysis of variance based on range.

*Table* 31b. Upper percentage points of the ratio $w_{\text{max.}} \Big/ \sum_{t=1}^{k} w_t$.

*Table* 31c. Upper percentage points of the ratio $w_{\text{max.}}/w_{\text{min.}}$.

It has been established from a number of investigations (e.g. Lord, 1950; Moore, 1957; Harter, 1963) that provided the ranges have been determined from small samples—preferably $n \leqslant 10$—these 'quick' tests based on the range are not seriously less effective in establishing departure from hypothesis (i.e. less powerful) than the more orthodox tests using root-mean-square estimators.

### 14·1 *The studentized range: definition and tables (Tables 29 and 30)*

If in the standardized range, $W_n = w_n/\sigma$, we replace the unknown population standard deviation $\sigma$ by the square root, $s_\nu$, of an independent mean-square estimate of $\sigma^2$ based on $\nu$ degrees of freedom, we obtain the *studentized range**

$$q = w_n/s_\nu.$$

---

* The term *studentized* has been gradually accepted into current usuage and we have ventured to drop both the capital $S$ and the inverted commas. The word may well have been first coined by W. S. Gosset himself; he certainly used it in correspondence as early as 1932 in connexion with this same problem of range (see letter quoted by E. S. Pearson, 1938, pp. 245–6).

The probability integral of this statistic is given by the integral

$$\Pr\{w_n/s_\nu \leqslant q\} = \int_0^\infty [\Gamma(\tfrac{1}{2}\nu)]^{-1}\, 2^{-\frac{1}{2}\nu+1}\, \nu^{\frac{1}{2}\nu}\, s^{\nu-1} \exp\{-\tfrac{1}{2}\nu s^2\}\, P(qs\mid n)\, ds, \tag{71}$$

where $P(w\mid n)$ is the probability integral of range (Table 23). For large $\nu$, this integral tends to $P(w\mid n)$ taken at argument $w=q$ and can, in fact, be evaluated as a series in powers of $\nu^{-1}$ (Hartley, 1944); thus

where
$$\left.\begin{aligned}
\Pr\{w_n/s_\nu \leqslant q\} &= P + a_1\nu^{-1} + a_2\nu^{-2} + \dots, \\
a_1 &= \tfrac{1}{4}\{q^2 P'' - q P'\}, \\
a_2 &= \tfrac{1}{96}\{3q^4 P^{\mathrm{iv}} - 2q^3 P'''\} - \tfrac{1}{8}a_1
\end{aligned}\right\} \tag{72}$$

and $P$ and its derivatives $P'$, ..., $P^{\mathrm{iv}}$ are taken at argument $w=q$. Table 29, as published in the earlier editions of this volume, was obtained partly from an evaluation of (72) and, when this became inadequate for small $\nu$ and large $q$, by numerical quadrature of (71). More accurate later work by Pachares (1959) and Harter *et al.* (1959) has made it possible to remove a number of last figure errors in our original table and to add a table of upper 10 % points for $q$. At the same time we have omitted the tables of lower 5 % and 1 % points. Harter's (1959) Tables give: (*a*) the probability integral of $q$ to six decimal places for $n=2$ (1) 20 (2) 40 (10) 100; $\nu=1$ (1) 20, 24, 30, 40, 60, 120; (*b*) a table to four significant figures of the percentage points of $q$ for $P=0{\cdot}001$, $0{\cdot}005$, $0{\cdot}010$, $0{\cdot}025$, $0{\cdot}05$, $0{\cdot}10$, $(0{\cdot}1)$, $0{\cdot}90$, $0{\cdot}95$, $0{\cdot}975$, $0{\cdot}99$, $0{\cdot}995$, $0{\cdot}999$.

### 14·2 *The studentized range: applications of Tables* 29 *and* 30. *Short-cut tests in the analysis of variance*

Although the control limits for range used in quality control are usually computed from *estimates* of $\sigma$, these are commonly based on so many observations that the use of the studentized range in place of range is not required and the procedure given in Example 21 (p. 45) is adequate.

The main use of this statistic is, therefore, in analysis of variance where $q$:

(*a*) is the basic statistic used in various 'multiple contrast' comparison procedures concerned with contrasts between treatment means, and in the construction of simultaneous confidence intervals for such contrasts;

(*b*) may be used as an alternative, short-cut, statistic in place of the $F$-test.

In the simplest form we can take $q$ as the ratio of (i) the range of $k$ 'treatment' means each based on $n$ observations, to (ii) an estimate of the error standard deviation divided by $\sqrt{n}$, where this estimate is determined in the usual way from the within-treatment sum of squares. In this form $q$ may provide a more powerful means than $F$ of detecting, say, the difference between the best yielding treatment and the poorest treatment (which is often the experimental 'control' treatment), particularly in situations in which the gain of most of the treatments over the control is insignificant.

However, we may go further than this and use Table 29 and its companion Table 30 to provide short-cut tests in which both of the variance components are estimated from ranges or mean ranges instead of mean squares, so that the formation of sums of squares is avoided altogether. Patnaik (1950) has described the most straightforward of such tests. The procedure makes use of the fact that the mean value, $\overline{w}_n$, of the ranges in $k$ samples, each containing $n$

observations, from normal populations having a common variance $\sigma^2$, is distributed approximately (see E. S. Pearson, 1952) as $c\chi\sigma/\sqrt{\nu}$, where the *scale factor c* and the *equivalent degrees of freedom ν* are functions of $n$ and $k$. These functions are shown in Table 30A for $n = 2\,(1)\,10$, $k = 1\,(1)\,5, 10$, (and $\infty$ for $c$). Extrapolation for $\nu$ beyond $k = 5$ (or 10 for Table B) may be carried out by adding to the value of $\nu$ at $k = 5$ the 'constant difference' (c.d.) multiplied by $(k-5)$.

Patnaik applied the method to the case of a simple classification, such as the analysis of tensile strength records of rubber specimens (Example 15, p. 37) into between- and within-batch components. In this case, we proceed as follows:

(*a*) Estimate the within-batch variance from the mean of the batch ranges, $\overline{w}_n$.

(*b*) Estimate the between-batch variance from the range, say, $\overline{x}_{\max.} - \overline{x}_{\min.}$ of the batch means $\overline{x}_t$.

(*c*) Calculate the ratio
$$q = (\overline{x}_{\max.} - \overline{x}_{\min.})\,c\,\sqrt{n}/\overline{w}_n. \tag{73}$$

Since the estimates (*a*) and (*b*) are independent, the expression $q$ of equation (73) is approximately distributed as a studentized range for sample size $k$ (in place of the tabular $n$ of Table 29) and having the equivalent degrees of freedom $\nu$, of Table 30A, for the $s$-estimate.

*Example* 26. Applying this test to the data of Example 15 (p. 37), the five-batch ranges give a mean $\overline{w}_6 = 246/5 = 49\cdot2$. Entering Table 30A with 'sample size', $n = 6$ and 'number of samples', $k = 5$, we find $\nu = 22\cdot6$ and $c = 2\cdot56$, so that

$$q = (194\cdot3 - 158\cdot3)\,2\cdot56\,\sqrt{6}/49\cdot2 = 4\cdot59.$$

This value can be referred directly to the upper percentage points of $q$ (Table 29). Entering the table with a 'sample size' of 5 (the number of batch means, $k = 5$, plays the role of the 'sample size' in the numerator of $q$) and degrees of freedom $\nu = 22\cdot6$, we find that the observed value of $4\cdot59$ falls between the 5 % point at $4\cdot2$ and the 1 % point at $5\cdot2$. A similar result was obtained in the application of the $F$-test. It will also be noted that our estimate of the within-batch standard deviation, $\overline{w}_6/c = 19\cdot2$, based on the equivalent of $22\cdot6$ degrees of freedom, is close to the square root of the 'within-batch mean square', $s_2 = \sqrt{367\cdot1} = 19\cdot16$, based on 25 degrees of freedom quoted on p. 38; the loss of the equivalent of about 2 degrees of freedom is due to the short-cut procedure. It should be remembered that the squares of both these estimates, $19\cdot2^2$ and $19\cdot16^2$, are unbiased estimates of $\sigma^2$, in contrast to the estimate

$$\overline{w}_6/d_6 = 49\cdot2/2\cdot534 = 19\cdot42,$$

which is an unbiased estimate of $\sigma$ ($d_6 = 2\cdot534$ from Table 20).

In the case of $k$ samples with ranges $w_t$ based on unequal sample sizes $n_t$ ($t = 1, 2, \ldots, k$), an estimate of $\sigma$ may be obtained (H. A. David, 1951) from the weighted mean range

$$\frac{\sum\limits_t w_t(d_{n_t}/V_{n_t})}{\sum\limits_t (d_{n_t}^2/V_{n_t}) + \frac{1}{2}}.$$

The factors $d_{n_t}/V_{n_t}$ and $d_{n_t}^2/V_{n_t}$ are given in Table 20.* This quantity is distributed approximately as the root-mean-square estimator, $s$, for $\nu = \frac{1}{2}\Sigma d_{n_t}^2/V_{n_t}$ degrees of freedom.

In the case of a double classification the procedure has to be modified (Hartley, 1950) as shown by the following example.

---

\* $V_{n_t}$ is the variance of the standardized range $w/\sigma$ for sample size $n_t$.

*Example* 27. We again use Snedecor's data tabled in Example 25 (p. 50), giving yields of four strains of wheat planted in five randomized blocks. In order to estimate the error standard deviation, we first form differences of individual yields from their respective strain means (strain residuals) and then form ranges of these residuals for each of the five blocks. This work is shown below:

*Strain residuals and their block ranges*

| Block | Strain | | | | Range |
|-------|--------|--------|--------|--------|-------|
|       | A | B | C | D | |
| 1 | −2·1 | −1·5 | −2·9 | 0·9 | 3·8 |
| 2 | −0·4 | −1·8 | 0·6 | −2·4 | 3·0 |
| 3 | −0·1 | 1·5 | 1·6 | 1·4 | 1·7 |
| 4 | 0·6 | 2·0 | −1·4 | −0·4 | 3·4 |
| 5 | 2·1 | −0·3 | 2·1 | 0·4 | 2·4 |
| Total | — | — | — | — | 14·3 |

The procedure is now exactly the same as in the single classification except that Table 30 B must be used,[†] with

$$\text{number of ranges} = 5, \quad \text{sample size (for range)} = 4.$$

We find: mean range $\overline{w} = 14\cdot3/5 = 2\cdot86$, $\nu = 10\cdot9$, $c = 1\cdot88$,

and hence $q = (34\cdot8 - 28\cdot4)\,1\cdot88\,\sqrt{5}/2\cdot86 = 9\cdot4$.

Referring this value to the upper percentage points of $q$ in Table 29, with sample size (for range) = 4 and degrees of freedom 10·9, we find that it exceeds the 1 % point which is 5·6, a highly significant result similar to that obtained previously from the $F$-test. The estimate of the error standard deviation is $2\cdot86/1\cdot88 = 1\cdot52$, which agrees well with that obtained from the analysis of variance table given on p. 51, namely, $\sqrt{2\cdot19} = 1\cdot48$.

The method of estimation in the present double classification is, of course, unsymmetrical, as we have taken residuals from strain means and the five ranges of four such residuals in each of five blocks. Alternatively, we could have taken four ranges of five residuals from block means. This latter method would here have given the same estimate of 1·52, but may in general differ slightly, the one based on the larger sample sizes usually having a larger $\nu$ (see Table 30 B), and therefore being more precise. However, one would normally take residuals about 'treatment' means as these means are usually required for individual comparison of treatments (see § 14·3 below).

If a test for block differences is desired, we would have to form the means of the five blocks which are found to be 31·4, 31·8, 33·9, 33·0 and 33·9 respectively. The range of these is $33\cdot9 - 31\cdot4 = 2\cdot5$, so that $q = 2\cdot5 \times 1\cdot88\,\sqrt{4}/2\cdot86 = 3\cdot3$. Entering Table 29 with a sample size of 5 and $\nu = 10\cdot9$, we find for $q$ a 5 % value of 4·6 which is not exceeded, so that there are no significant block differences.

*Generalizations to higher designs.* A table making provision for applying the range method to the split plot experiment is given by H. A. David (1951), who also discusses other designs.

* Table 30 B takes account of the correlation between the ranges of residuals. For details, see Hartley (1950).

### 14·3  *Use of range estimators in the comparison of two means* (*Table* 29 *a*)

A natural extension of the use of range is to introduce this estimator of the population standard deviation in place of the root-mean-square estimator, $s$, in Student's $t$-tests, remembering that $w$, just as $s$, is independent of the mean in sampling from a normal population. Lord (1947) published tables of the percentage points of

$$(a)\ \ (\bar{x} - \mu)/w \quad \text{and} \quad (b)\ \ (\bar{x}_1 - \bar{x}_2)/\{\tfrac{1}{2}(w_1 + w_2)\},$$

where $w$ is the range and $\bar{x}$ the mean in a sample of $n$ observations from a normal population having mean $\mu$. Similarly $\bar{x}_t$, $w_t$ ($t = 1, 2$) are the means and ranges in independent samples of equal size $n$ from two normal populations with a common mean and variance. The first ratio, (*a*), provides a test of significance for the mean in a single sample, while the second ratio, (*b*), is appropriately used in comparing the means of two independent samples, each containing the same number of observations. Further, in the case of $n$ paired observations the ratio (*a*) may be applied to the mean $\bar{x}$ and the range $w$ of the $n$ paired differences.

(*a*) *Single sample case.* On noting that the range in a sample of two observations is distributed as half a normal curve having standard deviation $\sqrt{2}\sigma$, it will be seen that the upper percentage points of $|\bar{x} - \mu|/w$ may be obtained from Table 29 *b* described below, by entering the table with $n_1 = 2$, $n_2 = n$ and dividing the tabular entry by $\sqrt{(2n)}$. For a single-tail test at level $\alpha'$, Table 29 *b* should be entered in the column $\alpha = 2\alpha'$.

As an illustration we may go back to Examples 5 and 6 (pp. 18, 20) and ask whether the 12 values of breaking strength of cotton fabric are consistent with the hypothesis that the average strength of this material is $\mu = 171 \cdot 5$. We find that

$$|\bar{x} - \mu|/w = |167 \cdot 08 - 171 \cdot 5|/27 = 0 \cdot 164.$$

Table 29 *b* entered with $n_1 = 2$, $n_2 = 12$ gives a 10 % point for $w_1/w_2$ of $0 \cdot 7726$ and a 5 % point of $0 \cdot 9513$; dividing these values by $\sqrt{24} = 4 \cdot 899$ we obtain the corresponding values $0 \cdot 158$ and $0 \cdot 194$ for a double-tail test of the ratio $|\bar{x} - \mu|/w$. Thus the observed value falls between the 10 % and 5 % points as was the case when applying the standard Student $t$-test.

(*b*) *Two sample case.* (Table 29 *a*). In the general case where $n_1 \neq n_2$, Moore (1957) suggested that the ratio $u = (\bar{x}_1 - \bar{x}_2)/(w_1 + w_2)$ might still be used as a test statistic although in theory the most effective test would now give different weights to the sample ranges, $w_1$ and $w_2$, depending on $n_1$ and $n_2$. He compared his test with one in which the denominator of the ratio had the value $\sum_{t=1}^{2} (w_t d_{n_t}/V_{n_t})$, the multiplying factors being the weights defined in §14·2 and given in Table 20. As a result of the comparison, he did not consider that the small gain in power when using the weighted range estimator justified the additional complication introduced into the test.

Table 29 *a*, gives upper significance points for Moore's ratio, $u$, for all combinations of sample sizes $2 \leqslant n_1, n_2 \leqslant 20$. When divided by two, the table entries for $n_1 = n_2$ correspond to those given by Lord (1947). Apart from the case $n_1 = n_2$, the tabular entries are not exact as Moore used a $\chi$-approximation for the distribution of $(w_1 + w_2)/\sigma$ on the lines suggested in §14·2. The few comparisons made with exact results obtained by quadrature did not show errors in the approximation of more than two units in the third decimal place.

*Example* 28. The following illustration is taken from Moore's (1957) paper. Two operators,

$A$ and $B$, make determinations of the percentage of ammonia in plant gas, with the following results:

| | | | | | | | | |
|---|---|---|---|---|---|---|---|---|
| Operator $A$ | 43 | 44 | 56 | 63 | 46 | | | |
| Operator $B$ | 39 | 35 | 43 | 32 | 36 | 48 | 33 | 33 |

From these figures can it be said that the operators are consistently measuring the same thing? The data give

| | $n_t$ | $\bar{x}_t$ | $w_t$ | $w_t/d_{n_t}$ | $\sum_i (x_{ti} - \bar{x}_t)^2$ | $s_t^2$ | $s_t$ |
|---|---|---|---|---|---|---|---|
| Operator $A$ $(t=1)$ | 5 | 50·4 | 20 | 8·60 | 305·2 | 76·30 | 8·73 |
| Operator $B$ $(t=2)$ | 8 | 37·375 | 16 | 5·62 | 221·875 | 31·70 | 5·63 |

It follows that $|\bar{x}_1 - \bar{x}_2|/(w_1 + w_2) = 13·025/36 = 0·362$, a value which Table 29$a$ shows to be just beyond the 1 % level of significance, remembering that we are here using a double-tail test. The usual form of $t$-test gives $t = 3·301$ which for $\nu = 11$ degrees of freedom is found from Table 12 to be also significant at the 1 % level. In view of the unusually close correspondence between the range and root-mean-square estimates of $\sigma$ shown in the 4th and 7th columns of the table above, agreement between the two tests was to be expected.

### 14·4 *Use of range estimators in comparing the variances in two populations (Table 29b)*

It is natural to proceed from a range-based 'substitute' $t$-test to a range-based $F$-test. Table 29$b$ prepared by Harter (1963), considerably extending earlier tables by Link (1950) and Pillai & Buenaventura (1961), gives upper percentage points of the distribution of the ratio $F' = w_1/w_2$ of ranges determined from two independent samples of $n_1$ and $n_2$ observations drawn from normal populations having a common variance. To find the lower percentage points for $w_1/w_2$, we enter the table with $n_1$ and $n_2$ reversed and take the reciprocal of the figure extracted. For example, if $n_1 = 12$, $n_2 = 8$, the lower and upper 2·5 % points for $w_1/w_2$ are $1/1·807 = 0·553$ and $2·563$, respectively.

When dealing with two small samples the use of the range ratio clearly provides an extremely rapid method of assessing the significance of differences in variance. The test is of course somewhat less powerful for the detection of differences between variances than that based on $F = s_1^2/s_2^2$,* but if observations are not difficult to come by, the inclusion of between one and three additional observations in each sample, followed by the use of $w_1/w_2$ rather than $F$, might be considered worthwhile.

Harter made some detailed computations comparing the power of the two tests for the case of equal sample sizes, $n_1 = n_2$. The figures in the following table are taken from his results. It is supposed that in the two populations sampled, $\sigma_1 = \theta\sigma_2$, with $\theta > 1$; then the table shows the chances of establishing significance at the 5 % and 1 % levels ($\alpha = 0·05$ and $0·01$) for six different values of $\theta$.

---

* It should be noted that the loss in power when using range estimates of variability is a good deal less in tests for detecting 'non-centralities', i.e. differences between population means as in the linear comparisons of §14·2.

| $n_1 = n_2$ | $\alpha = 0.05$ | | | | | | $\alpha = 0.01$ | | | | | |
|---|---|---|---|---|---|---|---|---|---|---|---|---|
| | $\theta = 2$ | $\theta = 3$ | $\theta = 4$ | $\theta = 6$ | $\theta = 8$ | $\theta = 10$ | $\theta = 2$ | $\theta = 3$ | $\theta = 4$ | $\theta = 6$ | $\theta = 8$ | $\theta = 10$ |
| 3 | 0·174 | 0·321 | 0·456 | 0·653 | 0·769 | 0·839 | 0·039 | 0·083 | 0·139 | 0·266 | 0·391 | 0·501 |
| | ·174 | ·321 | ·457 | ·655 | ·771 | ·840 | ·039 | ·083 | ·139 | ·267 | ·393 | ·503 |
| 6 | 0·387 | 0·707 | 0·868 | 0·969 | 0·991 | 0·997 | 0·141 | 0·396 | 0·629 | 0·873 | 0·954 | 0·981 |
| | ·402 | ·729 | ·884 | ·975 | ·993 | ·997 | ·146 | ·417 | ·656 | ·891 | ·962 | ·985 |
| 9 | 0·537 | 0·869 | 0·966 | 0·997 | 1·000 | 1·000 | 0·257 | 0·649 | 0·866 | 0·981 | 0·997 | 0·999 |
| | ·582 | ·902 | ·978 | ·998 | 1·000 | 1·000 | ·288 | ·708 | ·905 | ·990 | ·998 | 1·000 |
| 12 | 0·642 | 0·938 | 0·990 | 1·000 | 1·000 | 1·000 | 0·360 | 0·796 | 0·950 | 0·997 | 1·000 | 1·000 |
| | ·714 | ·967 | ·996 | 1·000 | 1·000 | 1·000 | ·430 | ·870 | ·978 | ·999 | 1·000 | 1·000 |
| 15 | 0·717 | 0·969 | 0·997 | 1·000 | 1·000 | 1·000 | 0·447 | 0·879 | 0·981 | 0·999 | 1·000 | 1·000 |
| | ·808 | ·989 | ·999 | 1·000 | 1·000 | 1·000 | ·558 | ·946 | ·995 | 1·000 | 1·000 | 1·000 |

(The first line of each pair gives the power of the $F'$ test, the second line that of the $F$ test; $n_1$ and $n_2$ are sample sizes.)

Taking Harter's results as a whole, we find the following 'equivalent' sample sizes:

| $n$ for $F$-test | 2 | 3–9 | 10–11 | 12 |
|---|---|---|---|---|
| $n'$ for 'equivalent' range ratio $F'$-test | 2 | $n+1$ | $n+2$ | 15 |

In other words, the power of the $F'$-test with $n_1 = n_2 = n'$ is at least as great as that of the $F$-test with sample sizes $n_1 = n_2 = n$, $n'$ and $n$ being as above.

As an illustration consider the data of *Example* 28. Here $w_1/w_2 = 20/16 = 1·25$. Entering Table 29$b$ with $n_1 = 5$, $n_2 = 8$ we see that the observed ratio lies between the upper 25 % and 10 % points, which fall at 1·112 and 1·475, respectively. There is therefore no evidence that Operator $A$'s measurements are more variable than those of Operator $B$. If we use the standard test, $F = s_1^2/s_2^2 = 76·30/31·70 = 2·41$; Table 18 entered with $\nu_1 = 4$, $\nu_2 = 7$ shows again that this value lies between the 25 % and 10 % points which fall at 1·72 and 2·96.

14·5 *Range tests for heterogeneity of variance (Table 31b and 31c)*

It was suggested by Bliss, Cochran & Tukey (1956) that a very simple test based on the observed ranges in several samples of equal size might be used as a quick substitute for Cochran's test based on variances, described in §16·5 below. If $w_t$ $(t = 1, 2, ..., k)$ are the ranges in $k$ independent samples, each containing $n$ observations and drawn from normal populations having a common variance, then Table 31$b$ gives the upper 5 % points of the ratio of the largest range to the sum of all the ranges, i.e. of $w_{max.}/\sum w_t$. The test was originally developed to meet the need for a simple rejection criterion for use with several bioassays in the U.S. Pharmacopeia XV (1955). If the observed ratio exceeded the tabular value, the set of assays represented by this largest range was assumed to contain an aberrant observation or outlier, which was identified by inspection and rejected.

This test is exactly parallel with that suggested by Cochran (1941) in which sample variances are used instead of ranges and we calculate the ratio $s_{max.}^2/\sum s_t^2$ for which upper 5 % and 1 % points are given in Table 31$a$. A further alternative test is based on the ratio $w_{max.}/w_{min.}$, for which upper percentages are given in Table 31$c$ (see pp. 202, 264–5).

As an illustration we may use the data of *Example* 15 (pp. 37–8) for measurements on tensile strength of rubber. Here

$$w_{max.} = 66, \quad \sum w_l = 246 \quad \text{and} \quad w_{max.}/\sum w_l = 0.268; \quad w_{min.} = 27, \quad w_{max.}/w_{min.} = 2.44;$$

for $k = 5$, $n = 6$ Table 31$b$ and 31$c$ give upper 5% points of 0.351 and 4.187, respectively. Similarly

$$s^2_{max.} = 653.1, \quad \sum s^2_l = 1835.5 \quad \text{and} \quad s^2_{max.}/\sum s^2_l = 0.356;$$

this is a value well short of the 5% point (0.506) of Table 31$a$, taking $\nu = n - 1 = 5$.

The three tests are therefore in agreement in providing no evidence suggesting a significant difference between batch variabilities. The same conclusion is reached in §16.3 using the $M$-test and in §16.5 using the ratio $s^2_{max.}/s^2_{min.}$. Of course these five tests will not always give the same verdict, their comparative powers depending on the alternative to variance homogeneity that holds good (see Pearson, 1966, *Biometrika*, **53**, 229–34).

For $k > 10$, the authors of the test suggest using the following supplementary table from which approximate 5% points can be obtained by dividing the tabled factors by $k + 2$:

| $k$ \ $n$ | 2 | 3 | 4 | 5 | 6 | 7 | 8 | 9 | 10 |
|---|---|---|---|---|---|---|---|---|---|
| 10 | 4.06 | 3.04 | 2.65 | $2.44_5$ | $2.30_5$ | 2.21 | $2.14_5$ | 2.09 | 2.05 |
| 12 | 4.06 | 3.03 | $2.63_5$ | $2.42_5$ | 2.29 | 2.20 | 2.13 | $2.07_5$ | 2.04 |
| 15 | 4.06 | 3.02 | $2.62_5$ | $2.41_5$ | 2.28 | $2.18_5$ | 2.12 | $2.06_5$ | $2.02_5$ |
| 20 | 4.13 | 3.03 | 2.62 | $2.41_5$ | 2.28 | $2.18_5$ | 2.11 | 2.05 | 2.01 |
| 50 | 4.26 | 3.11 | 2.67 | 2.44 | 2.29 | 2.19 | 2.11 | 2.06 | 2.01 |

Bliss *et al.* (1956) give an example from the turbidimetric assay of vitamin $B_{12}$. For purpose of illustration the essential data are the ranges of percentage transmission, read in a photometer, among 32 sets of 3 tubes, as tabled below:

| Observed range for $n = 3$ | 0 | 1 | 2 | 3 | 4 | 5 | 6 | 7 | 8 | 13 |
|---|---|---|---|---|---|---|---|---|---|---|
| No. of sets of tubes, total 32 | 1 | 5 | 6 | 8 | 4 | 2 | 3 | 1 | 1 | 1 |

The total of ranges is 113, $w$ (max.) is 13 and the ratio is 0.115. Since $k = 32$ the auxiliary table is entered with $(k + 2) \times 0.115 = 3.91$ which clearly exceeds the value 3.08 obtained by interpolation in the table. Thus on the basis of all 32 ranges, the range of 13 was attributed to an outlier which was then identified and rejected.

### 14.6 A test of internal consistency within a single univariate sample (*Table* 29$c$)

The studentized range, $w_n/s_\nu$, discussed in §§14.1 and 14.2, is the ratio of the range in a sample of $n$ observations to a completely independent estimate of $\sigma$ based on $\nu$ degrees of freedom. The ratio dealt with now, whose percentage points are given in Table 29$c$, is that of the range, $w$, to the standard deviation, $s$, where both are calculated from the same normal sample and are therefore highly correlated. The statistic can be useful in several ways in detecting what might be described as abnormality of sample pattern. Such abnormality might result from:

(*a*) various types of heterogeneity, e.g. if what has been termed slippage has occurred or if there has been a change in variability during the sampling;

(*b*) the presence of one or more rogue observations;

(*c*) a gross computing error in calculating the standard deviation;

(*d*) The population not following a normal distribution, being either platykurtic ($\beta_2 < 3$), when $w/s$ will tend to be too small, or leptokurtic ($\beta_2 > 3$) when $w/s$ will tend to be too great.

The methods employed in calculating the percentage points have been described by David, Hartley & Pearson (1954) and Pearson & Stephens (1964). The values given to three decimal places are exact; the remainder were obtained by fitting Pearson curves with the correct first four moments. These latter values should rarely be in error by more than two units in the second decimal place. The columns headed 0 % give the extreme lower and upper bounds for the ratio in samples of *n* observations from *any* distribution.

*Example* 28*a*. A report by Mahalanobis *et al.* (1949) describes an anthropometric survey of the United Provinces of India undertaken in 1941. From these data the frequency distributions of head length were taken for each of 23 racial groups and the values of $w/s$ calculated. The sample sizes, *n*, varied between 57 and 197 and Fig. 2*a* shows the values of $w/s$ plotted against *n*. Also drawn are the upper and lower 5 % and 1 % levels taken from Table 29*c*. It will be seen that for five of the 23 groups $w/s$ falls beyond the upper 5 % level, for two of these, well beyond the 1 % level.

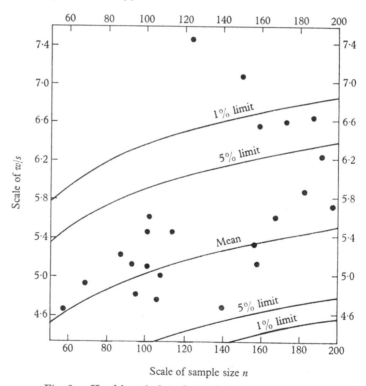

Fig. 2*a*. Head length data for 23 Indian racial groups.

On looking at the original frequency distributions it was found that in each of these five cases there was one or more than one divergent measurement, always in the sense of a small head length. Without further information it is not possible to say whether these outlying readings were due to faulty recording, but it is clear that the routine application of this simple check-test will from time to time provide a *prima facie* case for further scrutiny of data.

*Example* 28*b*. By considering the moment ratios $\sqrt{b_1}$ and $b_2$, it is shown below that the sample of 1000 measures of warp strength listed in the table of *Example* 35 (p. 69) are most unlikely to have been drawn randomly from a normal population. Could a quick pointer to this conclusion have been obtained from the ratio $w/s$?

As the data have been grouped, we cannot make a precise test. However, assuming that each observation falls at the centre of its group, we have $w = 95$ lb., $s = 17 \cdot 42$ lb. (not using Sheppard's correction for grouping). Hence $w/s = 5 \cdot 45$. Reference to Table 29$c$, with $n = 1000$, shows that the observed ratio falls below the lower 0·1 % point (at 5·50), certainly suggesting non-normality.

## 15. THE MEAN POSITION OF RANKED NORMAL DEVIATES (MEANS OF NORMAL ORDER STATISTICS) (TABLE 28)

### 15·1 Definitions

If we draw a sample of $n$ observations from a normal population with zero mean and standard deviation $\sigma$, we may arrange these in ascending order of magnitude, so that $x_1$ is the smallest and $x_n$ is the largest value. The $i$th value in the sequence, $X_i = x_i/\sigma$, may be termed the *i*th *ranked normal deviate*;* its expectation is

$$\xi(i \mid n) = \frac{n!}{(i-1)!\,(n-i)!} \int_{-\infty}^{\infty} Z P^{i-1} Q^{n-i} X \, dX, \tag{74}$$

where $Z$, $P$ and $Q$ are as defined in § 1·1. Table 28 gives $\xi(i \mid n)$ to 3 decimals for $n = 2\,(1)\,20$ and to 2 decimals for $n = 21\,(1)\,26\,(2)\,50$.

Since

$$\xi(i \mid n) = -\xi(n+1-i \mid n),$$

only positive values are tabled which may be regarded as the $[\frac{1}{2}n]$† largest ranks $\xi(n+1-i \mid n)$ or, with signs reversed, the $[\frac{1}{2}n]$ smallest ranks.

Reference to Table 27 will confirm that $|\xi(1 \mid n)| = \frac{1}{2}\bar{d}_n$, i.e. the mean extreme deviate equals half the mean range.

For odd values of $n$ between 26 and 50 linear interpolation between the neighbouring columns will give the value required with an error which should not be more than a unit in the second decimal. Note that for $n$ odd $\xi(\frac{1}{2}(n+1) \mid n) = 0$.

### 15·2 Applications

The table, in providing what may be called the average pattern of a normal sample, has applications in problems where ranked observations are selected for special study or where ranks must be translated into quantitative scores.

*Example* 29. In rearing a flock of thirty lambs it is decided to market the five heaviest at $2\frac{1}{2}$ months. We may wish to estimate their total weight. Taking from previous experience the information that the weights at $2\frac{1}{2}$ months follow a normal distribution with a mean of about 60 lb. and a standard deviation of about 4 lb., what would be the expected weight of the five heaviest lambs?

---

\* The term '$i$th normal order statistic' is current in American usage.
† $[x]$ stands for the largest integer smaller than or equal to $x$.

Entering Table 28 for $n = 30$, we find for this weight the estimate

$$5 \times 60 + 4(2 \cdot 04 + 1 \cdot 62 + 1 \cdot 36 + 1 \cdot 18 + 1 \cdot 03) = 329 \, \text{lb}.$$

In certain situations Table 28 may be used when estimating the parameters, $\mu$ and $\sigma$, of a normal population from the ordered observations of a random sample drawn from it. For example, the range estimate of $\sigma$, namely, $(x_n - x_1)/d_n$, may be calculated, but this would not normally be used for samples exceeding 20. For larger samples we may sometimes use the difference between the total of the $r$ largest observations $x_{n-r+1}, \ldots, x_n$ and that of the $r$ smallest observations $x_1, \ldots, x_r$ as an estimate of $\sigma$ (see Jones, 1946). Thus

$$S = \frac{x_{n-r+1} + \ldots + x_n - (x_1 + \ldots + x_r)}{2\{\xi(n \mid n) + \ldots + \xi(n - r + 1 \mid n)\}} \tag{75}$$

is an unbiased estimator of $\sigma$.

*Example* 30. Out of the fifty numbers in the first column of Wold's *Random Normal Deviates* (1948), the four largest are found to be $2 \cdot 82$, $2 \cdot 12$, $1 \cdot 98$ and $1 \cdot 39$, while the four smallest are $-2 \cdot 30$, $-2 \cdot 28$, $-1 \cdot 77$ and $-1 \cdot 00$. An estimate of $\sigma$ may therefore be computed from

$$S = \frac{2 \cdot 82 + 2 \cdot 12 + 1 \cdot 98 + 1 \cdot 39 + 1 \cdot 00 + 1 \cdot 77 + 2 \cdot 28 + 2 \cdot 30}{2(2 \cdot 25 + 1 \cdot 85 + 1 \cdot 63 + 1 \cdot 46)}$$

$$= 15 \cdot 66/(2 \times 7 \cdot 19) = 1 \cdot 089.$$

The usual root-mean-square estimate based on the whole fifty numbers is $s = 1 \cdot 003$. The population standard deviation for Wold's numbers is, of course, unity.

Jones (1946) has evaluated the required divisors $-2\{\xi(1 \mid n) + \ldots + \xi(r \mid n)\}$ for selected values of $n$ and $r$ as well as the variances of the estimates of $\sigma$. All his $n$ are $\geqslant 100$, but for $n \leqslant 10$ the variances may be obtained from the tables of variances and covariances of the $x_i$ calculated by Godwin (1949$b$). Figures for the efficiency of Jones's type of estimator were given by K. R. Nair (1950), while Godwin (1949$a$) discussed the problem of optimum 'linear estimators' of $\sigma$ based on the ordered sample values $x_i$. Similar questions were also considered by Mosteller (1946).

A further application of Table 28 is of the type described in Fisher & Yates's *Statistical Tables* (1963), p. 31 and Tables XX, XXI. If $n$ objects have been ranked (say in order of preference), but no quantitative values measuring this preference have been assigned by the experimenter, the score $\xi(i \mid n)$ may be given to the $i$th object and these scores may then be subjected to analysis. For example, they may form the basis for calculating a correlation coefficient (say, between two judges' rankings) or analysis of variance technique may be applied. In such applications it should be noted that whilst linear aggregates of the scores are unbiased estimators of the corresponding aggregates from observations drawn from the standard normal distribution, quadratic forms of the scores do not necessarily have this unbiased property. For example

$$\mathscr{E}\left(\sum_i x_i^2/\sigma^2\right) = n, \quad \text{while} \quad \sum_i \{\xi(i \mid n)\}^2 = n - \sum_i (\text{variance of } x_i/\sigma).$$

## 16. Test for Heterogeneity of Variance among Normally Distributed Observations (Tables 31, 32, 32a and 33)

### 16·1   Definitions

The statistical analysis of data often leads to the calculation of a number, say $k$, of independent mean-square estimates of variance, $s_t^2$, of which it is desired to test the homogeneity. In particular, one of the basic assumptions of the usual analysis of variance tests is that the population variances of all experimental groups can be taken as equal, and it is often desirable to check the justification for this assumption. Mathematically, we may define the problem as follows: the $s_t^2$ are distributed independently as $\chi^2 \sigma_t^2 / \nu_t$ with $\nu_t$ degrees of freedom, respectively, and we wish to test the hypothesis that the $\sigma_t^2$ have a common, though unknown, value $\sigma^2$.

The most useful test employs Bartlett's (1937) modification of Neyman & Pearson's (1931) likelihood ratio statistic. We use as criterion*

$$M = N \log_e \left\{ N^{-1} \sum_{t=1}^{k} \nu_t s_t^2 \right\} - \sum_{t=1}^{k} \nu_t \log_e s_t^2, \tag{76}$$

where $N = \sum_t \nu_t$. Provided that $\sigma_t^2 = \sigma^2$ for all $t$ and none of the degrees of freedom $\nu_t$ is small, $M$ is distributed approximately as $\chi^2$ with $k-1$ degrees of freedom.

For small samples, Bartlett showed that $M/C$, with

$$C = 1 + \frac{1}{3(k-1)} \left\{ \sum_t \frac{1}{\nu_t} - \frac{1}{N} \right\}, \tag{77}$$

is more closely approximated by $\chi^2$ for $k-1$ degrees of freedom. Investigations carried out by U. S. Nair (1938) and Bishop & Nair (1939) showed that the correction (77) is not always adequate if some of the $\nu_t$ are 1, 2 or 3.

In applying this test as well as the short-cut test described in § 16·5 below, it must be remembered that the theory is based on the assumption that the random variation within each of the $k$ groups follows the normal law. If this is not true a significant value of $M$, or of the ratio $s_{max.}^2 / s_{min.}^2$ of § 16·5, may indicate departure from normality rather than heterogeneity of variance. Tests of this kind are, indeed, more sensitive to departure from normality than the ordinary tests of the analysis of variance.

### 16·2   Description of Tables 32, 32a and 33

Table 32 is based on Hartley's (1940) $\chi^2$-series expansion of $M$, which is slightly more accurate than the expansion leading to (77) and permits the $\nu_t$ to drop as low as 2.† The truncated series used in this approximation depends on the three parameters

$$k, \quad c_1 = \sum_t \frac{1}{\nu_t} - \frac{1}{N} \quad \text{and} \quad c_3 = \sum_t \frac{1}{\nu_t^3} - \frac{1}{N^3}. \tag{78}$$

The 5 and 1 % significance points of $M$ are given in Table 32, whilst the auxiliary Table 33 is only required for accurate interpolation in Table 32. In Table 32, for each combination of

---

* $M$ corresponds to Bartlett's $-2 \log_e \mu$.

† Recently Box (1949) has re-examined this approximation. Whilst considerably improving current approximations to other likelihood criteria, Box did not materially improve on that for $M$.

$k$ and $c_1$ there are two percentage points denoted by $(a)$ and $(b)$. These are approximately maximum and minimum values of the true percentage point which will normally have an intermediate value, dependent on $c_3$. Provided the degrees of freedom are not very unequal, the correct value of $M$ will be close to the entry opposite $(a)$.

The table has been arranged to make its use as simple as possible. If in the table of 5 % points, say, all entries in the lines for the appropriate $k$ are greater than the value of $M$ derived from the data, this value is not significant at the 5 % level. On the other hand, if the calculated $M$ is larger than all entries for that $k$, then $M$ is significant at the 5 % level. In neither case is it necessary to calculate $c_1$ or $c_3$. When, however, $M$ falls within the range of values shown in the lines for the particular $k$, it is necessary to calculate $c_1$. Knowing this value, it will usually be possible to form an opinion on the significance of $M$ without proceeding to the calculation of $c_3$ needed for interpolation between the entries $(a)$ and $(b)$.

It will be noted that the entries in the tables under $c_1 = 0$ are simply the 5 and 1 % probability levels of $\chi^2$ with $k-1$ degrees of freedom, this being the limiting form approached when all the $\nu_t$ are large. On the other hand, for a given $k$, $c_1$ has its maximum value when all $\nu_t$ are unity and therefore $c_1 = k - 1/k$.*

Table 32a, due to Harsaae (*Biometrika*, 1969, **56,** 276-7) gives exact percentage points of $M$ in the case where all $\nu_t = \nu$, for $\nu = 1(1)10$, $k = 3(1)12$. Harsaae has confirmed that Table 32 should not be used when $\nu = 1$ and that there may be slight inaccuracy when $\nu = 2$.

### 16·3  Applications of Tables 31 and 32

*Example* 31. Column (3) of the table below gives a set of ten estimates of variance, calculated from ten samples of weight records of schoolboys of similar age, but from different forms. It is desired to test whether there are any real 'form differences' in the weight dispersion of the boys. The calculations for $M$ is as follows, using Table 53 to obtain natural logarithms:

| (1) Form no. $t$ | (2) No. of boys $n_t$ | (3) Weight variance $s_t^2$ (lb.²) | (4) $\nu_t$ | (5) $\log_e s_t^2$ | (6) $\nu_t \log_e s_t^2$ | (7) $1/\nu_t$ |
|---|---|---|---|---|---|---|
| 1 | 10 | 51 | 9 | 3·93 | 35·4 | 0·111 |
| 2 | 15 | 78 | 14 | 4·36 | 61·0 | 0·071 |
| 3 | 21 | 91 | 20 | 4·51 | 90·2 | 0·050 |
| 4 | 23 | 52 | 22 | 3·95 | 86·9 | 0·045 |
| 5 | 15 | 101 | 14 | 4·62 | 64·7 | 0·071 |
| 6 | 11 | 36 | 10 | 3·58 | 35·8 | 0·100 |
| 7 | 31 | 41 | 30 | 3·71 | 111·3 | 0·033 |
| 8 | 15 | 76 | 14 | 4·33 | 60·6 | 0·071 |
| 9 | 3 | 64 | 2 | 4·16 | 8·3 | 0·500 |
| 10 | 6 | 93 | 5 | 4·53 | 22·6 | 0·200 |
| Totals | 150 | — | 140 (= N) | — | 576·8 | 1·252 |

We obtain further

$$\Sigma \nu_t s_t^2 = 9176, \quad \Sigma(\nu_t s_t^2)/N = 65\cdot54, \quad \log_e\{\Sigma \nu_t s_t^2/N\} = 4\cdot183.$$

Hence
$$M = 140 \times 4\cdot183 - 576\cdot8 = 8\cdot8.$$

* Actually, the last entry in each line has been computed from the approximating function, putting $c_1 = k$.

The observed value of $M$ is therefore $8 \cdot 8$. This has to be compared with the appropriate tabulated $5\%$ (or $1\%$) point. It is seen from Table 32 ($5\%$ points) that all entries opposite $k = 10$ are greater than $8 \cdot 8$. Without further calculation it may therefore be concluded that $M$ is not significant at the $5\%$ level, and we may infer that no real differences are indicated in the weight dispersion among the ten forms of schoolboys.

Had the observed value of $M$ been $18 \cdot 8$ (instead of $8 \cdot 8$), the decision as to its significance would not have been obvious, since some of the $5\%$ points tabulated in the lines for $k = 10$ are smaller than $18 \cdot 8$.[*] It is now necessary to calculate $c_1$, defined by (78). Using the reciprocals of $\nu_t$ given in col. 7 of the table above, it is found that

$$c_1 = 1 \cdot 25.$$

Since the percentage points $(a)$ and $(b)$ for $k = 10$ and both $c_1 = 1 \cdot 0$ and $1 \cdot 5$ are less than $18 \cdot 8$, we can say that $M$ would now be significant at the $5\%$ level.

Had the data given a value of $17 \cdot 6$ for $M$, which lies between the four appropriate tabled entries, it would normally have satisfied our purpose merely to note that $M$ was on the border line of $5\%$ significance. If more precise information is needed, it will be necessary to proceed further by calculating $c_3$ and interpolating as follows.

It can be shown that, for a given $k$ and $c_1$, the range of $c_3$ is (to a first order of approximation)

$$c_3(a) = c_1^3/k^2 < c_3 < c_1 = c_3(b). \tag{79}$$

The lower bound is approached when all values of $\nu_t$ are equal and the upper bound when $j$, say, of the $\nu_t$ are each equal to unity and the $k - j$ remaining values all tend to infinity. In Table 32 the entry for the percentage point opposite $(a)$ is that for $c_3 = c_3(a)$; that opposite $(b)$ is for $c_3 = c_3(b)$. It will be seen that, at any rate throughout the tabulated range of values, the entry $(a)$ is greater than or equal to $(b)$. In using the former, therefore, we shall in rare cases fail to detect the significance of $M$.

If interpolation for $c_3$ is decided on, use may be made of the auxiliary Table 33. This gives for all the marginal entries $k$ and $c_1$ of Table 32 the two quantities

$$C = c_3(a) = c_1^3/k^2, \quad \Delta C = c_3(b) - c_3(a) = c_1 - c_1^3/k^2. \tag{80}$$

The procedure would then be first to interpolate linearly in the two nearest $c_1$ columns between the two percentage points $(a)$ and $(b)$, using the formula

Percentage point corresponding to $c_3$

$$= \frac{1}{\Delta C} \{(c_1 - c_3) \times \text{entry } (a) + (c_3 - C) \times \text{entry } (b)\}, \tag{81}$$

and then interpolating to the correct value of $c_1$.

*Illustration.* Suppose that $k = 10$ and the degrees of freedom are the ten values of $\nu_t$ given in col. 4 of the illustrative data tabled above. Here

$$c_1 = 1 \cdot 25, \quad c_3 = 0 \cdot 14.$$

For the interpolation process, we need the following entries:

| | | $c_1 = 1 \cdot 0$ | $c_1 = 1 \cdot 5$ |
|---|---|---|---|
| From Table 33 | $C$ | $0 \cdot 010$ | $0 \cdot 034$ |
| | $\Delta C$ | $0 \cdot 990$ | $1 \cdot 466$ |
| From Table 32 | Entry $(a)$ | $17 \cdot 54$ | $17 \cdot 83$ |
| | Entry $(b)$ | $17 \cdot 17$ | $17 \cdot 29$ |

[*] Reference to Table 32 ($1\%$ points) shows, however, that $M$ cannot be significant at the $1\%$ level.

Hence the 5 % point corresponding to $c_1 = 1 \cdot 0$, $c_3 = 0 \cdot 14$ is approximately, from equation (81),

$$\frac{1}{0 \cdot 99}\{0 \cdot 86 \times 17 \cdot 54 + 0 \cdot 13 \times 17 \cdot 17\} = 17 \cdot 49.$$

The 5 % point corresponding to $c_1 = 1 \cdot 5$ and $c_3 = 0 \cdot 14$ will be approximately

$$\frac{1}{1 \cdot 47}\{1 \cdot 36 \times 17 \cdot 83 + 0 \cdot 11 + 17 \cdot 29\} = 17 \cdot 79.$$

Interpolating between these two values for $c_1 = 1 \cdot 25$, we find finally a 5 % point for $M$ at $17 \cdot 64$. It will be seen that this value differs very little from that of $17 \cdot 68$ obtained by using the (a) entries only.

*Example* 32. As a second example, we may test the homogeneity of the $k = 5$ batch-variances quoted at the bottom of the table of tensile strength data presented in Example 15 (p. 38). Here, $\nu_t = \nu = 5$ for all $t$, so that the procedure used in the preceding example may be simplified by omitting the three columns headed $\nu_t$, $\nu_t \log_e s_t^2$ and $1/\nu_t$.

A summary of the calculation is as follows:

$$M = k\nu \log_e \{\Sigma s_t^2 / k\} - \nu \Sigma \log_e s_t^2 = 25 \log_e 367 - 5 \times 28 \cdot 63.$$

We find $M = 4 \cdot 5$ which, with $k = 5$, is clearly not significant.

### 16·4 *The relation between the M- and F-tests in the case of two groups*

It will be seen that Table 32 does not contain any entry for $k = 2$. This is because when two variance estimates $s_1^2$ and $s_2^2$ alone are available, we should normally test for the significance of their difference by calculating the variance ratio $F = s_1^2 / s_2^2$, and using a double-tail $F$-test as described in § 9·3. It is, however, of interest to consider the relation between the two tests in this special case. It is easily seen that

$$e^{-M} = \left(\frac{\nu_1 + \nu_2}{\nu_2 + \nu_1 F}\right)^{\nu_1 + \nu_2} F^{\nu_1}. \tag{82}$$

To $M = 0$ (when $s_1^2 = s_2^2$) corresponds the value $F = 1$, and for any value of $M > 0$ there will correspond two roots of (82), $F_1$ and $F_2$ (say), with $F_1 > 1$ and $F_2 < 1$. Thus the upper tail of the $M$-distribution for which $M \geqslant M(\alpha \mid \nu_t)$, where $\alpha$ is the significance level, will correspond to the two tails in the $F$-distribution, $F \geqslant F_1 = F(\alpha_1 \mid \nu_1, \nu_2)$ and $F \leqslant F_2 = F(1 - \alpha_2 \mid \nu_1, \nu_2)$. The total probability of falling in these tails will be $\alpha = \alpha_1 + \alpha_2$, e.g. $0 \cdot 05$ for the 5 % point of $M$, but this will not necessarily be divided equally between the tails. Only in the special case $\nu_1 = \nu_2$, where $F_2 = 1/F_1$ does the $M$-test correspond to the $F$-test with equal tails. It can be shown, however, that in the general case where $\nu_1 \neq \nu_2$, the $M$-test is approximated by the double-tail $F$-test for equal degrees of freedom $\nu$, given by $\nu = 1 \cdot 5 \left/ \left(\frac{1}{\nu_1} + \frac{1}{\nu_2} - \frac{1}{\nu_1 + \nu_2}\right)\right.$. This approximation is based on the assumption that the distribution of $M$ for $k = 2$ will depend only on $c_1$, and that we may therefore use an 'equivalent' common $\nu$, such that

$$\frac{2}{\nu} - \frac{1}{2\nu} = c_1 = \frac{1}{\nu_1} + \frac{1}{\nu_2} - \frac{1}{\nu_1 + \nu_2}.$$

### 16·5 *Short-cut tests for heterogeneity of variance (Tables 31 and 31a)*

The computation of the criterion $M$ as set out in *Example* 31 (p. 64) is comparatively laborious and often a deterrent in a rapid survey of data. For a quick assessment of heterogeneity in a set of mean squares we may compute the ratio of the largest to the smallest mean square $s^2_{\max.}/s^2_{\min.}$ or, alternatively, the ratio of the largest to the sum of the mean squares, $s^2_{\max.}\Big/\sum_{t=1}^{k} s^2_t$ (Cochran, 1941). Tables 31 and 31$a$ give 5 % and 1 % points of these ratios for the case where all $k$ mean squares are based on $\nu$ degrees of freedom.

*Example* 33. Suppose we take the five batch variances of *Example* 15 (p. 37), i.e. the mean squares 469, 653, 406, 196, 111, for which $s^2_{\max.} = 653$ and $s^2_{\min.} = 111$. Their ratio is about 6 and clearly does not exceed the 5 % value of 16·3 tabled for $k = 5$, $\nu = 5$. The application of Cochran's test to the same data has been given in §14·5 above. Both results confirm that of the $M$-test (*Example* 32, p. 66).

As an approximate procedure the tables may be used when the $\nu_t$ differ by entering them with the average of the $\nu_t$. In cases of doubt the $M$-criterion should be computed.

## 17. Tests for departure from normality (Tables 34A, B and C)

### 17·1  *Discussion of the problem*

If $n$ independent observations $x_i$ $(i = 1, 2, \ldots, n)$ of a random variable $x$ are available, we may wish to test the hypothesis that the population frequency function follows the normal law, i.e. that

$$f(x) = \frac{1}{\sqrt{(2\pi)}\,\sigma} \exp\left[ -\frac{1}{2}\left(\frac{x - \mu}{\sigma}\right)^2 \right].$$

Usually $\mu$ and $\sigma$ will be unknown and must be estimated from the data. It should be observed that by the very nature of the problem it is impossible to conclude definitely whether a given sample has been drawn from a particular kind of universe, normal or otherwise. The best that we can hope for is to be in a position to determine when the population is probably not normal, so that it would perhaps be more accurate to describe the tests considered below as *tests of non-normality*. Two methods of dealing with the problem are in common use:

(i) A normal curve is fitted to the sample data and the $\chi^2$-test for goodness of fit applied to the grouped frequencies.

(ii) Certain functions of the moments of the sample are calculated and the significance of their departure from the expected values for a normal population is examined.

While the procedure (i) has certain advantages, it may prove somewhat insensitive to real departures from normality, partly because the $\chi^2$-test only takes into account the magnitude of the differences between observed and expected group frequencies and not their sign and arrangement, and partly owing to the necessity of grouping together small tail frequencies when applying the test. If there are less than 50–100 observations, this loss of sensitivity through grouping will apply, indeed, to the whole range of the distribution. In the present discussion we are concerned only with procedure (ii).

If we define the moments of the observations as

$$\bar{x} = \sum_{i=1}^{n} \frac{x_i}{n}, \quad m_r = \sum_{i=1}^{n} \frac{(x_i - \bar{x})^r}{n} \quad (r \geqslant 2),$$

the well-known moment ratios are

$$\sqrt{b_1} = m_3/m_2^{\frac{3}{2}}, \quad b_2 = m_4/m_2^2.$$

Departure of $\sqrt{b_1}$ from the 'normal' value of zero is an indication of skewness in the frequency function of the sampled population, while departure in $b_2$ from the 'normal' value of 3 is an indication of kurtosis.* For large samples, rough tests of normality may be obtained by comparing $\sqrt{b_1}$ and $b_2 - 3$ with the approximate values of their standard errors, viz. $\sqrt{(6/n)}$ and $\sqrt{(24/n)}$ respectively. Work by R. A. Fisher (1929, 1930) and others has made it possible to calculate the higher sampling moments of $\sqrt{b_1}$ and $b_2$ for a normal universe. The upper and lower 5 and 1 % points (single-tail test) given in Tables 34 B and C, were computed by assuming that the distributions of $\sqrt{b_1}$ and $b_2$ can be represented approximately by Pearson-type curves having the correct first four moment coefficients (E. S. Pearson, 1930, 1931; and P. Williams, 1935). Further work (E. S. Pearson, 1963, 1965) has made it possible to improve the accuracy of the approximation and to provide significance levels for $b_2$ when $n < 200$.

R. C. Geary (1935, 1936) has suggested an alternative statistic which may be used for detecting changes in kurtosis, particularly when samples contain less than 50 observations, where owing to the asymmetry of the $b_2$-distribution the method employed in deriving Table 34C could not safely be used. This statistic is

$$a = \frac{\text{mean deviation}}{\text{standard deviation}} = \frac{\sum_i |x_i - \bar{x}|}{\{n \sum_i (x_i - \bar{x})^2\}^{\frac{1}{2}}}. \tag{83}$$

For the normal population itself, this ratio has the value $\sqrt{(2/\pi)} = 0.7979$; the ratio will be higher for platykurtic and lower for leptokurtic distributions.

Table 34A gives upper and lower 10, 5 and 1 % points for $a$ (single-tail test) as well as the expectation and standard deviation in sampling from a normal population. As $n \to \infty$ the expectation of $a$ tends to its normal population value of $0.7979$.

[Charts based on the tables for $a$ and $\sqrt{b_1}$ were published in *Biometrika* (1936), **28**, 304–7; these together with a similar chart of significance points for $b_2$, were reproduced by *Biometrika* as a 'separate', but they are not reproduced here.]

### 17·2 *Applications*

*Example* 34. The following table shows fifty observations of a variable $x$. Investigate whether it is likely that they have been drawn from a normal population. A rough plot in a dot diagram suggests a population distribution with marked positive skewness. However, it is desirable to establish a significant departure from normality on an objective basis. The sample size being small, we shall calculate $a$ and $\sqrt{b_1}$, not $b_2$.

| | | | | | | | | | |
|---|---|---|---|---|---|---|---|---|---|
| − 6 | − 14 | 19 | − 5 | − 15 | 4 | − 9 | − 7 | 5 | 29 |
| 0 | − 11 | 2 | − 12 | − 1 | − 16 | − 2 | 9 | − 8 | 6 |
| − 17 | 11 | 15 | 0 | − 10 | − 3 | 14 | 1 | 0 | 29 |
| − 9 | − 2 | − 13 | − 13 | − 14 | − 11 | − 7 | − 4 | 20 | − 8 |
| 11 | − 8 | − 13 | − 11 | 0 | − 15 | − 4 | − 2 | − 11 | − 6 |

The mean deviation is perhaps calculated most readily, using the formula

$$\sum_{i=1}^{n} |x_i - \bar{x}| = 2\{(sum \text{ of observations greater than } \bar{x})$$

$$-\bar{x} \times (number \text{ of observations greater than } \bar{x})\}.$$

---

* The symmetrical platykurtic distribution, with $\beta_2 < 3$, is characterized by a flatter top and more abrupt terminals than the normal curve; the symmetrical leptokurtic distribution, with $\beta_2 > 3$ has a sharper peak at the mean and more extended tails.

The computation will then proceed as follows:

For all observations $\quad \Sigma(x_i) = -112, \qquad \bar{x} = \quad -2\cdot24,$

$$\Sigma(x_i^2) = \ 6494, \quad \Sigma(x_i - \bar{x})^2 = \ 6243\cdot12,$$

$$\Sigma(x_i^3) = 33254, \quad \Sigma(x_i - \bar{x})^3 = 75769\cdot7376,$$

$$\sqrt{b_1} = 1\cdot086.$$

For observations greater than $\bar{x}$

$$\Sigma(x_i) = 168, \quad \text{number greater than } \bar{x} = 22.*$$

Hence $\qquad \sum_i |x_i - \bar{x}| = 2\{168 + 2\cdot24 \times 22\} = 434\cdot56,$

$$a = 0\cdot778.$$

Table 34 B shows that, for $n = 50$, $\sqrt{b_1}$ is well beyond the upper 1 % point at 0·787. Table 34 A indicates that $a$ is below the expected value for a normal population (0·802) but not significantly so. We should therefore conclude that the population has almost certainly considerable skewness, in the positive sense, i.e. with the longer tail towards increasing $x$.

The observations actually formed part of a sampling experiment (E. S. Pearson, 1935), the population distribution following a Pearson Type I curve for which $\sqrt{\beta_1} = 1\cdot0$, $\beta_2 = 3\cdot8$ and (mean deviation)/(standard deviation) = 0·797.

*Example* 35. Bayes (1937) has given the following distribution of 1000 observations made on the strength of the warp of a 12/20's duck cloth:

| Central value (lb.) | 400 | 405 | 410 | 415 | 420 | 425 | 430 | 435 | 440 | 445 |
|---|---|---|---|---|---|---|---|---|---|---|
| Observed frequency | 2 | 4 | 4 | 17 | 27 | 27 | 50 | 49 | 68 | 76 |
| Graduation | 2·6 | 3·8 | 7·4 | 13·0 | 20·7 | 30·8 | 43·1 | 57·0 | 71·7 | 85·9 |

| Central value (lb.) | 450 | 455 | 460 | 465 | 470 | 475 | 480 | 485 | 490 | 495 |
|---|---|---|---|---|---|---|---|---|---|---|
| Observed frequency | 95 | 113 | 125 | 105 | 97 | 73 | 38 | 19 | 10 | 1 |
| Graduation | 98·1 | 106·6 | 109·5 | 105·5 | 93·6 | 74·2 | 49·2 | 23·1 | 4·2 | 0·0 |

For these data Pearson & Welch (1937) give the following moment coefficients (using Sheppard's corrections for grouping):

$$\text{Mean} = 454\cdot09 \text{ lb.}, \quad \text{standard deviation} = 17\cdot358 \text{ lb.}$$

$$\sqrt{b_1} = -0\cdot421, \quad b_2 = 2\cdot748.$$

Tables 34 B and C, entered with $n = 1000$, show that $\sqrt{b_1}$ is clearly significant while $b_2$ is close to its lower 5 % point. In their further analysis of the problem, the authors represent the distribution by a Pearson Type I curve, the corresponding graduated frequencies obtained from which are shown in the bottom rows of the table. These data will be used again, below (see Examples 47 and 50, pp. 86, 89).

## IV. TABLES RELATING TO CERTAIN DISCRETE DISTRIBUTIONS
### (TABLES 36–41)

Included under this general heading is a group of six tables relating to the binomial series, the hypergeometric series and Poisson's limit to the binomial. The common element lies in the fact that the random variable is a 'count' which can only assume integral values $0, 1, 2, \ldots$.

* Note that there are three values of $-2$ and one of $-1$, all greater than $\bar{x} = -2\cdot24$, although negative.

Table 7, which gives the cumulative sum of the Poisson series, as well as the probability integral of $\chi^2$, and Table 16 giving the cumulative sum of binomial terms in the form of the incomplete B-function, have been printed more appropriately at an earlier stage.

## 18. TABLES GIVING THE INDIVIDUAL TERMS OF SELECTED BINOMIAL SERIES (TABLE 37)

The $(i+1)$th term in the expansion of the binomial $(q+p)^n$ may be written

$$f(i \mid n, p) = \binom{n}{i} p^i q^{n-i}$$

The table gives to 5 decimal places the values of $f(i \mid n, p)$, $i = 0, 1, \ldots, n$, for

$$n = 5,\ 10,\ 15,\ 20,\ 25,\ 30$$

and

$$p = 0\cdot01,\ 0\cdot02\ (0\cdot02)\ 0\cdot10\ (0\cdot10)\ 0\cdot50.$$

For $p > 0\cdot5$ the terms are obtained in reverse, using the arguments $i$ and $p$ printed in the last column but one and bottom row of each page.

The table is intended primarily for exploratory and illustrative purposes, e.g. in lecture or class work; the statistician who wishes to use a working table giving binomial terms over a wide range of values of $n$ and $p$, should consult *Tables of the Binomial Probability Distribution*, National Bureau of Standards, Applied Mathematics Series, no. 6 (1950). Alternatively, he may obtain the cumulative sums, and hence obtain the individual terms by differencing either from the *Tables of the Incomplete B-function* (Karl Pearson, 1934) or more approximately, from Table 16 (see §8·1 above), noting in both cases that

$$\sum_{i=0}^{a-1} f(i \mid n, p) = 1 - I_p(a, n-a+1) = 1 - \int_0^p u^{a-1}(1-u)^{n-a}\,du \Big/ \int_0^1 u^{a-1}(1-u)^{n-a}\,du. \quad (84)$$

*Example* 36. Suppose that we wish to find out what kind of errors are involved in using the normal probability integral as an approximation to the sums of the tail terms of certain binomial series in the neighbourhood of the 5 % points. Take the case of the binomial with $n = 30$, $p = 0\cdot2$. Using the correction for continuity, we compare:

(i) *For the lower tail*, the sums of terms from Table 37 corresponding to $i = 0, 1, \ldots, a$ with the integral of the normal distribution (obtained from Table 1) up to

$$X = (a + 0\cdot5 - np)/\sqrt{(npq)}.$$

(ii) *For the upper tail*, the sums of terms corresponding to $i = a, a+1, \ldots, n$ with the integral beyond

$$X = (a - 0\cdot5 - np)/\sqrt{(npq)},$$

where $np = 6\cdot0$, $\sqrt{(npq)} = 2\cdot191$. Results are shown in the following table:

| Terms | | Binomial | Normal approx. |
|---|---|---|---|
| Up to and including $\begin{cases} a=2 \\ a=3 \end{cases}$ | | 0·0442 <br> 0·1227 | 0·0551 <br> 0·1269 |
| Including and beyond $\begin{cases} a=10 \\ a=11 \end{cases}$ | | 0·0611 <br> 0·0256 | 0·0551 <br> 0·0200 |

The approximation is clearly rather rough, though it will be adequate for some practical purposes.

## 19. The test of significance in a $2 \times 2$ contingency table containing small frequencies (Table 38)

### 19·1 Description of the problem*

Suppose that in a group of $N = A + B$ individuals, $r$ possess a certain character, say $Y$, and $N - r$ do not. If now a sample of $A$ individuals is drawn randomly from the $N$, *without replacement*, the probability that $a$ of these possess the character $Y$ is

$$f(a \mid r, A, B) = \frac{A! \, B! \, r! \, (N-r)!}{a! \, b! \, (A-a)! \, (B-b)! \, N!}, \tag{85}$$

where $b = r - a$. This expression is proportional to the coefficient of $x^a$ in the hypergeometric series

$$F(\alpha, \beta, \gamma, x) = F(-r, -A, B-r+1, x).$$

If $A \geqslant B$, then $a$ can assume values

(i)    $0, 1, \ldots, r$            if   $r \leqslant B$,

(ii)   $r-B, r-B+1, \ldots, r$    if   $B < r \leqslant A$,

(iii)   $r-B, r-B+1, \ldots, A$    if   $r > A$.

For this probability distribution,

$$\text{Mean } a = rA/N, \tag{86}$$

$$\text{Variance of } a = \sigma_a^2 = ABr(N-r)/\{N^2(N-1)\}. \tag{87}$$

The result of the sampling described, which is equivalent to a random partition of the $N$ individuals into two groups, one of $A$ and the other of $B$, may be set down in the following $2 \times 2$ table:

|  | With $Y$ | Without $Y$ | Total |
|---|---|---|---|
| Sample or 1st group | $a$ | $A-a$ | $A$ |
| Remainder or 2nd group | $b$ | $B-b$ | $B$ |
| Total | $r$ | $N-r$ | $N$ |

If the partition is made at random, without any relation to the presence or absence of the character $Y$, then the expectation of $a$ is $rA/N$ and that of $b$ is $rB/N$; or, in other words, the expectation of the difference in proportions, $a/A - b/B$, is zero. In so far as some effect operates to make the presence of $Y$ more probable in one group than the other, $a$ will be more likely to differ from $rA/N$ and $a/A - b/B$ from zero, than would be expected under the random distribution law of equation (85). Table 38† is designed to assist in the decision as to whether this departure from expectation on the random hypothesis is significant. The form of the table may be explained with the help of Fig. 3, which shows for the particular values $A = 15$, $B = 12$ the relation between possible values of $a$, $b$ and $r = a + b$. For a given value of $r$, e.g. $r = 9$, the probabilities $f(a \mid 9, 15, 12)$ of equation (85) are associated with the $(a, b)$ values marked by circles along the line $r = 9$. Taking the upper tail of this distribution, the probabilities that $a$ is

---

* For rules applicable in routine tests of significance, see §19·2.

† This table is due to D. J. Finney (1948), and we are indebted to him for permission to reproduce it and to make very full use in this and the following section (19·2) of the explanatory comment which accompanied his original publication of the table.

7, 8 and 9 (and therefore that $b = 2$, 1 and 0) are respectively 0·091, 0·017 and 0·001. Thus using a single-tail test, i.e. asking whether $a/A$ is significantly greater than $b/B$, and working to a 5% level, we should conclude that there was a significant difference if $a = 8$, $b = 1$ ($\Pr\{a \geqslant 8\} = 0\cdot018$) but not if $a = 7$, $b = 2$ ($\Pr\{a \geqslant 7\} = 0\cdot109$).

If similar calculations are made for the cumulative sums of the terms in the upper tail of each of the hypergeometric series, for $r = 1, 2, \ldots, 26$, all the pairs of values $(a, b)$ to the right and below the stepped line in Fig. 3 will be judged significantly different at the 5% level.

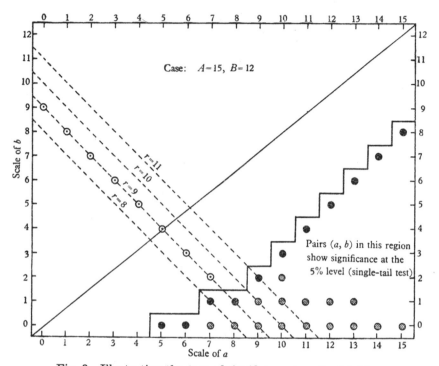

Fig. 3. Illustrating the test of significance in a $2 \times 2$ table.

Formally, this bounding line is placed above and to the left of points $(a_0, r - a_0)$, where

$$\sum_{a=a_0}^{k} f(a \mid r, A, B) \leqslant 0\cdot05 \quad \text{and} \quad \sum_{a=a_0-1}^{k} f(a \mid r, A, B) > 0\cdot05,$$

$k$ being the smaller of the quantities $r$ and $A$. Similar significance limits could be inserted in the diagram for other percentage levels, and lattice diagrams of this type could be drawn for other combinations of $A$ and $B$.

As arranged, Table 38 does not give significance levels for $a$ for fixed $r = a + b$, $A$ and $B$, but shows in bold type, for given $a$, $A$ and $B$, the highest value of $b$ ($< a$) which is just significant at the 5, 2·5, 1 and 0·5% levels. Thus for the special case illustrated in Fig. 3, the 5% values tabled for $(a, b)$ are those corresponding to the solid black circles. It will be seen that on this basis some entries, e.g. those for $a = 7$, $b = 0$ and for $a = 9$, $b = 1$ on the diagonals $r = 7$ and $r = 10$ respectively, are unnecessary and space is saved in tabulation.

The figures in small type following an entry, say $b = b_0$, are the sums along the diagonal of the hypergeometric terms for which $b \leqslant b_0$.

An extension of Table 38 for sample size combinations $B \leqslant A \leqslant 45$ has now been issued.*

* *Tables for Testing Significance in a $2 \times 2$ Contingency Table.* Compiled by D. J. Finney, R. Latscha, B. M. Bennett & P. Hsu with an Introduction by E. S. Pearson, 1963. Cambridge University Press.

Provided that none of the marginal totals $A$, $B$, $r$ or $N-r$ are very small, a good approximation to the sum of the tail terms of the hypergeometric series of equation (85) may be obtained from the integral under a normal curve, having the mean, $\bar{a}$, and variance, $\sigma_a^2$, of equations (86) and (87). Thus if $r \leqslant B \leqslant A$ and we want the sum of the first $a_0 + 1$ terms of $f(a \mid r, A, B)$, we use the following approximation

$$\sum_{a=0}^{a_0} f(a \mid r, A, B) = \int_{-\infty}^{X} \frac{1}{\sqrt{(2\pi)}} e^{-\frac{1}{2}u^2} du = P(X),$$

where

$$X = (a_0 + 0 \cdot 5 - \bar{a})/\sigma_a.$$

If we need an approximation to the sum of the terms corresponding to $a_0$ or *larger* integers, we use the complementary normal integral, $Q(X) = 1 - P(X)$ with $X = (a_0 - 0 \cdot 5 - \bar{a})/\sigma_a$. The half-unit added to or subtracted from $a_0$ is a correction introduced in approximating to the sum of a discrete distribution by a continuous integral.* Its use in connexion with the interpretation of $2 \times 2$ tables was first suggested by Yates (1934).

### 19·2   *Rules to follow in using Table* 38

Points to be noted are:

(i) The 'first group' in the sense of the $2 \times 2$ table on p. 71 is defined to be that for which $A \geqslant B$.

(ii) The type of observation which has been described conventionally in that table as possessing 'character $Y$', is that which makes $a/A \geqslant b/B$ (or $aB \geqslant bA$).

(iii) If $b$ is equal to or less than the integer in the column headed 0·05, 0·025, 0·01 or 0·005, $a/A$ is significantly greater than $b/B$ (single-tail test) at these probability levels. On the other hand, for the double-tail test, if $b$ is equal to or less than the integer in a given column, $a/A$ is significantly *different from* $b/B$ at a probability level equal to twice the figure heading that column, i.e. at the 0·10, 0·05, 0·02 and 0·01 levels, respectively.

(iv) A dash, or absence of an entry, for some combination of $A$, $B$ and $a$ indicates that no $2 \times 2$ table in that class can show a significant effect at that level.

(v) Owing to the discontinuous character of the hypergeometric distribution, the probability that, for given $r = a + b$, $b$ will be equal to or less than the value specified in bold type will generally be less, and often very considerably less, than that shown at the head of the column; the true numerical values are shown in small type.

(vi) From the mathematical point of view, the two pairs of marginal totals play equivalent roles in the test. Consequently, if only one set satisfies the condition that neither total exceeds 15, that margin may be conventionally regarded as giving $A$ and $B$. If both margins satisfy the condition, the two possible arrangements will lead to identical conclusions.

(vii) The use of the table presented here may be extended by noting that any $2 \times 2$ table more extreme than one known to show significant deviation from proportionality must itself be significant. Thus even though one of each pair of marginal totals exceeds 15, a test of significance without calculation may still be possible. In particular, if the standard arrangement of the table gives (1) below with $A > 15 \geqslant B$ and $aB \geqslant bA$, the deviation from proportionality will be significant if arrangement (2) is significant (but not necessarily non-significant

---

* This correction has also been made in Example 36 (p. 70), when using the normal probability integral to approximate to the sum of binomial terms.

otherwise), and the deviation will be non-significant if arrangement (3) is not significant (but not necessarily significant otherwise).

| | (1) | | | (2) | | | (3) | |
|---|---|---|---|---|---|---|---|---|
| $a$ | $A-a$ | $A$ | $15+a-A$ | $A-a$ | $15$ | $a$ | $15-a$ | $15$ |
| $b$ | $B-b$ | $B$ | $b$ | $B-b$ | $B$ | $b$ | $B-b$ | $B$ |
| $a+b$ | $A+B-a-b$ | $A+B$ | $15+a+b-A$ | $A+B-a-b$ | $15+B$ | $a+b$ | $15+B-a-b$ | $15+B$ |

### 19·3 *Applications of Table* 38

These may be usefully classified under several heads. While the basic mathematical distribution underlying the test (i.e. that given by equation (85)) is the same in all cases, there are differences of some importance in the way in which the random element may be introduced in collecting the data. We think it useful to accompany the illustrative examples with some account of these differences.

*Case* 1

The most direct application of the theory is to the type of experiment where (i) two 'treatments' are being compared, the response being a quantal one so that each individual either 'reacts' or 'fails to react'; (ii) the $N = A + B$ individuals to be used in the experiments are divided by a random partition (e.g. by using random numbers) into a group of $A$ receiving the first treatment and a group of $B$ receiving the second. It is then observed that proportions $a/A$ and $b/B$ react; the question asked is whether the difference in these proportions is statistically significant.

Note that in this situation where the random selection has been applied to a specified set of $N$ individuals, the experiment is self-contained and the reference set is strictly that which would be generated had different allocations of the treatments been made among the $N$ individuals.

*Example* 37. Suppose that it is desired to test the value of a period of 'preliminary training' in improving the subsequent performance of newly recruited operatives who are to be employed on a particular industrial process. Out of twenty-nine new recruits, a group of fourteen is selected randomly for this training. Subsequently all twenty-nine operatives are tested and the performance of each is classed as 'faulty' or 'correct', with the result shown below:

| | Performance | | Total |
|---|---|---|---|
| | Faulty | Correct | |
| No preliminary training | 9 (= $a$) | 6 | 15 (= $A$) |
| Preliminary training | 3 (= $b$) | 11 | 14 (= $B$) |
| Total | 12 | 17 | 29 |

The single-tail test is appropriate here; reference to Table 38 with $A = 15$, $B = 14$ and $a = 9$, shows that $b = 3$ is significant at the 5 % but not at the 2·5 % level. The figure in smaller type

74

indicates that if the preliminary training had no effect on performance, and twelve out of the twenty-nine operators would have shown a faulty performance whether they had a preliminary training or not, then the probability of a random partition putting $b \leqslant 3$ into one group and $a \geqslant 9$ into the other is 0·041.

As none of the marginal frequencies in the table are very small, we may expect to get a reasonable approximation to this probability of 0·041, using the normal probability integral as described at the end of §19·1. We have

$$\bar{a} = 15.12/29 = 6 \cdot 207, \quad \sigma_a^2 = 15.14.12.17/(29^2.28) = 1 \cdot 819, \quad \sigma_a = 1 \cdot 349.$$

Hence
$$X = (9 - 0 \cdot 5 - 6 \cdot 207)/1 \cdot 349 = 1 \cdot 70.$$

Since Table 1 shows that $Q(1 \cdot 70) = 1 - P(1 \cdot 70) = 0 \cdot 045$, the approximation can be regarded as satisfactory for our purpose.

*Case 2*

A second important type of application arises when we inquire whether the probability of an individual possessing a specified character $Y$ is the same in two large populations from which random samples of size $A$ and $B$, respectively, have been drawn. Here two separate random selections are involved, and the most natural reference set is one in which $a$ and $b$ (the number of individuals in the samples having the character $Y$) are no longer restricted to give a fixed total of $r$. Mathematically, the position may be defined briefly as follows.

If $p_1(Y)$ and $p_2(Y)$ are the probabilities in the two populations, the probability of obtaining a pair of samples with $a$ and $b$ individuals bearing the character $Y$, respectively, is

$$f(a, b \mid p_1, p_2) = \binom{A}{a} p_1^a (1 - p_1)^{A-a} \times \binom{B}{b} p_2^b (1 - p_2)^{B-b}.$$

If the hypothesis tested is true and $p_1 = p_2 = p$, then

$$f(a, b \mid p) = \binom{N}{r} p^r (1 - p)^{N-r} \times \frac{A! \, B! \, r! \, (N-r)!}{a! \, b! \, (A-a)! \, (B-b)! \, N!}. \tag{88}$$

The first term in (88) is the binomial probability of obtaining $r = a + b$ $Y$'s in a sample of $N = A + B$ when $p(Y) = p$; the second expression is the multinomial term already considered. Turning back to Fig. 3, the first term represents the probability that the point $(a, b)$ falls on a particular diagonal, $r = $ constant; this probability cannot be determined, since $p$ is essentially unknown. The second term is the conditional probability of $a$ (or $b$), given $r$ and is independent of the unknown $p$.

If we use the same test procedure as before, based on the sum of the tail terms of the hypergeometric series, e.g. reject the hypothesis of a common probability in the two populations when $(a, b)$ falls beyond the appropriate 5 % limit, we know that we shall be on the safe side, even in using the extended reference set, where $r$ is regarded as varying from one sampling to another. Under these conditions, using the nominal 5 % level, the proportion of occasions when we should reject the hypothesis $p_1(Y) = p_2(Y)$ when it is true cannot be determined. It is the sum of true tail terms (always $\leqslant 0 \cdot 05$) such as those given in small print in the table, weighted with the unknown binomial terms of equation (88). All that we can say is that this proportion will be considerably below the nominal 0·05.

Barnard (1947) has considered how a test might be developed providing an upper limit to this unknown proportion.

*Example* 38. The relative sensitivity of two mining explosives, C and D, was tested under controlled conditions. Ten cartridges of explosive C and six of explosive D were fired in turn in a standard gas chamber and a record was made of whether each shot resulted in an ignition or not. The results (taken from data quoted by E. S. Pearson, 1950) were as follows:

|  | Ignitions | Non-ignitions | Total |
|---|---|---|---|
| Explosive C | 0 | 10 ($=a$) | 10 ($=A$) |
| Explosive D | 4 | 2 ($=b$) | 6 ($=B$) |
| Total | 4 | 12 | 16 |

Is there clear evidence of a difference between the two explosives in liability to cause ignition? Table 38 shows the following figures for $A = 10$, $B = 6$, $a = 10$:

| Probability | 0·05 | 0·025 | 0·01 | 0·005 |
|---|---|---|---|---|
| $b$ | 3 | 2 | 2 | 1 |

Regarding the double-tail test as appropriate and remembering the rule (iii) of § 19·2 above, the observed result with $b = 2$ is significant at the 5 % level; it is also significant at the 2 % level.

*Case* 3

A third type of application is to the situation where the individuals in a population may possess two characters, $Y$ and $Z$, and we wish to determine, on the basis of a single sample of $N$, small compared to the population and randomly selected from it, whether the characters are independent or not. Writing $\bar{Y}$ and $\bar{Z}$ for the absence of $Y$ and $Z$, every individual may be classed in one or other of four categories and the probability scheme is as follows:

|  | $Y$ | $\bar{Y}$ | Total |
|---|---|---|---|
| $Z$ | $p(Y, Z)$ | $p(\bar{Y}, Z)$ | $p(Z)$ |
| $\bar{Z}$ | $p(Y, \bar{Z})$ | $p(\bar{Y}, \bar{Z})$ | $p(\bar{Z})$ |
| Total | $p(Y)$ | $p(\bar{Y})$ | 1 |

The condition for independence is that $p(YZ) = p(Y) \times p(Z)$. It follows at once that if this is satisfied and if the sample data are arranged in a $2 \times 2$ contingency table with the same notation as before, then

$$f(a, b \mid p(Y), p(Z)) = \binom{N}{r} p(Y)^r (1 - p(Y))^{N-r} \times \binom{N}{A} p(Z)^A (1 - p(Z))^{N-A}$$
$$\times \frac{A!\, B!\, r!\, (N-r)!}{a!\, b!\, (A-a)!\, (B-b)!\, N!}. \quad (89)$$

Thus the conditional probability distribution for $a$, given $r$ and $A$, is the same hypergeometric distribution as before. If we use the significance levels of this series, obtained from Table 38, rejecting the hypothesis of independence when $b$ for given $a$, $A$ and $B$ falls, say, beyond the appropriate 5 % level, we shall again be on the safe side, i.e. the risk of wrong rejection will be less than 0·05 in relation to the more extended reference set in which both $r$ and $A$ are regarded as varying from one sample to another.

*Example* 39. In an extensive inquiry into the relationship between intelligence and physical and mental characters (Karl Pearson, 1906, p. 144), data were given showing the relationship between teachers' estimates of intelligence and athleticism among 1708 schoolboys. Suppose that in a preliminary survey of the data, the records randomly selected for 30 boys had provided the following figures:

| Intelligence | Athletic | Not athletic | Total |
|---|---|---|---|
| Above average | 11 | 3 $(=b)$ | 14 $(=B)$ |
| Below average | 8 | 8 $(=a)$ | 16 $(=A)$ |
| Total | 19 | 11 | 30 |

Do these figures show any significant relationship between the two qualities? Since $A > 15$, we follow rule (vii) of § 19·2 and consider the tables

$$
\begin{array}{cc|c}
11 & 3 & 14 \\
8 & 7 & 15 \\
\hline
19 & 10 & 29
\end{array}
\quad \text{and} \quad
\begin{array}{cc|c}
11 & 3 & 14 \\
7 & 8 & 15 \\
\hline
18 & 11 & 29
\end{array}
$$

When Table 38 is entered with $A = 15$, $B = 14$, it is seen that in neither case is the arrangement significant, even at the 10 % level (double-tail test). This means that in the original table $a/A$ is not significantly different from $b/B$ at this level.

### 19·4 *The case of larger samples*

The scope of Table 38 is of course very limited.* When dealing with medium or large samples, using the mean and standard deviation of the hypergeometric series, we note that the ratio

$$
u = \frac{a - \mathscr{E}(a \mid r, A)}{\sigma(a \mid r, A)} = \frac{a - rA/N}{\left\{\dfrac{ABr(N-r)}{N^2(N-1)}\right\}^{\frac{1}{2}}} \tag{90}
$$

has expectation zero and unit standard deviation. This is true for the reference set of each of the three forms of application discussed, i.e. whether both margins, one margin or neither margin of the 2 × 2 table is regarded as fixed. The usual approximation is to regard the overall distribution of this ratio as roughly normal, i.e. to judge the significance of $u$ by reference to the normal probability scale of Table 1. Under these conditions it is clearly justifiable to substitute $N$ for $N - 1$, and the ratio is quoted under various alternative, but mathematically identical, forms, e.g. as

$$
\frac{a/A - b/B}{\left\{\dfrac{r}{N}\left(1 - \dfrac{r}{N}\right)\left(\dfrac{1}{A} + \dfrac{1}{B}\right)\right\}^{\frac{1}{2}}} \quad \text{or} \quad \frac{\{a(B-b) - b(A-a)\}\sqrt{N}}{\{ABr(N-r)\}^{\frac{1}{2}}}. \tag{90a}
$$

* For a reference to a more extensive table covering the range $B \leqslant A \leqslant 45$, see p. 72.

Assuming, on the hypothesis tested, that the ratio is a unit normal deviate, its square may be regarded as a value of $\chi^2$ based on $\nu = 1$ degree of freedom, and the test is often applied, making use of the $\chi^2$ tables. It should, however, be noted that in this form the test is automatically a double-tail one; by working with the square root as in equations (90) or (90$a$) and referring to the Normal tables, we do not lose sight of the sign of $a/A - b/B$ which may be particularly informative.

It is common practice to insert in the numerator of $u$ (equation (90)) the '$\frac{1}{2}$' correction for continuity referred to on p. 73 above, or to make the equivalent correction to the numerator of the ratios in equations (90$a$). In this way we shall in general get a more accurate approximation to the sum of the tail terms of the hypergeometric series from the integrals of the normal curve or of the $\chi^2$-distribution having one degree of freedom. However, it should be remembered that the expectation of $u^2$, when so corrected, is now less than unity, and as Lancaster (1949) has pointed out, this may result in considerable bias in any form of analysis which depends upon the combination of a number of independent values of $u^2$.

*Example* 40. When the full data for the 1708 schoolboys referred to in Example 39 (p. 77) were tabled, the following results were obtained:

| Intelligence | Athletic | Not athletic | Total |
|---|---|---|---|
| Above average<br>Below average | 581<br>567 | 209<br>351 | 790<br>918 |
| Total | 1148 | 560 | 1708 |

Using equation (90), or either of the alternative forms (90$a$), we find that $u = 5 \cdot 17$. Regarded as a standardized normal deviate, this value is clearly highly significant, so that there is little doubt that in the category of boys considered a positive relationship existed between 'intelligence' and skill in athletics.

## 20. TEST OF THE DIFFERENCE BETWEEN TWO POISSON EXPECTATIONS
### (TABLE 36)
### *Definition*

If $a$ and $b$ are two variables distributed independently in accordance with the Poisson law, with expectations $m_1$ and $m_2$ respectively, their joint probability function is

$$f(a, b \mid m_1, m_2) = m_1^a e^{-m_1}/a! \times m_2^b e^{-m_2}/b!$$

$$= M^r e^{-M}/r! \times \binom{r}{a} \theta^a (1-\theta)^b, \qquad (91)$$

where $\qquad r = a + b, \quad M = m_1 + m_2, \quad \theta = m_1/(m_1 + m_2)$.

The first term in (91) represents the probability that a Poisson variable with expectation $M$ has a value $r$, while the second expression is the term of a binomial. Thus the conditional probability distribution of $a$ (and therefore of $b = r - a$) for given $r$ and $\theta$ is a binomial. The position is very similar to that described in §19·1 above, and illustrated in Fig. 3, except that the lattice is no longer closed, $A$ and $B$ having become infinite. Further, the conditional distribution, along each diagonal, $r = $ constant, is now a binomial in place of a hypergeometric series.

In practical application, when $\theta = m_1/(m_1 + m_2)$ is specified by hypothesis, significance levels may be obtained for the conditional distribution from the tail sums of binomials, e.g. by use of the incomplete B-function relation (§ 8·1 and 18). In the special case where we wish to test whether the two Poisson expectations are the same, i.e. whether $m_1 = m_2$, so that $\theta = \frac{1}{2}$, we are concerned with the significance levels of the binomial $(\frac{1}{2} + \frac{1}{2})^r$.

Formally, Table 36 A shows for values of $r = a + b$ in the range 1 (1) 80, the values of $b$ for which

$$\sum_{i=0}^{b} \binom{r}{i} \left(\frac{1}{2}\right)^r \leqslant \alpha \quad \text{and} \quad \sum_{i=0}^{b+1} \binom{r}{i} \left(\frac{1}{2}\right)^r > \alpha,$$

for $\alpha = 0·10, 0·05, 0·025, 0·01$ and $0·005$.

If we denote by $b$ the smaller of the two observed frequencies $a$ and $b$, then if $b$ is equal to or less than the integer in the column headed $0·10, 0·05, 0·025, 0·01$ or $0·005$, $b$ is significantly *less than* $a$ (single-tail test) at these levels. Alternatively, if a double-tail test is appropriate, we should say that $b$ was significantly *different from* $a$ at the probability levels $0·20, 0·10, 0·05,$ $0·02$ or $0·01$ respectively. Absence of an entry indicates that at this level significance is not attainable for that value of $r$.

As in the case of Table 38, owing to the discontinuous character of the binomial distribution, the tail probability corresponding to a given critical value of $b$ will usually be considerably less than that shown at the head of the column. As a result, in the long run application of the test the proportion of times in which significance will be claimed, when in fact $m_1 = m_2$, will be considerably less than the nominal value defined by the probability level used. The extent of this over-estimation of the risk of error involved will depend on the value of the common expectation $m = m_1 = m_2$. To give some idea of the position, Table 36 B shows (for the single-tail test) for certain values of $m$ the probability of rejecting the hypothesis $m_1 = m_2$, when it is true, using the five nominal significance levels of Table 36 A. These probabilities were obtained from the double summation

$$\sum_{r=r_0}^{\infty} \left\{ (2m)^r e^{-2m}/r! \times \sum_{i=0}^{b} \binom{r}{i} \left(\frac{1}{2}\right)^r \right\},$$

where for given $r$, $b$ has the critical value given in Table 36 A, and where $r_0$ is the value of $r$ opposite the first entry of 0 in the appropriate $\alpha$-column.

It is seen that these true significance levels change systematically with $m$. In the nature of the problem, $m$ cannot be known, but within broad limits the table indicates how much on the safe side we shall be in using the nominal or upper bound significance values. The exceptionally low values of the probabilities in Table 36 B for $m = 2·5$ occur, of course, because with an expectation of this magnitude the two samples will often show frequencies $a$ and $b$ for which $a + b = r < r_0$. Significance is then not attainable, however different are $a$ and $b$. This effect, however, scarcely remains when $m = 5·0$.

The tables have been based on those given in a paper by Przyborowski & Wilenski (1940). These authors also gave tables and charts, not reproduced here, from which it is possible to assess the power of the test, i.e. the probability of establishing significance for given unequal values of the expectations $m_1$ and $m_2$.

*Example* 41. Maguire, Pearson & Wynn (1952) have quoted figures for the time intervals between explosions in coal mines in the United Kingdom involving more than ten men killed. If, starting from the beginning of the record, we take successive periods of 10 years, it is found that eight accidents occurred in the third of these periods and twenty accidents in the fourth period. If accidents occur randomly in time with a constant expectation per unit time, the frequency of accidents in a period of given length should follow the Poisson law. If it is questioned whether the difference between accident frequencies of eight and twenty is significant, we may use Table 36 A to test whether these two figures are consistent with sampling subject to a common Poisson law with expectation $m$.

Entering the table with $r = a + b = 28$ and using a double-tail test, i.e. doubling the probability at the top of the columns, we find that $b = 8$ is significant at the 5 % level. Thus there is some evidence for an increase in accident risk during the 20 years in question, although, of course, this is most unlikely to have taken the form of an increase from a constant expectation $m_1$ in the first period to another constant value $m_2$ in the second period.

It is seen from Table 36 B that when $m$ is in the neighbourhood of 12·5–15, the nominal 5 % level (double-tail test) corresponds to a true level of 0·030.

### 21. Individual terms of Poisson's limit to the binomial (Table 39)

If a variable $x$ follows the Poisson distribution law, with expectation $m$, the probability that $x = i$ will be

$$f(i \mid m) = m^i e^{-m}/i! \quad (i = 0, 1, \dots, \infty). \tag{92}$$

As described in § 3·3 above, use has been made of the relation between the $\chi^2$-integral and the cumulative sum of the terms of the Poisson series, to arrange the table of the former (Table 7) so that it can be used for the latter. Table 7, in fact, gives $\sum_{i=0}^{c-1} f(i \mid m)$ to 5-decimal accuracy.

The present Table 39, calculated at an earlier date, gives to 6-decimal accuracy the individual terms in the series (92) for $m = 0·1\,(0·1)\,15·0$. The two tables are complementary, and it will be found that sometimes one, sometimes the other is the more appropriate to use. The choice will depend partly on whether it is the cumulative sum or the individual probabilities that are required. But apart from this, from the point of view of interpolation between tabled values of $m$, the argument interval may be the controlling factor.

For $0 < m \leqslant 1·0$: Table 7 has the smaller interval, giving figures for 38 values of $m$ in this range, whereas Table 39 gives figures for only 10 values.

For $1·0 < m < 5·0$: both tables use the same argument interval, 0·1.

For $5·0 < m < 15·0$: Table 39 has the advantage, retaining the smaller interval of 0·1.

For $m > 15·0$: we are beyond the range of Table 39. While Table 7 gives cumulative sums up to $m = 67$ these are not carried further than the term $c = 35$, a fact which limits the usefulness of the extension.

An illustration of the use of Table 7 in fitting a Poisson distribution to a series of observed frequencies has already been given (Example 3, p. 11), and no further illustration is needed here.

### 22. The determination of confidence limits for the Poisson and binomial parameters

#### 22·1  General comment on the theory

If observations of random variables, $x_1, x_2, \dots, x_n$, are used to provide an estimate $T$ of a population parameter $\theta$, it is common practice to record with $T$ an estimate $s_T$ of its standard error. When dealing with samples containing many observations, the sampling distribution of $T$

will generally be approximately normal and the difference between $s_T$ and its true value $\sigma_T$ will usually be of smaller order than the difference between $T$ and $\theta$. Hence little ambiguity results from the various forms of putting on record the accuracy of the estimate $T$, e.g. from the statement that the odds are roughly 19 to 1 that the numerical value of the difference $T - \theta$ is less than $2s_T$.

The position, however, is different when the estimate is based on relatively few observations, since the sampling error in $s_T$ cannot then be overlooked. The fiducial theory of R. A. Fisher and the confidence interval theory of J. Neyman were developed to meet this situation. Both aim at providing means of calculating from the data intervals within which the unknown parameter $\theta$ may be expected to lie within a given measure of probability. While from the practical standpoint there is in most (though not in all) problems no difference between the result of applying the two methods, Fisher's approach introduces the concept of fiducial probability, while Neyman's employs only the classical concept of direct probability. The application of theory described here is in terms of Neyman's approach.

Several illustrations have been given earlier in this Introduction of the calculation of confidence limits: viz. (i) limits for the standard deviation, $\sigma$, of a normal population, based on the $\chi^2$ distribution (§ 4·3); (ii) limits for the population mean $\mu$, based on the $t$-distribution (§ 5·5); (iii) limits for the difference between the means of two normal populations having unequal variances, based on Welch's method (§ 6·2); (iv) limits for the correlation coefficient $\rho$ between two normal variables, based on the distribution of $r$ (§ 7·3). In all these cases the distributions of the sample statistics employed in the estimation were continuous. In the two following sections we are concerned with discontinuous distributions, and the meaning to be attached to the probability statement associated with the confidence interval needs rather careful definition; this is our reason for developing the argument in connexion with the Poisson parameter, $m$, in some detail.

### 22·2    Confidence limits for the expectation, $m$, of a Poisson variable (Table 40)

The general term of a Poisson series may be written as $e^{-m} m^i/i!$ $(i = 0, 1, 2, \ldots)$. For any given value $c$ and $\alpha < 0·5$, we may determine two values of $m$, say $m_A(c \mid \alpha) < m_B(c \mid \alpha)$, such that

$$\sum_{i=c}^{\infty} \frac{e^{-m_A} m_A^i}{i!} = \alpha, \qquad \sum_{i=0}^{c} \frac{e^{-m_B} m_B^i}{i!} = \alpha. \qquad (93)$$

Within the range of tabulation $m_A(c)$ and $m_B(c)$ may be readily determined from the table of percentage points of the $\chi^2$-distribution (Table 8) using the relation (18) of p. 10. Thus

$$m_B(c \mid \alpha) = \tfrac{1}{2}\chi_1^2, \quad \text{where} \quad Q(\chi_1^2 \mid \nu) = \alpha, \quad \nu = 2(c+1), \qquad (94)$$

$$m_A(c \mid \alpha) = \tfrac{1}{2}\chi_2^2, \quad \text{where} \quad 1 - Q(\chi_2^2 \mid \nu) = \alpha, \quad \nu = 2c. \qquad (95)$$

If, for example, we take $\alpha = 0·005$ and $c = 6$, we see from Table 8 that

(a) the upper $0·5\%$ point ($Q = 0·005$) for $\chi^2$ with $\nu = 14$ is $31·3193$ so that

$$m_B(6 \mid 0·005) = 15·66;$$

(b) the lower $0·5\%$ point ($Q = 0·995$) for $\chi^2$ with $\nu = 12$ is $3·07382$ so that

$$m_A(6 \mid 0·005) = 1·54.$$

If now we determine $m_B(c \mid \alpha)$ and $m_A(c \mid \alpha)$ for $c = 0, 1, 2, \ldots$ and plot their values as ordinates against $c$ as abscissa, we obtain the diagram shown in Fig. 4, where the two series of points have been connected by arbitrarily drawn smooth curves. The area between the curves is the so-called *confidence belt*. Suppose that for a particular observed value of $c$ we determine the limits $m_B(c)$ and $m_A(c)$, either from a chart or appropriate table, then the probability that the interval between these limits includes the true expectation $m$ is at least

$$1 - 2\alpha = 1 - 2 \times 0.005 = 0.99,$$

or
$$\Pr\{m_A(c \mid 0.005) \leqslant m \leqslant m_B(c \mid 0.005)\} \geqslant 0.99. \tag{96}$$

This result may be demonstrated as follows. If repeated observations are made of a Poisson variable having fixed but unknown expectation, say $m = m_0$, the points $(c, m_0)$ will lie along a line such as $CDEF$ in Fig. 4 (where, for illustration, $m_0 = 12$). This line is divided into three parts by the boundaries of the confidence belt:

(i) For observations with $c = 0, 1, \ldots$ on $CD$ the statement (96) will be incorrect because $m_B < m_0$; but from the nature of the construction the probability of $c$ falling in $CD$ is $\leqslant \alpha = 0.005$.

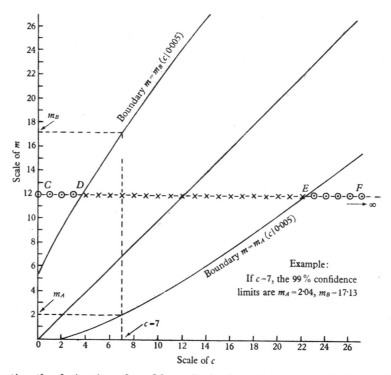

Fig. 4. Illustrating the derivation of confidence limits for a Poisson expectation with $1 - 2\alpha = 0.99$.

(ii) For observations with $c$ on $EF$ the statement (96) will be incorrect because $m_A > m_0$; the probability of $c$ falling in $EF$ is also $\leqslant \alpha = 0.005$.

(iii) For observations with $c$ on $DE$, the statement (96) will be correct; the probability of this occurring is therefore clearly $\geqslant 1 - 2\alpha = 0.99$.

This position will hold whatever be the expectation $m_0$, and thus in general (96) provides a relation in probability between two functions of any Poisson variable and its expectation.

Owing to the discontinuity in distribution, it is clear that in repeated sampling, particularly when $m$ is small, the proportion of occasions on which the interval includes the true expectation may be considerably in excess of the lower bound $1 - 2\alpha$. Thus it should be possible to find alternative methods of solution which would fix the confidence coefficient at exactly $1 - 2\alpha$ and at the same time narrow the interval. This matter has been discussed by W. L. Stevens (1950).

Table 40 gives values of $m_A(c \mid \alpha)$ and $m_B(c \mid \alpha)$ for $c = 0$ (1) 30 (5) 50 and $\alpha = 0.001, 0.005, 0.01$, 0.025 and 0.05. Beyond $c = 50$, the values of $m_A$ and $m_B$ may be computed using the relations (94) and (95) of p. 81, the required percentage points of $\chi^2$ being obtained from one of the approximate relations quoted under Table 8.

*Example* 42. A spot sample shows eighteen incoming calls received during an interval of 1 min. on a particular section of the equipment at a telephone exchange. What limits may be reasonably placed on the expected number of calls per $\frac{1}{4}$ hour?

Assuming that the rate of traffic remains reasonably constant during the period considered and that the distribution of calls received in an interval of constant length follows the Poisson law, we may obtain confidence limits from Table 40. For example, for $c = 18$ the lower and upper 95 % confidence limits are 10·67 and 28·45. For the average number of calls per $\frac{1}{4}$ hour we have, therefore, as limits

$$15 \times 10.67 = 160 \quad \text{and} \quad 15 \times 28.45 = 427.$$

In determining these values we are using a procedure giving limits which will include the true expectation, in the long run, at least 19 times out of 20. Clearly these are very wide limits, but it is a function of statistical method to emphasize that precise conclusions cannot be drawn from inadequate data.

### 22·3 *Confidence limits for p in binomial sampling (Table 41, two charts)*

The general term of the binomial expansion $(q+p)^n$ may be written as before

$$f(i \mid n, p) = \binom{n}{i} p^i (1-p)^{n-i}.$$

The value of $n$ is supposed known, and it is required to find confidence limits $p_A(c \mid n, \alpha)$ and $p_B(c \mid n, \alpha)$ for $p$ (where $p_A < p_B$) on the basis of an observed value $i = c$. The derivation proceeds on lines similar to those followed for the Poisson expectation (see § 22·2 above), except that the confidence belt of Fig. 4 is now 'closed', since $0 \leqslant c \leqslant n$ and $0 \leqslant p \leqslant 1$. For a given value of $i = c$, the values of $p_A$ and $p_B$ are defined by

$$\sum_{i=c}^{n} f(i \mid n, p_A) = \alpha, \quad \sum_{i=0}^{c} f(i \mid n, p_B) = \alpha, \tag{97}$$

where the cumulative sums may be conveniently expressed as in equation (84) in terms of the incomplete B-function integral.

Since there are now two parameters, $p$ (to be estimated) and $n$ (supposed known), no detailed tables have been given, but sufficient points $c$, $p_A(c \mid n, \alpha)$ and $c$, $p_B(c \mid n, \alpha)$ were calculated to draw smooth curves through them. By taking $c/n$ as abscissa and $p$ as ordinate these curves can be reproduced in a single diagram. The charts of Table 41 show confidence belts prepared in this way for

$$\alpha = 0.025 \quad \text{and} \quad 0.005 \quad \text{or} \quad 1 - 2\alpha = 0.95 \quad \text{and} \quad 0.99,$$

and for $\qquad n = 8, 10, 12, 16, 20, 24, 30, 40, 60, 100, 200, 400, 1000.$

The same limitation applies as in the case of the Poisson confidence limits; namely, the probability that the statement

$$p_A(c \mid n, \alpha) \leqslant p \leqslant p_B(c \mid n, \alpha) \tag{98}$$

is correct is likely to be considerably in excess of the lower bound, $1 - 2\alpha$.

The charts cannot and are not intended to provide very precise readings. The broad picture which they give of the relation between $p$ and $c/n$ will, however, be found of value in answering a variety of questions regarding probabilities, proportions and percentages. Some of these are illustrated in the following examples.

*Example* 43. The toxicity of a drug may be measured by the proportion, $p$, of mice in a standard laboratory population that will die after injection with a dose of given strength. Out of a sample of thirty mice randomly selected from the population, eight die after injection; within what limits may we expect that $p$ lies? Turning to the first chart of Table 41, and taking $n = 30$, $c/n = 8/30 = 0.267$, it will be seen that we may say that $0.12 < p < 0.46$, if we are prepared to accept a risk of error of not more than 1 in 20. To obtain greater confidence in prediction (risk of error 1 in 100) we must turn to the second chart and obtain $0.095 < p < 0.52$.*

*Example* 44. In a manufacturing process a crude index of quality, $P$, has been the percentage of articles which pass a certain test. This index has fluctuated in the past round $P = 60$, but it is proposed to make an intensive effort to improve quality (which will mean the raising of this percentage) by tightening the control of manufacture. Improvement is to be judged by studying the changes in the proportion of articles ($c/n$) passing the test in a random sample of $n$ articles. How large would $n$ need to be to obtain from the sample an estimate of $P$, with a range of uncertainty of not more than 5?

At the start, the value of $p = P/100$ in the material sampled is not more than 0.60, and we wish to determine $n$ so that the confidence belt will be of breadth about 0.05. On the assumption that a confidence coefficient of 0.95 is adequate, we may use the first chart. It will be seen that for $c/n$ having values between 0.6 and 0.8, $n$ must be more than 1000 for the interval $p_2 - p_1$ to be as small as 0.05.† In many cases the testing of so large a sample would be quite out of the question, and this result points to the fact that an index of this type is not an efficient measure of quality. Much more information of changes could probably be drawn from a smaller sample, if the index could be based on the mean value of some measured character determined for each article of the sample.

*Example* 45. There are two alternative hypotheses regarding the chance of an individual in a certain population bearing a given character; the alternatives are that $p = \frac{1}{4}$ or $p = \frac{1}{2}$. Such might be the case in some genetic investigation. How large a sample must be planned to make it practically certain that we can discriminate between the two hypotheses?

In this case we are concerned with the sampling variation of $c$ for $p = \frac{1}{4}$ and $p = \frac{1}{2}$, and $n$ should be chosen so large that there is no 'overlap' of any consequence between the two distributions. Suppose we choose $n$ so that the upper 0.005 point of the $c$ distribution for $p = \frac{1}{4}$, as judged from the curves of the second chart, corresponds to the lower 0.005 point of the distribution for $p = \frac{1}{2}$. This will occur when $n$ is slightly over 100, say 110.

If we were prepared to accept a greater risk of an inconclusive result, which we might well be prepared to do if the sample could be readily increased in size in a doubtful case, then we might choose $n$ so that the upper and lower 0.025 points of the $c$ distributions correspond. Turning to the first chart it is found that this occurs when $n$ is about 60.

* If interpolation is carried out in Table 16, it is found more precisely that the 95 % confidence limits fall at 0.123 and 0.459 while the 99 % limits fall at 0.093 and 0.516.

† Since for large values of $n$ the upper and lower bounds of the confidence belt are very nearly parallel lines making an angle of 45° with the axes, and the binomial may be represented by a normal curve, the breadth of the belt is approximately $4\{p(1-p)/n\}^{\frac{1}{2}}$, which if equated to 0.05 gives roughly $n = 1600$ for $p = 0.60$ and $n = 1000$ for $p = 0.80$.

# V. MISCELLANEOUS TABLES (PEARSON-TYPE CURVES, RANK CORRELATION, ORTHOGONAL POLYNOMIALS)

## 23. CHART RELATING THE TYPE OF PEARSON FREQUENCY CURVE TO THE VALUES OF $\beta_1$ AND $\beta_2$ (TABLE 43)

### 23·1  *Specification of the curves*

Karl Pearson's system of frequency curves (1895, 1901, 1916), $y = f(x)$, are obtained as solutions of the differential equation

$$\frac{1}{y}\frac{dy}{dx} = \frac{-(x+c_1)}{c_0 + c_1 x + c_2 x^2}, \tag{99}$$

where the origin for $x$ is at the mean. The form of the solution depends on the values of the constants $c_0$, $c_1$ and $c_2$, which may be shown to be related to the moments of the curve. If we write

$$\mu_r = \int_{l_1}^{l_2} x^r f(x)\, dx$$

for the $r$th moment about the mean ($\mu_0 = 1$, $\mu_1 = 0$), where $l_1$ and $l_2$ are the permissible lower and upper limits for $x$, and if

$$\sigma^2 = \mu_2, \quad \beta_1 = \mu_3^2/\mu_2^3, \quad \beta_2 = \mu_4/\mu_2^2,$$

then
$$c_0 = \frac{\sigma^2(4\beta_2 - 3\beta_1)}{2(5\beta_2 - 6\beta_1 - 9)}, \quad c_1 = \frac{\sigma\sqrt{\beta_1}(\beta_2 + 3)}{2(5\beta_2 - 6\beta_1 - 9)}, \quad c_2 = \frac{2\beta_2 - 3\beta_1 - 6}{2(5\beta_2 - 6\beta_1 - 9)}. \tag{100}$$

It follows that if a diagram is drawn plotting $\beta_1$, $\beta_2$ to rectangular axes, different areas, curves or points in the plane can be associated with particular types of curve. A chart of this kind is presented as Table 43, covering the main types of Pearson curves, i.e. Types I–VII. The line $\beta_2 - \beta_1 - 1 = 0$ forms an upper boundary above which, in the sense of the chart, the $\beta_1$, $\beta_2$ point of no real frequency distribution can fall, while for the Pearson system, $\mu_8$ is infinite on and below the line $8\beta_2 - 15\beta_1 - 36 = 0$ shown at the bottom of the chart. Using a standard notation, the equations to these seven curves may be expressed as follows:

| Type | Equation | Origin for $x$ | Limits for $x$ |
|------|----------|----------------|----------------|
| I* | $y = y_0\left(1 + \dfrac{x}{a_1}\right)^{m_1}\left(1 - \dfrac{x}{a_2}\right)^{m_2}$ | Mode | $-a_1 \leqslant x \leqslant a_2$ |
| II | $y = y_0\left(1 - \dfrac{x^2}{a^2}\right)^m$ | Mean ($=$mode) | $-a \leqslant x \leqslant a$ |
| III | $y = y_0 e^{-\gamma x}\left(1 + \dfrac{x}{a}\right)^{\gamma a}$ | Mode | $-a \leqslant x < \infty$ |
| IV | $y = y_0 e^{-\nu \tan^{-1} x/a}\left(1 + \dfrac{x^2}{a^2}\right)^{-m}$ | Mean $+\dfrac{\nu a}{r}$† | $-\infty < x < \infty$ |
| V | $y = y_0 e^{-\gamma/x} x^{-p}$ | At start of curve | $0 \leqslant x < \infty$ |
| VI | $y = y_0 (x-a)^{q_2} x^{-q_1}$ | At $a$ before start of curve | $a \leqslant x < \infty$ |
| VII | $y = y_0\left(1 + \dfrac{x^2}{a^2}\right)^{-m}$ | Mean ($=$mode) | $-\infty < x < \infty$ |

The notation used is that of W. P. Elderton (1953), whose book, *Frequency Curves and Correlation*, or the original papers of Pearson should be consulted for the relations between the moments and the parameters of the curves.

---

\* For the most common form of Type I curve of 'bell' shape (area I in chart), both $m_1$ and $m_2$ are positive; for J-shaped curves (area I($J$) in chart), either $m_1$ or $m_2$ is negative; for U-shaped curves (area I($U$) in chart), both are negative.

† $r = 6(\beta_2 - \beta_1 - 1)/(2\beta_2 - 3\beta_1 - 6) = 2m - 2$; this origin is chosen to simplify the form of the equation.

Historically this system of curves was developed to graduate frequency distributions of observational data which could not be represented by the Normal curve. Latterly, however, the system has been used increasingly to represent probability distributions whose moments are known but for which the mathematical equations are either undetermined or not expressible in simple form. Illustrations of this application are given in § 24·3 below.

*Example* 46. Moment ratios for the distribution of range in samples of $n$ observations from a normal population were evaluated approximately by L. H. C. Tippett (1925) and E. S. Pearson (1926) as follows:

| Sample size, $n$ | 6 | 10 | 20 | 60 | 100 |
|---|---|---|---|---|---|
| $\beta_1(w)$ | 0·189 | 0·156 | 0·161 | 0·201 | 0·223 |
| $\beta_2(w)$ | 3·17 | 3·22 | 3·26 | 3·35 | 3·39 |
| Type areas in which points fall | I | I | VI | VI | VI |

Determine which types of Pearson curve are likely to be most appropriate to use in approximating to the distribution of range. The first two $\beta_1, \beta_2$ points fall in the Type I area and the last three in the Type VI area, the Type III line, on which $2\beta_2 - 3\beta_1 - 6 = 0$, being crossed between $n = 10$ and 20.

The Type I and VI approximations were in fact used by E. S. Pearson (1932) to obtain rough percentage points for the distribution of range. The practical utility of this method is illustrated by the fact that the values so obtained were found to be scarcely in error when correct values for $n \leqslant 20$ were later derived from the true probability integral (see § 12·4 above). The discrepancy arose as much from the approximate nature of the $\beta_1, \beta_2$ values available in 1932 (compare the figures given above with those in Table 20) as from the use of Type I and VI curves.

*Example* 47. On p. 69 (Example 35) a frequency distribution has been given for 1000 observations on the warp strength of a duck cloth. The values of the moments and moment ratios for this distribution are

$$\text{Mean} = 454·09 \text{ lb.}, \quad \text{Standard deviation} = 17·358 \text{ lb.},$$

$$\sqrt{b_1} = -0·421, \quad b_1 = 0·1772, \quad b_2 = 2·748.$$

It has already been shown that the value of $\sqrt{b_1}$ establishes a significant departure from normality. Turning to the chart of Table 43 it will be seen that the point $(0·177, 2·748)$ lies clearly in the Type I area. Pearson & Welch (1937) fitted a Type I curve to the observed distribution, using the method of moments, and obtained the following equation, the origin being at zero lb.:

$$y = 21·9662(x - 370·02)^{5·1218}(495·59 - x)^{1·9805}.$$

The graduated frequencies obtained from this equation are shown in the table on p. 69. The fit appears good except towards the upper tail, where the curve comes down steeply to the terminal at $x = 495·59$ lb. An improved graduation could be obtained, no doubt, by applying corrections to the moment solution, so as to secure either a maximum-likelihood or minimum $\chi^2$ fit. Pearson & Welch were, however, concerned with the lower tail of the distribution corresponding to low breaking strengths and regarded the graduation as adequate. If the three frequency groups centred at 485, 490 and 495 lb. are combined into one group and those centred at 400 and 405 lb. into another, the value of $\chi^2$ based on seventeen groups is $14\cdot45$; for $\nu = 17 - 5 = 12$ degrees of freedom,* the probability of obtaining a worse fit through chance fluctuations (when the true law is of Type I form) equals $0\cdot27$.

## 24. TABLES OF CERTAIN PERCENTAGE POINTS OF PEARSON CURVES, FOR GIVEN $\beta_1$ AND $\beta_2$, EXPRESSED IN STANDARDIZED MEASURE (TABLE 42)

### 24·1 Definition

If $y = f(x)$, $l_1 \leqslant x \leqslant l_2$, is a frequency curve of the Pearson system (see § 23·1 above), having mean $\mu$ and standard deviation $\sigma$, so that $X = (x - \mu)/\sigma$ is a standardized deviate, then Table 42 gives values of
$$X_P = (x_P - \mu)/\sigma,$$
where
$$P = \int_{l_1}^{x_P} f(x)\,dx,$$

for $P = 0\cdot005,\ 0\cdot01,\ 0\cdot025,\ 0\cdot05,\ 0\cdot95,\ 0\cdot975,\ 0\cdot99$ and $0\cdot995$ and for values of $\beta_1$ and $\beta_2$ in the area of Fig. 5, lying below the line labelled Type IX. This diagram, taken from the paper by

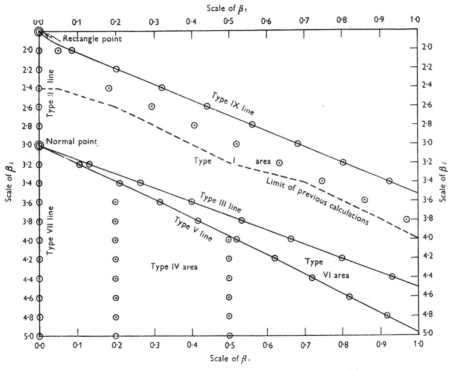

Fig. 5. Showing area in $\beta_1$, $\beta_2$ plane covered by Table 42.

Pearson & Merrington (1951), shows the points for which framework values of $X_P$ were computed in preparing the table.† The Type IX line, on which lie the $(\beta_1, \beta_2)$ points of the curves
$$y = y_0\left(1 + \frac{x}{a}\right)^m,$$

forms an upper boundary for the table entries; above this line (in the sense of the diagram) the $(\beta_1, \beta_2)$ points correspond to J-shaped and U-shaped curves.

* This involves an application of the $\chi^2$ test for goodness of fit referred to in § 3·2 above in connexion with Table 7. Since four moments have been used in the fitting and the total observed and theoretical frequencies are equal, five relations exist among the seventeen differences $(n_t - m_t)$. Hence $\nu = 12$. In theory, the fit should have been adjusted to obtain a 'minimum' $\chi^2$ before applying this test; in the present application this was unnecessary.

† A much fuller table has since been computed by Johnson et al. (1963). This gives the limits to three and sometimes four decimal places, adds 0·25, 10 and 25 % points and much extends the range of $\beta_1$ and $\beta_2$ covered.

To the accuracy justified, linear interpolation for $\beta_2$ and for $\beta_1$, except in the panel 0·00–0·01, is adequate. If at a given $(\beta_1, \beta_2)$ point the values of $X_P$ for several $P$ values are required, it is worth proceeding systematically using the formula

$$X(\theta, \phi) = X(0, 0) \times (1 - \theta - \phi + \theta\phi) + X(1, 0) \times (\theta - \theta\phi) + X(1, 1) \times \theta\phi + X(0, 1) \times (\phi - \theta\phi).$$

$$(101)$$

Here, as shown in Fig. 6, the four $X$-values are the four tabular entries at the corners of the panel in which the interpolate falls, and $\theta$ and $\phi$ are the appropriate fractions of the tabular intervals for $\beta_1$ and $\beta_2$ at the part of the table considered. For an illustration, see Example 48 (below).

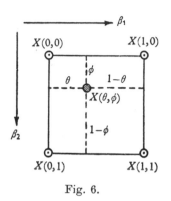

In the interval for $\beta_1$, 0·00–0·01, for a given $\beta_2$ a three-point Lagrangian formula may be used. Thus

$$X(\theta) = X(0) \times \tfrac{1}{3}(1 - \theta)(3 - \theta) + X(1) \times \tfrac{1}{2}\theta(3 - \theta) - X(3) \times \tfrac{1}{6}\theta(1 - \theta),$$

where $\theta = 100\beta_1$ and $X(0)$, $X(1)$ and $X(3)$ are the tabular entries for $\beta_1 = 0·00$, 0·01 and 0·03 respectively.

Fig. 6.

## 24·3 *Applications*

A considerable proportion of current statistical research is concerned with the determination of the sampling distributions of statistics required either as estimators or for use in tests of significance. It is often the case that while the distribution itself cannot be expressed in any simple form, the sampling moments can be derived and numerical values calculated either precisely or as approximations. In a great number of cases such investigation shows that the distribution tends to the normal form as the sample size is increased. However, this information regarding the limit is often not sufficient, and we require an answer to the question: what error is involved in assuming normality when the sample size has a specified value, $n$? In other words, to what extent in practice will the knowledge of the expectation and standard error of a particular statistic suffice?

In many instances experience has shown the value of the Pearson curves in approximating, on the basis of known moments, to the distributions of frequency functions which are either undetermined or are not readily expressed in simple form. In addition, these curves, of course, represent exactly the distributions of a number of the statistics in common use, e.g. $\chi^2$, $t$ and $F$.

*Example* 48. Bailey (1950), in considering the mathematical theory of what he terms a simple stochastic epidemic, gives a table of moments for the time of completion of an epidemic, when all available susceptibles have been exhausted. Thus if $\tau$ is the completion time in a community containing $n$ susceptibles, he shows that appreciable skewness and kurtosis remain in the distribution of $\tau$, even when $n$ is very large. With $n = 80$, he gives:

| $\gamma_1$ | $\gamma_2$ | $\beta_1 = \gamma_1^2$ | $\beta_2 = \gamma_2 + 3$ |
|---|---|---|---|
| 0·771 | 1·114 | 0·594 | 4·114 |

The following figures for percentage levels of $(\tau - \bar{\tau})/\sigma_\tau$ may be derived by interpolation in Table 42:

| | Lower | | Upper | |
|---|---|---|---|---|
| | 0·5% | 5·0% | 5% | 0·5% |
| Pearson curve (Type IV) approx. | −1·95 | −1·41 | 1·82 | 3·33 |
| From 'normal' probability scale | −2·58 | −1·64 | 1·64 | 2·58 |

The figures give added meaning to Bailey's measures of skewness and kurtosis, and a comparison with the normal scale percentage levels is instructive.

The interpolation was carried out systematically, using the formula (101). Thus $\theta = 0.94$, $\phi = 0.57$ and for $P = 0.005$

$$-X_{0.005}(0.94, 0.57) = 2.02 \times 0.026 + 1.90 \times 0.404 + 1.97 \times 0.536 + 2.09 \times 0.034 = 1.947.$$

*Example* 49. If we write $m = \sum\limits_{i=1}^{n} \dfrac{|x_i - \bar{x}|}{n}$ for the mean deviation in a random sample of observations $x_1, x_2, \ldots, x_n$ drawn from a normal population, the sampling moments of $m$ are known (see §10·1 and Table 20). The following are the appropriate values for the cases $n = 10$ and $20$:

| $n$ | $\bar{m}$ | $\sigma_m$ | $\beta_1(m)$ | $\beta_2(m)$ |
|---|---|---|---|---|
| 10 | 0·75694 | 0·1894 | 0·106 | 3·093 |
| 20 | 0·77768 | 0·1344 | 0·0513 | 3·045 |

We may now determine approximations to the lower and upper 0·5% points in these two sampling distributions, expressed in terms of the population standard deviation as unit. These will be given by $\bar{m} + X_P \sigma_m$, where the factors $X_P$ for $P = 0.005$ and $0.995$ are obtained by interpolation from Table 42. The results are as follows:

| $n$ | $X_{0.005}$ | $X_{0.995}$ | Lower 0·5% point | Upper 0·5% point |
|---|---|---|---|---|
| 10 | −2·24 | 2·86 | 0·333 | 1·299 |
| 20 | −2·35 | 2·78 | 0·462 | 1·151 |

The values for $n = 10$ correspond, to 3-decimal accuracy, with the exact percentage points derived from the probability integral of $m$ and given in Table 21. This integral has not been calculated beyond $n = 15$, but the accuracy of the approximation at $n = 10$ suggests that the values obtained at $n = 20$ should also be satisfactory, and that this method could be used to extend the table of percentage points of mean deviation (Table 21) beyond $n = 10$.

*Example* 50. The distribution of the warp strength, given in the table of Example 35 (p. 69), and discussed again in Example 47 (p. 86), is clearly not normal. Suppose it was desired to construct a control chart giving lower limits for the mean $\bar{x}_5$, of determinations of strength in $n = 5$ randomly selected test pieces of this type of cloth. We may ask how much error would be involved in subtracting from $\mu$ multiples of $\sigma(\bar{x}_5) = \sigma_x/\sqrt{5}$ obtained in the ordinary way from the *normal* probability scale.

Since $\sqrt{b_1}$ is negative, we shall obtain from Table 42 the upper 0·5 and 5 % values of $X_P$ for

$$\beta_1(\bar{x}_5) = \beta_1(x)/5 = 0\cdot1772/5 = 0\cdot035,$$

$$\beta_2(\bar{x}_5) = 3 + (\beta_2(x) - 3)/5 = 3 + (2\cdot748 - 3)/5 = 2\cdot95.$$

The appropriate panels of values of $X_P$, which will have negative signs, are:

for $P = 0\cdot05$:

|      | 0·03   | 0·05   |
| ---- | ------ | ------ |
| 2·8  | −1·70  | −1·72  |
| 3·0  | −1·69  | −1·71  |

and for $P = 0\cdot005$:

|      | 0·03   | 0·05   |
| ---- | ------ | ------ |
| 2·8  | −2·64  | −2·68  |
| 3·0  | −2·72  | −2·76  |

It is seen by inspection that $X_{0\cdot05} = -1\cdot70$, while linear interpolation for the two variables gives $X_{0\cdot005} = -2\cdot71$. The corresponding standardized deviates for a normal distribution are $-1\cdot64$ and $-2\cdot58$ respectively. Using these factors to obtain outer (0·005) and inner (0·05) limits in a control chart for $\bar{x}_5$, taking the mean level as 454·09 lb. and the standard error of $\bar{x}_5$ as $17\cdot358/\sqrt{5} = 7\cdot76$ lb., we find:

|                                                              | Outer limit | Inner limit |
| ------------------------------------------------------------ | ----------- | ----------- |
| Using observed $\beta_1$, $\beta_2$ for the 1000 values of $x$ | 433·1       | 440·9       |
| Assuming that $x$ is normally distributed                    | 434·1       | 441·4       |

As the limits would probably be required to the nearest 1 lb. only, it is seen that there would be no error involved in basing the inner limit on normal theory and only an error of 1 lb. in the case of the outer limit.

### 25. TABLES FOR USE IN CONNEXION WITH RANK CORRELATION
### (TABLES 44–46)

#### 25·1 *Definition of the coefficients*

The whole subject of rank correlation has been fully discussed in M. G. Kendall's *Rank Correlation Methods* (1962), and we are indebted to Professor Kendall and his publishers for permission to use some of his examples as well as extracts from his tables of probability values. Here we shall confine ourselves to a brief definition of the measures and some illustration of the use of the tables.

When a number of individuals are arranged in order according to some quality which they all possess to a varying degree, they are said to be *ranked*. In cases where each individual is ranked for two or more different qualities, it may be important to determine whether there is any association or correlation between the qualities and, if so, to calculate and compare measures of this relationship.

Spearman's coefficient of rank correlation, which has often been denoted by the letter $\rho$, and Kendall's coefficient $\tau$, both measure the correspondence between two rankings. Kendall and Babington Smith's coefficient of concordance $W$ is a measure of the correspondence between any number of rankings. To avoid confusion in notation, we shall here denote Spearman's and Kendall's coefficients by $r_s$ and $t_k$, respectively, retaining $W$ for the coefficient of concordance. The coefficients are most readily defined with the help of simple examples.

### (a) The coefficient $r_s$ (Spearman's $\rho$)

Suppose that a number of boys have been ranked according to their ability in mathematics and in music. Such a pair of rankings for $n = 10$ boys, denoted by the letters $A$ to $J$, might be as follows:

| Boy  ... | A | B | C | D | E | F | G | H | I | J |
|---|---|---|---|---|---|---|---|---|---|---|
| Rank for mathematics | 7 | 4 | 3 | 10 | 6 | 2 | 9 | 8 | 1 | 5 |
| Rank for music | 5 | 7 | 3 | 10 | 1 | 9 | 6 | 2 | 8 | 4 |
| Difference in ranks, $d$ | 2 | −3 | 0 | 0 | 5 | −7 | 3 | 6 | −7 | 1 |
| Squared difference, $d^2$ | 4 | 9 | 0 | 0 | 25 | 49 | 9 | 36 | 49 | 1 |

Spearman's coefficient, $r_s$, is obtained by treating the two series of ordinal numbers in the rankings as though they were cardinal numbers representing quality on two numerical scales, and then calculating the usual product-moment coefficient of correlation between the corresponding numbers in the two series. If $d_i$ is the difference in the ranking of the $i$th individual for the two qualities, then this coefficient may be shown to be given in simplest form by

$$r_s = 1 - 6 \sum_{i=1}^{n} (d_i^2)/(n^3 - n)$$
$$= 1 - 6 S_r/(n^3 - n), \tag{102}$$

where $S_r = \sum_i d_i^2$. For the figures given above, $n = 10$ and $\Sigma d_i^2 = 182$, so that $r_s = -0 \cdot 103$.

### (b) The coefficient $t_k$ (Kendall's $\tau$)

Suppose we consider any one of the $\frac{1}{2}n(n-1)$ possible pairs of the $n$ individuals and associate with this pair, (1) a score of $+1$ if the ranking for both qualities is the same order or (2) a score of $-1$ if the ranking is in different order. Thus in the illustration given above, the pair $AB$ scores $-1$, while $AC$ scores $+1$. Denote the sum of these scores for the $\frac{1}{2}n(n-1)$ pairs by $S_t$. It is seen that $S_t$ has a maximum value of $\frac{1}{2}n(n-1)$ if the two rankings are identical and a minimum value of $-\frac{1}{2}n(n-1)$ if the individuals are ranked in exactly opposite order. Kendall defines his coefficient as

$$t_k = \frac{S_t}{\frac{1}{2}n(n-1)}. \tag{103}$$

It is clear that $-1 \leqslant t_k \leqslant 1$.

Short-cut methods are available for calculating $S_t$; one of these commonly used is as follows. Since the scores will not be affected by any rearrangement of the individuals, we may order these so that one ranking is in the natural order. Thus the table on the preceding page may be written:

| Boy ... | I | F | C | B | J | E | A | H | G | D |
|---|---|---|---|---|---|---|---|---|---|---|
| Rank for mathematics | 1 | 2 | 3 | 4 | 5 | 6 | 7 | 8 | 9 | 10 |
| Rank for music | 8 | 9 | 3 | 7 | 4 | 1 | 5 | 2 | 6 | 10 |

Each pair of numbers in the second ranking which is in the right order will now contribute $+1$ to $S_t$. It is unnecessary to count the pairs in the wrong order, so that

$$S_t = N_+ \times (+1) + \{\tfrac{1}{2}n(n-1) - N_+\} \times (-1) = 2N_+ - \tfrac{1}{2}n(n-1),$$

$$t_k = \frac{4N_+}{n(n-1)} - 1,$$

where $N_+$ is the number of pairs in the second ranking which are in the right order.

For the illustration given, the computation of $N_+$ proceeds as follows. Consider first the pairs associated with the first member of the second ranking, namely 8; two members greater than 8 are on the right of it, so the contribution to $N_+$ is 2. Taking now the pairs associated with the next member 9 (other than 8, 9, which has already been taken into account), we find a contribution of 1. Similarly, the contribution from pairs associated with 3, arising from members to the right of it, is 5. Proceeding in this way, we find that

$$N_+ = 2 + 1 + 5 + 1 + 3 + 4 + 2 + 2 + 1 = 21.$$

Hence

$$S_t = 2 \times 21 - 45 = -3, \quad t_k = -0 \cdot 067.$$

### (c) The coefficient of concordance W

We now consider the case where there are several rankings, say $m$ in number, of $n$ individuals. Suppose, for example, that four observers rank six objects as follows (i.e. $m = 4$, $n = 6$):

| | Object | | | | | |
|---|---|---|---|---|---|---|
| | A | B | C | D | E | F |
| Observer I | 5 | 4 | 1 | 6 | 3 | 2 |
| Observer II | 2 | 3 | 1 | 5 | 6 | 4 |
| Observer III | 4 | 1 | 6 | 3 | 2 | 5 |
| Observer IV | 4 | 3 | 2 | 5 | 1 | 6 |
| Sum of ranks | 15 | 11 | 10 | 19 | 12 | 17 |
| Deviation of sum from average | 1 | −3 | −4 | 5 | −2 | 3 |

We may wish to measure the degree of consistency or concordance between the four observers' judgements. It would be possible to calculate a rank correlation coefficient between each pair of observers, but a single measure of the concordance of the observers, taken as a group, will usually be needed. The coefficient of concordance as defined by Kendall and Babington Smith is obtained as follows.

92

(1) The $n$ sums of the ranks allotted by each observer to an individual are found. These sums are shown in the bottom row of the table given above; they must add up to $\frac{1}{2}mn(n+1)$, or 84 in the case illustrated.

(2) The deviations of these sums from their mean value of $\frac{1}{2}m(n+1)$ are then found; the sum of the squares of these deviations will be denoted by $S_W$. In the example, the mean is 14 and $S_W = 64$.

(3) $S_W$ cannot be less than zero and has a maximum value of $\frac{1}{12}m^2(n^3-n)$ when all the rankings are identical; the coefficient of concordance is obtained by dividing $S_W$ by its maximum value, i.e.

$$W = \frac{12S_W}{m^2(n^3-n)}. \tag{104}$$

In the example, $W = 12 \times 64/(16 \times 210) = 0.229$. It may be shown that if the Spearman coefficient, $r_s$, is calculated for each of the $\frac{1}{2}m(m-1)$ possible pairs of observers, then

$$\text{Average } r_s = \frac{mW-1}{m-1}.$$

In the special case when there are only two observers,

$$r_s = 2W - 1.$$

### (d) The case of tied ranks

In the practical application of ranking methods cases will arise in which two or more individuals are so similar that no preference can be expressed between them. The members are then said to be *tied*. For the appropriate modification of the coefficients and the effect on the tests of significance described below, the reader may consult Kendall (1962), where the subject is fully discussed.

### 25·2   Tests of significance (Tables 44–46)

If the sample of individuals whose qualities are ranked has been drawn randomly from a much larger population, the question will arise as to whether the two or more qualities are correlated in this population. To test for significance, the observed value of the coefficient is referred to the distribution of values it would have in random samples from a population in which the qualities are completely uncorrelated. The scores $S_r$, $S_t$ and $S_W$, which can assume integer values only, are the basic quantities in the three coefficients, and for small values of $n$ (and $m$) it has been found possible to calculate the exact probabilities associated with each of their possible values, on the hypothesis of no correlation. These calculations form the basis of the tables. A brief statement follows regarding the distribution and the probability table for each score, $S$; some indication will also be given of how a test may be carried out when the numbers are beyond the range of the table.

### (a) The coefficient $r_s$ (Spearman's $\rho$)

When the qualities ranked are independent, $S_r$, which can assume only even integer values, is distributed symmetrically about $\frac{1}{6}(n^3-n)$. The figures in Table 44, covering the range $n = 4\,(1)\,10$, have been taken from the complete tables given by Kendall (1948) and David, Kendall & Stuart (1951). $Q = 1 - P(S_r \mid n)$ is the probability that $S_r$ is equalled or exceeded. Since the lower and upper limits for $S_r$ are 0 and $\frac{1}{3}(n^3-n)$ respectively, the probability is also $Q$ that the sum of squares of the rank differences is less than or equal to $\frac{1}{3}(n^3-n) - S_r$. To facilitate computation of the lower tail significance levels of the distribution of $S_r$, values of $\frac{1}{3}(n^3-n)$ are given in the bottom row of the table.

Owing to the rapid increase with $n$ of the range of the distribution, the argument interval for $S_r$ has been changed progressively across the table. Complete results are given for $n = 4, 5$; afterwards selected values only are quoted, ranging from near the 20 % level to near the 0·1 % level. It should be remembered that the upper percentage points for $S_r$ correspond to the lower points for $r_s$ and vice versa.

*Example* 51. We may ask whether there is any significant association between the rankings for mathematics and music for the ten boys considered in the table on p. 91. Here

$$r_s = -0·103, \quad S_r = 182, \quad n = 10.$$

Turning to the columns headed $n = 10$ in Table 44, we see that if the two qualities were independent, the expectation of $S_r$ is 165, half the figure entered in the bottom line of the table, while there is a probability of 0·235 that $S_r \geqslant 208$. Clearly $r_s$ does not differ significantly from zero.

Had the score for two other subjects, say mathematics and physics, been found to be $S_r = 52$, giving a rank correlation $r_s = 0·685$, we might again apply the test. $S_r$ is now below expectation, so that

$$\Pr\{r_s \geqslant 0·685\} = \Pr\{S_r \leqslant 52\} = \Pr\{S_r \geqslant 330 - 52 = 278\}.$$

The table shows this probability to be 0·017. Whether we regard a single-tail or double-tail test as appropriate, the correlation is certainly significant at the 5 % level.

*Tests for the significance of $r_s$ when $n > 10$.* If the two qualities are independent, the expectation of $r_s$ is zero and its standard error is $(n-1)^{-\frac{1}{2}}$. In samples with $n > 20$ an adequate test of significance may generally be obtained by referring the ratio of $r_s$ to its standard error, i.e. $r_s \sqrt{(n-1)}$, to the normal probability scale. For $10 < n < 20$, Kendall has shown that a good approximation will be obtained by treating $r_s$ as a product moment coefficient of correlation between normally distributed variables (§ 7·1) and making use of the significance points of Table 13, with degrees of freedom $\nu = n - 2$. Alternatively the use of the transformation $t = r_s\{(n-2)/(1-r_s^2)\}^{\frac{1}{2}}$, obtained by inverting equation (46), makes it possible to use Table 9.

To illustrate the accuracy of the $t$-approximation, we may use it in the case just considered, where it was supposed that a coefficient of $r_s = 0·685$ was found for ten rankings in mathematics and physics. We compute

$$t = 0·685\{8/(1 - 0·685^2)\}^{\frac{1}{2}} = 2·66.$$

Entering Table 9 with $\nu = n - 2 = 8$, we find that $\Pr\{t \leqslant 2·66\} = 0·9855$. Thus $\Pr\{r_s \geqslant 0·685\}$ approximately equals 0·0145. The correct value, we have seen, is 0·017. If we used the cruder normal approximation, we should refer $r_s \sqrt{(n-1)} = 0·685\sqrt{9} = 2·055$ to the table of the normal probability integral (Table 1) and find a probability of 0·020. In this case there is little to choose between the two approximations, but Kendall has shown that the $t$-approximation will in general be the more accurate.

### (b) *The coefficient $t_k$ (Kendall's $\tau$)*

When the qualities ranked are independent, $S_t$, which can assume only integer values,* is distributed symmetrically about zero. Table 45, which is reproduced in full from Kendall (1962), shows for $S_t \geqslant 0$ the probability $Q = 1 - P(S_t \mid n)$, i.e. the probability that $S_t$ is equalled or exceeded. $Q$ is also the probability that the score is less than or equal to $-S_t$. The upper percentage points for $S_t$ correspond to the upper percentage points for $t_k$. The table deals with sample sizes for which $4 \leqslant n \leqslant 10$.

* If $\frac{1}{2}n(n-1)$ is even, $S_t$ can take only even values; otherwise it can take only odd values.

94

For the illustration of mathematics and music ranking already considered, we found
$$t_s = -0.067, \quad S_t = -3, \quad \text{with} \quad n = 10.$$
It is at once clear from Table 45 that this result is quite insignificant, since $\Pr\{S_t \leqslant -3\} = 0.431$.

*Tests for significance of $t_k$ when $n > 10$.* In the case of independence, $t_k$ and $S_t$ vary about zero with standard errors
$$\sigma(t_k) = \left\{\frac{2(2n+5)}{9n(n-1)}\right\}^{\frac{1}{2}}, \quad \sigma(S_t) = \{\tfrac{1}{18}n(n-1)(2n+5)\}^{\frac{1}{2}}.$$

As $n$ increases, the sampling distribution approaches normality more rapidly than does the distribution of $r_s$. A test of significance may therefore be obtained by comparing the ratio of the observed $t_k$ (or $S_t$) to its standard error with the normal probability scale.

For values of $n$ between 10 and 30, some improvement in accuracy will be obtained by introducing a correction for continuity of the type used when the cumulative sum of binomial terms is approximated by the integral of the normal curve. Since $S_t$ increases by discrete steps of 2 units, this correction is applied by subtracting 1 from the observed $S_t$ if $S_t > 0$ (and adding 1 if $S_t < 0$), and then dividing the result by the standard error, $\sigma(S_t)$.

*Illustration of the use of correction for continuity.* Suppose $n = 10$ and the observed value of $S_t$ is 19. From the expression given above we see that
$$\sigma(S_t) = \{10 \times 9 \times 25/18\}^{\frac{1}{2}} = 11.18.$$
Our approximation, therefore, consists in determining the integral under the normal curve beyond a standardized deviate of
$$X = (S_t - 1)/\sigma(S_t) = (19 - 1)/11.18 = 1.61.$$
Table 1 gives this probability as 0.054, a figure which to 3 decimals corresponds exactly with the true probability given in Table 45. Had no correction for continuity been used, the ratio would have been 1.70, giving a probability of 0.045.

*(c) The coefficient of concordance, W (Table 46)*

For the case of independence, exact values of the probability $Q = 1 - P(S_W \mid n, m)$ that a specified value of $S_W$ will be attained or exceeded are given in Table 46 for $n = 3$, $m = 3(1)10$; $n = 4$, $m = 3(1)6$; $n = 5$, $m = 3$. The figures are taken from Kendall (1962). $S_W$ can assume only certain integral values, the range of possibilities increasing rapidly as $m$ increases; the distributions are not symmetrical. For $n = 3$, $m = 3(1)6$ and for $n = 4$, $m = 3$, we have given the complete results for $S_W$ greater than the lowest value shown in the table. In other cases a selection has been made, covering a range from near the upper 20% level to near the upper 0.1% level.

*Approximation beyond the range of the tables.* It may be shown that for independence
$$\mathscr{E}(W) = 1/m, \quad \sigma_W = \{2(m-1)/(m^3(n-1))\}^{\frac{1}{2}}. \tag{105}$$
Since $0 \leqslant W \leqslant 1$ an approximation to the distribution of $W$ may be obtained as suggested in § 8·4 above, that is, by using a Pearson Type I curve having the correct terminals and the mean and standard deviation given in (105). Thus
$$\Pr\{W \geqslant W_0\} \sim I_{1-W_0}(a, b), \tag{106}$$
where
$$b = \tfrac{1}{2}(n-1) - 1/m, \quad a = (m-1)b, \tag{107}$$
and $I$ is the incomplete B-function integral for which the percentage points are given in Table 16 for
$$\nu_1 = 2b, \quad \nu_2 = 2a.*$$

\* Alternatively, the chart of Table 17 could be used.

It has been suggested by Kendall & Babington Smith (1939) that an improved approximation will be obtained by using a correction for continuity, which involves setting

$$\Pr\{W \geqslant W_0'\} \sim I_{1-W_0'}(a, b),\qquad(108)$$

where $a$ and $b$ are as given in (107) and

$$W_0' = (S_{W_0} - 1)/\{\tfrac{1}{12}m^2(n^3 - n) + 2\},\qquad(109)$$

$S_{W_0}$ being the observed score.*

An alternative approximation has been suggested by Friedman (1940) which makes use of the fact that the distribution of a Type I or 'B' variable tends to that of $\chi^2$ as $a = 2\nu_2$ increases, for a given $b = 2\nu_1$. Equating $W$ to $c\chi^2$, and determining the *scale factor* $c$ and the *equivalent degrees of freedom*, $\nu$, so that the first two moments of $W$ and $c\chi^2$ agree, we find that

$$m(n-1)\, W = S_W/\{\tfrac{1}{12}mn(n+1)\}\qquad(110)$$

will be distributed approximately as $\chi^2$, with degrees of freedom $\nu = n - 1$. In reaching this simplest form of the result a factor $m/(m-1)$ has been written as 1.

*Example* 52. Consider first the results given on p. 93, where

$$m = 4, \quad n = 6, \quad S_{W_0} = 64, \quad W_0 = 0.229.$$

Is the coefficient of concordance significant? Since for independence, $\mathscr{E}(W) = 1/m = 0.25$, it is clear that the result is not significant and no further analysis is necessary.

Suppose, however, that we required an approximation to the upper 5 % point for $W$ in this case. We find from (107) that $b = 2.25$, $a = 6.75$. Interpolating in the 5 % points of Table 16 with $\nu_1 = 2b = 4.5$, $\nu_2 = 2a = 13.5$, we find $x = 0.496$. This puts the 5 % point for $W$ at 0.504. If we use the correction for continuity, the observed coefficient to be compared with this limit would be calculated from equation (109).

*Example* 53. Suppose that three assessors, I–III, had ranked five objects, $A$–$E$, in the following orders:

|     | $A$ | $B$ | $C$ | $D$ | $E$ |
|-----|-----|-----|-----|-----|-----|
| I   | 1 | 3 | 2 | 4 | 5 |
| II  | 2 | 4 | 1 | 5 | 3 |
| III | 1 | 3 | 2 | 4 | 5 |
| Sum of ranks | 4 | 10 | 5 | 13 | 13 |
| Deviation of sum from 9 | $-5$ | 1 | $-4$ | 4 | 4 |

We have

$$m = 3, \quad n = 5, \quad S_W = 74, \quad W = 0.822.$$

Is the concordance significant? We can here use Table 46, and see that $\Pr\{S_W \geqslant 74\} = 0.015$. The result is therefore significant at the 5 % level, but not at the 1 % level.

Now consider the approximation. We find

$$\nu_1 = 2b = 3\tfrac{1}{3}, \quad \nu_2 = 2a = 6\tfrac{2}{3}.$$

Interpolating in the 1 % points of Table 16, we find that $x = 0.189$, suggesting an approximate 1 % significance point for $W$ of 0.811. The observed $W_0 = 0.822$ falls beyond this point, but if we apply the correction for continuity, we obtain from equation (109)

$$W_0' = (74 - 1)/\{\tfrac{1}{12} \times 9 \times 120 + 2\} = 73/92 = 0.793.$$

This value falls short of 0.811, and we should conclude that the concordance was just not significant at the 1 % level, an answer agreeing with that obtained exactly from Table 46.

* Strictly speaking this correction for continuity is only correct when the interval in $S_W$ is 2, which is the interval most frequently met with when $n \geqslant 4$.

## 26. Orthogonal polynomials (Table 47)

### 26·1 *Description of the method of fitting and definition of the functions tabled*

When determining the regression law of a 'dependent' variable $y$ on an 'independent' variable $x$, a linear relationship between the two variables is often found to be inadequate. Unless some special regression law is suggested by theoretical considerations, a polynomial of the form

$$Y(x) = a_0 + a_1 x + a_2 x^2 + \ldots + a_k x^k \tag{111}$$

is often found to be a convenient curvilinear representation of $y$ as a function of $x$ and is fitted to observed pairs of associated values $y_t$, $x_t$. With such data the $x_t$ are often equidistant, as, for example, when $n$ observations $y_t$ ($t = 1, 2, \ldots, n$) are made at times $x_t$ progressing by constant intervals. In such cases it is convenient to standardize the $x$-scale so that

$$x_t = t - \tfrac{1}{2}(n+1) \quad (t = 1, 2, \ldots, n),$$

and to fit $Y(x)$ as a weighted sum of orthogonal polynomials,

$$Y(x) = A_0 \phi_0(x) + A_1 \phi_1(x) + \ldots + A_k \phi_k(x). \tag{112}$$

Here $\phi_i(x)$ is, apart from a constant factor, the $i$th degree Tchebycheff polynomial.*

Any pair of these polynomials $\phi_i(x)$, $\phi_j(x)$ ($i \neq j$) satisfies the orthogonality condition

$$\sum_{t=1}^{n} \phi_i(x_t) \phi_j(x_t) = 0, \tag{113}$$

which uniquely determines all $\phi_i(x)$, apart from a constant factor. In particular, we have

$$\left.\begin{aligned}
&\phi_0(x) = 1, \quad \phi_1(x) = \lambda_1 x, \quad \phi_2(x) = \lambda_2\{x^2 - \tfrac{1}{12}(n^2 - 1)\}, \\
&\phi_3(x) = \lambda_3\{x^3 - \tfrac{1}{20}(3n^2 - 7)\,x\}, \quad \phi_4(x) = \lambda_4\{x^4 - \tfrac{1}{14}(3n^2 - 13)\,x^2 + \tfrac{3}{560}(n^2 - 1)\,(n^2 - 9)\}, \\
&\phi_5(x) = \lambda_5\{x^5 - \tfrac{5}{18}(n^2 - 7)\,x^3 + \tfrac{1}{1008}(15n^4 - 230n^2 + 407)\,x\}, \\
&\phi_6(x) = \lambda_6\{x^6 - \tfrac{5}{44}(3n^2 - 31)\,x^4 + \tfrac{1}{176}(5n^4 - 110n^2 + 329)\,x^2 - \tfrac{5}{14784}(n^2 - 1)\,(n^2 - 9)\,(n^2 - 25)\},
\end{aligned}\right\} \tag{114}$$

where the $\lambda_i$ are chosen such that the $\phi_i(x_t)$ are positive or negative integers throughout.†

If we assume that the true regression law is a polynomial

$$\eta(x) = \sum_{i=0}^{k} \alpha_i \phi_i(x),$$

from which the observed $y_t$ differ by independent normal deviates $z_t$ having a common variance $\sigma^2$, i.e. if we assume that $y_t = \eta(x_t) + z_t$, then the orthogonality condition (113) implies that the least-square estimators $A_i$ of the $\alpha_i$ are given by the familiar formulae for ordinary regression coefficients, viz.

$$A_i = \sum_t y_t \phi_i(x_t) \Big/ \sum_t \{\phi_i(x_t)\}^2. \tag{115}$$

Further, the coefficients $A_i$, which can be computed from (115) for any $i \leqslant n - 1$, are independent normal variates with means (i) $\alpha_i$ for $i \leqslant k$, and (ii) 0 for $i > k$ and with variances

---

\* P. L. Tchebycheff's classical papers on the problem of interpolation by means of orthogonal functions appeared between 1854 and 1875. Statisticians will be familiar with R. A. Fisher's (1921 b) application of these polynomials to the statistical field and with A. C. Aitken's (1933) concise proof of their mathematical properties.

† The choice of these computationally most convenient factors was first introduced by R. A. Fisher, who denoted the Tchebycheff polynomials, so modified, by $\xi'_i$ in contrast to his earlier polynomials $\xi_i$ in which the factors $\lambda_i$ were omitted.

$\sigma^2/\sum\limits_t \{\phi_i(x_t)\}^2$. A mean-square estimate of $\sigma^2$ (independent of the $A_i$ for $i \leqslant k$) is provided by the residual mean square

$$s^2 = \left(\sum_{t=1}^{n} y_t^2 - \sum_{i=0}^{k} \left\{A_i^2 \sum_{t=1}^{n} [\phi_i(x_t)]^2\right\}\right)\Big/(n-k-1). \tag{116}$$

Thus the ratios $(A_i - \alpha_i)\sqrt{\sum\limits_t \{\phi_i(x_t)\}^2}/s$, with $\alpha_i = 0$ for $i > k$, follow Student's $t$-distribution (§ 5·1) for $\nu = n-k-1$ degrees of freedom. To facilitate these calculations, Table 47 provides the exact values of $\phi_i(x_t)$ for $n = 3\,(1)\,52$ and $i = 1\,(1)\,6$, except for small $n$ $(n < 7)$ when some of the higher order $\phi_i(x_t)$ are omitted. Since for $i$ even, $\phi_i(x_t) = \phi_i(x_{n-t+1})$ and for $i$ odd, $\phi_i(x_t) = -\phi_i(x_{n-t+1})$, values of $\phi$ for $n > 12$ are tabled only for $x_t \leqslant 0$. The two values given at the foot of each column are, respectively, the sum of squares $\sum\limits_{t=1}^{n} \{\phi_i(x_t)\}^2$ which is required for equations (115) and (116) and the factor $\lambda_i$ which is the coefficient of the highest power in each polynomial.

Values of the functions $\phi_i(x_t)$ have been tabled by: Fisher & Yates (1938, 1953) for $i = 1\,(1)\,5$, $n = 3\,(1)\,75$; Anderson & Houseman (1942) for $i = 1\,(1)\,5$, $n = 3\,(1)\,104$; van der Reyden (1943) for $i = 1\,(1)\,9$, $n = 5\,(1)\,52$.* The present Table 47 has been reproduced from van der Reyden's table with permission of the author and the Editor of the *Onderstepoort Journal of Veterinary Science and Animal Husbandry*. We have therefore used van der Reyden's notation of $\phi_i$ in place of Fisher's $\xi_i'$.

### 26·2  Illustration of the use of Table 47

*Example* 54. To illustrate the use of the table we choose the example given by van der Reyden (1943, p. 377) dealing with the average diurnal variation of atmospheric temperature, $y_t$, during December 1940 at Armoedsvlakte, Bechuanaland. A plot of the data suggests that at least a cubic will be required to represent the temperature trend, and in order to investigate the matter fully, all terms up to the sixth degree were computed. The work is set out in the table following.

*Fitting of sixth-degree polynomial to twenty-four observations of temperature*
*(in degrees Fahrenheit)*

| (1) $t$ | (2) $y_t$ | (3) $y_t$ | (4) $t$ | (5) Sum $y_t$ | (6) $\phi_2$ | (7) $\phi_4$ | (8) $\phi_6$ | (9) Diff. $y_t$ | (10) $\phi_1$ | (11) $\phi_3$ | (12) $\phi_5$ |
|---|---|---|---|---|---|---|---|---|---|---|---|
| (1) | 65·25 | 65·88 | (24) | 131·13 | 253 | 253 | 4807 | −0·63 | −23 | −1771 | −4807 |
| (2) | 69·37 | 66·71 | (23) | 136·08 | 187 | 33 | −3971 | 2·66 | −21 | −847 | 1463 |
| (3) | 74·44 | 67·09 | (22) | 141·53 | 127 | −97 | −4769 | 7·35 | −19 | −133 | 3743 |
| (4) | 79·00 | 68·12 | (21) | 147·12 | 73 | −157 | −2147 | 10·88 | −17 | 391 | 3553 |
| (5) | 82·72 | 69·08 | (20) | 151·80 | 25 | −165 | 1045 | 13·64 | −15 | 745 | 2071 |
| (6) | 85·97 | 70·57 | (19) | 156·54 | −17 | −137 | 3271 | 15·40 | −13 | 949 | 169 |
| (7) | 88·11 | 71·90 | (18) | 160·01 | −53 | −87 | 3957 | 16·21 | −11 | 1023 | −1551 |
| (8) | 89·67 | 73·13 | (17) | 162·80 | −83 | −27 | 3183 | 16·54 | −9 | 987 | −2721 |
| (9) | 90·36 | 74·07 | (16) | 164·43 | −107 | 33 | 1419 | 16·29 | −7 | 861 | −3171 |
| (10) | 90·35 | 76·15 | (15) | 166·50 | −125 | 85 | −695 | 14·20 | −5 | 665 | −2893 |
| (11) | 88·92 | 80·41 | (14) | 169·33 | −137 | 123 | −2525 | 8·51 | −3 | 419 | −2005 |
| (12) | 87·81 | 84·95 | (13) | 172·76 | −143 | 143 | −3575 | 2·86 | −1 | 143 | −715 |
| Total | 991·97 | 868·06 | | 1860·03 | | | | 123·91 | | | |

* In all cases, for small values of $n$ the range of $i$ is restricted.

The series of 24 observed temperature values is given in cols. 2 and 3; the first 12 values are found by descending col. 2 and the last 12 values by ascending col. 3. This arrangement facilitates the formation of the sums $y_t + y_{25-t}$ (entered in col. 5) and differences $y_t - y_{25-}$ (entered in col. 9). When computing $A_i$ from equation (115), the former are required as multipliers for $\phi_2$, $\phi_4$ and $\phi_6$ and the latter as multipliers for $\phi_1$, $\phi_3$ and $\phi_5$. The required values of the $\phi_i$ for $t = 1, 2, \ldots, 12$ are shown in cols. 6, 7, 8 and 10, 11, 12, but would normally not be copied out from Table 47.

Calculating the product sums and dividing by the appropriate values of $\Sigma\phi_i^2$, we obtain the seven values of $A_i$ as follows:

$$A_0 = 77{\cdot}50125, \qquad A_4 = 0{\cdot}0028930,$$
$$A_1 = -0{\cdot}2850804, \qquad A_5 = -0{\cdot}00043867,$$
$$A_2 = -0{\cdot}05024726, \qquad A_6 = -0{\cdot}000025491,$$
$$A_3 = 0{\cdot}004913506,$$

To obtain the actual values, $Y(x)$, from the fitted polynomial, we would have to multiply these values of $A_i$ by the corresponding $\phi_i(x_t)$ tabled above in accordance with formula (112).

### 26·3  *Tests of significance*

With the assumptions made regarding the random errors

$$z_t = y_t - \eta(x_t),$$

a variety of tests regarding polynomial regressions will follow on similar lines to those used elsewhere in the analysis of variance.

(a) *A general test*

If we are *prepared to assume* that

$$\eta(x) = \sum_{i=0}^{k+l} \alpha_i \phi_i(x), \quad \text{with} \quad \alpha_i = 0 \text{ for } i > k+l,$$

and wish to *test the hypothesis* that

$$\alpha_i = 0, \quad i = k+1, k+2, \ldots, k+l,$$

we may obtain our residual estimate of $\sigma^2$ from

$$s^2 = \left( \sum_t y_t^2 - \sum_{i=0}^{k+l} \{A_i^2 \sum_t [\phi_i(x_t)]^2\} \right) \Big/ (n-k-l-1). \tag{117}$$

Since on the hypothesis tested $\displaystyle\sum_{i=k+1}^{k+l} \{A_i^2 \sum_t [\phi_i(x_t)]^2\}$

is distributed as the sum of $l$ independent normal deviates each with variance $\sigma^2$, we may complete the test by calculating the variance ratio

$$F = \sum_{i=k+1}^{k+l} \frac{A_i^2 \sum_t [\phi_i(x_t)]^2}{ls^2}, \tag{118}$$

and entering Table 18 with $\nu_1 = l$, $\nu_2 = n-k-l-1$.

If, for example, in the case of the temperature data of Example **54** (p. 98), we were prepared to assume that the trend could certainly be represented by a polynomial of fifth degree

($\alpha_i = 0$ for $i > 5$), and wished to test whether a third-degree polynomial sufficed (i.e. to test whether $\alpha_4 = 0 = \alpha_5$), we could use the $F$ of equation (118) with $k = 3$, $l = 2$ as a comprehensive test statistic. Since from van der Reyder (1943, p. 378) we have $s^2 = 12 \cdot 738/18$, it is found that
$$F = 18 \times 37 \cdot 542/(2 \times 12 \cdot 738) = 26 \cdot 53,$$
a value which clearly exceeds the $0 \cdot 1 \%$ point of $F$ given in Table 18 for $\nu_1 = 2$, $\nu_2 = 18$ degrees of freedom. Thus a third-degree polynomial is not adequate in this case.

### (b) Case $k = 0$

A special case of the test described under (a) occurs when $k = 0$. This case arises when, from theoretical considerations, it is known that if the data have a trend at all, this must be some polynomial of the $l$th degree and the test is for the significance of this polynomial as a whole.

For example, if for the above data we suspected from theoretical considerations that the diurnal temperature variation might follow a law representable by a fifth-degree polynomial, we could test this hypothesis by computing the $F$ ratio of (118) for $k = 0$, $l = 5$. We then obtain
$$18 \times 1836 \cdot 66/(5 \times 12 \cdot 738) = 519 \cdot 1,$$
which clearly exceeds all tabulated percentage points of $F$ for $\nu_1 = 5$ and $\nu_2 = 18$ degrees of freedom; thus the theory would be confirmed.

### (c) Case $l = 1$

In this case we assume that the significance of a polynomial regression of degree $k$ has already been established and we desire to test whether the next higher term, i.e. that of $(k+1)$th degree, is required for the representation of the real law.

This test is often used in a hierarchical sequence, starting from $k = 0$ and testing in turn the significance of each term until an insignificant coefficient is reached. With such a procedure it should be remembered that: (i) A coefficient $\alpha_i$ of $\phi_i(x)$ in the real law may well be 0, or small although some higher coefficient is large; if this is the case, the residual variance $s^2$ calculated after fitting the $i$th degree polynomial will no longer be a correct estimate of $\sigma^2$. (ii) The chance of returning an observed $A_i$ as significant by the $i$th test in the sequence is no longer equal to the nominal level of significance in the $i$th $F$-test employed and may, in fact, be considerably smaller. For details of this test procedure in the present example see van der Reyden (1943).

It is clear that, in the case of equidistant $x_i$, the use of orthogonal polynomials considerably simplifies both the estimation of the polynomial regression of a given degree and also the tests of significance which may be required to decide between alternative polynomial regressions of different degree. In such tests, no recalculation of the estimates $A_i$ ($i \leqslant k$) is required if the degree of the fitted polynomial is increased from $k$ to $k + l$.

### 26·4  *Fitting polynomials to series with missing values*

It is worth noting that the present tables can still be used if the $x_i$ are equidistant except for a number of gaps, as, for instance, in experiments in which it was planned to make observations at a regular time interval but a number of omissions have occurred. The procedure is similar to the missing-plot technique of the analysis of variance, but we shall describe it in detail by means of an example.

*Illustration of fitting a fifth-degree polynomial for a series of $n = 24$ values,
with gaps at $t = 6$ and $t = 18$*

| (1) | Polynomial values for the gaps | | | | | | y-estimates and corrections | | | |
|---|---|---|---|---|---|---|---|---|---|---|
| | $\phi_0$ (2) | $\phi_1$ (3) | $\phi_2$ (4) | $\phi_3$ (5) | $\phi_4$ (6) | $\phi_5$ (7) | $_0 y_t$ (8) | $_1\Delta y_t$ (9) | $_2\Delta y_t$ (10) | Final $y_t$ (11) |
| (1) Gap at $t=6$ | 1 | −13 | −17 | 949 | −137 | 169 | 85 | 1·08 | 0·20 | 86·28 |
| (2) Gap at $t=18$ | 1 | 11 | −53 | −1023 | −87 | 1551 | 72 | −0·90 | −0·16 | 70·94 |
| (3) $\Sigma\phi_i^2$ (all $t$) | 24 | 4 600 | 394 680 | $10^3 \times 17\ 761$ | 394 680 | $10^3 \times 177\ 929$ | | | | |
| (4) $_0 A_i$ | 77·465 | −0·2821 | −0·050 219 | 0·004 856 | 0·003 208 | −0·000 4387 | | | | |
| (5) $_1\Delta A_i$ | 0·0075 | −0·0052 | 0·000 074 | 0·000 110 | −0·000 176 | −0·000 0068 | | | | |
| (6) $_2\Delta A_i$ | 0·002 | −0·0009 | 0·000 013 | 0·000 020 | −0·000 034 | −0·000 0012 | | | | |
| (7) Final $A_i$ | 77·47 | −0·288 | −0·050 13 | 0·004 99 | 0·003 00 | −0·000 447 | | | | |

*Example* 55. Let us suppose that the sixth and eighteenth temperature values were missing from the data used in Example 54, and that we wish to fit a fifth-degree polynomial to the remaining values. We first 'guess' values ($_0 y_t$, say) for the two missing temperatures; let these be $_0 y_6 = 85$ and $_0 y_{18} = 72$. Using these $_0 y_t$ in (115), we compute trial values $_0 A_i$ for the $A_i$. These are shown in line 4 of the table above. Using these trial $_0 A_i$ we compute corrected values, $_1 y_t$, from (112), but only at the gaps, $t = 6$ and $t = 18$. The corrections

$$_1\Delta y_6 = _1 y_6 - _0 y_6, \quad _1\Delta y_{18} = _1 y_{18} - _0 y_{18}$$

are shown in col. 9 of the table. These corrections are now used in turn to obtain corrections, $_1\Delta A_i$, for the $A_i$ from

$$_1\Delta A_i = \sum_{t=6,18} \{_1\Delta y_t \phi_i(x_t)\} \bigg/ \left\{ \sum_{t=1}^{24} [\phi_i(x_t)]^2 \right\}$$

and are shown in line 5 of the table; the remainder of the iteration process will be apparent. The final values obtained after the second iteration, viz. 86·28 and 70·94, should be compared with the graduated values, 86·25 and 71·07, obtained by van der Reyden (1943, p. 379) after fitting a fifth-degree polynomial to the complete data.

Usually one or two cycles of the iteration will suffice. The appropriate tests of significance are described by Hartley (1951) who also shows that the solution of the iteration described above is identical with the least squares fit to the observed $y_t$.

# VI. AUXILIARY TABLES

## 27. TABLES OF MISCELLANEOUS MATHEMATICAL QUANTITIES AND CONVERSION FACTORS (TABLES 48–54)

In this final section we have assembled a number of auxiliary tables giving some of the more general mathematical quantities which are used incidentally in statistical work. The applications are extremely varied and we shall select only a few examples to illustrate the use of the tables.

Table 48 gives the powers of natural numbers $n = 1\,(1)\,100$ up to $n^7$, and Table 49 gives the cumulative sums of these powers, $\sum\limits_{n=1}^{s} n^r$.* There are obvious uses of the former in the evaluation of moments, polynomials and power series. The computation of special tables to assist in fitting orthogonal polynomials to ordinates spaced at equal intervals has removed one of the more common uses for Table 49, but this will still be useful when fitting laws involving isolated powers, e.g. the law of heat loss through radiation $y = ct^4$.

Table 48 is also helpful in the computation of the general roots (fractional powers) of numbers. Thus if we need to find
$$x = y^{1/r}$$
from a given $y$, we may proceed as follows:

(a) Determine a first approximation, $x_0$, to $x$ by selecting the argument $x_0 = n$ such that $n^r$ is the nearest entry to $y$ in the appropriate column.

(b) Compute an improved approximation from
$$x_1 = \{(r-1)\,x_0 + y/x_0^{r-1}\}/r, \tag{119}$$
where $x_0^{r-1} = n^{r-1}$ is the number immediately preceding $n^r$ in the same line of the table.

This method gives as a rule 4-figure accuracy and, certainly, 3-figure accuracy.

*Illustration.* Find $(30068)^{\frac{1}{3}}$.

Entering the column headed $n^3$, we find that the entry $29791 = 31^3$ is nearest to $y = x^3 = 30068$, so that $x_0 = 31$. An improved value is then computed from
$$x_1 = \tfrac{1}{3}\{2 \times 31 + 30068/961\} = 31{\cdot}096.$$
This happens to be accurate to 5 figures.

Table 50 giving the squares of natural numbers, $n^2$, for $n = 1\,(1)\,999$, has been included mainly to assist in the evaluation of the sums of squares required in computing standard deviations or components in the analysis of variance when a calculating machine is not to hand. It may also be used for obtaining square roots (beyond the range of those given in Table 51) by the method just described for finding $x = y^{1/r}$, when $r = 2$. Equation (119) now becomes
$$x_1 = \tfrac{1}{2}\{x_0 + y/x_0\}, \tag{120}$$
and the use of Table 50 rather than Table 48 is now preferable, since it gives squares for 3-figure arguments. Equation (120) will yield square roots of 5–6-figure accuracy.

Table 51 gives, for $n = 1\,(1)\,100$, the three quantities $\sqrt{n}$, $1/\sqrt{n}$ and $1/n$, expressions frequently needed in the analysis of small samples.

## 27·2  *Factorials, $\Gamma$-functions and their logarithms to base 10*

Factorials are required in the evaluation of the terms of numerous statistical series of which it is sufficient to mention the binomial and hypergeometric. The $\Gamma$-function appears in the moments of many well-known probability distributions; in particular, it arises in the calculation of parameters for all the Pearson frequency curves (§ 23·1).

Table 51 gives $n!$ as an exact integer for $n = 1\,(1)\,9$; beyond this, for $n = 10\,(1)\,250$, the 5-decimal quantity tabled must be multiplied by $10^c$, where $c$ is the characteristic of $\log n!$

---

* For $r > 7$ Dr John Wishart has suggested that the relation $\sum\limits_{n=1}^{s} n^r = \sum\limits_{i=1}^{r} \binom{s+1}{i+1} \Delta^i O^r$ may be found useful, particularly if tables of the binomial coefficients and of the differences of the powers of zero are available.

shown alongside in the next column. Similarly the entry for $1/n!$ must be multiplied by $10^{-c}$ for all $n$. For $n = 251\,(1)\,1000$, only $\log n!$ is tabled. Throughout, this function is tabled to 7 decimals.

Table 52 gives $\Gamma(1+p)$ and $\log\Gamma(1+p)$ to 7 decimals for $p = 0\cdot00\,(0\cdot01)\,1\cdot00$. More generally, $\log\Gamma(n+p)$ with $n$ an integer and $0 < p < 1$ may be found as follows:*

(a) For $n = 1$; linear interpolation in Table 52 yields a maximum error of a unit in the fifth decimal.

(b) For $n = 2\,(1)\,6$; values may be obtained from the formula

$$\log\Gamma(n+p) = \log(n-1+p) + \log(n-2+p) + \ldots + \log(1+p) + \log\Gamma(1+p),$$

using ordinary tables of logarithms and Table 52.

(c) For $n > 6$; remembering that for integer $n$, $\log\Gamma(n) = \log(n-1)!$, we may interpolate in Table 51. Four-point Lagrangian interpolation yields 4-decimal accuracy for small $n$ with a progressive improvement until, near $n = 1000$, 7 accurate decimals are obtained.

### 27·3   *Functions of $p$ and $q = 1 - p$ $(0 < p < 1)$*

The later columns of Table 52 give to 4 or 5 decimal places values of the auxiliary functions $1 - p^2$, $(1-p^2)^{\frac{1}{2}}$, $(1-p^2)^{-\frac{1}{2}}$, $pq$, $(pq)^{\frac{1}{2}}$ and $p^2 + q^2$. Much fuller tables of some of these functions have been given by Kelley (1948). The following are some illustrations of the use of these functions:

$1 - p^2$. Problems of correlation, with $p = \rho$; for reducing a variance to a residual variance after removing a linear regression term; for use in a large sample approximation to the sampling variance of a product moment correlation coefficient, $r$ (normally distributed variables).

$(1-p^2)^{\frac{1}{2}}$. As above, for standard deviation instead of variance.

$(1-p^2)^{-\frac{1}{2}}$. For the evaluation of partial correlation coefficients by continued multiplication.

$pq$ and $(pq)^{\frac{1}{2}}$. For computing the binomial variance and standard deviation.

$p^2 + q^2$. For evaluating the variance of a weighted mean from

$$\operatorname{var}(px_1 + qx_2) = (p^2 + q^2)\,\sigma^2,$$

where $\sigma^2$ is the variance of independent variables $x_1$ and $x_2$.

### 27·4   *Natural logarithms (Table 53)*

Natural logarithms are provided for the decade $1 \leqslant x < 10$; if $x$ lies outside this range, the logarithm may be found by adding the appropriate value of $\log_e 10^n$ shown at the bottom of the table. However, in many calculations it is unnecessary to add the constant $\log_e 10^n$, as this cancels out in the course of the computation; such is the case when calculating the statistic $M$ (§ 16·1) used in testing for variance heterogeneity.

If proportional parts are used for interpolation, they should be added to, or subtracted from, the nearest tabular value. Examples are given at the foot of the table. This method will yield 5-decimal accuracy for $x > 5\cdot0$, but for $1\cdot0 < x < 5\cdot0$ errors of up to 4 units in the fifth decimal may occur and to obtain 5-decimal accuracy, more exact interpolation must be used.

### 27·5   *Miscellaneous constants (Table 54)*

Only mathematical constants and conversion factors for weights and measures are given here; for other physical constants, etc., the reader must consult standard works of reference.

---

\* For fuller tables see Brownlee (1923), Davis (1933), Pearson, E. S. (1922).

# APPENDIX I

## LIST OF REFERENCES

AITKEN, A. C. (1933). *Proc. Roy. Soc. Edinb.* **53**, 54–78.

ANDERSON, R. L. & HOUSEMAN, E. E. (1942). *Res. Bull., Iowa Agric. Exp. Sta.* no. 297.

ASPIN, A. A. (1949). *Biometrika*, **36**, 290–3.

BAILEY, N. T. J. (1950). *Biometrika*, **37**, 193–202.

BARNARD, G. A. (1947). *Biometrika*, **34**, 123–38.

BARTLETT, M. S. (1937). *Proc. Roy. Soc.* A, **160**, 268–82.

BAYES, A. W. (1937). *Suppl. J.R. Statist. Soc.* **4**, 61–80.

BISHOP, D. J. (1939). *Biometrika*, **31**, 31–55.

BISHOP, D. J. & NAIR, U. S. (1939). *Suppl. J.R. Statist. Soc.* **6**, 89–99.

BLISS, C. I. (1952). *The Statistics of Bio-assay, with special reference to Vitamins.* New York: Academic Press.

BLISS, C. I., COCHRAN, W. G. & TUKEY, J. W. (1956). *Biometrika*, **43**, 418–22.

BOX, G. E. P. (1949). *Biometrika*, **36**, 317–46.

BROWNLEE, J. (1923). Log $\Gamma(x)$ *from* $x = 1$ *to* $50 \cdot 9$ *by intervals of* $0 \cdot 01$. Tracts for Computers, no. IX. Cambridge University Press.

CADWELL, J. H. (1953). *Biometrika*, **40**, 336–46.

CARTER, A. H. (1947). *Biometrika*, **34**, 352–8.

COCHRAN, W. G. (1940). *Ann. Math. Statist.* **11**, 93–5.

COCHRAN, W. G. (1941). *Ann. Eugen., Lond.,* **11**, 47–52.

COLCORD, C. G. & DEMING, L. S. (1935). *Sankhyā*, **2**, 423–4.

COMRIE, L. J. (1936). *Interpolation and Allied Tables.* London: H.M. Stationery Office.

COMRIE, L. J. (1950). *Chambers' Shorter Six-figure Mathematical Tables.*

COMRIE, L. J. & HARTLEY, H. O. (1941). *Biometrika*, **32**, 183–6.

DAVID, F. N. (1938). *Tables of the Ordinates and Probability Integral of the Distribution of the Correlation Coefficient in Small Samples.* Cambridge University Press for the Biometrika Trustees.

DAVID, H. A. (1951). *Biometrika*, **38**, 393–409.

DAVID, H. A. (1952). *Biometrika*, **39**, 422–4.

DAVID, H. A. (1956). *Biometrika*, **43**, 449–51.

DAVID, H. A., HARTLEY, H. O. & PEARSON, E. S. (1954). *Biometrika*, **41**, 482–93.

DAVID, S. T., KENDALL, M. G. & STUART, A. (1951). *Biometrika*, **38**, 131–40.

DAVIS, H. T. (1933). *Tables of the Higher Mathematical Functions,* **1**. Bloomington, Indiana: Principia Press.

EISENHART, C., HASTAY, M. W. & WALLIS, W. A. (1947). *Techniques of Statistical Analysis.* New York: McGraw Hill Book Company.

ELDERTON, W. P. (1953). *Frequency Curves and Correlation,* 4th ed. Cambridge University Press.

FINNEY, D. J. (1941). *Ann. Eugen., Lond.,* **11**, 136–40.

FINNEY, D. J. (1948). *Biometrika*, **35**, 145–56.

FINNEY, D. J. (1952). *Probit Analysis. A Statistical Treatment of the Sigmoid Response Curve,* 2nd ed. Cambridge University Press.

FINNEY, D. J. & STEVENS, W. L. (1948). *Biometrika*, **35**, 191–201.

FISHER, R. A. (1915). *Biometrika*, **10**, 507–21.

FISHER, R. A. (1920). *Mon. Not. R. Astr. Soc.* **80**, 758–70.

FISHER, R. A. (1921a). *Metron.* **1**, Part 4, 3–32.

FISHER, R. A. (1921b). *J. Agric. Sci.* **11**, 107–35.

FISHER, R. A. (1929). *Proc. Lond. Math. Soc.,* Series 2, **30**, 199–238.

FISHER, R. A. (1930). *Proc. Roy. Soc.* A, **130**, 16–28.

FISHER, R. A. & YATES, F. (1963). *Statistical Tables for Biological, Agricultural and Medical Research,* 6th ed. (1st ed. 1938). Edinburgh: Oliver and Boyd.

FRIEDMAN, M. (1940). *Ann. Math. Statist.* **11**, 86–92.

GAYEN, A. K. (1951). *Biometrika*, **38**, 219–47.

GEARY, R. C. (1935). *Biometrika*, **27**, 310–32.

GEARY, R. C. (1936). *Biometrika*, **28**, 295–307.

GODWIN, H. J. (1945). *Biometrika*, **33**, 254–6.

GODWIN, H. J. (1949a). *Biometrika*, **36**, 92–100.

GODWIN, H. J. (1949b). *Ann. Math. Statist.* **20**, 279–85.

GOSSET, W. S. ('Student') (1908). *Biometrika*, **6**, 1–25.

GREENWOOD, J. A. & HARTLEY, H. O. (1962). *Guide to Tables in Mathematical Statistics*. Princeton University Press.

GUMBEL, E. J. (1949). *Biometrika*, **36**, 142–8.

HALTON THOMSON, D. (1947). *Biometrika*, **34**, 368–72.

HARLEY, B. I. & PEARSON, E. S. (1957). *Biometrika*, **44**, 257–60.

HARTER, H. L. (1963). *Biometrika*, **50**, 187–94.

HARTER, H. L. (1964). *Biometrika*, **51**, 231–39.

HARTER, H. L., CLEMM, D. S. & GUTHRIE, E. H. (1959). *The Probability Integrals of the Range and of the Studentized Range*. **1** and **2**. Wright Air Development Center, Ohio, Tech. Report 58–484.

HARTLEY, H. O. (1938). *Suppl. J.R. Statist. Soc.* **5**, 80–8.

HARTLEY, H. O. (1940). *Biometrika*, **31**, 249–55.

HARTLEY, H. O. (1941). *Biometrika*, **32**, 161–7.

HARTLEY, H. O. (1942). *Biometrika*, **32**, 309–10.

HARTLEY, H. O. (1944). *Biometrika*, **33**, 173–80.

HARTLEY, H. O. (1945). *Biometrika*, **33**, 257–8.

HARTLEY, H. O. (1950). *Biometrika*, **37**, 271–80.

HARTLEY, H. O. (1951). *Biometrika*, **38**, 410–13.

HELMERT, F. R. (1876). *Astr. Nachr.* **88**, no. 2096.

HOOKE, B. G. E. (1926). *Biometrika*, **18**, 1–55.

JOHNSON, N. L., NIXON, ERIC, AMOS, D. E. & PEARSON, E. S. (1963). *Biometrika*, **50**, 459–98.

JONES, A. E. (1946). *Biometrika*, **33**, 274–82.

KELLEY, T. L. (1948). *The Kelley Statistical Tables*, 2nd ed. Harvard University Press.

KENDALL, M. G. (1962). *Rank Correlation Methods*, 3rd ed. London: Chas. Griffin and Co. Ltd.

KENDALL, M. G. & BABINGTON SMITH, B. (1939). *Ann. Math. Statist.* **10**, 275–87.

LANCASTER, H. O. (1949). *Biometrika*, **36**, 370–82.

LATTER, O. H. (1906). *Biometrika*, **4**, 363–73.

LEGGATT, C. W. (1935). *Proc. Int. Seed Test. Ass.* **7**, 27–37.

LINK, R. F. (1950). *Ann. Math. Statist.* **21**, 112–16.

LORD, E. (1947). *Biometrika*, **34**, 41–67.

LORD, E. (1950). *Biometrika*, **37**, 64–77.

MAGUIRE, B. A., PEARSON, E. S. & WYNN, A. H. A. (1952). *Biometrika*, **39**, 168–80.

MAHALANOBIS, P. C., MAJUMDAR, D. N. & RAO, C. R. (1949). *Sankhyā*, **9**, 89.

McKAY, A. T. (1935). *Biometrika*, **27**, 466–71.

MERRINGTON, M. & THOMPSON, C. M. (1943). *Biometrika*, **33**, 73–88.

MOORE, P. G. (1957). *Biometrika*, **44**, 482–89.

MOSTELLER, F. (1946). *Ann. Math. Statist.* **17**, 377–408.

NAIR, K. R. (1948a). *Biometrika*, **35**, 16–31.

NAIR, K. R. (1948b). *Biometrika*, **35**, 118–44.

NAIR, K. R. (1950). *Biometrika*, **37**, 182–3.

NAIR, K. R. (1952). *Biometrika*, **39**, 189–91.

NAIR, U. S. (1938). *Biometrika*, **30**, 274–94.

NATIONAL BUREAU OF STANDARDS (1950). *Tables of the Binomial Probability Distribution*. Applied Maths. series no. 6.

NEYMAN, J. & PEARSON, E. S. (1931). *Bull. Int. Acad. Cracovie*, A, 460–81.

NORTON, H. W. (1952). *Math. Tab., Wash.*, **6**, 35–8.

PACHARES, J. (1959). *Biometrika*, **46**, 461–4.

PATNAIK, P. B. (1949). *Biometrika*, **36**, 202–32.

PATNAIK, P. B. (1950). *Biometrika*, **37**, 78–87.

PEARSON, E. S. (1922). *Table of Logarithms of the Complete Gamma-function (to 10 decimal places) for Argument 2–1200*. Tracts for Computers, no. VIII. Cambridge University Press.

PEARSON, E. S. (1930). *Biometrika*, **22**, 239–49.

PEARSON, E. S. (1931). *Biometrika*, **22**, 423–4.

PEARSON, E. S. (1932). *Biometrika*, **24**, 404–17.

PEARSON, E. S. (1935a). *Biometrika*, **27**, 333–47.

PEARSON, E. S. (1935b). *The Application of Statistical Methods to Industrial Standardisation and Quality Control*. British Standards Institution No. 600. 1935.

PEARSON, E. S. (1938). *Biometrika*, **30**, 210–50.

PEARSON, E. S. (1945). *Biometrika*, **33**, 252–3.

PEARSON, E. S. (1948). *Biometrika*, **35**, 424.

PEARSON, E. S. (1950). *Biometrika*, **37**, 383–98.

PEARSON, E. S. (1952). *Biometrika*, **39**, 130–6.

105

PEARSON, E. S. (1963). *Biometrika*, **50**, 95–112.

PEARSON, E. S. (1965), *Biometrika*, **52**, 282–5.

PEARSON, E. S. & CHANDRA SEKAR, C. (1936). *Biometrika*, **28**, 308–20.

PEARSON, E. S. & HARTLEY, H. O. (1951). *Biometrika*, **38**, 112–30.

PEARSON, E. S. & MERRINGTON, M. (1951). *Biometrika*, **38**, 4–10.

PEARSON, E. S. & STEPHENS, M. A. (1964). *Biometrika*, **51**, 484–6.

PEARSON, E. S. & WELCH, B. L. (1937). *Suppl. J.R. Statist. Soc.* **4**, 94–101.

PEARSON, K. (1895). *Phil. Trans.* A, **186**, 343–414.

PEARSON, K. (1901). *Phil. Trans.* A, **197**, 443–59.

PEARSON, K. (1902). *Biometrika*, **1**, 390–9.

PEARSON, K. (1906). *Biometrika*, **5**, 105–46.

PEARSON, K. (1914). *Tables for Statisticians and Biometricians*, Part 1. Cambridge University Press for the Biometrika Trustees.

PEARSON, K. (1916). *Phil. Trans.* A, **216**, 429–57.

PEARSON, K. (1922). *Tables of the Incomplete Γ-function*. Cambridge University Press for the Biometrika Trustees.

PEARSON, K. (1931). *Tables for Statisticians and Biometricians*, Part 2. Cambridge University Press for the Biometrika Trustees.

PEARSON, K. (1934). *Tables of the Incomplete B-function*. Cambridge University Press for the Biometrika Trustees.

PILLAI, K. C. S. (1959). *Biometrika*, **46**, 473–4.

PILLAI, K. C. S. & BUENAVENTURA, A. R. (1961). *Biometrika*, **48**, 195–6.

PRZYBOROWSKI, J. & WILENSKI, H. (1940). *Biometrika*, **31**, 313–23.

QUESENBERRY, C. P. & DAVID, H. A. (1961). *Biometrika*, **48**, 379–90.

REYDEN, VAN DER, D. (1943). *Onderstepoort J. Vet. Sci.* **18**, 355–404.

SHEPPARD, W. F. (1902). *Biometrika*, **2**, 174–90.

SIMAIKA, J. B. (1942). *Biometrika*, **32**, 263–76.

SNEDECOR, G. W. (1946). *Statistical Methods*, 4th ed. Ames, Iowa: Collegiate Press, Inc.

SOPER, H. E. (1921). *The Numerical Evaluation of the Incomplete B-function*. Tracts for Computers, no. VII. Cambridge University Press.

STEVENS, W. L. (1950). *Biometrika*, **37**, 117–29.

THOMPSON, W. R. (1935). *Ann. Math. Statist.* **6**, 214–19.

TIPPETT, L. H. C. (1925). *Biometrika*, **17**, 364–87.

TIPPETT, L. H. C. (1952). *The Methods of Statistics*, 4th ed. Williams and Norgate Ltd.

TSCHEPOURKOWSKY, E. (1905). *Biometrika*, **4**, 286–312.

WELCH, B. L. (1947). *Biometrika*, **34**, 28–35.

WILLIAMS, P. (1935). *Biometrika*, **27**, 269–71.

WISE, M. E. (1950). *Biometrika*, **37**, 208–18.

WISHART, J. (1927). *Biometrika*, **19**, 1–38.

WISHART, J. (1938). *J. Agric. Sci.* **28**, 299–306.

WOLD, H. (1948). *Random Normal Deviates*. Tracts for Computers, no. XXV. Cambridge University Press.

YATES, F. (1934). *Suppl. J.R. Statist. Soc.* **1**, 217–35.

# APPENDIX II

## ORIGIN OF TABLES

The following list shows the source or sources from which each of the tables in the present volume has been taken as well as the names of their computers where these are known to us. As statisticians, as well as editors, we should like to put on record our gratitude for these labours, spread over fifty years. The statistician's debt of thanks is, indeed, due not only to the contributors whose tables we are reissuing or expect to reissue, but to all those others whose work we are omitting because changes in statistical techniques have called for new forms of tabular aid. With few exceptions, their work can be found if required in the past volumes of *Biometrika*.

The great majority of the present tables have also appeared in *Biometrika* or have been computed recently under *Biometrika* auspices, but in a few cases referred to below we have drawn from outside sources, as stated in the Preface. The page numbers of a journal in the 'source' column is that of the first page of a table.

## ORIGIN OF INDIVIDUAL TABLES

| | SOURCE | COMPUTER |
|---|---|---|
| 1 | *Biometrika*, **2**, 182. *T.S.B.* **1**, II* | W. F. Sheppard |
| 2 | *Drapers Co. Research Memoirs*, Biometric Series, **8**, 27. *T.S.B.* **1**, IV | Julia Bell |
| 3 | *The Kelley Statistical Tables* (1948), Table I | |
| 4 | *Biometrika*, **5**, 405. *T.S.B.* **1**, I | W. F. Sheppard |
| 5 | *Biometrika*, **13**, 428. *T.S.B.* **2**, I | Derived from work of W. F. Sheppard by H. E. Soper and others |
| 6 | *Biometrika*, **35**, 193 | D. J. Finney and W. L. Stevens |
| 7 | *Biometrika*, **37**, 318 | Editorial and Mathematics Division, National Physical Laboratory |
| 8 | *Biometrika*, **32**, 188 (with the addition of a 0·1% column). Corrections: Harter (1963); D. B. Owen | Catherine M. Thompson (Jean H. Thompson) |
| 9 | *Biometrika*, **37**, 170 | Editorial and Mathematics Division, National Physical Laboratory |
| 10 | *Biometrika*, **38**, 115 | Jean H. Thompson and Mathematics Division, National Physical Laboratory |
| 11 | *Biometrika*, **36**, 291; *Biometrika*, **43**, 204 | Alice A. Aspin; W. H. Trickett, B. L. Welch and G. S. James |
| 12 13 | Freshly compiled, partly using *Biometrika*, **32**, 168, 300 and partly from Fisher & Yates, *Statistical Tables* (1953), Tables III and VI | |
| 14 | Freshly compiled from standard sources | |
| 15 | *Tables of the Ordinates and Probability Integral of the Distribution of the Correlation Coefficient* (1938), Charts II and IV | Florence N. David |
| 16 | *Biometrika*, **32**, 168; *Biometrika*, **50**, 452 | Catherine M. Thompson; D. E. Amos |
| 17 | *Biometrika*, **38**, 424 | H. O. Hartley and Elaine R. Fitch |
| 18 | Reduced from *Biometrika*, **33**, 74 with 0·1% points compiled from various sources | Maxime Merrington and Catherine M. Thompson |
| 19 | *Biometrika*, **35**, 26 | K. R. Nair |
| 20 | Mean deviation: freshly compiled / Range: *Biometrika*, **38**, 463 (derived from 5 decimal MS. of Table 23)† | Joyce M. May / Mathematics Division, National Physical Laboratory |

* *T.S.B.* **1** or **2** indicates *Tables for Statisticians and Biometricians*, parts 1 or 2, with table number following in Roman figures.

† The later and fuller tables computed by Harter *et al.* (1959) have made it possible to remove a number of last-figure errors from these three tables.

| | | |
|---|---|---|
| 21 | *Biometrika*, **33**, 265 | Scientific Computing Service Ltd., M. Sumner |
| 22 | *Biometrika*, **32**, 308 (freshly compiled for $n > 12$)* | Scientific Computing Service Ltd. |
| 23 | *Biometrika*, **32**, 302* | Scientific Computing Service Ltd. |
| 24 | Freshly compiled | Jean H. Thompson and Joyce M. May |
| 25 | *Biometrika*, **35**, 140 | K. R. Nair |
| 26 | *Biometrika*, **35**, 143; **43**, 450; **46**, 473 | K. R. Nair; H. A. David; K. C. S. Pillai |
| 26a | *Biometrika*, **48**, 388 | } C. P. Quesenberry and H. A. David |
| 26b | *Biometrika*, **48**, 389 (after condensation) | |
| 27 | *Biometrika*, **17**, 386. *T.S.B.* **2**, XXII | L. H. C. Tippett |
| 28 | Compiled from *Biometrika*, **36**, 98 ($n \leqslant 10$); Fisher & Yates, *Statistical Tables* (1953) ($n > 20$); with some fresh calculations ($10 < n < 20$) | In part, H. J. Godwin, Jean H. Thompson |
| 29 | *Biometrika*, **46**, 464 | H. L. Harter; J. Pachares |
| 29a | *Biometrika*, **44**, 487 | P. G. Moore |
| 29b | *Biometrika*, **50**, 191 | H. L. Harter |
| 29c | *Biometrika*, **41**, 491; *Biometrika*, **51**, 486 | H. A. David, H. O. Hartley and E. S. Pearson; E. S. Pearson and M. A. Stephens |
| 30 | *Biometrika*, **38**, 408 | H. A. David |
| 31 | *Biometrika*, **37**, 310; **39**, 424 | H. O. Hartley; H. A. David and Joyce M. May |
| 31a | Abridged from C. Eisenhart, M. W. Hastay and W. A. Wallis (1947). *Techniques of Statistical Analysis*, Table 15·1. See also W. G. Cochran (1941) | |
| 31b | *Biometrika*, **43**, 420 | C. I. Bliss, W. G. Cochran and J. W. Tukey |
| 32 33 | *Biometrika*, **33**, 302, 304 | } Catherine M. Thompson and Maxine Merrington |
| 34 | (A)   $a$ *Biometrika*, **28**, 303 | R. C. Geary |
| | (B)  $\sqrt{b_1}$ *Biometrika*, **28**, 306. *T.S.B.* **2**, XXXVII *bis* | E. S. Pearson and P. Williams |
| | (C)  $b_2$ *Biometrika*, **22**, 248. *T.S.B.* **2**, XXXVII *bis* | E. S. Pearson |
| 35 | Freshly compiled, using *Biometrika*, **10**, 529. *T.S.B.* **2**, XVII | Joyce M. May and H. O. Hartley |
| 36 | Enlarged, from *Biometrika*, **31**, 320 | J. Przyborowski and H. Wilenski; E. S. Pearson |
| 37 | Derived from *Tables of the Incomplete* B-*function*; see also National Bureau of Standards, Applied Mathematics Series, no. 6 | |
| 38 | *Biometrika*, **35**, 149 | D. J. Finney |
| 39 | *Biometrika*, **10**, 27. *T.S.B.* **1**, LI | H. E. Soper |
| 40 | Enlarged from *Biometrika*, **28**, 439 | F. Garwood |
| 41 | Enlarged from *Biometrika*, **26**, 410 | J. C. Clopper and E. S. Pearson |
| 42 | *Biometrika*, **38**, 6, with fresh calculations for 2·5 and 1 % points | Maxine Merrington and E. S. Pearson |
| 43 | Redrawn from *Biometrika*, **7**, 131. *T.S.B.* **1**, XXXV | A. Rhind |
| 44 45 46 | Reduced from M. G. Kendall, *Rank Correlation Methods* (1962), Tables 1, 2 and 5, and *Biometrika*, **38**, 132 | } M. G. Kendall |
| 47 | Based on tables published by D. van der Reyden, *Onderstepoort J. Vet. Sci.* (1943), **18**, 383 | D. F. I. van Heerden |
| 48 | *Biometrika*, **2**, 477. *T.S.B.* **1**, XXVII | W. P. Elderton |
| 49 | *Biometrika*, **2**, 479. *T.S.B.* **1**, XXVIII | W. P. Elderton |
| 50 | From standard sources | |
| 51 | Enlarged from an earlier table. *T.S.B.* **1**, XLIX | Julia Bell |
| 52 | Freshly compiled; partly based on *The Kelley Statistical Tables* (1948), Table I | |
| 53 | Freshly compiled from standard sources | |
| 54 | Freshly compiled; largely based on L. J. Comrie, *Chambers' Shorter Six-figure Mathematical Tables* (1950) | |

* See footnote † on page 107.

# TABLES

# Table 1. *The Normal probability function. The integral P(X) and ordinate Z(X) in terms of the standardized deviate X*

| X | P(X) | δ + | δ² − | Z(X) | δ − | δ² − |
|---|---|---|---|---|---|---|
| ·00 | ·5000000 | | 0 | ·3989423 | | 399 |
| | | 39894 | | | 199 | |
| ·01 | ·5039894 | | 4 | ·3989223 | | 399 |
| | | 39890 | | | 598 | |
| ·02 | ·5079783 | | 8 | ·3988625 | | 399 |
| | | 39882 | | | 997 | |
| ·03 | ·5119665 | | 12 | ·3987628 | | 398 |
| | | 39870 | | | 1395 | |
| ·04 | ·5159534 | | 16 | ·3986233 | | 398 |
| | | 39854 | | | 1793 | |
| ·05 | ·5199388 | | 20 | ·3984439 | | 397 |
| | | 39834 | | | 2191 | |
| ·06 | ·5239222 | | 24 | ·3982248 | | 397 |
| | | 39810 | | | 2588 | |
| ·07 | ·5279032 | | 28 | ·3979661 | | 396 |
| | | 39782 | | | 2984 | |
| ·08 | ·5318814 | | 32 | ·3976677 | | 395 |
| | | 39750 | | | 3379 | |
| ·09 | ·5358564 | | 36 | ·3973298 | | 394 |
| | | 39714 | | | 3773 | |
| ·10 | ·5398278 | | 40 | ·3969525 | | 393 |
| | | 39675 | | | 4166 | |
| ·11 | ·5437953 | | 44 | ·3965360 | | 392 |
| | | 39631 | | | 4558 | |
| ·12 | ·5477584 | | 48 | ·3960802 | | 390 |
| | | 39584 | | | 4948 | |
| ·13 | ·5517168 | | 51 | ·3955854 | | 389 |
| | | 39532 | | | 5337 | |
| ·14 | ·5556700 | | 55 | ·3950517 | | 387 |
| | | 39477 | | | 5724 | |
| ·15 | ·5596177 | | 59 | ·3944793 | | 386 |
| | | 39418 | | | 6110 | |
| ·16 | ·5635595 | | 63 | ·3938684 | | 384 |
| | | 39355 | | | 6493 | |
| ·17 | ·5674949 | | 67 | ·3932190 | | 382 |
| | | 39288 | | | 6875 | |
| ·18 | ·5714237 | | 71 | ·3925315 | | 380 |
| | | 39217 | | | 7255 | |
| ·19 | ·5753454 | | 74 | ·3918060 | | 378 |
| | | 39143 | | | 7633 | |
| ·20 | ·5792597 | | 78 | ·3910427 | | 375 |
| | | 39065 | | | 8008 | |
| ·21 | ·5831662 | | 82 | ·3902419 | | 373 |
| | | 38983 | | | 8381 | |
| ·22 | ·5870644 | | 86 | ·3894038 | | 371 |
| | | 38897 | | | 8752 | |
| ·23 | ·5909541 | | 89 | ·3885286 | | 368 |
| | | 38808 | | | 9120 | |
| ·24 | ·5948349 | | 93 | ·3876166 | | 365 |
| | | 38715 | | | 9485 | |
| ·25 | ·5987063 | | 97 | ·3866681 | | 362 |
| | | 38618 | | | 9847 | |
| ·26 | ·6025681 | | 100 | ·3856834 | | 360 |
| | | 38518 | | | 10207 | |
| ·27 | ·6064199 | | 104 | ·3846627 | | 357 |
| | | 38414 | | | 10564 | |
| ·28 | ·6102612 | | 107 | ·3836063 | | 354 |
| | | 38306 | | | 10917 | |
| ·29 | ·6140919 | | 111 | ·3825146 | | 350 |
| | | 38195 | | | 11268 | |
| ·30 | ·6179114 | | 114 | ·3813878 | | 347 |
| | | 38081 | | | 11615 | |
| ·31 | ·6217195 | | 118 | ·3802264 | | 344 |
| | | 37963 | | | 11958 | |
| ·32 | ·6255158 | | 121 | ·3790305 | | 340 |
| | | 37842 | | | 12298 | |
| ·33 | ·6293000 | | 125 | ·3778007 | | 337 |
| | | 37717 | | | 12635 | |
| ·34 | ·6330717 | | 128 | ·3765372 | | 333 |
| | | 37589 | | | 12968 | |
| ·35 | ·6368307 | | 131 | ·3752403 | | 329 |
| | | 37458 | | | 13297 | |
| ·36 | ·6405764 | | 135 | ·3739106 | | 325 |
| | | 37323 | | | 13623 | |
| ·37 | ·6443088 | | 138 | ·3725483 | | 322 |
| | | 37185 | | | 13944 | |
| ·38 | ·6480273 | | 141 | ·3711539 | | 318 |
| | | 37044 | | | 14262 | |
| ·39 | ·6517317 | | 144 | ·3697277 | | 313 |
| | | 36900 | | | 14575 | |
| ·40 | ·6554217 | | 147 | ·3682701 | | 309 |
| | | 36753 | | | 14885 | |
| ·41 | ·6590970 | | 150 | ·3667817 | | 305 |
| | | 36602 | | | 15190 | |
| ·42 | ·6627573 | | 153 | ·3652627 | | 301 |
| | | 36449 | | | 15491 | |
| ·43 | ·6664022 | | 156 | ·3637136 | | 296 |
| | | 36293 | | | 15787 | |
| ·44 | ·6700314 | | 159 | ·3621349 | | 292 |
| | | 36133 | | | 16079 | |
| ·45 | ·6736448 | | 162 | ·3605270 | | 288 |
| | | 35971 | | | 16367 | |
| ·46 | ·6772419 | | 165 | ·3588903 | | 283 |
| | | 35806 | | | 16650 | |
| ·47 | ·6808225 | | 168 | ·3572253 | | 278 |
| | | 35638 | | | 16928 | |
| ·48 | ·6843863 | | 171 | ·3555325 | | 274 |
| | | 35467 | | | 17202 | |
| ·49 | ·6879331 | | 173 | ·3538124 | | 269 |
| | | 35294 | | | 17470 | |
| ·50 | ·6914625 | | 176 | ·3520653 | | 264 |

| X | P(X) | δ + | δ² − |
|---|---|---|---|
| ·50 | ·6914625 | | 176 |
| | | 35118 | |
| ·51 | ·6949743 | | 179 |
| | | 34939 | |
| ·52 | ·6984682 | | 181 |
| | | 34758 | |
| ·53 | ·7019440 | | 184 |
| | | 34574 | |
| ·54 | ·7054015 | | 186 |
| | | 34388 | |
| ·55 | ·7088403 | | 189 |
| | | 34200 | |
| ·56 | ·7122603 | | 191 |
| | | 34009 | |
| ·57 | ·7156612 | | 193 |
| | | 33815 | |
| ·58 | ·7190427 | | 196 |
| | | 33620 | |
| ·59 | ·7224047 | | 198 |
| | | 33422 | |
| ·60 | ·7257469 | | 200 |
| | | 33222 | |
| ·61 | ·7290691 | | 202 |
| | | 33020 | |
| ·62 | ·7323711 | | 204 |
| | | 32816 | |
| ·63 | ·7356527 | | 206 |
| | | 32610 | |
| ·64 | ·7389137 | | 208 |
| | | 32402 | |
| ·65 | ·7421539 | | 210 |
| | | 32192 | |
| ·66 | ·7453731 | | 212 |
| | | 31980 | |
| ·67 | ·7485711 | | 214 |
| | | 31767 | |
| ·68 | ·7517478 | | 215 |
| | | 31551 | |
| ·69 | ·7549029 | | 217 |
| | | 31334 | |
| ·70 | ·7580363 | | 219 |
| | | 31116 | |
| ·71 | ·7611479 | | 220 |
| | | 30896 | |
| ·72 | ·7642375 | | 222 |
| | | 30674 | |
| ·73 | ·7673049 | | 223 |
| | | 30451 | |
| ·74 | ·7703500 | | 225 |
| | | 30226 | |
| ·75 | ·7733726 | | 226 |
| | | 30001 | |
| ·76 | ·7763727 | | 227 |
| | | 29773 | |
| ·77 | ·7793501 | | 228 |
| | | 29545 | |
| ·78 | ·7823046 | | 230 |
| | | 29316 | |
| ·79 | ·7852361 | | 231 |
| | | 29085 | |
| ·80 | ·7881446 | | 232 |
| | | 28853 | |
| ·81 | ·7910299 | | 233 |
| | | 28620 | |
| ·82 | ·7938919 | | 234 |
| | | 28387 | |
| ·83 | ·7967306 | | 235 |
| | | 28152 | |
| ·84 | ·7995458 | | 235 |
| | | 27917 | |
| ·85 | ·8023375 | | 236 |
| | | 27680 | |
| ·86 | ·8051055 | | 237 |
| | | 27443 | |
| ·87 | ·8078498 | | 238 |
| | | 27205 | |
| ·88 | ·8105703 | | 238 |
| | | 26967 | |
| ·89 | ·8132671 | | 239 |
| | | 26728 | |
| ·90 | ·8159399 | | 239 |
| | | 26489 | |
| ·91 | ·8185887 | | 240 |
| | | 26249 | |
| ·92 | ·8212136 | | 240 |
| | | 26008 | |
| ·93 | ·8238145 | | 241 |
| | | 25768 | |
| ·94 | ·8263912 | | 241 |
| | | 25527 | |
| ·95 | ·8289439 | | 241 |
| | | 25285 | |
| ·96 | ·8314724 | | 242 |
| | | 25044 | |
| ·97 | ·8339768 | | 242 |
| | | 24802 | |
| ·98 | ·8364569 | | 242 |
| | | 24560 | |
| ·99 | ·8389129 | | 242 |
| | | 24318 | |
| 1·00 | ·8413447 | | 242 |

$$Z(X) = e^{-\frac{1}{2}X^2}/\sqrt{(2\pi)}, \quad P(X) = 1 - Q(X) = \int_{-\infty}^{X} Z(u)\, du.$$

Table 1 (*continued*)

| Z(X) | δ − | δ² − |
|---|---|---|
| ·3520653 | | 264 |
| | 17734 | |
| ·3502919 | | 259 |
| | 17994 | |
| ·3484925 | | 254 |
| | 18248 | |
| ·3466677 | | 249 |
| | 18497 | |
| ·3448180 | | 244 |
| | 18741 | |
| ·3429439 | | 239 |
| | 18981 | |
| ·3410458 | | 234 |
| | 19215 | |
| ·3391243 | | 229 |
| | 19444 | |
| ·3371799 | | 224 |
| | 19667 | |
| ·3352132 | | 219 |
| | 19886 | |
| ·3332246 | | 213 |
| | 20099 | |
| ·3312147 | | 208 |
| | 20307 | |
| ·3291840 | | 203 |
| | 20510 | |
| ·3271330 | | 197 |
| | 20707 | |
| ·3250623 | | 192 |
| | 20899 | |
| ·3229724 | | 187 |
| | 21086 | |
| ·3208638 | | 181 |
| | 21267 | |
| ·3187371 | | 176 |
| | 21442 | |
| ·3165929 | | 170 |
| | 21613 | |
| ·3144317 | | 165 |
| | 21777 | |
| ·3122539 | | 159 |
| | 21936 | |
| ·3100603 | | 154 |
| | 22090 | |
| ·3078513 | | 148 |
| | 22239 | |
| ·3056274 | | 143 |
| | 22381 | |
| ·3033893 | | 137 |
| | 22519 | |
| ·3011374 | | 132 |
| | 22650 | |
| ·2988724 | | 126 |
| | 22777 | |
| ·2965948 | | 121 |
| | 22897 | |
| ·2943050 | | 115 |
| | 23013 | |
| ·2920038 | | 110 |
| | 23122 | |
| ·2896916 | | 104 |
| | 23227 | |
| ·2873689 | | 99 |
| | 23325 | |
| ·2850364 | | 93 |
| | 23419 | |
| ·2826945 | | 88 |
| | 23507 | |
| ·2803438 | | 83 |
| | 23589 | |
| ·2779849 | | 77 |
| | 23666 | |
| ·2756182 | | 72 |
| | 23738 | |
| ·2732444 | | 66 |
| | 23805 | |
| ·2708640 | | 61 |
| | 23866 | |
| ·2684774 | | 56 |
| | 23922 | |
| ·2660852 | | 51 |
| | 23972 | |
| ·2636880 | | 45 |
| | 24017 | |
| ·2612863 | | 40 |
| | 24058 | |
| ·2588805 | | 35 |
| | 24093 | |
| ·2564713 | | 30 |
| | 24122 | |
| ·2540591 | | 25 |
| | 24147 | |
| ·2516443 | | 20 |
| | 24167 | |
| ·2492277 | | 15 |
| | 24182 | |
| ·2468095 | | 10 |
| | 24191 | |
| ·2443904 | | 5 |
| | 24196 | |
| ·2419707 | | 0 |

| X | P (X) | δ + | δ² − | Z (X) | δ − | δ² + |
|---|---|---|---|---|---|---|
| 1·00 | ·8413447 | | 242 | ·2419707 | | 0 |
| | | 24076 | | | 24196 | |
| 1·01 | ·8437524 | | 242 | ·2395511 | | 5 |
| | | 23834 | | | 24191 | |
| 1·02 | ·8461358 | | 242 | ·2371320 | | 10 |
| | | 23592 | | | 24182 | |
| 1·03 | ·8484950 | | 242 | ·2347138 | | 14 |
| | | 23351 | | | 24168 | |
| 1·04 | ·8508300 | | 242 | ·2322970 | | 19 |
| | | 23109 | | | 24149 | |
| 1·05 | ·8531409 | | 241 | ·2298821 | | 24 |
| | | 22868 | | | 24125 | |
| 1·06 | ·8554277 | | 241 | ·2274696 | | 28 |
| | | 22626 | | | 24097 | |
| 1·07 | ·8576903 | | 241 | ·2250599 | | 33 |
| | | 22386 | | | 24064 | |
| 1·08 | ·8599289 | | 240 | ·2226535 | | 37 |
| | | 22145 | | | 24027 | |
| 1·09 | ·8621434 | | 240 | ·2202508 | | 41 |
| | | 21905 | | | 23986 | |
| 1·10 | ·8643339 | | 240 | ·2178522 | | 46 |
| | | 21665 | | | 23940 | |
| 1·11 | ·8665005 | | 239 | ·2154582 | | 50 |
| | | 21426 | | | 23890 | |
| 1·12 | ·8686431 | | 239 | ·2130691 | | 54 |
| | | 21188 | | | 23836 | |
| 1·13 | ·8707619 | | 238 | ·2106856 | | 58 |
| | | 20950 | | | 23778 | |
| 1·14 | ·8728568 | | 237 | ·2083078 | | 62 |
| | | 20712 | | | 23715 | |
| 1·15 | ·8749281 | | 237 | ·2059363 | | 66 |
| | | 20475 | | | 23649 | |
| 1·16 | ·8769756 | | 236 | ·2035714 | | 70 |
| | | 20239 | | | 23578 | |
| 1·17 | ·8789995 | | 235 | ·2012135 | | 74 |
| | | 20004 | | | 23504 | |
| 1·18 | ·8809999 | | 235 | ·1988631 | | 78 |
| | | 19769 | | | 23426 | |
| 1·19 | ·8829768 | | 234 | ·1965205 | | 82 |
| | | 19535 | | | 23344 | |
| 1·20 | ·8849303 | | 233 | ·1941861 | | 85 |
| | | 19302 | | | 23259 | |
| 1·21 | ·8868606 | | 232 | ·1918602 | | 89 |
| | | 19070 | | | 23170 | |
| 1·22 | ·8887676 | | 231 | ·1895432 | | 93 |
| | | 18839 | | | 23077 | |
| 1·23 | ·8906514 | | 230 | ·1872354 | | 96 |
| | | 18609 | | | 22981 | |
| 1·24 | ·8925123 | | 229 | ·1849373 | | 99 |
| | | 18379 | | | 22882 | |
| 1·25 | ·8943502 | | 228 | ·1826491 | | 103 |
| | | 18151 | | | 22779 | |
| 1·26 | ·8961653 | | 227 | ·1803712 | | 106 |
| | | 17924 | | | 22673 | |
| 1·27 | ·8979577 | | 226 | ·1781038 | | 109 |
| | | 17697 | | | 22564 | |
| 1·28 | ·8997274 | | 225 | ·1758474 | | 112 |
| | | 17472 | | | 22452 | |
| 1·29 | ·9014747 | | 224 | ·1736022 | | 115 |
| | | 17248 | | | 22337 | |
| 1·30 | ·9031995 | | 223 | ·1713686 | | 118 |
| | | 17026 | | | 22218 | |
| 1·31 | ·9049021 | | 222 | ·1691468 | | 121 |
| | | 16804 | | | 22097 | |
| 1·32 | ·9065825 | | 220 | ·1669370 | | 124 |
| | | 16584 | | | 21973 | |
| 1·33 | ·9082409 | | 219 | ·1647397 | | 127 |
| | | 16365 | | | 21847 | |
| 1·34 | ·9098773 | | 218 | ·1625551 | | 129 |
| | | 16147 | | | 21717 | |
| 1·35 | ·9114920 | | 217 | ·1603833 | | 132 |
| | | 15930 | | | 21585 | |
| 1·36 | ·9130850 | | 215 | ·1582248 | | 134 |
| | | 15715 | | | 21451 | |
| 1·37 | ·9146565 | | 214 | ·1560797 | | 137 |
| | | 15501 | | | 21314 | |
| 1·38 | ·9162067 | | 212 | ·1539483 | | 139 |
| | | 15289 | | | 21175 | |
| 1·39 | ·9177356 | | 211 | ·1518308 | | 142 |
| | | 15078 | | | 21033 | |
| 1·40 | ·9192433 | | 210 | ·1497275 | | 144 |
| | | 14868 | | | 20890 | |
| 1·41 | ·9207302 | | 208 | ·1476385 | | 146 |
| | | 14660 | | | 20744 | |
| 1·42 | ·9221962 | | 207 | ·1455641 | | 148 |
| | | 14453 | | | 20596 | |
| 1·43 | ·9236415 | | 205 | ·1435046 | | 150 |
| | | 14248 | | | 20446 | |
| 1·44 | ·9250663 | | 204 | ·1414600 | | 152 |
| | | 14044 | | | 20294 | |
| 1·45 | ·9264707 | | 202 | ·1394306 | | 154 |
| | | 13842 | | | 20140 | |
| 1·46 | ·9278550 | | 201 | ·1374165 | | 155 |
| | | 13642 | | | 19985 | |
| 1·47 | ·9292191 | | 199 | ·1354181 | | 157 |
| | | 13443 | | | 19828 | |
| 1·48 | ·9305634 | | 197 | ·1334353 | | 159 |
| | | 13245 | | | 19669 | |
| 1·49 | ·9318879 | | 196 | ·1314684 | | 160 |
| | | 13049 | | | 19508 | |
| 1·50 | ·9331928 | | 194 | ·1295176 | | 162 |

Note sign of second difference, δ².

111

Table 1. *The Normal probability function (continued)*

| X | P(X) | δ + | δ² − | Z(X) | δ − | δ² + |
|---|---|---|---|---|---|---|
| 1·50 | ·9331928 | 12855 | 194 | ·1295176 | 19346 | 162 |
| 1·51 | ·9344783 | 12662 | 193 | ·1275830 | 19183 | 163 |
| 1·52 | ·9357445 | 12471 | 191 | ·1256646 | 19018 | 165 |
| 1·53 | ·9369916 | 12282 | 189 | ·1237628 | 18853 | 166 |
| 1·54 | ·9382198 | 12094 | 188 | ·1218775 | 18685 | 167 |
| 1·55 | ·9394292 | 11908 | 186 | ·1200090 | 18517 | 168 |
| 1·56 | ·9406201 | 11724 | 184 | ·1181573 | 18348 | 169 |
| 1·57 | ·9417924 | 11541 | 183 | ·1163225 | 18177 | 170 |
| 1·58 | ·9429466 | 11360 | 181 | ·1145048 | 18006 | 171 |
| 1·59 | ·9440826 | 11181 | 179 | ·1127042 | 17834 | 172 |
| 1·60 | ·9452007 | 11004 | 177 | ·1109208 | 17661 | 173 |
| 1·61 | ·9463011 | 10828 | 176 | ·1091548 | 17487 | 174 |
| 1·62 | ·9473839 | 10654 | 174 | ·1074061 | 17312 | 174 |
| 1·63 | ·9484493 | 10482 | 172 | ·1056748 | 17137 | 175 |
| 1·64 | ·9494974 | 10311 | 170 | ·1039611 | 16962 | 176 |
| 1·65 | ·9505285 | 10142 | 169 | ·1022649 | 16786 | 176 |
| 1·66 | ·9515428 | 9975 | 167 | ·1005864 | 16609 | 177 |
| 1·67 | ·9525403 | 9810 | 165 | ·0989255 | 16432 | 177 |
| 1·68 | ·9535213 | 9647 | 163 | ·0972823 | 16255 | 177 |
| 1·69 | ·9544860 | 9485 | 162 | ·0956568 | 16077 | 178 |
| 1·70 | ·9554345 | 9325 | 160 | ·0940491 | 15899 | 178 |
| 1·71 | ·9563671 | 9167 | 158 | ·0924591 | 15722 | 178 |
| 1·72 | ·9572838 | 9011 | 156 | ·0908870 | 15544 | 178 |
| 1·73 | ·9581849 | 8856 | 155 | ·0893326 | 15366 | 178 |
| 1·74 | ·9590705 | 8704 | 153 | ·0877961 | 15188 | 178 |
| 1·75 | ·9599408 | 8553 | 151 | ·0862773 | 15010 | 178 |
| 1·76 | ·9607961 | 8403 | 149 | ·0847764 | 14832 | 178 |
| 1·77 | ·9616364 | 8256 | 147 | ·0832932 | 14654 | 178 |
| 1·78 | ·9624620 | 8110 | 146 | ·0818278 | 14477 | 177 |
| 1·79 | ·9632730 | 7966 | 144 | ·0803801 | 14300 | 177 |
| 1·80 | ·9640697 | 7824 | 142 | ·0789502 | 14123 | 177 |
| 1·81 | ·9648521 | 7684 | 140 | ·0775379 | 13946 | 176 |
| 1·82 | ·9656205 | 7545 | 139 | ·0761433 | 13770 | 176 |
| 1·83 | ·9663750 | 7409 | 137 | ·0747663 | 13594 | 176 |
| 1·84 | ·9671159 | 7273 | 135 | ·0734068 | 13419 | 175 |
| 1·85 | ·9678432 | 7140 | 133 | ·0720649 | 13245 | 175 |
| 1·86 | ·9685572 | 7009 | 132 | ·0707404 | 13071 | 174 |
| 1·87 | ·9692581 | 6879 | 130 | ·0694333 | 12897 | 173 |
| 1·88 | ·9699460 | 6751 | 128 | ·0681436 | 12725 | 173 |
| 1·89 | ·9706210 | 6624 | 126 | ·0668711 | 12553 | 172 |
| 1·90 | ·9712834 | 6500 | 125 | ·0656158 | 12382 | 171 |
| 1·91 | ·9719334 | 6377 | 123 | ·0643777 | 12211 | 170 |
| 1·92 | ·9725711 | 6255 | 121 | ·0631566 | 12041 | 170 |
| 1·93 | ·9731966 | 6136 | 120 | ·0619524 | 11873 | 169 |
| 1·94 | ·9738102 | 6018 | 118 | ·0607652 | 11705 | 168 |
| 1·95 | ·9744119 | 5902 | 116 | ·0595947 | 11538 | 167 |
| 1·96 | ·9750021 | 5787 | 115 | ·0584409 | 11372 | 166 |
| 1·97 | ·9755808 | 5674 | 113 | ·0573038 | 11206 | 165 |
| 1·98 | ·9761482 | 5563 | 111 | ·0561831 | 11042 | 164 |
| 1·99 | ·9767045 | 5453 | 110 | ·0550789 | 10879 | 163 |
| 2·00 | ·9772499 |  | 108 | ·0539910 |  | 162 |

| X | P(X) | δ + | δ² − |
|---|---|---|---|
| 2·00 | ·9772499 | 5345 | 108 |
| 2·01 | ·9777844 | 5239 | 106 |
| 2·02 | ·9783083 | 5134 | 105 |
| 2·03 | ·9788217 | 5031 | 103 |
| 2·04 | ·9793248 | 4929 | 102 |
| 2·05 | ·9798178 | 4829 | 100 |
| 2·06 | ·9803007 | 4731 | 98 |
| 2·07 | ·9807738 | 4634 | 97 |
| 2·08 | ·9812372 | 4539 | 95 |
| 2·09 | ·9816911 | 4445 | 94 |
| 2·10 | ·9821356 | 4352 | 92 |
| 2·11 | ·9825708 | 4262 | 91 |
| 2·12 | ·9829970 | 4172 | 89 |
| 2·13 | ·9834142 | 4084 | 88 |
| 2·14 | ·9838226 | 3998 | 86 |
| 2·15 | ·9842224 | 3913 | 85 |
| 2·16 | ·9846137 | 3829 | 84 |
| 2·17 | ·9849966 | 3747 | 82 |
| 2·18 | ·9853713 | 3666 | 81 |
| 2·19 | ·9857379 | 3587 | 79 |
| 2·20 | ·9860966 | 3509 | 78 |
| 2·21 | ·9864474 | 3432 | 77 |
| 2·22 | ·9867906 | 3357 | 75 |
| 2·23 | ·9871263 | 3283 | 74 |
| 2·24 | ·9874545 | 3210 | 73 |
| 2·25 | ·9877755 | 3138 | 71 |
| 2·26 | ·9880894 | 3068 | 70 |
| 2·27 | ·9883962 | 2999 | 69 |
| 2·28 | ·9886962 | 2932 | 68 |
| 2·29 | ·9889893 | 2865 | 66 |
| 2·30 | ·9892759 | 2800 | 65 |
| 2·31 | ·9895559 | 2736 | 64 |
| 2·32 | ·9898296 | 2674 | 63 |
| 2·33 | ·9900969 | 2612 | 62 |
| 2·34 | ·9903581 | 2552 | 60 |
| 2·35 | ·9906133 | 2492 | 59 |
| 2·36 | ·9908625 | 2434 | 58 |
| 2·37 | ·9911060 | 2377 | 57 |
| 2·38 | ·9913437 | 2321 | 56 |
| 2·39 | ·9915758 | 2267 | 55 |
| 2·40 | ·9918025 | 2213 | 54 |
| 2·41 | ·9920237 | 2160 | 53 |
| 2·42 | ·9922397 | 2108 | 52 |
| 2·43 | ·9924506 | 2058 | 51 |
| 2·44 | ·9926564 | 2008 | 50 |
| 2·45 | ·9928572 | 1960 | 49 |
| 2·46 | ·9930531 | 1912 | 48 |
| 2·47 | ·9932443 | 1865 | 47 |
| 2·48 | ·9934309 | 1820 | 46 |
| 2·49 | ·9936128 | 1775 | 45 |
| 2·50 | ·9937903 |  | 44 |

$$Z(X) = e^{-\frac{1}{2}X^2}/\surd(2\pi), \quad P(X) = 1 - Q(X) = \int_{-\infty}^{X} Z(u)\, du.$$

# Table 1 (continued)

| Z(X) | δ − | δ² + |
|---|---|---|
| ·0539910 | | 162 |
| | 10717 | |
| ·0529192 | | 161 |
| | 10557 | |
| ·0518636 | | 160 |
| | 10397 | |
| ·0508239 | | 159 |
| | 10238 | |
| ·0498001 | | 157 |
| | 10081 | |
| ·0487920 | | 156 |
| | 9924 | |
| ·0477996 | | 155 |
| | 9769 | |
| ·0468226 | | 154 |
| | 9616 | |
| ·0458611 | | 153 |
| | 9463 | |
| ·0449148 | | 151 |
| | 9312 | |
| ·0439836 | | 150 |
| | 9162 | |
| ·0430674 | | 149 |
| | 9013 | |
| ·0421661 | | 147 |
| | 8866 | |
| ·0412795 | | 146 |
| | 8720 | |
| ·0404076 | | 145 |
| | 8575 | |
| ·0395500 | | 143 |
| | 8432 | |
| ·0387069 | | 142 |
| | 8290 | |
| ·0378779 | | 140 |
| | 8149 | |
| ·0370629 | | 139 |
| | 8010 | |
| ·0362619 | | 138 |
| | 7873 | |
| ·0354746 | | 136 |
| | 7737 | |
| ·0347009 | | 135 |
| | 7602 | |
| ·0339408 | | 133 |
| | 7468 | |
| ·0331939 | | 132 |
| | 7337 | |
| ·0324603 | | 130 |
| | 7206 | |
| ·0317397 | | 129 |
| | 7077 | |
| ·0310319 | | 127 |
| | 6950 | |
| ·0303370 | | 126 |
| | 6824 | |
| ·0296546 | | 125 |
| | 6699 | |
| ·0289847 | | 123 |
| | 6576 | |
| ·0283270 | | 122 |
| | 6455 | |
| ·0276816 | | 120 |
| | 6335 | |
| ·0270481 | | 119 |
| | 6216 | |
| ·0264265 | | 117 |
| | 6099 | |
| ·0258166 | | 116 |
| | 5984 | |
| ·0252182 | | 114 |
| | 5870 | |
| ·0246313 | | 113 |
| | 5757 | |
| ·0240556 | | 111 |
| | 5646 | |
| ·0234910 | | 110 |
| | 5536 | |
| ·0229374 | | 108 |
| | 5428 | |
| ·0223945 | | 107 |
| | 5322 | |
| ·0218624 | | 105 |
| | 5217 | |
| ·0213407 | | 104 |
| | 5113 | |
| ·0208294 | | 102 |
| | 5011 | |
| ·0203284 | | 101 |
| | 4910 | |
| ·0198374 | | 99 |
| | 4811 | |
| ·0193563 | | 98 |
| | 4713 | |
| ·0188850 | | 96 |
| | 4617 | |
| ·0184233 | | 95 |
| | 4522 | |
| ·0179711 | | 93 |
| | 4428 | |
| ·0175283 | | 92 |

| X | P(X) | δ + | δ² − | Z(X) | δ − | δ² + |
|---|---|---|---|---|---|---|
| 2·50 | ·9937903 | | 44 | ·0175283 | | 92 |
| | | 1731 | | | 4336 | |
| 2·51 | ·9939634 | | 43 | ·0170947 | | 91 |
| | | 1688 | | | 4246 | |
| 2·52 | ·9941323 | | 42 | ·0166701 | | 89 |
| | | 1646 | | | 4157 | |
| 2·53 | ·9942969 | | 41 | ·0162545 | | 88 |
| | | 1605 | | | 4069 | |
| 2·54 | ·9944574 | | 40 | ·0158476 | | 86 |
| | | 1565 | | | 3982 | |
| 2·55 | ·9946139 | | 39 | ·0154493 | | 85 |
| | | 1525 | | | 3897 | |
| 2·56 | ·9947664 | | 39 | ·0150596 | | 84 |
| | | 1487 | | | 3814 | |
| 2·57 | ·9949151 | | 38 | ·0146782 | | 82 |
| | | 1449 | | | 3731 | |
| 2·58 | ·9950600 | | 37 | ·0143051 | | 81 |
| | | 1412 | | | 3650 | |
| 2·59 | ·9952012 | | 36 | ·0139401 | | 80 |
| | | 1376 | | | 3571 | |
| 2·60 | ·9953388 | | 35 | ·0135830 | | 78 |
| | | 1341 | | | 3493 | |
| 2·61 | ·9954729 | | 35 | ·0132337 | | 77 |
| | | 1306 | | | 3416 | |
| 2·62 | ·9956035 | | 34 | ·0128921 | | 76 |
| | | 1272 | | | 3340 | |
| 2·63 | ·9957308 | | 33 | ·0125581 | | 74 |
| | | 1239 | | | 3266 | |
| 2·64 | ·9958547 | | 32 | ·0122315 | | 73 |
| | | 1207 | | | 3193 | |
| 2·65 | ·9959754 | | 32 | ·0119122 | | 72 |
| | | 1176 | | | 3121 | |
| 2·66 | ·9960930 | | 31 | ·0116001 | | 70 |
| | | 1145 | | | 3051 | |
| 2·67 | ·9962074 | | 30 | ·0112951 | | 69 |
| | | 1115 | | | 2981 | |
| 2·68 | ·9963189 | | 29 | ·0109969 | | 68 |
| | | 1085 | | | 2913 | |
| 2·69 | ·9964274 | | 29 | ·0107056 | | 67 |
| | | 1056 | | | 2847 | |
| 2·70 | ·9965330 | | 28 | ·0104209 | | 66 |
| | | 1028 | | | 2781 | |
| 2·71 | ·9966358 | | 27 | ·0101428 | | 64 |
| | | 1001 | | | 2717 | |
| 2·72 | ·9967359 | | 27 | ·0098712 | | 63 |
| | | 974 | | | 2654 | |
| 2·73 | ·9968333 | | 26 | ·0096058 | | 62 |
| | | 948 | | | 2592 | |
| 2·74 | ·9969280 | | 26 | ·0093466 | | 61 |
| | | 922 | | | 2531 | |
| 2·75 | ·9970202 | | 25 | ·0090936 | | 60 |
| | | 897 | | | 2471 | |
| 2·76 | ·9971099 | | 24 | ·0088465 | | 59 |
| | | 873 | | | 2413 | |
| 2·77 | ·9971972 | | 24 | ·0086052 | | 57 |
| | | 849 | | | 2355 | |
| 2·78 | ·9972821 | | 23 | ·0083697 | | 56 |
| | | 825 | | | 2299 | |
| 2·79 | ·9973646 | | 23 | ·0081398 | | 55 |
| | | 803 | | | 2244 | |
| 2·80 | ·9974449 | | 22 | ·0079155 | | 54 |
| | | 781 | | | 2189 | |
| 2·81 | ·9975229 | | 22 | ·0076965 | | 53 |
| | | 759 | | | 2136 | |
| 2·82 | ·9975988 | | 21 | ·0074829 | | 52 |
| | | 738 | | | 2084 | |
| 2·83 | ·9976726 | | 21 | ·0072744 | | 51 |
| | | 717 | | | 2033 | |
| 2·84 | ·9977443 | | 20 | ·0070711 | | 50 |
| | | 697 | | | 1983 | |
| 2·85 | ·9978140 | | 20 | ·0068728 | | 49 |
| | | 678 | | | 1934 | |
| 2·86 | ·9978818 | | 19 | ·0066793 | | 48 |
| | | 658 | | | 1886 | |
| 2·87 | ·9979476 | | 19 | ·0064907 | | 47 |
| | | 640 | | | 1839 | |
| 2·88 | ·9980116 | | 18 | ·0063067 | | 46 |
| | | 622 | | | 1793 | |
| 2·89 | ·9980738 | | 18 | ·0061274 | | 45 |
| | | 604 | | | 1748 | |
| 2·90 | ·9981342 | | 17 | ·0059525 | | 44 |
| | | 587 | | | 1704 | |
| 2·91 | ·9981929 | | 17 | ·0057821 | | 43 |
| | | 570 | | | 1661 | |
| 2·92 | ·9982498 | | 16 | ·0056160 | | 42 |
| | | 553 | | | 1619 | |
| 2·93 | ·9983052 | | 16 | ·0054541 | | 41 |
| | | 537 | | | 1578 | |
| 2·94 | ·9983589 | | 16 | ·0052963 | | 40 |
| | | 522 | | | 1537 | |
| 2·95 | ·9984111 | | 15 | ·0051426 | | 40 |
| | | 507 | | | 1497 | |
| 2·96 | ·9984618 | | 15 | ·0049929 | | 39 |
| | | 492 | | | 1459 | |
| 2·97 | ·9985110 | | 14 | ·0048470 | | 38 |
| | | 478 | | | 1421 | |
| 2·98 | ·9985588 | | 14 | ·0047050 | | 37 |
| | | 464 | | | 1384 | |
| 2·99 | ·9986051 | | 14 | ·0045666 | | 36 |
| | | 450 | | | 1347 | |
| 3·00 | ·9986501 | | 13 | ·0044318 | | 35 |

Note sign of second difference, δ².

# Table 1. *The Normal probability function (continued)*

| X | P(X) | δ+ | δ²− | Z(X) | δ− | δ²+ |
|---|---|---|---|---|---|---|
| 3·00 | ·9986501 |  | 13 | ·0044318 |  | 35 |
|  |  | 437 |  |  | 1312 |  |
| 3·01 | ·9986938 |  | 13 | ·0043007 |  | 35 |
|  |  | 424 |  |  | 1277 |  |
| 3·02 | ·9987361 |  | 13 | ·0041729 |  | 34 |
|  |  | 411 |  |  | 1243 |  |
| 3·03 | ·9987772 |  | 12 | ·0040486 |  | 33 |
|  |  | 399 |  |  | 1210 |  |
| 3·04 | ·9988171 |  | 12 | ·0039276 |  | 32 |
|  |  | 387 |  |  | 1178 |  |
| 3·05 | ·9988558 |  | 12 | ·0038098 |  | 32 |
|  |  | 375 |  |  | 1146 |  |
| 3·06 | ·9988933 |  | 11 | ·0036951 |  | 31 |
|  |  | 364 |  |  | 1115 |  |
| 3·07 | ·9989297 |  | 11 | ·0035836 |  | 30 |
|  |  | 353 |  |  | 1085 |  |
| 3·08 | ·9989650 |  | 11 | ·0034751 |  | 29 |
|  |  | 342 |  |  | 1056 |  |
| 3·09 | ·9989992 |  | 10 | ·0033695 |  | 29 |
|  |  | 332 |  |  | 1027 |  |
| 3·10 | ·9990324 |  | 10 | ·0032668 |  | 28 |
|  |  | 322 |  |  | 999 |  |
| 3·11 | ·9990646 |  | 10 | ·0031669 |  | 27 |
|  |  | 312 |  |  | 971 |  |
| 3·12 | ·9990957 |  | 10 | ·0030698 |  | 27 |
|  |  | 302 |  |  | 944 |  |
| 3·13 | ·9991260 |  | 9 | ·0029754 |  | 26 |
|  |  | 293 |  |  | 918 |  |
| 3·14 | ·9991553 |  | 9 | ·0028835 |  | 26 |
|  |  | 284 |  |  | 893 |  |
| 3·15 | ·9991836 |  | 9 | ·0027943 |  | 25 |
|  |  | 275 |  |  | 868 |  |
| 3·16 | ·9992112 |  | 9 | ·0027075 |  | 24 |
|  |  | 267 |  |  | 843 |  |
| 3·17 | ·9992378 |  | 8 | ·0026231 |  | 24 |
|  |  | 258 |  |  | 820 |  |
| 3·18 | ·9992636 |  | 8 | ·0025412 |  | 23 |
|  |  | 250 |  |  | 797 |  |
| 3·19 | ·9992886 |  | 8 | ·0024615 |  | 23 |
|  |  | 242 |  |  | 774 |  |
| 3·20 | ·9993129 |  | 8 | ·0023841 |  | 22 |
|  |  | 235 |  |  | 752 |  |
| 3·21 | ·9993363 |  | 7 | ·0023089 |  | 21 |
|  |  | 227 |  |  | 731 |  |
| 3·22 | ·9993590 |  | 7 | ·0022358 |  | 21 |
|  |  | 220 |  |  | 710 |  |
| 3·23 | ·9993810 |  | 7 | ·0021649 |  | 20 |
|  |  | 213 |  |  | 689 |  |
| 3·24 | ·9994024 |  | 7 | ·0020960 |  | 20 |
|  |  | 206 |  |  | 669 |  |
| 3·25 | ·9994230 |  | 7 | ·0020290 |  | 19 |
|  |  | 200 |  |  | 650 |  |
| 3·26 | ·9994429 |  | 6 | ·0019641 |  | 19 |
|  |  | 193 |  |  | 631 |  |
| 3·27 | ·9994623 |  | 6 | ·0019010 |  | 18 |
|  |  | 187 |  |  | 612 |  |
| 3·28 | ·9994810 |  | 6 | ·0018397 |  | 18 |
|  |  | 181 |  |  | 595 |  |
| 3·29 | ·9994991 |  | 6 | ·0017803 |  | 17 |
|  |  | 175 |  |  | 577 |  |
| 3·30 | ·9995166 |  | 6 | ·0017226 |  | 17 |
|  |  | 169 |  |  | 560 |  |
| 3·31 | ·9995335 |  | 6 | ·0016666 |  | 17 |
|  |  | 164 |  |  | 543 |  |
| 3·32 | ·9995499 |  | 5 | ·0016122 |  | 16 |
|  |  | 159 |  |  | 527 |  |
| 3·33 | ·9995658 |  | 5 | ·0015595 |  | 16 |
|  |  | 153 |  |  | 512 |  |
| 3·34 | ·9995811 |  | 5 | ·0015084 |  | 15 |
|  |  | 148 |  |  | 496 |  |
| 3·35 | ·9995959 |  | 5 | ·0014587 |  | 15 |
|  |  | 143 |  |  | 481 |  |
| 3·36 | ·9996103 |  | 5 | ·0014106 |  | 15 |
|  |  | 139 |  |  | 467 |  |
| 3·37 | ·9996242 |  | 5 | ·0013639 |  | 14 |
|  |  | 134 |  |  | 453 |  |
| 3·38 | ·9996376 |  | 4 | ·0013187 |  | 14 |
|  |  | 130 |  |  | 439 |  |
| 3·39 | ·9996505 |  | 4 | ·0012748 |  | 13 |
|  |  | 125 |  |  | 426 |  |
| 3·40 | ·9996631 |  | 4 | ·0012322 |  | 13 |
|  |  | 121 |  |  | 413 |  |
| 3·41 | ·9996752 |  | 4 | ·0011910 |  | 13 |
|  |  | 117 |  |  | 400 |  |
| 3·42 | ·9996869 |  | 4 | ·0011510 |  | 12 |
|  |  | 113 |  |  | 388 |  |
| 3·43 | ·9996982 |  | 4 | ·0011122 |  | 12 |
|  |  | 109 |  |  | 376 |  |
| 3·44 | ·9997091 |  | 4 | ·0010747 |  | 12 |
|  |  | 106 |  |  | 364 |  |
| 3·45 | ·9997197 |  | 4 | ·0010383 |  | 11 |
|  |  | 102 |  |  | 353 |  |
| 3·46 | ·9997299 |  | 3 | ·0010030 |  | 11 |
|  |  | 99 |  |  | 342 |  |
| 3·47 | ·9997398 |  | 3 | ·0009689 |  | 11 |
|  |  | 95 |  |  | 331 |  |
| 3·48 | ·9997493 |  | 3 | ·0009358 |  | 10 |
|  |  | 92 |  |  | 320 |  |
| 3·49 | ·9997585 |  | 3 | ·0009037 |  | 10 |
|  |  | 89 |  |  | 310 |  |
| 3·50 | ·9997674 |  | 3 | ·0008727 |  | 10 |

| X | P(X) | δ+ | δ²− |
|---|---|---|---|
| 3·50 | ·9997674 |  | 3 |
|  |  | 86 |  |
| 3·51 | ·9997759 |  | 3 |
|  |  | 83 |  |
| 3·52 | ·9997842 |  | 3 |
|  |  | 80 |  |
| 3·53 | ·9997922 |  | 3 |
|  |  | 77 |  |
| 3·54 | ·9997999 |  | 3 |
|  |  | 74 |  |
| 3·55 | ·9998074 |  | 3 |
|  |  | 72 |  |
| 3·56 | ·9998146 |  | 3 |
|  |  | 69 |  |
| 3·57 | ·9998215 |  | 2 |
|  |  | 67 |  |
| 3·58 | ·9998282 |  | 2 |
|  |  | 65 |  |
| 3·59 | ·9998347 |  | 2 |
|  |  | 62 |  |
| 3·60 | ·9998409 |  | 2 |
|  |  | 60 |  |
| 3·61 | ·9998469 |  | 2 |
|  |  | 58 |  |
| 3·62 | ·9998527 |  | 2 |
|  |  | 56 |  |
| 3·63 | ·9998583 |  | 2 |
|  |  | 54 |  |
| 3·64 | ·9998637 |  | 2 |
|  |  | 52 |  |
| 3·65 | ·9998689 |  | 2 |
|  |  | 50 |  |
| 3·66 | ·9998739 |  | 2 |
|  |  | 48 |  |
| 3·67 | ·9998787 |  | 2 |
|  |  | 47 |  |
| 3·68 | ·9998834 |  | 2 |
|  |  | 45 |  |
| 3·69 | ·9998879 |  | 2 |
|  |  | 43 |  |
| 3·70 | ·9998922 |  | 2 |
|  |  | 42 |  |
| 3·71 | ·9998964 |  | 2 |
|  |  | 40 |  |
| 3·72 | ·9999004 |  | 1 |
|  |  | 39 |  |
| 3·73 | ·9999043 |  | 1 |
|  |  | 37 |  |
| 3·74 | ·9999080 |  | 1 |
|  |  | 36 |  |
| 3·75 | ·9999116 |  | 1 |
|  |  | 35 |  |
| 3·76 | ·9999150 |  | 1 |
|  |  | 33 |  |
| 3·77 | ·9999184 |  | 1 |
|  |  | 32 |  |
| 3·78 | ·9999216 |  | 1 |
|  |  | 31 |  |
| 3·79 | ·9999247 |  | 1 |
|  |  | 30 |  |
| 3·80 | ·9999277 |  | 1 |
|  |  | 29 |  |
| 3·81 | ·9999305 |  | 1 |
|  |  | 28 |  |
| 3·82 | ·9999333 |  | 1 |
|  |  | 27 |  |
| 3·83 | ·9999359 |  | 1 |
|  |  | 26 |  |
| 3·84 | ·9999385 |  | 1 |
|  |  | 25 |  |
| 3·85 | ·9999409 |  | 1 |
|  |  | 24 |  |
| 3·86 | ·9999433 |  | 1 |
|  |  | 23 |  |
| 3·87 | ·9999456 |  | 1 |
|  |  | 22 |  |
| 3·88 | ·9999478 |  | 1 |
|  |  | 21 |  |
| 3·89 | ·9999499 |  | 1 |
|  |  | 20 |  |
| 3·90 | ·9999519 |  | 1 |
|  |  | 19 |  |
| 3·91 | ·9999539 |  | 1 |
|  |  | 19 |  |
| 3·92 | ·9999557 |  | 1 |
|  |  | 18 |  |
| 3·93 | ·9999575 |  | 1 |
|  |  | 17 |  |
| 3·94 | ·9999593 |  | 1 |
|  |  | 17 |  |
| 3·95 | ·9999609 |  | 1 |
|  |  | 16 |  |
| 3·96 | ·9999625 |  | 1 |
|  |  | 15 |  |
| 3·97 | ·9999641 |  | 1 |
|  |  | 15 |  |
| 3·98 | ·9999655 |  | 1 |
|  |  | 14 |  |
| 3·99 | ·9999670 |  | 1 |
|  |  | 14 |  |
| 4·00 | ·9999683 |  | 1 |

$$Z(X) = e^{-\frac{1}{2}X^2}/\sqrt{(2\pi)}, \quad P(X) = 1 - Q(X) = \int_{-\infty}^{X} Z(u)\,du.$$

# Table 1 (continued)

| Z(X) | δ − | δ² + |
|---|---|---|
| ·0008727 | | |
| | 301 | 10 |
| ·0008426 | | |
| | 291 | 10 |
| ·0008135 | | |
| | 282 | 9 |
| ·0007853 | | |
| | 273 | 9 |
| ·0007581 | | |
| | 264 | 9 |
| ·0007317 | | |
| | 256 | 8 |
| ·0007061 | | |
| | 247 | 8 |
| ·0006814 | | |
| | 239 | 8 |
| ·0006575 | | |
| | 232 | 8 |
| ·0006343 | | |
| | 224 | 8 |
| ·0006119 | | |
| | 217 | 7 |
| ·0005902 | | |
| | 210 | 7 |
| ·0005693 | | |
| | 203 | 7 |
| ·0005490 | | |
| | 196 | 7 |
| ·0005294 | | |
| | 189 | 6 |
| ·0005105 | | |
| | 183 | 6 |
| ·0004921 | | |
| | 177 | 6 |
| ·0004744 | | |
| | 171 | 6 |
| ·0004573 | | |
| | 165 | 6 |
| ·0004408 | | |
| | 160 | 6 |
| ·0004248 | | |
| | 155 | 5 |
| ·0004093 | | |
| | 149 | 5 |
| ·0003944 | | |
| | 144 | 5 |
| ·0003800 | | |
| | 139 | 5 |
| ·0003661 | | |
| | 135 | 5 |
| ·0003526 | | |
| | 130 | 5 |
| ·0003396 | | |
| | 125 | 4 |
| ·0003271 | | |
| | 121 | 4 |
| ·0003149 | | |
| | 117 | 4 |
| ·0003032 | | |
| | 113 | 4 |
| ·0002919 | | |
| | 109 | 4 |
| ·0002810 | | |
| | 105 | 4 |
| ·0002705 | | |
| | 102 | 4 |
| ·0002604 | | |
| | 98 | 4 |
| ·0002506 | | |
| | 95 | 3 |
| ·0002411 | | |
| | 91 | 3 |
| ·0002320 | | |
| | 88 | 3 |
| ·0002232 | | |
| | 85 | 3 |
| ·0002147 | | |
| | 82 | 3 |
| ·0002065 | | |
| | 79 | 3 |
| ·0001987 | | |
| | 76 | 3 |
| ·0001910 | | |
| | 73 | 3 |
| ·0001837 | | |
| | 71 | 3 |
| ·0001766 | | |
| | 68 | 3 |
| ·0001698 | | |
| | 66 | 2 |
| ·0001633 | | |
| | 63 | 2 |
| ·0001569 | | |
| | 61 | 2 |
| ·0001508 | | |
| | 59 | 2 |
| ·0001449 | | |
| | 57 | 2 |
| ·0001393 | | |
| | 55 | 2 |
| ·0001338 | | 2 |

| X | P(X) | δ + | δ² − |
|---|---|---|---|
| 4·00 | ·9999683 | | |
| | | 13 | 1 |
| 4·01 | ·9999696 | | |
| | | 13 | 1 |
| 4·02 | ·9999709 | | |
| | | 12 | 0 |
| 4·03 | ·9999721 | | |
| | | 12 | |
| 4·04 | ·9999733 | | |
| | | 11 | |
| 4·05 | ·9999744 | | |
| | | 11 | |
| 4·06 | ·9999755 | | |
| | | 10 | |
| 4·07 | ·9999765 | | |
| | | 10 | |
| 4·08 | ·9999775 | | |
| | | 9 | |
| 4·09 | ·9999784 | | |
| | | 9 | |
| 4·10 | ·9999793 | | |
| | | 9 | |
| 4·11 | ·9999802 | | |
| | | 8 | |
| 4·12 | ·9999811 | | |
| | | 8 | |
| 4·13 | ·9999819 | | |
| | | 8 | |
| 4·14 | ·9999826 | | |
| | | 7 | |
| 4·15 | ·9999834 | | |
| | | 7 | |
| 4·16 | ·9999841 | | |
| | | 7 | |
| 4·17 | ·9999848 | | |
| | | 7 | |
| 4·18 | ·9999854 | | |
| | | 6 | |
| 4·19 | ·9999861 | | |
| | | 6 | |
| 4·20 | ·9999867 | | |
| | | 6 | |
| 4·21 | ·9999872 | | |
| | | 6 | |
| 4·22 | ·9999878 | | |
| | | 5 | |
| 4·23 | ·9999883 | | |
| | | 5 | |
| 4·24 | ·9999888 | | |
| | | 5 | |
| 4·25 | ·9999893 | | |
| | | 5 | |
| 4·26 | ·9999898 | | |
| | | 4 | |
| 4·27 | ·9999902 | | |
| | | 4 | |
| 4·28 | ·9999907 | | |
| | | 4 | |
| 4·29 | ·9999911 | | |
| | | 4 | |
| 4·30 | ·9999915 | | |
| | | 4 | |
| 4·31 | ·9999918 | | |
| | | 4 | |
| 4·32 | ·9999922 | | |
| | | 3 | |
| 4·33 | ·9999925 | | |
| | | 3 | |
| 4·34 | ·9999929 | | |
| | | 3 | |
| 4·35 | ·9999932 | | |
| | | 3 | |
| 4·36 | ·9999935 | | |
| | | 3 | |
| 4·37 | ·9999938 | | |
| | | 3 | |
| 4·38 | ·9999941 | | |
| | | 3 | |
| 4·39 | ·9999943 | | |
| | | 3 | |
| 4·40 | ·9999946 | | |
| | | 2 | |
| 4·41 | ·9999948 | | |
| | | 2 | |
| 4·42 | ·9999951 | | |
| | | 2 | |
| 4·43 | ·9999953 | | |
| | | 2 | |
| 4·44 | ·9999955 | | |
| | | 2 | |
| 4·45 | ·9999957 | | |
| | | 2 | |
| 4·46 | ·9999959 | | |
| | | 2 | |
| 4·47 | ·9999961 | | |
| | | 2 | |
| 4·48 | ·9999963 | | |
| | | 2 | |
| 4·49 | ·9999964 | | |
| | | 2 | |
| 4·50 | ·9999966 | | |

| Z(X) | δ − | δ² + |
|---|---|---|
| ·0001338 | | |
| | 53 | 2 |
| ·0001286 | | |
| | 51 | 2 |
| ·0001235 | | |
| | 49 | 2 |
| ·0001186 | | |
| | 47 | 2 |
| ·0001140 | | |
| | 45 | 2 |
| ·0001094 | | |
| | 43 | 2 |
| ·0001051 | | |
| | 42 | 2 |
| ·0001009 | | |
| | 40 | 2 |
| ·0000969 | | |
| | 39 | 1 |
| ·0000930 | | |
| | 37 | 1 |
| ·0000893 | | |
| | 36 | 1 |
| ·0000857 | | |
| | 35 | 1 |
| ·0000822 | | |
| | 33 | 1 |
| ·0000789 | | |
| | 32 | 1 |
| ·0000757 | | |
| | 31 | 1 |
| ·0000726 | | |
| | 30 | 1 |
| ·0000697 | | |
| | 28 | 1 |
| ·0000668 | | |
| | 27 | 1 |
| ·0000641 | | |
| | 26 | 1 |
| ·0000615 | | |
| | 25 | 1 |
| ·0000589 | | |
| | 24 | 1 |
| ·0000565 | | |
| | 23 | 1 |
| ·0000542 | | |
| | 22 | 1 |
| ·0000519 | | |
| | 22 | 1 |
| ·0000498 | | |
| | 21 | 1 |
| ·0000477 | | |
| | 20 | 1 |
| ·0000457 | | |
| | 19 | 1 |
| ·0000438 | | |
| | 18 | 1 |
| ·0000420 | | |
| | 18 | 1 |
| ·0000402 | | |
| | 17 | 1 |
| ·0000385 | | |
| | 16 | 1 |
| ·0000369 | | |
| | 16 | 1 |
| ·0000354 | | |
| | 15 | 1 |
| ·0000339 | | |
| | 14 | 1 |
| ·0000324 | | |
| | 14 | 1 |
| ·0000310 | | |
| | 13 | 1 |
| ·0000297 | | |
| | 13 | 1 |
| ·0000284 | | |
| | 12 | 0 |
| ·0000272 | | |
| | 12 | |
| ·0000261 | | |
| | 11 | |
| ·0000249 | | |
| | 11 | |
| ·0000239 | | |
| | 10 | |
| ·0000228 | | |
| | 10 | |
| ·0000218 | | |
| | 9 | |
| ·0000209 | | |
| | 9 | |
| ·0000200 | | |
| | 9 | |
| ·0000191 | | |
| | 8 | |
| ·0000183 | | |
| | 8 | |
| ·0000175 | | |
| | 8 | |
| ·0000167 | | |
| | 7 | |
| ·0000160 | | |

Note sign of second difference, δ².

Table 1. *The Normal probability function (continued)*

| X | P(X)* | Z(X)* | X | P(X)* | Z(X)* | X | P(X)* | Z(X)* |
|---|---|---|---|---|---|---|---|---|
| 4·50 | 66023 | 159837 | 5·00 | 97133 | 14867 | 5·50 | 99810 | 1077 |
| 4·51 | 67586 | 152797 | 5·01 | 97278 | 14141 | 5·51 | 99821 | 1019 |
| 4·52 | 69080 | 146051 | 5·02 | 97416 | 13450 | 5·52 | 99831 | 965 |
| 4·53 | 70508 | 139590 | 5·03 | 97548 | 12791 | 5·53 | 99840 | 913 |
| 4·54 | 71873 | 133401 | 5·04 | 97672 | 12162 | 5·54 | 99849 | 864 |
| 4·55 | 73177 | 127473 | 5·05 | 97791 | 11564 | 5·55 | 99857 | 817 |
| 4·56 | 74423 | 121797 | 5·06 | 97904 | 10994 | 5·56 | 99865 | 773 |
| 4·57 | 75614 | 116362 | 5·07 | 98011 | 10451 | 5·57 | 99873 | 731 |
| 4·58 | 76751 | 111159 | 5·08 | 98113 | 9934 | 5·58 | 99880 | 691 |
| 4·59 | 77838 | 106177 | 5·09 | 98210 | 9441 | 5·59 | 99886 | 654 |
| 4·60 | 78875 | 101409 | 5·10 | 98302 | 8972 | 5·60 | 99893 | 618 |
| 4·61 | 79867 | 96845 | 5·11 | 98389 | 8526 | 5·61 | 99899 | 585 |
| 4·62 | 80813 | 92477 | 5·12 | 98472 | 8101 | 5·62 | 99905 | 553 |
| 4·63 | 81717 | 88297 | 5·13 | 98551 | 7696 | 5·63 | 99910 | 522 |
| 4·64 | 82580 | 84298 | 5·14 | 98626 | 7311 | 5·64 | 99915 | 494 |
| 4·65 | 83403 | 80472 | 5·15 | 98698 | 6944 | 5·65 | 99920 | 467 |
| 4·66 | 84190 | 76812 | 5·16 | 98765 | 6595 | 5·66 | 99924 | 441 |
| 4·67 | 84940 | 73311 | 5·17 | 98830 | 6263 | 5·67 | 99929 | 417 |
| 4·68 | 85656 | 69962 | 5·18 | 98891 | 5947 | 5·68 | 99933 | 394 |
| 4·69 | 86340 | 66760 | 5·19 | 98949 | 5647 | 5·69 | 99936 | 372 |
| 4·70 | 86992 | 63698 | 5·20 | 99004 | 5361 | 5·70 | 99940 | 351 |
| 4·71 | 87614 | 60771 | 5·21 | 99056 | 5089 | 5·71 | 99944 | 332 |
| 4·72 | 88208 | 57972 | 5·22 | 99105 | 4831 | 5·72 | 99947 | 313 |
| 4·73 | 88774 | 55296 | 5·23 | 99152 | 4585 | 5·73 | 99950 | 296 |
| 4·74 | 89314 | 52739 | 5·24 | 99197 | 4351 | 5·74 | 99953 | 280 |
| 4·75 | 89829 | 50295 | 5·25 | 99240 | 4128 | 5·75 | 99955 | 264 |
| 4·76 | 90320 | 47960 | 5·26 | 99280 | 3917 | 5·76 | 99958 | 249 |
| 4·77 | 90789 | 45728 | 5·27 | 99318 | 3716 | 5·77 | 99960 | 235 |
| 4·78 | 91235 | 43596 | 5·28 | 99354 | 3525 | 5·78 | 99963 | 222 |
| 4·79 | 91661 | 41559 | 5·29 | 99388 | 3344 | 5·79 | 99965 | 210 |
| 4·80 | 92067 | 39613 | 5·30 | 99421 | 3171 | 5·80 | 99967 | 198 |
| 4·81 | 92453 | 37755 | 5·31 | 99452 | 3007 | 5·81 | 99969 | 187 |
| 4·82 | 92822 | 35980 | 5·32 | 99481 | 2852 | 5·82 | 99971 | 176 |
| 4·83 | 93173 | 34285 | 5·33 | 99509 | 2704 | 5·83 | 99972 | 166 |
| 4·84 | 93508 | 32667 | 5·34 | 99535 | 2563 | 5·84 | 99974 | 157 |
| 4·85 | 93827 | 31122 | 5·35 | 99560 | 2430 | 5·85 | 99975 | 148 |
| 4·86 | 94131 | 29647 | 5·36 | 99584 | 2303 | 5·86 | 99977 | 139 |
| 4·87 | 94420 | 28239 | 5·37 | 99606 | 2183 | 5·87 | 99978 | 131 |
| 4·88 | 94696 | 26895 | 5·38 | 99628 | 2069 | 5·88 | 99979 | 124 |
| 4·89 | 94958 | 25613 | 5·39 | 99648 | 1960 | 5·89 | 99981 | 117 |
| 4·90 | 95208 | 24390 | 5·40 | 99667 | 1857 | 5·90 | 99982 | 110 |
| 4·91 | 95446 | 23222 | 5·41 | 99685 | 1760 | 5·91 | 99983 | 104 |
| 4·92 | 95673 | 22108 | 5·42 | 99702 | 1667 | 5·92 | 99984 | 98 |
| 4·93 | 95889 | 21046 | 5·43 | 99718 | 1579 | 5·93 | 99985 | 92 |
| 4·94 | 96094 | 20033 | 5·44 | 99734 | 1495 | 5·94 | 99986 | 87 |
| 4·95 | 96289 | 19066 | 5·45 | 99748 | 1416 | 5·95 | 99987 | 82 |
| 4·96 | 96475 | 18144 | 5·46 | 99762 | 1341 | 5·96 | 99987 | 77 |
| 4·97 | 96652 | 17265 | 5·47 | 99775 | 1270 | 5·97 | 99988 | 73 |
| 4·98 | 96821 | 16428 | 5·48 | 99787 | 1202 | 5·98 | 99989 | 68 |
| 4·99 | 96981 | 15629 | 5·49 | 99799 | 1138 | 5·99 | 99990 | 65 |
|  |  |  |  |  |  | 6·00 | 99990 | 61 |

$$Z(X) = e^{-\frac{1}{2}X^2}/\sqrt{(2\pi)}, \quad P(X) = 1 - Q(X) = \int_{-\infty}^{X} Z(u)\, du.$$

* The entries for P(X) and Z(X) on this page are given to 10 decimal places; thus 0·99999 should be prefixed to each entry for P(X) and a decimal point, followed by four, five, ..., eight zeros, as appropriate, to Z(X).

Table 2. *The Normal probability function. Values of* $-\log Q(X) = -\log \{1 - P(X)\}$
*for large values of* $X$ *(extension of Table 1)*

| X | $-\log Q(X)$ | X | $-\log Q(X)$ | X | $-\log Q(X)$ |
|---|---|---|---|---|---|
| 5 | 6·54265 | 30 | 197·30921 | 50 | 544·96634 |
| 6 | 9·00586 | 31 | 210·56940 | 60 | 783·90743 |
| 7 | 11·89285 | 32 | 224·26344 | 70 | 1066·26576 |
| 8 | 15·20614 | 33 | 238·39135 | 80 | 1392·04459 |
| 9 | 18·94746 | 34 | 252·95315 | 90 | 1761·24604 |
| 10 | 23·11805 | 35 | 267·94888 | 100 | 2173·87154 |
| 11 | 27·71882 | 36 | 283·37855 | 150 | 4888·38812 |
| 12 | 32·75044 | 37 | 299·24218 | 200 | 8688·58977 |
| 13 | 38·21345 | 38 | 315·53979 | 250 | 13574·49960 |
| 14 | 44·10827 | 39 | 332·27139 | 300 | 19546·12790 |
| 15 | 50·43522 | 40 | 349·43701 | 350 | 26603·48018 |
| 16 | 57·19458 | 41 | 367·03664 | 400 | 34746·55970 |
| 17 | 64·38658 | 42 | 385·07032 | 450 | 43975·36860 |
| 18 | 72·01140 | 43 | 403·53804 | 500 | 54289·90830 |
| 19 | 80·06919 | 44 | 422·43983 | | |
| 20 | 88·56010 | 45 | 441·77568 | | |
| 21 | 97·48422 | 46 | 461·54561 | | |
| 22 | 106·84167 | 47 | 481·74964 | | |
| 23 | 116·63253 | 48 | 502·38776 | | |
| 24 | 126·85686 | 49 | 523·45999 | | |
| 25 | 137·51475 | 50 | 544·96634 | | |
| 26 | 148·60624 | | | | |
| 27 | 160·13139 | | | | |
| 28 | 172·09024 | | | | |
| 29 | 184·48283 | | | | |
| 30 | 197·30921 | | | | |

N.B. To obtain anything but a rough appreciation after $X = 50$, the table would require much extension, but for many practical problems it suffices to take after $X = 50$:

$$Q(X) = \frac{1}{\sqrt{(2\pi)}} \frac{1}{X} e^{-\frac{1}{2}X^2}$$

Table 3. *The Normal probability function. Values of* $X$ *for extreme values of* $Q$ *and* $P$
*(extension of Table 4)*

| Q | 0·0000 | 0·0001 | 0·0002 | 0·0003 | 0·0004 | 0·0005 | 0·0006 | 0·0007 | 0·0008 | 0·0009 | 0·0010 | |
|---|---|---|---|---|---|---|---|---|---|---|---|---|
| 0·000 | ∞ | 3·7190 | 3·5401 | 3·4316 | 3·3528 | 3·2905 | 3·2389 | 3·1947 | 3·1559 | 3·1214 | 3·0902 | 0·999 |
| ·001 | 3·0902 | 3·0618 | 3·0357 | 3·0115 | 2·9889 | 2·9677 | 2·9478 | 2·9290 | 2·9112 | 2·8943 | 2·8782 | ·998 |
| ·002 | 2·8782 | 2·8627 | 2·8480 | 2·8338 | 2·8202 | 2·8070 | 2·7944 | 2·7822 | 2·7703 | 2·7589 | 2·7478 | ·997 |
| ·003 | 2·7478 | 2·7370 | 2·7266 | 2·7164 | 2·7065 | 2·6968 | 2·6874 | 2·6783 | 2·6693 | 2·6606 | 2·6521 | ·996 |
| ·004 | 2·6521 | 2·6437 | 2·6356 | 2·6276 | 2·6197 | 2·6121 | 2·6045 | 2·5972 | 2·5899 | 2·5828 | 2·5758 | ·995 |
| 0·005 | 2·5758 | 2·5690 | 2·5622 | 2·5556 | 2·5491 | 2·5427 | 2·5364 | 2·5302 | 2·5241 | 2·5181 | 2·5121 | 0·994 |
| ·006 | 2·5121 | 2·5063 | 2·5006 | 2·4949 | 2·4893 | 2·4838 | 2·4783 | 2·4730 | 2·4677 | 2·4624 | 2·4573 | ·993 |
| ·007 | 2·4573 | 2·4522 | 2·4471 | 2·4422 | 2·4372 | 2·4324 | 2·4276 | 2·4228 | 2·4181 | 2·4135 | 2·4089 | ·992 |
| ·008 | 2·4089 | 2·4044 | 2·3999 | 2·3954 | 2·3911 | 2·3867 | 2·3824 | 2·3781 | 2·3739 | 2·3698 | 2·3656 | ·991 |
| ·009 | 2·3656 | 2·3615 | 2·3575 | 2·3535 | 2·3495 | 2·3455 | 2·3416 | 2·3378 | 2·3339 | 2·3301 | 2·3263 | ·990 |
| 0·010 | 2·3263 | 2·3226 | 2·3189 | 2·3152 | 2·3116 | 2·3080 | 2·3044 | 2·3009 | 2·2973 | 2·2938 | 2·2904 | 0·989 |
| ·011 | 2·2904 | 2·2869 | 2·2835 | 2·2801 | 2·2768 | 2·2734 | 2·2701 | 2·2668 | 2·2636 | 2·2603 | 2·2571 | ·988 |
| ·012 | 2·2571 | 2·2539 | 2·2508 | 2·2476 | 2·2445 | 2·2414 | 2·2383 | 2·2353 | 2·2322 | 2·2292 | 2·2262 | ·987 |
| ·013 | 2·2262 | 2·2232 | 2·2203 | 2·2173 | 2·2144 | 2·2115 | 2·2086 | 2·2058 | 2·2029 | 2·2001 | 2·1973 | ·986 |
| ·014 | 2·1973 | 2·1945 | 2·1917 | 2·1890 | 2·1862 | 2·1835 | 2·1808 | 2·1781 | 2·1754 | 2·1727 | 2·1701 | ·985 |
| 0·015 | 2·1701 | 2·1675 | 2·1648 | 2·1622 | 2·1596 | 2·1571 | 2·1545 | 2·1520 | 2·1494 | 2·1469 | 2·1444 | 0·984 |
| ·016 | 2·1444 | 2·1419 | 2·1394 | 2·1370 | 2·1345 | 2·1321 | 2·1297 | 2·1272 | 2·1248 | 2·1224 | 2·1201 | ·983 |
| ·017 | 2·1201 | 2·1177 | 2·1154 | 2·1130 | 2·1107 | 2·1084 | 2·1061 | 2·1038 | 2·1015 | 2·0992 | 2·0969 | ·982 |
| ·018 | 2·0969 | 2·0947 | 2·0924 | 2·0902 | 2·0880 | 2·0858 | 2·0836 | 2·0814 | 2·0792 | 2·0770 | 2·0749 | ·981 |
| ·019 | 2·0749 | 2·0727 | 2·0706 | 2·0684 | 2·0663 | 2·0642 | 2·0621 | 2·0600 | 2·0579 | 2·0558 | 2·0537 | ·980 |
| | 0·0010 | 0·0009 | 0·0008 | 0·0007 | 0·0006 | 0·0005 | 0·0004 | 0·0003 | 0·0002 | 0·0001 | 0·0000 | P |

Table 4. *The Normal probability function. Values of X in terms of Q and P*

| Q | ·000 | ·001 | ·002 | ·003 | ·004 | ·005 | ·006 | ·007 | ·008 | ·009 | ·010 | |
|---|------|------|------|------|------|------|------|------|------|------|------|---|
| ·00 | ∞ | 3·0902 | 2·8782 | 2·7478 | 2·6521 | 2·5758 | 2·5121 | 2·4573 | 2·4089 | 2·3656 | 2·3263 | ·99 |
| ·01 | 2·3263 | 2·2904 | 2·2571 | 2·2262 | 2·1973 | 2·1701 | 2·1444 | 2·1201 | 2·0969 | 2·0749 | 2·0537 | ·98 |
| ·02 | 2·0537 | 2·0335 | 2·0141 | 1·9954 | 1·9774 | 1·9600 | 1·9431 | 1·9268 | 1·9110 | 1·8957 | 1·8808 | ·97 |
| ·03 | 1·8808 | 1·8663 | 1·8522 | 1·8384 | 1·8250 | 1·8119 | 1·7991 | 1·7866 | 1·7744 | 1·7624 | 1·7507 | ·96 |
| ·04 | 1·7507 | 1·7392 | 1·7279 | 1·7169 | 1·7060 | 1·6954 | 1·6849 | 1·6747 | 1·6646 | 1·6546 | 1·6449 | ·95 |
| ·05 | 1·6449 | 1·6352 | 1·6258 | 1·6164 | 1·6072 | 1·5982 | 1·5893 | 1·5805 | 1·5718 | 1·5632 | 1·5548 | ·94 |
| ·06 | 1·5548 | 1·5464 | 1·5382 | 1·5301 | 1·5220 | 1·5141 | 1·5063 | 1·4985 | 1·4909 | 1·4833 | 1·4758 | ·93 |
| ·07 | 1·4758 | 1·4684 | 1·4611 | 1·4538 | 1·4466 | 1·4395 | 1·4325 | 1·4255 | 1·4187 | 1·4118 | 1·4051 | ·92 |
| ·08 | 1·4051 | 1·3984 | 1·3917 | 1·3852 | 1·3787 | 1·3722 | 1·3658 | 1·3595 | 1·3532 | 1·3469 | 1·3408 | ·91 |
| ·09 | 1·3408 | 1·3346 | 1·3285 | 1·3225 | 1·3165 | 1·3106 | 1·3047 | 1·2988 | 1·2930 | 1·2873 | 1·2816 | ·90 |
| ·10 | 1·2816 | 1·2759 | 1·2702 | 1·2646 | 1·2591 | 1·2536 | 1·2481 | 1·2426 | 1·2372 | 1·2319 | 1·2265 | ·89 |
| ·11 | 1·2265 | 1·2212 | 1·2160 | 1·2107 | 1·2055 | 1·2004 | 1·1952 | 1·1901 | 1·1850 | 1·1800 | 1·1750 | ·88 |
| ·12 | 1·1750 | 1·1700 | 1·1650 | 1·1601 | 1·1552 | 1·1503 | 1·1455 | 1·1407 | 1·1359 | 1·1311 | 1·1264 | ·87 |
| ·13 | 1·1264 | 1·1217 | 1·1170 | 1·1123 | 1·1077 | 1·1031 | 1·0985 | 1·0939 | 1·0893 | 1·0848 | 1·0803 | ·86 |
| ·14 | 1·0803 | 1·0758 | 1·0714 | 1·0669 | 1·0625 | 1·0581 | 1·0537 | 1·0494 | 1·0450 | 1·0407 | 1·0364 | ·85 |
| ·15 | 1·0364 | 1·0322 | 1·0279 | 1·0237 | 1·0194 | 1·0152 | 1·0110 | 1·0069 | 1·0027 | 0·9986 | 0·9945 | ·84 |
| ·16 | 0·9945 | 0·9904 | 0·9863 | 0·9822 | 0·9782 | 0·9741 | 0·9701 | 0·9661 | 0·9621 | 0·9581 | 0·9542 | ·83 |
| ·17 | 0·9542 | 0·9502 | 0·9463 | 0·9424 | 0·9385 | 0·9346 | 0·9307 | 0·9269 | 0·9230 | 0·9192 | 0·9154 | ·82 |
| ·18 | 0·9154 | 0·9116 | 0·9078 | 0·9040 | 0·9002 | 0·8965 | 0·8927 | 0·8890 | 0·8853 | 0·8816 | 0·8779 | ·81 |
| ·19 | 0·8779 | 0·8742 | 0·8705 | 0·8669 | 0·8633 | 0·8596 | 0·8560 | 0·8524 | 0·8488 | 0·8452 | 0·8416 | ·80 |
| ·20 | 0·8416 | 0·8381 | 0·8345 | 0·8310 | 0·8274 | 0·8239 | 0·8204 | 0·8169 | 0·8134 | 0·8099 | 0·8064 | ·79 |
| ·21 | 0·8064 | 0·8030 | 0·7995 | 0·7961 | 0·7926 | 0·7892 | 0·7858 | 0·7824 | 0·7790 | 0·7756 | 0·7722 | ·78 |
| ·22 | 0·7722 | 0·7688 | 0·7655 | 0·7621 | 0·7588 | 0·7554 | 0·7521 | 0·7488 | 0·7454 | 0·7421 | 0·7388 | ·77 |
| ·23 | 0·7388 | 0·7356 | 0·7323 | 0·7290 | 0·7257 | 0·7225 | 0·7192 | 0·7160 | 0·7128 | 0·7095 | 0·7063 | ·76 |
| ·24 | 0·7063 | 0·7031 | 0·6999 | 0·6967 | 0·6935 | 0·6903 | 0·6871 | 0·6840 | 0·6808 | 0·6776 | 0·6745 | ·75 |
| ·25 | 0·6745 | 0·6713 | 0·6682 | 0·6651 | 0·6620 | 0·6588 | 0·6557 | 0·6526 | 0·6495 | 0·6464 | 0·6433 | ·74 |
| ·26 | 0·6433 | 0·6403 | 0·6372 | 0·6341 | 0·6311 | 0·6280 | 0·6250 | 0·6219 | 0·6189 | 0·6158 | 0·6128 | ·73 |
| ·27 | 0·6128 | 0·6098 | 0·6068 | 0·6038 | 0·6008 | 0·5978 | 0·5948 | 0·5918 | 0·5888 | 0·5858 | 0·5828 | ·72 |
| ·28 | 0·5828 | 0·5799 | 0·5769 | 0·5740 | 0·5710 | 0·5681 | 0·5651 | 0·5622 | 0·5592 | 0·5563 | 0·5534 | ·71 |
| ·29 | 0·5534 | 0·5505 | 0·5476 | 0·5446 | 0·5417 | 0·5388 | 0·5359 | 0·5330 | 0·5302 | 0·5273 | 0·5244 | ·70 |
| ·30 | 0·5244 | 0·5215 | 0·5187 | 0·5158 | 0·5129 | 0·5101 | 0·5072 | 0·5044 | 0·5015 | 0·4987 | 0·4959 | ·69 |
| ·31 | 0·4959 | 0·4930 | 0·4902 | 0·4874 | 0·4845 | 0·4817 | 0·4789 | 0·4761 | 0·4733 | 0·4705 | 0·4677 | ·68 |
| ·32 | 0·4677 | 0·4649 | 0·4621 | 0·4593 | 0·4565 | 0·4538 | 0·4510 | 0·4482 | 0·4454 | 0·4427 | 0·4399 | ·67 |
| ·33 | 0·4399 | 0·4372 | 0·4344 | 0·4316 | 0·4289 | 0·4261 | 0·4234 | 0·4207 | 0·4179 | 0·4152 | 0·4125 | ·66 |
| ·34 | 0·4125 | 0·4097 | 0·4070 | 0·4043 | 0·4016 | 0·3989 | 0·3961 | 0·3934 | 0·3907 | 0·3880 | 0·3853 | ·65 |
| ·35 | 0·3853 | 0·3826 | 0·3799 | 0·3772 | 0·3745 | 0·3719 | 0·3692 | 0·3665 | 0·3638 | 0·3611 | 0·3585 | ·64 |
| ·36 | 0·3585 | 0·3558 | 0·3531 | 0·3505 | 0·3478 | 0·3451 | 0·3425 | 0·3398 | 0·3372 | 0·3345 | 0·3319 | ·63 |
| ·37 | 0·3319 | 0·3292 | 0·3266 | 0·3239 | 0·3213 | 0·3186 | 0·3160 | 0·3134 | 0·3107 | 0·3081 | 0·3055 | ·62 |
| ·38 | 0·3055 | 0·3029 | 0·3002 | 0·2976 | 0·2950 | 0·2924 | 0·2898 | 0·2871 | 0·2845 | 0·2819 | 0·2793 | ·61 |
| ·39 | 0·2793 | 0·2767 | 0·2741 | 0·2715 | 0·2689 | 0·2663 | 0·2637 | 0·2611 | 0·2585 | 0·2559 | 0·2533 | ·60 |
| ·40 | 0·2533 | 0·2508 | 0·2482 | 0·2456 | 0·2430 | 0·2404 | 0·2378 | 0·2353 | 0·2327 | 0·2301 | 0·2275 | ·59 |
| ·41 | 0·2275 | 0·2250 | 0·2224 | 0·2198 | 0·2173 | 0·2147 | 0·2121 | 0·2096 | 0·2070 | 0·2045 | 0·2019 | ·58 |
| ·42 | 0·2019 | 0·1993 | 0·1968 | 0·1942 | 0·1917 | 0·1891 | 0·1866 | 0·1840 | 0·1815 | 0·1789 | 0·1764 | ·57 |
| ·43 | 0·1764 | 0·1738 | 0·1713 | 0·1687 | 0·1662 | 0·1637 | 0·1611 | 0·1586 | 0·1560 | 0·1535 | 0·1510 | ·56 |
| ·44 | 0·1510 | 0·1484 | 0·1459 | 0·1434 | 0·1408 | 0·1383 | 0·1358 | 0·1332 | 0·1307 | 0·1282 | 0·1257 | ·55 |
| ·45 | 0·1257 | 0·1231 | 0·1206 | 0·1181 | 0·1156 | 0·1130 | 0·1105 | 0·1080 | 0·1055 | 0·1030 | 0·1004 | ·54 |
| ·46 | 0·1004 | 0·0979 | 0·0954 | 0·0929 | 0·0904 | 0·0878 | 0·0853 | 0·0828 | 0·0803 | 0·0778 | 0·0753 | ·53 |
| ·47 | 0·0753 | 0·0728 | 0·0702 | 0·0677 | 0·0652 | 0·0627 | 0·0602 | 0·0577 | 0·0552 | 0·0527 | 0·0502 | ·52 |
| ·48 | 0·0502 | 0·0476 | 0·0451 | 0·0426 | 0·0401 | 0·0376 | 0·0351 | 0·0326 | 0·0301 | 0·0276 | 0·0251 | ·51 |
| ·49 | 0·0251 | 0·0226 | 0·0201 | 0·0175 | 0·0150 | 0·0125 | 0·0100 | 0·0075 | 0·0050 | 0·0025 | 0·0000 | ·50 |
| | ·010 | ·009 | ·008 | ·007 | ·006 | ·005 | ·004 | ·003 | ·002 | ·001 | ·000 | P |

Extreme values:

| Q | $10^{-4}$ | $10^{-5}$ | $10^{-6}$ | $10^{-7}$ | $10^{-8}$ | $10^{-9}$ |
|---|-----------|-----------|-----------|-----------|-----------|-----------|
| X | 3·7190 | 4·2649 | 4·7534 | 5·1993 | 5·6120 | 5·9978 |

For an extension in the range Q = 0·0000 (0·0001) 0·0200, see Table 3; also see Table 2.

# Table 5. *The Normal probability function. Values of Z in terms of Q and P*

| Q | ·000 | ·001 | ·002 | ·003 | ·004 | ·005 | ·006 | ·007 | ·008 | ·009 | ·010 | |
|---|------|------|------|------|------|------|------|------|------|------|------|---|
| ·00 | ·00000 | ·00337 | ·00634 | ·00915− | ·01185− | ·01446 | ·01700 | ·01949 | ·02192 | ·02431 | ·02665+ | ·99 |
| ·01 | ·02665+ | ·02896 | ·03123 | ·03348 | ·03569 | ·03787 | ·04003 | ·04216 | ·04427 | ·04635+ | ·04842 | ·98 |
| ·02 | ·04842 | ·05046 | ·05249 | ·05449 | ·05648 | ·05845+ | ·06040 | ·06233 | ·06425+ | ·06615+ | ·06804 | ·97 |
| ·03 | ·06804 | ·06992 | ·07177 | ·07362 | ·07545+ | ·07727 | ·07908 | ·08087 | ·08265+ | ·08442 | ·08617 | ·96 |
| ·04 | ·08617 | ·08792 | ·08965+ | ·09137 | ·09309 | ·09479 | ·09648 | ·09816 | ·09983 | ·10149 | ·10314 | ·95 |
| ·05 | ·10314 | ·10478 | ·10641 | ·10803 | ·10964 | ·11124 | ·11284 | ·11442 | ·11600 | ·11756 | ·11912 | ·94 |
| ·06 | ·11912 | ·12067 | ·12222 | ·12375− | ·12528 | ·12679 | ·12830 | ·12981 | ·13130 | ·13279 | ·13427 | ·93 |
| ·07 | ·13427 | ·13574 | ·13720 | ·13866 | ·14011 | ·14156 | ·14299 | ·14442 | ·14584 | ·14726 | ·14867 | ·92 |
| ·08 | ·14867 | ·15007 | ·15146 | ·15285+ | ·15423 | ·15561 | ·15698 | ·15834 | ·15970 | ·16105− | ·16239 | ·91 |
| ·09 | ·16239 | ·16373 | ·16506 | ·16639 | ·16770 | ·16902 | ·17033 | ·17163 | ·17292 | ·17421 | ·17550 | ·90 |
| ·10 | ·17550 | ·17678 | ·17805− | ·17932 | ·18058 | ·18184 | ·18309 | ·18433 | ·18557 | ·18681 | ·18804 | ·89 |
| ·11 | ·18804 | ·18926 | ·19048 | ·19169 | ·19290 | ·19410 | ·19530 | ·19649 | ·19768 | ·19886 | ·20004 | ·88 |
| ·12 | ·20004 | ·20121 | ·20238 | ·20354 | ·20470 | ·20585+ | ·20700 | ·20814 | ·20928 | ·21042 | ·21155− | ·87 |
| ·13 | ·21155− | ·21267 | ·21379 | ·21490 | ·21601 | ·21712 | ·21822 | ·21932 | ·22041 | ·22149 | ·22258 | ·86 |
| ·14 | ·22258 | ·22365+ | ·22473 | ·22580 | ·22686 | ·22792 | ·22898 | ·23003 | ·23108 | ·23212 | ·23316 | ·85 |
| ·15 | ·23316 | ·23419 | ·23522 | ·23625− | ·23727 | ·23829 | ·23930 | ·24031 | ·24131 | ·24232 | ·24331 | ·84 |
| ·16 | ·24331 | ·24430 | ·24529 | ·24627 | ·24726 | ·24823 | ·24921 | ·25017 | ·25114 | ·25210 | ·25305+ | ·83 |
| ·17 | ·25305+ | ·25401 | ·25495+ | ·25590 | ·25684 | ·25778 | ·25871 | ·25964 | ·26056 | ·26148 | ·26240 | ·82 |
| ·18 | ·26240 | ·26331 | ·26422 | ·26513 | ·26603 | ·26693 | ·26782 | ·26871 | ·26960 | ·27049 | ·27137 | ·81 |
| ·19 | ·27137 | ·27224 | ·27311 | ·27398 | ·27485− | ·27571 | ·27657 | ·27742 | ·27827 | ·27912 | ·27996 | ·80 |
| ·20 | ·27996 | ·28080 | ·28164 | ·28247 | ·28330 | ·28413 | ·28495− | ·28577 | ·28658 | ·28739 | ·28820 | ·79 |
| ·21 | ·28820 | ·28901 | ·28981 | ·29060 | ·29140 | ·29219 | ·29298 | ·29376 | ·29454 | ·29532 | ·29609 | ·78 |
| ·22 | ·29609 | ·29686 | ·29763 | ·29840 | ·29916 | ·29991 | ·30067 | ·30142 | ·30216 | ·30291 | ·30365− | ·77 |
| ·23 | ·30365− | ·30439 | ·30512 | ·30585− | ·30658 | ·30730 | ·30802 | ·30874 | ·30945+ | ·31017 | ·31087 | ·76 |
| ·24 | ·31087 | ·31158 | ·31228 | ·31298 | ·31367 | ·31436 | ·31505+ | ·31574 | ·31642 | ·31710 | ·31778 | ·75 |
| ·25 | ·31778 | ·31845− | ·31912 | ·31979 | ·32045− | ·32111 | ·32177 | ·32242 | ·32307 | ·32372 | ·32437 | ·74 |
| ·26 | ·32437 | ·32501 | ·32565− | ·32628 | ·32691 | ·32754 | ·32817 | ·32879 | ·32941 | ·33003 | ·33065− | ·73 |
| ·27 | ·33065− | ·33126 | ·33187 | ·33247 | ·33307 | ·33367 | ·33427 | ·33486 | ·33545+ | ·33604 | ·33662 | ·72 |
| ·28 | ·33662 | ·33720 | ·33778 | ·33836 | ·33893 | ·33950 | ·34007 | ·34063 | ·34119 | ·34175− | ·34230 | ·71 |
| ·29 | ·34230 | ·34286 | ·34341 | ·34395+ | ·34449 | ·34503 | ·34557 | ·34611 | ·34664 | ·34717 | ·34769 | ·70 |
| ·30 | ·34769 | ·34822 | ·34874 | ·34925+ | ·34977 | ·35028 | ·35079 | ·35129 | ·35180 | ·35230 | ·35279 | ·69 |
| ·31 | ·35279 | ·35329 | ·35378 | ·35427 | ·35475+ | ·35524 | ·35572 | ·35620 | ·35667 | ·35714 | ·35761 | ·68 |
| ·32 | ·35761 | ·35808 | ·35854 | ·35900 | ·35946 | ·35991 | ·36037 | ·36082 | ·36126 | ·36171 | ·36215− | ·67 |
| ·33 | ·36215− | ·36259 | ·36302 | ·36346 | ·36389 | ·36431 | ·36474 | ·36516 | ·36558 | ·36600 | ·36641 | ·66 |
| ·34 | ·36641 | ·36682 | ·36723 | ·36764 | ·36804 | ·36844 | ·36884 | ·36923 | ·36962 | ·37001 | ·37040 | ·65 |
| ·35 | ·37040 | ·37078 | ·37116 | ·37154 | ·37192 | ·37229 | ·37266 | ·37303 | ·37340 | ·37376 | ·37412 | ·64 |
| ·36 | ·37412 | ·37447 | ·37483 | ·37518 | ·37553 | ·37588 | ·37622 | ·37656 | ·37690 | ·37724 | ·37757 | ·63 |
| ·37 | ·37757 | ·37790 | ·37823 | ·37855+ | ·37888 | ·37920 | ·37951 | ·37983 | ·38014 | ·38045− | ·38076 | ·62 |
| ·38 | ·38076 | ·38106 | ·38136 | ·38166 | ·38196 | ·38225+ | ·38254 | ·38283 | ·38312 | ·38340 | ·38368 | ·61 |
| ·39 | ·38368 | ·38396 | ·38423 | ·38451 | ·38478 | ·38504 | ·38531 | ·38557 | ·38583 | ·38609 | ·38634 | ·60 |
| ·40 | ·38634 | ·38659 | ·38684 | ·38709 | ·38734 | ·38758 | ·38782 | ·38805+ | ·38829 | ·38852 | ·38875− | ·59 |
| ·41 | ·38875− | ·38897 | ·38920 | ·38942 | ·38964 | ·38986 | ·39007 | ·39028 | ·39048 | ·39069 | ·39089 | ·58 |
| ·42 | ·39089 | ·39109 | ·39129 | ·39149 | ·39168 | ·39187 | ·39206 | ·39224 | ·39243 | ·39261 | ·39279 | ·57 |
| ·43 | ·39279 | ·39296 | ·39313 | ·39330 | ·39347 | ·39364 | ·39380 | ·39396 | ·39411 | ·39427 | ·39442 | ·56 |
| ·44 | ·39442 | ·39457 | ·39472 | ·39486 | ·39501 | ·39514 | ·39528 | ·39542 | ·39555− | ·39568 | ·39580 | ·55 |
| ·45 | ·39580 | ·39593 | ·39605+ | ·39617 | ·39629 | ·39640 | ·39651 | ·39662 | ·39673 | ·39683 | ·39694 | ·54 |
| ·46 | ·39694 | ·39703 | ·39713 | ·39723 | ·39732 | ·39741 | ·39749 | ·39758 | ·39766 | ·39774 | ·39781 | ·53 |
| ·47 | ·39781 | ·39789 | ·39796 | ·39803 | ·39809 | ·39816 | ·39822 | ·39828 | ·39834 | ·39839 | ·39844 | ·52 |
| ·48 | ·39844 | ·39849 | ·39854 | ·39858 | ·39862 | ·39866 | ·39870 | ·39873 | ·39876 | ·39879 | ·39882 | ·51 |
| ·49 | ·39882 | ·39884 | ·39886 | ·39888 | ·39890 | ·39891 | ·39892 | ·39893 | ·39894 | ·39894 | ·39894 | ·50 |
| | ·010 | ·009 | ·008 | ·007 | ·006 | ·005 | ·004 | ·003 | ·002 | ·001 | ·000 | P |

Table 6. *The Normal probability function. Table for probit analysis*

| Proportion P | Expected probit Y | Maximum working probit Y+Q/Z | Minimum working probit Y−P/Z | Range 1/Z | Weighting coefficient Z²/PQ | | | |
|---|---|---|---|---|---|---|---|---|
| 0·500 | 5·00 | 6·2533 | 3·7467 | 2·5066 | 0·6366 | 6·2533 | 3·7467 | 5·00 |
| ·504 | ·01 | ·2534 | ·7466 | ·5068 | ·6366 | ·2534 | ·7466 | 4·99 |
| ·508 | ·02 | ·2536 | ·7465 | ·5071 | ·6365 | ·2535 | ·7464 | ·98 |
| ·512 | ·03 | ·2539 | ·7461 | ·5078 | ·6364 | ·2539 | ·7461 | ·97 |
| ·516 | ·04 | ·2543 | ·7457 | ·5086 | ·6362 | ·2543 | ·7457 | ·96 |
| 0·520 | 5·05 | 6·2548 | 3·7450 | 2·5098 | 0·6360 | 6·2550 | 3·7452 | 4·95 |
| ·524 | ·06 | ·2555 | ·7444 | ·5111 | ·6358 | ·2556 | ·7445 | ·94 |
| ·528 | ·07 | ·2563 | ·7435 | ·5128 | ·6355 | ·2565 | ·7437 | ·93 |
| ·532 | ·08 | ·2572 | ·7425 | ·5147 | ·6351 | ·2575 | ·7428 | ·92 |
| ·536 | ·09 | ·2582 | ·7414 | ·5168 | ·6347 | ·2586 | ·7418 | ·91 |
| 0·540 | 5·10 | 6·2593 | 3·7401 | 2·5192 | 0·6343 | 6·2599 | 3·7407 | 4·90 |
| ·544 | ·11 | ·2605 | ·7387 | ·5218 | ·6338 | ·2613 | ·7395 | ·89 |
| ·548 | ·12 | ·2618 | ·7371 | ·5247 | ·6333 | ·2629 | ·7382 | ·88 |
| ·552 | ·13 | ·2632 | ·7353 | ·5279 | ·6327 | ·2647 | ·7368 | ·87 |
| ·556 | ·14 | ·2647 | ·7334 | ·5313 | ·6321 | ·2666 | ·7353 | ·86 |
| 0·560 | 5·15 | 6·2664 | 3·7314 | 2·5350 | 0·6314 | 6·2686 | 3·7336 | 4·85 |
| ·564 | ·16 | ·2681 | ·7292 | ·5389 | ·6307 | ·2708 | ·7319 | ·84 |
| ·567 | ·17 | ·2699 | ·7268 | ·5431 | ·6300 | ·2732 | ·7301 | ·83 |
| ·571 | ·18 | ·2718 | ·7242 | ·5476 | ·6292 | ·2758 | ·7282 | ·82 |
| ·575 | ·19 | ·2738 | ·7215 | ·5523 | ·6283 | ·2785 | ·7262 | ·81 |
| 0·579 | 5·20 | 6·2759 | 3·7186 | 2·5573 | 0·6274 | 6·2814 | 3·7241 | 4·80 |
| ·583 | ·21 | ·2781 | ·7156 | ·5625 | ·6265 | ·2844 | ·7219 | ·79 |
| ·587 | ·22 | ·2804 | ·7124 | ·5680 | ·6255 | ·2876 | ·7196 | ·78 |
| ·591 | ·23 | ·2828 | ·7090 | ·5738 | ·6245 | ·2910 | ·7172 | ·77 |
| ·595 | ·24 | ·2853 | ·7054 | ·5799 | ·6234 | ·2946 | ·7147 | ·76 |
| 0·599 | 5·25 | 6·2878 | 3·7016 | 2·5862 | 0·6223 | 6·2984 | 3·7122 | 4·75 |
| ·603 | ·26 | ·2905 | ·6977 | ·5928 | ·6211 | ·3023 | ·7095 | ·74 |
| ·606 | ·27 | ·2932 | ·6935 | ·5997 | ·6199 | ·3065 | ·7068 | ·73 |
| ·610 | ·28 | ·2960 | ·6892 | ·6068 | ·6187 | ·3108 | ·7040 | ·72 |
| ·614 | ·29 | ·2989 | ·6846 | ·6143 | ·6174 | ·3154 | ·7011 | ·71 |
| 0·618 | 5·30 | 6·3018 | 3·6798 | 2·6220 | 0·6161 | 6·3202 | 3·6982 | 4·70 |
| ·622 | ·31 | ·3049 | ·6749 | ·6300 | ·6147 | ·3251 | ·6951 | ·69 |
| ·626 | ·32 | ·3080 | ·6697 | ·6383 | ·6133 | ·3303 | ·6920 | ·68 |
| ·629 | ·33 | ·3112 | ·6643 | ·6469 | ·6119 | ·3357 | ·6888 | ·67 |
| ·633 | ·34 | ·3145 | ·6587 | ·6558 | ·6104 | ·3413 | ·6855 | ·66 |
| 0·637 | 5·35 | 6·3178 | 3·6528 | 2·6650 | 0·6088 | 6·3472 | 3·6822 | 4·65 |
| ·641 | ·36 | ·3213 | ·6469 | ·6744 | ·6072 | ·3531 | ·6787 | ·64 |
| ·644 | ·37 | ·3248 | ·6406 | ·6842 | ·6056 | ·3594 | ·6752 | ·63 |
| ·648 | ·38 | ·3283 | ·6340 | ·6943 | ·6040 | ·3660 | ·6717 | ·62 |
| ·652 | ·39 | ·3320 | ·6273 | ·7047 | ·6023 | ·3727 | ·6680 | ·61 |
| 0·655 | 5·40 | 6·3357 | 3·6203 | 2·7154 | 0·6005 | 6·3797 | 3·6643 | 4·60 |
| ·659 | ·41 | ·3394 | ·6130 | ·7264 | ·5987 | ·3870 | ·6606 | ·59 |
| ·663 | ·42 | ·3433 | ·6055 | ·7378 | ·5969 | ·3945 | ·6567 | ·58 |
| ·666 | ·43 | ·3472 | ·5978 | ·7494 | ·5951 | ·4022 | ·6528 | ·57 |
| ·670 | ·44 | ·3512 | ·5898 | ·7614 | ·5932 | ·4102 | ·6488 | ·56 |
| 0·674 | 5·45 | 6·3552 | 3·5815 | 2·7737 | 0·5912 | 6·4185 | 3·6448 | 4·55 |
| ·677 | ·46 | ·3593 | ·5729 | ·7864 | ·5893 | ·4271 | ·6407 | ·54 |
| ·681 | ·47 | ·3635 | ·5641 | ·7994 | ·5872 | ·4359 | ·6365 | ·53 |
| ·684 | ·48 | ·3677 | ·5550 | ·8127 | ·5852 | ·4450 | ·6323 | ·52 |
| ·688 | ·49 | ·3720 | ·5456 | ·8264 | ·5831 | ·4544 | ·6280 | ·51 |
| 0·691 | 5·50 | 6·3764 | 3·5360 | 2·8404 | 0·5810 | 6·4640 | 3·6236 | 4·50 |

$Z = e^{-\frac{1}{2}X^2}/\sqrt{(2\pi)}$

$Y = X + 5$

$P = 1 - Q = \int_{-\infty}^{X} Z(u)\,du$

| 1/Z Range | Z²/PQ Weighting coefficient | Y+Q/Z Maximum working probit | Y−P/Z Minimum working probit | Y Expected probit |
|---|---|---|---|---|

# Table 6 (continued)

| Proportion P | Expected probit Y | Maximum working probit Y+Q/Z | Minimum working probit Y−P/Z | Range 1/Z | Weighting coefficient Z²/PQ | | | |
|---|---|---|---|---|---|---|---|---|
| 0·691 | 5·50 | 6·3764 | 3·5360 | 2·8404 | 0·5810 | 6·4640 | 3·6236 | 4·50 |
| ·695 | ·51 | ·3808 | ·5260 | ·8548 | ·5788 | ·4740 | ·6192 | ·49 |
| ·698 | ·52 | ·3852 | ·5157 | ·8695 | ·5766 | ·4843 | ·6148 | ·48 |
| ·702 | ·53 | ·3898 | ·5052 | ·8846 | ·5744 | ·4948 | ·6102 | ·47 |
| ·705 | ·54 | ·3944 | ·4943 | ·9001 | ·5722 | ·5057 | ·6056 | ·46 |
| 0·709 | 5·55 | 6·3990 | 3·4831 | 2·9159 | 0·5699 | 6·5169 | 3·6010 | 4·45 |
| ·712 | ·56 | ·4037 | ·4715 | ·9322 | ·5675 | ·5285 | ·5963 | ·44 |
| ·716 | ·57 | ·4085 | ·4597 | ·9488 | ·5652 | ·5403 | ·5915 | ·43 |
| ·719 | ·58 | ·4133 | ·4475 | ·9658 | ·5628 | ·5525 | ·5867 | ·42 |
| ·722 | ·59 | ·4181 | ·4349 | ·9832 | ·5603 | ·5651 | ·5819 | ·41 |
| 0·726 | 5·60 | 6·4230 | 3·4220 | 3·0010 | 0·5579 | 6·5780 | 3·5770 | 4·40 |
| ·729 | ·61 | ·4280 | ·4088 | ·0192 | ·5554 | ·5912 | ·5720 | ·39 |
| ·732 | ·62 | ·4330 | ·3952 | ·0378 | ·5529 | ·6048 | ·5670 | ·38 |
| ·736 | ·63 | ·4381 | ·3812 | ·0569 | ·5503 | ·6188 | ·5619 | ·37 |
| ·739 | ·64 | ·4432 | ·3669 | ·0763 | ·5477 | ·6331 | ·5568 | ·36 |
| 0·742 | 5·65 | 6·4484 | 3·3522 | 3·0962 | 0·5451 | 6·6478 | 3·5516 | 4·35 |
| ·745 | ·66 | ·4536 | ·3370 | ·1166 | ·5425 | ·6630 | ·5464 | ·34 |
| ·749 | ·67 | ·4588 | ·3214 | ·1374 | ·5398 | ·6786 | ·5412 | ·33 |
| ·752 | ·68 | ·4641 | ·3055 | ·1586 | ·5371 | ·6945 | ·5359 | ·32 |
| ·755 | ·69 | ·4695 | ·2892 | ·1803 | ·5343 | ·7108 | ·5305 | ·31 |
| 0·758 | 5·70 | 6·4749 | 3·2724 | 3·2025 | 0·5316 | 6·7276 | 3·5251 | 4·30 |
| ·761 | ·71 | ·4803 | ·2551 | ·2252 | ·5288 | ·7449 | ·5197 | ·29 |
| ·764 | ·72 | ·4858 | ·2375 | ·2483 | ·5260 | ·7625 | ·5142 | ·28 |
| ·767 | ·73 | ·4914 | ·2194 | ·2720 | ·5232 | ·7806 | ·5086 | ·27 |
| ·770 | ·74 | ·4969 | ·2008 | ·2961 | ·5203 | ·7992 | ·5031 | ·26 |
| 0·773 | 5·75 | 6·5026 | 3·1819 | 3·3207 | 0·5174 | 6·8181 | 3·4974 | 4·25 |
| ·776 | ·76 | ·5082 | ·1623 | ·3459 | ·5145 | ·8377 | ·4918 | ·24 |
| ·779 | ·77 | ·5139 | ·1423 | ·3716 | ·5116 | ·8577 | ·4861 | ·23 |
| ·782 | ·78 | ·5197 | ·1219 | ·3978 | ·5086 | ·8781 | ·4803 | ·22 |
| ·785 | ·79 | ·5255 | ·1009 | ·4246 | ·5056 | ·8991 | ·4745 | ·21 |
| 0·788 | 5·80 | 6·5313 | 3·0794 | 3·4519 | 0·5026 | 6·9206 | 3·4687 | 4·20 |
| ·791 | ·81 | ·5372 | ·0574 | ·4798 | ·4996 | ·9426 | ·4628 | ·19 |
| ·794 | ·82 | ·5431 | ·0348 | ·5083 | ·4965 | ·9652 | ·4569 | ·18 |
| ·797 | ·83 | ·5490 | ·0116 | ·5374 | ·4935 | ·9884 | ·4510 | ·17 |
| ·800 | ·84 | ·5550 | 2·9880 | ·5670 | ·4904 | 7·0120 | ·4450 | ·16 |
| 0·802 | 5·85 | 6·5611 | 2·9638 | 3·5973 | 0·4873 | 7·0362 | 3·4389 | 4·15 |
| ·805 | ·86 | ·5671 | ·9389 | ·6282 | ·4841 | ·0611 | ·4329 | ·14 |
| ·808 | ·87 | ·5732 | ·9135 | ·6597 | ·4810 | ·0865 | ·4268 | ·13 |
| ·811 | ·88 | ·5794 | ·8875 | ·6919 | ·4778 | ·1125 | ·4206 | ·12 |
| ·813 | ·89 | ·5855 | ·8608 | ·7247 | ·4746 | ·1392 | ·4145 | ·11 |
| 0·816 | 5·90 | 6·5917 | 2·8335 | 3·7582 | 0·4714 | 7·1665 | 3·4083 | 4·10 |
| ·819 | ·91 | ·5980 | ·8056 | ·7924 | ·4682 | ·1944 | ·4020 | ·09 |
| ·821 | ·92 | ·6043 | ·7771 | ·8272 | ·4650 | ·2229 | ·3957 | ·08 |
| ·824 | ·93 | ·6106 | ·7478 | ·8628 | ·4617 | ·2522 | ·3894 | ·07 |
| ·826 | ·94 | ·6169 | ·7178 | ·8991 | ·4585 | ·2822 | ·3831 | ·06 |
| 0·829 | 5·95 | 6·6233 | 2·6872 | 3·9361 | 0·4552 | 7·3128 | 3·3767 | 4·05 |
| ·831 | ·96 | ·6297 | ·6558 | ·9739 | ·4519 | ·3442 | ·3703 | ·04 |
| ·834 | ·97 | ·6362 | ·6238 | 4·0124 | ·4486 | ·3762 | ·3638 | ·03 |
| ·836 | ·98 | ·6426 | ·5909 | ·0517 | ·4453 | ·4091 | ·3574 | ·02 |
| ·839 | ·99 | ·6491 | ·5573 | ·0918 | ·4420 | ·4427 | ·3509 | ·01 |
| 0·841 | 6·00 | 6·6557 | 2·5230 | 4·1327 | 0·4386 | 7·4770 | 3·3443 | 4·00 |
| | | | | 1/Z Range | Z²/PQ Weighting coefficient | Y+Q/Z Maximum working probit | Y−P/Z Minimum working probit | Y Expected probit |

$$Z = e^{-\frac{1}{2}X^2}/\sqrt{(2\pi)}$$
$$Y = X + 5$$
$$P = 1 - Q = \int_{-\infty}^{X} Z(u)\, du$$

Table 6. *Table for probit analysis (continued)*

| Proportion P | Expected probit Y | Maximum working probit Y+Q/Z | Minimum working probit Y−P/Z | Range 1/Z | Weighting coefficient Z²/PQ | Y+Q/Z | Y−P/Z | Y |
|---|---|---|---|---|---|---|---|---|
| 0·841 | 6·00 | 6·6557 | 2·5230 | 4·1327 | 0·4386 | 7·4770 | 3·3443 | 4·00 |
| ·844 | ·01 | ·6623 | ·4878 | ·1745 | ·4353 | ·5122 | ·3377 | 3·99 |
| ·846 | ·02 | ·6689 | ·4518 | ·2171 | ·4319 | ·5482 | ·3311 | ·98 |
| ·848 | ·03 | ·6755 | ·4150 | ·2605 | ·4285 | ·5850 | ·3245 | ·97 |
| ·851 | ·04 | ·6822 | ·3774 | ·3048 | ·4252 | ·6226 | ·3178 | ·96 |
| 0·853 | 6·05 | 6·6888 | 2·3387 | 4·3501 | 0·4218 | 7·6613 | 3·3112 | 3·95 |
| ·855 | ·06 | ·6956 | ·2994 | ·3962 | ·4184 | ·7006 | ·3044 | ·94 |
| ·858 | ·07 | ·7023 | ·2590 | ·4433 | ·4150 | ·7410 | ·2977 | ·93 |
| ·860 | ·08 | ·7091 | ·2178 | ·4913 | ·4116 | ·7822 | ·2909 | ·92 |
| ·862 | ·09 | ·7159 | ·1756 | ·5403 | ·4082 | ·8244 | ·2841 | ·91 |
| 0·864 | 6·10 | 6·7227 | 2·1324 | 4·5903 | 0·4047 | 7·8676 | 3·2773 | 3·90 |
| ·867 | ·11 | ·7296 | ·0883 | ·6413 | ·4013 | ·9117 | ·2704 | ·89 |
| ·869 | ·12 | ·7365 | ·0432 | ·6933 | ·3979 | ·9568 | ·2635 | ·88 |
| ·871 | ·13 | ·7434 | 1·9970 | ·7464 | ·3944 | 8·0030 | ·2566 | ·87 |
| ·873 | ·14 | ·7504 | ·9498 | ·8006 | ·3910 | ·0502 | ·2496 | ·86 |
| 0·875 | 6·15 | 6·7573 | 1·9014 | 4·8559 | 0·3876 | 8·0986 | 3·2427 | 3·85 |
| ·877 | ·16 | ·7643 | ·8520 | ·9123 | ·3841 | ·1480 | ·2357 | ·84 |
| ·879 | ·17 | ·7714 | ·8016 | ·9698 | ·3807 | ·1984 | ·2286 | ·83 |
| ·881 | ·18 | ·7784 | ·7498 | 5·0286 | ·3772 | ·2502 | ·2216 | ·82 |
| ·883 | ·19 | ·7855 | ·6970 | ·0885 | ·3738 | ·3030 | ·2145 | ·81 |
| 0·885 | 6·20 | 6·7926 | 1·6429 | 5·1497 | 0·3703 | 8·3571 | 3·2074 | 3·80 |
| ·887 | ·21 | ·7997 | ·5876 | ·2121 | ·3669 | ·4124 | ·2003 | ·79 |
| ·889 | ·22 | ·8068 | ·5310 | ·2758 | ·3634 | ·4690 | ·1932 | ·78 |
| ·891 | ·23 | ·8140 | ·4731 | ·3409 | ·3600 | ·5269 | ·1860 | ·77 |
| ·893 | ·24 | ·8212 | ·4140 | ·4072 | ·3565 | ·5860 | ·1788 | ·76 |
| 0·894 | 6·25 | 6·8284 | 1·3534 | 5·4750 | 0·3531 | 8·6466 | 3·1716 | 3·75 |
| ·896 | ·26 | ·8357 | ·2916 | ·5441 | ·3496 | ·7084 | ·1643 | ·74 |
| ·898 | ·27 | ·8429 | ·2282 | ·6147 | ·3462 | ·7718 | ·1571 | ·73 |
| ·900 | ·28 | ·8502 | ·1635 | ·6867 | ·3428 | ·8365 | ·1498 | ·72 |
| ·901 | ·29 | ·8575 | ·0972 | ·7603 | ·3393 | ·9028 | ·1425 | ·71 |
| 0·903 | 6·30 | 6·8649 | 1·0295 | 5·8354 | 0·3359 | 8·9705 | 3·1351 | 3·70 |
| ·905 | ·31 | ·8722 | 0·9602 | ·9120 | ·3325 | 9·0398 | ·1278 | ·69 |
| ·907 | ·32 | ·8796 | ·8893 | ·9903 | ·3291 | ·1107 | ·1204 | ·68 |
| ·908 | ·33 | ·8870 | ·8168 | 6·0702 | ·3256 | ·1832 | ·1130 | ·67 |
| ·910 | ·34 | ·8944 | ·7426 | ·1518 | ·3222 | ·2574 | ·1056 | ·66 |
| 0·911 | 6·35 | 6·9019 | 0·6668 | 6·2351 | 0·3188 | 9·3332 | 3·0981 | 3·65 |
| ·913 | ·36 | ·9093 | ·5892 | ·3201 | ·3155 | ·4108 | ·0907 | ·64 |
| ·915 | ·37 | ·9168 | ·5098 | ·4070 | ·3121 | ·4902 | ·0832 | ·63 |
| ·916 | ·38 | ·9243 | ·4286 | ·4957 | ·3087 | ·5714 | ·0757 | ·62 |
| ·918 | ·39 | ·9318 | ·3455 | ·5863 | ·3053 | ·6545 | ·0682 | ·61 |
| 0·919 | 6·40 | 6·9394 | 0·2606 | 6·6788 | 0·3020 | 9·7394 | 3·0606 | 3·60 |
| ·921 | ·41 | ·9469 | ·1736 | ·7733 | ·2986 | ·8264 | ·0531 | ·59 |
| ·922 | ·42 | ·9545 | ·0847 | ·8698 | ·2953 | ·9153 | ·0455 | ·58 |
| ·924 | ·43 | ·9621 | | ·9684 | ·2920 | | ·0379 | ·57 |
| ·925 | ·44 | ·9697 | | 7·0691 | ·2887 | | ·0303 | ·56 |
| 0·926 | 6·45 | 6·9774 | | 7·1720 | 0·2854 | | 3·0226 | 3·55 |
| ·928 | ·46 | ·9850 | | ·2771 | ·2821 | | ·0150 | ·54 |
| ·929 | ·47 | 6·9927 | | ·3845 | ·2788 | | ·0073 | ·53 |
| ·931 | ·48 | 7·0004 | | ·4943 | ·2756 | | 2·9996 | ·52 |
| ·932 | ·49 | ·0081 | | ·6064 | ·2723 | | ·9919 | ·51 |
| 0·933 | 6·50 | 7·0158 | | 7·7210 | 0·2691 | | 2·9842 | 3·50 |

$$Z = e^{-\frac{1}{2}X^2}/\surd(2\pi)$$
$$Y = X + 5$$
$$P = 1 - Q = \int_{-\infty}^{X} Z(u)\,du$$

| 1/Z Range | Z²/PQ Weighting coefficient | Y+Q/Z Maximum working probit | Y−P/Z Minimum working probit | Y Expected probit |
|---|---|---|---|---|

Table 6 (continued)

| Proportion $P$ | Expected probit $Y$ | Maximum working probit $Y + Q/Z$ | Range $1/Z$ | Weighting coefficient $Z^2/PQ$ | | |
|---|---|---|---|---|---|---|
| 0·9332 | 6·50 | 7·0158 | 7·7210 | 0·2691 | 2·9842 | 3·50 |
| 345 | ·51 | ·0236 | ·8380 | ·2658 | ·9764 | ·49 |
| 357 | ·52 | ·0313 | ·9577 | ·2626 | ·9687 | ·48 |
| 370 | ·53 | ·0391 | 8·0800 | ·2594 | ·9609 | ·47 |
| 382 | ·54 | ·0469 | ·2050 | ·2563 | ·9531 | ·46 |
| 0·9394 | 6·55 | 7·0547 | 8·3327 | 0·2531 | 2·9453 | 3·45 |
| 406 | ·56 | ·0625 | ·4633 | ·2500 | ·9375 | ·44 |
| 418 | ·57 | ·0704 | ·5968 | ·2468 | ·9296 | ·43 |
| 429 | ·58 | ·0783 | ·7333 | ·2437 | ·9217 | ·42 |
| 441 | ·59 | ·0861 | ·8728 | ·2406 | ·9139 | ·41 |
| 0·9452 | 6·60 | 7·0940 | 9·0154 | 0·2375 | 2·9060 | 3·40 |
| 463 | ·61 | ·1020 | ·1613 | ·2345 | ·8980 | ·39 |
| 474 | ·62 | ·1099 | ·3105 | ·2314 | ·8901 | ·38 |
| 484 | ·63 | ·1178 | ·4630 | ·2284 | ·8822 | ·37 |
| 495 | ·64 | ·1258 | ·6190 | ·2254 | ·8742 | ·36 |
| 0·9505 | 6·65 | 7·1338 | 9·7785 | 0·2224 | 2·8662 | 3·35 |
| 515 | ·66 | ·1417 | ·9417 | ·2194 | ·8583 | ·34 |
| 525 | ·67 | ·1498 | 10·1086 | ·2165 | ·8502 | ·33 |
| 535 | ·68 | ·1578 | 10·2794 | ·2135 | ·8422 | ·32 |
| 545 | ·69 | ·1658 | 10·4540 | ·2106 | ·8342 | ·31 |
| 0·9554 | 6·70 | 7·1739 | 10·6327 | 0·2077 | 2·8261 | 3·30 |
| 564 | ·71 | ·1819 | 10·8156 | ·2049 | ·8181 | ·29 |
| 573 | ·72 | ·1900 | 11·0027 | ·2020 | ·8100 | ·28 |
| 582 | ·73 | ·1981 | 11·1941 | ·1992 | ·8019 | ·27 |
| 591 | ·74 | ·2062 | 11·3900 | ·1964 | ·7938 | ·26 |
| 0·9599 | 6·75 | 7·2143 | 11·5905 | 0·1936 | 2·7857 | 3·25 |
| 608 | ·76 | ·2224 | 11·7957 | ·1908 | ·7776 | ·24 |
| 616 | ·77 | ·2306 | 12·0058 | ·1881 | ·7694 | ·23 |
| 625 | ·78 | ·2387 | 12·2208 | ·1853 | ·7613 | ·22 |
| 633 | ·79 | ·2469 | 12·4409 | ·1826 | ·7531 | ·21 |
| 0·9641 | 6·80 | 7·2551 | 12·6662 | 0·1799 | 2·7449 | 3·20 |
| 649 | ·81 | ·2633 | 12·8969 | ·1773 | ·7367 | ·19 |
| 656 | ·82 | ·2715 | 13·1331 | ·1746 | ·7285 | ·18 |
| 664 | ·83 | ·2797 | 13·3750 | ·1720 | ·7203 | ·17 |
| 671 | ·84 | ·2880 | 13·6227 | ·1694 | ·7120 | ·16 |
| 0·9678 | 6·85 | 7·2962 | 13·8764 | 0·1669 | 2·7038 | 3·15 |
| 686 | ·86 | ·3045 | 14·1362 | ·1643 | ·6955 | ·14 |
| 693 | ·87 | ·3128 | 14·4023 | ·1618 | ·6872 | ·13 |
| 699 | ·88 | ·3210 | 14·6749 | ·1593 | ·6790 | ·12 |
| 706 | ·89 | ·3293 | 14·9541 | ·1568 | ·6707 | ·11 |
| 0·9713 | 6·90 | 7·3376 | 15·2402 | 0·1544 | 2·6624 | 3·10 |
| 719 | ·91 | ·3460 | 15·5333 | ·1519 | ·6540 | ·09 |
| 726 | ·92 | ·3543 | 15·8337 | ·1495 | ·6457 | ·08 |
| 732 | ·93 | ·3626 | 16·1414 | ·1471 | ·6374 | ·07 |
| 738 | ·94 | ·3710 | 16·4568 | ·1448 | ·6290 | ·06 |
| 0·9744 | 6·95 | 7·3794 | 16·7800 | 0·1424 | 2·6206 | 3·05 |
| 750 | ·96 | ·3877 | 17·1113 | ·1401 | ·6123 | ·04 |
| 756 | ·97 | ·3961 | 17·4509 | ·1378 | ·6039 | ·03 |
| 761 | ·98 | ·4045 | 17·7989 | ·1356 | ·5955 | ·02 |
| 767 | ·99 | ·4129 | 18·1558 | ·1333 | ·5871 | ·01 |
| 0·9772 | 7·00 | 7·4214 | 18·5216 | 0·1311 | 2·5786 | 3·00 |
| | $Z = e^{-\frac{1}{2}X^2}/\sqrt{(2\pi)}$ $Y = X + 5$ $P = 1 - Q = \int_{-\infty}^{X} Z(u)\,du$ | | $1/Z$ Range | $Z^2/PQ$ Weighting coefficient | $Y - P/Z$ Minimum working probit | $Y$ Expected probit |

16-2

Table 6. *Table for probit analysis (continued)*

| Proportion $P$ | Expected probit $Y$ | Maximum working probit $Y+Q/Z$ | Range $1/Z$ | Weighting coefficient $Z^2/PQ$ | | |
|---|---|---|---|---|---|---|
| 0·9772 | **7·00** | 7·4214 | 18·5216 | 0·1311 | 2·5786 | **3·00** |
| 778 | ·01 | ·4298 | 18·8967 | ·1289 | ·5702 | 2·99 |
| 783 | ·02 | ·4382 | 19·2814 | ·1268 | ·5618 | ·98 |
| 788 | ·03 | ·4467 | 19·6758 | ·1246 | ·5533 | ·97 |
| 793 | ·04 | ·4552 | 20·0803 | ·1225 | ·5448 | ·96 |
| 0·9798 | **7·05** | 7·4636 | 20·4952 | 0·1204 | 2·5364 | **2·95** |
| 803 | ·06 | ·4721 | 20·9207 | ·1183 | ·5279 | ·94 |
| 808 | ·07 | ·4806 | 21·3572 | ·1163 | ·5194 | ·93 |
| 812 | ·08 | ·4891 | 21·8050 | ·1142 | ·5109 | ·92 |
| 817 | ·09 | ·4976 | 22·2644 | ·1122 | ·5024 | ·91 |
| 0·9821 | **7·10** | 7·5062 | 22·7357 | 0·1103 | 2·4938 | **2·90** |
| 826 | ·11 | ·5147 | 23·2194 | ·1083 | ·4853 | ·89 |
| 830 | ·12 | ·5232 | 23·7157 | ·1064 | ·4768 | ·88 |
| 834 | ·13 | ·5318 | 24·2251 | ·1045 | ·4682 | ·87 |
| 838 | ·14 | ·5404 | 24·7478 | ·1026 | ·4596 | ·86 |
| 0·9842 | **7·15** | 7·5489 | 25·2844 | 0·1007 | 2·4511 | **2·85** |
| 846 | ·16 | ·5575 | 25·8352 | ·0989 | ·4425 | ·84 |
| 850 | ·17 | ·5661 | 26·4006 | ·0971 | ·4339 | ·83 |
| 854 | ·18 | ·5747 | 26·9812 | ·0953 | ·4253 | ·82 |
| 857 | ·19 | ·5833 | 27·5772 | ·0935 | ·4167 | ·81 |
| 0·9861 | **7·20** | 7·5919 | 28·1892 | 0·0918 | 2·4081 | **2·80** |
| 864 | ·21 | ·6006 | 28·8177 | ·0901 | ·3994 | ·79 |
| 868 | ·22 | ·6092 | 29·4631 | ·0884 | ·3908 | ·78 |
| 871 | ·23 | ·6178 | 30·1260 | ·0867 | ·3822 | ·77 |
| 875 | ·24 | ·6265 | 30·8069 | ·0851 | ·3735 | ·76 |
| 0·9878 | **7·25** | 7·6351 | 31·5063 | 0·0834 | 2·3649 | **2·75** |
| 881 | ·26 | ·6438 | 32·2249 | ·0818 | ·3562 | ·74 |
| 884 | ·27 | ·6525 | 32·9631 | ·0802 | ·3475 | ·73 |
| 887 | ·28 | ·6612 | 33·7216 | ·0787 | ·3388 | ·72 |
| 890 | ·29 | ·6699 | 34·5010 | ·0771 | ·3301 | ·71 |
| 0·9893 | **7·30** | 7·6786 | 35·3020 | 0·0756 | 2·3214 | **2·70** |
| 896 | ·31 | ·6873 | 36·1251 | ·0741 | ·3127 | ·69 |
| 898 | ·32 | ·6960 | 36·9712 | ·0727 | ·3040 | ·68 |
| 901 | ·33 | ·7047 | 37·8408 | ·0712 | ·2953 | ·67 |
| 904 | ·34 | ·7135 | 38·7348 | ·0698 | ·2865 | ·66 |
| 0·9906 | **7·35** | 7·7222 | 39·6539 | 0·0684 | 2·2778 | **2·65** |
| 909 | ·36 | ·7310 | 40·5988 | ·0671 | ·2690 | ·64 |
| 911 | ·37 | ·7397 | 41·5704 | ·0656 | ·2603 | ·63 |
| 913 | ·38 | ·7485 | 42·5695 | ·0643 | ·2515 | ·62 |
| 916 | ·39 | ·7573 | 43·5970 | ·0630 | ·2427 | ·61 |
| 0·9918 | **7·40** | 7·7661 | 44·6538 | 0·0617 | 2·2339 | **2·60** |
| 920 | ·41 | ·7748 | 45·7407 | ·0604 | ·2252 | ·59 |
| 922 | ·42 | ·7836 | 46·8588 | ·0591 | ·2164 | ·58 |
| 925 | ·43 | ·7924 | 48·0090 | ·0579 | ·2076 | ·57 |
| 927 | ·44 | ·8013 | 49·1924 | ·0567 | ·1987 | ·56 |
| 0·9929 | **7·45** | 7·8101 | 50·4099 | 0·0555 | 2·1899 | **2·55** |
| 931 | ·46 | ·8189 | 51·6628 | ·0543 | ·1811 | ·54 |
| 932 | ·47 | ·8277 | 52·9521 | ·0532 | ·1723 | ·53 |
| 934 | ·48 | ·8366 | 54·2791 | ·0520 | ·1634 | ·52 |
| 936 | ·49 | ·8454 | 55·6448 | ·0509 | ·1546 | ·51 |
| 0·9938 | **7·50** | 7·8543 | 57·0506 | 0·0498 | 2·1457 | **2·50** |

$$Z = e^{-\frac{1}{2}X^2}/\sqrt{(2\pi)}$$
$$Y = X + 5$$
$$P = 1 - Q = \int_{-\infty}^{X} Z(u)\,du$$

| | | | $1/Z$ Range | $Z^2/PQ$ Weighting coefficient | $Y - P/Z$ Minimum working probit | $Y$ Expected probit |
|---|---|---|---|---|---|---|

Table 6 (*continued*)

| Proportion P | Expected probit Y | Maximum working probit Y+Q/Z | Range 1/Z | Weighting coefficient Z²/PQ | | |
|---|---|---|---|---|---|---|
| 0·99379 | 7·50 | 7·8543 | 57·0506 | 0·0498 | 2·1457 | 2·50 |
| 396 | ·51 | ·8631 | 58·4978 | ·0487 | ·1369 | ·49 |
| 413 | ·52 | ·8720 | 59·9876 | ·0476 | ·1280 | ·48 |
| 430 | ·53 | ·8809 | 61·5216 | ·0466 | ·1191 | ·47 |
| 446 | ·54 | ·8897 | 63·1011 | ·0456 | ·1103 | ·46 |
| 0·99461 | 7·55 | 7·8986 | 64·7277 | 0·0446 | 2·1014 | 2·45 |
| 477 | ·56 | ·9075 | 66·4028 | ·0436 | ·0925 | ·44 |
| 492 | ·57 | ·9164 | 68·1280 | ·0426 | ·0836 | ·43 |
| 506 | ·58 | ·9253 | 69·9051 | ·0416 | ·0747 | ·42 |
| 520 | ·59 | ·9342 | 71·7357 | ·0407 | ·0658 | ·41 |
| 0·99534 | 7·60 | 7·9432 | 73·6216 | 0·0398 | 2·0568 | 2·40 |
| 547 | ·61 | ·9521 | 75·5646 | ·0389 | ·0479 | ·39 |
| 560 | ·62 | ·9610 | 77·5667 | ·0380 | ·0390 | ·38 |
| 573 | ·63 | ·9700 | 79·6298 | ·0371 | ·0300 | ·37 |
| 585 | ·64 | ·9789 | 81·7559 | ·0362 | ·0211 | ·36 |
| 0·99598 | 7·65 | 7·9879 | 83·9472 | 0·0354 | 2·0121 | 2·35 |
| 609 | ·66 | ·9968 | 86·2059 | ·0346 | ·0032 | ·34 |
| 621 | ·67 | 8·0058 | 88·5342 | ·0338 | 1·9942 | ·33 |
| 632 | ·68 | ·0147 | 90·9344 | ·0330 | ·9853 | ·32 |
| 643 | ·69 | ·0237 | 93·4091 | ·0322 | ·9763 | ·31 |
| 0·99653 | 7·70 | 8·0327 | 95·9607 | 0·0314 | 1·9673 | 2·30 |
| 664 | ·71 | ·0417 | 98·5918 | ·0307 | ·9583 | ·29 |
| 674 | ·72 | ·0507 | 101·3053 | ·0300 | ·9493 | ·28 |
| 683 | ·73 | ·0597 | 104·1038 | ·0292 | ·9403 | ·27 |
| 693 | ·74 | ·0687 | 106·9903 | ·0285 | ·9313 | ·26 |
| 0·99702 | 7·75 | 8·0777 | 109·9679 | 0·0278 | 1·9223 | 2·25 |
| 711 | ·76 | ·0867 | 113·0396 | ·0272 | ·9133 | ·24 |
| 720 | ·77 | ·0957 | 116·2088 | ·0265 | ·9043 | ·23 |
| 728 | ·78 | ·1047 | 119·4788 | ·0258 | ·8953 | ·22 |
| 736 | ·79 | ·1138 | 122·8530 | ·0252 | ·8862 | ·21 |
| 0·99744 | 7·80 | 8·1228 | 126·3352 | 0·0246 | 1·8772 | 2·20 |
| 752 | ·81 | ·1318 | 129·9290 | ·0240 | ·8682 | ·19 |
| 760 | ·82 | ·1409 | 133·6385 | ·0234 | ·8591 | ·18 |
| 767 | ·83 | ·1499 | 137·4676 | ·0228 | ·8501 | ·17 |
| 774 | ·84 | ·1590 | 141·4206 | ·0222 | ·8410 | ·16 |
| 0·99781 | 7·85 | 8·1681 | 145·5018 | 0·0217 | 1·8319 | 2·15 |
| 788 | ·86 | ·1771 | 149·7158 | ·0211 | ·8229 | ·14 |
| 795 | ·87 | ·1862 | 154·0671 | ·0206 | ·8138 | ·13 |
| 801 | ·88 | ·1953 | 158·5609 | ·0200 | ·8047 | ·12 |
| 807 | ·89 | ·2044 | 163·2020 | ·0195 | ·7956 | ·11 |
| 0·99813 | 7·90 | 8·2134 | 167·9957 | 0·0190 | 1·7866 | 2·10 |
| 819 | ·91 | ·2225 | 172·9476 | ·0185 | ·7775 | ·09 |
| 825 | ·92 | ·2316 | 178·0632 | ·0181 | ·7684 | ·08 |
| 831 | ·93 | ·2407 | 183·3485 | ·0176 | ·7593 | ·07 |
| 836 | ·94 | ·2498 | 188·8095 | ·0171 | ·7502 | ·06 |
| 0·99841 | 7·95 | 8·2590 | 194·4526 | 0·0167 | 1·7410 | 2·05 |
| 846 | ·96 | ·2681 | 200·2844 | ·0162 | ·7319 | ·04 |
| 851 | ·97 | ·2772 | 206·3118 | ·0158 | ·7228 | ·03 |
| 856 | ·98 | ·2863 | 212·5418 | ·0154 | ·7137 | ·02 |
| 861 | ·99 | ·2955 | 218·9818 | ·0150 | ·7045 | ·01 |
| 0·99865 | 8·00 | 8·3046 | 225·6395 | 0·0146 | 1·6954 | 2·00 |

$Z = e^{-\frac{1}{2}X^2}/\sqrt{(2\pi)}$

$Y = X + 5$

$P = 1 - Q = \int_{-\infty}^{X} Z(u)\, du$

| | | | 1/Z Range | Z²/PQ Weighting coefficient | Y−P/Z Minimum working probit | Y Expected probit |
|---|---|---|---|---|---|---|

125

Table 6. *Table for probit analysis (continued)*

| Proportion P | Expected probit Y | Maximum working probit $Y + Q/Z$ | Range $1/Z$ | Weighting coefficient $Z^2/PQ$ | | |
|---|---|---|---|---|---|---|
| 0.99865 | 8.00 | 8.3046 | 225.6395 | 0.0146 | 1.6954 | 2.00 |
| 869 | .01 | .3137 | 232.5229 | .0142 | .6863 | 1.99 |
| 874 | .02 | .3229 | 239.6402 | .0138 | .6771 | .98 |
| 878 | .03 | .3320 | 247.0000 | .0134 | .6680 | .97 |
| 882 | .04 | .3412 | 254.6114 | .0131 | .6588 | .96 |
| 0.99886 | 8.05 | 8.3503 | 262.4836 | 0.0127 | 1.6497 | 1.95 |
| 889 | .06 | .3595 | 270.6262 | .0124 | .6405 | .94 |
| 893 | .07 | .3687 | 279.0493 | .0120 | .6313 | .93 |
| 896 | .08 | .3778 | 287.7634 | .0117 | .6222 | .92 |
| 900 | .09 | .3870 | 296.7792 | .0114 | .6130 | .91 |
| 0.99903 | 8.10 | 8.3962 | 306.1082 | 0.0110 | 1.6038 | 1.90 |
| 906 | .11 | .4054 | 315.7619 | .0107 | .5946 | .89 |
| 910 | .12 | .4146 | 325.7527 | .0104 | .5854 | .88 |
| 913 | .13 | .4238 | 336.0932 | .0101 | .5762 | .87 |
| 916 | .14 | .4330 | 346.7966 | .0099 | .5670 | .86 |
| 0.99918 | 8.15 | 8.4422 | 357.8732 | 0.0096 | 1.5578 | 1.85 |
| 921 | .16 | .4514 | 369.3477 | .0093 | .5486 | .84 |
| 924 | .17 | .4606 | 381.2245 | .0090 | .5394 | .83 |
| 926 | .18 | .4698 | 393.5226 | .0088 | .5302 | .82 |
| 929 | .19 | .4790 | 406.2580 | .0085 | .5210 | .81 |
| 0.99931 | 8.20 | 8.4882 | 419.4476 | 0.0083 | 1.5118 | 1.80 |
| 934 | .21 | .4974 | 433.1086 | .0080 | .5026 | .79 |
| 936 | .22 | .5067 | 447.2593 | .0078 | .4933 | .78 |
| 938 | .23 | .5159 | 461.9185 | .0076 | .4841 | .77 |
| 940 | .24 | .5251 | 477.1059 | .0074 | .4749 | .76 |
| 0.99942 | 8.25 | 8.5344 | 492.8419 | 0.0071 | 1.4656 | 1.75 |
| 944 | .26 | .5436 | 509.1479 | .0069 | .4564 | .74 |
| 946 | .27 | .5529 | 526.0459 | .0067 | .4471 | .73 |
| 948 | .28 | .5621 | 543.5592 | .0065 | .4379 | .72 |
| 950 | .29 | .5714 | 561.7116 | .0063 | .4286 | .71 |
| 0.99952 | 8.30 | 8.5806 | 580.5283 | 0.0061 | 1.4194 | 1.70 |
| 953 | .31 | .5899 | 600.0353 | .0060 | .4101 | .69 |
| 955 | .32 | .5992 | 620.2599 | .0058 | .4008 | .68 |
| 957 | .33 | .6084 | 641.2302 | .0056 | .3916 | .67 |
| 958 | .34 | .6177 | 662.9758 | .0054 | .3823 | .66 |
| 0.99960 | 8.35 | 8.6270 | 685.5274 | 0.0053 | 1.3730 | 1.65 |
| 961 | .36 | .6363 | 708.9171 | .0051 | .3637 | .64 |
| 962 | .37 | .6456 | 733.1780 | .0050 | .3544 | .63 |
| 964 | .38 | .6548 | 758.3451 | .0048 | .3452 | .62 |
| 965 | .39 | .6641 | 784.4545 | .0047 | .3359 | .61 |
| 0.99966 | 8.40 | 8.6734 | 811.5439 | 0.0045 | 1.3266 | 1.60 |
| 968 | .41 | .6827 | 839.6528 | .0044 | .3173 | .59 |
| 969 | .42 | .6920 | 868.8222 | .0042 | .3080 | .58 |
| 970 | .43 | .7013 | 899.0948 | .0041 | .2987 | .57 |
| 971 | .44 | .7106 | 930.5153 | .0040 | .2894 | .56 |
| 0.99972 | 8.45 | 8.7200 | 963.1301 | 0.0038 | 1.2800 | 1.55 |
| 973 | .46 | .7293 | 996.9878 | .0037 | .2707 | .54 |
| 974 | .47 | .7386 | 1032.1389 | .0036 | .2614 | .53 |
| 975 | .48 | .7479 | 1068.6362 | .0035 | .2521 | .52 |
| 976 | .49 | .7572 | 1106.5347 | .0034 | .2428 | .51 |
| 0.99977 | 8.50 | 8.7666 | 1145.8919 | 0.0033 | 1.2334 | 1.50 |

$$Z = e^{-\frac{1}{2}X^2}/\sqrt{(2\pi)}$$
$$Y = X + 5$$
$$P = 1 - Q = \int_{-\infty}^{X} Z(u)\,du$$

| | | | $1/Z$ Range | $Z^2/PQ$ Weighting coefficient | $Y - P/Z$ Minimum working probit | Y Expected probit |
|---|---|---|---|---|---|---|

Table 6 (*continued*)

| Proportion P | Expected probit Y | Maximum working probit $Y + Q/Z$ | Range $1/Z$ | Weighting coefficient $Z^2/PQ$ | | |
|---|---|---|---|---|---|---|
| 0·999767 | 8·50 | 8·7666 | 1145·8919 | 0·0033 | 1·2334 | 1·50 |
| 776 | ·51 | ·7759 | 1186·7675 | ·0032 | ·2241 | ·49 |
| 784 | ·52 | ·7852 | 1229·2242 | ·0031 | ·2148 | ·48 |
| 792 | ·53 | ·7946 | 1273·3271 | ·0030 | ·2054 | ·47 |
| 800 | ·54 | ·8039 | 1319·1443 | ·0029 | ·1961 | ·46 |
| 0·999807 | 8·55 | 8·8133 | 1366·7467 | 0·0028 | 1·1867 | 1·45 |
| 815 | ·56 | ·8226 | 1416·2085 | ·0027 | ·1774 | ·44 |
| 822 | ·57 | ·8320 | 1467·6071 | ·0026 | ·1680 | ·43 |
| 828 | ·58 | ·8413 | 1521·0232 | ·0025 | ·1587 | ·42 |
| 835 | ·59 | ·8507 | 1576·5411 | ·0024 | ·1493 | ·41 |
| 0·999841 | 8·60 | 8·8600 | 1634·2488 | 0·0024 | 1·1400 | 1·40 |
| 847 | ·61 | ·8694 | 1694·2383 | ·0023 | ·1306 | ·39 |
| 853 | ·62 | ·8788 | 1756·6055 | ·0022 | ·1212 | ·38 |
| 858 | ·63 | ·8881 | 1821·4507 | ·0021 | ·1119 | ·37 |
| 864 | ·64 | ·8975 | 1888·8785 | ·0021 | ·1025 | ·36 |
| 0·999869 | 8·65 | 8·9069 | 1958·9983 | 0·0020 | 1·0931 | 1·35 |
| 874 | ·66 | ·9162 | 2031·9243 | ·0019 | ·0838 | ·34 |
| 879 | ·67 | ·9256 | 2107·7758 | ·0019 | ·0744 | ·33 |
| 883 | ·68 | ·9350 | 2186·6775 | ·0018 | ·0650 | ·32 |
| 888 | ·69 | ·9444 | 2268·7596 | ·0017 | ·0556 | ·31 |
| 0·999892 | 8·70 | 8·9538 | 2354·1583 | 0·0017 | 1·0462 | 1·30 |
| 896 | ·71 | ·9632 | 2443·0158 | ·0016 | ·0368 | ·29 |
| 900 | ·72 | ·9726 | 2535·4807 | ·0016 | ·0274 | ·28 |
| 904 | ·73 | ·9820 | 2631·7085 | ·0015 | ·0180 | ·27 |
| 908 | ·74 | ·9914 | 2731·8615 | ·0015 | ·0086 | ·26 |
| 0·999912 | 8·75 | 9·0008 | 2836·1096 | 0·0014 | 0·9992 | 1·25 |
| 915 | ·76 | ·0102 | 2944·6302 | ·0014 | ·9898 | ·24 |
| 918 | ·77 | ·0196 | 3057·6091 | ·0013 | ·9804 | ·23 |
| 922 | ·78 | ·0290 | 3175·2401 | ·0013 | ·9710 | ·22 |
| 925 | ·79 | ·0384 | 3297·7264 | ·0012 | ·9616 | ·21 |
| 0·999928 | 8·80 | 9·0478 | 3425·2801 | 0·0012 | 0·9522 | 1·20 |
| 931 | ·81 | ·0572 | 3558·1233 | ·0011 | ·9428 | ·19 |
| 933 | ·82 | ·0667 | 3696·4883 | ·0011 | ·9333 | ·18 |
| 936 | ·83 | ·0761 | 3840·6179 | ·0011 | ·9239 | ·17 |
| 938 | ·84 | ·0855 | 3990·7662 | ·0010 | ·9145 | ·16 |
| 0·999941 | 8·85 | 9·0949 | 4147·1994 | 0·0010 | 0·9051 | 1·15 |
| 943 | ·86 | ·1044 | 4310·1955 | ·0010 | ·8956 | ·14 |
| 946 | ·87 | ·1138 | 4480·0457 | ·0009 | ·8862 | ·13 |
| 948 | ·88 | ·1232 | 4657·0549 | ·0009 | ·8768 | ·12 |
| 950 | ·89 | ·1327 | 4841·5419 | ·0009 | ·8673 | ·11 |
| 0·999952 | 8·90 | 9·1421 | 5033·8407 | 0·0008 | 0·8579 | 1·10 |
| 954 | ·91 | ·1516 | 5234·3007 | ·0008 | ·8484 | ·09 |
| 956 | ·92 | ·1610 | 5443·2878 | ·0008 | ·8390 | ·08 |
| 958 | ·93 | ·1704 | 5661·1851 | ·0007 | ·8296 | ·07 |
| 959 | ·94 | ·1799 | 5888·3938 | ·0007 | ·8201 | ·06 |
| 0·999961 | 8·95 | 9·1894 | 6125·3338 | 0·0007 | 0·8106 | 1·05 |
| 963 | ·96 | ·1988 | 6372·4452 | ·0007 | ·8012 | ·04 |
| 964 | ·97 | ·2083 | 6630·1886 | ·0006 | ·7917 | ·03 |
| 966 | ·98 | ·2177 | 6899·0468 | ·0006 | ·7823 | ·02 |
| 967 | ·99 | ·2272 | 7179·5252 | ·0006 | ·7728 | ·01 |
| 0·999968 | 9·00 | 9·2367 | 7472·1536 | 0·0006 | 0·7633 | 1·00 |
| | $Z = e^{-\frac{1}{2}X^2}/\sqrt{(2\pi)}$ $Y = X + 5$ $P = 1 - Q = \int_{-\infty}^{X} Z(u)\,du$ | | $1/Z$ Range | $Z^2/PQ$ Weighting coefficient | $Y - P/Z$ Minimum working probit | Y Expected probit |

## Table 7. *Probability integral of the χ²-distribution and the cumulative sum of the Poisson distribution*

| $\nu$ | $\chi^2=0.001$ $m=0.0005$ | 0.002 0.0010 | 0.003 0.0015 | 0.004 0.0020 | 0.005 0.0025 | 0.006 0.0030 | 0.007 0.0035 | 0.008 0.0040 | 0.009 0.0045 | 0.010 0.0050 | c |
|---|---|---|---|---|---|---|---|---|---|---|---|
| 1 | 0.97477 | 0.96433 | 0.95632 | 0.94957 | 0.94363 | 0.93826 | 0.93332 | 0.92873 | 0.92442 | 0.92034 |   |
| 2 | ·99950 | ·99900 | ·99850 | ·99800 | ·99750 | ·99700 | ·99651 | ·99601 | ·99551 | ·99501 | 1 |
| 3 | ·99999 | ·99998 | ·99996 | ·99993 | ·99991 | ·99988 | ·99984 | ·99981 | ·99977 | ·99973 |   |
| 4 |   |   |   |   |   |   | ·99999 | ·99999 | ·99999 | ·99999 | 2 |

| $\nu$ | $\chi^2=10.5$ $m=5.25$ | 11.0 5.5 | 11.5 5.75 | 12.0 6.0 | 12.5 6.25 | 13.0 6.5 | 13.5 6.75 | 14.0 7.0 | 14.5 7.25 | 15.0 7.5 | c |
|---|---|---|---|---|---|---|---|---|---|---|---|
| 1 | 0.00119 | 0.00091 | 0.00070 | 0.00053 | 0.00041 | 0.00031 | 0.00024 | 0.00018 | 0.00014 | 0.00011 |   |
| 2 | ·00525 | ·00409 | ·00318 | ·00248 | ·00193 | ·00150 | ·00117 | ·00091 | ·00071 | ·00055 | 1 |
| 3 | ·01476 | ·01173 | ·00931 | ·00738 | ·00585 | ·00464 | ·00367 | ·00291 | ·00230 | ·00182 |   |
| 4 | ·03280 | ·02656 | ·02148 | ·01735 | ·01400 | ·01128 | ·00907 | ·00730 | ·00586 | ·00470 | 2 |
| 5 | ·06225 | ·05138 | ·04232 | ·03479 | ·02854 | ·02338 | ·01912 | ·01561 | ·01273 | ·01036 |   |
| 6 | ·10511 | ·08838 | ·07410 | ·06197 | ·05170 | ·04304 | ·03575 | ·02964 | ·02452 | ·02026 | 3 |
| 7 | 0.16196 | 0.13862 | 0.11825 | 0.10056 | 0.08527 | 0.07211 | 0.06082 | 0.05118 | 0.04297 | 0.03600 |   |
| 8 | ·23167 | ·20170 | ·17495 | ·15120 | ·13025 | ·11185 | ·09577 | ·08177 | ·06963 | ·05915 | 4 |
| 9 | ·31154 | ·27571 | ·24299 | ·21331 | ·18657 | ·16261 | ·14126 | ·12233 | ·10562 | ·09094 |   |
| 10 | ·39777 | ·35752 | ·31991 | ·28506 | ·25299 | ·22367 | ·19704 | ·17299 | ·15138 | ·13206 | 5 |
| 11 | ·48605 | ·44326 | ·40237 | ·36364 | ·32726 | ·29333 | ·26190 | ·23299 | ·20655 | ·18250 |   |
| 12 | ·57218 | ·52892 | ·48662 | ·44568 | ·40640 | ·36904 | ·33377 | ·30071 | ·26992 | ·24144 | 6 |
| 13 | 0.65263 | 0.61082 | 0.56901 | 0.52764 | 0.48713 | 0.44781 | 0.40997 | 0.37384 | 0.33960 | 0.30735 |   |
| 14 | ·72479 | ·68604 | ·64639 | ·60630 | ·56622 | ·52652 | ·48759 | ·44971 | ·41316 | ·37815 | 7 |
| 15 | ·78717 | ·75259 | ·71641 | ·67903 | ·64086 | ·60230 | ·56374 | ·52553 | ·48800 | ·45142 |   |
| 16 | ·83925 | ·80949 | ·77762 | ·74398 | ·70890 | ·67276 | ·63591 | ·59871 | ·56152 | ·52464 | 8 |
| 17 | ·88135 | ·85656 | ·82942 | ·80014 | ·76896 | ·73619 | ·70212 | ·66710 | ·63145 | ·59548 |   |
| 18 | ·91436 | ·89436 | ·87195 | ·84724 | ·82038 | ·79157 | ·76106 | ·72909 | ·69596 | ·66197 | 9 |
| 19 | 0.93952 | 0.92384 | 0.90587 | 0.88562 | 0.86316 | 0.83857 | 0.81202 | 0.78369 | 0.75380 | 0.72260 |   |
| 20 | ·95817 | ·94622 | ·93221 | ·91608 | ·89779 | ·87738 | ·85492 | ·83050 | ·80427 | ·77641 | 10 |
| 21 | ·97166 | ·96279 | ·95214 | ·93962 | ·92513 | ·90862 | ·89010 | ·86960 | ·84718 | ·82295 |   |
| 22 | ·98118 | ·97475 | ·96686 | ·95738 | ·94618 | ·93316 | ·91827 | ·90148 | ·88279 | ·86224 | 11 |
| 23 | ·98773 | ·98319 | ·97748 | ·97047 | ·96201 | ·95199 | ·94030 | ·92687 | ·91165 | ·89463 |   |
| 24 | ·99216 | ·98901 | ·98498 | ·97991 | ·97367 | ·96612 | ·95715 | ·94665 | ·93454 | ·92076 | 12 |
| 25 | 0.99507 | 0.99295 | 0.99015 | 0.98657 | 0.98206 | 0.97650 | 0.96976 | 0.96173 | 0.95230 | 0.94138 |   |
| 26 | ·99696 | ·99555 | ·99366 | ·99117 | ·98798 | ·98397 | ·97902 | ·97300 | ·96581 | ·95733 | 13 |
| 27 | ·99815 | ·99724 | ·99598 | ·99429 | ·99208 | ·98925 | ·98567 | ·98125 | ·97588 | ·96943 |   |
| 28 | ·99890 | ·99831 | ·99749 | ·99637 | ·99487 | ·99290 | ·99037 | ·98719 | ·98324 | ·97844 | 14 |
| 29 | ·99935 | ·99899 | ·99846 | ·99773 | ·99672 | ·99538 | ·99363 | ·99138 | ·98854 | ·98502 |   |
| 30 | 0.99963 | 0.99940 | 0.99907 | 0.99860 | 0.99794 | 0.99704 | 0.99585 | 0.99428 | 0.99227 | 0.98974 | 15 |
| 32 | ·99988 | ·99980 | ·99968 | ·99949 | ·99922 | ·99884 | ·99831 | ·99759 | ·99664 | ·99539 | 16 |
| 34 | ·99996 | ·99994 | ·99989 | ·99983 | ·99972 | ·99957 | ·99935 | ·99904 | ·99862 | ·99804 | 17 |
| 36 | ·99999 | ·99998 | ·99997 | ·99994 | ·99991 | ·99985 | ·99976 | ·99964 | ·99946 | ·99921 | 18 |
| 38 |   |   | ·99999 | ·99998 | ·99997 | ·99995 | ·99992 | ·99987 | ·99980 | ·99970 | 19 |
| 40 |   |   |   |   | 0.99999 | 0.99998 | 0.99997 | 0.99996 | 0.99993 | 0.99989 | 20 |
| 42 |   |   |   |   |   | ·99999 | ·99999 | ·99998 | ·99996 | 21 |
| 44 |   |   |   |   |   |   |   |   | ·99999 | ·99999 | 22 |

The quantity tabled is

$$Q(\chi^2 \mid \nu) = 1 - P(\chi^2 \mid \nu) = 2^{-\frac{1}{2}\nu}\,\{\Gamma(\tfrac{1}{2}\nu)\}^{-1}\int_{\chi^2}^{\infty} e^{-\frac{1}{2}x}\,x^{\frac{1}{2}\nu-1}\,dx,$$

which is equal to $\sum_{j=0}^{c-1} e^{-m}\,m^j/j!$, if $\nu$ is even and $c=\tfrac{1}{2}\nu$, $m=\tfrac{1}{2}\chi^2$.

128

Table 7 (*continued*)

| ν | $\chi^2=0.01$ $m=0.005$ | 0.02 0.010 | 0.03 0.015 | 0.04 0.020 | 0.05 0.025 | 0.06 0.030 | 0.07 0.035 | 0.08 0.040 | 0.09 0.045 | 0.10 0.050 | c |
|---|---|---|---|---|---|---|---|---|---|---|---|
| 1 | 0·92034 | 0·88754 | 0·86249 | 0·84148 | 0·82306 | 0·80650 | 0·79134 | 0·77730 | 0·76418 | 0·75183 | |
| 2 | ·99501 | ·99005 | ·98511 | ·98020 | ·97531 | ·97045 | ·96561 | ·96079 | ·95600 | ·95123 | 1 |
| 3 | ·99973 | ·99925 | ·99863 | ·99790 | ·99707 | ·99616 | ·99518 | ·99412 | ·99301 | ·99184 | |
| 4 | ·99999 | ·99995 | ·99989 | ·99980 | ·99969 | ·99956 | ·99940 | ·99922 | ·99902 | ·99879 | 2 |
| 5 | | | ·99999 | ·99998 | ·99997 | ·99995 | ·99993 | ·99991 | ·99987 | ·99984 | |
| 6 | | | | | | | ·99999 | ·99999 | ·99999 | ·99998 | 3 |

| ν | $\chi^2=15.5$ $m=7.75$ | 16·0 8·0 | 16·5 8·25 | 17·0 8·5 | 17·5 8·75 | 18·0 9·0 | 18·5 9·25 | 19·0 9·5 | 19·5 9·75 | 20·0 10·0 | c |
|---|---|---|---|---|---|---|---|---|---|---|---|
| 1 | 0·00008 | 0·00006 | 0·00005 | 0·00004 | 0·00003 | 0·00002 | 0·00002 | 0·00001 | 0·00001 | 0·00001 | |
| 2 | ·00043 | ·00034 | ·00026 | ·00020 | ·00016 | ·00012 | ·00010 | ·00008 | ·00006 | ·00005 | 1 |
| 3 | ·00144 | ·00113 | ·00090 | ·00071 | ·00056 | ·00044 | ·00035 | ·00027 | ·00022 | ·00017 | |
| 4 | ·00377 | ·00302 | ·00242 | ·00193 | ·00154 | ·00123 | ·00099 | ·00079 | ·00063 | ·00050 | 2 |
| 5 | ·00843 | ·00684 | ·00555 | ·00450 | ·00364 | ·00295 | ·00238 | ·00192 | ·00155 | ·00125 | |
| 6 | ·01670 | ·01375 | ·01131 | ·00928 | ·00761 | ·00623 | ·00510 | ·00416 | ·00340 | ·00277 | 3 |
| 7 | 0·03010 | 0·02512 | 0·02092 | 0·01740 | 0·01444 | 0·01197 | 0·00991 | 0·00819 | 0·00676 | 0·00557 | |
| 8 | ·05012 | ·04238 | ·03576 | ·03011 | ·02530 | ·02123 | ·01777 | ·01486 | ·01240 | ·01034 | 4 |
| 9 | ·07809 | ·06688 | ·05715 | ·04872 | ·04144 | ·03517 | ·02980 | ·02519 | ·02126 | ·01791 | |
| 10 | ·11487 | ·09963 | ·08619 | ·07436 | ·06401 | ·05496 | ·04709 | ·04026 | ·03435 | ·02925 | 5 |
| 11 | ·16073 | ·14113 | ·12356 | ·10788 | ·09393 | ·08158 | ·07068 | ·06109 | ·05269 | ·04534 | |
| 12 | ·21522 | ·19124 | ·16939 | ·14960 | ·13174 | ·11569 | ·10133 | ·08853 | ·07716 | ·06709 | 6 |
| 13 | 0·27719 | 0·24913 | 0·22318 | 0·19930 | 0·17744 | 0·15752 | 0·13944 | 0·12310 | 0·10840 | 0·09521 | |
| 14 | ·34485 | ·31337 | ·28380 | ·25618 | ·23051 | ·20678 | ·18495 | ·16495 | ·14671 | ·13014 | 7 |
| 15 | ·41604 | ·38205 | ·34962 | ·31886 | ·28986 | ·26267 | ·23729 | ·21373 | ·19196 | ·17193 | |
| 16 | ·48837 | ·45296 | ·41864 | ·38560 | ·35398 | ·32390 | ·29544 | ·26866 | ·24359 | ·22022 | 8 |
| 17 | ·55951 | ·52383 | ·48871 | ·45437 | ·42102 | ·38884 | ·35797 | ·32853 | ·30060 | ·27423 | |
| 18 | ·62740 | ·59255 | ·55770 | ·52311 | ·48902 | ·45565 | ·42320 | ·39182 | ·36166 | ·33282 | 9 |
| 19 | 0·69033 | 0·65728 | 0·62370 | 0·58987 | 0·55603 | 0·52244 | 0·48931 | 0·45684 | 0·42521 | 0·39458 | |
| 20 | ·74712 | ·71662 | ·68516 | ·65297 | ·62031 | ·58741 | ·55451 | ·52183 | ·48957 | ·45793 | 10 |
| 21 | ·79705 | ·76965 | ·74093 | ·71111 | ·68039 | ·64900 | ·61718 | ·58514 | ·55310 | ·52126 | |
| 22 | ·83990 | ·81589 | ·79032 | ·76336 | ·73519 | ·70599 | ·67597 | ·64533 | ·61428 | ·58304 | 11 |
| 23 | ·87582 | ·85527 | ·83304 | ·80925 | ·78402 | ·75749 | ·72983 | ·70122 | ·67185 | ·64191 | |
| 24 | ·90527 | ·88808 | ·86919 | ·84866 | ·82657 | ·80301 | ·77810 | ·75199 | ·72483 | ·69678 | 12 |
| 25 | 0·92891 | 0·91483 | 0·89912 | 0·88179 | 0·86287 | 0·84239 | 0·82044 | 0·79712 | 0·77254 | 0·74683 | |
| 26 | ·94749 | ·93620 | ·92341 | ·90908 | ·89320 | ·87577 | ·85683 | ·83643 | ·81464 | ·79156 | 13 |
| 27 | ·96182 | ·95295 | ·94274 | ·93112 | ·91806 | ·90352 | ·88750 | ·87000 | ·85107 | ·83076 | |
| 28 | ·97266 | ·96582 | ·95782 | ·94859 | ·93805 | ·92615 | ·91285 | ·89814 | ·88200 | ·86446 | 14 |
| 29 | ·98071 | ·97554 | ·96939 | ·96218 | ·95383 | ·94427 | ·93344 | ·92129 | ·90779 | ·89293 | |
| 30 | 0·98659 | 0·98274 | 0·97810 | 0·97258 | 0·96608 | 0·95853 | 0·94986 | 0·94001 | 0·92891 | 0·91654 | 15 |
| 32 | ·99379 | ·99177 | ·98925 | ·98617 | ·98243 | ·97796 | ·97269 | ·96653 | ·95941 | ·95126 | 16 |
| 34 | ·99728 | ·99628 | ·99500 | ·99339 | ·99137 | ·98889 | ·98588 | ·98227 | ·97799 | ·97296 | 17 |
| 36 | ·99887 | ·99841 | ·99779 | ·99700 | ·99597 | ·99468 | ·99306 | ·99107 | ·98864 | ·98572 | 18 |
| 38 | ·99955 | ·99935 | ·99907 | ·99870 | ·99821 | ·99757 | ·99675 | ·99572 | ·99442 | ·99281 | 19 |
| 40 | 0·99983 | 0·99975 | 0·99963 | 0·99947 | 0·99924 | 0·99894 | 0·99855 | 0·99804 | 0·99738 | 0·99655 | 20 |
| 42 | ·99994 | ·99991 | ·99986 | ·99979 | ·99969 | ·99956 | ·99938 | ·99914 | ·99882 | ·99841 | 21 |
| 44 | ·99998 | ·99997 | ·99995 | ·99992 | ·99988 | ·99983 | ·99975 | ·99964 | ·99949 | ·99930 | 22 |
| 46 | ·99999 | ·99999 | ·99998 | ·99997 | ·99996 | ·99993 | ·99990 | ·99986 | ·99979 | ·99970 | 23 |
| 48 | | | ·99999 | ·99999 | ·99998 | ·99998 | ·99996 | ·99994 | ·99992 | ·99988 | 24 |
| 50 | | | | | 0·99999 | 0·99999 | 0·99999 | ·99998 | ·99997 | ·99995 | 25 |
| 52 | | | | | | | | ·99999 | ·99999 | ·99998 | 26 |
| 54 | | | | | | | | | | ·99999 | 27 |

# Table 7. *Probability integral of the $\chi^2$-distribution (continued)*

| $\nu$ | $\chi^2=0.1$ m=0.05 | 0.2 0.10 | 0.3 0.15 | 0.4 0.20 | 0.5 0.25 | 0.6 0.30 | 0.7 0.35 | 0.8 0.40 | 0.9 0.45 | 1.0 0.50 | c |
|---|---|---|---|---|---|---|---|---|---|---|---|
| 1 | 0.75183 | 0.65472 | 0.58388 | 0.52709 | 0.47950 | 0.43858 | 0.40278 | 0.37109 | 0.34278 | 0.31731 | |
| 2 | .95123 | .90484 | .86071 | .81873 | .77880 | .74082 | .70469 | .67032 | .63763 | .60653 | 1 |
| 3 | .99184 | .97759 | .96003 | .94024 | .91889 | .89643 | .87320 | .84947 | .82543 | .80125 | |
| 4 | .99879 | .99532 | .98981 | .98248 | .97350 | .96306 | .95133 | .93845 | .92456 | .90980 | 2 |
| 5 | .99984 | .99911 | .99764 | .99533 | .99212 | .98800 | .98297 | .97703 | .97022 | .96257 | |
| 6 | .99998 | .99985 | .99950 | .99885 | .99784 | .99640 | .99449 | .99207 | .98912 | .98561 | 3 |
| 7 | | 0.99997 | 0.99990 | 0.99974 | 0.99945 | 0.99899 | 0.99834 | 0.99744 | 0.99628 | 0.99483 | |
| 8 | | | .99998 | .99994 | .99987 | .99973 | .99953 | .99922 | .99880 | .99825 | 4 |
| 9 | | | | .99999 | .99997 | .99993 | .99987 | .99978 | .99964 | .99944 | |
| 10 | | | | | .99999 | .99998 | .99997 | .99994 | .99989 | .99983 | 5 |
| 11 | | | | | | .99999 | .99999 | .99998 | .99997 | .99995 | |
| 12 | | | | | | | | | .99999 | .99999 | 6 |

| $\nu$ | $\chi^2=21$ m=10.5 | 22 11.0 | 23 11.5 | 24 12.0 | 25 12.5 | 26 13.0 | 27 13.5 | 28 14.0 | 29 14.5 | 30 15.0 | c |
|---|---|---|---|---|---|---|---|---|---|---|---|
| 1 | 0.00001 | | | | | | | | | | |
| 2 | .00003 | 0.00002 | 0.00001 | 0.00001 | | | | | | | 1 |
| 3 | .00011 | .00007 | .00004 | .00003 | 0.00002 | 0.00001 | 0.00001 | | | | |
| 4 | .00032 | .00020 | .00013 | .00008 | .00005 | .00003 | .00002 | 0.00001 | 0.00001 | 0.00001 | 2 |
| 5 | .00081 | .00052 | .00034 | .00022 | .00014 | .00009 | .00006 | .00004 | .00002 | .00002 | |
| 6 | .00184 | .00121 | .00080 | .00052 | .00034 | .00022 | .00015 | .00009 | .00006 | .00004 | 3 |
| 7 | 0.00377 | 0.00254 | 0.00171 | 0.00114 | 0.00076 | 0.00050 | 0.00033 | 0.00022 | 0.00015 | 0.00010 | |
| 8 | .00715 | .00492 | .00336 | .00229 | .00155 | .00105 | .00071 | .00047 | .00032 | .00021 | 4 |
| 9 | .01265 | .00888 | .00620 | .00430 | .00297 | .00204 | .00140 | .00095 | .00065 | .00044 | |
| 10 | .02109 | .01511 | .01075 | .00760 | .00535 | .00374 | .00260 | .00181 | .00125 | .00086 | 5 |
| 11 | .03337 | .02437 | .01768 | .01273 | .00912 | .00649 | .00460 | .00324 | .00227 | .00159 | |
| 12 | .05038 | .03752 | .02773 | .02034 | .01482 | .01073 | .00773 | .00553 | .00394 | .00279 | 6 |
| 13 | 0.07293 | 0.05536 | 0.04168 | 0.03113 | 0.02308 | 0.01700 | 0.01244 | 0.00905 | 0.00655 | 0.00471 | |
| 14 | .10163 | .07861 | .06027 | .04582 | .03457 | .02589 | .01925 | .01423 | .01045 | .00763 | 7 |
| 15 | .13683 | .10780 | .08414 | .06509 | .04994 | .03802 | .02874 | .02157 | .01609 | .01192 | |
| 16 | .17851 | .14319 | .11374 | .08950 | .06982 | .05403 | .04148 | .03162 | .02394 | .01800 | 8 |
| 17 | .22629 | .18472 | .14925 | .11944 | .09471 | .07446 | .05807 | .04494 | .03453 | .02635 | |
| 18 | .27941 | .23199 | .19059 | .15503 | .12492 | .09976 | .07900 | .06206 | .04838 | .03745 | 9 |
| 19 | 0.33680 | 0.28426 | 0.23734 | 0.19615 | 0.16054 | 0.13019 | 0.10465 | 0.08343 | 0.06599 | 0.05180 | |
| 20 | .39713 | .34051 | .28880 | .24239 | .20143 | .16581 | .13526 | .10940 | .08776 | .06985 | 10 |
| 21 | .45894 | .39951 | .34398 | .29306 | .24716 | .20645 | .17085 | .14015 | .11400 | .09199 | |
| 22 | .52074 | .45989 | .40173 | .34723 | .29707 | .25168 | .21123 | .17568 | .14486 | .11846 | 11 |
| 23 | .58109 | .52025 | .46077 | .40381 | .35029 | .30087 | .25597 | .21578 | .18031 | .14940 | |
| 24 | .63873 | .57927 | .51980 | .46160 | .40576 | .35317 | .30445 | .26004 | .22013 | .18475 | 12 |
| 25 | 0.69261 | 0.63574 | 0.57756 | 0.51937 | 0.46237 | 0.40760 | 0.35588 | 0.30785 | 0.26392 | 0.22429 | |
| 26 | .74196 | .68870 | .63295 | .57597 | .51898 | .46311 | .40933 | .35846 | .31108 | .26761 | 13 |
| 27 | .78629 | .73738 | .68501 | .63032 | .57446 | .51860 | .46379 | .41097 | .36090 | .31415 | |
| 28 | .82535 | .78129 | .73304 | .68154 | .62784 | .57305 | .51825 | .46445 | .41253 | .36322 | 14 |
| 29 | .85915 | .82019 | .77654 | .72893 | .67825 | .62549 | .57171 | .51791 | .46507 | .41400 | |
| 30 | 0.88789 | 0.85404 | 0.81526 | 0.77203 | 0.72503 | 0.67513 | 0.62327 | 0.57044 | 0.51760 | 0.46565 | 15 |
| 32 | .93167 | .90740 | .87830 | .84442 | .80603 | .76361 | .71779 | .66936 | .61916 | .56809 | 16 |
| 34 | .96039 | .94408 | .92360 | .89871 | .86931 | .83549 | .79755 | .75592 | .71121 | .66412 | 17 |
| 36 | .97814 | .96781 | .95425 | .93703 | .91584 | .89047 | .86088 | .82720 | .78972 | .74886 | 18 |
| 38 | .98849 | .98231 | .97383 | .96258 | .94815 | .93017 | .90838 | .88264 | .85296 | .81947 | 19 |
| 40 | 0.99421 | 0.99071 | 0.98568 | 0.97872 | 0.96941 | 0.95733 | 0.94213 | 0.92350 | 0.90122 | 0.87522 | 20 |
| 42 | .99721 | .99533 | .99250 | .98840 | .98269 | .97499 | .96491 | .95209 | .93622 | .91703 | 21 |
| 44 | .99871 | .99775 | .99623 | .99394 | .99060 | .98592 | .97955 | .97116 | .96038 | .94689 | 22 |
| 46 | .99943 | .99896 | .99818 | .99695 | .99509 | .99238 | .98854 | .98329 | .97630 | .96726 | 23 |
| 48 | .99976 | .99954 | .99916 | .99853 | .99754 | .99603 | .99382 | .99067 | .98634 | .98054 | 24 |
| 50 | 0.99990 | 0.99980 | 0.99962 | 0.99931 | 0.99881 | 0.99801 | 0.99678 | 0.99498 | 0.99241 | 0.98884 | 25 |
| 52 | .99996 | .99992 | .99984 | .99969 | .99944 | .99903 | .99839 | .99739 | .99592 | .99382 | 26 |
| 54 | .99999 | .99997 | .99993 | .99987 | .99975 | .99955 | .99922 | .99869 | .99789 | .99669 | 27 |
| 56 | | .99999 | .99997 | .99994 | .99989 | .99980 | .99963 | .99937 | .99894 | .99828 | 28 |
| 58 | | | .99999 | .99998 | .99995 | .99991 | .99983 | .99970 | .99949 | .99914 | 29 |
| 60 | | | | 0.99999 | 0.99998 | 0.99996 | 0.99993 | 0.99986 | 0.99976 | 0.99958 | 30 |
| 62 | | | | | .99999 | .99998 | .99997 | .99994 | .99989 | .99980 | 31 |
| 64 | | | | | | .99999 | .99999 | .99997 | .99995 | .99991 | 32 |
| 66 | | | | | | | | .99999 | .99998 | .99996 | 33 |
| 68 | | | | | | | | | .99999 | .99998 | 34 |
| 70 | | | | | | | | | | 0.99999 | 35 |

## Table 7 (continued)

| ν | χ²=1·1 m=0·55 | 1·2 0·60 | 1·3 0·65 | 1·4 0·70 | 1·5 0·75 | 1·6 0·80 | 1·7 0·85 | 1·8 0·90 | 1·9 0·95 | 2·0 1·00 | c |
|---|---|---|---|---|---|---|---|---|---|---|---|
| 1 | 0·29427 | 0·27332 | 0·25421 | 0·23672 | 0·22067 | 0·20590 | 0·19229 | 0·17971 | 0·16808 | 0·15730 | |
| 2 | ·57695 | ·54881 | ·52205 | ·49659 | ·47237 | ·44933 | ·42741 | ·40657 | ·38674 | ·36788 | 1 |
| 3 | ·77707 | ·75300 | ·72913 | ·70553 | ·68227 | ·65939 | ·63693 | ·61493 | ·59342 | ·57241 | |
| 4 | ·89427 | ·87810 | ·86138 | ·84420 | ·82664 | ·80879 | ·79072 | ·77248 | ·75414 | ·73576 | 2 |
| 5 | ·95410 | ·94488 | ·93493 | ·92431 | ·91307 | ·90125 | ·88890 | ·87607 | ·86280 | ·84915 | |
| 6 | ·98154 | ·97689 | ·97166 | ·96586 | ·95949 | ·95258 | ·94512 | ·93714 | ·92866 | ·91970 | 3 |
| 7 | 0·99305 | 0·99093 | 0·98844 | 0·98557 | 0·98231 | 0·97864 | 0·97457 | 0·97008 | 0·96517 | 0·95984 | |
| 8 | ·99753 | ·99664 | ·99555 | ·99425 | ·99271 | ·99092 | ·98887 | ·98654 | ·98393 | ·98101 | 4 |
| 9 | ·99917 | ·99882 | ·99838 | ·99782 | ·99715 | ·99633 | ·99537 | ·99425 | ·99295 | ·99147 | |
| 10 | ·99973 | ·99961 | ·99944 | ·99921 | ·99894 | ·99859 | ·99817 | ·99766 | ·99705 | ·99634 | 5 |
| 11 | ·99992 | ·99987 | ·99981 | ·99973 | ·99962 | ·99948 | ·99930 | ·99908 | ·99882 | ·99850 | |
| 12 | ·99998 | ·99996 | ·99994 | ·99991 | ·99987 | ·99982 | ·99975 | ·99966 | ·99954 | ·99941 | 6 |
| 13 | 0·99999 | 0·99999 | 0·99998 | 0·99997 | 0·99996 | 0·99994 | 0·99991 | 0·99988 | 0·99983 | 0·99977 | 7 |
| 14 | | | | ·99999 | ·99999 | ·99998 | ·99997 | ·99996 | ·99994 | ·99992 | |
| 15 | | | | | | ·99999 | ·99999 | ·99999 | ·99998 | ·99997 | 8 |
| 16 | | | | | | | | | ·99999 | ·99999 | |

| ν | χ²=31 m=15·5 | 32 16·0 | 33 16·5 | 34 17·0 | 35 17·5 | 36 18·0 | 37 18·5 | 38 19·0 | 39 19·5 | 40 20·0 | c |
|---|---|---|---|---|---|---|---|---|---|---|---|
| 5 | 0·00001 | 0·00001 | | | | | | | | | |
| 6 | ·00003 | ·00002 | 0·00001 | 0·00001 | | | | | | | 3 |
| 7 | 0·00006 | 0·00004 | 0·00003 | 0·00002 | 0·00001 | 0·00001 | | | | | |
| 8 | ·00014 | ·00009 | ·00006 | ·00004 | ·00003 | ·00002 | 0·00001 | 0·00001 | | | 4 |
| 9 | ·00030 | ·00020 | ·00013 | ·00009 | ·00006 | ·00004 | ·00003 | ·00002 | 0·00001 | 0·00001 | |
| 10 | ·00059 | ·00040 | ·00027 | ·00019 | ·00012 | ·00008 | ·00006 | ·00004 | ·00003 | ·00002 | 5 |
| 11 | ·00110 | ·00076 | ·00053 | ·00036 | ·00025 | ·00017 | ·00012 | ·00008 | ·00005 | ·00004 | |
| 12 | ·00197 | ·00138 | ·00097 | ·00068 | ·00047 | ·00032 | ·00022 | ·00015 | ·00011 | ·00007 | 6 |
| 13 | 0·00337 | 0·00240 | 0·00170 | 0·00120 | 0·00085 | 0·00059 | 0·00041 | 0·00029 | 0·00020 | 0·00014 | |
| 14 | ·00554 | ·00401 | ·00288 | ·00206 | ·00147 | ·00104 | ·00074 | ·00052 | ·00036 | ·00026 | 7 |
| 15 | ·00878 | ·00644 | ·00469 | ·00341 | ·00246 | ·00177 | ·00127 | ·00090 | ·00064 | ·00045 | |
| 16 | ·01346 | ·01000 | ·00739 | ·00543 | ·00397 | ·00289 | ·00210 | ·00151 | ·00109 | ·00078 | 8 |
| 17 | ·01997 | ·01505 | ·01127 | ·00840 | ·00622 | ·00459 | ·00337 | ·00246 | ·00179 | ·00129 | |
| 18 | ·02879 | ·02199 | ·01669 | ·01260 | ·00945 | ·00706 | ·00524 | ·00387 | ·00285 | ·00209 | 9 |
| 19 | 0·04037 | 0·03125 | 0·02404 | 0·01838 | 0·01397 | 0·01056 | 0·00793 | 0·00593 | 0·00442 | 0·00327 | |
| 20 | ·05519 | ·04330 | ·03374 | ·02613 | ·02010 | ·01538 | ·01170 | ·00886 | ·00667 | ·00500 | 10 |
| 21 | ·07366 | ·05855 | ·04622 | ·03624 | ·02824 | ·02187 | ·01683 | ·01289 | ·00981 | ·00744 | |
| 22 | ·09612 | ·07740 | ·06187 | ·04912 | ·03875 | ·03007 | ·02366 | ·01832 | ·01411 | ·01081 | 11 |
| 23 | ·12279 | ·10014 | ·08107 | ·06516 | ·05202 | ·04125 | ·03251 | ·02547 | ·01984 | ·01537 | |
| 24 | ·15378 | ·12699 | ·10407 | ·08467 | ·06840 | ·05489 | ·04376 | ·03467 | ·02731 | ·02139 | 12 |
| 25 | 0·18902 | 0·15801 | 0·13107 | 0·10791 | 0·08820 | 0·07160 | 0·05774 | 0·04626 | 0·03684 | 0·02916 | |
| 26 | ·22827 | ·19312 | ·16210 | ·13502 | ·11165 | ·09167 | ·07475 | ·06056 | ·04875 | ·03901 | 13 |
| 27 | ·27114 | ·23208 | ·19707 | ·16605 | ·13887 | ·11530 | ·09507 | ·07786 | ·06336 | ·05124 | |
| 28 | ·31708 | ·27451 | ·23574 | ·20087 | ·16987 | ·14260 | ·11886 | ·09840 | ·08092 | ·06613 | 14 |
| 29 | ·36542 | ·31987 | ·27774 | ·23926 | ·20454 | ·17356 | ·14622 | ·12234 | ·10166 | ·08394 | |
| 30 | 0·41541 | 0·36753 | 0·32254 | 0·28083 | 0·24264 | 0·20808 | 0·17714 | 0·14975 | 0·12573 | 0·10486 | 15 |
| 32 | ·51701 | ·46675 | ·41802 | ·37145 | ·32754 | ·28665 | ·24903 | ·21479 | ·18398 | ·15651 | 16 |
| 34 | ·61544 | ·56596 | ·51648 | ·46774 | ·42040 | ·37505 | ·33214 | ·29203 | ·25497 | ·22107 | 17 |
| 36 | ·70518 | ·65934 | ·61205 | ·56402 | ·51600 | ·46865 | ·42259 | ·37836 | ·33639 | ·29703 | 18 |
| 38 | ·78246 | ·74235 | ·69965 | ·65496 | ·60893 | ·56225 | ·51555 | ·46948 | ·42461 | ·38142 | 19 |
| 40 | 0·84551 | 0·81225 | 0·77572 | 0·73632 | 0·69453 | 0·65092 | 0·60607 | 0·56061 | 0·51514 | 0·47026 | 20 |
| 42 | ·89437 | ·86817 | ·83848 | ·80548 | ·76943 | ·73072 | ·68979 | ·64717 | ·60342 | ·55909 | 21 |
| 44 | ·93043 | ·91077 | ·88780 | ·86147 | ·83185 | ·79912 | ·76355 | ·72550 | ·68538 | ·64370 | 22 |
| 46 | ·95584 | ·94176 | ·92478 | ·90473 | ·88150 | ·85509 | ·82558 | ·79314 | ·75804 | ·72061 | 23 |
| 48 | ·97296 | ·96331 | ·95131 | ·93670 | ·91928 | ·89889 | ·87547 | ·84902 | ·81963 | ·78749 | 24 |
| 50 | 0·98402 | 0·97769 | 0·96955 | 0·95935 | 0·94682 | 0·93174 | 0·91392 | 0·89325 | 0·86968 | 0·84323 | 25 |
| 52 | ·99087 | ·98688 | ·98159 | ·97476 | ·96611 | ·95539 | ·94238 | ·92687 | ·90872 | ·88782 | 26 |
| 54 | ·99496 | ·99254 | ·98923 | ·98483 | ·97908 | ·97177 | ·96263 | ·95144 | ·93800 | ·92211 | 27 |
| 56 | ·99731 | ·99590 | ·99390 | ·99117 | ·98750 | ·98268 | ·97650 | ·96873 | ·95914 | ·94752 | 28 |
| 58 | ·99861 | ·99781 | ·99665 | ·99502 | ·99275 | ·98970 | ·98567 | ·98046 | ·97387 | ·96567 | 29 |
| 60 | 0·99930 | 0·99887 | 0·99822 | 0·99727 | 0·99593 | 0·99406 | 0·99152 | 0·98815 | 0·98377 | 0·97818 | 30 |
| 62 | ·99966 | ·99943 | ·99908 | ·99855 | ·99778 | ·99667 | ·99512 | ·99302 | ·99021 | ·98653 | 31 |
| 64 | ·99984 | ·99972 | ·99954 | ·99925 | ·99882 | ·99819 | ·99728 | ·99600 | ·99425 | ·99191 | 32 |
| 66 | ·99993 | ·99987 | ·99978 | ·99963 | ·99939 | ·99904 | ·99852 | ·99777 | ·99672 | ·99527 | 33 |
| 68 | ·99997 | ·99994 | ·99989 | ·99982 | ·99970 | ·99951 | ·99922 | ·99879 | ·99818 | ·99731 | 34 |
| 70 | 0·99999 | 0·99997 | 0·99995 | 0·99991 | 0·99985 | 0·99975 | 0·99960 | 0·99936 | 0·99902 | 0·99851 | 35 |

## Table 7. *Probability integral of the χ²-distribution (continued)*

| ν | χ²=2.2 m=1.1 | 2.4 1.2 | 2.6 1.3 | 2.8 1.4 | 3.0 1.5 | 3.2 1.6 | 3.4 1.7 | 3.6 1.8 | 3.8 1.9 | 4.0 2.0 | c |
|---|---|---|---|---|---|---|---|---|---|---|---|
| 1 | 0·13801 | 0·12134 | 0·10686 | 0·09426 | 0·08327 | 0·07364 | 0·06520 | 0·05778 | 0·05125 | 0·04550 | |
| 2 | ·33287 | ·30119 | ·27253 | ·24660 | ·22313 | ·20190 | ·18268 | ·16530 | ·14957 | ·13534 | 1 |
| 3 | ·53195 | ·49363 | ·45749 | ·42350 | ·39163 | ·36181 | ·33397 | ·30802 | ·28389 | ·26146 | |
| 4 | ·69903 | ·66263 | ·62682 | ·59183 | ·55783 | ·52493 | ·49325 | ·46284 | ·43375 | ·40601 | 2 |
| 5 | ·82084 | ·79147 | ·76137 | ·73079 | ·69999 | ·66918 | ·63857 | ·60831 | ·57856 | ·54942 | |
| 6 | ·90042 | ·87949 | ·85711 | ·83350 | ·80885 | ·78336 | ·75722 | ·73062 | ·70372 | ·67668 | 3 |
| 7 | 0·94795 | 0·93444 | 0·91938 | 0·90287 | 0·88500 | 0·86590 | 0·84570 | 0·82452 | 0·80250 | 0·77978 | |
| 8 | ·97426 | ·96623 | ·95691 | ·94628 | ·93436 | ·92119 | ·90681 | ·89129 | ·87470 | ·85712 | 4 |
| 9 | ·98790 | ·98345 | ·97807 | ·97170 | ·96430 | ·95583 | ·94631 | ·93572 | ·92408 | ·91141 | |
| 10 | ·99457 | ·99225 | ·98934 | ·98575 | ·98142 | ·97632 | ·97039 | ·96359 | ·95592 | ·94735 | 5 |
| 11 | ·99766 | ·99652 | ·99503 | ·99311 | ·99073 | ·98781 | ·98431 | ·98019 | ·97541 | ·96992 | |
| 12 | ·99903 | ·99850 | ·99777 | ·99680 | ·99554 | ·99396 | ·99200 | ·98962 | ·98678 | ·98344 | 6 |
| 13 | 0·99961 | 0·99938 | 0·99903 | 0·99856 | 0·99793 | 0·99711 | 0·99606 | 0·99475 | 0·99314 | 0·99119 | |
| 14 | ·99985 | ·99975 | ·99960 | ·99938 | ·99907 | ·99866 | ·99813 | ·99743 | ·99655 | ·99547 | 7 |
| 15 | ·99994 | ·99990 | ·99984 | ·99974 | ·99960 | ·99940 | ·99913 | ·99878 | ·99832 | ·99774 | |
| 16 | ·99998 | ·99996 | ·99994 | ·99989 | ·99983 | ·99974 | ·99961 | ·99944 | ·99921 | ·99890 | 8 |
| 17 | ·99999 | ·99999 | ·99998 | ·99996 | ·99993 | ·99989 | ·99983 | ·99975 | ·99964 | ·99948 | |
| 18 | | | ·99999 | ·99998 | ·99997 | ·99995 | ·99993 | ·99989 | ·99984 | ·99976 | 9 |
| 19 | | | | 0·99999 | 0·99999 | 0·99998 | 0·99997 | 0·99995 | 0·99993 | 0·99989 | |
| 20 | | | | | | ·99999 | ·99999 | ·99998 | ·99997 | ·99995 | 10 |
| 21 | | | | | | | | ·99999 | ·99999 | ·99998 | |
| 22 | | | | | | | | | | ·99999 | 11 |

| ν | χ²=42 m=21 | 44 22 | 46 23 | 48 24 | 50 25 | 52 26 | 54 27 | 56 28 | 58 29 | 60 30 | c |
|---|---|---|---|---|---|---|---|---|---|---|---|
| 10 | 0·00001 | | | | | | | | | | 5 |
| 11 | ·00002 | 0·00001 | | | | | | | | | |
| 12 | ·00003 | ·00002 | 0·00001 | | | | | | | | 6 |
| 13 | 0·00006 | 0·00003 | 0·00001 | 0·00001 | | | | | | | |
| 14 | ·00012 | ·00006 | ·00003 | ·00001 | 0·00001 | | | | | | 7 |
| 15 | ·00023 | ·00011 | ·00005 | ·00003 | ·00001 | 0·00001 | | | | | |
| 16 | ·00040 | ·00020 | ·00010 | ·00005 | ·00002 | ·00001 | 0·00001 | | | | 8 |
| 17 | ·00067 | ·00034 | ·00017 | ·00009 | ·00004 | ·00002 | ·00001 | 0·00001 | | | |
| 18 | ·00111 | ·00058 | ·00030 | ·00015 | ·00008 | ·00004 | ·00002 | ·00001 | | | 9 |
| 19 | 0·00177 | 0·00094 | 0·00050 | 0·00026 | 0·00013 | 0·00007 | 0·00003 | 0·00002 | 0·00001 | | |
| 20 | ·00277 | ·00151 | ·00081 | ·00043 | ·00022 | ·00011 | ·00006 | ·00003 | ·00001 | 0·00001 | 10 |
| 21 | ·00421 | ·00234 | ·00128 | ·00069 | ·00036 | ·00019 | ·00010 | ·00005 | ·00003 | ·00001 | |
| 22 | ·00625 | ·00355 | ·00198 | ·00109 | ·00059 | ·00031 | ·00016 | ·00009 | ·00004 | ·00002 | 11 |
| 23 | ·00908 | ·00526 | ·00299 | ·00167 | ·00092 | ·00050 | ·00027 | ·00014 | ·00007 | ·00004 | |
| 24 | ·01291 | ·00763 | ·00443 | ·00252 | ·00142 | ·00078 | ·00043 | ·00023 | ·00012 | ·00006 | 12 |
| 25 | 0·01797 | 0·01085 | 0·00642 | 0·00373 | 0·00213 | 0·00120 | 0·00066 | 0·00036 | 0·00020 | 0·00011 | |
| 26 | ·02455 | ·01512 | ·00912 | ·00540 | ·00314 | ·00180 | ·00102 | ·00056 | ·00031 | ·00017 | 13 |
| 27 | ·03292 | ·02068 | ·01272 | ·00768 | ·00455 | ·00265 | ·00152 | ·00086 | ·00048 | ·00026 | |
| 28 | ·04336 | ·02779 | ·01743 | ·01072 | ·00647 | ·00384 | ·00224 | ·00129 | ·00073 | ·00041 | 14 |
| 29 | ·05616 | ·03670 | ·02346 | ·01470 | ·00903 | ·00545 | ·00324 | ·00189 | ·00109 | ·00062 | |
| 30 | 0·07157 | 0·04769 | 0·03107 | 0·01983 | 0·01240 | 0·00762 | 0·00460 | 0·00273 | 0·00160 | 0·00092 | 15 |
| 32 | ·11108 | ·07689 | ·05200 | ·03440 | ·02229 | ·01417 | ·00884 | ·00543 | ·00328 | ·00195 | 16 |
| 34 | ·16292 | ·11704 | ·08208 | ·05627 | ·03775 | ·02482 | ·01601 | ·01014 | ·00632 | ·00387 | 17 |
| 36 | ·22696 | ·16900 | ·12277 | ·08713 | ·06048 | ·04111 | ·02739 | ·01791 | ·01151 | ·00727 | 18 |
| 38 | ·30168 | ·23250 | ·17477 | ·12828 | ·09204 | ·06463 | ·04446 | ·03000 | ·01987 | ·01293 | 19 |
| 40 | 0·38426 | 0·30603 | 0·23771 | 0·18026 | 0·13358 | 0·09682 | 0·06872 | 0·04781 | 0·03263 | 0·02187 | 20 |
| 42 | ·47097 | ·38691 | ·31010 | ·24264 | ·18549 | ·13867 | ·10147 | ·07274 | ·05114 | ·03529 | 21 |
| 44 | ·55769 | ·47164 | ·38938 | ·31393 | ·24730 | ·19048 | ·14357 | ·10599 | ·07669 | ·05444 | 22 |
| 46 | ·64046 | ·55637 | ·47227 | ·39170 | ·31753 | ·25172 | ·19525 | ·14830 | ·11038 | ·08057 | 23 |
| 48 | ·71603 | ·63742 | ·55515 | ·47285 | ·39388 | ·32094 | ·25591 | ·19981 | ·15285 | ·11465 | 24 |
| 50 | 0·78216 | 0·71172 | 0·63458 | 0·55400 | 0·47340 | 0·39593 | 0·32416 | 0·25990 | 0·20417 | 0·15724 | 25 |
| 52 | ·83770 | ·77710 | ·70766 | ·63191 | ·55292 | ·47392 | ·39786 | ·32721 | ·26371 | ·20836 | 26 |
| 54 | ·88257 | ·83242 | ·77230 | ·70382 | ·62939 | ·55190 | ·47440 | ·39970 | ·33011 | ·26734 | 27 |
| 56 | ·91746 | ·87750 | ·82737 | ·76774 | ·70019 | ·62700 | ·55094 | ·47486 | ·40143 | ·33287 | 28 |
| 58 | ·94363 | ·91291 | ·87260 | ·82253 | ·76340 | ·69674 | ·62475 | ·55003 | ·47530 | ·40308 | 29 |
| 60 | 0·96258 | 0·93978 | 0·90848 | 0·86788 | 0·81790 | 0·75926 | 0·69347 | 0·62261 | 0·54917 | 0·47572 | 30 |
| 62 | ·97585 | ·95949 | ·93598 | ·90415 | ·86331 | ·81345 | ·75531 | ·69035 | ·62058 | ·54835 | 31 |
| 64 | ·98483 | ·97347 | ·95639 | ·93224 | ·89993 | ·85889 | ·80917 | ·75153 | ·68738 | ·61864 | 32 |
| 66 | ·99073 | ·98308 | ·97106 | ·95330 | ·92854 | ·89582 | ·85462 | ·80507 | ·74792 | ·68454 | 33 |
| 68 | ·99448 | ·98949 | ·98128 | ·96862 | ·95022 | ·92491 | ·89181 | ·85049 | ·80112 | ·74445 | 34 |
| 70 | 0·99680 | 0·99364 | 0·98819 | 0·97943 | 0·96616 | 0·94716 | 0·92134 | 0·88790 | 0·84649 | 0·79731 | 35 |

Table 7 (*continued*)

| ν | $\chi^2=4.2$ m=2.1 | 4.4 2.2 | 4.6 2.3 | 4.8 2.4 | 5.0 2.5 | 5.2 2.6 | 5.4 2.7 | 5.6 2.8 | 5.8 2.9 | 6.0 3.0 | c |
|---|---|---|---|---|---|---|---|---|---|---|---|
| 1 | 0·04042 | 0·03594 | 0·03197 | 0·02846 | 0·02535 | 0·02259 | 0·02014 | 0·01796 | 0·01603 | 0·01431 | 1 |
| 2 | ·12246 | ·11080 | ·10026 | ·09072 | ·08208 | ·07427 | ·06721 | ·06081 | ·05502 | ·04979 | |
| 3 | ·24066 | ·22139 | ·20354 | ·18704 | ·17180 | ·15772 | ·14474 | ·13278 | ·12176 | ·11161 | 1 |
| 4 | ·37962 | ·35457 | ·33085 | ·30844 | ·28730 | ·26739 | ·24866 | ·23108 | ·21459 | ·19915 | 2 |
| 5 | ·52099 | ·49337 | ·46662 | ·44077 | ·41588 | ·39196 | ·36904 | ·34711 | ·32617 | ·30622 | |
| 6 | ·64963 | ·62271 | ·59604 | ·56971 | ·54381 | ·51843 | ·49363 | ·46945 | ·44596 | ·42319 | 3 |
| 7 | 0·75647 | 0·73272 | 0·70864 | 0·68435 | 0·65996 | 0·63557 | 0·61127 | 0·58715 | 0·56329 | 0·53975 | |
| 8 | ·83834 | ·81935 | ·79935 | ·77872 | ·75758 | ·73600 | ·71409 | ·69194 | ·66962 | ·64723 | 4 |
| 9 | ·89776 | ·88317 | ·86769 | ·85138 | ·83431 | ·81654 | ·79814 | ·77919 | ·75976 | ·73992 | |
| 10 | ·93787 | ·92750 | ·91625 | ·90413 | ·89118 | ·87742 | ·86291 | ·84768 | ·83178 | ·81526 | 5 |
| 11 | ·96370 | ·95672 | ·94898 | ·94046 | ·93117 | ·92109 | ·91026 | ·89868 | ·88637 | ·87337 | |
| 12 | ·97955 | ·97509 | ·97002 | ·96433 | ·95798 | ·95096 | ·94327 | ·93489 | ·92583 | ·91603 | 6 |
| 13 | 0·98887 | 0·98614 | 0·98298 | 0·97934 | 0·97519 | 0·97052 | 0·96530 | 0·95951 | 0·95313 | 0·94615 | |
| 14 | ·99414 | ·99254 | ·99064 | ·98841 | ·98581 | ·98283 | ·97943 | ·97559 | ·97128 | ·96649 | 7 |
| 15 | ·99701 | ·99610 | ·99501 | ·99369 | ·99213 | ·99029 | ·98816 | ·98571 | ·98291 | ·97975 | |
| 16 | ·99851 | ·99802 | ·99741 | ·99666 | ·99575 | ·99467 | ·99338 | ·99187 | ·99012 | ·98810 | 8 |
| 17 | ·99928 | ·99902 | ·99869 | ·99828 | ·99777 | ·99715 | ·99639 | ·99550 | ·99443 | ·99319 | |
| 18 | ·99966 | ·99953 | ·99936 | ·99914 | ·99886 | ·99851 | ·99809 | ·99757 | ·99694 | ·99620 | 9 |
| 19 | 0·99985 | 0·99978 | 0·99969 | 0·99958 | 0·99943 | 0·99924 | 0·99901 | 0·99872 | 0·99836 | 0·99793 | |
| 20 | ·99993 | ·99990 | ·99986 | ·99980 | ·99972 | ·99962 | ·99950 | ·99934 | ·99914 | ·99890 | 10 |
| 21 | ·99997 | ·99995 | ·99993 | ·99991 | ·99987 | ·99982 | ·99975 | ·99967 | ·99956 | ·99943 | |
| 22 | ·99999 | ·99998 | ·99997 | ·99996 | ·99994 | ·99991 | ·99988 | ·99984 | ·99978 | ·99971 | 11 |
| 23 | ·99999 | ·99999 | ·99999 | ·99998 | ·99997 | ·99996 | ·99994 | ·99992 | ·99989 | ·99986 | 12 |
| 24 | | ·99999 | ·99999 | ·99999 | ·99999 | ·99998 | ·99997 | ·99996 | ·99995 | ·99993 | |
| 25 | | | | | 0·99999 | 0·99999 | 0·99999 | 0·99998 | 0·99998 | 0·99997 | |
| 26 | | | | | | | | ·99999 | ·99999 | ·99998 | 13 |
| 27 | | | | | | | | | ·99999 | ·99999 | |

| ν | $\chi^2=62$ m=31 | 64 32 | 66 33 | 68 34 | 70 35 | 72 36 | 74 37 | 76 38 | 78 39 | 80 40 | c |
|---|---|---|---|---|---|---|---|---|---|---|---|
| 21 | 0·00001 | | | | | | | | | | |
| 22 | ·00001 | 0·00001 | | | | | | | | | 11 |
| 23 | ·00002 | ·00001 | 0·00001 | | | | | | | | |
| 24 | ·00003 | ·00002 | ·00001 | | | | | | | | 12 |
| 25 | 0·00006 | 0·00003 | 0·00002 | 0·00001 | | | | | | | |
| 26 | ·00009 | ·00005 | ·00003 | ·00001 | 0·00001 | | | | | | 13 |
| 27 | ·00014 | ·00008 | ·00004 | ·00002 | ·00001 | 0·00001 | | | | | |
| 28 | ·00023 | ·00012 | ·00007 | ·00004 | ·00002 | ·00001 | 0·00001 | | | | 14 |
| 29 | ·00035 | ·00019 | ·00011 | ·00006 | ·00003 | ·00002 | ·00001 | | | | |
| 30 | 0·00052 | 0·00029 | 0·00016 | 0·00009 | 0·00005 | 0·00003 | 0·00001 | 0·00001 | | | 15 |
| 32 | ·00114 | ·00066 | ·00038 | ·00021 | ·00012 | ·00007 | ·00004 | ·00002 | 0·00001 | 0·00001 | 16 |
| 34 | ·00234 | ·00139 | ·00082 | ·00047 | ·00027 | ·00015 | ·00009 | ·00005 | ·00003 | ·00001 | 17 |
| 36 | ·00452 | ·00277 | ·00167 | ·00100 | ·00059 | ·00034 | ·00020 | ·00011 | ·00006 | ·00004 | 18 |
| 38 | ·00828 | ·00522 | ·00324 | ·00198 | ·00120 | ·00071 | ·00042 | ·00025 | ·00014 | ·00008 | 19 |
| 40 | 0·01441 | 0·00934 | 0·00596 | 0·00375 | 0·00233 | 0·00142 | 0·00086 | 0·00051 | 0·00030 | 0·00018 | 20 |
| 42 | ·02392 | ·01594 | ·01045 | ·00675 | ·00430 | ·00270 | ·00167 | ·00102 | ·00062 | ·00037 | 21 |
| 44 | ·03795 | ·02600 | ·01751 | ·01161 | ·00758 | ·00488 | ·00310 | ·00194 | ·00120 | ·00073 | 22 |
| 46 | ·05772 | ·04062 | ·02810 | ·01912 | ·01281 | ·00846 | ·00550 | ·00353 | ·00224 | ·00140 | 23 |
| 48 | ·08437 | ·06097 | ·04329 | ·03023 | ·02077 | ·01405 | ·00937 | ·00616 | ·00399 | ·00256 | 24 |
| 50 | 0·11880 | 0·08810 | 0·06418 | 0·04596 | 0·03237 | 0·02245 | 0·01533 | 0·01032 | 0·00685 | 0·00448 | 25 |
| 52 | ·16148 | ·12283 | ·09175 | ·06736 | ·04862 | ·03453 | ·02415 | ·01664 | ·01130 | ·00757 | 26 |
| 54 | ·21237 | ·16557 | ·12675 | ·09533 | ·07049 | ·05127 | ·03670 | ·02587 | ·01797 | ·01231 | 27 |
| 56 | ·27080 | ·21623 | ·16953 | ·13057 | ·09884 | ·07358 | ·05390 | ·03888 | ·02762 | ·01934 | 28 |
| 58 | ·33550 | ·27412 | ·21994 | ·17335 | ·13428 | ·10227 | ·07663 | ·05652 | ·04105 | ·02933 | 29 |
| 60 | 0·40465 | 0·33801 | 0·27730 | 0·22351 | 0·17705 | 0·13789 | 0·10563 | 0·07964 | 0·05912 | 0·04323 | 30 |
| 62 | ·47611 | ·40615 | ·34040 | ·28035 | ·22694 | ·18063 | ·14140 | ·10893 | ·08260 | ·06169 | 31 |
| 64 | ·54757 | ·47649 | ·40758 | ·34270 | ·28328 | ·23026 | ·18409 | ·14482 | ·11215 | ·08552 | 32 |
| 66 | ·61680 | ·54683 | ·47685 | ·40894 | ·34490 | ·28609 | ·23346 | ·18745 | ·14816 | ·11530 | 33 |
| 68 | ·68183 | ·61504 | ·54612 | ·47719 | ·41025 | ·34700 | ·28880 | ·23654 | ·19071 | ·15140 | 34 |
| 70 | 0·74112 | 0·67923 | 0·61335 | 0·54544 | 0·47752 | 0·41150 | 0·34903 | 0·29141 | 0·23953 | 0·19388 | 35 |

Table 7. *Probability integral of the χ²-distribution (continued)*

| ν | $\chi^2=6.2$ $m=3.1$ | 6.4 3.2 | 6.6 3.3 | 6.8 3.4 | 7.0 3.5 | 7.2 3.6 | 7.4 3.7 | 7.6 3.8 | 7.8 3.9 | 8.0 4.0 | c |
|---|---|---|---|---|---|---|---|---|---|---|---|
| 1 | 0.01278 | 0.01141 | 0.01020 | 0.00912 | 0.00815 | 0.00729 | 0.00652 | 0.00584 | 0.00522 | 0.00468 | |
| 2 | ·04505 | ·04076 | ·03688 | ·03337 | ·03020 | ·02732 | ·02472 | ·02237 | ·02024 | ·01832 | 1 |
| 3 | ·10228 | ·09369 | ·08580 | ·07855 | ·07190 | ·06579 | ·06018 | ·05504 | ·05033 | ·04601 | |
| 4 | ·18470 | ·17120 | ·15860 | ·14684 | ·13589 | ·12569 | ·11620 | ·10738 | ·09919 | ·09158 | 2 |
| 5 | ·28724 | ·26922 | ·25213 | ·23595 | ·22064 | ·20619 | ·19255 | ·17970 | ·16761 | ·15624 | |
| 6 | ·40116 | ·37990 | ·35943 | ·33974 | ·32085 | ·30275 | ·28543 | ·26890 | ·25313 | ·23810 | 3 |
| 7 | 0.51660 | 0.49390 | 0.47168 | 0.45000 | 0.42888 | 0.40836 | 0.38845 | 0.36918 | 0.35056 | 0.33259 | |
| 8 | ·62484 | ·60252 | ·58034 | ·55836 | ·53663 | ·51522 | ·49415 | ·47349 | ·45325 | ·43347 | 4 |
| 9 | ·71975 | ·69931 | ·67869 | ·65793 | ·63712 | ·61631 | ·59555 | ·57490 | ·55442 | ·53415 | |
| 10 | ·79819 | ·78061 | ·76259 | ·74418 | ·72544 | ·70644 | ·68722 | ·66784 | ·64837 | ·62884 | 5 |
| 11 | ·85969 | ·84539 | ·83049 | ·81504 | ·79908 | ·78266 | ·76583 | ·74862 | ·73110 | ·71330 | |
| 12 | ·90567 | ·89459 | ·88288 | ·87054 | ·85761 | ·84412 | ·83009 | ·81556 | ·80056 | ·78513 | 6 |
| 13 | 0.93857 | 0.93038 | 0.92157 | 0.91216 | 0.90215 | 0.89155 | 0.88038 | 0.86865 | 0.85638 | 0.84360 | |
| 14 | ·96120 | ·95538 | ·94903 | ·94215 | ·93471 | ·92673 | ·91819 | ·90911 | ·89948 | ·88933 | 7 |
| 15 | ·97619 | ·97222 | ·96782 | ·96296 | ·95765 | ·95186 | ·94559 | ·93882 | ·93155 | ·92378 | |
| 16 | ·98579 | ·98317 | ·98022 | ·97693 | ·97326 | ·96921 | ·96476 | ·95989 | ·95460 | ·94887 | 8 |
| 17 | ·99174 | ·99007 | ·98816 | ·98599 | ·98355 | ·98081 | ·97775 | ·97437 | ·97064 | ·96655 | |
| 18 | ·99532 | ·99429 | ·99309 | ·99171 | ·99013 | ·98833 | ·98630 | ·98402 | ·98147 | ·97864 | 9 |
| 19 | 0.99741 | 0.99679 | 0.99606 | 0.99521 | 0.99421 | 0.99307 | 0.99176 | 0.99026 | 0.98857 | 0.98667 | |
| 20 | ·99860 | ·99824 | ·99781 | ·99729 | ·99669 | ·99598 | ·99515 | ·99420 | ·99311 | ·99187 | 10 |
| 21 | ·99926 | ·99905 | ·99880 | ·99850 | ·99814 | ·99771 | ·99721 | ·99662 | ·99594 | ·99514 | |
| 22 | ·99962 | ·99950 | ·99936 | ·99919 | ·99898 | ·99873 | ·99843 | ·99807 | ·99765 | ·99716 | 11 |
| 23 | ·99981 | ·99974 | ·99967 | ·99957 | ·99945 | ·99931 | ·99913 | ·99892 | ·99867 | ·99837 | |
| 24 | ·99990 | ·99987 | ·99983 | ·99978 | ·99971 | ·99963 | ·99953 | ·99941 | ·99926 | ·99908 | 12 |
| 25 | 0.99995 | 0.99994 | 0.99991 | 0.99989 | 0.99985 | 0.99981 | 0.99975 | 0.99968 | 0.99960 | 0.99949 | |
| 26 | ·99998 | ·99997 | ·99996 | ·99994 | ·99992 | ·99990 | ·99987 | ·99983 | ·99978 | ·99973 | 13 |
| 27 | ·99999 | ·99999 | ·99998 | ·99997 | ·99996 | ·99995 | ·99993 | ·99991 | ·99989 | ·99985 | |
| 28 | | ·99999 | ·99999 | ·99999 | ·99998 | ·99998 | ·99997 | ·99996 | ·99994 | ·99992 | 14 |
| 29 | | | | | ·99999 | ·99999 | ·99999 | ·99998 | ·99998 | ·99996 | |
| 30 | | | | | | 0.99999 | 0.99999 | 0.99999 | 0.99999 | 0.99998 | 15 |

| ν | $\chi^2=82$ $m=41$ | 84 42 | 86 43 | 88 44 | 90 45 | 92 46 | 94 47 | 96 48 | 98 49 | 100 50 | c |
|---|---|---|---|---|---|---|---|---|---|---|---|
| 34 | 0.00001 | | | | | | | | | | 17 |
| 36 | ·00002 | 0.00001 | | | | | | | | | 18 |
| 38 | ·00004 | ·00002 | 0.00001 | 0.00001 | | | | | | | 19 |
| 40 | 0.00010 | 0.00006 | 0.00003 | 0.00002 | 0.00001 | 0.00001 | | | | | 20 |
| 42 | ·00022 | ·00013 | ·00007 | ·00004 | ·00002 | ·00001 | 0.00001 | | | | 21 |
| 44 | ·00044 | ·00026 | ·00016 | ·00009 | ·00005 | ·00002 | ·00002 | 0.00001 | | | 22 |
| 46 | ·00086 | ·00053 | ·00032 | ·00019 | ·00011 | ·00007 | ·00004 | ·00002 | 0.00001 | 0.00001 | 23 |
| 48 | ·00162 | ·00101 | ·00062 | ·00038 | ·00023 | ·00014 | ·00008 | ·00005 | ·00003 | ·00002 | 24 |
| 50 | 0.00290 | 0.00185 | 0.00117 | 0.00073 | 0.00045 | 0.00027 | 0.00017 | 0.00010 | 0.00006 | 0.00003 | 25 |
| 52 | ·00500 | ·00326 | ·00210 | ·00134 | ·00084 | ·00053 | ·00032 | ·00020 | ·00012 | ·00007 | 26 |
| 54 | ·00832 | ·00555 | ·00365 | ·00238 | ·00153 | ·00097 | ·00061 | ·00038 | ·00023 | ·00014 | 27 |
| 56 | ·01335 | ·00910 | ·00612 | ·00406 | ·00267 | ·00173 | ·00111 | ·00070 | ·00044 | ·00027 | 28 |
| 58 | ·02073 | ·01442 | ·00990 | ·00671 | ·00450 | ·00298 | ·00195 | ·00126 | ·00081 | ·00051 | 29 |
| 60 | 0.03115 | 0.02214 | 0.01552 | 0.01074 | 0.00734 | 0.00495 | 0.00330 | 0.00218 | 0.00142 | 0.00092 | 30 |
| 62 | ·04540 | ·03294 | ·02357 | ·01664 | ·01160 | ·00798 | ·00543 | ·00365 | ·00242 | ·00159 | 31 |
| 64 | ·06425 | ·04757 | ·03473 | ·02502 | ·01778 | ·01248 | ·00865 | ·00592 | ·00401 | ·00269 | 32 |
| 66 | ·08839 | ·06678 | ·04974 | ·03653 | ·02648 | ·01894 | ·01338 | ·00934 | ·00644 | ·00439 | 33 |
| 68 | ·11839 | ·09122 | ·06928 | ·05189 | ·03834 | ·02795 | ·02012 | ·01431 | ·01005 | ·00698 | 34 |
| 70 | 0.15457 | 0.12142 | 0.09401 | 0.07176 | 0.05404 | 0.04015 | 0.02944 | 0.02132 | 0.01525 | 0.01078 | 35 |

## Table 7 (*continued*)

| ν | χ²=8·2 m=4·1 | 8·4 4·2 | 8·6 4·3 | 8·8 4·4 | 9·0 4·5 | 9·2 4·6 | 9·4 4·7 | 9·6 4·8 | 9·8 4·9 | 10·0 5·0 | c |
|---|---|---|---|---|---|---|---|---|---|---|---|
| 1 | 0.00419 | 0.00375 | 0.00336 | 0.00301 | 0.00270 | 0.00242 | 0.00217 | 0.00195 | 0.00175 | 0.00157 | |
| 2 | ·01657 | ·01500 | ·01357 | ·01228 | ·01111 | ·01005 | ·00910 | ·00823 | ·00745 | ·00674 | 1 |
| 3 | ·04205 | ·03843 | ·03511 | ·03207 | ·02929 | ·02675 | ·02442 | ·02229 | ·02034 | ·01857 | |
| 4 | ·08452 | ·07798 | ·07191 | ·06630 | ·06110 | ·05629 | ·05184 | ·04773 | ·04394 | ·04043 | 2 |
| 5 | ·14555 | ·13553 | ·12612 | ·11731 | ·10906 | ·10135 | ·09413 | ·08740 | ·08110 | ·07524 | |
| 6 | ·22381 | ·21024 | ·19736 | ·18514 | ·17358 | ·16264 | ·15230 | ·14254 | ·13333 | ·12465 | 3 |
| 7 | 0.31529 | 0.29865 | 0.28266 | 0.26734 | 0.25266 | 0.23861 | 0.22520 | 0.21240 | 0.20019 | 0.18857 | |
| 8 | ·41418 | ·39540 | ·37715 | ·35945 | ·34230 | ·32571 | ·30968 | ·29423 | ·27935 | ·26503 | 4 |
| 9 | ·51412 | ·49439 | ·47499 | ·45594 | ·43727 | ·41902 | ·40120 | ·38383 | ·36692 | ·35049 | |
| 10 | ·60931 | ·58983 | ·57044 | ·55118 | ·53210 | ·51323 | ·49461 | ·47626 | ·45821 | ·44049 | 5 |
| 11 | ·69528 | ·67709 | ·65876 | ·64035 | ·62189 | ·60344 | ·58502 | ·56669 | ·54846 | ·53039 | |
| 12 | ·76931 | ·75314 | ·73666 | ·71991 | ·70293 | ·68576 | ·66844 | ·65101 | ·63350 | ·61596 | 6 |
| 13 | 0.83033 | 0.81660 | 0.80244 | 0.78788 | 0.77294 | 0.75768 | 0.74211 | 0.72627 | 0.71020 | 0.69393 | |
| 14 | ·87865 | ·86746 | ·85579 | ·84365 | ·83105 | ·81803 | ·80461 | ·79081 | ·77666 | ·76218 | 7 |
| 15 | ·91551 | ·90675 | ·89749 | ·88774 | ·87752 | ·86683 | ·85569 | ·84412 | ·83213 | ·81974 | |
| 16 | ·94269 | ·93606 | ·92897 | ·92142 | ·91341 | ·90495 | ·89603 | ·88667 | ·87686 | ·86663 | 8 |
| 17 | ·96208 | ·95723 | ·95198 | ·94633 | ·94026 | ·93378 | ·92687 | ·91954 | ·91179 | ·90361 | |
| 18 | ·97551 | ·97207 | ·96830 | ·96420 | ·95974 | ·95493 | ·94974 | ·94418 | ·93824 | ·93191 | 9 |
| 19 | 0.98454 | 0.98217 | 0.97955 | 0.97666 | 0.97348 | 0.97001 | 0.96623 | 0.96213 | 0.95771 | 0.95295 | |
| 20 | ·99046 | ·98887 | ·98709 | ·98511 | ·98291 | ·98047 | ·97779 | ·97486 | ·97166 | ·96817 | 10 |
| 21 | ·99424 | ·99320 | ·99203 | ·99070 | ·98921 | ·98755 | ·98570 | ·98365 | ·98139 | ·97891 | |
| 22 | ·99659 | ·99593 | ·99518 | ·99431 | ·99333 | ·99222 | ·99098 | ·98958 | ·98803 | ·98630 | 11 |
| 23 | ·99802 | ·99761 | ·99714 | ·99659 | ·99596 | ·99524 | ·99442 | ·99349 | ·99245 | ·99128 | |
| 24 | ·99888 | ·99863 | ·99833 | ·99799 | ·99760 | ·99714 | ·99661 | ·99601 | ·99532 | ·99455 | 12 |
| 25 | 0.99937 | 0.99922 | 0.99905 | 0.99884 | 0.99860 | 0.99831 | 0.99798 | 0.99760 | 0.99716 | 0.99665 | |
| 26 | ·99966 | ·99957 | ·99947 | ·99934 | ·99919 | ·99902 | ·99882 | ·99858 | ·99830 | ·99798 | 13 |
| 27 | ·99981 | ·99977 | ·99971 | ·99963 | ·99955 | ·99944 | ·99932 | ·99917 | ·99900 | ·99880 | |
| 28 | ·99990 | ·99987 | ·99984 | ·99980 | ·99975 | ·99969 | ·99962 | ·99953 | ·99942 | ·99930 | 14 |
| 29 | ·99995 | ·99993 | ·99991 | ·99989 | ·99986 | ·99983 | ·99979 | ·99973 | ·99967 | ·99960 | |
| 30 | 0.99997 | 0.99997 | 0.99996 | 0.99994 | 0.99993 | 0.99991 | 0.99988 | 0.99985 | 0.99982 | ·99977 | 15 |
| 32 | ·99999 | ·99999 | ·99999 | ·00008 | ·99998 | ·99997 | ·99997 | ·99996 | ·99995 | ·99993 | 16 |
| 34 | | | | | | ·99999 | ·99999 | ·99999 | ·99999 | ·99998 | 17 |

| ν | χ²=102 m=51 | 104 52 | 106 53 | 108 54 | 110 55 | 112 56 | 114 57 | 116 58 | 118 59 | 120 60 | c |
|---|---|---|---|---|---|---|---|---|---|---|---|
| 48 | 0.00001 | | | | | | | | | | 24 |
| 50 | 0.00002 | 0.00001 | 0.00001 | | | | | | | | 25 |
| 52 | ·00004 | ·00002 | ·00001 | 0.00001 | | | | | | | 26 |
| 54 | ·00009 | ·00005 | ·00003 | ·00002 | 0.00001 | 0.00001 | | | | | 27 |
| 56 | ·00017 | ·00010 | ·00006 | ·00004 | ·00002 | ·00001 | 0.00001 | | | | 28 |
| 58 | ·00032 | ·00020 | ·00012 | ·00007 | ·00004 | ·00003 | ·00002 | 0.00001 | 0.00001 | | 29 |
| 60 | 0.00059 | 0.00037 | 0.00023 | 0.00014 | 0.00009 | 0.00005 | 0.00003 | 0.00002 | 0.00001 | 0.00001 | 30 |
| 62 | ·00104 | ·00067 | ·00043 | ·00027 | ·00017 | ·00010 | ·00006 | ·00004 | ·00002 | ·00001 | 31 |
| 64 | ·00178 | ·00117 | ·00076 | ·00049 | ·00031 | ·00019 | ·00012 | ·00008 | ·00005 | ·00003 | 32 |
| 66 | ·00296 | ·00198 | ·00130 | ·00085 | ·00055 | ·00035 | ·00022 | ·00014 | ·00009 | ·00005 | 33 |
| 68 | ·00479 | ·00325 | ·00219 | ·00145 | ·00095 | ·00062 | ·00040 | ·00026 | ·00016 | ·00010 | 34 |
| 70 | 0.00753 | 0.00521 | 0.00356 | 0.00241 | 0.00161 | 0.00107 | 0.00070 | 0.00046 | 0.00029 | 0.00019 | 35 |

| ν | χ²=122 m=61 | 124 62 | 126 63 | 128 64 | 130 65 | 132 66 | 134 67 | | | | c |
|---|---|---|---|---|---|---|---|---|---|---|---|
| 62 | 0.00001 | | | | | | | | | | 31 |
| 64 | ·00002 | 0.00001 | 0.00001 | | | | | | | | 32 |
| 66 | ·00003 | ·00002 | ·00001 | 0.00001 | | | | | | | 33 |
| 68 | ·00006 | ·00004 | ·00002 | ·00002 | 0.00001 | | | | | | 34 |
| 70 | 0.00012 | 0.00008 | 0.00005 | 0.00003 | 0.00002 | 0.00001 | 0.00001 | | | | 35 |

## Table 8. *Percentage points of the χ²-distribution*

| ν \ Q | 0·995 | 0·990 | 0·975 | 0·950 | 0·900 | 0·750 | 0·500 |
|---|---|---|---|---|---|---|---|
| 1 | 392704.10⁻¹⁰ | 157088.10⁻⁹ | 982069.10⁻⁹ | 393214.10⁻⁸ | 0·0157908 | 0·1015308 | 0·454936 |
| 2 | 0·0100251 | 0·0201007 | 0·0506356 | 0·102587 | 0·210721 | 0·575364 | 1·38629 |
| 3 | 0·0717218 | 0·114832 | 0·215795 | 0·351846 | 0·584374 | 1·212534 | 2·36597 |
| 4 | 0·206989 | 0·297109 | 0·484419 | 0·710723 | 1·063623 | 1·92256 | 3·35669 |
| 5 | 0·411742 | 0·554298 | 0·831212 | 1·145476 | 1·61031 | 2·67460 | 4·35146 |
| 6 | 0·675727 | 0·872090 | 1·23734 | 1·63538 | 2·20413 | 3·45460 | 5·34812 |
| 7 | 0·989256 | 1·239043 | 1·68987 | 2·16735 | 2·83311 | 4·25485 | 6·34581 |
| 8 | 1·34441 | 1·64650 | 2·17973 | 2·73264 | 3·48954 | 5·07064 | 7·34412 |
| 9 | 1·73493 | 2·08790 | 2·70039 | 3·32511 | 4·16816 | 5·89883 | 8·34283 |
| 10 | 2·15586 | 2·55821 | 3·24697 | 3·94030 | 4·86518 | 6·73720 | 9·34182 |
| 11 | 2·60322 | 3·05348 | 3·81575 | 4·57481 | 5·57778 | 7·58414 | 10·3410 |
| 12 | 3·07382 | 3·57057 | 4·40379 | 5·22603 | 6·30380 | 8·43842 | 11·3403 |
| 13 | 3·56503 | 4·10692 | 5·00875 | 5·89186 | 7·04150 | 9·29907 | 12·3398 |
| 14 | 4·07467 | 4·66043 | 5·62873 | 6·57063 | 7·78953 | 10·1653 | 13·3393 |
| 15 | 4·60092 | 5·22935 | 6·26214 | 7·26094 | 8·54676 | 11·0365 | 14·3389 |
| 16 | 5·14221 | 5·81221 | 6·90766 | 7·96165 | 9·31224 | 11·9122 | 15·3385 |
| 17 | 5·69722 | 6·40776 | 7·56419 | 8·67176 | 10·0852 | 12·7919 | 16·3382 |
| 18 | 6·26480 | 7·01491 | 8·23075 | 9·39046 | 10·8649 | 13·6753 | 17·3379 |
| 19 | 6·84397 | 7·63273 | 8·90652 | 10·1170 | 11·6509 | 14·5620 | 18·3377 |
| 20 | 7·43384 | 8·26040 | 9·59078 | 10·8508 | 12·4426 | 15·4518 | 19·3374 |
| 21 | 8·03365 | 8·89720 | 10·28293 | 11·5913 | 13·2396 | 16·3444 | 20·3372 |
| 22 | 8·64272 | 9·54249 | 10·9823 | 12·3380 | 14·0415 | 17·2396 | 21·3370 |
| 23 | 9·26043 | 10·19567 | 11·6886 | 13·0905 | 14·8480 | 18·1373 | 22·3369 |
| 24 | 9·88623 | 10·8564 | 12·4012 | 13·8484 | 15·6587 | 19·0373 | 23·3367 |
| 25 | 10·5197 | 11·5240 | 13·1197 | 14·6114 | 16·4734 | 19·9393 | 24·3366 |
| 26 | 11·1602 | 12·1981 | 13·8439 | 15·3792 | 17·2919 | 20·8434 | 25·3365 |
| 27 | 11·8076 | 12·8785 | 14·5734 | 16·1514 | 18·1139 | 21·7494 | 26·3363 |
| 28 | 12·4613 | 13·5647 | 15·3079 | 16·9279 | 18·9392 | 22·6572 | 27·3362 |
| 29 | 13·1211 | 14·2565 | 16·0471 | 17·7084 | 19·7677 | 23·5666 | 28·3361 |
| 30 | 13·7867 | 14·9535 | 16·7908 | 18·4927 | 20·5992 | 24·4776 | 29·3360 |
| 40 | 20·7065 | 22·1643 | 24·4330 | 26·5093 | 29·0505 | 33·6603 | 39·3353 |
| 50 | 27·9907 | 29·7067 | 32·3574 | 34·7643 | 37·6886 | 42·9421 | 49·3349 |
| 60 | 35·5345 | 37·4849 | 40·4817 | 43·1880 | 46·4589 | 52·2938 | 59·3347 |
| 70 | 43·2752 | 45·4417 | 48·7576 | 51·7393 | 55·3289 | 61·6983 | 69·3345 |
| 80 | 51·1719 | 53·5401 | 57·1532 | 60·3915 | 64·2778 | 71·1445 | 79·3343 |
| 90 | 59·1963 | 61·7541 | 65·6466 | 69·1260 | 73·2911 | 80·6247 | 89·3342 |
| 100 | 67·3276 | 70·0649 | 74·2219 | 77·9295 | 82·3581 | 90·1332 | 99·3341 |
| X | − 2·5758 | − 2·3263 | − 1·9600 | − 1·6449 | − 1·2816 | − 0·6745 | 0·0000 |

$$Q = Q(\chi^2 \,|\, \nu) = 1 - P(\chi^2 \,|\, \nu) = 2^{-\frac{1}{2}\nu} \{\Gamma(\tfrac{1}{2}\nu)\}^{-1} \int_{\chi^2}^{\infty} e^{-\frac{1}{2}x} x^{\frac{1}{2}\nu - 1} \, dx.$$

Table 8 (*continued*)

| $\nu$ \ $Q$ | 0·250 | 0·100 | 0·050 | 0·025 | 0·010 | 0·005 | 0·001 |
|---|---|---|---|---|---|---|---|
| 1 | 1·32330 | 2·70554 | 3·84146 | 5·02389 | 6·63490 | 7·87944 | 10·828 |
| 2 | 2·77259 | 4·60517 | 5·99146 | 7·37776 | 9·21034 | 10·5966 | 13·816 |
| 3 | 4·10834 | 6·25139 | 7·81473 | 9·34840 | 11·3449 | 12·8382 | 16·266 |
| 4 | 5·38527 | 7·77944 | 9·48773 | 11·1433 | 13·2767 | 14·8603 | 18·467 |
| 5 | 6·62568 | 9·23636 | 11·0705 | 12·8325 | 15·0863 | 16·7496 | 20·515 |
| 6 | 7·84080 | 10·6446 | 12·5916 | 14·4494 | 16·8119 | 18·5476 | 22·458 |
| 7 | 9·03715 | 12·0170 | 14·0671 | 16·0128 | 18·4753 | 20·2777 | 24·322 |
| 8 | 10·2189 | 13·3616 | 15·5073 | 17·5345 | 20·0902 | 21·9550 | 26·125 |
| 9 | 11·3888 | 14·6837 | 16·9190 | 19·0228 | 21·6660 | 23·5894 | 27·877 |
| 10 | 12·5489 | 15·9872 | 18·3070 | 20·4832 | 23·2093 | 25·1882 | 29·588 |
| 11 | 13·7007 | 17·2750 | 19·6751 | 21·9200 | 24·7250 | 26·7568 | 31·264 |
| 12 | 14·8454 | 18·5493 | 21·0261 | 23·3367 | 26·2170 | 28·2995 | 32·909 |
| 13 | 15·9839 | 19·8119 | 22·3620 | 24·7356 | 27·6882 | 29·8195 | 34·528 |
| 14 | 17·1169 | 21·0641 | 23·6848 | 26·1189 | 29·1412 | 31·3194 | 36·123 |
| 15 | 18·2451 | 22·3071 | 24·9958 | 27·4884 | 30·5779 | 32·8013 | 37·697 |
| 16 | 19·3689 | 23·5418 | 26·2962 | 28·8454 | 31·9999 | 34·2672 | 39·252 |
| 17 | 20·4887 | 24·7690 | 27·5871 | 30·1910 | 33·4087 | 35·7185 | 40·790 |
| 18 | 21·6049 | 25·9894 | 28·8693 | 31·5264 | 34·8053 | 37·1565 | 42·312 |
| 19 | 22·7178 | 27·2036 | 30·1435 | 32·8523 | 36·1909 | 38·5823 | 43·820 |
| 20 | 23·8277 | 28·4120 | 31·4104 | 34·1696 | 37·5662 | 39·9968 | 45·315 |
| 21 | 24·9348 | 29·6151 | 32·6706 | 35·4789 | 38·9322 | 41·4011 | 46·797 |
| 22 | 26·0393 | 30·8133 | 33·9244 | 36·7807 | 40·2894 | 42·7957 | 48·268 |
| 23 | 27·1413 | 32·0069 | 35·1725 | 38·0756 | 41·6384 | 44·1813 | 49·728 |
| 24 | 28·2412 | 33·1962 | 36·4150 | 39·3641 | 42·9798 | 45·5585 | 51·179 |
| 25 | 29·3389 | 34·3816 | 37·6525 | 40·6465 | 44·3141 | 46·9279 | 52·618 |
| 26 | 30·4346 | 35·5632 | 38·8851 | 41·9232 | 45·6417 | 48·2899 | 54·052 |
| 27 | 31·5284 | 36·7412 | 40·1133 | 43·1945 | 46·9629 | 49·6449 | 55·476 |
| 28 | 32·6205 | 37·9159 | 41·3371 | 44·4608 | 48·2782 | 50·9934 | 56·892 |
| 29 | 33·7109 | 39·0875 | 42·5570 | 45·7223 | 49·5879 | 52·3356 | 58·301 |
| 30 | 34·7997 | 40·2560 | 43·7730 | 46·9792 | 50·8922 | 53·6720 | 59·703 |
| 40 | 45·6160 | 51·8051 | 55·7585 | 59·3417 | 63·6907 | 66·7660 | 73·402 |
| 50 | 56·3336 | 63·1671 | 67·5048 | 71·4202 | 76·1539 | 79·4900 | 86·661 |
| 60 | 66·9815 | 74·3970 | 79·0819 | 83·2977 | 88·3794 | 91·9517 | 99·607 |
| 70 | 77·5767 | 85·5270 | 90·5312 | 95·0232 | 100·425 | 104·215 | 112·317 |
| 80 | 88·1303 | 96·5782 | 101·879 | 106·629 | 112·329 | 116·321 | 124·839 |
| 90 | 98·6499 | 107·565 | 113·145 | 118·136 | 124·116 | 128·299 | 137·208 |
| 100 | 109·141 | 118·498 | 124·342 | 129·561 | 135·807 | 140·169 | 149·449 |
| $X$ | $+0\cdot6745$ | $+1\cdot2816$ | $+1\cdot6449$ | $+1\cdot9600$ | $+2\cdot3263$ | $+2\cdot5758$ | $+3\cdot0902$ |

For $\nu > 100$ take

$$\chi^2 = \nu\left(1 - \frac{2}{9\nu} + X\sqrt{\frac{2}{9\nu}}\right)^3 \quad \text{or} \quad \chi^2 = \tfrac{1}{2}\{X + \sqrt{(2\nu - 1)}\}^2,$$

according to the degree of accuracy required. $X$ is the standardized normal deviate corresponding to $P = 1 - Q$, and is shown in the bottom line of the table.

# Table 9. *Probability integral, $P(t \mid \nu)$, of the t-distribution*

| $t$ \\ $\nu$ | 1 | 2 | 3 | 4 | 5 | 6 | 7 | 8 | 9 | 10 |
|---|---|---|---|---|---|---|---|---|---|---|
| 0·0 | 0·50000 | 0·50000 | 0·50000 | 0·50000 | 0·50000 | 0·50000 | 0·50000 | 0·50000 | 0·50000 | 0·50000 |
| 0·1 | ·53173 | ·53527 | ·53667 | ·53742 | ·53788 | ·53820 | ·53843 | ·53860 | ·53873 | ·53884 |
| 0·2 | ·56283 | ·57002 | ·57286 | ·57438 | ·57532 | ·57596 | ·57642 | ·57676 | ·57704 | ·57726 |
| 0·3 | ·59277 | ·60376 | ·60812 | ·61044 | ·61188 | ·61285 | ·61356 | ·61409 | ·61450 | ·61484 |
| 0·4 | ·62112 | ·63608 | ·64203 | ·64520 | ·64716 | ·64850 | ·64946 | ·65019 | ·65076 | ·65122 |
| 0·5 | 0·64758 | 0·66667 | 0·67428 | 0·67834 | 0·68085 | 0·68256 | 0·68380 | 0·68473 | 0·68546 | 0·68605 |
| 0·6 | ·67202 | ·69529 | ·70460 | ·70958 | ·71267 | ·71477 | ·71629 | ·71745 | ·71835 | ·71907 |
| 0·7 | ·69440 | ·72181 | ·73284 | ·73875 | ·74243 | ·74493 | ·74674 | ·74811 | ·74919 | ·75006 |
| 0·8 | ·71478 | ·74618 | ·75890 | ·76574 | ·76999 | ·77289 | ·77500 | ·77659 | ·77784 | ·77885 |
| 0·9 | ·73326 | ·76845 | ·78277 | ·79050 | ·79531 | ·79860 | ·80099 | ·80280 | ·80422 | ·80536 |
| 1·0 | 0·75000 | 0·78868 | 0·80450 | 0·81305 | 0·81839 | 0·82204 | 0·82469 | 0·82670 | 0·82828 | 0·82955 |
| 1·1 | ·76515 | ·80698 | ·82416 | ·83346 | ·83927 | ·84325 | ·84614 | ·84834 | ·85006 | ·85145 |
| 1·2 | ·77886 | ·82349 | ·84187 | ·85182 | ·85805 | ·86232 | ·86541 | ·86777 | ·86961 | ·87110 |
| 1·3 | ·79129 | ·83838 | ·85777 | ·86827 | ·87485 | ·87935 | ·88262 | ·88510 | ·88705 | ·88862 |
| 1·4 | ·80257 | ·85177 | ·87200 | ·88295 | ·88980 | ·89448 | ·89788 | ·90046 | ·90249 | ·90412 |
| 1·5 | 0·81283 | 0·86380 | 0·88471 | 0·89600 | 0·90305 | 0·90786 | 0·91135 | 0·91400 | 0·91608 | 0·91775 |
| 1·6 | ·82219 | ·87464 | ·89605 | ·90758 | ·91475 | ·91964 | ·92318 | ·92587 | ·92797 | ·92966 |
| 1·7 | ·83075 | ·88439 | ·90615 | ·91782 | ·92506 | ·92998 | ·93354 | ·93622 | ·93833 | ·94002 |
| 1·8 | ·83859 | ·89317 | ·91516 | ·92688 | ·93412 | ·93902 | ·94256 | ·94522 | ·94731 | ·94897 |
| 1·9 | ·84579 | ·90109 | ·92318 | ·93488 | ·94207 | ·94691 | ·95040 | ·95302 | ·95506 | ·95669 |
| 2·0 | 0·85242 | 0·90825 | 0·93034 | 0·94194 | 0·94903 | 0·95379 | 0·95719 | 0·95974 | 0·96172 | 0·96331 |
| 2·1 | ·85854 | ·91473 | ·93672 | ·94817 | ·95512 | ·95976 | ·96306 | ·96553 | ·96744 | ·96896 |
| 2·2 | ·86420 | ·92060 | ·94241 | ·95367 | ·96045 | ·96495 | ·96813 | ·97050 | ·97233 | ·97378 |
| 2·3 | ·86945 | ·92593 | ·94751 | ·95853 | ·96511 | ·96945 | ·97250 | ·97476 | ·97650 | ·97787 |
| 2·4 | ·87433 | ·93077 | ·95206 | ·96282 | ·96919 | ·97335 | ·97627 | ·97841 | ·98005 | ·98134 |
| 2·5 | 0·87888 | 0·93519 | 0·95615 | 0·96662 | 0·97275 | 0·97674 | 0·97950 | 0·98153 | 0·98307 | 0·98428 |
| 2·6 | ·88313 | ·93923 | ·95981 | ·96998 | ·97587 | ·97967 | ·98229 | ·98419 | ·98563 | ·98675 |
| 2·7 | ·88709 | ·94292 | ·96311 | ·97295 | ·97861 | ·98221 | ·98468 | ·98646 | ·98780 | ·98884 |
| 2·8 | ·89081 | ·94630 | ·96607 | ·97559 | ·98100 | ·98442 | ·98674 | ·98840 | ·98964 | ·99060 |
| 2·9 | ·89430 | ·94941 | ·96875 | ·97794 | ·98310 | ·98633 | ·98851 | ·99005 | ·99120 | ·99208 |
| 3·0 | 0·89758 | 0·95227 | 0·97116 | 0·98003 | 0·98495 | 0·98800 | 0·99003 | 0·99146 | 0·99252 | 0·99333 |
| 3·1 | ·90067 | ·95490 | ·97335 | ·98189 | ·98657 | ·98944 | ·99134 | ·99267 | ·99364 | ·99437 |
| 3·2 | ·90359 | ·95733 | ·97533 | ·98355 | ·98800 | ·99070 | ·99247 | ·99369 | ·99459 | ·99525 |
| 3·3 | ·90634 | ·95958 | ·97713 | ·98503 | ·98926 | ·99180 | ·99344 | ·99457 | ·99539 | ·99599 |
| 3·4 | ·90895 | ·96166 | ·97877 | ·98636 | ·99037 | ·99275 | ·99428 | ·99532 | ·99606 | ·99661 |
| 3·5 | 0·91141 | 0·96358 | 0·98026 | 0·98755 | 0·99136 | 0·99359 | 0·99500 | 0·99596 | 0·99664 | 0·99714 |
| 3·6 | ·91376 | ·96538 | ·98162 | ·98862 | ·99223 | ·99432 | ·99563 | ·99651 | ·99713 | ·99758 |
| 3·7 | ·91598 | ·96705 | ·98286 | ·98958 | ·99300 | ·99496 | ·99617 | ·99698 | ·99754 | ·99795 |
| 3·8 | ·91809 | ·96860 | ·98400 | ·99045 | ·99369 | ·99552 | ·99664 | ·99738 | ·99789 | ·99826 |
| 3·9 | ·92010 | ·97005 | ·98504 | ·99123 | ·99430 | ·99601 | ·99705 | ·99773 | ·99819 | ·99852 |
| 4·0 | 0·92202 | 0·97141 | 0·98600 | 0·99193 | 0·99484 | 0·99644 | 0·99741 | 0·99803 | 0·99845 | 0·99874 |
| 4·2 | ·92560 | ·97386 | ·98768 | ·99315 | ·99575 | ·99716 | ·99798 | ·99850 | ·99885 | ·99909 |
| 4·4 | ·92887 | ·97602 | ·98912 | ·99415 | ·99649 | ·99772 | ·99842 | ·99886 | ·99914 | ·99933 |
| 4·6 | ·93186 | ·97792 | ·99034 | ·99498 | ·99708 | ·99815 | ·99876 | ·99912 | ·99936 | ·99951 |
| 4·8 | ·93462 | ·97962 | ·99140 | ·99568 | ·99756 | ·99850 | ·99902 | ·99932 | ·99951 | ·99964 |
| 5·0 | 0·93717 | 0·98113 | 0·99230 | 0·99625 | 0·99795 | 0·99877 | 0·99922 | 0·99947 | 0·99963 | 0·99973 |
| 5·2 | ·93952 | ·98248 | ·99309 | ·99674 | ·99827 | ·99899 | ·99937 | ·99959 | ·99972 | ·99980 |
| 5·4 | ·94171 | ·98369 | ·99378 | ·99715 | ·99853 | ·99917 | ·99950 | ·99968 | ·99978 | ·99985 |
| 5·6 | ·94375 | ·98478 | ·99437 | ·99750 | ·99875 | ·99931 | ·99959 | ·99975 | ·99983 | ·99989 |
| 5·8 | ·94565 | ·98577 | ·99490 | ·99780 | ·99893 | ·99942 | ·99967 | ·99980 | ·99987 | ·99991 |
| 6·0 | 0·94743 | 0·98666 | 0·99536 | 0·99806 | 0·99908 | 0·99952 | 0·99973 | 0·99984 | 0·99990 | 0·99993 |
| 6·2 | ·94910 | ·98748 | ·99577 | ·99828 | ·99920 | ·99959 | ·99978 | ·99987 | ·99992 | ·99995 |
| 6·4 | ·95066 | ·98822 | ·99614 | ·99847 | ·99931 | ·99966 | ·99982 | ·99990 | ·99994 | ·99996 |
| 6·6 | ·95214 | ·98890 | ·99646 | ·99863 | ·99940 | ·99971 | ·99985 | ·99992 | ·99995 | ·99997 |
| 6·8 | ·95352 | ·98953 | ·99675 | ·99878 | ·99948 | ·99975 | ·99987 | ·99993 | ·99996 | ·99998 |
| 7·0 | 0·95483 | 0·99010 | 0·99701 | 0·99890 | 0·99954 | 0·99979 | 0·99990 | 0·99994 | 0·99997 | 0·99998 |
| 7·2 | ·95607 | ·99063 | ·99724 | ·99901 | ·99960 | ·99982 | ·99991 | ·99995 | ·99997 | ·99999 |
| 7·4 | ·95724 | ·99111 | ·99745 | ·99911 | ·99964 | ·99984 | ·99993 | ·99996 | ·99998 | ·99999 |
| 7·6 | ·95836 | ·99156 | ·99764 | ·99920 | ·99969 | ·99986 | ·99994 | ·99997 | ·99998 | ·99999 |
| 7·8 | ·95941 | ·99198 | ·99781 | ·99927 | ·99972 | ·99988 | ·99995 | ·99997 | ·99999 | ·99999 |
| 8·0 | 0·96042 | 0·99237 | 0·99796 | 0·99934 | 0·99975 | 0·99990 | 0·99996 | 0·99998 | 0·99999 | 0·99999 |

Table 9 (*continued*)

| $t$ \ $\nu$ | 11 | 12 | 13 | 14 | 15 | 16 | 17 | 18 | 19 | 20 |
|---|---|---|---|---|---|---|---|---|---|---|
| 0·0 | 0·50000 | 0·50000 | 0·50000 | 0·50000 | 0·50000 | 0·50000 | 0·50000 | 0·50000 | 0·50000 | 0·50000 |
| 0·1 | ·53893 | ·53900 | ·53907 | ·53912 | ·53917 | ·53921 | ·53924 | ·53928 | ·53930 | ·53933 |
| 0·2 | ·57744 | ·57759 | ·57771 | ·57782 | ·57792 | ·57800 | ·57807 | ·57814 | ·57820 | ·57825 |
| 0·3 | ·61511 | ·61534 | ·61554 | ·61571 | ·61585 | ·61598 | ·61609 | ·61619 | ·61628 | ·61636 |
| 0·4 | ·65159 | ·65191 | ·65217 | ·65240 | ·65260 | ·65278 | ·65293 | ·65307 | ·65319 | ·65330 |
| 0·5 | 0·68654 | 0·68694 | 0·68728 | 0·68758 | 0·68783 | 0·68806 | 0·68826 | 0·68843 | 0·68859 | 0·68873 |
| 0·6 | ·71967 | ·72017 | ·72059 | ·72095 | ·72127 | ·72155 | ·72179 | ·72201 | ·72220 | ·72238 |
| 0·7 | ·75077 | ·75136 | ·75187 | ·75230 | ·75268 | ·75301 | ·75330 | ·75356 | ·75380 | ·75400 |
| 0·8 | ·77968 | ·78037 | ·78096 | ·78146 | ·78190 | ·78229 | ·78263 | ·78293 | ·78320 | ·78344 |
| 0·9 | ·80630 | ·80709 | ·80776 | ·80833 | ·80883 | ·80927 | ·80965 | ·81000 | ·81031 | ·81058 |
| 1·0 | 0·83060 | 0·83148 | 0·83222 | 0·83286 | 0·83341 | 0·83390 | 0·83433 | 0·83472 | 0·83506 | 0·83537 |
| 1·1 | ·85259 | ·85355 | ·85436 | ·85506 | ·85566 | ·85620 | ·85667 | ·85709 | ·85746 | ·85780 |
| 1·2 | ·87233 | ·87335 | ·87422 | ·87497 | ·87562 | ·87620 | ·87670 | ·87715 | ·87756 | ·87792 |
| 1·3 | ·88991 | ·89099 | ·89191 | ·89270 | ·89339 | ·89399 | ·89452 | ·89500 | ·89542 | ·89581 |
| 1·4 | ·90546 | ·90658 | ·90754 | ·90836 | ·90907 | ·90970 | ·91025 | ·91074 | ·91118 | ·91158 |
| 1·5 | 0·91912 | 0·92027 | 0·92125 | 0·92209 | 0·92282 | 0·92346 | 0·92402 | 0·92452 | 0·92498 | 0·92538 |
| 1·6 | ·93105 | ·93221 | ·93320 | ·93404 | ·93478 | ·93542 | ·93599 | ·93650 | ·93695 | ·93736 |
| 1·7 | ·94140 | ·94256 | ·94354 | ·94439 | ·94512 | ·94576 | ·94632 | ·94683 | ·94728 | ·94768 |
| 1·8 | ·95034 | ·95148 | ·95245 | ·95328 | ·95400 | ·95463 | ·95518 | ·95568 | ·95612 | ·95652 |
| 1·9 | ·95802 | ·95914 | ·96008 | ·96089 | ·96158 | ·96220 | ·96273 | ·96321 | ·96364 | ·96403 |
| 2·0 | 0·96460 | 0·96567 | 0·96658 | 0·96736 | 0·96803 | 0·96861 | 0·96913 | 0·96959 | 0·97000 | 0·97037 |
| 2·1 | ·97020 | ·97123 | ·97209 | ·97283 | ·97347 | ·97403 | ·97452 | ·97495 | ·97534 | ·97569 |
| 2·2 | ·97496 | ·97593 | ·97675 | ·97745 | ·97805 | ·97858 | ·97904 | ·97945 | ·97981 | ·98014 |
| 2·3 | ·97898 | ·97990 | ·98067 | ·98132 | ·98189 | ·98238 | ·98281 | ·98319 | ·98352 | ·98383 |
| 2·4 | ·98238 | ·98324 | ·98396 | ·98457 | ·98509 | ·98554 | ·98594 | ·98629 | ·98660 | ·98688 |
| 2·5 | 0·98525 | 0·98604 | 0·98671 | 0·98727 | 0·98775 | 0·98816 | 0·98853 | 0·98885 | 0·98913 | 0·98938 |
| 2·6 | ·98765 | ·98839 | ·98900 | ·98951 | ·98995 | ·99033 | ·99066 | ·99095 | ·99121 | ·99144 |
| 2·7 | ·98967 | ·99035 | ·99090 | ·99137 | ·99177 | ·99211 | ·99241 | ·99267 | ·99290 | ·99311 |
| 2·8 | ·99130 | ·99193 | 00240 | 00201 | ·99327 | ·99358 | ·99385 | ·99408 | ·99429 | ·99447 |
| 2·9 | ·99278 | ·99334 | ·99380 | ·99418 | ·99450 | ·99478 | ·99502 | ·99523 | ·99541 | ·99557 |
| 3·0 | 0·99396 | 0·99447 | 0·99488 | 0·99522 | 0·99551 | 0·99576 | 0·99597 | 0·99616 | 0·99632 | 0·99646 |
| 3·1 | ·99495 | ·99541 | ·99578 | ·99608 | ·99634 | ·99656 | ·99675 | ·99691 | ·99705 | ·99718 |
| 3·2 | ·99577 | ·99618 | ·99652 | ·99679 | ·99702 | ·99721 | ·99738 | ·99752 | ·99764 | ·99775 |
| 3·3 | ·99646 | ·99683 | ·99713 | ·99737 | ·99757 | ·99774 | ·99789 | ·99801 | ·99812 | ·99821 |
| 3·4 | ·99703 | ·99737 | ·99763 | ·99784 | ·99802 | ·99817 | ·99830 | ·99840 | ·99850 | ·99858 |
| 3·5 | 0·99751 | 0·99781 | 0·99804 | 0·99823 | 0·99839 | 0·99852 | 0·99863 | 0·99872 | 0·99880 | 0·99887 |
| 3·6 | ·99791 | ·99818 | ·99838 | ·99855 | ·99869 | ·99880 | ·99890 | ·99898 | ·99905 | ·99911 |
| 3·7 | ·99825 | ·99848 | ·99867 | ·99881 | ·99893 | ·99903 | ·99911 | ·99918 | ·99924 | ·99929 |
| 3·8 | ·99853 | ·99874 | ·99890 | ·99902 | ·99913 | ·99921 | ·99928 | ·99934 | ·99939 | ·99944 |
| 3·9 | ·99876 | ·99895 | ·99909 | ·99920 | ·99929 | ·99936 | ·99942 | ·99948 | ·99952 | ·99956 |
| 4·0 | 0·99896 | 0·99912 | 0·99924 | 0·99934 | 0·99942 | 0·99948 | 0·99954 | 0·99958 | 0·99962 | 0·99965 |
| 4·2 | ·99926 | ·99938 | ·99948 | ·99955 | ·99961 | ·99966 | ·99970 | ·99973 | ·99976 | ·99978 |
| 4·4 | ·99947 | ·99957 | ·99964 | ·99970 | ·99974 | ·99978 | ·99980 | ·99983 | ·99985 | ·99986 |
| 4·6 | ·99962 | ·99969 | ·99975 | ·99979 | ·99983 | ·99985 | ·99987 | ·99989 | ·99990 | ·99991 |
| 4·8 | ·99972 | ·99978 | ·99983 | ·99986 | ·99988 | ·99990 | ·99992 | ·99993 | ·99994 | ·99995 |
| 5·0 | 0·99980 | 0·99985 | 0·99988 | 0·99990 | 0·99992 | 0·99993 | 0·99995 | 0·99995 | 0·99996 | 0·99997 |
| 5·2 | ·99985 | ·99989 | ·99992 | ·99993 | ·99995 | ·99996 | ·99996 | ·99997 | ·99997 | ·99998 |
| 5·4 | ·99989 | ·99992 | ·99994 | ·99995 | ·99996 | ·99997 | ·99998 | ·99998 | ·99999 | ·99999 |
| 5·6 | ·99992 | ·99994 | ·99996 | ·99997 | ·99997 | ·99998 | ·99998 | ·99999 | ·99999 | ·99999 |
| 5·8 | ·99994 | ·99996 | ·99997 | ·99998 | ·99998 | ·99999 | ·99999 | ·99999 | ·99999 | ·99999 |
| 6·0 | 0·99995 | 0·99997 | 0·99998 | 0·99998 | 0·99999 | 0·99999 | 0·99999 | 0·99999 | | |
| 6·2 | ·99997 | ·99998 | ·99998 | ·99999 | ·99999 | ·99999 | | | | |
| 6·4 | ·99997 | ·99998 | ·99999 | ·99999 | ·99999 | | | | | |
| 6·6 | ·99998 | ·99999 | ·99999 | ·99999 | | | | | | |
| 6·8 | ·99998 | ·99999 | ·99999 | | | | | | | |
| 7·0 | 0·99999 | 0·99999 | | | | | | | | |

*Upper percentage points of t*

| $1 - P(t \mid \nu)$ | $\nu = 1$ | 2 | 3 | 4 | 5 | 6 | 7 | 8 | 9 | 10 |
|---|---|---|---|---|---|---|---|---|---|---|
| $10^{-3}$ | 318·3 | 22·33 | 10·21 | 7·17 | 5·89 | 5·21 | 4·79 | 4·50 | 4·30 | 4·14 |
| $10^{-4}$ | 3183 | 70·7 | 22·20 | 13·03 | 9·68 | 8·02 | 7·06 | 6·44 | 6·01 | 5·69 |
| $10^{-5}$ | 31831 | 224 | 47·91 | 23·33 | 15·54 | 12·03 | 10·11 | 8·90 | 8·10 | 7·53 |
| $5 \times 10^{-6}$ | 63652 | 316 | 60·40 | 27·82 | 17·89 | 13·55 | 11·22 | 9·79 | 8·83 | 8·15 |

## Table 9. *Probability integral of the t-distribution (continued)*

| t \ ν | 20 | 21 | 22 | 23 | 24 | 30 | 40 | 60 | 120 | ∞ |
|---|---|---|---|---|---|---|---|---|---|---|
| 0·00 | 0·50000 | 0·50000 | 0·50000 | 0·50000 | 0·50000 | 0·50000 | 0·50000 | 0·50000 | 0·50000 | 0·50000 |
| 0·05 | ·51969 | ·51970 | ·51971 | ·51972 | ·51973 | ·51977 | ·51981 | ·51986 | ·51990 | ·51994 |
| 0·10 | ·53933 | ·53935 | ·53938 | ·53939 | ·53941 | ·53950 | ·53958 | ·53966 | ·53974 | ·53983 |
| 0·15 | ·55887 | ·55890 | ·55893 | ·55896 | ·55899 | ·55912 | ·55924 | ·55937 | ·55949 | ·55962 |
| 0·20 | ·57825 | ·57830 | ·57834 | ·57838 | ·57842 | ·57858 | ·57875 | ·57892 | ·57909 | ·57926 |
| 0·25 | 0·59743 | 0·59749 | 0·59755 | 0·59760 | 0·59764 | 0·59785 | 0·59807 | 0·59828 | 0·59849 | 0·59871 |
| 0·30 | ·61636 | ·61644 | ·61650 | ·61656 | ·61662 | ·61688 | ·61713 | ·61739 | ·61765 | ·61791 |
| 0·35 | ·63500 | ·63509 | ·63517 | ·63524 | ·63530 | ·63561 | ·63591 | ·63622 | ·63652 | ·63683 |
| 0·40 | ·65330 | ·65340 | ·65349 | ·65358 | ·65365 | ·65400 | ·65436 | ·65471 | ·65507 | ·65542 |
| 0·45 | ·67122 | ·67134 | ·67144 | ·67154 | ·67163 | ·67203 | ·67243 | ·67283 | ·67324 | ·67364 |
| 0·50 | 0·68873 | 0·68886 | 0·68898 | 0·68909 | 0·68919 | 0·68964 | 0·69009 | 0·69055 | 0·69100 | 0·69146 |
| 0·55 | ·70579 | ·70594 | ·70607 | ·70619 | ·70630 | ·70680 | ·70731 | ·70782 | ·70833 | ·70884 |
| 0·60 | ·72238 | ·72254 | ·72268 | ·72281 | ·72294 | ·72349 | ·72405 | ·72462 | ·72518 | ·72575 |
| 0·65 | ·73846 | ·73863 | ·73879 | ·73893 | ·73907 | ·73968 | ·74030 | ·74091 | ·74153 | ·74215 |
| 0·70 | ·75400 | ·75419 | ·75437 | ·75453 | ·75467 | ·75534 | ·75601 | ·75668 | ·75736 | ·75804 |
| 0·75 | 0·76901 | 0·76921 | 0·76940 | 0·76957 | 0·76973 | 0·77045 | 0·77118 | 0·77191 | 0·77264 | 0·77337 |
| 0·80 | ·78344 | ·78367 | ·78387 | ·78405 | ·78422 | ·78500 | ·78578 | ·78657 | ·78735 | ·78814 |
| 0·85 | ·79731 | ·79754 | ·79776 | ·79796 | ·79814 | ·79897 | ·79981 | ·80065 | ·80149 | ·80234 |
| 0·90 | ·81058 | ·81084 | ·81107 | ·81128 | ·81147 | ·81236 | ·81325 | ·81414 | ·81504 | ·81594 |
| 0·95 | ·82327 | ·82354 | ·82378 | ·82401 | ·82421 | ·82515 | ·82609 | ·82704 | ·82799 | ·82894 |
| 1·00 | 0·83537 | 0·83565 | 0·83591 | 0·83614 | 0·83636 | 0·83735 | 0·83834 | 0·83934 | 0·84034 | 0·84134 |
| 1·05 | ·84688 | ·84717 | ·84744 | ·84769 | ·84791 | ·84895 | ·84999 | ·85104 | ·85209 | ·85314 |
| 1·10 | ·85780 | ·85811 | ·85839 | ·85864 | ·85888 | ·85996 | ·86105 | ·86214 | ·86323 | ·86433 |
| 1·15 | ·86814 | ·86846 | ·86875 | ·86902 | ·86926 | ·87039 | ·87151 | ·87265 | ·87378 | ·87493 |
| 1·20 | ·87792 | ·87825 | ·87855 | ·87882 | ·87907 | ·88023 | ·88140 | ·88257 | ·88375 | ·88493 |
| 1·25 | 0·88714 | 0·88747 | 0·88778 | 0·88807 | 0·88832 | 0·88952 | 0·89072 | 0·89192 | 0·89313 | 0·89435 |
| 1·30 | ·89581 | ·89616 | ·89647 | ·89676 | ·89703 | ·89825 | ·89948 | ·90071 | ·90195 | ·90320 |
| 1·35 | ·90395 | ·90431 | ·90463 | ·90492 | ·90519 | ·90644 | ·90770 | ·90896 | ·91022 | ·91149 |
| 1·40 | ·91158 | ·91194 | ·91227 | ·91257 | ·91285 | ·91411 | ·91539 | ·91667 | ·91795 | ·91924 |
| 1·45 | ·91872 | ·91908 | ·91942 | ·91972 | ·92000 | ·92128 | ·92257 | ·92387 | ·92517 | ·92647 |
| 1·50 | 0·92538 | 0·92575 | 0·92608 | 0·92639 | 0·92667 | 0·92797 | 0·92927 | 0·93057 | 0·93188 | 0·93319 |
| 1·55 | ·93159 | ·93196 | ·93230 | ·93260 | ·93289 | ·93419 | ·93549 | ·93680 | ·93811 | ·93943 |
| 1·60 | ·93736 | ·93773 | ·93807 | ·93838 | ·93866 | ·93996 | ·94127 | ·94257 | ·94389 | ·94520 |
| 1·65 | ·94272 | ·94309 | ·94342 | ·94373 | ·94401 | ·94531 | ·94661 | ·94792 | ·94922 | ·95053 |
| 1·70 | ·94768 | ·94805 | ·94839 | ·94869 | ·94897 | ·95026 | ·95155 | ·95284 | ·95414 | ·95543 |
| 1·75 | 0·95228 | 0·95264 | 0·95297 | 0·95327 | 0·95355 | 0·95483 | 0·95611 | 0·95738 | 0·95866 | 0·95994 |
| 1·80 | ·95652 | ·95688 | ·95720 | ·95750 | ·95778 | ·95904 | ·96030 | ·96156 | ·96281 | ·96407 |
| 1·85 | ·96043 | ·96078 | ·96110 | ·96140 | ·96167 | ·96291 | ·96414 | ·96538 | ·96661 | ·96784 |
| 1·90 | ·96403 | ·96437 | ·96469 | ·96498 | ·96524 | ·96646 | ·96767 | ·96888 | ·97008 | ·97128 |
| 1·95 | ·96733 | ·96767 | ·96798 | ·96827 | ·96852 | ·96971 | ·97089 | ·97207 | ·97325 | ·97441 |
| 2·0 | 0·97037 | 0·97070 | 0·97100 | 0·97128 | 0·97153 | 0·97269 | 0·97384 | 0·97498 | 0·97612 | 0·97725 |
| 2·1 | ·97569 | ·97601 | ·97629 | ·97655 | ·97679 | ·97788 | ·97896 | ·98003 | ·98109 | ·98214 |
| 2·2 | ·98014 | ·98043 | ·98070 | ·98094 | ·98116 | ·98218 | ·98318 | ·98416 | ·98514 | ·98610 |
| 2·3 | ·98383 | ·98410 | ·98435 | ·98457 | ·98478 | ·98571 | ·98663 | ·98753 | ·98841 | ·98928 |
| 2·4 | ·98688 | ·98712 | ·98735 | ·98756 | ·98774 | ·98860 | ·98943 | ·99024 | ·99103 | ·99180 |
| 2·5 | 0·98938 | 0·98961 | 0·98982 | 0·99000 | 0·99017 | 0·99094 | 0·99169 | 0·99241 | 0·99312 | 0·99379 |
| 2·6 | ·99144 | ·99164 | ·99183 | ·99200 | ·99215 | ·99284 | ·99350 | ·99414 | ·99475 | ·99534 |
| 2·7 | ·99311 | ·99329 | ·99346 | ·99361 | ·99375 | ·99436 | ·99494 | ·99550 | ·99603 | ·99653 |
| 2·8 | ·99447 | ·99463 | ·99478 | ·99492 | ·99504 | ·99557 | ·99608 | ·99657 | ·99702 | ·99744 |
| 2·9 | ·99557 | ·99572 | ·99585 | ·99596 | ·99607 | ·99654 | ·99698 | ·99740 | ·99778 | ·99813 |
| 3·0 | 0·99646 | 0·99659 | 0·99670 | 0·99681 | 0·99690 | 0·99730 | 0·99768 | 0·99804 | 0·99836 | 0·99865 |
| 3·1 | ·99718 | ·99729 | ·99739 | ·99748 | ·99756 | ·99791 | ·99823 | ·99853 | ·99879 | ·99903 |
| 3·2 | ·99775 | ·99785 | ·99793 | ·99801 | ·99808 | ·99838 | ·99865 | ·99890 | ·99912 | ·99931 |
| 3·3 | ·99821 | ·99829 | ·99837 | ·99844 | ·99849 | ·99875 | ·99898 | ·99918 | ·99936 | ·99952 |
| 3·4 | ·99858 | ·99865 | ·99871 | ·99877 | ·99882 | ·99904 | ·99923 | ·99940 | ·99954 | ·99966 |
| 3·5 | 0·99887 | 0·99893 | 0·99899 | 0·99904 | 0·99908 | 0·99926 | 0·99942 | 0·99956 | 0·99967 | 0·99977 |
| 3·6 | ·99911 | ·99916 | ·99920 | ·99925 | ·99928 | ·99943 | ·99957 | ·99968 | ·99977 | ·99984 |
| 3·7 | ·99929 | ·99933 | ·99937 | ·99941 | ·99944 | ·99957 | ·99967 | ·99976 | ·99984 | ·99989 |
| 3·8 | ·99944 | ·99948 | ·99951 | ·99954 | ·99956 | ·99967 | ·99976 | ·99983 | ·99989 | ·99993 |
| 3·9 | ·99956 | ·99959 | ·99961 | ·99964 | ·99966 | ·99975 | ·99982 | ·99988 | ·99992 | ·99995 |
| 4·0 | 0·99965 | 0·99967 | 0·99970 | 0·99972 | 0·99974 | 0·99981 | 0·99987 | 0·99991 | 0·99995 | 0·99997 |
| 5·0 | 0·99997 | 0·99997 | 0·99998 | 0·99998 | 0·99998 | 0·99999 | 0·99999 | | | |

Table 10. *Chart for determining the power function of the t-test*

If $y'$ is a normal variable with $\mathscr{E}(y') = \Delta$ and if $s_\nu^2$ is an independent mean-square estimate of its variance, $\sigma_\nu^2$, based on $\nu$ degrees of freedom, then $t' = y'/s_\nu$ is distributed as a non-central $t$. The chart shows on a logarithmic scale the chance of establishing significance according to the value of $\phi = \Delta/\sigma_\nu \times 1/\sqrt{2}$, using a two-tail $t$-test, at either the 5 or 1 % levels ($\alpha = 0.05$ or $0.01$). If a single-tail $t$-test is appropriate, then the curves marked $\alpha = 0.05$ and $0.01$ give, respectively, the chance of establishing significance at the 2·5 and 0·5 % levels.

141

Table 11. *Test for comparisons involving two variances which must be separately estimated*

Upper 5 % critical values of $v = \dfrac{(y - \eta)}{\sqrt{(\lambda_1 s_1^2 + \lambda_2 s_2^2)}}$

(*i.e. upper* 10 % *critical values of* $|v|$)*

| $\nu_2$ | $\nu_1$ | $\dfrac{\lambda_1 s_1^2}{\lambda_1 s_1^2 + \lambda_2 s_2^2}$ 0·0 | 0·1 | 0·2 | 0·3 | 0·4 | 0·5 | 0·6 | 0·7 | 0·8 | 0·9 | 1·0 |
|---|---|---|---|---|---|---|---|---|---|---|---|---|
| 6 | 6 | 1·94 | 1·90 | 1·85 | 1·80 | 1·76 | 1·74 | 1·76 | 1·80 | 1·85 | 1·90 | 1·94 |
|  | 8 | 1·94 | 1·90 | 1·85 | 1·80 | 1·76 | 1·73 | 1·74 | 1·76 | 1·79 | 1·82 | 1·86 |
|  | 10 | 1·94 | 1·90 | 1·85 | 1·80 | 1·76 | 1·73 | 1·73 | 1·74 | 1·76 | 1·78 | 1·81 |
|  | 15 | 1·94 | 1·90 | 1·85 | 1·80 | 1·76 | 1·73 | 1·71 | 1·71 | 1·72 | 1·73 | 1·75 |
|  | 20 | 1·94 | 1·90 | 1·85 | 1·80 | 1·76 | 1·73 | 1·71 | 1·70 | 1·70 | 1·71 | 1·72 |
|  | ∞ | 1·94 | 1·90 | 1·85 | 1·80 | 1·76 | 1·72 | 1·69 | 1·67 | 1·66 | 1·65 | 1·64 |
| 8 | 6 | 1·86 | 1·82 | 1·79 | 1·76 | 1·74 | 1·73 | 1·76 | 1·80 | 1·85 | 1·90 | 1·94 |
|  | 8 | 1·86 | 1·82 | 1·79 | 1·76 | 1·73 | 1·73 | 1·73 | 1·76 | 1·79 | 1·82 | 1·86 |
|  | 10 | 1·86 | 1·82 | 1·79 | 1·76 | 1·73 | 1·72 | 1·72 | 1·74 | 1·76 | 1·78 | 1·81 |
|  | 15 | 1·86 | 1·82 | 1·79 | 1·76 | 1·73 | 1·71 | 1·71 | 1·71 | 1·72 | 1·73 | 1·75 |
|  | 20 | 1·86 | 1·82 | 1·79 | 1·76 | 1·73 | 1·71 | 1·70 | 1·70 | 1·70 | 1·71 | 1·72 |
|  | ∞ | 1·86 | 1·82 | 1·79 | 1·75 | 1·72 | 1·70 | 1·68 | 1·66 | 1·65 | 1·65 | 1·64 |
| 10 | 6 | 1·81 | 1·78 | 1·76 | 1·74 | 1·73 | 1·73 | 1·76 | 1·80 | 1·85 | 1·90 | 1·94 |
|  | 8 | 1·81 | 1·78 | 1·76 | 1·74 | 1·72 | 1·72 | 1·73 | 1·76 | 1·79 | 1·82 | 1·86 |
|  | 10 | 1·81 | 1·78 | 1·76 | 1·73 | 1·72 | 1·71 | 1·72 | 1·73 | 1·76 | 1·78 | 1·81 |
|  | 15 | 1·81 | 1·78 | 1·76 | 1·73 | 1·72 | 1·70 | 1·70 | 1·71 | 1·72 | 1·73 | 1·75 |
|  | 20 | 1·81 | 1·78 | 1·76 | 1·73 | 1·71 | 1·70 | 1·69 | 1·69 | 1·70 | 1·71 | 1·72 |
|  | ∞ | 1·81 | 1·78 | 1·76 | 1·73 | 1·71 | 1·69 | 1·67 | 1·66 | 1·65 | 1·65 | 1·64 |
| 15 | 6 | 1·75 | 1·73 | 1·72 | 1·71 | 1·71 | 1·73 | 1·76 | 1·80 | 1·85 | 1·90 | 1·94 |
|  | 8 | 1·75 | 1·73 | 1·72 | 1·71 | 1·71 | 1·71 | 1·73 | 1·76 | 1·79 | 1·82 | 1·86 |
|  | 10 | 1·75 | 1·73 | 1·72 | 1·71 | 1·70 | 1·70 | 1·72 | 1·73 | 1·76 | 1·78 | 1·81 |
|  | 15 | 1·75 | 1·73 | 1·72 | 1·70 | 1·70 | 1·69 | 1·70 | 1·70 | 1·72 | 1·73 | 1·75 |
|  | 20 | 1·75 | 1·73 | 1·72 | 1·70 | 1·69 | 1·69 | 1·69 | 1·69 | 1·70 | 1·71 | 1·72 |
|  | ∞ | 1·75 | 1·73 | 1·72 | 1·70 | 1·68 | 1·67 | 1·66 | 1·65 | 1·65 | 1·65 | 1·64 |
| 20 | 6 | 1·72 | 1·71 | 1·70 | 1·70 | 1·71 | 1·73 | 1·76 | 1·80 | 1·85 | 1·90 | 1·94 |
|  | 8 | 1·72 | 1·71 | 1·70 | 1·70 | 1·70 | 1·71 | 1·73 | 1·76 | 1·79 | 1·82 | 1·86 |
|  | 10 | 1·72 | 1·71 | 1·70 | 1·69 | 1·69 | 1·70 | 1·71 | 1·73 | 1·76 | 1·78 | 1·81 |
|  | 15 | 1·72 | 1·71 | 1·70 | 1·69 | 1·69 | 1·69 | 1·69 | 1·70 | 1·72 | 1·73 | 1·75 |
|  | 20 | 1·72 | 1·71 | 1·70 | 1·69 | 1·68 | 1·68 | 1·68 | 1·69 | 1·70 | 1·71 | 1·72 |
|  | ∞ | 1·72 | 1·71 | 1·70 | 1·68 | 1·67 | 1·66 | 1·66 | 1·65 | 1·65 | 1·65 | 1·64 |
| ∞ | 6 | 1·64 | 1·65 | 1·66 | 1·67 | 1·69 | 1·72 | 1·76 | 1·80 | 1·85 | 1·90 | 1·94 |
|  | 8 | 1·64 | 1·65 | 1·65 | 1·66 | 1·68 | 1·70 | 1·72 | 1·75 | 1·79 | 1·82 | 1·86 |
|  | 10 | 1·64 | 1·65 | 1·65 | 1·66 | 1·67 | 1·69 | 1·71 | 1·73 | 1·76 | 1·78 | 1·81 |
|  | 15 | 1·64 | 1·65 | 1·65 | 1·65 | 1·66 | 1·67 | 1·68 | 1·70 | 1·72 | 1·73 | 1·75 |
|  | 20 | 1·64 | 1·65 | 1·65 | 1·65 | 1·66 | 1·66 | 1·67 | 1·68 | 1·70 | 1·71 | 1·72 |
|  | ∞ | 1·64 | 1·64 | 1·64 | 1·64 | 1·64 | 1·64 | 1·64 | 1·64 | 1·64 | 1·64 | 1·64 |

\* $y$ is normally distributed about $\eta$ with variance $\lambda_1 \sigma_1^2 + \lambda_2 \sigma_2^2$, and $s_1^2$ and $s_2^2$ are independent estimates of $\sigma_1^2$ and $\sigma_2^2$, based on $\nu_1$ and $\nu_2$ degrees of freedom, respectively. $\lambda_1$ and $\lambda_2$ are known constants.

In the problem of comparing the means of samples taken from two normal populations, put $y = (\bar{x}_1 - \bar{x}_2)$, $\nu_1 = (n_1 - 1)$, $\nu_2 = (n_2 - 1)$, $\lambda_1 = 1/n_1$ and $\lambda_2 = 1/n_2$, where $n_1$ and $n_2$ are the sample sizes.

Table 11 (*continued*)

Upper $2 \cdot 5 \%$ *critical values of* $v = \dfrac{(y - \eta)}{\sqrt{(\lambda_1 s_1^2 + \lambda_2 s_2^2)}}$

(*i.e. upper* $5 \%$ *critical values of* $|v|$)

| $\nu_2$ | $\nu_1$ | $\dfrac{\lambda_1 s_1^2}{(\lambda_1 s_1^2 + \lambda_2 s_2^2)}$ 0·0 | 0·1 | 0·2 | 0·3 | 0·4 | 0·5 | 0·6 | 0·7 | 0·8 | 0·9 | 1·0 |
|---|---|---|---|---|---|---|---|---|---|---|---|---|
| 8 | 8 | 2·31 | 2·25 | 2·20 | 2·14 | 2·10 | 2·08 | 2·10 | 2·14 | 2·20 | 2·25 | 2·31 |
| | 10 | 2·31 | 2·25 | 2·20 | 2·15 | 2·10 | 2·08 | 2·08 | 2·11 | 2·14 | 2·19 | 2·23 |
| | 12 | 2·31 | 2·25 | 2·20 | 2·15 | 2·10 | 2·07 | 2·07 | 2·08 | 2·11 | 2·14 | 2·18 |
| | 15 | 2·31 | 2·25 | 2·20 | 2·15 | 2·10 | 2·07 | 2·05 | 2·06 | 2·08 | 2·10 | 2·13 |
| | 20 | 2·31 | 2·25 | 2·20 | 2·15 | 2·10 | 2·06 | 2·04 | 2·04 | 2·05 | 2·07 | 2·09 |
| | ∞ | 2·31 | 2·25 | 2·20 | 2·14 | 2·09 | 2·05 | 2·01 | 1·99 | 1·97 | 1·96 | 1·96 |
| 10 | 8 | 2·23 | 2·19 | 2·14 | 2·11 | 2·08 | 2·08 | 2·10 | 2·15 | 2·20 | 2·25 | 2·31 |
| | 10 | 2·23 | 2·18 | 2·14 | 2·11 | 2·08 | 2·06 | 2·08 | 2·11 | 2·14 | 2·18 | 2·23 |
| | 12 | 2·23 | 2·18 | 2·14 | 2·10 | 2·07 | 2·06 | 2·06 | 2·08 | 2·11 | 2·14 | 2·18 |
| | 15 | 2·23 | 2·18 | 2·14 | 2·10 | 2·07 | 2·05 | 2·05 | 2·06 | 2·08 | 2·10 | 2·13 |
| | 20 | 2·23 | 2·18 | 2·14 | 2·10 | 2·07 | 2·05 | 2·04 | 2·04 | 2·05 | 2·06 | 2·09 |
| | ∞ | 2·23 | 2·18 | 2·14 | 2·10 | 2·06 | 2·03 | 2·00 | 1·98 | 1·97 | 1·96 | 1·96 |
| 12 | 8 | 2·18 | 2·14 | 2·11 | 2·08 | 2·07 | 2·07 | 2·10 | 2·15 | 2·20 | 2·25 | 2·31 |
| | 10 | 2·18 | 2·14 | 2·11 | 2·08 | 2·06 | 2·06 | 2·07 | 2·10 | 2·14 | 2·18 | 2·23 |
| | 12 | 2·18 | 2·14 | 2·11 | 2·08 | 2·06 | 2·05 | 2·06 | 2·08 | 2·11 | 2·14 | 2·18 |
| | 15 | 2·18 | 2·14 | 2·11 | 2·08 | 2·06 | 2·04 | 2·04 | 2·06 | 2·08 | 2·10 | 2·13 |
| | 20 | 2·18 | 2·14 | 2·11 | 2·08 | 2·05 | 2·04 | 2·03 | 2·03 | 2·05 | 2·06 | 2·09 |
| | ∞ | 2·18 | 2·14 | 2·11 | 2·07 | 2·04 | 2·02 | 1·99 | 1·98 | 1·97 | 1·96 | 1·96 |
| 15 | 8 | 2·13 | 2·10 | 2·08 | 2·06 | 2·05 | 2·07 | 2·10 | 2·15 | 2·20 | 2·25 | 2·31 |
| | 10 | 2·13 | 2·10 | 2·08 | 2·06 | 2·05 | 2·05 | 2·07 | 2·10 | 2·14 | 2·18 | 2·23 |
| | 12 | 2·13 | 2·10 | 2·08 | 2·06 | 2·04 | 2·04 | 2·06 | 2·08 | 2·11 | 2·14 | 2·18 |
| | 15 | 2·13 | 2·10 | 2·08 | 2·05 | 2·04 | 2·03 | 2·04 | 2·05 | 2·08 | 2·10 | 2·13 |
| | 20 | 2·13 | 2·10 | 2·08 | 2·05 | 2·04 | 2·03 | 2·03 | 2·03 | 2·05 | 2·06 | 2·09 |
| | ∞ | 2·13 | 2·10 | 2·07 | 2·05 | 2·02 | 2·00 | 1·99 | 1·97 | 1·97 | 1·96 | 1·96 |
| 20 | 8 | 2·09 | 2·07 | 2·05 | 2·04 | 2·04 | 2·06 | 2·10 | 2·15 | 2·20 | 2·25 | 2·31 |
| | 10 | 2·09 | 2·06 | 2·05 | 2·04 | 2·04 | 2·05 | 2·07 | 2·10 | 2·14 | 2·18 | 2·23 |
| | 12 | 2·09 | 2·06 | 2·05 | 2·03 | 2·03 | 2·04 | 2·05 | 2·08 | 2·11 | 2·14 | 2·18 |
| | 15 | 2·09 | 2·06 | 2·05 | 2·03 | 2·03 | 2·03 | 2·04 | 2·05 | 2·08 | 2·10 | 2·13 |
| | 20 | 2·09 | 2·06 | 2·05 | 2·03 | 2·02 | 2·02 | 2·02 | 2·03 | 2·05 | 2·06 | 2·09 |
| | ∞ | 2·09 | 2·06 | 2·04 | 2·02 | 2·01 | 1·99 | 1·98 | 1·97 | 1·96 | 1·96 | 1·96 |
| ∞ | 8 | 1·96 | 1·96 | 1·97 | 1·99 | 2·01 | 2·05 | 2·09 | 2·14 | 2·20 | 2·25 | 2·31 |
| | 10 | 1·96 | 1·96 | 1·97 | 1·98 | 2·00 | 2·03 | 2·06 | 2·10 | 2·14 | 2·18 | 2·23 |
| | 12 | 1·96 | 1·96 | 1·97 | 1·98 | 1·99 | 2·02 | 2·04 | 2·07 | 2·11 | 2·14 | 2·18 |
| | 15 | 1·96 | 1·96 | 1·97 | 1·97 | 1·99 | 2·00 | 2·02 | 2·05 | 2·07 | 2·10 | 2·13 |
| | 20 | 1·96 | 1·96 | 1·96 | 1·97 | 1·98 | 1·99 | 2·01 | 2·02 | 2·04 | 2·06 | 2·09 |
| | ∞ | 1·96 | 1·96 | 1·96 | 1·96 | 1·96 | 1·96 | 1·96 | 1·96 | 1·96 | 1·96 | 1·96 |

Table 11 *(continued)*. *Test for comparisons involving two variances which must be separately estimated*

Upper 1 % critical values of $v = \dfrac{(y - \eta)}{\sqrt{(\lambda_1 s_1^2 + \lambda_2 s_2^2)}}$

(*i.e. upper 2 % critical values of* $|v|$)*

| $\nu_2$ | $\nu_1$ | $\dfrac{\lambda_1 s_1^2}{\lambda_1 s_1^2 + \lambda_2 s_2^2}$ 0·0 | 0·1 | 0·2 | 0·3 | 0·4 | 0·5 | 0·6 | 0·7 | 0·8 | 0·9 | 1·0 |
|---|---|---|---|---|---|---|---|---|---|---|---|---|
| 10 | 10 | 2·76 | 2·70 | 2·63 | 2·56 | 2·51 | 2·50 | 2·51 | 2·56 | 2·63 | 2·70 | 2·76 |
|  | 12 | 2·76 | 2·70 | 2·63 | 2·56 | 2·51 | 2·49 | 2·49 | 2·52 | 2·57 | 2·62 | 2·68 |
|  | 15 | 2·76 | 2·70 | 2·63 | 2·56 | 2·51 | 2·48 | 2·47 | 2·48 | 2·52 | 2·56 | 2·60 |
|  | 20 | 2·76 | 2·70 | 2·63 | 2·56 | 2·51 | 2·47 | 2·45 | 2·45 | 2·47 | 2·49 | 2·53 |
|  | 30 | 2·76 | 2·70 | 2·63 | 2·56 | 2·50 | 2·46 | 2·43 | 2·42 | 2·42 | 2·44 | 2·46 |
|  | ∞ | 2·76 | 2·70 | 2·63 | 2·56 | 2·50 | 2·44 | 2·40 | 2·36 | 2·34 | 2·33 | 2·33 |
| 12 | 10 | 2·68 | 2·62 | 2·57 | 2·52 | 2·49 | 2·49 | 2·51 | 2·56 | 2·63 | 2·70 | 2·76 |
|  | 12 | 2·68 | 2·62 | 2·57 | 2·52 | 2·48 | 2·47 | 2·48 | 2·52 | 2·57 | 2·62 | 2·68 |
|  | 15 | 2·68 | 2·62 | 2·57 | 2·52 | 2·48 | 2·46 | 2·46 | 2·48 | 2·52 | 2·56 | 2·60 |
|  | 20 | 2·68 | 2·62 | 2·57 | 2·52 | 2·48 | 2·45 | 2·44 | 2·45 | 2·47 | 2·49 | 2·53 |
|  | 30 | 2·68 | 2·62 | 2·57 | 2·52 | 2·47 | 2·44 | 2·42 | 2·41 | 2·42 | 2·44 | 2·46 |
|  | ∞ | 2·68 | 2·62 | 2·57 | 2·51 | 2·46 | 2·42 | 2·38 | 2·36 | 2·34 | 2·33 | 2·33 |
| 15 | 10 | 2·60 | 2·56 | 2·52 | 2·48 | 2·47 | 2·48 | 2·51 | 2·56 | 2·63 | 2·70 | 2·76 |
|  | 12 | 2·60 | 2·56 | 2·52 | 2·48 | 2·46 | 2·46 | 2·48 | 2·52 | 2·57 | 2·62 | 2·68 |
|  | 15 | 2·60 | 2·56 | 2·51 | 2·48 | 2·45 | 2·45 | 2·45 | 2·48 | 2·51 | 2·56 | 2·60 |
|  | 20 | 2·60 | 2·56 | 2·51 | 2·48 | 2·45 | 2·43 | 2·43 | 2·44 | 2·46 | 2·49 | 2·53 |
|  | 30 | 2·60 | 2·56 | 2·51 | 2·47 | 2·44 | 2·42 | 2·41 | 2·41 | 2·42 | 2·44 | 2·46 |
|  | ∞ | 2·60 | 2·56 | 2·51 | 2·47 | 2·43 | 2·40 | 2·37 | 2·35 | 2·34 | 2·33 | 2·33 |
| 20 | 10 | 2·53 | 2·49 | 2·47 | 2·45 | 2·45 | 2·47 | 2·51 | 2·56 | 2·63 | 2·70 | 2·76 |
|  | 12 | 2·53 | 2·49 | 2·47 | 2·45 | 2·44 | 2·45 | 2·48 | 2·52 | 2·57 | 2·62 | 2·68 |
|  | 15 | 2·53 | 2·49 | 2·46 | 2·44 | 2·43 | 2·43 | 2·45 | 2·48 | 2·51 | 2·56 | 2·60 |
|  | 20 | 2·53 | 2·49 | 2·46 | 2·44 | 2·42 | 2·42 | 2·42 | 2·44 | 2·46 | 2·49 | 2·53 |
|  | 30 | 2·53 | 2·49 | 2·46 | 2·44 | 2·42 | 2·40 | 2·40 | 2·40 | 2·42 | 2·43 | 2·46 |
|  | ∞ | 2·53 | 2·49 | 2·46 | 2·43 | 2·40 | 2·38 | 2·36 | 2·34 | 2·33 | 2·33 | 2·33 |
| 30 | 10 | 2·46 | 2·44 | 2·42 | 2·42 | 2·43 | 2·46 | 2·50 | 2·56 | 2·63 | 2·70 | 2·76 |
|  | 12 | 2·46 | 2·44 | 2·42 | 2·41 | 2·42 | 2·44 | 2·47 | 2·52 | 2·57 | 2·62 | 2·68 |
|  | 15 | 2·46 | 2·44 | 2·42 | 2·41 | 2·41 | 2·42 | 2·44 | 2·47 | 2·51 | 2·56 | 2·60 |
|  | 20 | 2·46 | 2·43 | 2·42 | 2·40 | 2·40 | 2·40 | 2·42 | 2·44 | 2·46 | 2·49 | 2·53 |
|  | 30 | 2·46 | 2·43 | 2·42 | 2·40 | 2·39 | 2·39 | 2·39 | 2·40 | 2·42 | 2·43 | 2·46 |
|  | ∞ | 2·46 | 2·43 | 2·41 | 2·39 | 2·37 | 2·36 | 2·35 | 2·34 | 2·33 | 2·33 | 2·33 |
| ∞ | 10 | 2·33 | 2·33 | 2·34 | 2·36 | 2·40 | 2·44 | 2·50 | 2·56 | 2·63 | 2·70 | 2·76 |
|  | 12 | 2·33 | 2·33 | 2·34 | 2·36 | 2·38 | 2·42 | 2·46 | 2·51 | 2·57 | 2·62 | 2·68 |
|  | 15 | 2·33 | 2·33 | 2·34 | 2·35 | 2·37 | 2·40 | 2·43 | 2·47 | 2·51 | 2·56 | 2·60 |
|  | 20 | 2·33 | 2·33 | 2·33 | 2·34 | 2·36 | 2·38 | 2·40 | 2·43 | 2·46 | 2·49 | 2·53 |
|  | 30 | 2·33 | 2·33 | 2·33 | 2·34 | 2·35 | 2·36 | 2·37 | 2·39 | 2·41 | 2·43 | 2·46 |
|  | ∞ | 2·33 | 2·33 | 2·33 | 2·33 | 2·33 | 2·33 | 2·33 | 2·33 | 2·33 | 2·33 | 2·33 |

* $y$ is normally distributed about $\eta$ with variance $\lambda_1 \sigma_1^2 + \lambda_2 \sigma_2^2$, and $s_1^2$ and $s_2^2$ are independent estimates of $\sigma_1^2$ and $\sigma_2^2$, based on $\nu_1$ and $\nu_2$ degrees of freedom, respectively. $\lambda_1$ and $\lambda_2$ are known constants.
In the problem of comparing the means of samples taken from two normal populations, put $y = (\bar{x}_1 - \bar{x}_2)$, $\nu_1 = (n_1 - 1)$, $\nu_2 = (n_2 - 1)$, $\lambda_1 = 1/n_1$ and $\lambda_2 = 1/n_2$, where $n_1$ and $n_2$ are the sample sizes.

Table 11 (*continued*)

Upper 0·5 % critical values of $v = \dfrac{y - \eta}{\sqrt{(\lambda_1 s_1^2 + \lambda_2 s_2^2)}}$

(*i.e. upper* 1 % *critical values of* $|v|$)

| $\dfrac{\lambda_1 s_1^2}{(\lambda_1 s_1^2 + \lambda_2 s_2^2)}$ | 0·0 | 0·1 | 0·2 | 0·3 | 0·4 | 0·5 | 0·6 | 0·7 | 0·8 | 0·9 | 1·0 |
|---|---|---|---|---|---|---|---|---|---|---|---|
| $\nu_2$  $\nu_1$ | | | | | | | | | | | |
| 10  10 | 3·17 | 3·08 | 3·00 | 2·90 | 2·82 | 2·79 | 2·82 | 2·90 | 3·00 | 3·08 | 3·17 |
| 12 | 3·17 | 3·08 | 3·00 | 2·91 | 2·82 | 2·78 | 2·79 | 2·84 | 2·91 | 2·98 | 3·05 |
| 15 | 3·17 | 3·08 | 3·00 | 2·91 | 2·82 | 2·77 | 2·76 | 2·78 | 2·83 | 2·89 | 2·95 |
| 20 | 3·17 | 3·08 | 3·00 | 2·91 | 2·82 | 2·76 | 2·73 | 2·74 | 2·76 | 2·80 | 2·85 |
| 30 | 3·17 | 3·08 | 3·00 | 2·91 | 2·82 | 2·75 | 2·71 | 2·69 | 2·70 | 2·72 | 2·75 |
| ∞ | 3·17 | 3·08 | 2·99 | 2·91 | 2·82 | 2·74 | 2·67 | 2·63 | 2·60 | 2·58 | 2·58 |
| 12  10 | 3·05 | 2·98 | 2·91 | 2·84 | 2·79 | 2·78 | 2·82 | 2·91 | 3·00 | 3·08 | 3·17 |
| 12 | 3·05 | 2·98 | 2·91 | 2·84 | 2·78 | 2·76 | 2·78 | 2·84 | 2·91 | 2·98 | 3·05 |
| 15 | 3·05 | 2·98 | 2·91 | 2·84 | 2·78 | 2·75 | 2·75 | 2·78 | 2·83 | 2·89 | 2·95 |
| 20 | 3·05 | 2·98 | 2·91 | 2·84 | 2·78 | 2·74 | 2·72 | 2·73 | 2·76 | 2·80 | 2·85 |
| 30 | 3·05 | 2·98 | 2·91 | 2·84 | 2·77 | 2·73 | 2·70 | 2·69 | 2·70 | 2·72 | 2·75 |
| ∞ | 3·05 | 2·98 | 2·91 | 2·84 | 2·77 | 2·71 | 2·65 | 2·62 | 2·59 | 2·58 | 2·58 |
| 15  10 | 2·95 | 2·89 | 2·83 | 2·78 | 2·76 | 2·77 | 2·82 | 2·91 | 3·00 | 3·08 | 3·17 |
| 12 | 2·95 | 2·89 | 2·83 | 2·78 | 2·75 | 2·75 | 2·78 | 2·84 | 2·91 | 2·98 | 3·05 |
| 15 | 2·95 | 2·89 | 2·83 | 2·78 | 2·74 | 2·73 | 2·74 | 2·78 | 2·83 | 2·89 | 2·95 |
| 20 | 2·95 | 2·89 | 2·83 | 2·78 | 2·74 | 2·71 | 2·71 | 2·73 | 2·76 | 2·80 | 2·85 |
| 30 | 2·95 | 2·89 | 2·83 | 2·78 | 2·73 | 2·70 | 2·68 | 2·68 | 2·70 | 2·72 | 2·75 |
| ∞ | 2·95 | 2·89 | 2·83 | 2·77 | 2·72 | 2·67 | 2·64 | 2·61 | 2·59 | 2·58 | 2·58 |
| 20  10 | 2·85 | 2·80 | 2·76 | 2·74 | 2·73 | 2·76 | 2·82 | 2·91 | 3·00 | 3·08 | 3·17 |
| 12 | 2·85 | 2·80 | 2·76 | 2·73 | 2·72 | 2·74 | 2·78 | 2·84 | 2·91 | 2·98 | 3·05 |
| 15 | 2·85 | 2·80 | 2·76 | 2·73 | 2·71 | 2·71 | 2·74 | 2·78 | 2·83 | 2·89 | 2·95 |
| 20 | 2·85 | 2·80 | 2·76 | 2·73 | 2·70 | 2·70 | 2·70 | 2·73 | 2·76 | 2·80 | 2·85 |
| 30 | 2·85 | 2·80 | 2·76 | 2·72 | 2·69 | 2·68 | 2·67 | 2·68 | 2·70 | 2·72 | 2·75 |
| ∞ | 2·85 | 2·80 | 2·76 | 2·72 | 2·68 | 2·65 | 2·62 | 2·60 | 2·59 | 2·58 | 2·58 |
| 30  10 | 2·75 | 2·72 | 2·70 | 2·69 | 2·71 | 2·75 | 2·82 | 2·91 | 3·00 | 3·08 | 3·17 |
| 12 | 2·75 | 2·72 | 2·70 | 2·69 | 2·70 | 2·73 | 2·77 | 2·84 | 2·91 | 2·98 | 3·05 |
| 15 | 2·75 | 2·72 | 2·70 | 2·68 | 2·68 | 2·70 | 2·73 | 2·78 | 2·83 | 2·89 | 2·95 |
| 20 | 2·75 | 2·72 | 2·70 | 2·68 | 2·67 | 2·68 | 2·69 | 2·72 | 2·76 | 2·80 | 2·85 |
| 30 | 2·75 | 2·72 | 2·69 | 2·67 | 2·66 | 2·66 | 2·66 | 2·67 | 2·69 | 2·72 | 2·75 |
| ∞ | 2·75 | 2·72 | 2·69 | 2·66 | 2·64 | 2·62 | 2·60 | 2·59 | 2·58 | 2·58 | 2·58 |
| ∞  10 | 2·58 | 2·58 | 2·60 | 2·63 | 2·67 | 2·74 | 2·82 | 2·91 | 2·99 | 3·08 | 3·17 |
| 12 | 2·58 | 2·58 | 2·59 | 2·62 | 2·65 | 2·71 | 2·77 | 2·84 | 2·91 | 2·98 | 3·05 |
| 15 | 2·58 | 2·58 | 2·59 | 2·61 | 2·64 | 2·67 | 2·72 | 2·77 | 2·83 | 2·89 | 2·95 |
| 20 | 2·58 | 2·58 | 2·59 | 2·60 | 2·62 | 2·65 | 2·68 | 2·72 | 2·76 | 2·80 | 2·85 |
| 30 | 2·58 | 2·58 | 2·58 | 2·59 | 2·60 | 2·62 | 2·64 | 2·66 | 2·69 | 2·72 | 2·75 |
| ∞ | 2·58 | 2·58 | 2·58 | 2·58 | 2·58 | 2·58 | 2·58 | 2·58 | 2·58 | 2·58 | 2·58 |

Table 12. *Percentage points of the t-distribution*

| ν | Q=0.4 2Q=0.8 | 0.25 0.5 | 0.1 0.2 | 0.05 0.1 | 0.025 0.05 | 0.01 0.02 | 0.005 0.01 | 0.0025 0.005 | 0.001 0.002 | 0.0005 0.001 |
|---|---|---|---|---|---|---|---|---|---|---|
| 1 | 0.325 | 1.000 | 3.078 | 6.314 | 12.706 | 31.821 | 63.657 | 127.32 | 318.31 | 636.62 |
| 2 | ·289 | 0.816 | 1.886 | 2.920 | 4.303 | 6.965 | 9.925 | 14.089 | 22.327 | 31.598 |
| 3 | ·277 | ·765 | 1.638 | 2.353 | 3.182 | 4.541 | 5.841 | 7.453 | 10.214 | 12.924 |
| 4 | ·271 | ·741 | 1.533 | 2.132 | 2.776 | 3.747 | 4.604 | 5.598 | 7.173 | 8.610 |
| 5 | 0.267 | 0.727 | 1.476 | 2.015 | 2.571 | 3.365 | 4.032 | 4.773 | 5.893 | 6.869 |
| 6 | ·265 | ·718 | 1.440 | 1.943 | 2.447 | 3.143 | 3.707 | 4.317 | 5.208 | 5.959 |
| 7 | ·263 | ·711 | 1.415 | 1.895 | 2.365 | 2.998 | 3.499 | 4.029 | 4.785 | 5.408 |
| 8 | ·262 | ·706 | 1.397 | 1.860 | 2.306 | 2.896 | 3.355 | 3.833 | 4.501 | 5.041 |
| 9 | ·261 | ·703 | 1.383 | 1.833 | 2.262 | 2.821 | 3.250 | 3.690 | 4.297 | 4.781 |
| 10 | 0.260 | 0.700 | 1.372 | 1.812 | 2.228 | 2.764 | 3.169 | 3.581 | 4.144 | 4.587 |
| 11 | ·260 | ·697 | 1.363 | 1.796 | 2.201 | 2.718 | 3.106 | 3.497 | 4.025 | 4.437 |
| 12 | ·259 | ·695 | 1.356 | 1.782 | 2.179 | 2.681 | 3.055 | 3.428 | 3.930 | 4.318 |
| 13 | ·259 | ·694 | 1.350 | 1.771 | 2.160 | 2.650 | 3.012 | 3.372 | 3.852 | 4.221 |
| 14 | ·258 | ·692 | 1.345 | 1.761 | 2.145 | 2.624 | 2.977 | 3.326 | 3.787 | 4.140 |
| 15 | 0.258 | 0.691 | 1.341 | 1.753 | 2.131 | 2.602 | 2.947 | 3.286 | 3.733 | 4.073 |
| 16 | ·258 | ·690 | 1.337 | 1.746 | 2.120 | 2.583 | 2.921 | 3.252 | 3.686 | 4.015 |
| 17 | ·257 | ·689 | 1.333 | 1.740 | 2.110 | 2.567 | 2.898 | 3.222 | 3.646 | 3.965 |
| 18 | ·257 | ·688 | 1.330 | 1.734 | 2.101 | 2.552 | 2.878 | 3.197 | 3.610 | 3.922 |
| 19 | ·257 | ·688 | 1.328 | 1.729 | 2.093 | 2.539 | 2.861 | 3.174 | 3.579 | 3.883 |
| 20 | 0.257 | 0.687 | 1.325 | 1.725 | 2.086 | 2.528 | 2.845 | 3.153 | 3.552 | 3.850 |
| 21 | ·257 | ·686 | 1.323 | 1.721 | 2.080 | 2.518 | 2.831 | 3.135 | 3.527 | 3.819 |
| 22 | ·256 | ·686 | 1.321 | 1.717 | 2.074 | 2.508 | 2.819 | 3.119 | 3.505 | 3.792 |
| 23 | ·256 | ·685 | 1.319 | 1.714 | 2.069 | 2.500 | 2.807 | 3.104 | 3.485 | 3.767 |
| 24 | ·256 | ·685 | 1.318 | 1.711 | 2.064 | 2.492 | 2.797 | 3.091 | 3.467 | 3.745 |
| 25 | 0.256 | 0.684 | 1.316 | 1.708 | 2.060 | 2.485 | 2.787 | 3.078 | 3.450 | 3.725 |
| 26 | ·256 | ·684 | 1.315 | 1.706 | 2.056 | 2.479 | 2.779 | 3.067 | 3.435 | 3.707 |
| 27 | ·256 | ·684 | 1.314 | 1.703 | 2.052 | 2.473 | 2.771 | 3.057 | 3.421 | 3.690 |
| 28 | ·256 | ·683 | 1.313 | 1.701 | 2.048 | 2.467 | 2.763 | 3.047 | 3.408 | 3.674 |
| 29 | ·256 | ·683 | 1.311 | 1.699 | 2.045 | 2.462 | 2.756 | 3.038 | 3.396 | 3.659 |
| 30 | 0.256 | 0.683 | 1.310 | 1.697 | 2.042 | 2.457 | 2.750 | 3.030 | 3.385 | 3.646 |
| 40 | ·255 | ·681 | 1.303 | 1.684 | 2.021 | 2.423 | 2.704 | 2.971 | 3.307 | 3.551 |
| 60 | ·254 | ·679 | 1.296 | 1.671 | 2.000 | 2.390 | 2.660 | 2.915 | 3.232 | 3.460 |
| 120 | ·254 | ·677 | 1.289 | 1.658 | 1.980 | 2.358 | 2.617 | 2.860 | 3.160 | 3.373 |
| ∞ | ·253 | ·674 | 1.282 | 1.645 | 1.960 | 2.326 | 2.576 | 2.807 | 3.090 | 3.291 |

$Q = 1 - P(t|\nu)$ is the upper-tail area of the distribution for $\nu$ degrees of freedom, appropriate for use in a single-tail test. For a two-tail test, $2Q$ must be used.

Table 13. *Percentage points for the distribution of the correlation coefficient, r, when $\rho = 0$*

| ν | Q=0.05 2Q=0.1 | 0.025 0.05 | 0.01 0.02 | 0.005 0.01 | 0.0025 0.005 | 0.0005 0.001 | ν | Q=0.05 2Q=0.1 | 0.025 0.05 | 0.01 0.02 | 0.005 0.01 | 0.0025 0.005 | 0.0005 0.001 |
|---|---|---|---|---|---|---|---|---|---|---|---|---|---|
| 1 | 0.9877 | $0.9^2692$ | $0.9^3507$ | $0.9^3877$ | $0.9^4692$ | $0.9^5877$ | 16 | 0.400 | 0.468 | 0.543 | 0.590 | 0.631 | 0.708 |
| 2 | ·9000 | ·9500 | ·9800 | $·9^2000$ | $·9^2500$ | $·9^3000$ | 17 | ·389 | ·456 | ·529 | ·575 | ·616 | ·693 |
| 3 | ·805 | ·878 | ·9343 | ·9587 | ·9740 | $·9^3114$ | 18 | ·378 | ·444 | ·516 | ·561 | ·602 | ·679 |
| 4 | ·729 | ·811 | ·882 | ·9172 | ·9417 | ·9741 | 19 | ·369 | ·433 | ·503 | ·549 | ·589 | ·665 |
| 5 | ·669 | ·754 | ·833 | ·875 | ·9056 | ·9509 | 20 | ·360 | ·423 | ·492 | ·537 | ·576 | ·652 |
| 6 | 0.621 | 0.707 | 0.789 | 0.834 | 0.870 | 0.9249 | 25 | 0.323 | 0.381 | 0.445 | 0.487 | 0.524 | 0.597 |
| 7 | ·582 | ·666 | ·750 | ·798 | ·836 | ·898 | 30 | ·296 | ·349 | ·409 | ·449 | ·484 | ·554 |
| 8 | ·549 | ·632 | ·715 | ·765 | ·805 | ·872 | 35 | ·275 | ·325 | ·381 | ·418 | ·452 | ·519 |
| 9 | ·521 | ·602 | ·685 | ·735 | ·776 | ·847 | 40 | ·257 | ·304 | ·358 | ·393 | ·425 | ·490 |
| 10 | ·497 | ·576 | ·658 | ·708 | ·750 | ·823 | 45 | ·243 | ·288 | ·338 | ·372 | ·403 | ·465 |
| 11 | 0.476 | 0.553 | 0.634 | 0.684 | 0.726 | 0.801 | 50 | 0.231 | 0.273 | 0.322 | 0.354 | 0.384 | 0.443 |
| 12 | ·457 | ·532 | ·612 | ·661 | ·703 | ·780 | 60 | ·211 | ·250 | ·295 | ·325 | ·352 | ·408 |
| 13 | ·441 | ·514 | ·592 | ·641 | ·683 | ·760 | 70 | ·195 | ·232 | ·274 | ·302 | ·327 | ·380 |
| 14 | ·426 | ·497 | ·574 | ·623 | ·664 | ·742 | 80 | ·183 | ·217 | ·257 | ·283 | ·307 | ·357 |
| 15 | ·412 | ·482 | ·558 | ·606 | ·647 | ·725 | 90 | ·173 | ·205 | ·242 | ·267 | ·290 | ·338 |
|  |  |  |  |  |  |  | 100 | ·164 | ·195 | ·230 | ·254 | ·276 | ·321 |

$Q = 1 - P(r|\nu, \rho = 0)$ is the upper-tail area of the distribution of $r$ appropriate for use in a single-tail test. For a two-tail test, $2Q$ must be used. If $r$ is calculated from $n$ paired observations, enter the table with $\nu = n - 2$. For partial correlations enter with $\nu = n - k - 2$, where $k$ is the number of variables held constant.

The columns for $2Q = 0.2$, 0.02 and 0.001 in Table 12 and $2Q = 0.02$ and 0.001 in Table 13 have been taken from *Statistical Tables for Biological, Agricultural and Medical Research*, Tables III and VI (Fisher & Yates, 1963) by permission of the authors and the publishers, Messrs Oliver and Boyd.

# Table 14. *The z-transformation of the correlation coefficient, $z = \tanh^{-1} r$*

| r | .000 | .002 | .004 | .006 | .008 | 1 | 2 | 3 | 4 | 5 | 6 | 7 | 8 | 9 | 10 | .000 | .002 | .004 | .006 | .008 | r |
|---|---|---|---|---|---|---|---|---|---|---|---|---|---|---|---|---|---|---|---|---|---|
| | *r* (3rd decimal) | | | | | Proportional parts, for right side→ | | | | | | | | | | *r* (3rd decimal) | | | | | |
| ·00 | ·0000 | ·0020 | ·0040 | ·0060 | ·0080 | 1 | 3 | 4 | 5 | 7 | 8 | 9 | 11 | 12 | 13 | ·5493 | ·5520 | ·5547 | ·5573 | ·5600 | ·50 |
| 1 | ·0100 | ·0120 | ·0140 | ·0160 | ·0180 | 1 | 3 | 4 | 5 | 7 | 8 | 10 | 11 | 12 | 14 | ·5627 | ·5654 | ·5682 | ·5709 | ·5736 | 1 |
| 2 | ·0200 | ·0220 | ·0240 | ·0260 | ·0280 | 1 | 3 | 4 | 6 | 7 | 8 | 10 | 11 | 13 | 14 | ·5763 | ·5791 | ·5818 | ·5846 | ·5874 | 2 |
| 3 | ·0300 | ·0320 | ·0340 | ·0360 | ·0380 | 1 | 3 | 4 | 6 | 7 | 8 | 10 | 11 | 13 | 14 | ·5901 | ·5929 | ·5957 | ·5985 | ·6013 | 3 |
| 4 | ·0400 | ·0420 | ·0440 | ·0460 | ·0480 | 1 | 3 | 4 | 6 | 7 | 9 | 10 | 11 | 13 | 14 | ·6042 | ·6070 | ·6098 | ·6127 | ·6155 | 4 |
| ·05 | ·0500 | ·0520 | ·0541 | ·0561 | ·0581 | 1 | 3 | 4 | 6 | 7 | 9 | 10 | 12 | 13 | 14 | ·6184 | ·6213 | ·6241 | ·6270 | ·6299 | ·55 |
| 6 | ·0601 | ·0621 | ·0641 | ·0661 | ·0681 | 1 | 3 | 4 | 6 | 7 | 9 | 10 | 12 | 13 | 15 | ·6328 | ·6358 | ·6387 | ·6416 | ·6446 | 6 |
| 7 | ·0701 | ·0721 | ·0741 | ·0761 | ·0782 | 1 | 3 | 4 | 6 | 7 | 9 | 10 | 12 | 14 | 15 | ·6475 | ·6505 | ·6535 | ·6565 | ·6595 | 7 |
| 8 | ·0802 | ·0822 | ·0842 | ·0862 | ·0882 | 2 | 3 | 5 | 6 | 8 | 9 | 11 | 12 | 14 | 15 | ·6625 | ·6655 | ·6685 | ·6716 | ·6746 | 8 |
| 9 | ·0902 | ·0923 | ·0943 | ·0963 | ·0983 | 2 | 3 | 5 | 6 | 8 | 9 | 11 | 12 | 14 | 15 | ·6777 | ·6807 | ·6838 | ·6869 | ·6900 | 9 |
| ·10 | ·1003 | ·1024 | ·1044 | ·1064 | ·1084 | 2 | 3 | 5 | 6 | 8 | 9 | 11 | 13 | 14 | 16 | ·6931 | ·6963 | ·6994 | ·7026 | ·7057 | ·60 |
| 1 | ·1104 | ·1125 | ·1145 | ·1165 | ·1186 | 2 | 3 | 5 | 6 | 8 | 10 | 11 | 13 | 14 | 16 | ·7089 | ·7121 | ·7153 | ·7185 | ·7218 | 1 |
| 2 | ·1206 | ·1226 | ·1246 | ·1267 | ·1287 | 2 | 3 | 5 | 7 | 8 | 10 | 11 | 13 | 15 | 16 | ·7250 | ·7283 | ·7315 | ·7348 | ·7381 | 2 |
| 3 | ·1307 | ·1328 | ·1348 | ·1368 | ·1389 | 2 | 3 | 5 | 7 | 8 | 10 | 12 | 13 | 15 | 17 | ·7414 | ·7447 | ·7481 | ·7514 | ·7548 | 3 |
| 4 | ·1409 | ·1430 | ·1450 | ·1471 | ·1491 | 2 | 3 | 5 | 7 | 9 | 10 | 12 | 14 | 15 | 17 | ·7582 | ·7616 | ·7650 | ·7684 | ·7718 | 4 |
| ·15 | ·1511 | ·1532 | ·1552 | ·1573 | ·1593 | 2 | 4 | 5 | 7 | 9 | 11 | 12 | 14 | 16 | 18 | ·7753 | ·7788 | ·7823 | ·7858 | ·7893 | ·65 |
| 6 | ·1614 | ·1634 | ·1655 | ·1676 | ·1696 | 2 | 4 | 5 | 7 | 9 | 11 | 13 | 14 | 16 | 18 | ·7928 | ·7964 | ·7999 | ·8035 | ·8071 | 6 |
| 7 | ·1717 | ·1737 | ·1758 | ·1779 | ·1799 | 2 | 4 | 6 | 7 | 9 | 11 | 13 | 15 | 17 | 18 | ·8107 | ·8144 | ·8180 | ·8217 | ·8254 | 7 |
| 8 | ·1820 | ·1841 | ·1861 | ·1882 | ·1903 | 2 | 4 | 6 | 8 | 9 | 11 | 13 | 15 | 17 | 19 | ·8291 | ·8328 | ·8366 | ·8404 | ·8441 | 8 |
| 9 | ·1923 | ·1944 | ·1965 | ·1986 | ·2007 | 2 | 4 | 6 | 8 | 10 | 12 | 14 | 15 | 17 | 19 | ·8480 | ·8518 | ·8556 | ·8595 | ·8634 | 9 |
| ·20 | ·2027 | ·2048 | ·2069 | ·2090 | ·2111 | 2 | 4 | 6 | 8 | 10 | 12 | 14 | 16 | 18 | 20 | ·8673 | ·8712 | ·8752 | ·8792 | ·8832 | ·70 |
| 1 | ·2132 | ·2153 | ·2174 | ·2195 | ·2216 | 2 | 4 | 6 | 8 | 10 | 12 | 15 | 16 | 18 | 20 | ·8872 | ·8912 | ·8953 | ·8994 | ·9035 | 1 |
| 2 | ·2237 | ·2258 | ·2279 | ·2300 | ·2321 | 2 | 4 | 6 | 8 | 11 | 13 | 15 | 17 | 19 | 21 | ·9076 | ·9118 | ·9160 | ·9202 | ·9245 | 2 |
| 3 | ·2342 | ·2363 | ·2384 | ·2405 | ·2427 | 2 | 4 | 7 | 9 | 11 | 13 | 15 | 17 | 20 | 22 | ·9287 | ·9330 | ·9373 | ·9417 | ·9461 | 3 |
| 4 | ·2448 | ·2469 | ·2490 | ·2512 | ·2533 | 2 | 4 | 7 | 9 | 11 | 13 | 16 | 18 | 20 | 22 | ·9505 | ·9549 | ·9594 | ·9639 | ·9684 | 4 |
| ·25 | ·2554 | ·2575 | ·2597 | ·2618 | ·2640 | 1 | 2 | 3 | 4 | 5 | 6 | 7 | 9 | 10 | 11 | 0·973 | 0·978 | 0·982 | 0·987 | 0·991 | ·75 |
| 6 | ·2661 | ·2683 | ·2704 | ·2726 | ·2747 | 1 | 2 | 3 | 4 | 5 | 6 | 8 | 9 | 10 | 11 | 0·996 | 1·001 | 1·006 | 1·011 | 1·015 | 6 |
| 7 | ·2769 | ·2790 | ·2812 | ·2833 | ·2855 | 1 | 2 | 3 | 4 | 5 | 6 | 8 | 9 | 10 | 11 | 1·020 | 1·025 | 1·030 | 1·035 | 1·040 | 7 |
| 8 | ·2877 | ·2899 | ·2920 | ·2942 | ·2964 | 1 | 2 | 3 | 4 | 5 | 7 | 8 | 9 | 10 | 11 | 1·045 | 1·050 | 1·056 | 1·061 | 1·066 | 8 |
| 9 | ·2986 | ·3008 | ·3029 | ·3051 | ·3073 | 1 | 2 | 3 | 4 | 5 | 7 | 8 | 9 | 10 | 11 | 1·071 | 1·077 | 1·082 | 1·088 | 1·093 | 9 |
| ·30 | ·3095 | ·3117 | ·3139 | ·3161 | ·3183 | 1 | 2 | 3 | 4 | 6 | 7 | 8 | 9 | 10 | 11 | 1·099 | 1·104 | 1·110 | 1·116 | 1·121 | ·80 |
| 1 | ·3205 | ·3228 | ·3250 | ·3272 | ·3294 | 1 | 2 | 3 | 4 | 6 | 7 | 8 | 9 | 10 | 11 | 1·127 | 1·133 | 1·139 | 1·145 | 1·151 | 1 |
| 2 | ·3316 | ·3339 | ·3361 | ·3383 | ·3406 | 1 | 2 | 3 | 4 | 6 | 7 | 8 | 9 | 10 | 11 | 1·157 | 1·163 | 1·169 | 1·175 | 1·182 | 2 |
| 3 | ·3428 | ·3451 | ·3473 | ·3496 | ·3518 | 1 | 2 | 3 | 5 | 6 | 7 | 8 | 9 | 10 | 11 | 1·188 | 1·195 | 1·201 | 1·208 | 1·214 | 3 |
| 4 | ·3541 | ·3564 | ·3586 | ·3609 | ·3632 | 1 | 2 | 3 | 5 | 6 | 7 | 8 | 9 | 10 | 11 | 1·221 | 1·228 | 1·235 | 1·242 | 1·249 | 4 |
| ·35 | ·3654 | ·3677 | ·3700 | ·3723 | ·3746 | 1 | 2 | 3 | 5 | 6 | 7 | 8 | 9 | 10 | 11 | 1·256 | 1·263 | 1·271 | 1·278 | 1·286 | ·85 |
| 6 | ·3769 | ·3792 | ·3815 | ·3838 | ·3861 | 1 | 2 | 3 | 5 | 6 | 7 | 8 | 9 | 10 | 12 | 1·293 | 1·301 | 1·309 | 1·317 | 1·325 | 6 |
| 7 | ·3884 | ·3907 | ·3931 | ·3954 | ·3977 | 1 | 2 | 3 | 5 | 6 | 7 | 8 | 9 | 10 | 12 | 1·333 | 1·341 | 1·350 | 1·358 | 1·367 | 7 |
| 8 | ·4001 | ·4024 | ·4047 | ·4071 | ·4094 | 1 | 2 | 4 | 5 | 6 | 7 | 8 | 9 | 11 | 12 | 1·376 | 1·385 | 1·394 | 1·403 | 1·412 | 8 |
| 9 | ·4118 | ·4142 | ·4165 | ·4189 | ·4213 | 1 | 2 | 4 | 5 | 6 | 7 | 8 | 9 | 11 | 12 | 1·422 | 1·432 | 1·442 | 1·452 | 1·462 | 9 |
| ·40 | ·4236 | ·4260 | ·4284 | ·4308 | ·4332 | 1 | 2 | 4 | 5 | 6 | 7 | 8 | 10 | 11 | 12 | 1·472 | 1·483 | 1·494 | 1·505 | 1·516 | ·90 |
| 1 | ·4356 | ·4380 | ·4404 | ·4428 | ·4453 | 1 | 2 | 4 | 5 | 6 | 7 | 8 | 10 | 11 | 12 | 1·528 | 1·539 | 1·551 | 1·564 | 1·576 | 1 |
| 2 | ·4477 | ·4501 | ·4526 | ·4550 | ·4574 | 1 | 2 | 4 | 5 | 6 | 7 | 9 | 10 | 11 | 12 | 1·589 | 1·602 | 1·616 | 1·630 | 1·644 | 2 |
| 3 | ·4599 | ·4624 | ·4648 | ·4673 | ·4698 | 1 | 2 | 4 | 5 | 6 | 7 | 9 | 10 | 11 | 12 | 1·658 | 1·673 | 1·689 | 1·705 | 1·721 | 3 |
| 4 | ·4722 | ·4747 | ·4772 | ·4797 | ·4822 | 1 | 2 | 4 | 5 | 6 | 7 | 9 | 10 | 11 | 12 | 1·738 | 1·756 | 1·774 | 1·792 | 1·812 | 4 |
| ·45 | ·4847 | ·4872 | ·4897 | ·4922 | ·4948 | 1 | 3 | 4 | 5 | 6 | 8 | 9 | 10 | 11 | 13 | 1·832 | 1·853 | 1·874 | 1·897 | 1·921 | ·95 |
| 6 | ·4973 | ·4999 | ·5024 | ·5049 | ·5075 | 1 | 3 | 4 | 5 | 6 | 8 | 9 | 10 | 11 | 13 | 1·946 | 1·972 | 2·000 | 2·029 | 2·060 | 6 |
| 7 | ·5101 | ·5126 | ·5152 | ·5178 | ·5204 | 1 | 3 | 4 | 5 | 6 | 8 | 9 | 10 | 12 | 13 | 2·092 | 2·127 | 2·165 | 2·205 | 2·249 | 7 |
| 8 | ·5230 | ·5256 | ·5282 | ·5308 | ·5334 | 1 | 3 | 4 | 5 | 7 | 8 | 9 | 10 | 12 | 13 | 2·298 | 2·351 | 2·410 | 2·477 | 2·555 | 8 |
| 9 | ·5361 | ·5387 | ·5413 | ·5440 | ·5466 | 1 | 3 | 4 | 5 | 7 | 8 | 9 | 11 | 12 | 13 | 2·647 | 2·759 | 2·903 | 3·106 | 3·453 | 9 |
| r | ·000 | ·002 | ·004 | ·006 | ·008 | 1 | 2 | 3 | 4 | 5 | 6 | 7 | 8 | 9 | 10 | ·000 | ·002 | ·004 | ·006 | ·008 | r |
| | *r* (3rd decimal) | | | | | ←Proportional parts, for left side | | | | | | | | | | *r* (3rd decimal) | | | | | |

## Interpolation

(1) $0 \leqslant r \leqslant 0.25$: find argument $r_0$ nearest to $r$ and form $z = z(r_0) + \Delta r$ (where $\Delta r = r - r_0$), e.g. for $r = 0.2042$, $z = 0.2069 + 0.0002 = 0.2071$.

(2) $0.25 \leqslant r \leqslant 0.75$: find argument $r_0$ nearest to $r$ and form $z = z(r_0) \pm P$, where $P$ is the proportional part for $\Delta r = r - r_0$, e.g. for $r = 0.5146$, $z = 0.5682 + 0.0008 = 0.5690$; for $r = 0.5372$, $z = 0.6013 - 0.0011 = 0.6002$.

(3) $0.75 \leqslant r \leqslant 0.98$: use linear interpolation to get 3-decimal place accuracy.

(4) $0.98 \leqslant r < 1$: form $z = -\frac{1}{2}\log_e(1-r) + 0.097 + \frac{1}{4}r$, with the help of Table 53.

147

## Table 15. *Chart giving confidence limits for the population correlation coefficient, ρ, given the sample coefficient, r. Confidence coefficient, $1 - 2\alpha = 0.95$*

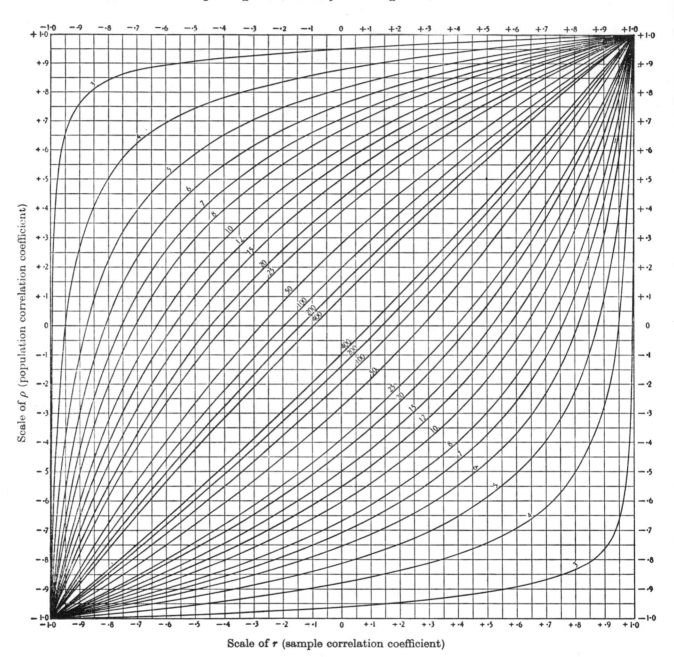

Scale of ρ (population correlation coefficient)

Scale of *r* (sample correlation coefficient)

The numbers on the curves indicate sample size. The chart can also be used to determine upper and lower 2·5 % significance points for *r*, given ρ.

Table 15 (*continued*). *Confidence coefficient*, $1 - 2\alpha = 0.99$

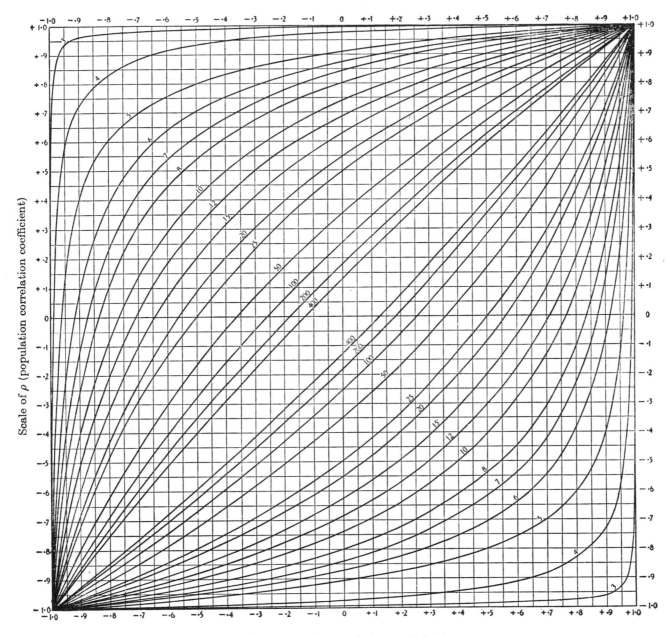

Scale of *r* (sample correlation coefficient)

**The numbers on the curves indicate sample size. The chart can also be used to determine upper and lower 0·5 % significance points for *r*, given *ρ*.**

Table 16. *Percentage points of the B-distribution*

50% *points for x*

$$\nu_1 = 2b, \quad \nu_2 = 2a$$

| $\nu_2$ \ $\nu_1$ | 1 | 2 | 3 | 4 | 5 | 6 | 7 | 8 | 9 |
|---|---|---|---|---|---|---|---|---|---|
| 1 | 0·50000 | 0·25000 | 0·16319 | 0·12061 | 0·095526 | 0·079033 | 0·067378 | 0·058711 | 0·052015 |
| 2 | ·75000 | ·50000 | ·37004 | ·29289 | ·24214 | ·20630 | ·17966 | ·15910 | ·14276 |
| 3 | ·83681 | ·62996 | ·50000 | ·41363 | ·35245 | ·30695 | ·27181 | ·24386 | ·22112 |
| 4 | ·87939 | ·70711 | ·58637 | ·50000 | ·43555 | ·38573 | ·34609 | ·31381 | ·28703 |
| 5 | 0·90447 | 0·75786 | 0·64755 | 0·56445 | 0·50000 | 0·44867 | 0·40684 | 0·37213 | 0·34286 |
| 6 | ·92097 | ·79370 | ·69305 | ·61427 | ·55133 | ·50000 | ·45737 | ·42141 | ·39068 |
| 7 | ·93262 | ·82034 | ·72819 | ·65391 | ·59316 | ·54263 | ·50000 | ·46355 | ·43205 |
| 8 | ·94129 | ·84090 | ·75614 | ·68619 | ·62787 | ·57859 | ·53645 | ·50000 | ·46818 |
| 9 | ·94799 | ·85724 | ·77888 | ·71297 | ·65714 | ·60932 | ·56795 | ·53182 | ·50000 |
| 10 | 0·95331 | 0·87055 | 0·79775 | 0·73555 | 0·68214 | 0·63588 | 0·59546 | 0·55984 | 0·52824 |
| 11 | ·95765 | ·88159 | ·81366 | ·75484 | ·70376 | ·65907 | ·61968 | ·58471 | ·55346 |
| 12 | ·96125 | ·89090 | ·82725 | ·77151 | ·72262 | ·67948 | ·64116 | ·60692 | ·57613 |
| 13 | ·96429 | ·89885 | ·83899 | ·78606 | ·73923 | ·69759 | ·66035 | ·62687 | ·59661 |
| 14 | ·96689 | ·90572 | ·84924 | ·79887 | ·75396 | ·71376 | ·67760 | ·64490 | ·61520 |
| 15 | 0·96913 | 0·91172 | 0·85827 | 0·81023 | 0·76712 | 0·72830 | 0·69318 | 0·66127 | 0·63216 |
| 16 | ·97109 | ·91700 | ·86627 | ·82038 | ·77894 | ·74143 | ·70732 | ·67620 | ·64768 |
| 17 | ·97282 | ·92169 | ·87342 | ·82950 | ·78963 | ·75334 | ·72022 | ·68986 | ·66195 |
| 18 | ·97435 | ·92587 | ·87985 | ·83774 | ·79932 | ·76421 | ·73203 | ·70242 | ·67511 |
| 19 | ·97572 | ·92964 | ·88565 | ·84522 | ·80817 | ·77417 | ·74288 | ·71401 | ·68729 |
| 20 | 0·97695 | 0·93303 | 0·89092 | 0·85204 | 0·81626 | 0·78331 | 0·75289 | 0·72472 | 0·69858 |
| 21 | ·97806 | ·93612 | ·89573 | ·85828 | ·82371 | ·79175 | ·76215 | ·73467 | ·70909 |
| 22 | ·97907 | ·93893 | ·90013 | ·86402 | ·83057 | ·79955 | ·77074 | ·74392 | ·71889 |
| 23 | ·97999 | ·94151 | ·90417 | ·86931 | ·83692 | ·80679 | ·77873 | ·75254 | ·72805 |
| 24 | ·98083 | ·94387 | ·90790 | ·87421 | ·84281 | ·81353 | ·78619 | ·76061 | ·73663 |
| 25 | 0·98161 | 0·94606 | 0·91135 | 0·87875 | 0·84828 | 0·81981 | 0·79315 | 0·76816 | 0·74469 |
| 26 | ·98232 | ·94808 | ·91455 | ·88298 | ·85340 | ·82568 | ·79968 | ·77526 | ·75227 |
| 27 | ·98298 | ·94995 | ·91753 | ·88692 | ·85817 | ·83118 | ·80581 | ·78193 | ·75941 |
| 28 | ·98360 | ·95170 | ·92031 | ·89060 | ·86265 | ·83635 | ·81157 | ·78821 | ·76615 |
| 29 | ·98417 | ·95332 | ·92290 | ·89406 | ·86685 | ·84120 | ·81701 | ·79415 | ·77253 |
| 30 | 0·98470 | 0·95484 | 0·92534 | 0·89730 | 0·87080 | 0·84578 | 0·82214 | 0·79976 | 0·77857 |
| 40 | ·98855 | ·96594 | ·94324 | ·92136 | ·90038 | ·88030 | ·86107 | ·84266 | ·82501 |
| 60 | ·99238 | ·97716 | ·96164 | ·94645 | ·93166 | ·91731 | ·90338 | ·88985 | ·87672 |
| 120 | ·99620 | ·98851 | ·98056 | ·97264 | ·96482 | ·95710 | ·94951 | ·94202 | ·93465 |
| ∞ | 1·00000 | 1·00000 | 1·00000 | 1·00000 | 1·00000 | 1·00000 | 1·00000 | 1·00000 | 1·00000 |

This table gives the values of $x$ for which

$$I_x(a, b) = \int_0^x u^{a-1}(1-u)^{b-1}\, du \Big/ \int_0^1 u^{a-1}(1-u)^{b-1}\, du = 0.50,$$

where $a = \frac{1}{2}\nu_2$, $b = \frac{1}{2}\nu_1$.

Table 16 (*continued*)

50% *points for x*

$$\nu_1 = 2b, \quad \nu_2 = 2a$$

| $\nu_1$ \ $\nu_2$ | 10 | 12 | 15 | 20 | 24 | 30 | 40 | 60 | 120 |
|---|---|---|---|---|---|---|---|---|---|
| 1 | 0·046687 | 0·038746 | 0·030867 | 0·023051 | 0·019168 | 0·015301 | 0·011450 | 0·0076165 | 0·0037997 |
| 2 | ·12945 | ·10910 | ·088278 | ·066967 | ·056126 | ·045158 | ·034064 | ·022840 | ·011486 |
| 3 | ·20225 | ·17275 | ·14173 | ·10908 | ·092099 | ·074664 | ·056756 | ·038355 | ·019444 |
| 4 | ·26445 | ·22849 | ·18977 | ·14796 | ·12579 | ·10270 | ·078644 | ·053552 | ·027361 |
| 5 | 0·31786 | 0·27738 | 0·23288 | 0·18374 | 0·15719 | 0·12920 | 0·099622 | 0·068335 | 0·035184 |
| 6 | ·36412 | ·32052 | ·27170 | ·21669 | ·18647 | ·15422 | ·11970 | ·082690 | ·042896 |
| 7 | ·40454 | ·35884 | ·30682 | ·24711 | ·21381 | ·17786 | ·13893 | ·096624 | ·050494 |
| 8 | ·44016 | ·39308 | ·33873 | ·27528 | ·23939 | ·20024 | ·15734 | ·11015 | ·057977 |
| 9 | ·47176 | ·42387 | ·36784 | ·30142 | ·26337 | ·22143 | ·17499 | ·12328 | ·065345 |
| 10 | 0·50000 | 0·45169 | 0·39451 | 0·32575 | 0·28589 | 0·24154 | 0·19192 | 0·13603 | 0·072602 |
| 11 | ·52538 | ·47696 | ·41902 | ·34845 | ·30707 | ·26064 | ·20818 | ·14842 | ·079747 |
| 12 | ·54831 | ·50000 | ·44162 | ·36967 | ·32704 | ·27880 | ·22379 | ·16046 | ·086785 |
| 13 | ·56912 | ·52110 | ·46254 | ·38956 | ·34589 | ·29610 | ·23880 | ·17217 | ·093716 |
| 14 | ·58811 | ·54049 | ·48194 | ·40823 | ·36371 | ·31258 | ·25325 | ·18355 | ·10054 |
| 15 | 0·60549 | 0·55838 | 0·50000 | 0·42579 | 0·38059 | 0·32832 | 0·26715 | 0·19463 | 0·10727 |
| 16 | ·62147 | ·57492 | ·51684 | ·44234 | ·39660 | ·34334 | ·28055 | ·20541 | ·11390 |
| 17 | ·63621 | ·59027 | ·53258 | ·45797 | ·41181 | ·35772 | ·29347 | ·21591 | ·12043 |
| 18 | ·64984 | ·60456 | ·54733 | ·47274 | ·42626 | ·37147 | ·30593 | ·22613 | ·12686 |
| 19 | ·66248 | ·61788 | ·56118 | ·48673 | ·44002 | ·38465 | ·31796 | ·23609 | ·13320 |
| 20 | 0·67425 | 0·63033 | 0·57421 | 0·50000 | 0·45314 | 0·39729 | 0·32958 | 0·24580 | 0·13945 |
| 21 | ·68522 | ·64200 | ·58649 | ·51260 | ·46566 | ·40942 | ·34082 | ·25527 | ·14561 |
| 22 | ·69548 | ·65295 | ·59807 | ·52458 | ·47762 | ·42108 | ·35168 | ·26450 | ·15168 |
| 23 | ·70509 | ·66325 | ·60903 | ·53599 | ·48905 | ·43228 | ·36219 | ·27350 | ·15767 |
| 24 | ·71411 | ·67296 | ·61941 | ·54686 | ·50000 | ·44305 | ·37237 | ·28229 | ·16357 |
| 25 | 0·72260 | 0·68213 | 0·62924 | 0·55723 | 0·51049 | 0·45343 | 0·38222 | 0·29086 | 0·16939 |
| 26 | ·73060 | ·69079 | ·63859 | ·56714 | ·52054 | ·46342 | ·39177 | ·29924 | ·17513 |
| 27 | ·73815 | ·69900 | ·64747 | ·57662 | ·53019 | ·47306 | ·40103 | ·30741 | ·18080 |
| 28 | ·74529 | ·70678 | ·65593 | ·58569 | ·53946 | ·48236 | ·41001 | ·31540 | ·18638 |
| 29 | ·75205 | ·71417 | ·66399 | ·59438 | ·54837 | ·49133 | ·41873 | ·32321 | ·19189 |
| 30 | 0·75846 | 0·72120 | 0·67168 | 0·60271 | 0·55695 | 0·50000 | 0·42720 | 0·33084 | 0·19732 |
| 40 | ·80808 | ·77621 | ·73285 | ·67042 | ·62763 | ·57280 | ·50000 | ·39866 | ·24791 |
| 60 | ·86397 | ·83954 | ·80537 | ·75420 | ·71771 | ·66916 | ·60134 | ·50000 | ·33209 |
| 120 | ·92740 | ·91321 | ·89273 | ·86055 | ·83643 | ·80268 | ·75209 | ·66791 | ·50000 |
| ∞ | 1·00000 | 1·00000 | 1·00000 | 1·00000 | 1·00000 | 1·00000 | 1·00000 | 1·00000 | 1·00000 |

For $\nu_1 = \infty$, $x = 0$

Table 16. *Percentage points of the B-distribution (continued)*

Lower 25% points for x

$$\nu_1 = 2b, \quad \nu_2 = 2a$$

| $\nu_2$ \ $\nu_1$ | 1 | 2 | 3 | 4 | 5 | 6 | 7 | 8 | 9 |
|---|---|---|---|---|---|---|---|---|---|
| 1 | 0.14645 | 0.062500 | 0.039063 | 0.028310 | 0.022173 | 0.018215 | 0.015452 | 0.013416 | 0.011853 |
| 2 | ·43750 | ·25000 | ·17452 | ·13397 | ·10870 | ·091440 | ·078908 | ·069395 | ·061929 |
| 3 | ·59715 | ·39685 | ·29801 | ·23885 | ·19937 | ·17113 | ·14991 | ·13339 | ·12015 |
| 4 | ·68878 | ·50000 | ·39448 | ·32635 | ·27852 | ·24302 | ·21560 | ·19376 | ·17596 |
| 5 | 0·74711 | 0·57435 | 0·46936 | 0·39775 | 0·34546 | 0·30550 | 0·27390 | 0·24828 | 0·22707 |
| 6 | ·78726 | ·62996 | ·52848 | ·45632 | ·40198 | ·35944 | ·32516 | ·29692 | ·27323 |
| 7 | ·81650 | ·67295 | ·57609 | ·50494 | ·45001 | ·40614 | ·37021 | ·34022 | ·31478 |
| 8 | ·83872 | ·70711 | ·61516 | ·54582 | ·49117 | ·44680 | ·40996 | ·37885 | ·35219 |
| 9 | ·85616 | ·73487 | ·64773 | ·58060 | ·52678 | ·48245 | ·44521 | ·41343 | ·38597 |
| 10 | 0·87021 | 0·75786 | 0·67529 | 0·61052 | 0·55783 | 0·51390 | 0·47662 | 0·44451 | 0·41655 |
| 11 | ·88177 | ·77720 | ·69888 | ·63651 | ·58513 | ·54184 | ·50475 | ·47257 | ·44435 |
| 12 | ·89144 | ·79370 | ·71931 | ·65929 | ·60930 | ·56679 | ·53009 | ·49801 | ·46970 |
| 13 | ·89966 | ·80793 | ·73716 | ·67941 | ·63085 | ·58921 | ·55300 | ·52116 | ·49289 |
| 14 | ·90672 | ·82034 | ·75288 | ·69730 | ·65017 | ·60946 | ·57382 | ·54230 | ·51419 |
| 15 | 0·91285 | 0·83124 | 0·76684 | 0·71332 | 0·66758 | 0·62782 | 0·59282 | 0·56169 | 0·53380 |
| 16 | ·91823 | ·84090 | ·77932 | ·72773 | ·68336 | ·64456 | ·61021 | ·57953 | ·55192 |
| 17 | ·92298 | ·84951 | ·79053 | ·74077 | ·69772 | ·65986 | ·62619 | ·59599 | ·56870 |
| 18 | ·92721 | ·85724 | ·80066 | ·75263 | ·71084 | ·67391 | ·64093 | ·61122 | ·58428 |
| 19 | ·93100 | ·86422 | ·80986 | ·76345 | ·72287 | ·68686 | ·65456 | ·62536 | ·59879 |
| 20 | 0·93442 | 0·87055 | 0·81825 | 0·77337 | 0·73395 | 0·69882 | 0·66720 | 0·63852 | 0·61234 |
| 21 | ·93751 | ·87632 | ·82593 | ·78250 | ·74418 | ·70991 | ·67895 | ·65079 | ·62500 |
| 22 | ·94033 | ·88159 | ·83299 | ·79092 | ·75366 | ·72021 | ·68991 | ·66226 | ·63688 |
| 23 | ·94290 | ·88644 | ·83950 | ·79871 | ·76246 | ·72981 | ·70015 | ·67300 | ·64803 |
| 24 | ·94526 | ·89090 | ·84553 | ·80595 | ·77066 | ·73878 | ·70973 | ·68309 | ·65852 |
| 25 | 0·94744 | 0·89503 | 0·85112 | 0·81268 | 0·77831 | 0·74717 | 0·71873 | 0·69258 | 0·66841 |
| 26 | ·94944 | ·89885 | ·85632 | ·81896 | ·78547 | ·75505 | ·72719 | ·70152 | ·67774 |
| 27 | ·95130 | ·90241 | ·86116 | ·82484 | ·79218 | ·76244 | ·73515 | ·70995 | ·68657 |
| 28 | ·95303 | ·90572 | ·86570 | ·83035 | ·79848 | ·76941 | ·74267 | ·71793 | ·69492 |
| 29 | ·95464 | ·90882 | ·86994 | ·83552 | ·80442 | ·77598 | ·74977 | ·72548 | ·70285 |
| 30 | 0·95614 | 0·91172 | 0·87393 | 0·84039 | 0·81002 | 0·78219 | 0·75649 | 0·73263 | 0·71038 |
| 40 | ·96706 | ·93303 | ·90351 | ·87685 | ·85230 | ·82947 | ·80809 | ·78797 | ·76896 |
| 60 | ·97801 | ·95484 | ·93434 | ·91548 | ·89782 | ·88113 | ·86525 | ·85009 | ·83557 |
| 120 | ·98899 | ·97716 | ·96648 | ·95647 | ·94692 | ·93774 | ·92887 | ·92025 | ·91187 |
| ∞ | 1·00000 | 1·00000 | 1·00000 | 1·00000 | 1·00000 | 1·00000 | 1·00000 | 1·00000 | 1·00000 |

This table gives the values of x for which

$$I_x(a, b) = \int_0^x u^{a-1}(1-u)^{b-1}\, du \bigg/ \int_0^1 u^{a-1}(1-u)^{b-1}\, du = 0.25,$$

where $a = \frac{1}{2}\nu_2$, $b = \frac{1}{2}\nu_1$.

Table 16 (*continued*)

## Lower 25% points for $x$

$$\nu_1 = 2b, \quad \nu_2 = 2a$$

| $\nu_1$ / $\nu_2$ | 10 | 12 | 15 | 20 | 24 | 30 | 40 | 60 | 120 |
|---|---|---|---|---|---|---|---|---|---|
| 1 | 0·010616 | 0·0087814 | 0·0069734 | 0·0051914 | 0·0043101 | 0·0034353 | 0·0025669 | 0·0017049 | 0·0$^3$84926 |
| 2 | ·055912 | ·046816 | ·037631 | ·028358 | ·023688 | ·018996 | ·014281 | ·0095436 | ·0047832 |
| 3 | ·10930 | ·092592 | ·075324 | ·057467 | ·048307 | ·038986 | ·029500 | ·019844 | ·010012 |
| 4 | ·16116 | ·13797 | ·11350 | ·087610 | ·074095 | ·060174 | ·045827 | ·031031 | ·015764 |
| 5 | 0·20922 | 0·18082 | 0·15026 | 0·11726 | 0·099749 | 0·081498 | 0·062458 | 0·042571 | 0·021774 |
| 6 | ·25307 | ·22058 | ·18500 | ·14585 | ·12475 | ·10251 | ·079043 | ·054222 | ·027923 |
| 7 | ·29291 | ·25724 | ·21758 | ·17316 | ·14887 | ·12301 | ·095405 | ·065857 | ·034143 |
| 8 | ·32908 | ·29099 | ·24802 | ·19913 | ·17203 | ·14289 | ·11145 | ·077403 | ·040396 |
| 9 | ·36198 | ·32205 | ·27644 | ·22376 | ·19420 | ·16211 | ·12712 | ·088814 | ·046656 |
| 10 | 0·39196 | 0·35068 | 0·30297 | 0·24710 | 0·21538 | 0·18064 | 0·14240 | 0·10006 | 0·052904 |
| 11 | ·41938 | ·37712 | ·32776 | ·26921 | ·23562 | ·19850 | ·15726 | ·11113 | ·059127 |
| 12 | ·44451 | ·40158 | ·35094 | ·29017 | ·25493 | ·21570 | ·17171 | ·12200 | ·065317 |
| 13 | ·46762 | ·42426 | ·37265 | ·31004 | ·27338 | ·23226 | ·18575 | ·13267 | ·071466 |
| 14 | ·48893 | ·44534 | ·39302 | ·32889 | ·29100 | ·24819 | ·19938 | ·14314 | ·077570 |
| 15 | 0·50863 | 0·46497 | 0·41215 | 0·34679 | 0·30784 | 0·26353 | 0·21261 | 0·15341 | 0·083624 |
| 16 | ·52691 | ·48330 | ·43016 | ·36380 | ·32395 | ·27831 | ·22546 | ·16347 | ·089625 |
| 17 | ·54389 | ·50043 | ·44712 | ·37998 | ·33936 | ·29254 | ·23793 | ·17332 | ·095571 |
| 18 | ·55972 | ·51649 | ·46312 | ·39539 | ·35411 | ·30625 | ·25004 | ·18298 | ·10146 |
| 19 | ·57449 | ·53156 | ·47825 | ·41008 | ·36824 | ·31946 | ·26179 | ·19244 | ·10729 |
| 20 | 0·58832 | 0·54574 | 0·49256 | 0·42409 | 0·38179 | 0·33221 | 0·27321 | 0·20170 | 0·11307 |
| 21 | ·60129 | ·55909 | ·50613 | ·43746 | ·39478 | ·34450 | ·28430 | ·21078 | ·11878 |
| 22 | ·61348 | ·57169 | ·51900 | ·45025 | ·40726 | ·35637 | ·29507 | ·21966 | ·12443 |
| 23 | ·62495 | ·58360 | ·53122 | ·46247 | ·41925 | ·36783 | ·30554 | ·22837 | ·13003 |
| 24 | ·63576 | ·59487 | ·54285 | ·47418 | ·43078 | ·37891 | ·31572 | ·23690 | ·13556 |
| 25 | 0·64597 | 0·60556 | 0·55392 | 0·48539 | 0·44186 | 0·38961 | 0·32561 | 0·24525 | 0·14103 |
| 26 | ·65563 | ·61570 | ·56447 | ·49615 | ·45253 | ·39996 | ·33524 | ·25343 | ·14645 |
| 27 | ·66478 | ·62533 | ·57455 | ·50647 | ·46281 | ·40997 | ·34460 | ·26145 | ·15180 |
| 28 | ·67346 | ·63450 | ·58417 | ·51639 | ·47272 | ·41967 | ·35371 | ·26931 | ·15710 |
| 29 | ·68170 | ·64323 | ·59337 | ·52591 | ·48228 | ·42906 | ·36259 | ·27701 | ·16234 |
| 30 | 0·68954 | 0·65156 | 0·60217 | 0·53508 | 0·49150 | 0·43815 | 0·37122 | 0·28455 | 0·16752 |
| 40 | ·75095 | ·71758 | ·67308 | ·61054 | ·56853 | ·51555 | ·44650 | ·35245 | ·21626 |
| 60 | ·82163 | ·79529 | ·75915 | ·70620 | ·66914 | ·62056 | ·55390 | ·45636 | ·29913 |
| 120 | ·90370 | ·88794 | ·86554 | ·83103 | ·80557 | ·77041 | ·71852 | ·63381 | ·46918 |
| $\infty$ | 1·00000 | 1·00000 | 1·00000 | 1·00000 | 1·00000 | 1·00000 | 1·00000 | 1·00000 | 1·00000 |

For $\nu_1 = \infty$, $x = 0$

Table 16. *Percentage points of the B-distribution (continued)*

### Lower 10% points for $x$

$$\nu_1 = 2b, \quad \nu_2 = 2a$$

| $\nu_2$ \ $\nu_1$ | 1 | 2 | 3 | 4 | 5 | 6 | 7 | 8 | 9 |
|---|---|---|---|---|---|---|---|---|---|
| 1 | 0·024472 | 0·010000 | 0·0061812 | 0·0044577 | 0·0034819 | 0·0028553 | 0·0024193 | 0·0020986 | 0·0018528 |
| 2 | ·19000 | ·10000 | ·067830 | ·051317 | ·041268 | ·034511 | ·029654 | ·025996 | ·023141 |
| 3 | ·35136 | ·21544 | ·15648 | ·12310 | ·10154 | ·086434 | ·075257 | ·066647 | ·059809 |
| 4 | ·46812 | ·31623 | ·24136 | ·19580 | ·16493 | ·14256 | ·12558 | ·11223 | ·10147 |
| 5 | 0·55185 | 0·39811 | 0·31529 | 0·26204 | 0·22457 | 0·19664 | 0·17498 | 0·15766 | 0·14349 |
| 6 | ·61375 | ·46416 | ·37816 | ·32046 | ·27858 | ·24664 | ·22139 | ·20091 | ·18394 |
| 7 | ·66104 | ·51795 | ·43151 | ·37151 | ·32685 | ·29210 | ·26421 | ·24127 | ·22207 |
| 8 | ·69821 | ·56234 | ·47700 | ·41611 | ·36982 | ·33319 | ·30339 | ·27860 | ·25764 |
| 9 | ·72814 | ·59948 | ·51610 | ·45522 | ·40811 | ·37029 | ·33915 | ·31299 | ·29067 |
| 10 | 0·75273 | 0·63096 | 0·54996 | 0·48968 | 0·44232 | 0·40382 | 0·37178 | 0·34462 | 0·32128 |
| 11 | ·77328 | ·65793 | ·57954 | ·52022 | ·47300 | ·43419 | ·40159 | ·37374 | ·34963 |
| 12 | ·79069 | ·68129 | ·60555 | ·54744 | ·50062 | ·46178 | ·42889 | ·40058 | ·37592 |
| 13 | ·80564 | ·70170 | ·62860 | ·57181 | ·52560 | ·48693 | ·45393 | ·42535 | ·40032 |
| 14 | ·81861 | ·71969 | ·64915 | ·59375 | ·54827 | ·50992 | ·47697 | ·44827 | ·42299 |
| 15 | 0·82996 | 0·73564 | 0·66758 | 0·61360 | 0·56893 | 0·53100 | 0·49822 | 0·46951 | 0·44410 |
| 16 | ·83998 | ·74989 | ·68419 | ·63164 | ·58783 | ·55040 | ·51787 | ·48924 | ·46380 |
| 17 | ·84889 | ·76270 | ·69923 | ·64809 | ·60517 | ·56829 | ·53608 | ·50760 | ·48219 |
| 18 | ·85686 | ·77426 | ·71293 | ·66315 | ·62114 | ·58484 | ·55300 | ·52473 | ·49942 |
| 19 | ·86403 | ·78476 | ·72544 | ·67699 | ·63588 | ·60020 | ·56876 | ·54074 | ·51557 |
| 20 | 0·87052 | 0·79433 | 0·73691 | 0·68976 | 0·64954 | 0·61448 | 0·58347 | 0·55574 | 0·53073 |
| 21 | ·87643 | ·80309 | ·74747 | ·70156 | ·66222 | ·62779 | ·59722 | ·56980 | ·54500 |
| 22 | ·88181 | ·81113 | ·75722 | ·71250 | ·67403 | ·64022 | ·61011 | ·58302 | ·55845 |
| 23 | ·88675 | ·81855 | ·76625 | ·72268 | ·68504 | ·65187 | ·62222 | ·59547 | ·57115 |
| 24 | ·89129 | ·82540 | ·77464 | ·73216 | ·69535 | ·66279 | ·63361 | ·60721 | ·58314 |
| 25 | 0·89549 | 0·83176 | 0·78245 | 0·74103 | 0·70500 | 0·67305 | 0·64434 | 0·61829 | 0·59450 |
| 26 | ·89937 | ·83768 | ·78973 | ·74933 | ·71407 | ·68271 | ·65446 | ·62878 | ·60526 |
| 27 | ·90297 | ·84319 | ·79655 | ·75711 | ·72260 | ·69183 | ·66403 | ·63871 | ·61548 |
| 28 | ·90633 | ·84834 | ·80294 | ·76443 | ·73064 | ·70044 | ·67310 | ·64813 | ·62518 |
| 29 | ·90946 | ·85317 | ·80894 | ·77132 | ·73823 | ·70858 | ·68168 | ·65708 | ·63442 |
| 30 | 0·91239 | 0·85770 | 0·81459 | 0·77783 | 0·74541 | 0·71630 | 0·68984 | 0·66559 | 0·64322 |
| 40 | ·93381 | ·89125 | ·85693 | ·82706 | ·80025 | ·77578 | ·75319 | ·73219 | ·71255 |
| 60 | ·95555 | ·92612 | ·90182 | ·88023 | ·86048 | ·84213 | ·82490 | ·80864 | ·79321 |
| 120 | ·97761 | ·96235 | ·94944 | ·93773 | ·92679 | ·91643 | ·90653 | ·89702 | ·88785 |
| ∞ | 1·00000 | 1·00000 | 1·00000 | 1·00000 | 1·00000 | 1·00000 | 1·00000 | 1·00000 | 1·00000 |

This table gives the values of $x$ for which

$$I_x(a, b) = \int_0^x u^{a-1}(1-u)^{b-1}\, du \Big/ \int_0^1 u^{a-1}(1-u)^{b-1}\, du = 0.10,$$

where $a = \tfrac{1}{2}\nu_2,\; b = \tfrac{1}{2}\nu_1.$

Table 16 (*continued*)

## Lower 10% points for $x$

$$\nu_1 = 2b, \quad \nu_2 = 2a$$

| $\nu_2$ \ $\nu_1$ | 10 | 12 | 15 | 20 | 24 | 30 | 40 | 60 | 120 |
|---|---|---|---|---|---|---|---|---|---|
| 1 | 0·0016585 | 0·0013709 | 0·0010878 | 0·0³80919 | 0·0³67157 | 0·0³53506 | 0·0³39965 | 0·0³26535 | 0·0³13213 |
| 2 | ·020852 | ·017407 | ·013950 | ·010481 | ·0087416 | ·0069994 | ·0052542 | ·0035059 | ·0017545 |
| 3 | ·054246 | ·045740 | ·037035 | ·028119 | ·023579 | ·018982 | ·014327 | ·0096132 | ·0048379 |
| 4 | ·092595 | ·078823 | ·064459 | ·049452 | ·041691 | ·033749 | ·025617 | ·017288 | ·0087521 |
| 5 | 0·13167 | 0·11307 | 0·093336 | 0·072324 | 0·061295 | 0·049889 | 0·038083 | 0·025851 | 0·013167 |
| 6 | ·16964 | ·14685 | ·12228 | ·095653 | ·081477 | ·066668 | ·051174 | ·034941 | ·017906 |
| 7 | ·20573 | ·17941 | ·15059 | ·11886 | ·10173 | ·083668 | ·064573 | ·044345 | ·022866 |
| 8 | ·23966 | ·21040 | ·17792 | ·14161 | ·12177 | ·10064 | ·078083 | ·053928 | ·027978 |
| 9 | ·27139 | ·23970 | ·20411 | ·16374 | ·14141 | ·11743 | ·091577 | ·063600 | ·033197 |
| 10 | 0·30097 | 0·26732 | 0·22908 | 0·18513 | 0·16056 | 0·13394 | 0·10497 | 0·073298 | 0·038489 |
| 11 | ·32853 | ·29330 | ·25284 | ·20576 | ·17915 | ·15010 | ·11820 | ·082977 | ·043832 |
| 12 | ·35422 | ·31772 | ·27540 | ·22559 | ·19716 | ·16587 | ·13123 | ·092604 | ·049206 |
| 13 | ·37817 | ·34068 | ·29682 | ·24464 | ·21457 | ·18124 | ·14403 | ·10216 | ·054597 |
| 14 | ·40053 | ·36228 | ·31715 | ·26292 | ·23139 | ·19619 | ·15659 | ·11161 | ·059993 |
| 15 | 0·42143 | 0·38261 | 0·33645 | 0·28045 | 0·24762 | 0·21072 | 0·16889 | 0·12096 | 0·065386 |
| 16 | ·44100 | ·40176 | ·35478 | ·29726 | ·26327 | ·22483 | ·18093 | ·13019 | ·070768 |
| 17 | ·45934 | ·41983 | ·37219 | ·31338 | ·27837 | ·23853 | ·19270 | ·13930 | ·076134 |
| 18 | ·47657 | ·43689 | ·38875 | ·32885 | ·29293 | ·25182 | ·20420 | ·14828 | ·081478 |
| 19 | ·49277 | ·45302 | ·40451 | ·34369 | ·30697 | ·26471 | ·21544 | ·15712 | ·086796 |
| 20 | 0·50803 | 0·46829 | 0·41952 | 0·35793 | 0·32051 | 0·27721 | 0·22642 | 0·16583 | 0·092085 |
| 21 | ·52243 | ·48276 | ·43382 | ·37161 | ·33358 | ·28934 | ·23713 | ·17440 | ·097342 |
| 22 | ·53603 | ·49649 | ·44747 | ·38475 | ·34619 | ·30111 | ·24759 | ·18283 | ·10257 |
| 23 | ·54889 | ·50953 | ·46049 | ·39738 | ·35836 | ·31253 | ·25781 | ·19112 | ·10775 |
| 24 | ·56108 | ·52193 | ·47294 | ·40954 | ··37012 | ·32361 | ·26778 | ·19928 | ·11290 |
| 25 | 0·57264 | 0·53373 | 0·48485 | 0·42123 | 0·38147 | 0·33437 | 0·27751 | 0·20730 | 0·11801 |
| 26 | ·58361 | ·54498 | ·49624 | ·43248 | ·39245 | ·34481 | ·28701 | ·21518 | ·12308 |
| 27 | ·59405 | ·55571 | ·50716 | ·44333 | ·40306 | ·35495 | ·29629 | ·22293 | ·12811 |
| 28 | ·60398 | ·56595 | ·51763 | ·45378 | ·41332 | ·36479 | ·30534 | ·23054 | ·13310 |
| 29 | ·61344 | ·57574 | ·52767 | ·46386 | ·42325 | ·37436 | ·31419 | ·23803 | ·13804 |
| 30 | 0·62247 | 0·58511 | 0·53731 | 0·47359 | 0·43286 | 0·38366 | 0·32283 | 0·24539 | 0·14295 |
| 40 | ·69412 | ·66034 | ·61599 | ·55476 | ·51428 | ·46386 | ·39910 | ·31243 | ·18960 |
| 60 | ·77851 | ·75104 | ·71386 | ·66029 | ·62333 | ·57545 | ·51067 | ·41750 | ·27063 |
| 120 | ·87897 | ·86198 | ·83814 | ·80192 | ·77553 | ·73946 | ·68688 | ·60235 | ·44158 |
| $\infty$ | 1·00000 | 1·00000 | 1·00000 | 1·00000 | 1·00000 | 1·00000 | 1·00000 | 1·00000 | 1·00000 |

For $\nu_1 = \infty$, $x = 0$

Table 16. *Percentage points of the B-distribution (continued)*

## Lower 5 % points for $x$

$$\nu_1 = 2b, \quad \nu_2 = 2a$$

| $\nu_2$ \ $\nu_1$ | 1 | 2 | 3 | 4 | 5 | 6 | 7 | 8 | 9 |
|---|---|---|---|---|---|---|---|---|---|
| 1 | 0·0061558 | 0·0025000 | 0·0015429 | 0·0011119 | 0·0$^3$86820 | 0·0$^3$71179 | 0·0$^3$60300 | 0·0$^3$52300 | 0·0$^3$46170 |
| 2 | ·097500 | ·050000 | ·033617 | ·025321 | ·020308 | ·016952 | ·014548 | ·012741 | ·011334 |
| 3 | ·22852 | ·13572 | ·097308 | ·076010 | ·062413 | ·052962 | ·046007 | ·040671 | ·036447 |
| 4 | ·34163 | ·22361 | ·16825 | ·13535 | ·11338 | ·097611 | ·085727 | ·076440 | ·068979 |
| 5 | 0·43074 | 0·30171 | 0·23553 | 0·19403 | 0·16528 | 0·14409 | 0·12778 | 0·11482 | 0·10427 |
| 6 | ·50053 | ·36840 | ·29599 | ·24860 | ·21477 | ·18926 | ·16927 | ·15316 | ·13989 |
| 7 | ·55593 | ·42489 | ·34929 | ·29811 | ·26063 | ·23182 | ·20890 | ·19019 | ·17461 |
| 8 | ·60071 | ·47287 | ·39607 | ·34259 | ·30260 | ·27134 | ·24613 | ·22532 | ·20783 |
| 9 | ·63751 | ·51390 | ·43716 | ·38245 | ·34080 | ·30777 | ·28082 | ·25835 | ·23930 |
| 10 | 0·66824 | 0·54928 | 0·47338 | 0·41820 | 0·37553 | 0·34126 | 0·31301 | 0·28924 | 0·26894 |
| 11 | ·69425 | ·58003 | ·50546 | ·45033 | ·40712 | ·37203 | ·34283 | ·31807 | ·29677 |
| 12 | ·71654 | ·60696 | ·53402 | ·47930 | ·43590 | ·40031 | ·37044 | ·34494 | ·32286 |
| 13 | ·73583 | ·63073 | ·55958 | ·50551 | ·46219 | ·42635 | ·39604 | ·37000 | ·34732 |
| 14 | ·75268 | ·65184 | ·58256 | ·52932 | ·48626 | ·45036 | ·41980 | ·39338 | ·37025 |
| 15 | 0·76754 | 0·67070 | 0·60333 | 0·55102 | 0·50836 | 0·47255 | 0·44187 | 0·41521 | 0·39176 |
| 16 | ·78072 | ·68766 | ·62217 | ·57086 | ·52872 | ·49310 | ·46242 | ·43563 | ·41196 |
| 17 | ·79249 | ·70297 | ·63933 | ·58907 | ·54750 | ·51217 | ·48159 | ·45474 | ·43094 |
| 18 | ·80307 | ·71687 | ·65503 | ·60584 | ·56490 | ·52991 | ·49949 | ·47267 | ·44880 |
| 19 | ·81263 | ·72954 | ·66944 | ·62131 | ·58103 | ·54645 | ·51624 | ·48951 | ·46564 |
| 20 | 0·82131 | 0·74113 | 0·68271 | 0·63564 | 0·59605 | 0·56189 | 0·53194 | 0·50535 | 0·48152 |
| 21 | ·82923 | ·75178 | ·69496 | ·64894 | ·61004 | ·57635 | ·54669 | ·52027 | ·49652 |
| 22 | ·83647 | ·76160 | ·70632 | ·66132 | ·62312 | ·58990 | ·56056 | ·53434 | ·51071 |
| 23 | ·84313 | ·77067 | ·71687 | ·67287 | ·63536 | ·60263 | ·57363 | ·54764 | ·52415 |
| 24 | ·84927 | ·77908 | ·72669 | ·68366 | ·64684 | ·61461 | ·58596 | ·56022 | ·53689 |
| 25 | 0·85494 | 0·78690 | 0·73586 | 0·69377 | 0·65764 | 0·62590 | 0·59761 | 0·57213 | 0·54898 |
| 26 | ·86021 | ·79418 | ·74444 | ·70327 | ·66780 | ·63656 | ·60864 | ·58343 | ·56048 |
| 27 | ·86511 | ·80099 | ·75249 | ·71219 | ·67738 | ·64663 | ·61909 | ·59416 | ·57141 |
| 28 | ·86967 | ·80736 | ·76004 | ·72060 | ·68643 | ·65617 | ·62900 | ·60436 | ·58183 |
| 29 | ·87394 | ·81334 | ·76715 | ·72854 | ·69499 | ·66522 | ·63842 | ·61407 | ·59177 |
| 30 | 0·87794 | 0·81896 | 0·77386 | 0·73604 | 0·70311 | 0·67381 | 0·64738 | 0·62332 | 0·60125 |
| 40 | ·90734 | ·86089 | ·82447 | ·79327 | ·76559 | ·74053 | ·71758 | ·69636 | ·67663 |
| 60 | ·93748 | ·90497 | ·87881 | ·85591 | ·83517 | ·81606 | ·79824 | ·78150 | ·76569 |
| 120 | ·96837 | ·95130 | ·93720 | ·92458 | ·91290 | ·90192 | ·89148 | ·88150 | ·87191 |
| ∞ | 1·00000 | 1·00000 | 1·00000 | 1·00000 | 1·00000 | 1·00000 | 1·00000 | 1·00000 | 1·00000 |

This table gives the values of $x$ for which

$$I_x(a, b) = \int_0^x u^{a-1}(1-u)^{b-1}\, du \Big/ \int_0^1 u^{a-1}(1-u)^{b-1}\, du = 0.05,$$

where $a = \tfrac{1}{2}\nu_2$, $b = \tfrac{1}{2}\nu_1$.

Table 16 (*continued*)

*Lower 5 % points for x*

$$\nu_1 = 2b, \quad \nu_2 = 2a$$

| $\nu_2$ \ $\nu_1$ | 10 | 12 | 15 | 20 | 24 | 30 | 40 | 60 | 120 |
|---|---|---|---|---|---|---|---|---|---|
| 1 | $0.0^341325$ | $0.0^334154$ | $0.0^327098$ | $0.0^320156$ | $0.0^316727$ | $0.0^313326$ | $0.0^499535$ | $0.0^466082$ | $0.0^432904$ |
| 2 | ·010206 | ·0085124 | ·0068158 | ·0051162 | ·0042653 | ·0034137 | ·0025614 | ·0017083 | $0.0^385452$ |
| 3 | ·033020 | ·027794 | ·022465 | ·017026 | ·014264 | ·011472 | ·0086511 | ·0057991 | ·0029157 |
| 4 | ·062850 | ·053376 | ·043541 | ·033319 | ·028053 | ·022679 | ·017191 | ·011585 | ·0058568 |
| 5 | 0·095510 | 0·081790 | 0·067312 | 0·051995 | 0·043994 | 0·035747 | 0·027240 | 0·018458 | 0·0093841 |
| 6 | ·12876 | ·11111 | ·092207 | ·071870 | ·061103 | ·049898 | ·038224 | ·026043 | ·013317 |
| 7 | ·16142 | ·14029 | ·11733 | ·092238 | ·078783 | ·064651 | ·049781 | ·034103 | ·017540 |
| 8 | ·19290 | ·16875 | ·14216 | ·11267 | ·096658 | ·079695 | ·061676 | ·042481 | ·021976 |
| 9 | ·22292 | ·19618 | ·16638 | ·13288 | ·11449 | ·094827 | ·073748 | ·051068 | ·026572 |
| 10 | 0·25137 | 0·22244 | 0·18984 | 0·15272 | 0·13211 | 0·10991 | 0·085885 | 0·059786 | 0·031288 |
| 11 | ·27823 | ·24746 | ·21244 | ·17207 | ·14943 | ·12484 | ·098008 | ·068575 | ·036094 |
| 12 | ·30354 | ·27125 | ·23413 | ·19086 | ·16636 | ·13955 | ·11006 | ·077394 | ·040967 |
| 13 | ·32737 | ·29383 | ·25492 | ·20908 | ·18288 | ·15401 | ·12199 | ·086209 | ·045889 |
| 14 | ·34981 | ·31524 | ·27481 | ·22669 | ·19895 | ·16818 | ·13377 | ·094994 | ·050847 |
| 15 | 0·37095 | 0·33554 | 0·29382 | 0·24370 | 0·21457 | 0·18203 | 0·14539 | 0·10373 | 0·055827 |
| 16 | ·39086 | ·35480 | ·31199 | ·26011 | ·22972 | ·19556 | ·15682 | ·11240 | ·060821 |
| 17 | ·40965 | ·37307 | ·32936 | ·27594 | ·24441 | ·20877 | ·16805 | ·12099 | ·065820 |
| 18 | ·42738 | ·39041 | ·34596 | ·29120 | ·25865 | ·22164 | ·17908 | ·12950 | ·070818 |
| 19 | ·44414 | ·40689 | ·36183 | ·30591 | ·27244 | ·23418 | ·18989 | ·13791 | ·075809 |
| 20 | 0·45999 | 0·42256 | 0·37701 | 0·32009 | 0·28580 | 0·24639 | 0·20050 | 0·14622 | 0·080789 |
| 21 | ·47501 | ·43746 | ·39154 | ·33375 | ·29874 | ·25828 | ·21088 | ·15442 | ·085753 |
| 22 | ·48925 | ·45165 | ·40544 | ·34693 | ·31126 | ·26985 | ·22106 | ·16252 | ·090698 |
| 23 | ·50276 | ·46518 | ·41877 | ·35964 | ·32340 | ·28112 | ·23102 | ·17051 | ·095622 |
| 24 | ·51560 | ·47808 | ·43154 | ·37190 | ·33515 | ·29208 | ·24077 | ·17838 | ·10052 |
| 25 | 0·52782 | 0·49040 | 0·44379 | 0·38373 | 0·34653 | 0·30275 | 0·25032 | 0·18615 | 0·10539 |
| 26 | ·53945 | ·50217 | ·45554 | ·39516 | ·35756 | ·31314 | ·25966 | ·19379 | ·11024 |
| 27 | ·55054 | ·51343 | ·46683 | ·40619 | ·36826 | ·32325 | ·26880 | ·20133 | ·11505 |
| 28 | ·56112 | ·52420 | ·47768 | ·41685 | ·37862 | ·33309 | ·27775 | ·20875 | ·11983 |
| 29 | ·57122 | ·53452 | ·48812 | ·42715 | ·38867 | ·34267 | ·28650 | ·21606 | ·12458 |
| 30 | 0·58088 | 0·54442 | 0·49816 | 0·43711 | 0·39842 | 0·35200 | 0·29507 | 0·22326 | 0·12930 |
| 40 | ·65819 | ·62459 | ·58083 | ·52099 | ·48175 | ·43321 | ·37136 | ·28936 | ·17453 |
| 60 | ·75070 | ·72282 | ·68535 | ·63185 | ·59522 | ·54807 | ·48477 | ·39458 | ·25416 |
| 120 | ·86266 | ·84504 | ·82047 | ·78342 | ·75661 | ·72016 | ·66738 | ·58326 | ·42519 |
| ∞ | 1·00000 | 1·00000 | 1·00000 | 1·00000 | 1·00000 | 1·00000 | 1·00000 | 1·00000 | 1·00000 |

For $\nu_1 = \infty$, $x = 0$

157

Table 16. *Percentage points of the B-distribution (continued)*

Lower 2·5 % points for x

$$\nu_1 = 2b, \quad \nu_2 = 2a$$

| $\nu_2$ \ $\nu_1$ | 1 | 2 | 3 | 4 | 5 | 6 | 7 | 8 | 9 |
|---|---|---|---|---|---|---|---|---|---|
| 1 | 0·0015413 | 0·0²62500 | 0·0³38558 | 0·0³27783 | 0·0³21691 | 0·0³17782 | 0·0³15064 | 0·0³13065 | 0·0³11533 |
| 2 | ·049375 | ·025000 | ·016737 | ·012579 | ·010076 | ·0084038 | ·0072076 | ·0063095 | ·0056104 |
| 3 | ·14675 | ·085499 | ·060830 | ·047316 | ·038748 | ·032820 | ·028471 | ·025143 | ·022513 |
| 4 | ·24664 | ·15811 | ·11786 | ·094299 | ·078706 | ·067586 | ·059243 | ·052745 | ·047539 |
| 5 | 0·33318 | 0·22865 | 0·17674 | 0·14471 | 0·12275 | 0·10669 | 0·094390 | 0·084663 | 0·076770 |
| 6 | ·40505 | ·29240 | ·23259 | ·19412 | ·16696 | ·14663 | ·13081 | ·11812 | ·10770 |
| 7 | ·46442 | ·34855 | ·28375 | ·24063 | ·20942 | ·18562 | ·16681 | ·15153 | ·13886 |
| 8 | ·51378 | ·39764 | ·32993 | ·28358 | ·24933 | ·22278 | ·20151 | ·18405 | ·16944 |
| 9 | ·55524 | ·44054 | ·37137 | ·32290 | ·28642 | ·25774 | ·23450 | ·21523 | ·19897 |
| 10 | 0·59043 | 0·47818 | 0·40855 | 0·35877 | 0·32071 | 0·29042 | 0·26561 | 0·24486 | 0·22722 |
| 11 | ·62062 | ·51135 | ·44194 | ·39146 | ·35234 | ·32085 | ·29482 | ·27288 | ·25409 |
| 12 | ·64677 | ·54074 | ·47202 | ·42128 | ·38149 | ·34914 | ·32219 | ·29930 | ·27957 |
| 13 | ·66961 | ·56693 | ·49920 | ·44853 | ·40838 | ·37545 | ·34779 | ·32416 | ·30368 |
| 14 | ·68973 | ·59038 | ·52385 | ·47349 | ·43321 | ·39991 | ·37175 | ·34755 | ·32646 |
| 15 | 0·70756 | 0·61149 | 0·54628 | 0·49641 | 0·45618 | 0·42268 | 0·39418 | 0·36955 | 0·34799 |
| 16 | ·72349 | ·63058 | ·56676 | ·51750 | ·47746 | ·44390 | ·41520 | ·39026 | ·36833 |
| 17 | ·73778 | ·64792 | ·58553 | ·53697 | ·49723 | ·46372 | ·43490 | ·40976 | ·38756 |
| 18 | ·75069 | ·66373 | ·60278 | ·55498 | ·51561 | ·48224 | ·45341 | ·42814 | ·40575 |
| 19 | ·76239 | ·67821 | ·61869 | ·57169 | ·53276 | ·49959 | ·47081 | ·44549 | ·42297 |
| 20 | 0·77305 | 0·69150 | 0·63339 | 0·58722 | 0·54877 | 0·51586 | 0·48719 | 0·46187 | 0·43928 |
| 21 | ·78280 | ·70376 | ·64702 | ·60169 | ·56375 | ·53115 | ·50263 | ·47736 | ·45475 |
| 22 | ·79176 | ·71509 | ·65970 | ·61520 | ·57780 | ·54553 | ·51720 | ·49202 | ·46943 |
| 23 | ·80001 | ·72559 | ·67150 | ·62785 | ·59099 | ·55908 | ·53098 | ·50592 | ·48338 |
| 24 | ·80763 | ·73535 | ·68253 | ·63970 | ·60341 | ·57187 | ·54401 | ·51911 | ·49664 |
| 25 | 0·81469 | 0·74445 | 0·69285 | 0·65084 | 0·61511 | 0·58396 | 0·55636 | 0·53163 | 0·50927 |
| 26 | ·82126 | ·75295 | ·70253 | ·66132 | ·62615 | ·59540 | ·56808 | ·54354 | ·52130 |
| 27 | ·82738 | ·76090 | ·71162 | ·67119 | ·63658 | ·60624 | ·57921 | ·55488 | ·53278 |
| 28 | ·83310 | ·76836 | ·72018 | ·68052 | ·64646 | ·61652 | ·58980 | ·56568 | ·54373 |
| 29 | ·83845 | ·77538 | ·72825 | ·68933 | ·65582 | ·62630 | ·59988 | ·57599 | ·55420 |
| 30 | 0·84347 | 0·78198 | 0·73587 | 0·69768 | 0·66471 | 0·63559 | 0·60948 | 0·58582 | 0·56421 |
| 40 | ·88059 | ·83157 | ·79381 | ·76184 | ·73369 | ·70839 | ·68533 | ·66411 | ·64446 |
| 60 | ·91904 | ·88430 | ·85681 | ·83298 | ·81156 | ·79193 | ·77372 | ·75668 | ·74065 |
| 120 | ·95883 | ·94037 | ·92535 | ·91201 | ·89975 | ·88828 | ·87743 | ·86708 | ·85717 |
| ∞ | 1·00000 | 1·00000 | 1·00000 | 1·00000 | 1·00000 | 1·00000 | 1·00000 | 1·00000 | 1·00000 |

This table gives the values of $x$ for which

$$I_x(a,\ b) = \int_0^x u^{a-1}(1-u)^{b-1}\,du \bigg/ \int_0^1 u^{a-1}(1-u)^{b-1}\,du = 0.025,$$

where $a = \tfrac{1}{2}\nu_2,\ b = \tfrac{1}{2}\nu_1$.

Table 16 (*continued*)

## Lower 2·5 % points for x

$$\nu_1 = 2b, \quad \nu_2 = 2a$$

| $\nu_2$ \ $\nu_1$ | 10 | 12 | 15 | 20 | 24 | 30 | 40 | 60 | 120 |
|---|---|---|---|---|---|---|---|---|---|
| 1 | 0·0³10323 | 0·0⁴85313 | 0·0⁴67686 | 0·0⁴50345 | 0·0⁴41780 | 0·0⁴33285 | 0·0⁴24860 | 0·0⁴16505 | 0·0⁵82180 |
| 2 | ·0050508 | ·0042107 | ·0033700 | ·0025286 | ·0021076 | ·0016864 | ·0012651 | ·0³84357 | ·0³42187 |
| 3 | ·020382 | ·017139 | ·013838 | ·010477 | ·0087725 | ·0070519 | ·0053148 | ·0035607 | ·0017893 |
| 4 | ·043272 | ·036693 | ·029885 | ·022831 | ·019207 | ·015514 | ·011749 | ·0079110 | ·0039956 |
| 5 | 0·070233 | 0·060028 | 0·049302 | 0·038002 | 0·032119 | 0·026068 | 0·019841 | 0·013428 | 0·0068184 |
| 6 | ·098988 | ·085233 | ·070563 | ·054861 | ·046579 | ·037985 | ·029056 | ·019767 | ·010092 |
| 7 | ·12818 | ·11113 | ·092695 | ·072663 | ·061969 | ·050772 | ·039029 | ·026691 | ·013702 |
| 8 | ·15701 | ·13700 | ·11508 | ·090920 | ·077872 | ·064092 | ·049508 | ·034033 | ·017569 |
| 9 | ·18504 | ·16240 | ·13732 | ·10931 | ·094004 | ·077712 | ·060314 | ·041675 | ·021634 |
| 10 | 0·21201 | 0·18709 | 0·15917 | 0·12760 | 0·11017 | 0·091466 | 0·071319 | 0·049528 | 0·025854 |
| 11 | ·23780 | ·21091 | ·18048 | ·14565 | ·12623 | ·10523 | ·082426 | ·057528 | ·030196 |
| 12 | ·26238 | ·23379 | ·20115 | ·16336 | ·14210 | ·11893 | ·093564 | ·065622 | ·034634 |
| 13 | ·28574 | ·25571 | ·22112 | ·18067 | ·15770 | ·13249 | ·10468 | ·073771 | ·039147 |
| 14 | ·30790 | ·27667 | ·24039 | ·19753 | ·17299 | ·14588 | ·11573 | ·081944 | ·043718 |
| 15 | 0·32893 | 0·29668 | 0·25893 | 0·21392 | 0·18793 | 0·15905 | 0·12669 | 0·090115 | 0·048335 |
| 16 | ·34888 | ·31578 | ·27676 | ·22983 | ·20252 | ·17198 | ·13753 | ·098266 | ·052985 |
| 17 | ·36779 | ·33400 | ·29389 | ·24525 | ·21674 | ·18466 | ·14823 | ·10638 | ·057659 |
| 18 | ·38574 | ·35138 | ·31034 | ·26019 | ·23058 | ·19708 | ·15878 | ·11444 | ·062348 |
| 19 | ·40278 | ·36797 | ·32614 | ·27465 | ·24404 | ·20922 | ·16916 | ·12244 | ·067047 |
| 20 | 0·41896 | 0·38380 | 0·34132 | 0·28864 | 0·25713 | 0·22110 | 0·17938 | 0·13038 | 0·071749 |
| 21 | ·43435 | ·39893 | ·35589 | ·30218 | ·26985 | ·23270 | ·18943 | ·13823 | ·076449 |
| 22 | ·44900 | ·41338 | ·36990 | ·31528 | ·28221 | ·24402 | ·19930 | ·14601 | ·081144 |
| 23 | ·46294 | ·42720 | ·38335 | ·32795 | ·29422 | ·25508 | ·20899 | ·15370 | ·085828 |
| 24 | ·47623 | ·44042 | ·39629 | ·34021 | ·30588 | ·26587 | ·21850 | ·16130 | ·090500 |
| 25 | 0·48891 | 0·45307 | 0·40874 | 0·35207 | 0·31721 | 0·27640 | 0·22783 | 0·16881 | 0·095156 |
| 26 | ·50101 | ·46520 | ·42071 | ·36355 | ·32821 | ·28667 | ·23698 | ·17622 | ·099794 |
| 27 | ·51257 | ·47682 | ·43223 | ·37466 | ·33890 | ·29669 | ·24596 | ·18354 | ·10441 |
| 28 | ·52363 | ·48797 | ·44333 | ·38542 | ·34928 | ·30647 | ·25476 | ·19076 | ·10901 |
| 29 | ·53421 | ·49867 | ·45403 | ·39584 | ·35937 | ·31601 | ·26339 | ·19789 | ·11358 |
| 30 | 0·54435 | 0·50895 | 0·46434 | 0·40594 | 0·36918 | 0·32531 | 0·27185 | 0·20492 | 0·11812 |
| 40 | ·62616 | ·59296 | ·54999 | ·49168 | ·45370 | ·40697 | ·34780 | ·26997 | ·16201 |
| 60 | ·72550 | ·69743 | ·65992 | ·60674 | ·57056 | ·52422 | ·46239 | ·37498 | ·24027 |
| 120 | ·84764 | ·82954 | ·80442 | ·76678 | ·73968 | ·70299 | ·65017 | ·56658 | ·41107 |
| ∞ | 1·00000 | 1·00000 | 1·00000 | 1·00000 | 1·00000 | 1·00000 | 1·00000 | 1·00000 | 1·00000 |

For $\nu_1 = \infty$, $x = 0$

Table 16. *Percentage points of the B-distribution* (*continued*)

### Lower 1 % points for $x$

$$\nu_1 = 2b, \quad \nu_2 = 2a$$

| $\nu_2$ \ $\nu_1$ | 1 | 2 | 3 | 4 | 5 | 6 | 7 | 8 | 9 |
|---|---|---|---|---|---|---|---|---|---|
| 1 | $0 \cdot 0^3 24672$ | $0 \cdot 0^3 10000$ | $0 \cdot 0^4 61686$ | $0 \cdot 0^4 44446$ | $0 \cdot 0^4 34699$ | $0 \cdot 0^4 28446$ | $0 \cdot 0^4 24097$ | $0 \cdot 0^4 20899$ | $0 \cdot 0^4 18449$ |
| 2 | ·019900 | ·010000 | ·0066778 | ·0050126 | ·0040121 | ·0033445 | ·0028674 | ·0025094 | ·0022309 |
| 3 | ·080827 | ·046416 | ·032834 | ·025458 | ·020807 | ·017599 | ·015252 | ·013458 | ·012043 |
| 4 | ·15874 | ·10000 | ·073960 | ·058903 | ·049014 | ·041999 | ·036754 | ·032682 | ·029426 |
| 5 | 0·23520 | 0·15849 | 0·12142 | 0·098877 | 0·083563 | 0·072429 | 0·063948 | 0·057264 | 0·051857 |
| 6 | ·30387 | ·21544 | ·16979 | ·14087 | ·12065 | ·10564 | ·094014 | ·084730 | ·077136 |
| 7 | ·36370 | ·26827 | ·21636 | ·18236 | ·15801 | ·13959 | ·12511 | ·11341 | ·10375 |
| 8 | ·41540 | ·31623 | ·25997 | ·22207 | ·19437 | ·17307 | ·15612 | ·14227 | ·13073 |
| 9 | ·46009 | ·35938 | ·30024 | ·25945 | ·22910 | ·20543 | ·18637 | ·17066 | ·15745 |
| 10 | 0·49890 | 0·39811 | 0·33719 | 0·29431 | 0·26191 | 0·23632 | 0·21551 | 0·19820 | 0·18355 |
| 11 | ·53279 | ·43288 | ·37099 | ·32667 | ·29271 | ·26560 | ·24335 | ·22469 | ·20879 |
| 12 | ·56258 | ·46416 | ·40191 | ·35664 | ·32153 | ·29323 | ·26981 | ·25003 | ·23307 |
| 13 | ·58893 | ·49239 | ·43021 | ·38437 | ·34845 | ·31924 | ·29487 | ·27417 | ·25631 |
| 14 | ·61238 | ·51795 | ·45615 | ·41006 | ·37358 | ·34369 | ·31858 | ·29712 | ·27851 |
| 15 | 0·63336 | 0·54117 | 0·47999 | 0·43387 | 0·39706 | 0·36666 | 0·34098 | 0·31891 | 0·29968 |
| 16 | ·65224 | ·56234 | ·50193 | ·45597 | ·41899 | ·38826 | ·36214 | ·33958 | ·31985 |
| 17 | ·66930 | ·58171 | ·52219 | ·47651 | ·43951 | ·40857 | ·38213 | ·35920 | ·33905 |
| 18 | ·68479 | ·59948 | ·54094 | ·49565 | ·45872 | ·42768 | ·40103 | ·37781 | ·35733 |
| 19 | ·69892 | ·61585 | ·55832 | ·51350 | ·47674 | ·44568 | ·41890 | ·39547 | ·37473 |
| 20 | 0·71185 | 0·63096 | 0·57447 | 0·53018 | 0·49366 | 0·46266 | 0·43581 | 0·41224 | 0·39131 |
| 21 | ·72372 | ·64495 | ·58952 | ·54581 | ·50958 | ·47868 | ·45184 | ·42818 | ·40711 |
| 22 | ·73467 | ·65793 | ·60357 | ·56046 | ·52456 | ·49383 | ·46703 | ·44333 | ·42217 |
| 23 | ·74479 | ·67002 | ·61671 | ·57422 | ·53869 | ·50816 | ·48144 | ·45775 | ·43653 |
| 24 | ·75417 | ·68129 | ·62903 | ·58717 | ·55204 | ·52174 | ·49514 | ·47149 | ·45025 |
| 25 | 0·76290 | 0·69183 | 0·64059 | 0·59938 | 0·56466 | 0·53461 | 0·50816 | 0·48458 | 0·46335 |
| 26 | ·77103 | ·70170 | ·65147 | ·61090 | ·57660 | ·54683 | ·52055 | ·49706 | ·47587 |
| 27 | ·77862 | ·71097 | ·66172 | ·62180 | ·58793 | ·55845 | ·53236 | ·50899 | ·48785 |
| 28 | ·78573 | ·71969 | ·67139 | ·63211 | ·59868 | ·56951 | ·54362 | ·52038 | ·49932 |
| 29 | ·79240 | ·72790 | ·68054 | ·64188 | ·60890 | ·58004 | ·55437 | ·53127 | ·51031 |
| 30 | 0·79867 | 0·73564 | 0·68919 | 0·65116 | 0·61862 | 0·59008 | 0·56464 | 0·54170 | 0·52085 |
| 40 | ·84541 | ·79433 | ·75561 | ·72316 | ·69482 | ·66950 | ·64656 | ·62555 | ·60617 |
| 60 | ·89449 | ·85770 | ·82898 | ·80433 | ·78233 | ·76227 | ·74376 | ·72651 | ·71034 |
| 120 | ·94599 | ·92612 | ·91014 | ·89607 | ·88321 | ·87124 | ·85995 | ·84924 | ·83900 |
| $\infty$ | 1·00000 | 1·00000 | 1·00000 | 1·00000 | 1·00000 | 1·00000 | 1·00000 | 1·00000 | 1·00000 |

This table gives the values of $x$ for which

$$I_x(a, b) = \int_0^x u^{a-1}(1-u)^{b-1}\, du \Big/ \int_0^1 u^{a-1}(1-u)^{b-1}\, du = 0.01,$$

where $a = \frac{1}{2}\nu_2$, $b = \frac{1}{2}\nu_1$.

Table 16 (continued)

## Lower 1 % points for x

$$\nu_1 = 2b, \quad \nu_2 = 2a$$

| $\nu_2$ \ $\nu_1$ | 10 | 12 | 15 | 20 | 24 | 30 | 40 | 60 | 120 |
|---|---|---|---|---|---|---|---|---|---|
| 1 | $0\cdot0^4 16513$ | $0\cdot0^4 13647$ | $0\cdot0^4 10827$ | $0\cdot0^5 80531$ | $0\cdot0^5 66831$ | $0\cdot0^5 53242$ | $0\cdot0^5 39766$ | $0\cdot0^5 26400$ | $0\cdot0^5 13145$ |
| 2 | ·0020080 | ·0016737 | ·0013391 | ·0010045 | $·0^3 83718$ | $·0^3 66980$ | $·0^3 50239$ | $·0^3 33496$ | $·0^3 16749$ |
| 3 | ·010898 | ·0091569 | ·0073877 | ·0055887 | ·0046777 | ·0037588 | ·0028317 | ·0018964 | $·0^3 95252$ |
| 4 | ·026763 | ·022665 | ·018435 | ·014065 | ·011824 | ·0095436 | ·0072226 | ·0048595 | ·0024525 |
| 5 | 0·047389 | 0·040434 | 0·033149 | 0·025503 | 0·021534 | 0·017459 | 0·013275 | 0·0089747 | 0·0045520 |
| 6 | ·070804 | ·060840 | ·050258 | ·038982 | ·033057 | ·026923 | ·020567 | ·013973 | ·0071235 |
| 7 | ·095628 | ·082714 | ·068820 | ·053801 | ·045816 | ·037481 | ·028767 | ·019640 | ·010065 |
| 8 | ·12095 | ·10526 | ·088177 | ·069455 | ·059390 | ·048797 | ·037625 | ·025815 | ·013300 |
| 9 | ·14619 | ·12796 | ·10787 | ·085584 | ·073472 | ·060623 | ·046957 | ·032376 | ·016768 |
| 10 | 0·17097 | 0·15044 | 0·12760 | 0·10193 | 0·087838 | 0·072776 | 0·056621 | 0·039229 | 0·020426 |
| 11 | ·19506 | ·17250 | ·14713 | ·11830 | ·10232 | ·085117 | ·066512 | ·046303 | ·024237 |
| 12 | ·21834 | ·19398 | ·16633 | ·13458 | ·11681 | ·097542 | ·076547 | ·053541 | ·028173 |
| 13 | ·24073 | ·21479 | ·18510 | ·15065 | ·13120 | ·10997 | ·086660 | ·060896 | ·032212 |
| 14 | ·26220 | ·23489 | ·20338 | ·16646 | ·14544 | ·12235 | ·096802 | ·068334 | ·036335 |
| 15 | 0·28276 | 0·25426 | 0·22113 | 0·18196 | 0·15948 | 0·13462 | 0·10693 | 0·075823 | 0·040526 |
| 16 | ·30240 | ·27289 | ·23833 | ·19711 | ·17327 | ·14676 | ·11702 | ·083341 | ·044772 |
| 17 | ·32117 | ·29079 | ·25497 | ·21189 | ·18680 | ·15873 | ·12704 | ·090866 | ·049062 |
| 18 | ·33910 | ·30797 | ·27105 | ·22630 | ·20005 | ·17053 | ·13697 | ·098383 | ·053386 |
| 19 | ·35622 | ·32446 | ·28658 | ·24032 | ·21301 | ·18212 | ·14680 | ·10588 | ·057738 |
| 20 | 0·37257 | 0·34029 | 0·30157 | 0·25395 | 0·22567 | 0·19351 | 0·15651 | 0·11334 | 0·062109 |
| 21 | ·38818 | ·35548 | ·31603 | ·26721 | ·23803 | ·20468 | ·16609 | ·12076 | ·066494 |
| 22 | ·40311 | ·37005 | ·32999 | ·28008 | ·25008 | ·21563 | ·17554 | ·12812 | ·070888 |
| 23 | ·41738 | ·38405 | ·34345 | ·29258 | ·26184 | ·22637 | ·18486 | ·13543 | ·075285 |
| 24 | ·43103 | ·39749 | ·35645 | ·30472 | ·27329 | ·23687 | ·19403 | ·14268 | ·079683 |
| 25 | 0·44410 | 0·41040 | 0·36899 | 0·31651 | 0·28446 | 0·24716 | 0·20305 | 0·14986 | 0·084077 |
| 26 | ·45661 | ·42280 | ·38109 | ·32795 | ·29534 | ·25723 | ·21193 | ·15697 | ·088464 |
| 27 | ·46861 | ·43473 | ·39278 | ·33906 | ·30594 | ·26707 | ·22066 | ·16401 | ·092842 |
| 28 | ·48011 | ·44621 | ·40407 | ·34985 | ·31626 | ·27670 | ·22925 | ·17096 | ·097209 |
| 29 | ·49115 | ·45726 | ·41498 | ·36032 | ·32632 | ·28612 | ·23768 | ·17785 | ·10156 |
| 30 | 0·50175 | 0·46789 | 0·42552 | 0·37049 | 0·33612 | 0·29534 | 0·24597 | 0·18465 | 0·10590 |
| 40 | ·58819 | ·55573 | ·51398 | ·45778 | ·42144 | ·37700 | ·32111 | ·24819 | ·14811 |
| 60 | ·69511 | ·66701 | ·62969 | ·57717 | ·54167 | ·49647 | ·43655 | ·35258 | ·22459 |
| 120 | ·82918 | ·81062 | ·78497 | ·74677 | ·71942 | ·68259 | ·62988 | ·54709 | ·39479 |
| ∞ | 1·00000 | 1·00000 | 1·00000 | 1·00000 | 1·00000 | 1·00000 | 1·00000 | 1·00000 | 1·00000 |

For $\nu_1 = \infty$, $x = 0$

Table 16. *Percentage points of the B-distribution (continued)*

## Lower 0·5 % points for x

$$\nu_1 = 2b, \quad \nu_2 = 2a$$

| $\nu_2$ \ $\nu_1$ | 1 | 2 | 3 | 4 | 5 | 6 | 7 | 8 | 9 |
|---|---|---|---|---|---|---|---|---|---|
| 1 | $0\cdot0^461684$ | $0\cdot0^425000$ | $0\cdot0^415421$ | $0\cdot0^411111$ | $0\cdot0^586745$ | $0\cdot0^571112$ | $0\cdot0^560240$ | $0\cdot0^552245$ | $0\cdot0^546121$ |
| 2 | ·0099750 | ·0050000 | ·0033361 | ·0025031 | ·0020030 | ·0016695 | ·0014311 | ·0012524 | ·0011133 |
| 3 | ·051237 | ·029240 | ·020632 | ·015976 | ·013046 | ·011028 | ·0095530 | ·0084269 | ·0075388 |
| 4 | ·11321 | ·070711 | ·052099 | ·041400 | ·034399 | ·029445 | ·025748 | ·022881 | ·020592 |
| 5 | 0·17995 | 0·12011 | 0·091593 | 0·074378 | 0·062737 | 0·054301 | 0·047891 | 0·042849 | 0·038776 |
| 6 | ·24356 | ·17100 | ·13408 | ·11088 | ·094759 | ·082829 | ·073618 | ·066279 | ·060287 |
| 7 | ·30126 | ·22007 | ·17656 | ·14830 | ·12818 | ·11303 | ·10116 | ·091593 | ·083708 |
| 8 | ·35261 | ·26591 | ·21745 | ·18510 | ·16159 | ·14360 | ·12933 | ·11770 | ·10804 |
| 9 | ·39799 | ·30808 | ·25604 | ·22046 | ·19415 | ·17373 | ·15736 | ·14389 | ·13261 |
| 10 | 0·43809 | 0·34657 | 0·29204 | 0·25399 | 0·22542 | 0·20297 | 0·18478 | 0·16970 | 0·15697 |
| 11 | ·47360 | ·38162 | ·32543 | ·28554 | ·25517 | ·23105 | ·21132 | ·19484 | ·18083 |
| 12 | ·50517 | ·41352 | ·35632 | ·31509 | ·28332 | ·25783 | ·23682 | ·21914 | ·20401 |
| 13 | ·53337 | ·44258 | ·38487 | ·34270 | ·30986 | ·28328 | ·26120 | ·24250 | ·22642 |
| 14 | ·55865 | ·46912 | ·41127 | ·36848 | ·33484 | ·30739 | ·28444 | ·26489 | ·24798 |
| 15 | 0·58144 | 0·49340 | 0·43569 | 0·39255 | 0·35833 | 0·33022 | 0·30656 | 0·28629 | 0·26869 |
| 16 | ·60206 | ·51567 | ·45832 | ·41503 | ·38042 | ·35180 | ·32757 | ·30672 | ·28852 |
| 17 | ·62080 | ·53616 | ·47932 | ·43605 | ·40120 | ·37221 | ·34754 | ·32620 | ·30752 |
| 18 | ·63789 | ·55505 | ·49885 | ·45571 | ·42076 | ·39151 | ·36650 | ·34478 | ·32568 |
| 19 | ·65354 | ·57251 | ·51703 | ·47414 | ·43917 | ·40976 | ·38451 | ·36248 | ·34305 |
| 20 | 0·66791 | 0·58870 | 0·53400 | 0·49144 | 0·45654 | 0·42705 | 0·40162 | 0·37936 | 0·35966 |
| 21 | ·68117 | ·60375 | ·54987 | ·50768 | ·47293 | ·44343 | ·41789 | ·39546 | ·37554 |
| 22 | ·69341 | ·61775 | ·56472 | ·52297 | ·48841 | ·45896 | ·43337 | ·41082 | ·39073 |
| 23 | ·70477 | ·63083 | ·57866 | ·53738 | ·50306 | ·47369 | ·44810 | ·42547 | ·40527 |
| 24 | ·71532 | ·64305 | ·59176 | ·55098 | ·51693 | ·48769 | ·46213 | ·43947 | ·41918 |
| 25 | 0·72516 | 0·65451 | 0·60409 | 0·56382 | 0·53007 | 0·50100 | 0·47551 | 0·45285 | 0·43251 |
| 26 | ·73434 | ·66527 | ·61572 | ·57597 | ·54255 | ·51367 | ·48827 | ·46564 | ·44528 |
| 27 | ·74294 | ·67539 | ·62669 | ·58749 | ·55440 | ·52574 | ·50045 | ·47788 | ·45752 |
| 28 | ·75100 | ·68492 | ·63707 | ·59841 | ·56568 | ·53724 | ·51210 | ·48960 | ·46927 |
| 29 | ·75857 | ·69392 | ·64690 | ·60878 | ·57642 | ·54822 | ·52324 | ·50083 | ·48054 |
| 30 | 0·76570 | 0·70242 | 0·65622 | 0·61864 | 0·58665 | 0·55871 | 0·53389 | 0·51159 | 0·49137 |
| 40 | ·81920 | ·76727 | ·72823 | ·69571 | ·66744 | ·64229 | ·61956 | ·59882 | ·57973 |
| 60 | ·87598 | ·83811 | ·80877 | ·78370 | ·76142 | ·74119 | ·72256 | ·70526 | ·68907 |
| 120 | ·93619 | ·91548 | ·89893 | ·88442 | ·87120 | ·85892 | ·84739 | ·83645 | ·82602 |
| ∞ | 1·00000 | 1·00000 | 1·00000 | 1·00000 | 1·00000 | 1·00000 | 1·00000 | 1·00000 | 1·00000 |

This table gives the values of $x$ for which

$$I_x(a, b) = \int_0^x u^{a-1}(1-u)^{b-1}\, du \Big/ \int_0^1 u^{a-1}(1-u)^{b-1}\, du = 0 \cdot 005,$$

where $a = \tfrac{1}{2}\nu_2$, $b = \tfrac{1}{2}\nu_1$.

## Table 16 (*continued*)

### Lower 0·5 % points for x

$$\nu_1 = 2b, \quad \nu_2 = 2a$$

| $\nu_2$ \ $\nu_1$ | 10 | 12 | 15 | 20 | 24 | 30 | 40 | 60 | 120 |
|---|---|---|---|---|---|---|---|---|---|
| 1 | 0·0⁵41280 | 0·0⁵34116 | 0·0⁵27067 | 0·0⁵20132 | 0·0⁵16707 | 0·0⁵13310 | 0·0⁶99411 | 0·0⁶65998 | 0·0⁶32862 |
| 2 | ·0010020 | ·0³83507 | ·0³66812 | ·0³50113 | ·0³41762 | ·0³33411 | ·0³25060 | ·0³16707 | ·0⁴83539 |
| 3 | ·0068204 | ·0057290 | ·0046206 | ·0034943 | ·0029242 | ·0023493 | ·0017696 | ·0011848 | ·0³59503 |
| 4 | ·018721 | ·015844 | ·012879 | ·0098197 | ·0082522 | ·0066584 | ·0050373 | ·0033880 | ·0017093 |
| 5 | 0·035415 | 0·030191 | 0·024729 | 0·019006 | 0·016040 | 0·012998 | 0·0098777 | 0·0066743 | 0·0033833 |
| 6 | ·055299 | ·047464 | ·039162 | ·030337 | ·025709 | ·020924 | ·015973 | ·010844 | ·0055240 |
| 7 | ·077090 | ·066592 | ·055329 | ·043189 | ·036749 | ·030038 | ·023034 | ·015712 | ·0080441 |
| 8 | ·099867 | ·086788 | ·072586 | ·057076 | ·048759 | ·040023 | ·030828 | ·021129 | ·010873 |
| 9 | ·12300 | ·10749 | ·090464 | ·071635 | ·061433 | ·050635 | ·039174 | ·026976 | ·013953 |
| 10 | 0·14606 | 0·12831 | 0·10862 | 0·086595 | 0·074540 | 0·061684 | 0·047930 | 0·033162 | 0·017241 |
| 11 | ·16876 | ·14898 | ·12683 | ·10175 | ·087903 | ·073027 | ·056985 | ·039611 | ·020700 |
| 12 | ·19092 | ·16931 | ·14489 | ·11696 | ·10139 | ·084550 | ·066252 | ·046265 | ·024302 |
| 13 | ·21242 | ·18919 | ·16270 | ·13211 | ·11490 | ·096167 | ·075662 | ·053076 | ·028022 |
| 14 | ·23320 | ·20853 | ·18017 | ·14710 | ·12835 | ·10781 | ·085158 | ·060005 | ·031841 |
| 15 | 0·25323 | 0·22728 | 0·19725 | 0·16190 | 0·14170 | 0·11942 | 0·094697 | 0·067019 | 0·035743 |
| 16 | ·27248 | ·24543 | ·21388 | ·17644 | ·15488 | ·13097 | ·10424 | ·074093 | ·039714 |
| 17 | ·29098 | ·26295 | ·23006 | ·19070 | ·16787 | ·14241 | ·11377 | ·081204 | ·043741 |
| 18 | ·30872 | ·27986 | ·24576 | ·20465 | ·18065 | ·15373 | ·12324 | ·088333 | ·047815 |
| 19 | ·32574 | ·29615 | ·26099 | ·21829 | ·19319 | ·16489 | ·13265 | ·095466 | ·051927 |
| 20 | 0·34206 | 0·31184 | 0·27575 | 0·23160 | 0·20549 | 0·17590 | 0·14198 | 0·10259 | 0·056070 |
| 21 | ·35770 | ·32696 | ·29004 | ·24458 | ·21753 | ·18673 | ·15122 | ·10969 | ·060237 |
| 22 | ·37269 | ·34151 | ·30387 | ·25723 | ·22932 | ·19738 | ·16036 | ·11676 | ·064421 |
| 23 | ·38707 | ·35552 | ·31725 | ·26954 | ·24084 | ·20784 | ·16938 | ·12380 | ·068619 |
| 24 | ·40087 | ·36901 | ·33020 | ·28153 | ·25210 | ·21811 | ·17829 | ·13078 | ·072825 |
| 25 | 0·41411 | 0·38200 | 0·34272 | 0·29320 | 0·26309 | 0·22818 | 0·18707 | 0·13772 | 0·077035 |
| 26 | ·42682 | ·39452 | ·35484 | ·30456 | ·27383 | ·23806 | ·19573 | ·14461 | ·081247 |
| 27 | ·43903 | ·40658 | ·36657 | ·31560 | ·28432 | ·24775 | ·20426 | ·15143 | ·085457 |
| 28 | ·45076 | ·41821 | ·37792 | ·32635 | ·29455 | ·25724 | ·21266 | ·15819 | ·089662 |
| 29 | ·46204 | ·42942 | ·38891 | ·33681 | ·30454 | ·26654 | ·22093 | ·16489 | ·093860 |
| 30 | 0·47289 | 0·44024 | 0·39954 | 0·34698 | 0·31429 | 0·27565 | 0·22907 | 0·17152 | 0·098048 |
| 40 | ·56205 | ·53024 | ·48950 | ·43493 | ·39980 | ·35700 | ·30341 | ·23388 | ·13907 |
| 60 | ·67384 | ·64584 | ·60879 | ·55688 | ·52194 | ·47762 | ·41913 | ·33759 | ·21421 |
| 120 | ·81604 | ·79720 | ·77125 | ·73277 | ·70531 | ·66845 | ·61590 | ·53378 | ·38380 |
| ∞ | 1·00000 | 1·00000 | 1·00000 | 1·00000 | 1·00000 | 1·00000 | 1·00000 | 1·00000 | 1·00000 |

For $\nu_1 = \infty$, $x = 0$

## Table 16. *Percentage points of the B-distribution (continued)*
### Lower 0·25 % points for x

$$\nu_1 = 2b, \quad \nu_2 = 2a$$

| $\nu_1$ / $\nu_2$ | 1 | 2 | 3 | 4 | 5 | 6 | 7 | 8 | 9 |
|---|---|---|---|---|---|---|---|---|---|
| 1 | $0\cdot0^415421$ | $0\cdot0^562500$ | $0\cdot0^538553$ | $0\cdot0^527778$ | $0\cdot0^521686$ | $0\cdot0^517778$ | $0\cdot0^515060$ | $0\cdot0^513061$ | $0\cdot0^511530$ |
| 2 | ·0049938 | ·0025000 | ·0016674 | ·0012508 | ·0010008 | $0\cdot0^383403$ | $0\cdot0^371492$ | $0\cdot0^362559$ | $0\cdot0^355610$ |
| 3 | ·032403 | ·018420 | ·012978 | ·010040 | ·0081943 | ·0069244 | ·0059966 | ·0052886 | ·0047305 |
| 4 | ·080525 | ·050000 | ·036742 | ·029152 | ·024198 | ·020698 | ·018089 | ·016069 | ·014456 |
| 5 | 0·13734 | 0·091028 | 0·069178 | 0·056059 | 0·047218 | 0·040827 | 0·035979 | 0·032171 | 0·029099 |
| 6 | ·19476 | ·13572 | ·10601 | ·087454 | ·074607 | ·065131 | ·057831 | ·052024 | ·047291 |
| 7 | ·24902 | ·18053 | ·14424 | ·12083 | ·10424 | ·091778 | ·082047 | ·074220 | ·067778 |
| 8 | ·29873 | ·22361 | ·18208 | ·15455 | ·13464 | ·11946 | ·10745 | ·097696 | ·089597 |
| 9 | ·34367 | ·26410 | ·21856 | ·18764 | ·16489 | ·14730 | ·13324 | ·12170 | ·11205 |
| 10 | 0·38408 | 0·30171 | 0·25316 | 0·21954 | 0·19441 | 0·17475 | 0·15887 | 0·14573 | 0·13466 |
| 11 | ·42037 | ·33643 | ·28571 | ·24995 | ·22287 | ·20145 | ·18398 | ·16943 | ·15708 |
| 12 | ·45301 | ·36840 | ·31616 | ·27876 | ·25010 | ·22719 | ·20837 | ·19258 | ·17910 |
| 13 | ·48243 | ·39782 | ·34458 | ·30594 | ·27601 | ·25188 | ·23191 | ·21504 | ·20056 |
| 14 | ·50904 | ·42489 | ·37107 | ·33153 | ·30060 | ·27547 | ·25452 | ·23673 | ·22138 |
| 15 | 0·53319 | 0·44984 | 0·39575 | 0·35558 | 0·32388 | 0·29794 | 0·27619 | 0·25760 | 0·24150 |
| 16 | ·55517 | ·47287 | ·41876 | ·37819 | ·34591 | ·31932 | ·29690 | ·27765 | ·26089 |
| 17 | ·57525 | ·49417 | ·44023 | ·39943 | ·36674 | ·33965 | ·31668 | ·29687 | ·27956 |
| 18 | ·59365 | ·51390 | ·46029 | ·41941 | ·38644 | ·35897 | ·33555 | ·31528 | ·29749 |
| 19 | ·61057 | ·53223 | ·47906 | ·43822 | ·40508 | ·37732 | ·35356 | ·33290 | ·31471 |
| 20 | 0·62617 | 0·54928 | 0·49664 | 0·45593 | 0·42272 | 0·39476 | 0·37074 | 0·34976 | 0·33124 |
| 21 | ·64060 | ·56518 | ·51313 | ·47264 | ·43943 | ·41135 | ·38712 | ·36590 | ·34711 |
| 22 | ·65398 | ·58003 | ·52863 | ·48841 | ·45526 | ·42713 | ·40276 | ·38135 | ·36233 |
| 23 | ·66641 | ·59393 | ·54321 | ·50331 | ·47029 | ·44214 | ·41769 | ·39614 | ·37693 |
| 24 | ·67800 | ·60696 | ·55695 | ·51741 | ·48455 | ·45645 | ·43195 | ·41029 | ·39095 |
| 25 | 0·68882 | 0·61921 | 0·56991 | 0·53076 | 0·49811 | 0·47008 | 0·44558 | 0·42386 | 0·40441 |
| 26 | ·69895 | ·63073 | ·58216 | ·54343 | ·51100 | ·48309 | ·45861 | ·43686 | ·41734 |
| 27 | ·70845 | ·64159 | ·59375 | ·55545 | ·52328 | ·49550 | ·47108 | ·44933 | ·42976 |
| 28 | ·71737 | ·65184 | ·60473 | ·56688 | ·53498 | ·50736 | ·48302 | ·46129 | ·44170 |
| 29 | ·72577 | ·66153 | ·61515 | ·57776 | ·54615 | ·51870 | ·49446 | ·47277 | ·45319 |
| 30 | 0·73369 | 0·67070 | 0·62505 | 0·58811 | 0·55680 | 0·52956 | 0·50543 | 0·48380 | 0·46423 |
| 40 | ·79348 | ·74113 | ·70204 | ·66963 | ·64157 | ·61667 | ·59425 | ·57382 | ·55507 |
| 60 | ·85761 | ·81896 | ·78919 | ·76385 | ·74141 | ·72108 | ·70241 | ·68511 | ·66895 |
| 120 | ·92636 | ·90497 | ·88794 | ·87306 | ·85954 | ·84702 | ·83527 | ·82416 | ·81357 |
| ∞ | 1·00000 | 1·00000 | 1·00000 | 1·00000 | 1·00000 | 1·00000 | 1·00000 | 1·00000 | 1·00000 |

This tables gives the values of $x$ for which

$$I_x(a, b) = \int_0^x u^{a-1}(1-u)^{b-1}\, du \Big/ \int_0^1 u^{a-1}(1-u)^{b-1}\, du = 0.0025,$$

where $a = \tfrac{1}{2}\nu_2$, $b = \tfrac{1}{2}\nu_1$.

Table 16 (continued).  *Lower 0·25 % points for x*

$$\nu_1 = 2b, \quad \nu_2 = 2a$$

| $\nu_2$ \ $\nu_1$ | 10 | 12 | 15 | 20 | 24 | 30 | 40 | 60 | 120 |
|---|---|---|---|---|---|---|---|---|---|
| 1 | $0\cdot0^510320$ | $0\cdot0^685289$ | $0\cdot0^667667$ | $0\cdot0^650330$ | $0\cdot0^641767$ | $0\cdot0^633275$ | $0\cdot0^624852$ | $0\cdot0^616499$ | $0\cdot0^782154$ |
| 2 | $\cdot0^350050$ | $\cdot0^341710$ | $\cdot0^333370$ | $\cdot0^325028$ | $\cdot0^320857$ | $\cdot0^316686$ | $\cdot0^312515$ | $\cdot0^483434$ | $\cdot0^441718$ |
| 3 | $\cdot0042791$ | $\cdot0035937$ | $\cdot0028978$ | $\cdot0021910$ | $\cdot0018333$ | $\cdot0014727$ | $\cdot0011092$ | $\cdot0^374260$ | $\cdot0^337289$ |
| 4 | $\cdot013139$ | $\cdot011115$ | $\cdot0090313$ | $\cdot0068827$ | $\cdot0057826$ | $\cdot0046647$ | $\cdot0035282$ | $\cdot0023724$ | $\cdot0011966$ |
| 5 | $0\cdot026565$ | $0\cdot022632$ | $0\cdot018524$ | $0\cdot014228$ | $0\cdot012002$ | $0\cdot0097228$ | $0\cdot0073857$ | $0\cdot0049884$ | $0\cdot0025277$ |
| 6 | $\cdot043354$ | $\cdot037180$ | $\cdot030649$ | $\cdot023720$ | $\cdot020091$ | $\cdot016343$ | $\cdot012469$ | $\cdot0084602$ | $\cdot0043072$ |
| 7 | $\cdot062379$ | $\cdot053830$ | $\cdot044676$ | $\cdot034832$ | $\cdot029620$ | $\cdot024195$ | $\cdot018541$ | $\cdot012638$ | $\cdot0064653$ |
| 8 | $\cdot082760$ | $\cdot071838$ | $\cdot060007$ | $\cdot047120$ | $\cdot040224$ | $\cdot032992$ | $\cdot025391$ | $\cdot017387$ | $\cdot0089391$ |
| 9 | $\cdot10385$ | $\cdot090643$ | $\cdot076179$ | $\cdot060230$ | $\cdot051609$ | $\cdot042499$ | $\cdot032849$ | $\cdot022598$ | $\cdot011676$ |
| 10 | $0\cdot12520$ | $0\cdot10983$ | $0\cdot092843$ | $0\cdot073889$ | $0\cdot063544$ | $0\cdot052533$ | $0\cdot040776$ | $0\cdot028181$ | $0\cdot014633$ |
| 11 | $\cdot14647$ | $\cdot12912$ | $\cdot10974$ | $\cdot087888$ | $\cdot075849$ | $\cdot062945$ | $\cdot049062$ | $\cdot034061$ | $\cdot017776$ |
| 12 | $\cdot16745$ | $\cdot14828$ | $\cdot12668$ | $\cdot10206$ | $\cdot088383$ | $\cdot073619$ | $\cdot057615$ | $\cdot040179$ | $\cdot021074$ |
| 13 | $\cdot18799$ | $\cdot16717$ | $\cdot14352$ | $\cdot11630$ | $\cdot10104$ | $\cdot084463$ | $\cdot066365$ | $\cdot046487$ | $\cdot024504$ |
| 14 | $\cdot20799$ | $\cdot18569$ | $\cdot16016$ | $\cdot13049$ | $\cdot11373$ | $\cdot095402$ | $\cdot075252$ | $\cdot052943$ | $\cdot028046$ |
| 15 | $0\cdot22739$ | $0\cdot20377$ | $0\cdot17652$ | $0\cdot14458$ | $0\cdot12638$ | $0\cdot10638$ | $0\cdot084228$ | $0\cdot059513$ | $0\cdot031682$ |
| 16 | $\cdot24616$ | $\cdot22136$ | $\cdot19255$ | $\cdot15849$ | $\cdot13896$ | $\cdot11734$ | $\cdot093255$ | $\cdot066170$ | $\cdot035399$ |
| 17 | $\cdot26427$ | $\cdot23843$ | $\cdot20822$ | $\cdot17221$ | $\cdot15140$ | $\cdot12826$ | $\cdot10230$ | $\cdot072890$ | $\cdot039183$ |
| 18 | $\cdot28173$ | $\cdot25498$ | $\cdot22349$ | $\cdot18569$ | $\cdot16370$ | $\cdot13910$ | $\cdot11133$ | $\cdot079652$ | $\cdot043025$ |
| 19 | $\cdot29855$ | $\cdot27099$ | $\cdot23837$ | $\cdot19891$ | $\cdot17581$ | $\cdot14984$ | $\cdot12034$ | $\cdot086441$ | $\cdot046915$ |
| 20 | $0\cdot31473$ | $0\cdot28647$ | $0\cdot25283$ | $0\cdot21187$ | $0\cdot18773$ | $0\cdot16045$ | $0\cdot12930$ | $0\cdot093240$ | $0\cdot050844$ |
| 21 | $\cdot33030$ | $\cdot30143$ | $\cdot26689$ | $\cdot22454$ | $\cdot19944$ | $\cdot17093$ | $\cdot13819$ | $\cdot10004$ | $\cdot054807$ |
| 22 | $\cdot34527$ | $\cdot31588$ | $\cdot28053$ | $\cdot23692$ | $\cdot21093$ | $\cdot18127$ | $\cdot14701$ | $\cdot10682$ | $\cdot058795$ |
| 23 | $\cdot35968$ | $\cdot32983$ | $\cdot29377$ | $\cdot24901$ | $\cdot22219$ | $\cdot19145$ | $\cdot15574$ | $\cdot11359$ | $\cdot062805$ |
| 24 | $\cdot37353$ | $\cdot34330$ | $\cdot30661$ | $\cdot26082$ | $\cdot23322$ | $\cdot20146$ | $\cdot16438$ | $\cdot12033$ | $\cdot066831$ |
| 25 | $0\cdot38686$ | $0\cdot35631$ | $0\cdot31907$ | $0\cdot27233$ | $0\cdot24403$ | $0\cdot21131$ | $0\cdot17292$ | $0\cdot12703$ | $0\cdot070869$ |
| 26 | $\cdot39968$ | $\cdot36886$ | $\cdot33115$ | $\cdot28356$ | $\cdot25460$ | $\cdot22099$ | $\cdot18136$ | $\cdot13369$ | $\cdot074915$ |
| 27 | $\cdot41203$ | $\cdot38099$ | $\cdot34286$ | $\cdot29451$ | $\cdot26494$ | $\cdot23050$ | $\cdot18968$ | $\cdot14031$ | $\cdot078965$ |
| 28 | $\cdot42391$ | $\cdot39270$ | $\cdot35422$ | $\cdot30518$ | $\cdot27506$ | $\cdot23983$ | $\cdot19790$ | $\cdot14687$ | $\cdot083017$ |
| 29 | $\cdot43536$ | $\cdot40402$ | $\cdot36523$ | $\cdot31558$ | $\cdot28495$ | $\cdot24899$ | $\cdot20600$ | $\cdot15339$ | $\cdot087068$ |
| 30 | $0\cdot44640$ | $0\cdot41496$ | $0\cdot37591$ | $0\cdot32571$ | $0\cdot29462$ | $0\cdot25798$ | $0\cdot21398$ | $0\cdot15985$ | $0\cdot091115$ |
| 40 | $\cdot53774$ | $\cdot50663$ | $\cdot46693$ | $\cdot41399$ | $\cdot38004$ | $\cdot33882$ | $\cdot28740$ | $\cdot22099$ | $\cdot13099$ |
| 60 | $\cdot65378$ | $\cdot62595$ | $\cdot58923$ | $\cdot53801$ | $\cdot50367$ | $\cdot46023$ | $\cdot40313$ | $\cdot32392$ | $\cdot20483$ |
| 120 | $\cdot80346$ | $\cdot78440$ | $\cdot75823$ | $\cdot71954$ | $\cdot69203$ | $\cdot65519$ | $\cdot60285$ | $\cdot52143$ | $\cdot37370$ |
| $\infty$ | $1\cdot00000$ | $1\cdot00000$ | $1\cdot00000$ | $1\cdot00000$ | $1\cdot00000$ | $1\cdot00000$ | $1\cdot00000$ | $1\cdot00000$ | $1\cdot00000$ |

For $\nu_1 = \infty$, $x = 0$.

## Table 16. *Percentage points of the B-distribution (continued)*
### *Lower 0·1 % points for x*

$$\nu_1 = 2b, \quad \nu_2 = 2a$$

| $\nu_2$ \ $\nu_1$ | 1 | 2 | 3 | 4 | 5 | 6 | 7 | 8 | 9 |
|---|---|---|---|---|---|---|---|---|---|
| 1 | $0\cdot0^5 24674$ | $0\cdot0^5 10000$ | $0\cdot0^6 61685$ | $0\cdot0^6 44444$ | $0\cdot0^6 34698$ | $0\cdot0^6 28444$ | $0\cdot0^6 24096$ | $0\cdot0^6 20898$ | $0\cdot0^6 18448$ |
| 2 | ·0019990 | ·0010000 | $\cdot0^3 66678$ | $\cdot0^3 50013$ | $\cdot0^3 40012$ | $\cdot0^3 33344$ | $\cdot0^3 28582$ | $\cdot0^3 25009$ | $\cdot0^3 22231$ |
| 3 | ·017644 | ·010000 | ·0070369 | ·0054407 | ·0044385 | ·0037496 | ·0032465 | ·0028627 | ·0025603 |
| 4 | ·051192 | ·031623 | ·023184 | ·018370 | ·015235 | ·013023 | ·011376 | ·010102 | ·0090853 |
| 5 | 0·095821 | 0·063096 | 0·047798 | 0·038658 | 0·032518 | 0·028089 | 0·024736 | 0·022105 | 0·019984 |
| 6 | ·14455 | ·10000 | ·077811 | ·064038 | ·054539 | ·047552 | ·042181 | ·037916 | ·034444 |
| 7 | ·19313 | ·13895 | ·11056 | ·092358 | ·079519 | ·069913 | ·062428 | ·056419 | ·051482 |
| 8 | ·23942 | ·17783 | ·14417 | ·12201 | ·10607 | ·093954 | ·084400 | ·076655 | ·070238 |
| 9 | ·28251 | ·21544 | ·17750 | ·15192 | ·13320 | ·11878 | ·10729 | ·097886 | ·090036 |
| 10 | 0·32217 | 0·25119 | 0·20983 | 0·18139 | 0·16025 | 0·14377 | 0·13051 | 0·11957 | 0·11037 |
| 11 | ·35846 | ·28480 | ·24079 | ·20999 | ·18678 | ·16851 | ·15366 | ·14132 | ·13088 |
| 12 | ·39160 | ·31623 | ·27019 | ·23748 | ·21254 | ·19270 | ·17645 | ·16286 | ·15129 |
| 13 | ·42187 | ·34551 | ·29798 | ·26374 | ·23735 | ·21618 | ·19872 | ·18401 | ·17142 |
| 14 | ·44953 | ·37276 | ·32416 | ·28872 | ·26115 | ·23885 | ·22033 | ·20464 | ·19114 |
| 15 | 0·47487 | 0·39811 | 0·34879 | 0·31243 | 0·28389 | 0·26064 | 0·24121 | 0·22467 | 0·21037 |
| 16 | ·49813 | ·42170 | ·37194 | ·33489 | ·30558 | ·28154 | ·26134 | ·24405 | ·22905 |
| 17 | ·51952 | ·44367 | ·39370 | ·35615 | ·32624 | ·30155 | ·28070 | ·26277 | ·24714 |
| 18 | ·53926 | ·46416 | ·41415 | ·37628 | ·34590 | ·32069 | ·29928 | ·28080 | ·26464 |
| 19 | ·55750 | ·48329 | ·43340 | ·39532 | ·36460 | ·33897 | ·31711 | ·29816 | ·28153 |
| 20 | 0·57440 | 0·50119 | 0·45152 | 0·41336 | 0·38239 | 0·35643 | 0·33420 | 0·31486 | 0·29783 |
| 21 | ·59011 | ·51795 | ·46860 | ·43044 | ·39932 | ·37311 | ·35058 | ·33091 | ·31354 |
| 22 | ·60472 | ·53367 | ·48471 | ·44664 | ·41543 | ·38905 | ·36628 | ·34634 | ·32867 |
| 23 | ·61836 | ·54844 | ·49993 | ·46201 | ·43078 | ·40428 | ·38133 | ·36117 | ·34325 |
| 24 | ·63111 | ·56234 | ·51432 | ·47660 | ·44540 | ·41883 | ·39575 | ·37541 | ·35729 |
| 25 | 0·64306 | 0·57544 | 0·52795 | 0·49046 | 0·45934 | 0·43275 | 0·40958 | 0·38910 | 0·37082 |
| 26 | ·65427 | ·58780 | ·54086 | ·50365 | ·47265 | ·44607 | ·42284 | ·40227 | ·38385 |
| 27 | ·66481 | ·59948 | ·55311 | ·51621 | ·48535 | ·45882 | ·43557 | ·41493 | ·39641 |
| 28 | ·67474 | ·61054 | ·56475 | ·52817 | ·49749 | ·47103 | ·44779 | ·42710 | ·40851 |
| 29 | ·68410 | ·62102 | ·57582 | ·53958 | ·50910 | ·48273 | ·45952 | ·43882 | ·42017 |
| 30 | 0·69295 | 0·63096 | 0·58636 | 0·55048 | 0·52021 | 0·49396 | 0·47080 | 0·45010 | 0·43142 |
| 40 | ·76032 | ·70795 | ·66908 | ·63702 | ·60937 | ·58494 | ·56299 | ·54306 | ·52481 |
| 60 | ·83365 | ·79433 | ·76420 | ·73867 | ·71614 | ·69579 | ·67716 | ·65993 | ·64388 |
| 120 | ·91338 | ·89125 | ·87372 | ·85844 | ·84460 | ·83182 | ·81985 | ·80854 | ·79780 |
| $\infty$ | 1·00000 | 1·00000 | 1·00000 | 1·00000 | 1·00000 | 1·00000 | 1·00000 | 1·00000 | 1·00000 |

This table gives the values of $x$ for which

$$I_x(a, b) = \int_0^x u^{a-1}(1-u)^{b-1}\, du \Big/ \int_0^1 u^{a-1}(1-u)^{b-1}\, du = 0\cdot001,$$

where $a = \tfrac{1}{2}\nu_2,\ b = \tfrac{1}{2}\nu_1$.

Table 16 (*continued*). *Lower* 0·1 % *points for* x

$$\nu_1 = 2b, \quad \nu_2 = 2a$$

| $\nu_2$ \ $\nu_1$ | 10 | 12 | 15 | 20 | 24 | 30 | 40 | 60 | 120 |
|---|---|---|---|---|---|---|---|---|---|
| 1 | 0.0$^6$16512 | 0.0$^6$13646 | 0.0$^6$10827 | 0.0$^7$80527 | 0.0$^7$66827 | 0.0$^7$53240 | 0.0$^7$39764 | 0.0$^7$26399 | 0.0$^7$13145 |
| 2 | ·0$^3$20008 | ·0$^3$16674 | ·0$^3$13339 | ·0$^3$10005 | ·0$^4$83372 | ·0$^4$66698 | ·0$^4$50024 | ·0$^4$33349 | ·0$^4$16675 |
| 3 | ·0023158 | ·0019445 | ·0015677 | ·0011851 | ·0$^3$99159 | ·0$^3$79650 | ·0$^3$59984 | ·0$^3$40156 | ·0$^3$20162 |
| 4 | ·0082555 | ·0069815 | ·0056704 | ·0043196 | ·0036285 | ·0029264 | ·0022129 | ·0014877 | ·0$^3$75019 |
| 5 | 0.018237 | 0.015527 | 0.012701 | 0.0097486 | 0.0082211 | 0.0066572 | 0.0050552 | 0.0034131 | 0.0017288 |
| 6 | ·031561 | ·027043 | ·022273 | ·017221 | ·014579 | ·011854 | ·0090391 | ·0061296 | ·0031189 |
| 7 | ·047351 | ·040819 | ·033840 | ·026352 | ·022395 | ·018281 | ·013999 | ·0095351 | ·0048744 |
| 8 | ·064830 | ·056206 | ·046888 | ·036766 | ·031361 | ·025702 | ·019764 | ·013522 | ·0069454 |
| 9 | ·083377 | ·072674 | ·060988 | ·048141 | ·041214 | ·033908 | ·026183 | ·017993 | ·0092863 |
| 10 | 0.10252 | 0.089813 | 0.075797 | 0.060214 | 0.051732 | 0.042723 | 0.033125 | 0.022865 | 0.011858 |
| 11 | ·12192 | ·10731 | ·091048 | ·072774 | ·062738 | ·052005 | ·040484 | ·028068 | ·014627 |
| 12 | ·14131 | ·12493 | ·10654 | ·085655 | ·074088 | ·061635 | ·048171 | ·033544 | ·017565 |
| 13 | ·16051 | ·14250 | ·12210 | ·098725 | ·085665 | ·071517 | ·056112 | ·039242 | ·020649 |
| 14 | ·17939 | ·15989 | ·13763 | ·11188 | ·097379 | ·081573 | ·064245 | ·045122 | ·023858 |
| 15 | 0.19787 | 0.17700 | 0.15302 | 0.12503 | 0.10915 | 0.091740 | 0.072521 | 0.051149 | 0.027174 |
| 16 | ·21588 | ·19378 | ·16821 | ·13813 | ·12093 | ·10196 | ·080896 | ·057292 | ·030584 |
| 17 | ·23338 | ·21018 | ·18316 | ·15111 | ·13266 | ·11221 | ·089336 | ·063528 | ·034073 |
| 18 | ·25035 | ·22616 | ·19781 | ·16394 | ·14431 | ·12243 | ·097811 | ·069833 | ·037632 |
| 19 | ·26678 | ·24171 | ·21216 | ·17659 | ·15585 | ·13260 | ·10630 | ·076190 | ·041249 |
| 20 | 0.28268 | 0.25682 | 0.22618 | 0.18904 | 0.16725 | 0.14270 | 0.11477 | 0.082583 | 0.044917 |
| 21 | ·29803 | ·27149 | ·23985 | ·20127 | ·17849 | ·15272 | ·12322 | ·088998 | ·048629 |
| 22 | ·31287 | ·28571 | ·25319 | ·21326 | ·18957 | ·16263 | ·13163 | ·005423 | ·052376 |
| 23 | ·32719 | ·29949 | ·26617 | ·22502 | ·20047 | ·17242 | ·13998 | ·10185 | ·056154 |
| 24 | ·34101 | ·31285 | ·27881 | ·23654 | ·21118 | ·18209 | ·14826 | ·10827 | ·059957 |
| 25 | 0.35435 | 0.32578 | 0.29110 | 0.24780 | 0.22169 | 0.19162 | 0.15648 | 0.11467 | 0.063780 |
| 26 | ·36723 | ·33831 | ·30306 | ·25882 | ·23202 | ·20102 | ·16461 | ·12104 | ·067620 |
| 27 | ·37966 | ·35044 | ·31469 | ·26959 | ·24214 | ·21027 | ·17266 | ·12739 | ·071472 |
| 28 | ·39166 | ·36218 | ·32599 | ·28011 | ·25206 | ·21937 | ·18062 | ·13370 | ·075333 |
| 29 | ·40324 | ·37356 | ·33698 | ·29039 | ·26179 | ·22833 | ·18848 | ·13998 | ·079199 |
| 30 | 0.41443 | 0.38458 | 0.34766 | 0.30043 | 0.27131 | 0.23713 | 0.19625 | 0.14621 | 0.083069 |
| 40 | ·50798 | ·47784 | ·43954 | ·38873 | ·35629 | ·31705 | ·26833 | ·20574 | ·12150 |
| 60 | ·62883 | ·60130 | ·56512 | ·51488 | ·48135 | ·43908 | ·38377 | ·30748 | ·19364 |
| 120 | ·78755 | ·76828 | ·74189 | ·70304 | ·67550 | ·63876 | ·58676 | ·50630 | ·36144 |
| ∞ | 1·00000 | 1·00000 | 1·00000 | 1·00000 | 1·00000 | 1·00000 | 1·00000 | 1·00000 | 1·00000 |

For $\nu_1 = \infty$, $x = 0$.

# Table 17. *Chart for determining the probability levels of the incomplete B-function, $I_x(a, b)$*

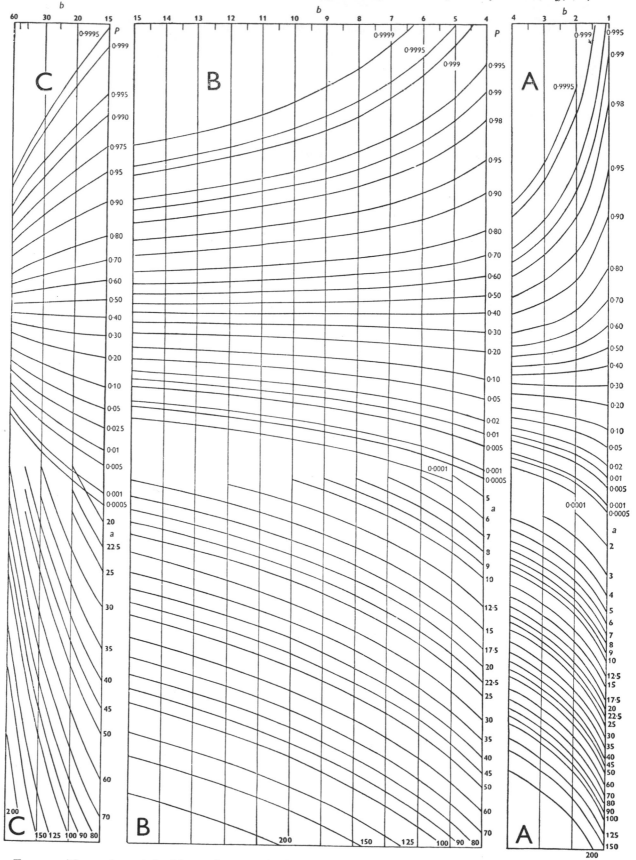

For use with $x$-scale contained in pocket at end of volume. In each section, each member of the lower family of curves corresponds to a constant value of $a$, and each member of the upper family to a constant value of $P = I_x(a, b)$. For directions as to use, see Introduction, pp. 33–4.

## Table 18. Percentage points of the F-distribution (variance ratio)

### Upper 25% points

| $\nu_2$ \ $\nu_1$ | 1 | 2 | 3 | 4 | 5 | 6 | 7 | 8 | 9 | 10 | 12 | 15 | 20 | 24 | 30 | 40 | 60 | 120 | ∞ |
|---|---|---|---|---|---|---|---|---|---|---|---|---|---|---|---|---|---|---|---|
| 1 | 5.83 | 7.50 | 8.20 | 8.58 | 8.82 | 8.98 | 9.10 | 9.19 | 9.26 | 9.32 | 9.41 | 9.49 | 9.58 | 9.63 | 9.67 | 9.71 | 9.76 | 9.80 | 9.85 |
| 2 | 2.57 | 3.00 | 3.15 | 3.23 | 3.28 | 3.31 | 3.34 | 3.35 | 3.37 | 3.38 | 3.39 | 3.41 | 3.43 | 3.43 | 3.44 | 3.45 | 3.46 | 3.47 | 3.48 |
| 3 | 2.02 | 2.28 | 2.36 | 2.39 | 2.41 | 2.42 | 2.43 | 2.44 | 2.44 | 2.44 | 2.45 | 2.46 | 2.46 | 2.46 | 2.47 | 2.47 | 2.47 | 2.47 | 2.47 |
| 4 | 1.81 | 2.00 | 2.05 | 2.06 | 2.07 | 2.08 | 2.08 | 2.08 | 2.08 | 2.08 | 2.08 | 2.08 | 2.08 | 2.08 | 2.08 | 2.08 | 2.08 | 2.08 | 2.08 |
| 5 | 1.69 | 1.85 | 1.88 | 1.89 | 1.89 | 1.89 | 1.89 | 1.89 | 1.89 | 1.89 | 1.89 | 1.89 | 1.88 | 1.88 | 1.88 | 1.88 | 1.87 | 1.87 | 1.87 |
| 6 | 1.62 | 1.76 | 1.78 | 1.79 | 1.79 | 1.78 | 1.78 | 1.78 | 1.77 | 1.77 | 1.77 | 1.76 | 1.76 | 1.75 | 1.75 | 1.75 | 1.74 | 1.74 | 1.74 |
| 7 | 1.57 | 1.70 | 1.72 | 1.72 | 1.71 | 1.71 | 1.70 | 1.70 | 1.69 | 1.69 | 1.68 | 1.68 | 1.67 | 1.67 | 1.66 | 1.66 | 1.65 | 1.65 | 1.65 |
| 8 | 1.54 | 1.66 | 1.67 | 1.66 | 1.66 | 1.65 | 1.64 | 1.64 | 1.63 | 1.63 | 1.62 | 1.62 | 1.61 | 1.60 | 1.60 | 1.59 | 1.59 | 1.58 | 1.58 |
| 9 | 1.51 | 1.62 | 1.63 | 1.63 | 1.62 | 1.61 | 1.60 | 1.60 | 1.59 | 1.59 | 1.58 | 1.57 | 1.56 | 1.56 | 1.55 | 1.54 | 1.54 | 1.53 | 1.53 |
| 10 | 1.49 | 1.60 | 1.60 | 1.59 | 1.59 | 1.58 | 1.57 | 1.56 | 1.56 | 1.55 | 1.54 | 1.53 | 1.52 | 1.52 | 1.51 | 1.51 | 1.50 | 1.49 | 1.48 |
| 11 | 1.47 | 1.58 | 1.58 | 1.57 | 1.56 | 1.55 | 1.54 | 1.53 | 1.53 | 1.52 | 1.51 | 1.50 | 1.49 | 1.49 | 1.48 | 1.47 | 1.47 | 1.46 | 1.45 |
| 12 | 1.46 | 1.56 | 1.56 | 1.55 | 1.54 | 1.53 | 1.52 | 1.51 | 1.51 | 1.50 | 1.49 | 1.48 | 1.47 | 1.46 | 1.45 | 1.45 | 1.44 | 1.43 | 1.42 |
| 13 | 1.45 | 1.55 | 1.55 | 1.53 | 1.52 | 1.51 | 1.50 | 1.49 | 1.49 | 1.48 | 1.47 | 1.46 | 1.45 | 1.44 | 1.43 | 1.42 | 1.42 | 1.41 | 1.40 |
| 14 | 1.44 | 1.53 | 1.53 | 1.52 | 1.51 | 1.50 | 1.49 | 1.48 | 1.47 | 1.46 | 1.45 | 1.44 | 1.43 | 1.42 | 1.41 | 1.41 | 1.40 | 1.39 | 1.38 |
| 15 | 1.43 | 1.52 | 1.52 | 1.51 | 1.49 | 1.48 | 1.47 | 1.46 | 1.46 | 1.45 | 1.44 | 1.43 | 1.41 | 1.41 | 1.40 | 1.39 | 1.38 | 1.37 | 1.36 |
| 16 | 1.42 | 1.51 | 1.51 | 1.50 | 1.48 | 1.47 | 1.46 | 1.45 | 1.44 | 1.44 | 1.43 | 1.41 | 1.40 | 1.39 | 1.38 | 1.37 | 1.36 | 1.35 | 1.34 |
| 17 | 1.42 | 1.51 | 1.50 | 1.49 | 1.47 | 1.46 | 1.45 | 1.44 | 1.43 | 1.43 | 1.41 | 1.40 | 1.39 | 1.38 | 1.37 | 1.36 | 1.35 | 1.34 | 1.33 |
| 18 | 1.41 | 1.50 | 1.49 | 1.48 | 1.46 | 1.45 | 1.44 | 1.43 | 1.42 | 1.42 | 1.40 | 1.39 | 1.38 | 1.37 | 1.36 | 1.35 | 1.34 | 1.33 | 1.32 |
| 19 | 1.41 | 1.49 | 1.49 | 1.47 | 1.46 | 1.44 | 1.43 | 1.42 | 1.41 | 1.41 | 1.40 | 1.38 | 1.37 | 1.36 | 1.35 | 1.34 | 1.33 | 1.32 | 1.30 |
| 20 | 1.40 | 1.49 | 1.48 | 1.47 | 1.45 | 1.44 | 1.43 | 1.42 | 1.41 | 1.40 | 1.39 | 1.37 | 1.36 | 1.35 | 1.34 | 1.33 | 1.32 | 1.31 | 1.29 |
| 21 | 1.40 | 1.48 | 1.48 | 1.46 | 1.44 | 1.43 | 1.42 | 1.41 | 1.40 | 1.39 | 1.38 | 1.37 | 1.35 | 1.34 | 1.33 | 1.32 | 1.31 | 1.30 | 1.28 |
| 22 | 1.40 | 1.48 | 1.47 | 1.45 | 1.44 | 1.42 | 1.41 | 1.40 | 1.39 | 1.39 | 1.37 | 1.36 | 1.34 | 1.33 | 1.32 | 1.31 | 1.30 | 1.29 | 1.28 |
| 23 | 1.39 | 1.47 | 1.47 | 1.45 | 1.43 | 1.42 | 1.41 | 1.40 | 1.39 | 1.38 | 1.37 | 1.35 | 1.34 | 1.33 | 1.32 | 1.31 | 1.30 | 1.28 | 1.27 |
| 24 | 1.39 | 1.47 | 1.46 | 1.44 | 1.43 | 1.41 | 1.40 | 1.39 | 1.38 | 1.38 | 1.36 | 1.35 | 1.33 | 1.32 | 1.31 | 1.30 | 1.29 | 1.28 | 1.26 |
| 25 | 1.39 | 1.47 | 1.46 | 1.44 | 1.42 | 1.41 | 1.40 | 1.39 | 1.38 | 1.37 | 1.36 | 1.34 | 1.33 | 1.32 | 1.31 | 1.29 | 1.28 | 1.27 | 1.25 |
| 26 | 1.38 | 1.46 | 1.45 | 1.44 | 1.42 | 1.41 | 1.39 | 1.38 | 1.37 | 1.37 | 1.35 | 1.34 | 1.32 | 1.31 | 1.30 | 1.29 | 1.28 | 1.26 | 1.25 |
| 27 | 1.38 | 1.46 | 1.45 | 1.43 | 1.42 | 1.40 | 1.39 | 1.38 | 1.37 | 1.36 | 1.35 | 1.33 | 1.32 | 1.31 | 1.30 | 1.28 | 1.27 | 1.26 | 1.24 |
| 28 | 1.38 | 1.46 | 1.45 | 1.43 | 1.41 | 1.40 | 1.39 | 1.38 | 1.37 | 1.36 | 1.34 | 1.33 | 1.31 | 1.30 | 1.29 | 1.28 | 1.27 | 1.25 | 1.24 |
| 29 | 1.38 | 1.45 | 1.45 | 1.43 | 1.41 | 1.40 | 1.38 | 1.37 | 1.36 | 1.35 | 1.34 | 1.32 | 1.31 | 1.30 | 1.29 | 1.27 | 1.26 | 1.25 | 1.23 |
| 30 | 1.38 | 1.45 | 1.44 | 1.42 | 1.41 | 1.39 | 1.38 | 1.37 | 1.36 | 1.35 | 1.34 | 1.32 | 1.30 | 1.29 | 1.28 | 1.27 | 1.26 | 1.24 | 1.23 |
| 40 | 1.36 | 1.44 | 1.42 | 1.40 | 1.39 | 1.37 | 1.36 | 1.35 | 1.34 | 1.33 | 1.31 | 1.30 | 1.28 | 1.26 | 1.25 | 1.24 | 1.22 | 1.21 | 1.19 |
| 60 | 1.35 | 1.42 | 1.41 | 1.38 | 1.37 | 1.35 | 1.33 | 1.32 | 1.31 | 1.30 | 1.29 | 1.27 | 1.25 | 1.24 | 1.22 | 1.21 | 1.19 | 1.17 | 1.15 |
| 120 | 1.34 | 1.40 | 1.39 | 1.37 | 1.35 | 1.33 | 1.31 | 1.30 | 1.29 | 1.28 | 1.26 | 1.24 | 1.22 | 1.21 | 1.19 | 1.18 | 1.16 | 1.13 | 1.10 |
| ∞ | 1.32 | 1.39 | 1.37 | 1.35 | 1.33 | 1.31 | 1.29 | 1.28 | 1.27 | 1.25 | 1.24 | 1.22 | 1.19 | 1.18 | 1.16 | 1.14 | 1.12 | 1.08 | 1.00 |

$F = \dfrac{s_1^2}{s_2^2} = \dfrac{S_1/\nu_1}{S_2/\nu_2}$, where $s_1^2 = S_1/\nu_1$ and $s_2^2 = S_2/\nu_2$ are independent mean squares estimating a common variance $\sigma^2$ and based on $\nu_1$ and $\nu_2$ degrees of freedom, respectively.

## Table 18. Percentage points of the F-distribution (continued)

### Upper 10 % points

| $\nu_2$ \ $\nu_1$ | 1 | 2 | 3 | 4 | 5 | 6 | 7 | 8 | 9 | 10 | 12 | 15 | 20 | 24 | 30 | 40 | 60 | 120 | ∞ |
|---|---|---|---|---|---|---|---|---|---|---|---|---|---|---|---|---|---|---|---|
| 1 | 39·86 | 49·50 | 53·59 | 55·83 | 57·24 | 58·20 | 58·91 | 59·44 | 59·86 | 60·19 | 60·71 | 61·22 | 61·74 | 62·00 | 62·26 | 62·53 | 62·79 | 63·06 | 63·33 |
| 2 | 8·53 | 9·00 | 9·16 | 9·24 | 9·29 | 9·33 | 9·35 | 9·37 | 9·38 | 9·39 | 9·41 | 9·42 | 9·44 | 9·45 | 9·46 | 9·47 | 9·47 | 9·48 | 9·49 |
| 3 | 5·54 | 5·46 | 5·39 | 5·34 | 5·31 | 5·28 | 5·27 | 5·25 | 5·24 | 5·23 | 5·22 | 5·20 | 5·18 | 5·18 | 5·17 | 5·16 | 5·15 | 5·14 | 5·13 |
| 4 | 4·54 | 4·32 | 4·19 | 4·11 | 4·05 | 4·01 | 3·98 | 3·95 | 3·94 | 3·92 | 3·90 | 3·87 | 3·84 | 3·83 | 3·82 | 3·80 | 3·79 | 3·78 | 3·76 |
| 5 | 4·06 | 3·78 | 3·62 | 3·52 | 3·45 | 3·40 | 3·37 | 3·34 | 3·32 | 3·30 | 3·27 | 3·24 | 3·21 | 3·19 | 3·17 | 3·16 | 3·14 | 3·12 | 3·10 |
| 6 | 3·78 | 3·46 | 3·29 | 3·18 | 3·11 | 3·05 | 3·01 | 2·98 | 2·96 | 2·94 | 2·90 | 2·87 | 2·84 | 2·82 | 2·80 | 2·78 | 2·76 | 2·74 | 2·72 |
| 7 | 3·59 | 3·26 | 3·07 | 2·96 | 2·88 | 2·83 | 2·78 | 2·75 | 2·72 | 2·70 | 2·67 | 2·63 | 2·59 | 2·58 | 2·56 | 2·54 | 2·51 | 2·49 | 2·47 |
| 8 | 3·46 | 3·11 | 2·92 | 2·81 | 2·73 | 2·67 | 2·62 | 2·59 | 2·56 | 2·54 | 2·50 | 2·46 | 2·42 | 2·40 | 2·38 | 2·36 | 2·34 | 2·32 | 2·29 |
| 9 | 3·36 | 3·01 | 2·81 | 2·69 | 2·61 | 2·55 | 2·51 | 2·47 | 2·44 | 2·42 | 2·38 | 2·34 | 2·30 | 2·28 | 2·25 | 2·23 | 2·21 | 2·18 | 2·16 |
| 10 | 3·29 | 2·92 | 2·73 | 2·61 | 2·52 | 2·46 | 2·41 | 2·38 | 2·35 | 2·32 | 2·28 | 2·24 | 2·20 | 2·18 | 2·16 | 2·13 | 2·11 | 2·08 | 2·06 |
| 11 | 3·23 | 2·86 | 2·66 | 2·54 | 2·45 | 2·39 | 2·34 | 2·30 | 2·27 | 2·25 | 2·21 | 2·17 | 2·12 | 2·10 | 2·08 | 2·05 | 2·03 | 2·00 | 1·97 |
| 12 | 3·18 | 2·81 | 2·61 | 2·48 | 2·39 | 2·33 | 2·28 | 2·24 | 2·21 | 2·19 | 2·15 | 2·10 | 2·06 | 2·04 | 2·01 | 1·99 | 1·96 | 1·93 | 1·90 |
| 13 | 3·14 | 2·76 | 2·56 | 2·43 | 2·35 | 2·28 | 2·23 | 2·20 | 2·16 | 2·14 | 2·10 | 2·05 | 2·01 | 1·98 | 1·96 | 1·93 | 1·90 | 1·88 | 1·85 |
| 14 | 3·10 | 2·73 | 2·52 | 2·39 | 2·31 | 2·24 | 2·19 | 2·15 | 2·12 | 2·10 | 2·05 | 2·01 | 1·96 | 1·94 | 1·91 | 1·89 | 1·86 | 1·83 | 1·80 |
| 15 | 3·07 | 2·70 | 2·49 | 2·36 | 2·27 | 2·21 | 2·16 | 2·12 | 2·09 | 2·06 | 2·02 | 1·97 | 1·92 | 1·90 | 1·87 | 1·85 | 1·82 | 1·79 | 1·76 |
| 16 | 3·05 | 2·67 | 2·46 | 2·33 | 2·24 | 2·18 | 2·13 | 2·09 | 2·06 | 2·03 | 1·99 | 1·94 | 1·89 | 1·87 | 1·84 | 1·81 | 1·78 | 1·75 | 1·72 |
| 17 | 3·03 | 2·64 | 2·44 | 2·31 | 2·22 | 2·15 | 2·10 | 2·06 | 2·03 | 2·00 | 1·96 | 1·91 | 1·86 | 1·84 | 1·81 | 1·78 | 1·75 | 1·72 | 1·69 |
| 18 | 3·01 | 2·62 | 2·42 | 2·29 | 2·20 | 2·13 | 2·08 | 2·04 | 2·00 | 1·98 | 1·93 | 1·89 | 1·84 | 1·81 | 1·78 | 1·75 | 1·72 | 1·69 | 1·66 |
| 19 | 2·99 | 2·61 | 2·40 | 2·27 | 2·18 | 2·11 | 2·06 | 2·02 | 1·98 | 1·96 | 1·91 | 1·86 | 1·81 | 1·79 | 1·76 | 1·73 | 1·70 | 1·67 | 1·63 |
| 20 | 2·97 | 2·59 | 2·38 | 2·25 | 2·16 | 2·09 | 2·04 | 2·00 | 1·96 | 1·94 | 1·89 | 1·84 | 1·79 | 1·77 | 1·74 | 1·71 | 1·68 | 1·64 | 1·61 |
| 21 | 2·96 | 2·57 | 2·36 | 2·23 | 2·14 | 2·08 | 2·02 | 1·98 | 1·95 | 1·92 | 1·87 | 1·83 | 1·78 | 1·75 | 1·72 | 1·69 | 1·66 | 1·62 | 1·59 |
| 22 | 2·95 | 2·56 | 2·35 | 2·22 | 2·13 | 2·06 | 2·01 | 1·97 | 1·93 | 1·90 | 1·86 | 1·81 | 1·76 | 1·73 | 1·70 | 1·67 | 1·64 | 1·60 | 1·57 |
| 23 | 2·94 | 2·55 | 2·34 | 2·21 | 2·11 | 2·05 | 1·99 | 1·95 | 1·92 | 1·89 | 1·84 | 1·80 | 1·74 | 1·72 | 1·69 | 1·66 | 1·62 | 1·59 | 1·55 |
| 24 | 2·93 | 2·54 | 2·33 | 2·19 | 2·10 | 2·04 | 1·98 | 1·94 | 1·91 | 1·88 | 1·83 | 1·78 | 1·73 | 1·70 | 1·67 | 1·64 | 1·61 | 1·57 | 1·53 |
| 25 | 2·92 | 2·53 | 2·32 | 2·18 | 2·09 | 2·02 | 1·97 | 1·93 | 1·89 | 1·87 | 1·82 | 1·77 | 1·72 | 1·69 | 1·66 | 1·63 | 1·59 | 1·56 | 1·52 |
| 26 | 2·91 | 2·52 | 2·31 | 2·17 | 2·08 | 2·01 | 1·96 | 1·92 | 1·88 | 1·86 | 1·81 | 1·76 | 1·71 | 1·68 | 1·65 | 1·61 | 1·58 | 1·54 | 1·50 |
| 27 | 2·90 | 2·51 | 2·30 | 2·17 | 2·07 | 2·00 | 1·95 | 1·91 | 1·87 | 1·85 | 1·80 | 1·75 | 1·70 | 1·67 | 1·64 | 1·60 | 1·57 | 1·53 | 1·49 |
| 28 | 2·89 | 2·50 | 2·29 | 2·16 | 2·06 | 2·00 | 1·94 | 1·90 | 1·87 | 1·84 | 1·79 | 1·74 | 1·69 | 1·66 | 1·63 | 1·59 | 1·56 | 1·52 | 1·48 |
| 29 | 2·89 | 2·50 | 2·28 | 2·15 | 2·06 | 1·99 | 1·93 | 1·89 | 1·86 | 1·83 | 1·78 | 1·73 | 1·68 | 1·65 | 1·62 | 1·58 | 1·55 | 1·51 | 1·47 |
| 30 | 2·88 | 2·49 | 2·28 | 2·14 | 2·05 | 1·98 | 1·93 | 1·88 | 1·85 | 1·82 | 1·77 | 1·72 | 1·67 | 1·64 | 1·61 | 1·57 | 1·54 | 1·50 | 1·46 |
| 40 | 2·84 | 2·44 | 2·23 | 2·09 | 2·00 | 1·93 | 1·87 | 1·83 | 1·79 | 1·76 | 1·71 | 1·66 | 1·61 | 1·57 | 1·54 | 1·51 | 1·47 | 1·42 | 1·38 |
| 60 | 2·79 | 2·39 | 2·18 | 2·04 | 1·95 | 1·87 | 1·82 | 1·77 | 1·74 | 1·71 | 1·66 | 1·60 | 1·54 | 1·51 | 1·48 | 1·44 | 1·40 | 1·35 | 1·29 |
| 120 | 2·75 | 2·35 | 2·13 | 1·99 | 1·90 | 1·82 | 1·77 | 1·72 | 1·68 | 1·65 | 1·60 | 1·55 | 1·48 | 1·45 | 1·41 | 1·37 | 1·32 | 1·26 | 1·19 |
| ∞ | 2·71 | 2·30 | 2·08 | 1·94 | 1·85 | 1·77 | 1·72 | 1·67 | 1·63 | 1·60 | 1·55 | 1·49 | 1·42 | 1·38 | 1·34 | 1·30 | 1·24 | 1·17 | 1·00 |

$F = \frac{s_1^2}{s_2^2} = \frac{S_1/\nu_1}{S_2/\nu_2}$, where $s_1^2 = S_1/\nu_1$ and $s_2^2 = S_2/\nu_2$ are independent mean squares estimating a common variance $\sigma^2$ and based on $\nu_1$ and $\nu_2$ degrees of freedom, respectively.

## Table 18 (*continued*)

### *Upper 5% points*

| $\nu_2$ \ $\nu_1$ | 1 | 2 | 3 | 4 | 5 | 6 | 7 | 8 | 9 | 10 | 12 | 15 | 20 | 24 | 30 | 40 | 60 | 120 | ∞ |
|---|---|---|---|---|---|---|---|---|---|---|---|---|---|---|---|---|---|---|---|
| 1 | 161·4 | 199·5 | 215·7 | 224·6 | 230·2 | 234·0 | 236·8 | 238·9 | 240·5 | 241·9 | 243·9 | 245·9 | 248·0 | 249·1 | 250·1 | 251·1 | 252·2 | 253·3 | 254·3 |
| 2 | 18·51 | 19·00 | 19·16 | 19·25 | 19·30 | 19·33 | 19·35 | 19·37 | 19·38 | 19·40 | 19·41 | 19·43 | 19·45 | 19·45 | 19·46 | 19·47 | 19·48 | 19·49 | 19·50 |
| 3 | 10·13 | 9·55 | 9·28 | 9·12 | 9·01 | 8·94 | 8·89 | 8·85 | 8·81 | 8·79 | 8·74 | 8·70 | 8·66 | 8·64 | 8·62 | 8·59 | 8·57 | 8·55 | 8·53 |
| 4 | 7·71 | 6·94 | 6·59 | 6·39 | 6·26 | 6·16 | 6·09 | 6·04 | 6·00 | 5·96 | 5·91 | 5·86 | 5·80 | 5·77 | 5·75 | 5·72 | 5·69 | 5·66 | 5·63 |
| 5 | 6·61 | 5·79 | 5·41 | 5·19 | 5·05 | 4·95 | 4·88 | 4·82 | 4·77 | 4·74 | 4·68 | 4·62 | 4·56 | 4·53 | 4·50 | 4·46 | 4·43 | 4·40 | 4·36 |
| 6 | 5·99 | 5·14 | 4·76 | 4·53 | 4·39 | 4·28 | 4·21 | 4·15 | 4·10 | 4·06 | 4·00 | 3·94 | 3·87 | 3·84 | 3·81 | 3·77 | 3·74 | 3·70 | 3·67 |
| 7 | 5·59 | 4·74 | 4·35 | 4·12 | 3·97 | 3·87 | 3·79 | 3·73 | 3·68 | 3·64 | 3·57 | 3·51 | 3·44 | 3·41 | 3·38 | 3·34 | 3·30 | 3·27 | 3·23 |
| 8 | 5·32 | 4·46 | 4·07 | 3·84 | 3·69 | 3·58 | 3·50 | 3·44 | 3·39 | 3·35 | 3·28 | 3·22 | 3·15 | 3·12 | 3·08 | 3·04 | 3·01 | 2·97 | 2·93 |
| 9 | 5·12 | 4·26 | 3·86 | 3·63 | 3·48 | 3·37 | 3·29 | 3·23 | 3·18 | 3·14 | 3·07 | 3·01 | 2·94 | 2·90 | 2·86 | 2·83 | 2·79 | 2·75 | 2·71 |
| 10 | 4·96 | 4·10 | 3·71 | 3·48 | 3·33 | 3·22 | 3·14 | 3·07 | 3·02 | 2·98 | 2·91 | 2·85 | 2·77 | 2·74 | 2·70 | 2·66 | 2·62 | 2·58 | 2·54 |
| 11 | 4·84 | 3·98 | 3·59 | 3·36 | 3·20 | 3·09 | 3·01 | 2·95 | 2·90 | 2·85 | 2·79 | 2·72 | 2·65 | 2·61 | 2·57 | 2·53 | 2·49 | 2·45 | 2·40 |
| 12 | 4·75 | 3·89 | 3·49 | 3·26 | 3·11 | 3·00 | 2·91 | 2·85 | 2·80 | 2·75 | 2·69 | 2·62 | 2·54 | 2·51 | 2·47 | 2·43 | 2·38 | 2·34 | 2·30 |
| 13 | 4·67 | 3·81 | 3·41 | 3·18 | 3·03 | 2·92 | 2·83 | 2·77 | 2·71 | 2·67 | 2·60 | 2·53 | 2·46 | 2·42 | 2·38 | 2·34 | 2·30 | 2·25 | 2·21 |
| 14 | 4·60 | 3·74 | 3·34 | 3·11 | 2·96 | 2·85 | 2·76 | 2·70 | 2·65 | 2·60 | 2·53 | 2·46 | 2·39 | 2·35 | 2·31 | 2·27 | 2·22 | 2·18 | 2·13 |
| 15 | 4·54 | 3·68 | 3·29 | 3·06 | 2·90 | 2·79 | 2·71 | 2·64 | 2·59 | 2·54 | 2·48 | 2·40 | 2·33 | 2·29 | 2·25 | 2·20 | 2·16 | 2·11 | 2·07 |
| 16 | 4·49 | 3·63 | 3·24 | 3·01 | 2·85 | 2·74 | 2·66 | 2·59 | 2·54 | 2·49 | 2·42 | 2·35 | 2·28 | 2·24 | 2·19 | 2·15 | 2·11 | 2·06 | 2·01 |
| 17 | 4·45 | 3·59 | 3·20 | 2·96 | 2·81 | 2·70 | 2·61 | 2·55 | 2·49 | 2·45 | 2·38 | 2·31 | 2·23 | 2·19 | 2·15 | 2·10 | 2·06 | 2·01 | 1·96 |
| 18 | 4·41 | 3·55 | 3·16 | 2·93 | 2·77 | 2·66 | 2·58 | 2·51 | 2·46 | 2·41 | 2·34 | 2·27 | 2·19 | 2·15 | 2·11 | 2·06 | 2·02 | 1·97 | 1·92 |
| 19 | 4·38 | 3·52 | 3·13 | 2·90 | 2·74 | 2·63 | 2·54 | 2·48 | 2·42 | 2·38 | 2·31 | 2·23 | 2·16 | 2·11 | 2·07 | 2·03 | 1·98 | 1·93 | 1·88 |
| 20 | 4·35 | 3·49 | 3·10 | 2·87 | 2·71 | 2·60 | 2·51 | 2·45 | 2·39 | 2·35 | 2·28 | 2·20 | 2·12 | 2·08 | 2·04 | 1·99 | 1·95 | 1·90 | 1·84 |
| 21 | 4·32 | 3·47 | 3·07 | 2·84 | 2·68 | 2·57 | 2·49 | 2·42 | 2·37 | 2·32 | 2·25 | 2·18 | 2·10 | 2·05 | 2·01 | 1·96 | 1·92 | 1·87 | 1·81 |
| 22 | 4·30 | 3·44 | 3·05 | 2·82 | 2·66 | 2·55 | 2·46 | 2·40 | 2·34 | 2·30 | 2·23 | 2·15 | 2·07 | 2·03 | 1·98 | 1·94 | 1·89 | 1·84 | 1·78 |
| 23 | 4·28 | 3·42 | 3·03 | 2·80 | 2·64 | 2·53 | 2·44 | 2·37 | 2·32 | 2·27 | 2·20 | 2·13 | 2·05 | 2·01 | 1·96 | 1·91 | 1·86 | 1·81 | 1·76 |
| 24 | 4·26 | 3·40 | 3·01 | 2·78 | 2·62 | 2·51 | 2·42 | 2·36 | 2·30 | 2·25 | 2·18 | 2·11 | 2·03 | 1·98 | 1·94 | 1·89 | 1·84 | 1·79 | 1·73 |
| 25 | 4·24 | 3·39 | 2·99 | 2·76 | 2·60 | 2·49 | 2·40 | 2·34 | 2·28 | 2·24 | 2·16 | 2·09 | 2·01 | 1·96 | 1·92 | 1·87 | 1·82 | 1·77 | 1·71 |
| 26 | 4·23 | 3·37 | 2·98 | 2·74 | 2·59 | 2·47 | 2·39 | 2·32 | 2·27 | 2·22 | 2·15 | 2·07 | 1·99 | 1·95 | 1·90 | 1·85 | 1·80 | 1·75 | 1·69 |
| 27 | 4·21 | 3·35 | 2·96 | 2·73 | 2·57 | 2·46 | 2·37 | 2·31 | 2·25 | 2·20 | 2·13 | 2·06 | 1·97 | 1·93 | 1·88 | 1·84 | 1·79 | 1·73 | 1·67 |
| 28 | 4·20 | 3·34 | 2·95 | 2·71 | 2·56 | 2·45 | 2·36 | 2·29 | 2·24 | 2·19 | 2·12 | 2·04 | 1·96 | 1·91 | 1·87 | 1·82 | 1·77 | 1·71 | 1·65 |
| 29 | 4·18 | 3·33 | 2·93 | 2·70 | 2·55 | 2·43 | 2·35 | 2·28 | 2·22 | 2·18 | 2·10 | 2·03 | 1·94 | 1·90 | 1·85 | 1·81 | 1·75 | 1·70 | 1·64 |
| 30 | 4·17 | 3·32 | 2·92 | 2·69 | 2·53 | 2·42 | 2·33 | 2·27 | 2·21 | 2·16 | 2·09 | 2·01 | 1·93 | 1·89 | 1·84 | 1·79 | 1·74 | 1·68 | 1·62 |
| 40 | 4·08 | 3·23 | 2·84 | 2·61 | 2·45 | 2·34 | 2·25 | 2·18 | 2·12 | 2·08 | 2·00 | 1·92 | 1·84 | 1·79 | 1·74 | 1·69 | 1·64 | 1·58 | 1·51 |
| 60 | 4·00 | 3·15 | 2·76 | 2·53 | 2·37 | 2·25 | 2·17 | 2·10 | 2·04 | 1·99 | 1·92 | 1·84 | 1·75 | 1·70 | 1·65 | 1·59 | 1·53 | 1·47 | 1·39 |
| 120 | 3·92 | 3·07 | 2·68 | 2·45 | 2·29 | 2·17 | 2·09 | 2·02 | 1·96 | 1·91 | 1·83 | 1·75 | 1·66 | 1·61 | 1·55 | 1·50 | 1·43 | 1·35 | 1·25 |
| ∞ | 3·84 | 3·00 | 2·60 | 2·37 | 2·21 | 2·10 | 2·01 | 1·94 | 1·88 | 1·83 | 1·75 | 1·67 | 1·57 | 1·52 | 1·46 | 1·39 | 1·32 | 1·22 | 1·00 |

$F = \dfrac{s_1^2}{s_2^2} = \dfrac{S_1}{\nu_1} \Big/ \dfrac{S_2}{\nu_2}$, where $s_1^2 = S_1/\nu_1$ and $s_2^2 = S_2/\nu_2$ are independent mean squares estimating a common variance $\sigma^2$ and based on $\nu_1$ and $\nu_2$ degrees of freedom, respectively.

## Table 18. *Percentage points of the F-distribution (continued)*

### Upper 2·5 % points

| $\nu_2 \backslash \nu_1$ | 1 | 2 | 3 | 4 | 5 | 6 | 7 | 8 | 9 | 10 | 12 | 15 | 20 | 24 | 30 | 40 | 60 | 120 | ∞ |
|---|---|---|---|---|---|---|---|---|---|---|---|---|---|---|---|---|---|---|---|
| 1 | 647·8 | 799·5 | 864·2 | 899·6 | 921·8 | 937·1 | 948·2 | 956·7 | 963·3 | 968·6 | 976·7 | 984·9 | 993·1 | 997·2 | 1001 | 1006 | 1010 | 1014 | 1018 |
| 2 | 38·51 | 39·00 | 39·17 | 39·25 | 39·30 | 39·33 | 39·36 | 39·37 | 39·39 | 39·40 | 39·41 | 39·43 | 39·45 | 39·46 | 39·46 | 39·47 | 39·48 | 39·49 | 39·50 |
| 3 | 17·44 | 16·04 | 15·44 | 15·10 | 14·88 | 14·73 | 14·62 | 14·54 | 14·47 | 14·42 | 14·34 | 14·25 | 14·17 | 14·12 | 14·08 | 14·04 | 14·04 | 13·95 | 13·90 |
| 4 | 12·22 | 10·65 | 9·98 | 9·60 | 9·36 | 9·20 | 9·07 | 8·98 | 8·90 | 8·84 | 8·75 | 8·66 | 8·56 | 8·51 | 8·46 | 8·41 | 8·36 | 8·31 | 8·26 |
| 5 | 10·01 | 8·43 | 7·76 | 7·39 | 7·15 | 6·98 | 6·85 | 6·76 | 6·68 | 6·62 | 6·52 | 6·43 | 6·33 | 6·28 | 6·23 | 6·18 | 6·12 | 6·07 | 6·02 |
| 6 | 8·81 | 7·26 | 6·60 | 6·23 | 5·99 | 5·82 | 5·70 | 5·60 | 5·52 | 5·46 | 5·37 | 5·27 | 5·17 | 5·12 | 5·07 | 5·01 | 4·96 | 4·90 | 4·85 |
| 7 | 8·07 | 6·54 | 5·89 | 5·52 | 5·29 | 5·12 | 4·99 | 4·90 | 4·82 | 4·76 | 4·67 | 4·57 | 4·47 | 4·42 | 4·36 | 4·31 | 4·25 | 4·20 | 4·14 |
| 8 | 7·57 | 6·06 | 5·42 | 5·05 | 4·82 | 4·65 | 4·53 | 4·43 | 4·36 | 4·30 | 4·20 | 4·10 | 4·00 | 3·95 | 3·89 | 3·84 | 3·78 | 3·73 | 3·67 |
| 9 | 7·21 | 5·71 | 5·08 | 4·72 | 4·48 | 4·32 | 4·20 | 4·10 | 4·03 | 3·96 | 3·87 | 3·77 | 3·67 | 3·61 | 3·56 | 3·51 | 3·45 | 3·39 | 3·33 |
| 10 | 6·94 | 5·46 | 4·83 | 4·47 | 4·24 | 4·07 | 3·95 | 3·85 | 3·78 | 3·72 | 3·62 | 3·52 | 3·42 | 3·37 | 3·31 | 3·26 | 3·20 | 3·14 | 3·08 |
| 11 | 6·72 | 5·26 | 4·63 | 4·28 | 4·04 | 3·88 | 3·76 | 3·66 | 3·59 | 3·53 | 3·43 | 3·33 | 3·23 | 3·17 | 3·12 | 3·06 | 3·00 | 2·94 | 2·88 |
| 12 | 6·55 | 5·10 | 4·47 | 4·12 | 3·89 | 3·73 | 3·61 | 3·51 | 3·44 | 3·37 | 3·28 | 3·18 | 3·07 | 3·02 | 2·96 | 2·91 | 2·85 | 2·79 | 2·72 |
| 13 | 6·41 | 4·97 | 4·35 | 4·00 | 3·77 | 3·60 | 3·48 | 3·39 | 3·31 | 3·25 | 3·15 | 3·05 | 2·95 | 2·89 | 2·84 | 2·78 | 2·72 | 2·66 | 2·60 |
| 14 | 6·30 | 4·86 | 4·24 | 3·89 | 3·66 | 3·50 | 3·38 | 3·29 | 3·21 | 3·15 | 3·05 | 2·95 | 2·84 | 2·79 | 2·73 | 2·67 | 2·61 | 2·55 | 2·49 |
| 15 | 6·20 | 4·77 | 4·15 | 3·80 | 3·58 | 3·41 | 3·29 | 3·20 | 3·12 | 3·06 | 2·96 | 2·86 | 2·76 | 2·70 | 2·64 | 2·59 | 2·52 | 2·46 | 2·40 |
| 16 | 6·12 | 4·69 | 4·08 | 3·73 | 3·50 | 3·34 | 3·22 | 3·12 | 3·05 | 2·99 | 2·89 | 2·79 | 2·68 | 2·63 | 2·57 | 2·51 | 2·45 | 2·38 | 2·32 |
| 17 | 6·04 | 4·62 | 4·01 | 3·66 | 3·44 | 3·28 | 3·16 | 3·06 | 2·98 | 2·92 | 2·82 | 2·72 | 2·62 | 2·56 | 2·50 | 2·44 | 2·38 | 2·32 | 2·25 |
| 18 | 5·98 | 4·56 | 3·95 | 3·61 | 3·38 | 3·22 | 3·10 | 3·01 | 2·93 | 2·87 | 2·77 | 2·67 | 2·56 | 2·50 | 2·44 | 2·38 | 2·32 | 2·26 | 2·19 |
| 19 | 5·92 | 4·51 | 3·90 | 3·56 | 3·33 | 3·17 | 3·05 | 2·96 | 2·88 | 2·82 | 2·72 | 2·62 | 2·51 | 2·45 | 2·39 | 2·33 | 2·27 | 2·20 | 2·13 |
| 20 | 5·87 | 4·46 | 3·86 | 3·51 | 3·29 | 3·13 | 3·01 | 2·91 | 2·84 | 2·77 | 2·68 | 2·57 | 2·46 | 2·41 | 2·35 | 2·29 | 2·22 | 2·16 | 2·09 |
| 21 | 5·83 | 4·42 | 3·82 | 3·48 | 3·25 | 3·09 | 2·97 | 2·87 | 2·80 | 2·73 | 2·64 | 2·53 | 2·42 | 2·37 | 2·31 | 2·25 | 2·18 | 2·11 | 2·04 |
| 22 | 5·79 | 4·38 | 3·78 | 3·44 | 3·22 | 3·05 | 2·93 | 2·84 | 2·76 | 2·70 | 2·60 | 2·50 | 2·39 | 2·33 | 2·27 | 2·21 | 2·14 | 2·08 | 2·00 |
| 23 | 5·75 | 4·35 | 3·75 | 3·41 | 3·18 | 3·02 | 2·90 | 2·81 | 2·73 | 2·67 | 2·57 | 2·47 | 2·36 | 2·30 | 2·24 | 2·18 | 2·11 | 2·04 | 1·97 |
| 24 | 5·72 | 4·32 | 3·72 | 3·38 | 3·15 | 2·99 | 2·87 | 2·78 | 2·70 | 2·64 | 2·54 | 2·44 | 2·33 | 2·27 | 2·21 | 2·15 | 2·08 | 2·01 | 1·94 |
| 25 | 5·69 | 4·29 | 3·69 | 3·35 | 3·13 | 2·97 | 2·85 | 2·75 | 2·68 | 2·61 | 2·51 | 2·41 | 2·30 | 2·24 | 2·18 | 2·12 | 2·05 | 1·98 | 1·91 |
| 26 | 5·66 | 4·27 | 3·67 | 3·33 | 3·10 | 2·94 | 2·82 | 2·73 | 2·65 | 2·59 | 2·49 | 2·39 | 2·28 | 2·22 | 2·16 | 2·09 | 2·03 | 1·95 | 1·88 |
| 27 | 5·63 | 4·24 | 3·65 | 3·31 | 3·08 | 2·92 | 2·80 | 2·71 | 2·63 | 2·57 | 2·47 | 2·36 | 2·25 | 2·19 | 2·13 | 2·07 | 2·00 | 1·93 | 1·85 |
| 28 | 5·61 | 4·22 | 3·63 | 3·29 | 3·06 | 2·90 | 2·78 | 2·69 | 2·61 | 2·55 | 2·45 | 2·34 | 2·23 | 2·17 | 2·11 | 2·05 | 1·98 | 1·91 | 1·83 |
| 29 | 5·59 | 4·20 | 3·61 | 3·27 | 3·04 | 2·88 | 2·76 | 2·67 | 2·59 | 2·53 | 2·43 | 2·32 | 2·21 | 2·15 | 2·09 | 2·03 | 1·96 | 1·89 | 1·81 |
| 30 | 5·57 | 4·18 | 3·59 | 3·25 | 3·03 | 2·87 | 2·75 | 2·65 | 2·57 | 2·51 | 2·41 | 2·31 | 2·20 | 2·14 | 2·07 | 2·01 | 1·94 | 1·87 | 1·79 |
| 40 | 5·42 | 4·05 | 3·46 | 3·13 | 2·90 | 2·74 | 2·62 | 2·53 | 2·45 | 2·39 | 2·29 | 2·18 | 2·07 | 2·01 | 1·94 | 1·88 | 1·80 | 1·72 | 1·64 |
| 60 | 5·29 | 3·93 | 3·34 | 3·01 | 2·79 | 2·63 | 2·51 | 2·41 | 2·33 | 2·27 | 2·17 | 2·06 | 1·94 | 1·88 | 1·82 | 1·74 | 1·67 | 1·58 | 1·48 |
| 120 | 5·15 | 3·80 | 3·23 | 2·89 | 2·67 | 2·52 | 2·39 | 2·30 | 2·22 | 2·16 | 2·05 | 1·94 | 1·82 | 1·76 | 1·69 | 1·61 | 1·53 | 1·43 | 1·31 |
| ∞ | 5·02 | 3·69 | 3·12 | 2·79 | 2·57 | 2·41 | 2·29 | 2·19 | 2·11 | 2·05 | 1·94 | 1·83 | 1·71 | 1·64 | 1·57 | 1·48 | 1·39 | 1·27 | 1·00 |

$F = \dfrac{s_1^2}{s_2^2} = \dfrac{S_1}{\nu_1} \bigg/ \dfrac{S_2}{\nu_2}$, where $s_1^2 = S_1/\nu_1$ and $s_2^2 = S_2/\nu_2$ are independent mean squares estimating a common variance $\sigma^2$ and based on $\nu_1$ and $\nu_2$ degrees of freedom, respectively.

## Table 18 (continued)
### Upper 1 % points

| $v_2$ \ $v_1$ | 1 | 2 | 3 | 4 | 5 | 6 | 7 | 8 | 9 | 10 | 12 | 15 | 20 | 24 | 30 | 40 | 60 | 120 | ∞ |
|---|---|---|---|---|---|---|---|---|---|---|---|---|---|---|---|---|---|---|---|
| 1 | 4052 | 4999·5 | 5403 | 5625 | 5764 | 5859 | 5928 | 5981 | 6022 | 6056 | 6106 | 6157 | 6209 | 6235 | 6261 | 6287 | 6313 | 6339 | 6366 |
| 2 | 98·50 | 99·00 | 99·17 | 99·25 | 99·30 | 99·33 | 99·36 | 99·37 | 99·39 | 99·40 | 99·42 | 99·43 | 99·45 | 99·46 | 99·47 | 99·47 | 99·48 | 99·49 | 99·50 |
| 3 | 34·12 | 30·82 | 29·46 | 28·71 | 28·24 | 27·91 | 27·67 | 27·49 | 27·35 | 27·23 | 27·05 | 26·87 | 26·69 | 26·60 | 26·50 | 26·41 | 26·32 | 26·22 | 26·13 |
| 4 | 21·20 | 18·00 | 16·69 | 15·98 | 15·52 | 15·21 | 14·98 | 14·80 | 14·66 | 14·55 | 14·37 | 14·20 | 14·02 | 13·93 | 13·84 | 13·75 | 13·65 | 13·56 | 13·46 |
| 5 | 16·26 | 13·27 | 12·06 | 11·39 | 10·97 | 10·67 | 10·46 | 10·29 | 10·16 | 10·05 | 9·89 | 9·72 | 9·55 | 9·47 | 9·38 | 9·29 | 9·20 | 9·11 | 9·02 |
| 6 | 13·75 | 10·92 | 9·78 | 9·15 | 8·75 | 8·47 | 8·26 | 8·10 | 7·98 | 7·87 | 7·72 | 7·56 | 7·40 | 7·31 | 7·23 | 7·14 | 7·06 | 6·97 | 6·88 |
| 7 | 12·25 | 9·55 | 8·45 | 7·85 | 7·46 | 7·19 | 6·99 | 6·84 | 6·72 | 6·62 | 6·47 | 6·31 | 6·16 | 6·07 | 5·99 | 5·91 | 5·82 | 5·74 | 5·65 |
| 8 | 11·26 | 8·65 | 7·59 | 7·01 | 6·63 | 6·37 | 6·18 | 6·03 | 5·91 | 5·81 | 5·67 | 5·52 | 5·36 | 5·28 | 5·20 | 5·12 | 5·03 | 4·95 | 4·86 |
| 9 | 10·56 | 8·02 | 6·99 | 6·42 | 6·06 | 5·80 | 5·61 | 5·47 | 5·35 | 5·26 | 5·11 | 4·96 | 4·81 | 4·73 | 4·65 | 4·57 | 4·48 | 4·40 | 4·31 |
| 10 | 10·04 | 7·56 | 6·55 | 5·99 | 5·64 | 5·39 | 5·20 | 5·06 | 4·94 | 4·85 | 4·71 | 4·56 | 4·41 | 4·33 | 4·25 | 4·17 | 4·08 | 4·00 | 3·91 |
| 11 | 9·65 | 7·21 | 6·22 | 5·67 | 5·32 | 5·07 | 4·89 | 4·74 | 4·63 | 4·54 | 4·40 | 4·25 | 4·10 | 4·02 | 3·94 | 3·86 | 3·78 | 3·69 | 3·60 |
| 12 | 9·33 | 6·93 | 5·95 | 5·41 | 5·06 | 4·82 | 4·64 | 4·50 | 4·39 | 4·30 | 4·16 | 4·01 | 3·86 | 3·78 | 3·70 | 3·62 | 3·54 | 3·45 | 3·36 |
| 13 | 9·07 | 6·70 | 5·74 | 5·21 | 4·86 | 4·62 | 4·44 | 4·30 | 4·19 | 4·10 | 3·96 | 3·82 | 3·66 | 3·59 | 3·51 | 3·43 | 3·34 | 3·25 | 3·17 |
| 14 | 8·86 | 6·51 | 5·56 | 5·04 | 4·69 | 4·46 | 4·28 | 4·14 | 4·03 | 3·94 | 3·80 | 3·66 | 3·51 | 3·43 | 3·35 | 3·27 | 3·18 | 3·09 | 3·00 |
| 15 | 8·68 | 6·36 | 5·42 | 4·89 | 4·56 | 4·32 | 4·14 | 4·00 | 3·89 | 3·80 | 3·67 | 3·52 | 3·37 | 3·29 | 3·21 | 3·13 | 3·05 | 2·96 | 2·87 |
| 16 | 8·53 | 6·23 | 5·29 | 4·77 | 4·44 | 4·20 | 4·03 | 3·89 | 3·78 | 3·69 | 3·55 | 3·41 | 3·26 | 3·18 | 3·10 | 3·02 | 2·93 | 2·84 | 2·75 |
| 17 | 8·40 | 6·11 | 5·18 | 4·67 | 4·34 | 4·10 | 3·93 | 3·79 | 3·68 | 3·59 | 3·46 | 3·31 | 3·16 | 3·08 | 3·00 | 2·92 | 2·83 | 2·75 | 2·65 |
| 18 | 8·29 | 6·01 | 5·09 | 4·58 | 4·25 | 4·01 | 3·84 | 3·71 | 3·60 | 3·51 | 3·37 | 3·23 | 3·08 | 3·00 | 2·92 | 2·84 | 2·75 | 2·66 | 2·57 |
| 19 | 8·18 | 5·93 | 5·01 | 4·50 | 4·17 | 3·94 | 3·77 | 3·63 | 3·52 | 3·43 | 3·30 | 3·15 | 3·00 | 2·92 | 2·84 | 2·76 | 2·67 | 2·58 | 2·49 |
| 20 | 8·10 | 5·85 | 4·94 | 4·43 | 4·10 | 3·87 | 3·70 | 3·56 | 3·46 | 3·37 | 3·23 | 3·09 | 2·94 | 2·86 | 2·78 | 2·69 | 2·61 | 2·52 | 2·42 |
| 21 | 8·02 | 5·78 | 4·87 | 4·37 | 4·04 | 3·81 | 3·64 | 3·51 | 3·40 | 3·31 | 3·17 | 3·03 | 2·88 | 2·80 | 2·72 | 2·64 | 2·55 | 2·46 | 2·36 |
| 22 | 7·95 | 5·72 | 4·82 | 4·31 | 3·99 | 3·76 | 3·59 | 3·45 | 3·35 | 3·26 | 3·12 | 2·98 | 2·83 | 2·75 | 2·67 | 2·58 | 2·50 | 2·40 | 2·31 |
| 23 | 7·88 | 5·66 | 4·76 | 4·26 | 3·94 | 3·71 | 3·54 | 3·41 | 3·30 | 3·21 | 3·07 | 2·93 | 2·78 | 2·70 | 2·62 | 2·54 | 2·45 | 2·35 | 2·26 |
| 24 | 7·82 | 5·61 | 4·72 | 4·22 | 3·90 | 3·67 | 3·50 | 3·36 | 3·26 | 3·17 | 3·03 | 2·89 | 2·74 | 2·66 | 2·58 | 2·49 | 2·40 | 2·31 | 2·21 |
| 25 | 7·77 | 5·57 | 4·68 | 4·18 | 3·85 | 3·63 | 3·46 | 3·32 | 3·22 | 3·13 | 2·99 | 2·85 | 2·70 | 2·62 | 2·54 | 2·45 | 2·36 | 2·27 | 2·17 |
| 26 | 7·72 | 5·53 | 4·64 | 4·14 | 3·82 | 3·59 | 3·42 | 3·29 | 3·18 | 3·09 | 2·96 | 2·81 | 2·66 | 2·58 | 2·50 | 2·42 | 2·33 | 2·23 | 2·13 |
| 27 | 7·68 | 5·49 | 4·60 | 4·11 | 3·78 | 3·56 | 3·39 | 3·26 | 3·15 | 3·06 | 2·93 | 2·78 | 2·63 | 2·55 | 2·47 | 2·38 | 2·29 | 2·20 | 2·10 |
| 28 | 7·64 | 5·45 | 4·57 | 4·07 | 3·75 | 3·53 | 3·36 | 3·23 | 3·12 | 3·03 | 2·90 | 2·75 | 2·60 | 2·52 | 2·44 | 2·35 | 2·26 | 2·17 | 2·06 |
| 29 | 7·60 | 5·42 | 4·54 | 4·04 | 3·73 | 3·50 | 3·33 | 3·20 | 3·09 | 3·00 | 2·87 | 2·73 | 2·57 | 2·49 | 2·41 | 2·33 | 2·23 | 2·14 | 2·03 |
| 30 | 7·56 | 5·39 | 4·51 | 4·02 | 3·70 | 3·47 | 3·30 | 3·17 | 3·07 | 2·98 | 2·84 | 2·70 | 2·55 | 2·47 | 2·39 | 2·30 | 2·21 | 2·11 | 2·01 |
| 40 | 7·31 | 5·18 | 4·31 | 3·83 | 3·51 | 3·29 | 3·12 | 2·99 | 2·89 | 2·80 | 2·66 | 2·52 | 2·37 | 2·29 | 2·20 | 2·11 | 2·02 | 1·92 | 1·80 |
| 60 | 7·08 | 4·98 | 4·13 | 3·65 | 3·34 | 3·12 | 2·95 | 2·82 | 2·72 | 2·63 | 2·50 | 2·35 | 2·20 | 2·12 | 2·03 | 1·94 | 1·84 | 1·73 | 1·60 |
| 120 | 6·85 | 4·79 | 3·95 | 3·48 | 3·17 | 2·96 | 2·79 | 2·66 | 2·56 | 2·47 | 2·34 | 2·19 | 2·03 | 1·95 | 1·86 | 1·76 | 1·66 | 1·53 | 1·38 |
| ∞ | 6·63 | 4·61 | 3·78 | 3·32 | 3·02 | 2·80 | 2·64 | 2·51 | 2·41 | 2·32 | 2·18 | 2·04 | 1·88 | 1·79 | 1·70 | 1·59 | 1·47 | 1·32 | 1·00 |

$F = \dfrac{s_1^2}{s_2^2} = \dfrac{S_1}{S_2}\Big/\dfrac{v_1}{v_2}$, where $s_1^2 = S_1/v_1$ and $s_2^2 = S_2/v_2$ are independent mean squares estimating a common variance $\sigma^2$ and based on $v_1$ and $v_2$ degrees of freedom, respectively.

173

## Table 18. *Percentage points of the F-distribution (continued)*

### Upper 0.5 % points

| $\nu_2$ \ $\nu_1$ | 1 | 2 | 3 | 4 | 5 | 6 | 7 | 8 | 9 | 10 | 12 | 15 | 20 | 24 | 30 | 40 | 60 | 120 | ∞ |
|---|---|---|---|---|---|---|---|---|---|---|---|---|---|---|---|---|---|---|---|
| 1 | 16211 | 20000 | 21615 | 22500 | 23056 | 23437 | 23715 | 23925 | 24091 | 24224 | 24426 | 24630 | 24836 | 24940 | 25044 | 25148 | 25253 | 25359 | 25465 |
| 2 | 198·5 | 199·0 | 199·2 | 199·2 | 199·3 | 199·3 | 199·4 | 199·4 | 199·4 | 199·4 | 199·4 | 199·4 | 199·4 | 199·5 | 199·5 | 199·5 | 199·5 | 199·5 | 199·5 |
| 3 | 55·55 | 49·80 | 47·47 | 46·19 | 45·39 | 44·84 | 44·43 | 44·13 | 43·88 | 43·69 | 43·39 | 43·08 | 42·78 | 42·62 | 42·47 | 42·31 | 42·15 | 41·99 | 41·83 |
| 4 | 31·33 | 26·28 | 24·26 | 23·15 | 22·46 | 21·97 | 21·62 | 21·35 | 21·14 | 20·97 | 20·70 | 20·44 | 20·17 | 20·03 | 19·89 | 19·75 | 19·61 | 19·47 | 19·32 |
| 5 | 22·78 | 18·31 | 16·53 | 15·56 | 14·94 | 14·51 | 14·20 | 13·96 | 13·77 | 13·62 | 13·38 | 13·15 | 12·90 | 12·78 | 12·66 | 12·53 | 12·40 | 12·27 | 12·14 |
| 6 | 18·63 | 14·54 | 12·92 | 12·03 | 11·46 | 11·07 | 10·79 | 10·57 | 10·39 | 10·25 | 10·03 | 9·81 | 9·59 | 9·47 | 9·36 | 9·24 | 9·12 | 9·00 | 8·88 |
| 7 | 16·24 | 12·40 | 10·88 | 10·05 | 9·52 | 9·16 | 8·89 | 8·68 | 8·51 | 8·38 | 8·18 | 7·97 | 7·75 | 7·65 | 7·53 | 7·42 | 7·31 | 7·19 | 7·08 |
| 8 | 14·69 | 11·04 | 9·60 | 8·81 | 8·30 | 7·95 | 7·69 | 7·50 | 7·34 | 7·21 | 7·01 | 6·81 | 6·61 | 6·50 | 6·40 | 6·29 | 6·18 | 6·06 | 5·95 |
| 9 | 13·61 | 10·11 | 8·72 | 7·96 | 7·47 | 7·13 | 6·88 | 6·69 | 6·54 | 6·42 | 6·23 | 6·03 | 5·83 | 5·73 | 5·62 | 5·52 | 5·41 | 5·30 | 5·19 |
| 10 | 12·83 | 9·43 | 8·08 | 7·34 | 6·87 | 6·54 | 6·30 | 6·12 | 5·97 | 5·85 | 5·66 | 5·47 | 5·27 | 5·17 | 5·07 | 4·97 | 4·86 | 4·75 | 4·64 |
| 11 | 12·23 | 8·91 | 7·60 | 6·88 | 6·42 | 6·10 | 5·86 | 5·68 | 5·54 | 5·42 | 5·24 | 5·05 | 4·86 | 4·76 | 4·65 | 4·55 | 4·44 | 4·34 | 4·23 |
| 12 | 11·75 | 8·51 | 7·23 | 6·52 | 6·07 | 5·76 | 5·52 | 5·35 | 5·20 | 5·09 | 4·91 | 4·72 | 4·53 | 4·43 | 4·33 | 4·23 | 4·12 | 4·01 | 3·90 |
| 13 | 11·37 | 8·19 | 6·93 | 6·23 | 5·79 | 5·48 | 5·25 | 5·08 | 4·94 | 4·82 | 4·64 | 4·46 | 4·27 | 4·17 | 4·07 | 3·97 | 3·87 | 3·76 | 3·65 |
| 14 | 11·06 | 7·92 | 6·68 | 6·00 | 5·56 | 5·26 | 5·03 | 4·86 | 4·72 | 4·60 | 4·43 | 4·25 | 4·06 | 3·96 | 3·86 | 3·76 | 3·66 | 3·55 | 3·44 |
| 15 | 10·80 | 7·70 | 6·48 | 5·80 | 5·37 | 5·07 | 4·85 | 4·67 | 4·54 | 4·42 | 4·25 | 4·07 | 3·88 | 3·79 | 3·69 | 3·58 | 3·48 | 3·37 | 3·26 |
| 16 | 10·58 | 7·51 | 6·30 | 5·64 | 5·21 | 4·91 | 4·69 | 4·52 | 4·38 | 4·27 | 4·10 | 3·92 | 3·73 | 3·64 | 3·54 | 3·44 | 3·33 | 3·22 | 3·11 |
| 17 | 10·38 | 7·35 | 6·16 | 5·50 | 5·07 | 4·78 | 4·56 | 4·39 | 4·25 | 4·14 | 3·97 | 3·79 | 3·61 | 3·51 | 3·41 | 3·31 | 3·21 | 3·10 | 2·98 |
| 18 | 10·22 | 7·21 | 6·03 | 5·37 | 4·96 | 4·66 | 4·44 | 4·28 | 4·14 | 4·03 | 3·86 | 3·68 | 3·50 | 3·40 | 3·30 | 3·20 | 3·10 | 2·99 | 2·87 |
| 19 | 10·07 | 7·09 | 5·92 | 5·27 | 4·85 | 4·56 | 4·34 | 4·18 | 4·04 | 3·93 | 3·76 | 3·59 | 3·40 | 3·31 | 3·21 | 3·11 | 3·00 | 2·89 | 2·78 |
| 20 | 9·94 | 6·99 | 5·82 | 5·17 | 4·76 | 4·47 | 4·26 | 4·09 | 3·96 | 3·85 | 3·68 | 3·50 | 3·32 | 3·22 | 3·12 | 3·02 | 2·92 | 2·81 | 2·69 |
| 21 | 9·83 | 6·89 | 5·73 | 5·09 | 4·68 | 4·39 | 4·18 | 4·01 | 3·88 | 3·77 | 3·60 | 3·43 | 3·24 | 3·15 | 3·05 | 2·95 | 2·84 | 2·73 | 2·61 |
| 22 | 9·73 | 6·81 | 5·65 | 5·02 | 4·61 | 4·32 | 4·11 | 3·94 | 3·81 | 3·70 | 3·54 | 3·36 | 3·18 | 3·08 | 2·98 | 2·88 | 2·77 | 2·66 | 2·55 |
| 23 | 9·63 | 6·73 | 5·58 | 4·95 | 4·54 | 4·26 | 4·05 | 3·88 | 3·75 | 3·64 | 3·47 | 3·30 | 3·12 | 3·02 | 2·92 | 2·82 | 2·71 | 2·60 | 2·48 |
| 24 | 9·55 | 6·66 | 5·52 | 4·89 | 4·49 | 4·20 | 3·99 | 3·83 | 3·69 | 3·59 | 3·42 | 3·25 | 3·06 | 2·97 | 2·87 | 2·77 | 2·66 | 2·55 | 2·43 |
| 25 | 9·48 | 6·60 | 5·46 | 4·84 | 4·43 | 4·15 | 3·94 | 3·78 | 3·64 | 3·54 | 3·37 | 3·20 | 3·01 | 2·92 | 2·82 | 2·72 | 2·61 | 2·50 | 2·38 |
| 26 | 9·41 | 6·54 | 5·41 | 4·79 | 4·38 | 4·10 | 3·89 | 3·73 | 3·60 | 3·49 | 3·33 | 3·15 | 2·97 | 2·87 | 2·77 | 2·67 | 2·56 | 2·45 | 2·33 |
| 27 | 9·34 | 6·49 | 5·36 | 4·74 | 4·34 | 4·06 | 3·85 | 3·69 | 3·56 | 3·45 | 3·28 | 3·11 | 2·93 | 2·83 | 2·73 | 2·63 | 2·52 | 2·41 | 2·29 |
| 28 | 9·28 | 6·44 | 5·32 | 4·70 | 4·30 | 4·02 | 3·81 | 3·65 | 3·52 | 3·41 | 3·25 | 3·07 | 2·89 | 2·79 | 2·69 | 2·59 | 2·48 | 2·37 | 2·25 |
| 29 | 9·23 | 6·40 | 5·28 | 4·66 | 4·26 | 3·98 | 3·77 | 3·61 | 3·48 | 3·38 | 3·21 | 3·04 | 2·86 | 2·76 | 2·66 | 2·56 | 2·45 | 2·33 | 2·21 |
| 30 | 9·18 | 6·35 | 5·24 | 4·62 | 4·23 | 3·95 | 3·74 | 3·58 | 3·45 | 3·34 | 3·18 | 3·01 | 2·82 | 2·73 | 2·63 | 2·52 | 2·42 | 2·30 | 2·18 |
| 40 | 8·83 | 6·07 | 4·98 | 4·37 | 3·99 | 3·71 | 3·51 | 3·35 | 3·22 | 3·12 | 2·95 | 2·78 | 2·60 | 2·50 | 2·40 | 2·30 | 2·18 | 2·06 | 1·93 |
| 60 | 8·49 | 5·79 | 4·73 | 4·14 | 3·76 | 3·49 | 3·29 | 3·13 | 3·01 | 2·90 | 2·74 | 2·57 | 2·39 | 2·29 | 2·19 | 2·08 | 1·96 | 1·83 | 1·69 |
| 120 | 8·18 | 5·54 | 4·50 | 3·92 | 3·55 | 3·28 | 3·09 | 2·93 | 2·81 | 2·71 | 2·54 | 2·37 | 2·19 | 2·09 | 1·98 | 1·87 | 1·75 | 1·61 | 1·43 |
| ∞ | 7·88 | 5·30 | 4·28 | 3·72 | 3·35 | 3·09 | 2·90 | 2·74 | 2·62 | 2·52 | 2·36 | 2·19 | 2·00 | 1·90 | 1·79 | 1·67 | 1·53 | 1·36 | 1·00 |

$F = \dfrac{s_1^2}{s_2^2} = \dfrac{S_1/S_2}{\nu_1/\nu_2}$, where $s_1^2 = S_1/\nu_1$ and $s_2^2 = S_2/\nu_2$ are independent mean squares estimating a common variance $\sigma^2$ and based on $\nu_1$ and $\nu_2$ degrees of freedom, respectively

## Table 18 (continued)
### Upper 0.1% points

| $\nu_1$ / $\nu_2$ | 1 | 2 | 3 | 4 | 5 | 6 | 7 | 8 | 9 | 10 | 12 | 15 | 20 | 24 | 30 | 40 | 60 | 120 | ∞ |
|---|---|---|---|---|---|---|---|---|---|---|---|---|---|---|---|---|---|---|---|
| 1 | 4053* | 5000* | 5404* | 5625* | 5764* | 5859* | 5929* | 5981* | 6023* | 6056* | 6107* | 6158* | 6209* | 6235* | 6261* | 6287* | 6313* | 6340* | 6366* |
| 2 | 998.5 | 999.0 | 999.2 | 999.2 | 999.3 | 999.3 | 999.4 | 999.4 | 999.4 | 999.4 | 999.4 | 999.4 | 999.4 | 999.5 | 999.5 | 999.5 | 999.5 | 999.5 | 999.5 |
| 3 | 167.0 | 148.5 | 141.1 | 137.1 | 134.6 | 132.8 | 131.6 | 130.6 | 129.9 | 129.2 | 128.3 | 127.4 | 126.4 | 125.9 | 125.4 | 125.0 | 124.5 | 124.0 | 123.5 |
| 4 | 74.14 | 61.25 | 56.18 | 53.44 | 51.71 | 50.53 | 49.66 | 49.00 | 48.47 | 48.05 | 47.41 | 46.76 | 46.10 | 45.77 | 45.43 | 45.09 | 44.75 | 44.40 | 44.05 |
| 5 | 47.18 | 37.12 | 33.20 | 31.09 | 29.75 | 28.84 | 28.16 | 27.64 | 27.24 | 26.92 | 26.42 | 25.91 | 25.39 | 25.14 | 24.87 | 24.60 | 24.33 | 24.06 | 23.79 |
| 6 | 35.51 | 27.00 | 23.70 | 21.92 | 20.81 | 20.03 | 19.46 | 19.03 | 18.69 | 18.41 | 17.99 | 17.56 | 17.12 | 16.89 | 16.67 | 16.44 | 16.21 | 15.99 | 15.75 |
| 7 | 29.25 | 21.69 | 18.77 | 17.19 | 16.21 | 15.52 | 15.02 | 14.63 | 14.33 | 14.08 | 13.71 | 13.32 | 12.93 | 12.73 | 12.53 | 12.33 | 12.12 | 11.91 | 11.70 |
| 8 | 25.42 | 18.49 | 15.83 | 14.39 | 13.49 | 12.86 | 12.40 | 12.04 | 11.77 | 11.54 | 11.19 | 10.84 | 10.48 | 10.30 | 10.11 | 9.92 | 9.73 | 9.53 | 9.33 |
| 9 | 22.86 | 16.39 | 13.90 | 12.56 | 11.71 | 11.13 | 10.70 | 10.37 | 10.11 | 9.89 | 9.57 | 9.24 | 8.90 | 8.72 | 8.55 | 8.37 | 8.19 | 8.00 | 7.81 |
| 10 | 21.04 | 14.91 | 12.55 | 11.28 | 10.48 | 9.92 | 9.52 | 9.20 | 8.96 | 8.75 | 8.45 | 8.13 | 7.80 | 7.64 | 7.47 | 7.30 | 7.12 | 6.94 | 6.76 |
| 11 | 19.69 | 13.81 | 11.56 | 10.35 | 9.58 | 9.05 | 8.66 | 8.35 | 8.12 | 7.92 | 7.63 | 7.32 | 7.01 | 6.85 | 6.68 | 6.52 | 6.35 | 6.17 | 6.00 |
| 12 | 18.64 | 12.97 | 10.80 | 9.63 | 8.89 | 8.38 | 8.00 | 7.71 | 7.48 | 7.29 | 7.00 | 6.71 | 6.40 | 6.25 | 6.09 | 5.93 | 5.76 | 5.59 | 5.42 |
| 13 | 17.81 | 12.31 | 10.21 | 9.07 | 8.35 | 7.86 | 7.49 | 7.21 | 6.98 | 6.80 | 6.52 | 6.23 | 5.93 | 5.78 | 5.63 | 5.47 | 5.30 | 5.14 | 4.97 |
| 14 | 17.14 | 11.78 | 9.73 | 8.62 | 7.92 | 7.43 | 7.08 | 6.80 | 6.58 | 6.40 | 6.13 | 5.85 | 5.56 | 5.41 | 5.25 | 5.10 | 4.94 | 4.77 | 4.60 |
| 15 | 16.59 | 11.34 | 9.34 | 8.25 | 7.57 | 7.09 | 6.74 | 6.47 | 6.26 | 6.08 | 5.81 | 5.54 | 5.25 | 5.10 | 4.95 | 4.80 | 4.64 | 4.47 | 4.31 |
| 16 | 16.12 | 10.97 | 9.00 | 7.94 | 7.27 | 6.81 | 6.46 | 6.19 | 5.98 | 5.81 | 5.55 | 5.27 | 4.99 | 4.85 | 4.70 | 4.54 | 4.39 | 4.23 | 4.06 |
| 17 | 15.72 | 10.66 | 8.73 | 7.68 | 7.02 | 6.56 | 6.22 | 5.96 | 5.75 | 5.58 | 5.32 | 5.05 | 4.78 | 4.63 | 4.48 | 4.33 | 4.18 | 4.02 | 3.85 |
| 18 | 15.38 | 10.39 | 8.49 | 7.46 | 6.81 | 6.35 | 6.02 | 5.76 | 5.56 | 5.39 | 5.13 | 4.87 | 4.59 | 4.45 | 4.30 | 4.15 | 4.00 | 3.84 | 3.67 |
| 19 | 15.08 | 10.16 | 8.28 | 7.26 | 6.62 | 6.18 | 5.85 | 5.59 | 5.39 | 5.22 | 4.97 | 4.70 | 4.43 | 4.29 | 4.14 | 3.99 | 3.84 | 3.68 | 3.51 |
| 20 | 14.82 | 9.95 | 8.10 | 7.10 | 6.46 | 6.02 | 5.69 | 5.44 | 5.24 | 5.08 | 4.82 | 4.56 | 4.29 | 4.15 | 4.00 | 3.86 | 3.70 | 3.54 | 3.38 |
| 21 | 14.59 | 9.77 | 7.94 | 6.95 | 6.32 | 5.88 | 5.56 | 5.31 | 5.11 | 4.95 | 4.70 | 4.44 | 4.17 | 4.03 | 3.88 | 3.74 | 3.58 | 3.42 | 3.26 |
| 22 | 14.38 | 9.61 | 7.80 | 6.81 | 6.19 | 5.76 | 5.44 | 5.19 | 4.99 | 4.83 | 4.58 | 4.33 | 4.06 | 3.92 | 3.78 | 3.63 | 3.48 | 3.32 | 3.15 |
| 23 | 14.19 | 9.47 | 7.67 | 6.69 | 6.08 | 5.65 | 5.33 | 5.09 | 4.89 | 4.73 | 4.48 | 4.23 | 3.96 | 3.82 | 3.68 | 3.53 | 3.38 | 3.22 | 3.05 |
| 24 | 14.03 | 9.34 | 7.55 | 6.59 | 5.98 | 5.55 | 5.23 | 4.99 | 4.80 | 4.64 | 4.39 | 4.14 | 3.87 | 3.74 | 3.59 | 3.45 | 3.29 | 3.14 | 2.97 |
| 25 | 13.88 | 9.22 | 7.45 | 6.49 | 5.88 | 5.46 | 5.15 | 4.91 | 4.71 | 4.56 | 4.31 | 4.06 | 3.79 | 3.66 | 3.52 | 3.37 | 3.22 | 3.06 | 2.89 |
| 26 | 13.74 | 9.12 | 7.36 | 6.41 | 5.80 | 5.38 | 5.07 | 4.83 | 4.64 | 4.48 | 4.24 | 3.99 | 3.72 | 3.59 | 3.44 | 3.30 | 3.15 | 2.99 | 2.82 |
| 27 | 13.61 | 9.02 | 7.27 | 6.33 | 5.73 | 5.31 | 5.00 | 4.76 | 4.57 | 4.41 | 4.17 | 3.92 | 3.66 | 3.52 | 3.38 | 3.23 | 3.08 | 2.92 | 2.75 |
| 28 | 13.50 | 8.93 | 7.19 | 6.25 | 5.66 | 5.24 | 4.93 | 4.69 | 4.50 | 4.35 | 4.11 | 3.86 | 3.60 | 3.46 | 3.32 | 3.18 | 3.02 | 2.86 | 2.69 |
| 29 | 13.39 | 8.85 | 7.12 | 6.19 | 5.59 | 5.18 | 4.87 | 4.64 | 4.45 | 4.29 | 4.05 | 3.80 | 3.54 | 3.41 | 3.27 | 3.12 | 2.97 | 2.81 | 2.64 |
| 30 | 13.29 | 8.77 | 7.05 | 6.12 | 5.53 | 5.12 | 4.82 | 4.58 | 4.39 | 4.24 | 4.00 | 3.75 | 3.49 | 3.36 | 3.22 | 3.07 | 2.92 | 2.76 | 2.59 |
| 40 | 12.61 | 8.25 | 6.60 | 5.70 | 5.13 | 4.73 | 4.44 | 4.21 | 4.02 | 3.87 | 3.64 | 3.40 | 3.15 | 3.01 | 2.87 | 2.73 | 2.57 | 2.41 | 2.23 |
| 60 | 11.97 | 7.76 | 6.17 | 5.31 | 4.76 | 4.37 | 4.09 | 3.87 | 3.69 | 3.54 | 3.31 | 3.08 | 2.83 | 2.69 | 2.55 | 2.41 | 2.25 | 2.08 | 1.89 |
| 120 | 11.38 | 7.32 | 5.79 | 4.95 | 4.42 | 4.04 | 3.77 | 3.55 | 3.38 | 3.24 | 3.02 | 2.78 | 2.53 | 2.40 | 2.26 | 2.11 | 1.95 | 1.76 | 1.54 |
| ∞ | 10.83 | 6.91 | 5.42 | 4.62 | 4.10 | 3.74 | 3.47 | 3.27 | 3.10 | 2.96 | 2.74 | 2.51 | 2.27 | 2.13 | 1.99 | 1.84 | 1.66 | 1.45 | 1.00 |

* Multiply these entries by 100.

This 0.1% table is based on the following sources: Colcord & Deming (1935); Fisher & Yates (1953, Table V) used with the permission of the authors and of Messrs Oliver and Boyd; Norton (1952).

175

## Table 19. *Percentage points of the largest variance ratio*, $s^2_{max.}/s^2_0$

### Upper 5 % points

| $\nu$ \ $k$ | 1 | 2 | 3 | 4 | 5 | 6 | 7 | 8 | 9 | 10 |
|---|---|---|---|---|---|---|---|---|---|---|
| 10 | 4·96 | 6·79 | 8·00 | 8·96 | 9·78 | 10·52 | 11·18 | 11·79 | 12·36 | 12·87 |
| 12 | 4·75 | 6·44 | 7·53 | 8·37 | 9·06 | 9·68 | 10·20 | 10·68 | 11·12 | 11·53 |
| 15 | 4·54 | 6·12 | 7·11 | 7·86 | 8·47 | 8·98 | 9·43 | 9·82 | 10·19 | 10·52 |
| 20 | 4·35 | 5·81 | 6·72 | 7·40 | 7·94 | 8·39 | 8·79 | 9·13 | 9·44 | 9·71 |
| 30 | 4·17 | 5·52 | 6·36 | 6·97 | 7·46 | 7·87 | 8·21 | 8·51 | 8·79 | 9·03 |
| 60 | 4·00 | 5·25 | 6·02 | 6·58 | 7·02 | 7·38 | 7·68 | 7·96 | 8·20 | 8·41 |
| ∞ | 3·84 | 5·00 | 5·70 | 6·21 | 6·60 | 6·92 | 7·20 | 7·44 | 7·65 | 7·84 |

### Upper 1 % points

| $\nu$ \ $k$ | 1 | 2 | 3 | 4 | 5 | 6 | 7 | 8 | 9 | 10 |
|---|---|---|---|---|---|---|---|---|---|---|
| 10 | 10·04 | 13·17 | 15·08 | 16·43 | 17·43 | 18·25 | 18·91 | 19·48 | 19·97 | 20·41 |
| 12 | 9·33 | 11·88 | 13·52 | 14·73 | 15·69 | 16·47 | 17·12 | 17·68 | 18·16 | 18·60 |
| 15 | 8·68 | 10·82 | 12·18 | 13·21 | 14·03 | 14·72 | 15·30 | 15·81 | 16·26 | 16·66 |
| 20 | 8·10 | 9·93 | 11·08 | 11·93 | 12·61 | 13·19 | 13·67 | 14·09 | 14·49 | 14·83 |
| 30 | 7·56 | 9·16 | 10·14 | 10·86 | 11·43 | 11·90 | 12·31 | 12·66 | 12·97 | 13·26 |
| 60 | 7·08 | 8·49 | 9·34 | 9·95 | 10·43 | 10·82 | 11·15 | 11·45 | 11·72 | 11·95 |
| ∞ | 6·63 | 7·88 | 8·61 | 9·15 | 9·54 | 9·87 | 10·16 | 10·41 | 10·62 | 10·82 |

$k$ is the number of independent variance estimates, each based on 1 degree of freedom, of which $s^2_{max.}$ is the largest. $\nu$ denotes the degrees of freedom of the independent 'error' mean square, $s^2_0$.

## Table 20. *Moment constants of the mean deviation and of the range*

| $n$ | Mean deviation, $m/\sigma$ | | | | | Range, $W = w/\sigma$ | | | | | | |
|---|---|---|---|---|---|---|---|---|---|---|---|---|
| | Expectation | S.D. | Variance | $\beta_1$ | $\beta_2$ | $\mathscr{E}(W_n) = d_n$ | S.D. | $V_n$ = variance | $\beta_1$ | $\beta_2$ | $d_n/V_n$ | $d_n^2/V_n$ |
| 2 | 0·564 190 | 0·4263 | 0·18169 | 0·991 | 3·869 | 1·12838 | 0·8525 | 0·72676 | 0·9906 | 3·869 | 1·55 | 1·75 |
| 3 | ·651 470 | ·3419 | ·11692 | ·417 | 3·286 | 1·69257 | ·8884 | ·78920 | ·4176 | 3·286 | 2·14 | 3·63 |
| 4 | ·690 988 | ·2970 | ·08822 | ·298 | 3·252 | 2·05875 | ·8798 | ·77406 | ·2735 | 3·188 | 2·66 | 5·48 |
| 5 | 0·713 650 | 0·2663 | 0·07094 | 0·230 | 3·197 | 2·32593 | 0·8641 | 0·74664 | 0·2167 | 3·169 | 3·12 | 7·25 |
| 6 | ·728 366 | ·2436 | ·05934 | ·187 | 3·161 | 2·53441 | ·8480 | ·71917 | ·1892 | 3·170 | 3·52 | 8·93 |
| 7 | ·738 698 | ·2258 | ·05101 | ·157 | 3·136 | 2·70436 | ·8332 | ·69423 | ·1743 | 3·176 | 3·90 | 10·53 |
| 8 | ·746 353 | ·2115 | ·04473 | ·136 | 3·118 | 2·84720 | ·8198 | ·67212 | ·1659 | 3·184 | 4·24 | 12·06 |
| 9 | ·752 253 | ·1996 | ·03982 | ·119 | 3·104 | 2·97003 | ·8078 | ·65260 | ·1609 | 3·192 | 4·55 | 13·52 |
| 10 | 0·756 940 | 0·1894 | 0·03589 | 0·106 | 3·0927 | 3·07751 | 0·7971 | 0·63529 | 0·1581 | 3·200 | 4·84 | 14·91 |
| 11 | ·760 753 | ·1807 | ·03266 | ·0961 | 3·0838 | 3·17287 | ·7873 | ·61986 | ·1566 | 3·207 | 5·12 | 16·2 |
| 12 | ·763 916 | ·1731 | ·02997 | ·0876 | 3·0765 | 3·25846 | ·7785 | ·60603 | ·1559 | 3·214 | 5·38 | 17·5 |
| 13 | ·766 583 | ·1664 | ·02769 | ·0805 | 3·0703 | 3·33598 | ·7704 | ·59354 | ·1559 | 3·221 | 5·62 | 18·8 |
| 14 | ·768 861 | ·1604 | ·02573 | ·0744 | 3·0650 | 3·40676 | ·7630 | ·58220 | ·1563 | 3·227 | 5·85 | 19·9 |
| 15 | 0·770 830 | 0·1550 | 0·02403 | 0·0692 | 3·0605 | 3·47183 | 0·7562 | 0·57186 | 0·1569 | 3·233 | 6·07 | 21·1 |
| 16 | ·772 548 | ·1501 | ·02254 | ·0647 | 3·0566 | 3·53198 | ·7499 | ·56236 | ·1578 | 3·238 | 6·28 | 22·2 |
| 17 | ·774 062 | ·1457 | ·02122 | ·0607 | 3·0531 | 3·58788 | ·7441 | ·55361 | ·1588 | 3·243 | 6·48 | 23·3 |
| 18 | ·775 404 | ·1416 | ·02005 | ·0572 | 3·0501 | 3·64006 | ·7386 | ·54552 | ·1598 | 3·248 | 6·67 | 24·3 |
| 19 | ·776 604 | ·1378 | ·01900 | ·0541 | 3·0473 | 3·68896 | ·7335 | ·53800 | ·1610 | 3·253 | 6·86 | 25·3 |
| 20 | 0·777 682 | 0·1344 | 0·01806 | 0·0513 | 3·0449 | 3·73495 | 0·7287 | 0·53098 | 0·1622 | 3·257 | 7·03 | 26·3 |
| 30 | ·784 474 | ·1098 | ·01206 | ·0338 | 3·0296 | | | | | | | |
| 60 | ·791 208 | ·0777 | ·00604 | ·0167 | 3·0146 | | | | | | | |

The unit is the population standard deviation.

Table 21. *Percentage points of the distribution of the mean deviation*

| Lower percentage points | | | | | | |
|---|---|---|---|---|---|---|
| Size of sample $n$ | 0·1 | 0·5 | 1·0 | 2·5 | 5·0 | 10·0 |
| 2 | 0·001 | 0·004 | 0·009 | 0·022 | 0·044 | 0·089 |
| 3 | 0·022 | 0·052 | 0·073 | 0·116 | 0·166 | 0·238 |
| 4 | 0·066 | 0·114 | 0·145 | 0·199 | 0·254 | 0·328 |
| 5 | 0·112 | 0·170 | 0·203 | 0·260 | 0·315 | 0·386 |
| 6 | 0·153 | 0·215 | 0·250 | 0·306 | 0·360 | 0·428 |
| 7 | 0·190 | 0·252 | 0·287 | 0·342 | 0·394 | 0·459 |
| 8 | 0·220 | 0·283 | 0·318 | 0·372 | 0·422 | 0·484 |
| 9 | 0·247 | 0·310 | 0·344 | 0·396 | 0·445 | 0·504 |
| 10 | 0·271 | 0·333 | 0·366 | 0·417 | 0·464 | 0·521 |
| Normal approximation | | | | | | |
| 10 | 0·171 | 0·269 | 0·316 | 0·386 | 0·445 | 0·514 |

| Upper percentage points | | | | | | |
|---|---|---|---|---|---|---|
| Size of sample $n$ | 10·0 | 5·0 | 2·5 | 1·0 | 0·5 | 0·1 |
| 2 | 1·163 | 1·386 | 1·585 | 1·821 | 1·985 | 2·327 |
| 3 | 1·117 | 1·276 | 1·417 | 1·586 | 1·703 | 1·949 |
| 4 | 1·089 | 1·224 | 1·344 | 1·489 | 1·590 | 1·806 |
| 5 | 1·069 | 1·187 | 1·292 | 1·419 | 1·507 | 1·693 |
| 6 | 1·052 | 1·158 | 1·253 | 1·366 | 1·445 | 1·613 |
| 7 | 1·038 | 1·135 | 1·222 | 1·325 | 1·397 | 1·550 |
| 8 | 1·026 | 1·116 | 1·196 | 1·292 | 1·358 | 1·499 |
| 9 | 1·016 | 1·100 | 1·175 | 1·264 | 1·326 | 1·457 |
| 10 | 1·007 | 1·086 | 1·156 | 1·240 | 1·299 | 1·422 |
| Normal approximation | | | | | | |
| 10 | 1·000 | 1·069 | 1·128 | 1·198 | 1·245 | 1·342 |

The unit is the population standard deviation. For $n > 10$, see Introduction, pp. 41–2, 83.

Table 22. *Percentage points of the distribution of the range*

| Size of sample $n$ | Factor $1/d_n$ | Lower percentage points | | | | | | Upper percentage points | | | | | |
|---|---|---|---|---|---|---|---|---|---|---|---|---|---|
| | | 0·1 | 0·5 | 1·0 | 2·5 | 5·0 | 10·0 | 10·0 | 5·0 | 2·5 | 1·0 | 0·5 | 0·1 |
| 2 | 0·8862 | 0·00 | 0·01 | 0·02 | 0·04 | 0·09 | 0·18 | 2·33 | 2·77 | 3·17 | 3·64 | 3·97 | 4·65 |
| 3 | ·5908 | 0·06 | 0·13 | 0·19 | 0·30 | 0·43 | 0·62 | 2·90 | 3·31 | 3·68 | 4·12 | 4·42 | 5·06 |
| 4 | ·4857 | 0·20 | 0·34 | 0·43 | 0·59 | 0·76 | 0·98 | 3·24 | 3·63 | 3·98 | 4·40 | 4·69 | 5·31 |
| 5 | ·4299 | 0·37 | 0·55 | 0·67 | 0·85 | 1·03 | 1·26 | 3·48 | 3·86 | 4·20 | 4·60 | 4·89 | 5·48 |
| 6 | 0·3946 | 0·53 | 0·75 | 0·87 | 1·07 | 1·25 | 1·49 | 3·66 | 4·03 | 4·36 | 4·76 | 5·03 | 5·62 |
| 7 | ·3698 | 0·69 | 0·92 | 1·05 | 1·25 | 1·44 | 1·68 | 3·81 | 4·17 | 4·49 | 4·88 | 5·15 | 5·73 |
| 8 | ·3512 | 0·83 | 1·08 | 1·20 | 1·41 | 1·60 | 1·84 | 3·93 | 4·29 | 4·60 | 4·99 | 5·25 | 5·82 |
| 9 | ·3367 | 0·97 | 1·21 | 1·34 | 1·55 | 1·74 | 1·97 | 4·04 | 4·39 | 4·70 | 5·08 | 5·34 | 5·90 |
| 10 | 0·3249 | 1·08 | 1·33 | 1·47 | 1·67 | 1·86 | 2·09 | 4·13 | 4·47 | 4·78 | 5·16 | 5·42 | 5·97 |
| 11 | ·3152 | 1·19 | 1·45 | 1·58 | 1·78 | 1·97 | 2·20 | 4·21 | 4·55 | 4·86 | 5·23 | 5·49 | 6·04 |
| 12 | ·3069 | 1·29 | 1·55 | 1·68 | 1·88 | 2·07 | 2·30 | 4·28 | 4·62 | 4·92 | 5·29 | 5·55 | 6·09 |
| 13 | ·2998 | 1·39 | 1·64 | 1·77 | 1·98 | 2·16 | 2·39 | 4·35 | 4·68 | 5·04 | 5·35 | 5·60 | 6·14 |
| 14 | ·2935 | 1·47 | 1·72 | 1·86 | 2·06 | 2·24 | 2·47 | 4·41 | 4·74 | 5·04 | 5·40 | 5·65 | 6·19 |
| 15 | 0·2880 | 1·55 | 1·80 | 1·93 | 2·14 | 2·32 | 2·54 | 4·47 | 4·80 | 5·09 | 5·45 | 5·70 | 6·23 |
| 16 | ·2831 | 1·62 | 1·88 | 2·01 | 2·21 | 2·39 | 2·61 | 4·52 | 4·85 | 5·14 | 5·49 | 5·74 | 6·27 |
| 17 | ·2787 | 1·69 | 1·94 | 2·07 | 2·27 | 2·45 | 2·67 | 4·57 | 4·89 | 5·18 | 5·54 | 5·78 | 6·31 |
| 18 | ·2747 | 1·76 | 2·01 | 2·14 | 2·34 | 2·52 | 2·73 | 4·61 | 4·93 | 5·22 | 5·57 | 5·82 | 6·35 |
| 19 | ·2711 | 1·82 | 2·07 | 2·20 | 2·39 | 2·57 | 2·79 | 4·65 | 4·97 | 5·26 | 5·61 | 5·86 | 6·38 |
| 20 | 0·2677 | 1·88 | 2·12 | 2·25 | 2·45 | 2·63 | 2·84 | 4·69 | 5·01 | 5·30 | 5·65 | 5·89 | 6·41 |

The unit is the population standard deviation.
Estimate of $\sigma$ = range (or mean range) in a sample of $n$ observations $\times 1/d_n$.

Table 23. *Probability integral of the range, W, in normal samples of size n*

| n / W | 2 | 3 | 4 | 5 | 6 | 7 | 8 | 9 | 10 |
|---|---|---|---|---|---|---|---|---|---|
| 0·00 | 0·0000 | 0·0000 | | | | | | | |
| 0·05 | ·0282 | ·0007 | 0·0000 | | | | | | |
| 0·10 | ·0564 | ·0028 | ·0001 | | | | | | |
| 0·15 | ·0845 | ·0062 | ·0004 | 0·0000 | | | | | |
| 0·20 | ·1125 | ·0110 | ·0010 | ·0001 | | | | | |
| 0·25 | 0·1403 | 0·0171 | 0·0020 | 0·0002 | 0·0000 | | | | |
| 0·30 | ·1680 | ·0245 | ·0034 | ·0004 | ·0001 | | | | |
| 0·35 | ·1955 | ·0332 | ·0053 | ·0008 | ·0001 | | | | |
| 0·40 | ·2227 | ·0431 | ·0079 | ·0014 | ·0002 | 0·0000 | | | |
| 0·45 | ·2497 | ·0543 | ·0111 | ·0022 | ·0004 | ·0001 | | | |
| 0·50 | 0·2763 | 0·0666 | 0·0152 | 0·0033 | 0·0007 | 0·0002 | 0·0000 | | |
| 0·55 | ·3027 | ·0800 | ·0200 | ·0048 | ·0011 | ·0003 | ·0001 | | |
| 0·60 | ·3286 | ·0944 | ·0257 | ·0068 | ·0017 | ·0004 | ·0001 | 0·0000 | |
| 0·65 | ·3542 | ·1099 | ·0322 | ·0092 | ·0026 | ·0007 | ·0002 | ·0001 | |
| 0·70 | ·3794 | ·1263 | ·0398 | ·0121 | ·0036 | ·0011 | ·0003 | ·0001 | |
| 0·75 | 0·4041 | 0·1436 | 0·0483 | 0·0157 | 0·0050 | 0·0016 | 0·0005 | 0·0002 | 0·0000 |
| 0·80 | ·4284 | ·1616 | ·0578 | ·0200 | ·0068 | ·0023 | ·0008 | ·0002 | ·0001 |
| 0·85 | ·4522 | ·1805 | ·0682 | ·0250 | ·0090 | ·0032 | ·0011 | ·0004 | ·0001 |
| 0·90 | ·4755 | ·2000 | ·0797 | ·0308 | ·0117 | ·0044 | ·0016 | ·0006 | ·0002 |
| 0·95 | ·4983 | ·2201 | ·0922 | ·0375 | ·0150 | ·0059 | ·0023 | ·0009 | ·0003 |
| 1·00 | 0·5205 | 0·2407 | 0·1057 | 0·0450 | 0·0188 | 0·0078 | 0·0032 | 0·0013 | 0·0005 |
| 1·05 | ·5422 | ·2618 | ·1201 | ·0535 | ·0234 | ·0101 | ·0043 | ·0018 | ·0008 |
| 1·10 | ·5633 | ·2833 | ·1355 | ·0629 | ·0287 | ·0129 | ·0058 | ·0025 | ·0011 |
| 1·15 | ·5839 | ·3052 | ·1517 | ·0733 | ·0348 | ·0163 | ·0075 | ·0035 | ·0016 |
| 1·20 | ·6039 | ·3272 | ·1688 | ·0847 | ·0417 | ·0203 | ·0098 | ·0047 | ·0022 |
| 1·25 | 0·6232 | 0·3495 | 0·1867 | 0·0970 | 0·0495 | 0·0249 | 0·0125 | 0·0062 | 0·0030 |
| 1·30 | ·6420 | ·3719 | ·2054 | ·1104 | ·0583 | ·0304 | ·0157 | ·0080 | ·0041 |
| 1·35 | ·6602 | ·3943 | ·2248 | ·1247 | ·0680 | ·0366 | ·0195 | ·0103 | ·0054 |
| 1·40 | ·6778 | ·4168 | ·2448 | ·1400 | ·0787 | ·0437 | ·0240 | ·0131 | ·0071 |
| 1·45 | ·6948 | ·4392 | ·2654 | ·1562 | ·0904 | ·0516 | ·0292 | ·0164 | ·0092 |
| 1·50 | 0·7112 | 0·4614 | 0·2865 | 0·1733 | 0·1031 | 0·0606 | 0·0353 | 0·0204 | 0·0117 |
| 1·55 | ·7269 | ·4835 | ·3080 | ·1913 | ·1168 | ·0705 | ·0421 | ·0250 | ·0148 |
| 1·60 | ·7421 | ·5053 | ·3299 | ·2101 | ·1315 | ·0814 | ·0499 | ·0304 | ·0184 |
| 1·65 | ·7567 | ·5269 | ·3521 | ·2296 | ·1473 | ·0934 | ·0587 | ·0366 | ·0227 |
| 1·70 | ·7707 | ·5481 | ·3745 | ·2498 | ·1639 | ·1064 | ·0684 | ·0437 | ·0278 |
| 1·75 | 0·7841 | 0·5690 | 0·3970 | 0·2706 | 0·1815 | 0·1204 | 0·0792 | 0·0517 | 0·0336 |
| 1·80 | ·7969 | ·5894 | ·4197 | ·2920 | ·2000 | ·1355 | ·0910 | ·0607 | ·0403 |
| 1·85 | ·8092 | ·6094 | ·4423 | ·3138 | ·2193 | ·1516 | ·1039 | ·0707 | ·0479 |
| 1·90 | ·8209 | ·6290 | ·4649 | ·3361 | ·2394 | ·1686 | ·1178 | ·0818 | ·0565 |
| 1·95 | ·8321 | ·6480 | ·4874 | ·3587 | ·2602 | ·1867 | ·1329 | ·0939 | ·0661 |
| 2·00 | 0·8427 | 0·6665 | 0·5096 | 0·3816 | 0·2816 | 0·2056 | 0·1489 | 0·1072 | 0·0768 |
| 2·05 | ·8528 | ·6845 | ·5317 | ·4046 | ·3035 | ·2254 | ·1661 | ·1216 | ·0886 |
| 2·10 | ·8624 | ·7019 | ·5534 | ·4277 | ·3260 | ·2460 | ·1842 | ·1371 | ·1015 |
| 2·15 | ·8716 | ·7187 | ·5748 | ·4508 | ·3489 | ·2673 | ·2032 | ·1536 | ·1155 |
| 2·20 | ·8802 | ·7349 | ·5957 | ·4739 | ·3720 | ·2893 | ·2232 | ·1712 | ·1307 |
| 2·25 | 0·8884 | 0·7505 | 0·6163 | 0·4969 | 0·3955 | 0·3118 | 0·2440 | 0·1899 | 0·1470 |
| 2·30 | ·8961 | ·7655 | ·6363 | ·5196 | ·4190 | ·3348 | ·2656 | ·2095 | ·1645 |
| 2·35 | ·9034 | ·7799 | ·6559 | ·5421 | ·4427 | ·3582 | ·2878 | ·2300 | ·1829 |
| 2·40 | ·9103 | ·7937 | ·6748 | ·5643 | ·4663 | ·3820 | ·3107 | ·2514 | ·2025 |
| 2·45 | ·9168 | ·8069 | ·6932 | ·5861 | ·4899 | ·4059 | ·3341 | ·2735 | ·2229 |
| 2·50 | 0·9229 | 0·8195 | 0·7110 | 0·6075 | 0·5132 | 0·4300 | 0·3579 | 0·2963 | 0·2443 |

Table 23 (*continued*)

| W \ n | 11 | 12 | 13 | 14 | 15 | 16 | 17 | 18 | 19 | 20 |
|---|---|---|---|---|---|---|---|---|---|---|
| **0·85** | 0·0000 | | | | | | | | | |
| **0·90** | ·0001 | | | | | | | | | |
| **0·95** | ·0001 | 0·0000 | | | | | | | | |
| **1·00** | 0·0002 | 0·0001 | 0·0000 | | | | | | | |
| **1·05** | ·0003 | ·0001 | ·0001 | | | | | | | |
| **1·10** | ·0005 | ·0002 | ·0001 | 0·0000 | | | | | | |
| **1·15** | ·0007 | ·0003 | ·0001 | ·0001 | 0·0000 | | | | | |
| **1·20** | ·0010 | ·0005 | ·0002 | ·0001 | ·0001 | | | | | |
| **1·25** | 0·0015 | 0·0007 | 0·0004 | 0·0002 | 0·0001 | 0·0000 | | | | |
| **1·30** | ·0021 | ·0010 | ·0005 | ·0003 | ·0001 | ·0001 | 0·0000 | | | |
| **1·35** | ·0028 | ·0015 | ·0008 | ·0004 | ·0002 | ·0001 | ·0001 | | | |
| **1·40** | ·0038 | ·0021 | ·0011 | ·0006 | ·0003 | ·0002 | ·0001 | 0·0000 | | |
| **1·45** | ·0051 | ·0028 | ·0016 | ·0009 | ·0005 | ·0003 | ·0001 | ·0001 | 0·0000 | |
| **1·50** | 0·0067 | 0·0038 | 0·0022 | 0·0012 | 0·0007 | 0·0004 | 0·0002 | 0·0001 | 0·0001 | 0·0000 |
| **1·55** | ·0087 | ·0051 | ·0030 | ·0017 | ·0010 | ·0006 | ·0003 | ·0002 | ·0001 | ·0001 |
| **1·60** | ·0111 | ·0067 | ·0040 | ·0024 | ·0014 | ·0008 | ·0005 | ·0003 | ·0002 | ·0001 |
| **1·65** | ·0140 | ·0086 | ·0053 | ·0032 | ·0020 | ·0012 | ·0007 | ·0004 | ·0003 | ·0002 |
| **1·70** | ·0176 | ·0111 | ·0070 | ·0044 | ·0027 | ·0017 | ·0011 | ·0007 | ·0004 | ·0003 |
| **1·75** | 0·0217 | 0·0140 | 0·0090 | 0·0058 | 0·0037 | 0·0023 | 0·0015 | 0·0010 | 0·0006 | 0·0004 |
| **1·80** | ·0266 | ·0175 | ·0115 | ·0075 | ·0049 | ·0032 | ·0021 | ·0014 | ·0009 | ·0006 |
| **1·85** | ·0323 | ·0217 | ·0145 | ·0097 | ·0065 | ·0043 | ·0029 | ·0019 | ·0013 | ·0008 |
| **1·90** | ·0388 | ·0266 | ·0182 | ·0124 | ·0084 | ·0057 | ·0039 | ·0026 | ·0018 | ·0012 |
| **1·95** | ·0463 | ·0323 | ·0225 | ·0156 | ·0108 | ·0075 | ·0052 | ·0036 | ·0024 | ·0017 |
| **2·00** | 0·0548 | 0·0389 | 0·0276 | 0·0195 | 0·0137 | 0·0097 | 0·0068 | 0·0048 | 0·0033 | 0·0023 |
| **2·05** | ·0643 | ·0465 | ·0335 | ·0241 | ·0173 | ·0124 | ·0088 | ·0063 | ·0045 | ·0032 |
| **2·10** | ·0748 | ·0550 | ·0403 | ·0295 | ·0215 | ·0156 | ·0114 | ·0082 | ·0060 | ·0043 |
| **2·15** | ·0866 | ·0646 | ·0481 | ·0357 | ·0265 | ·0196 | ·0144 | ·0106 | ·0078 | ·0058 |
| **2·20** | ·0994 | ·0753 | ·0569 | ·0429 | ·0323 | ·0242 | ·0182 | ·0136 | ·0102 | ·0076 |
| **2·25** | 0·1134 | 0·0872 | 0·0669 | 0·0511 | 0·0390 | 0·0297 | 0·0226 | 0·0172 | 0·0130 | 0·0099 |
| **2·30** | ·1286 | ·1003 | ·0779 | ·0604 | ·0468 | ·0361 | ·0279 | ·0214 | ·0165 | ·0127 |
| **2·35** | ·1450 | ·1145 | ·0902 | ·0709 | ·0556 | ·0435 | ·0340 | ·0265 | ·0207 | ·0161 |
| **2·40** | ·1624 | ·1299 | ·1036 | ·0825 | ·0655 | ·0519 | ·0411 | ·0325 | ·0256 | ·0202 |
| **2·45** | ·1810 | ·1466 | ·1183 | ·0953 | ·0766 | ·0615 | ·0493 | ·0394 | ·0315 | ·0251 |
| **2·50** | 0·2007 | 0·1643 | 0·1342 | 0·1094 | 0·0890 | 0·0722 | 0·0585 | 0·0474 | 0·0383 | 0·0309 |

## Table 23. *Probability integral of the range (continued)*

| W \ n | 2 | 3 | 4 | 5 | 6 | 7 | 8 | 9 | 10 |
|---|---|---|---|---|---|---|---|---|---|
| 2·50 | 0·9229 | 0·8195 | 0·7110 | 0·6075 | 0·5132 | 0·4300 | 0·3579 | 0·2963 | 0·2443 |
| 2·55 | ·9286 | ·8315 | ·7282 | ·6283 | ·5364 | ·4541 | ·3820 | ·3198 | ·2665 |
| 2·60 | ·9340 | ·8429 | ·7448 | ·6487 | ·5592 | ·4782 | ·4064 | ·3437 | ·2894 |
| 2·65 | ·9390 | ·8537 | ·7607 | ·6685 | ·5816 | ·5022 | ·4310 | ·3680 | ·3130 |
| 2·70 | ·9438 | ·8640 | ·7759 | ·6877 | ·6036 | ·5259 | ·4555 | ·3927 | ·3372 |
| 2·75 | 0·9482 | 0·8737 | 0·7905 | 0·7063 | 0·6252 | 0·5494 | 0·4801 | 0·4175 | 0·3617 |
| 2·80 | ·9523 | ·8828 | ·8045 | ·7242 | ·6461 | ·5725 | ·5045 | ·4425 | ·3867 |
| 2·85 | ·9561 | ·8915 | ·8177 | ·7415 | ·6665 | ·5952 | ·5286 | ·4675 | ·4119 |
| 2·90 | ·9597 | ·8996 | ·8304 | ·7581 | ·6863 | ·6174 | ·5525 | ·4923 | ·4372 |
| 2·95 | ·9630 | ·9073 | ·8424 | ·7739 | ·7055 | ·6391 | ·5760 | ·5171 | ·4625 |
| 3·00 | 0·9661 | 0·9145 | 0·8537 | 0·7891 | 0·7239 | 0·6601 | 0·5991 | 0·5415 | 0·4878 |
| 3·05 | ·9690 | ·9212 | ·8645 | ·8036 | ·7416 | ·6806 | ·6216 | ·5656 | ·5129 |
| 3·10 | ·9716 | ·9275 | ·8746 | ·8174 | ·7587 | ·7003 | ·6436 | ·5892 | ·5378 |
| 3·15 | ·9741 | ·9334 | ·8842 | ·8305 | ·7750 | ·7194 | ·6649 | ·6124 | ·5623 |
| 3·20 | ·9763 | ·9388 | ·8931 | ·8429 | ·7905 | ·7377 | ·6856 | ·6350 | ·5864 |
| 3·25 | 0·9784 | 0·9439 | 0·9016 | 0·8546 | 0·8053 | 0·7553 | 0·7055 | 0·6569 | 0·6099 |
| 3·30 | ·9804 | ·9487 | ·9095 | ·8657 | ·8194 | ·7721 | ·7248 | ·6782 | ·6329 |
| 3·35 | ·9822 | ·9531 | ·9168 | ·8761 | ·8327 | ·7881 | ·7432 | ·6988 | ·6553 |
| 3·40 | ·9838 | ·9572 | ·9237 | ·8859 | ·8454 | ·8034 | ·7609 | ·7186 | ·6769 |
| 3·45 | ·9853 | ·9610 | ·9302 | ·8951 | ·8573 | ·8179 | ·7778 | ·7376 | ·6978 |
| 3·50 | 0·9867 | 0·9644 | 0·9361 | 0·9037 | 0·8685 | 0·8316 | 0·7938 | 0·7558 | 0·7180 |
| 3·55 | ·9879 | ·9677 | ·9417 | ·9117 | ·8790 | ·8446 | ·8091 | ·7732 | ·7373 |
| 3·60 | ·9891 | ·9706 | ·9468 | ·9192 | ·8889 | ·8568 | ·8236 | ·7898 | ·7558 |
| 3·65 | ·9901 | ·9734 | ·9516 | ·9261 | ·8981 | ·8683 | ·8372 | ·8055 | ·7735 |
| 3·70 | ·9911 | ·9759 | ·9560 | ·9326 | ·9067 | ·8790 | ·8501 | ·8204 | ·7903 |
| 3·75 | 0·9920 | 0·9782 | 0·9600 | 0·9386 | 0·9147 | 0·8891 | 0·8622 | 0·8345 | 0·8062 |
| 3·80 | ·9928 | ·9803 | ·9637 | ·9441 | ·9222 | ·8985 | ·8736 | ·8477 | ·8212 |
| 3·85 | ·9935 | ·9822 | ·9672 | ·9493 | ·9291 | ·9073 | ·8842 | ·8602 | ·8355 |
| 3·90 | ·9942 | ·9840 | ·9703 | ·9540 | ·9355 | ·9155 | ·8941 | ·8718 | ·8488 |
| 3·95 | ·9948 | ·9856 | ·9732 | ·9583 | ·9415 | ·9230 | ·9034 | ·8827 | ·8614 |
| 4·00 | 0·9953 | 0·9870 | 0·9758 | 0·9623 | 0·9469 | 0·9300 | 0·9120 | 0·8929 | 0·8731 |
| 4·05 | ·9958 | ·9883 | ·9782 | ·9660 | ·9520 | ·9365 | ·9199 | ·9024 | ·8841 |
| 4·10 | ·9963 | ·9895 | ·9804 | ·9693 | ·9566 | ·9425 | ·9273 | ·9112 | ·8943 |
| 4·15 | ·9967 | ·9906 | ·9824 | ·9724 | ·9608 | ·9480 | ·9341 | ·9193 | ·9038 |
| 4·20 | ·9970 | ·9916 | ·9842 | ·9752 | ·9647 | ·9530 | ·9404 | ·9268 | ·9126 |
| 4·25 | 0·9973 | 0·9925 | 0·9859 | 0·9777 | 0·9682 | 0·9576 | 0·9461 | 0·9338 | 0·9208 |
| 4·30 | ·9976 | ·9933 | ·9874 | ·9800 | ·9715 | ·9619 | ·9514 | ·9402 | ·9283 |
| 4·35 | ·9979 | ·9941 | ·9887 | ·9821 | ·9744 | ·9657 | ·9562 | ·9460 | ·9352 |
| 4·40 | ·9981 | ·9947 | ·9899 | ·9840 | ·9771 | ·9692 | ·9607 | ·9514 | ·9416 |
| 4·45 | ·9983 | ·9953 | ·9910 | ·9857 | ·9795 | ·9724 | ·9647 | ·9563 | ·9474 |
| 4·50 | 0·9985 | 0·9958 | 0·9920 | 0·9873 | 0·9817 | 0·9754 | 0·9684 | 0·9608 | 0·9527 |
| 4·55 | ·9987 | ·9963 | ·9929 | ·9887 | ·9837 | ·9780 | ·9717 | ·9649 | ·9576 |
| 4·60 | ·9989 | ·9967 | ·9937 | ·9899 | ·9855 | ·9804 | ·9747 | ·9686 | ·9620 |
| 4·65 | ·9990 | ·9971 | ·9944 | ·9911 | ·9871 | ·9825 | ·9775 | ·9719 | ·9660 |
| 4·70 | ·9991 | ·9974 | ·9951 | ·9921 | ·9885 | ·9845 | ·9799 | ·9750 | ·9696 |
| 4·75 | 0·9992 | 0·9977 | 0·9956 | 0·9930 | 0·9898 | 0·9862 | 0·9822 | 0·9777 | 0·9729 |
| 4·80 | ·9993 | ·9980 | ·9962 | ·9938 | ·9910 | ·9878 | ·9842 | ·9802 | ·9759 |
| 4·85 | ·9994 | ·9982 | ·9966 | ·9945 | ·9920 | ·9892 | ·9860 | ·9824 | ·9786 |
| 4·90 | ·9995 | ·9985 | ·9970 | ·9952 | ·9930 | ·9904 | ·9876 | ·9844 | ·9810 |
| 4·95 | ·9995 | ·9986 | ·9974 | ·9958 | ·9938 | ·9916 | ·9890 | ·9862 | ·9832 |
| 5·00 | 0·9996 | 0·9988 | 0·9977 | 0·9963 | 0·9945 | 0·9926 | 0·9903 | 0·9878 | 0·9851 |

Table 23 (*continued*)

| W \ n | 11 | 12 | 13 | 14 | 15 | 16 | 17 | 18 | 19 | 20 |
|---|---|---|---|---|---|---|---|---|---|---|
| 2·50 | 0·2007 | 0·1643 | 0·1342 | 0·1094 | 0·0890 | 0·0722 | 0·0585 | 0·0474 | 0·0383 | 0·0309 |
| 2·55 | ·2213 | ·1833 | ·1513 | ·1247 | ·1025 | ·0842 | ·0690 | ·0565 | ·0462 | ·0377 |
| 2·60 | ·2429 | ·2032 | ·1696 | ·1413 | ·1174 | ·0974 | ·0807 | ·0668 | ·0552 | ·0455 |
| 2·65 | ·2653 | ·2243 | ·1891 | ·1590 | ·1335 | ·1119 | ·0937 | ·0783 | ·0654 | ·0545 |
| 2·70 | ·2885 | ·2462 | ·2096 | ·1780 | ·1509 | ·1278 | ·1080 | ·0911 | ·0768 | ·0647 |
| 2·75 | 0·3124 | 0·2690 | 0·2311 | 0·1981 | 0·1696 | 0·1449 | 0·1236 | 0·1053 | 0·0896 | 0·0761 |
| 2·80 | ·3368 | ·2926 | ·2536 | ·2194 | ·1894 | ·1632 | ·1405 | ·1208 | ·1037 | ·0889 |
| 2·85 | ·3618 | ·3169 | ·2770 | ·2416 | ·2103 | ·1828 | ·1587 | ·1376 | ·1191 | ·1031 |
| 2·90 | ·3870 | ·3417 | ·3011 | ·2647 | ·2323 | ·2036 | ·1782 | ·1557 | ·1360 | ·1186 |
| 2·95 | ·4125 | ·3670 | ·3258 | ·2887 | ·2553 | ·2255 | ·1989 | ·1752 | ·1541 | ·1355 |
| 3·00 | 0·4382 | 0·3927 | 0·3511 | 0·3134 | 0·2792 | 0·2484 | 0·2207 | 0·1959 | 0·1736 | 0·1537 |
| 3·05 | ·4639 | ·4186 | ·3769 | ·3387 | ·3039 | ·2723 | ·2436 | ·2177 | ·1944 | ·1733 |
| 3·10 | ·4895 | ·4446 | ·4029 | ·3645 | ·3292 | ·2969 | ·2675 | ·2407 | ·2163 | ·1942 |
| 3·15 | ·5150 | ·4706 | ·4291 | ·3907 | ·3551 | ·3223 | ·2922 | ·2646 | ·2394 | ·2163 |
| 3·20 | ·5401 | ·4965 | ·4554 | ·4171 | ·3814 | ·3483 | ·3177 | ·2894 | ·2634 | ·2395 |
| 3·25 | 0·5649 | 0·5222 | 0·4817 | 0·4437 | 0·4080 | 0·3748 | 0·3438 | 0·3151 | 0·2884 | 0·2638 |
| 3·30 | ·5893 | ·5475 | ·5078 | ·4703 | ·4348 | ·4016 | ·3704 | ·3413 | ·3142 | ·2890 |
| 3·35 | ·6131 | ·5725 | ·5337 | ·4967 | ·4617 | ·4286 | ·3974 | ·3681 | ·3407 | ·3150 |
| 3·40 | ·6363 | ·5970 | ·5592 | ·5230 | ·4885 | ·4557 | ·4246 | ·3953 | ·3676 | ·3416 |
| 3·45 | ·6589 | ·6209 | ·5842 | ·5489 | ·5150 | ·4827 | ·4519 | ·4227 | ·3950 | ·3688 |
| 3·50 | 0·6807 | 0·6442 | 0·6087 | 0·5744 | 0·5413 | 0·5096 | 0·4792 | 0·4502 | 0·4226 | 0·3964 |
| 3·55 | ·7017 | ·6668 | ·6326 | ·5994 | ·5672 | ·5362 | ·5063 | ·4777 | ·4504 | ·4242 |
| 3·60 | ·7220 | ·6886 | ·6558 | ·6237 | ·5926 | ·5624 | ·5332 | ·5051 | ·4781 | ·4522 |
| 3·65 | ·7414 | ·7096 | ·6782 | ·6474 | ·6173 | ·5881 | ·5597 | ·5322 | ·5056 | ·4801 |
| 3·70 | ·7600 | ·7298 | ·6999 | ·6704 | ·6414 | ·6132 | ·5856 | ·5588 | ·5329 | ·5078 |
| 3·75 | 0·7776 | 0·7491 | 0·7206 | 0·6925 | 0·6648 | 0·6376 | 0·6110 | 0·5850 | 0·5598 | 0·5352 |
| 3·80 | ·7944 | ·7675 | ·7406 | ·7138 | ·6874 | ·6613 | ·6357 | ·6106 | ·5861 | ·5622 |
| 3·85 | ·8103 | ·7850 | ·7596 | ·7342 | ·7090 | ·6842 | ·6596 | ·6355 | ·6118 | ·5887 |
| 3·90 | ·8254 | ·8016 | ·7777 | ·7537 | ·7298 | ·7062 | ·6827 | ·6596 | ·6369 | ·6145 |
| 3·95 | ·8395 | ·8173 | ·7948 | ·7723 | ·7497 | ·7273 | ·7050 | ·6829 | ·6611 | ·6397 |
| 4·00 | 0·8528 | 0·8321 | 0·8111 | 0·7899 | 0·7686 | 0·7474 | 0·7263 | 0·7053 | 0·6845 | 0·6640 |
| 4·05 | ·8653 | ·8460 | ·8264 | ·8066 | ·7866 | ·7666 | ·7466 | ·7268 | ·7070 | ·6874 |
| 4·10 | ·8769 | ·8590 | ·8408 | ·8223 | ·8036 | ·7848 | ·7660 | ·7472 | ·7285 | ·7099 |
| 4·15 | ·8878 | ·8712 | ·8543 | ·8371 | ·8196 | ·8021 | ·7844 | ·7667 | ·7491 | ·7315 |
| 4·20 | ·8978 | ·8826 | ·8669 | ·8509 | ·8347 | ·8183 | ·8018 | ·7852 | ·7686 | ·7520 |
| 4·25 | 0·9072 | 0·8931 | 0·8787 | 0·8639 | 0·8488 | 0·8336 | 0·8182 | 0·8027 | 0·7871 | 0·7715 |
| 4·30 | ·9158 | ·9029 | ·8896 | ·8760 | ·8620 | ·8479 | ·8336 | ·8191 | ·8046 | ·7899 |
| 4·35 | ·9238 | ·9120 | ·8998 | ·8872 | ·8744 | ·8613 | ·8480 | ·8346 | ·8210 | ·8074 |
| 4·40 | ·9312 | ·9204 | ·9092 | ·8976 | ·8858 | ·8737 | ·8615 | ·8490 | ·8364 | ·8237 |
| 4·45 | ·9379 | ·9281 | ·9178 | ·9073 | ·8964 | ·8853 | ·8740 | ·8625 | ·8508 | ·8391 |
| 4·50 | 0·9441 | 0·9352 | 0·9258 | 0·9162 | 0·9062 | 0·8960 | 0·8856 | 0·8750 | 0·8643 | 0·8534 |
| 4·55 | ·9498 | ·9417 | ·9332 | ·9244 | ·9153 | ·9060 | ·8964 | ·8867 | ·8768 | ·8667 |
| 4·60 | ·9550 | ·9476 | ·9399 | ·9319 | ·9236 | ·9151 | ·9064 | ·8975 | ·8884 | ·8791 |
| 4·65 | ·9597 | ·9530 | ·9460 | ·9388 | ·9313 | ·9235 | ·9155 | ·9074 | ·8991 | ·8906 |
| 4·70 | ·9639 | ·9579 | ·9516 | ·9451 | ·9382 | ·9312 | ·9240 | ·9165 | ·9089 | ·9012 |
| 4·75 | 0·9678 | 0·9624 | 0·9567 | 0·9508 | 0·9446 | 0·9383 | 0·9317 | 0·9249 | 0·9180 | 0·9110 |
| 4·80 | ·9713 | ·9665 | ·9614 | ·9560 | ·9505 | ·9447 | ·9387 | ·9326 | ·9263 | ·9199 |
| 4·85 | ·9745 | ·9702 | ·9656 | ·9608 | ·9557 | ·9505 | ·9452 | ·9396 | ·9339 | ·9281 |
| 4·90 | ·9774 | ·9735 | ·9694 | ·9650 | ·9605 | ·9559 | ·9510 | ·9460 | ·9409 | ·9356 |
| 4·95 | ·9799 | ·9765 | ·9728 | ·9689 | ·9649 | ·9607 | ·9563 | ·9518 | ·9472 | ·9424 |
| 5·00 | 0·9822 | 0·9791 | 0·9759 | 0·9724 | 0·9688 | 0·9650 | 0·9611 | 0·9571 | 0·9529 | 0·9486 |

Table 23. *Probability integral of the range (continued)*

| $W$ \ $n$ | 2 | 3 | 4 | 5 | 6 | 7 | 8 | 9 | 10 |
|---|---|---|---|---|---|---|---|---|---|
| 5·00 | 0·9996 | 0·9988 | 0·9977 | 0·9963 | 0·9945 | 0·9926 | 0·9903 | 0·9878 | 0·9851 |
| 5·05 | ·9996 | ·9990 | ·9980 | ·9967 | ·9952 | ·9935 | ·9915 | ·9893 | ·9869 |
| 5·10 | ·9997 | ·9991 | ·9982 | ·9971 | ·9958 | ·9942 | ·9925 | ·9906 | ·9884 |
| 5·15 | ·9997 | ·9992 | ·9985 | ·9975 | ·9963 | ·9950 | ·9934 | ·9917 | ·9898 |
| 5·20 | ·9998 | ·9993 | ·9987 | ·9978 | ·9968 | ·9956 | ·9942 | ·9927 | ·9911 |
| 5·25 | 0·9998 | 0·9994 | 0·9988 | 0·9981 | 0·9972 | 0·9961 | 0·9949 | ·09936 | 0·9922 |
| 5·30 | ·9998 | ·9995 | ·9990 | ·9983 | ·9975 | ·9966 | ·9956 | ·9944 | ·9931 |
| 5·35 | ·9998 | ·9995 | ·9991 | ·9985 | ·9979 | ·9971 | ·9961 | ·9951 | ·9940 |
| 5·40 | ·9999 | ·9996 | ·9992 | ·9987 | ·9981 | ·9974 | ·9966 | ·9957 | ·9948 |
| 5·45 | ·9999 | ·9997 | ·9993 | ·9989 | ·9984 | ·9978 | ·9971 | ·9963 | ·9954 |
| 5·50 | 0·9999 | 0·9997 | 0·9994 | 0·9990 | 0·9986 | 0·9981 | 0·9974 | 0·9968 | 0·9960 |
| 5·55 | ·9999 | ·9997 | ·9995 | ·9992 | ·9988 | ·9983 | ·9978 | ·9972 | ·9965 |
| 5·60 | ·9999 | ·9998 | ·9996 | ·9993 | ·9989 | ·9985 | ·9981 | ·9976 | ·9970 |
| 5·65 | ·9999 | ·9998 | ·9996 | ·9994 | ·9991 | ·9987 | ·9983 | ·9979 | ·9974 |
| 5·70 | 0·9999 | ·9998 | ·9997 | ·9995 | ·9992 | ·9989 | ·9986 | ·9982 | ·9977 |
| 5·75 | 1·0000 | 0·9999 | 0·9997 | 0·9995 | 0·9993 | 0·9991 | 0·9988 | 0·9984 | 0·9980 |
| 5·80 | | ·9999 | ·9998 | ·9996 | ·9994 | ·9992 | ·9989 | ·9986 | ·9983 |
| 5·85 | | ·9999 | ·9998 | ·9997 | ·9995 | ·9993 | ·9991 | ·9988 | ·9985 |
| 5·90 | | ·9999 | ·9998 | ·9997 | ·9996 | ·9994 | ·9992 | ·9990 | ·9988 |
| 5·95 | | ·9999 | ·9998 | ·9997 | ·9996 | ·9995 | ·9993 | ·9991 | ·9989 |
| 6·00 | | 0·9999 | 0·9999 | 0·9998 | 0·9997 | 0·9996 | 0·9994 | 0·9993 | 0·9991 |
| 6·05 | | 0·9999 | ·9999 | ·9998 | ·9997 | ·9996 | ·9995 | ·9994 | ·9992 |
| 6·10 | | 1·0000 | ·9999 | ·9998 | ·9998 | ·9997 | ·9996 | ·9995 | ·9993 |
| 6·15 | | | ·9999 | ·9999 | ·9998 | ·9997 | ·9996 | ·9995 | ·9994 |
| 6·20 | | | ·9999 | ·9999 | ·9998 | ·9998 | ·9997 | ·9996 | ·9995 |
| 6·25 | | | 0·9999 | 0·9999 | 0·9999 | 0·9998 | 0·9997 | 0·9997 | 0·9996 |
| 6·30 | | | 1·0000 | ·9999 | ·9999 | ·9998 | ·9998 | ·9997 | ·9996 |
| 6·35 | | | | ·9999 | ·9999 | ·9999 | ·9998 | ·9998 | ·9997 |
| 6·40 | | | | ·9999 | ·9999 | ·9999 | ·9998 | ·9998 | ·9997 |
| 6·45 | | | | 0·9999 | ·9999 | ·9999 | ·9999 | ·9998 | ·9998 |
| 6·50 | | | | 1·0000 | 0·9999 | 0·9999 | 0·9999 | 0·9999 | 0·9998 |
| 6·55 | | | | | 0·9999 | ·9999 | ·9999 | ·9999 | ·9998 |
| 6·60 | | | | | 1·0000 | ·9999 | ·9999 | ·9999 | ·9999 |
| 6·65 | | | | | | 0·9999 | ·9999 | ·9999 | ·9999 |
| 6·70 | | | | | | 1·0000 | 0·9999 | ·9999 | ·9999 |
| 6·75 | | | | | | | 1·0000 | 0·9999 | 0·9999 |
| 6·80 | | | | | | | | 0·9999 | ·9999 |
| 6·85 | | | | | | | | 1·0000 | 0·9999 |
| 6·90 | | | | | | | | | 1·0000 |
| 6·95 | | | | | | | | | |
| 7·00 | | | | | | | | | |
| 7·05 | | | | | | | | | |
| 7·10 | | | | | | | | | |
| 7·15 | | | | | | | | | |
| 7·20 | | | | | | | | | |
| 7·25 | | | | | | | | | |

Table 23 (*continued*)

| W \ n | 11 | 12 | 13 | 14 | 15 | 16 | 17 | 18 | 19 | 20 |
|---|---|---|---|---|---|---|---|---|---|---|
| 5·00 | 0·9822 | 0·9791 | 0·9759 | 0·9724 | 0·9688 | 0·9650 | 0·9611 | 0·9571 | 0·9529 | 0·9486 |
| 5·05 | ·9843 | ·9816 | ·9786 | ·9756 | ·9723 | ·9690 | ·9655 | ·9618 | ·9581 | ·9543 |
| 5·10 | ·9862 | ·9837 | ·9811 | ·9784 | ·9755 | ·9725 | ·9694 | ·9661 | ·9628 | ·9593 |
| 5·15 | ·9878 | ·9856 | ·9833 | ·9809 | ·9783 | ·9757 | ·9729 | ·9700 | ·9670 | ·9639 |
| 5·20 | ·9893 | ·9874 | ·9853 | ·9832 | ·9809 | ·9785 | ·9760 | ·9735 | ·9708 | ·9681 |
| 5·25 | 0·9906 | 0·9889 | 0·9871 | 0·9852 | 0·9832 | 0·9811 | 0·9789 | 0·9766 | 0·9742 | 0·9718 |
| 5·30 | ·9917 | ·9903 | ·9887 | ·9870 | ·9852 | ·9833 | ·9814 | ·9794 | ·9773 | ·9751 |
| 5·35 | ·9928 | ·9915 | ·9901 | ·9886 | ·9870 | ·9854 | ·9836 | ·9819 | ·9800 | ·9781 |
| 5·40 | ·9937 | ·9925 | ·9913 | ·9900 | ·9886 | ·9872 | ·9856 | ·9841 | ·9824 | ·9807 |
| 5·45 | ·9945 | ·9935 | ·9924 | ·9913 | ·9900 | ·9888 | ·9874 | ·9860 | ·9846 | ·9831 |
| 5·50 | 0·9952 | 0·9943 | 0·9934 | 0·9924 | 0·9913 | 0·9902 | 0·9890 | 0·9878 | 0·9865 | 0·9852 |
| 5·55 | ·9958 | ·9951 | ·9942 | ·9933 | ·9924 | ·9914 | ·9904 | ·9893 | ·9882 | ·9870 |
| 5·60 | ·9964 | ·9957 | ·9950 | ·9942 | ·9934 | ·9925 | ·9916 | ·9907 | ·9897 | ·9887 |
| 5·65 | ·9969 | ·9963 | ·9956 | ·9950 | ·9943 | ·9935 | ·9927 | ·9919 | ·9910 | ·9901 |
| 5·70 | ·9973 | ·9968 | ·9962 | ·9956 | ·9950 | ·9944 | ·9937 | ·9930 | ·9922 | ·9914 |
| 5·75 | 0·9976 | 0·9972 | 0·9967 | 0·9962 | 0·9957 | 0·9951 | 0·9945 | 0·9939 | 0·9932 | 0·9925 |
| 5·80 | ·9980 | ·9976 | ·9972 | ·9967 | ·9963 | ·9958 | ·9952 | ·9947 | ·9941 | ·9935 |
| 5·85 | ·9982 | ·9979 | ·9976 | ·9972 | ·9968 | ·9963 | ·9959 | ·9954 | ·9949 | ·9944 |
| 5·90 | ·9985 | ·9982 | ·9979 | ·9976 | ·9972 | ·9968 | ·9964 | ·9960 | ·9956 | ·9952 |
| 5·95 | ·9987 | ·9985 | ·9982 | ·9979 | ·9976 | ·9973 | ·9969 | ·9966 | ·9962 | ·9958 |
| 6·00 | 0·9989 | 0·9987 | 0·9984 | 0·9982 | 0·9979 | 0·9977 | 0·9974 | 0·9971 | 0·9967 | 0·9964 |
| 6·05 | ·9990 | ·9989 | ·9987 | ·9985 | ·9982 | ·9980 | ·9977 | ·9975 | ·9972 | ·9969 |
| 6·10 | ·9992 | ·9990 | ·9989 | ·9987 | ·9985 | ·9983 | ·9981 | ·9978 | ·9976 | ·9973 |
| 6·15 | ·9993 | ·9992 | ·9990 | ·9989 | ·9987 | ·9985 | ·9983 | ·9981 | ·9979 | ·9977 |
| 6·20 | ·9994 | ·9993 | ·9992 | ·9990 | ·9989 | ·9987 | ·9986 | ·9984 | ·9982 | ·9980 |
| 6·25 | 0·9995 | 0·9994 | 0·9993 | 0·9992 | 0·9990 | 0·9989 | 0·9988 | 0·9986 | 0·9985 | 0·9983 |
| 6·30 | ·9996 | ·9995 | ·9994 | ·9993 | ·9992 | ·9991 | ·9990 | ·9988 | ·9987 | ·9986 |
| 6·35 | ·9996 | ·9996 | ·9995 | ·9994 | ·9993 | ·9992 | ·9991 | ·9990 | ·9989 | ·9988 |
| 6·40 | ·9997 | ·9996 | ·9996 | ·9995 | ·9994 | ·9993 | ·9992 | ·9992 | ·9991 | ·9990 |
| 6·45 | ·9997 | ·9997 | ·9996 | ·9996 | ·9995 | ·9994 | ·9994 | ·9993 | ·9992 | ·9991 |
| 6·50 | 0·9998 | 0·9997 | 0·9997 | 0·9996 | 0·9996 | 0·9995 | 0·9995 | 0·9994 | 0·9993 | 0·9993 |
| 6·55 | ·9998 | ·9998 | ·9997 | ·9997 | ·9996 | ·9996 | ·9995 | ·9995 | ·9994 | ·9994 |
| 6·60 | ·9998 | ·9998 | ·9998 | ·9997 | ·9997 | ·9997 | ·9996 | ·9996 | ·9995 | ·9995 |
| 6·65 | ·9999 | ·9998 | ·9998 | ·9998 | ·9997 | ·9997 | ·9997 | ·9996 | ·9996 | ·9995 |
| 6·70 | ·9999 | ·9999 | ·9998 | ·9998 | ·9998 | ·9998 | ·9997 | ·9997 | ·9997 | ·9996 |
| 6·75 | 0·9999 | 0·9999 | 0·9999 | 0·9998 | 0·9998 | 0·9998 | 0·9998 | 0·9997 | 0·9997 | 0·9997 |
| 6·80 | ·9999 | ·9999 | ·9999 | ·9999 | ·9998 | ·9998 | ·9998 | ·9998 | ·9998 | ·9997 |
| 6·85 | ·9999 | ·9999 | ·9999 | ·9999 | ·9999 | ·9999 | ·9998 | ·9998 | ·9998 | ·9998 |
| 6·90 | 0·9999 | ·9999 | ·9999 | ·9999 | ·9999 | ·9999 | ·9999 | ·9998 | ·9998 | ·9998 |
| 6·95 | 1·0000 | 0·9999 | ·9999 | ·9999 | ·9999 | ·9999 | ·9999 | ·9999 | ·9999 | ·9998 |
| 7·00 | | 1·0000 | 0·9999 | 0·9999 | 0·9999 | 0·9999 | 0·9999 | 0·9999 | 0·9999 | 0·9999 |
| 7·05 | | | 1·0000 | 0·9999 | ·9999 | ·9999 | ·9999 | ·9999 | ·9999 | ·9999 |
| 7·10 | | | | 1·0000 | 0·9999 | 0·9999 | ·9999 | ·9999 | ·9999 | ·9999 |
| 7·15 | | | | | 1·0000 | 0·9999 | 0·9999 | ·9999 | ·9999 | ·9999 |
| 7·20 | | | | | | 1·0000 | 1·0000 | 0·9999 | 0·9999 | ·9999 |
| 7·25 | | | | | | | | 1·0000 | 1·0000 | 0·9999 |
| 7·30 | | | | | | | | | | 1·0000 |

Table 24. *Percentage points of the extreme standardized deviate from population mean,*
$$(x_n - \mu)/\sigma \text{ or } (\mu - x_1)/\sigma$$

| n | Lower percentage points | | | | | | Upper percentage points | | | | | |
|---|---|---|---|---|---|---|---|---|---|---|---|---|
| | 0·1 | 0·5 | 1·0 | 2·5 | 5·0 | 10·0 | 10·0 | 5·0 | 2·5 | 1·0 | 0·5 | 0·1 |
| 1 | −3·090 | −2·576 | −2·326 | −1·960 | −1·645 | −1·282 | 1·282 | 1·645 | 1·960 | 2·326 | 2·576 | 3·090 |
| 2 | −1·858 | −1·471 | −1·282 | −1·002 | −0·760 | −0·478 | 1·632 | 1·955 | 2·239 | 2·575 | 2·807 | 3·290 |
| 3 | −1·282 | −0·950 | −0·788 | −0·546 | −0·336 | −0·090 | 1·818 | 2·121 | 2·391 | 2·712 | 2·935 | 3·403 |
| 4 | −0·924 | −0·625 | −0·478 | −0·259 | −0·068 | 0·157 | 1·943 | 2·234 | 2·494 | 2·806 | 3·023 | 3·481 |
| 5 | −0·671 | −0·395 | −0·258 | −0·055 | 0·124 | 0·334 | 2·036 | 2·319 | 2·572 | 2·877 | 3·090 | 3·540 |
| 6 | −0·478 | −0·218 | −0·090 | 0·102 | 0·271 | 0·471 | 2·111 | 2·386 | 2·635 | 2·934 | 3·143 | 3·588 |
| 7 | −0·325 | −0·077 | 0·045 | ·229 | ·390 | ·582 | 2·172 | 2·442 | 2·687 | 2·981 | 3·188 | 3·628 |
| 8 | −0·198 | 0·039 | ·157 | ·333 | ·489 | ·674 | 2·224 | 2·490 | 2·731 | 3·022 | 3·227 | 3·662 |
| 9 | −0·090 | ·138 | ·252 | ·423 | ·574 | ·753 | 2·269 | 2·531 | 2·769 | 3·057 | 3·260 | 3·692 |
| 10 | 0·003 | ·224 | ·334 | ·500 | ·647 | ·822 | 2·309 | 2·568 | 2·803 | 3·089 | 3·290 | 3·719 |
| 11 | 0·084 | 0·300 | 0·407 | 0·568 | 0·711 | 0·882 | 2·344 | 2·601 | 2·834 | 3·117 | 3·317 | 3·743 |
| 12 | ·157 | ·367 | ·471 | ·629 | ·769 | ·936 | 2·376 | 2·630 | 2·862 | 3·143 | 3·341 | 3·765 |
| 13 | ·222 | ·427 | ·529 | ·684 | ·821 | ·985 | 2·406 | 2·657 | 2·887 | 3·166 | 3·363 | 3·785 |
| 14 | ·281 | ·482 | ·582 | ·733 | ·868 | 1·029 | 2·432 | 2·682 | 2·910 | 3·187 | 3·383 | 3·803 |
| 15 | ·334 | ·531 | ·630 | ·779 | ·911 | 1·070 | 2·457 | 2·705 | 2·932 | 3·207 | 3·402 | 3·820 |
| 16 | 0·384 | 0·577 | 0·674 | 0·821 | 0·951 | 1·107 | 2·480 | 2·726 | 2·952 | 3·226 | 3·420 | 3·836 |
| 17 | ·429 | ·620 | ·715 | ·859 | ·988 | 1·142 | 2·502 | 2·746 | 2·970 | 3·243 | 3·436 | 3·851 |
| 18 | ·471 | ·659 | ·753 | ·895 | 1·022 | 1·175 | 2·522 | 2·765 | 2·988 | 3·259 | 3·452 | 3·865 |
| 19 | ·511 | ·696 | ·788 | ·929 | 1·054 | 1·205 | 2·541 | 2·783 | 3·004 | 3·275 | 3·466 | 3·878 |
| 20 | ·547 | ·730 | ·822 | ·960 | 1·084 | 1·233 | 2·559 | 2·799 | 3·020 | 3·289 | 3·480 | 3·890 |
| 21 | 0·582 | 0·762 | 0·853 | 0·990 | 1·113 | 1·260 | 2·576 | 2·815 | 3·034 | 3·303 | 3·493 | 3·902 |
| 22 | ·614 | ·793 | ·882 | 1·018 | 1·139 | 1·285 | 2·592 | 2·830 | 3·049 | 3·316 | 3·506 | 3·914 |
| 23 | ·645 | ·821 | ·910 | 1·044 | 1·164 | 1·309 | 2·607 | 2·844 | 3·062 | 3·328 | 3·517 | 3·924 |
| 24 | ·674 | ·848 | ·936 | 1·069 | 1·188 | 1·332 | 2·621 | 2·857 | 3·075 | 3·340 | 3·529 | 3·934 |
| 25 | ·702 | ·874 | ·961 | 1·093 | 1·211 | 1·353 | 2·635 | 2·870 | 3·087 | 3·351 | 3·539 | 3·944 |
| 26 | 0·728 | 0·899 | 0·985 | 1·116 | 1·233 | 1·374 | 2·648 | 2·883 | 3·098 | 3·362 | 3·550 | 3·954 |
| 27 | ·753 | ·922 | 1·008 | 1·137 | 1·253 | 1·393 | 2·661 | 2·895 | 3·110 | 3·373 | 3·560 | 3·963 |
| 28 | ·777 | ·945 | 1·029 | 1·158 | 1·273 | 1·412 | 2·673 | 2·906 | 3·120 | 3·383 | 3·569 | 3·971 |
| 29 | ·800 | ·966 | 1·050 | 1·178 | 1·292 | 1·430 | 2·685 | 2·917 | 3·130 | 3·392 | 3·578 | 3·980 |
| 30 | ·822 | ·987 | 1·070 | 1·197 | 1·310 | 1·447 | 2·696 | 2·928 | 3·141 | 3·402 | 3·587 | 3·988 |

Table 25. *Percentage points of the extreme standardized deviate from sample mean,*
$$(x_n - \bar{x})/\sigma \text{ or } (\bar{x} - x_1)/\sigma$$

| Size of sample n | Lower percentage points | | | | | | Upper percentage points | | | | | |
|---|---|---|---|---|---|---|---|---|---|---|---|---|
| | 0·1 | 0·5 | 1·0 | 2·5 | 5·0 | 10·0 | 10·0 | 5·0 | 2·5 | 1·0 | 0·5 | 0·1 |
| 3 | 0·03 | 0·06 | 0·09 | 0·14 | 0·20 | 0·29 | 1·50 | 1·74 | 1·95 | 2·22 | 2·40 | 2·78 |
| 4 | 0·09 | 0·16 | 0·20 | 0·27 | 0·35 | 0·45 | 1·70 | 1·94 | 2·16 | 2·43 | 2·62 | 3·01 |
| 5 | 0·16 | 0·25 | 0·30 | 0·38 | 0·47 | 0·58 | 1·83 | 2·08 | 2·30 | 2·57 | 2·76 | 3·17 |
| 6 | 0·23 | 0·33 | 0·38 | 0·48 | 0·56 | 0·68 | 1·94 | 2·18 | 2·41 | 2·68 | 2·87 | 3·28 |
| 7 | 0·30 | 0·40 | 0·46 | 0·56 | 0·65 | 0·76 | 2·02 | 2·27 | 2·49 | 2·76 | 2·95 | 3·36 |
| 8 | 0·36 | 0·47 | 0·53 | 0·62 | 0·72 | 0·84 | 2·09 | 2·33 | 2·56 | 2·83 | 3·02 | 3·43 |
| 9 | 0·41 | 0·53 | 0·59 | 0·69 | 0·78 | 0·90 | 2·15 | 2·39 | 2·61 | 2·88 | 3·07 | 3·48 |

**Table 26.** *Upper percentage points of the extreme studentized deviate from the sample mean $(x_n - \bar{x})/s_\nu$ or $(\bar{x} - x_1)/s_\nu$*

| | $\nu$ \ $n$ | 3 | 4 | 5 | 6 | 7 | 8 | 9 | 10 | 12 |
|---|---|---|---|---|---|---|---|---|---|---|
| 10% points | 10 | 1·68 | 1·92 | 2·09 | 2·23 | 2·33 | 2·42 | 2·50 | 2·56 | 2·68 |
| | 11 | 1·66 | 1·90 | 2·07 | 2·20 | 2·30 | 2·39 | 2·46 | 2·53 | 2·64 |
| | 12 | 1·65 | 1·88 | 2·05 | 2·17 | 2·28 | 2·36 | 2·44 | 2·50 | 2·61 |
| | 13 | 1·63 | 1·86 | 2·03 | 2·16 | 2·26 | 2·34 | 2·41 | 2·47 | 2·58 |
| | 14 | 1·62 | 1·85 | 2·01 | 2·14 | 2·24 | 2·32 | 2·39 | 2·45 | 2·56 |
| | 15 | 1·61 | 1·84 | 2·00 | 2·12 | 2·22 | 2·31 | 2·38 | 2·44 | 2·54 |
| | 16 | 1·61 | 1·83 | 1·99 | 2·11 | 2·21 | 2·29 | 2·36 | 2·42 | 2·52 |
| | 17 | 1·60 | 1·82 | 1·98 | 2·10 | 2·20 | 2·28 | 2·35 | 2·41 | 2·51 |
| | 18 | 1·59 | 1·82 | 1·97 | 2·09 | 2·19 | 2·27 | 2·34 | 2·39 | 2·49 |
| | 19 | 1·59 | 1·81 | 1·96 | 2·08 | 2·18 | 2·26 | 2·33 | 2·38 | 2·48 |
| | 20 | 1·58 | 1·80 | 1·96 | 2·08 | 2·17 | 2·25 | 2·32 | 2·37 | 2·47 |
| | 24 | 1·57 | 1·78 | 1·94 | 2·05 | 2·15 | 2·22 | 2·29 | 2·34 | 2·44 |
| | 30 | 1·55 | 1·77 | 1·92 | 2·03 | 2·12 | 2·20 | 2·26 | 2·32 | 2·41 |
| | 40 | 1·54 | 1·75 | 1·90 | 2·01 | 2·10 | 2·17 | 2·23 | 2·29 | 2·38 |
| | 60 | 1·52 | 1·73 | 1·87 | 1·98 | 2·07 | 2·14 | 2·20 | 2·26 | 2·35 |
| | 120 | 1·51 | 1·71 | 1·85 | 1·96 | 2·05 | 2·12 | 2·18 | 2·23 | 2·32 |
| | ∞ | 1·50 | 1·70 | 1·83 | 1·94 | 2·02 | 2·09 | 2·15 | 2·20 | 2·28 |
| 5% points | 5 | 2·37 | 2·71 | 2·95 | 3·15 | 3·30 | 3·43 | 3·54 | 3·64 | 3·80 |
| | 6 | 2·24 | 2·55 | 2·78 | 2·95 | 3·09 | 3·21 | 3·31 | 3·39 | 3·54 |
| | 7 | 2·15 | 2·45 | 2·66 | 2·82 | 2·95 | 3·06 | 3·15 | 3·23 | 3·37 |
| | 8 | 2·09 | 2·37 | 2·57 | 2·72 | 2·85 | 2·95 | 3·04 | 3·12 | 3·25 |
| | 9 | 2·04 | 2·32 | 2·51 | 2·65 | 2·78 | 2·87 | 2·96 | 3·03 | 3·15 |
| | 10 | 2·01 | 2·27 | 2·46 | 2·60 | 2·72 | 2·81 | 2·89 | 2·96 | 3·08 |
| | 11 | 1·98 | 2·24 | 2·42 | 2·56 | 2·67 | 2·76 | 2·84 | 2·91 | 3·03 |
| | 12 | 1·96 | 2·21 | 2·39 | 2·52 | 2·63 | 2·72 | 2·80 | 2·87 | 2·98 |
| | 13 | 1·94 | 2·19 | 2·36 | 2·50 | 2·60 | 2·69 | 2·76 | 2·83 | 2·94 |
| | 14 | 1·93 | 2·17 | 2·34 | 2·47 | 2·57 | 2·66 | 2·74 | 2·80 | 2·91 |
| | 15 | 1·91 | 2·15 | 2·32 | 2·45 | 2·55 | 2·64 | 2·71 | 2·77 | 2·88 |
| | 16 | 1·90 | 2·14 | 2·31 | 2·43 | 2·53 | 2·62 | 2·69 | 2·75 | 2·86 |
| | 17 | 1·89 | 2·13 | 2·29 | 2·42 | 2·52 | 2·60 | 2·67 | 2·73 | 2·84 |
| | 18 | 1·88 | 2·11 | 2·28 | 2·40 | 2·50 | 2·58 | 2·65 | 2·71 | 2·82 |
| | 19 | 1·87 | 2·11 | 2·27 | 2·39 | 2·49 | 2·57 | 2·64 | 2·70 | 2·80 |
| | 20 | 1·87 | 2·10 | 2·26 | 2·38 | 2·47 | 2·56 | 2·63 | 2·68 | 2·78 |
| | 24 | 1·84 | 2·07 | 2·23 | 2·34 | 2·44 | 2·52 | 2·58 | 2·64 | 2·74 |
| | 30 | 1·82 | 2·04 | 2·20 | 2·31 | 2·40 | 2·48 | 2·54 | 2·60 | 2·69 |
| | 40 | 1·80 | 2·02 | 2·17 | 2·28 | 2·37 | 2·44 | 2·50 | 2·56 | 2·65 |
| | 60 | 1·78 | 1·99 | 2·14 | 2·25 | 2·33 | 2·41 | 2·47 | 2·52 | 2·61 |
| | 120 | 1·76 | 1·96 | 2·11 | 2·22 | 2·30 | 2·37 | 2·43 | 2·48 | 2·57 |
| | ∞ | 1·74 | 1·94 | 2·08 | 2·18 | 2·27 | 2·33 | 2·39 | 2·44 | 2·52 |
| 2·5% points | 10 | 2·34 | 2·63 | 2·83 | 2·98 | 3·10 | 3·20 | 3·29 | 3·36 | 3·49 |
| | 11 | 2·30 | 2·58 | 2·77 | 2·92 | 3·03 | 3·13 | 3·22 | 3·29 | 3·41 |
| | 12 | 2·27 | 2·54 | 2·73 | 2·87 | 2·98 | 3·08 | 3·16 | 3·23 | 3·35 |
| | 13 | 2·24 | 2·51 | 2·69 | 2·83 | 2·94 | 3·03 | 3·11 | 3·18 | 3·29 |
| | 14 | 2·22 | 2·48 | 2·66 | 2·79 | 2·90 | 2·99 | 3·07 | 3·14 | 3·25 |
| | 15 | 2·20 | 2·45 | 2·63 | 2·76 | 2·87 | 2·96 | 3·04 | 3·11 | 3·21 |
| | 16 | 2·18 | 2·43 | 2·61 | 2·74 | 2·84 | 2·93 | 3·01 | 3·08 | 3·18 |
| | 17 | 2·17 | 2·42 | 2·59 | 2·72 | 2·82 | 2·91 | 2·98 | 3·05 | 3·15 |
| | 18 | 2·15 | 2·40 | 2·57 | 2·70 | 2·80 | 2·89 | 2·96 | 3·02 | 3·12 |
| | 19 | 2·14 | 2·39 | 2·56 | 2·68 | 2·78 | 2·87 | 2·94 | 3·00 | 3·10 |
| | 20 | 2·13 | 2·37 | 2·54 | 2·67 | 2·77 | 2·85 | 2·92 | 2·98 | 3·08 |
| | 24 | 2·10 | 2·34 | 2·50 | 2·62 | 2·72 | 2·80 | 2·87 | 2·93 | 3·02 |
| | 30 | 2·07 | 2·30 | 2·46 | 2·58 | 2·67 | 2·75 | 2·81 | 2·87 | 2·96 |
| | 40 | 2·04 | 2·27 | 2·42 | 2·53 | 2·62 | 2·70 | 2·76 | 2·82 | 2·91 |
| | 60 | 2·01 | 2·23 | 2·38 | 2·49 | 2·58 | 2·65 | 2·71 | 2·76 | 2·85 |
| | 120 | 1·98 | 2·20 | 2·34 | 2·45 | 2·53 | 2·60 | 2·66 | 2·71 | 2·79 |
| | ∞ | 1·95 | 2·16 | 2·30 | 2·41 | 2·49 | 2·56 | 2·61 | 2·66 | 2·74 |

| | $n$ | 3 | 4 | 5 | 6 | 7 | 8 | 9 | 10 | 12 |
|---|---|---|---|---|---|---|---|---|---|---|
| | $\nu$ | | | | | | | | | |
| 1% points | 5 | 3·65 | 4·11 | 4·45 | 4·70 | 4·93 | 5·11 | 5·26 | 5·39 | 5·62 |
| | 6 | 3·32 | 3·72 | 4·02 | 4·24 | 4·43 | 4·58 | 4·71 | 4·82 | 5·01 |
| | 7 | 3·11 | 3·48 | 3·74 | 3·94 | 4·11 | 4·25 | 4·37 | 4·46 | 4·63 |
| | 8 | 2·96 | 3·31 | 3·56 | 3·74 | 3·89 | 4·02 | 4·13 | 4·22 | 4·38 |
| | 9 | 2·86 | 3·19 | 3·41 | 3·59 | 3·73 | 3·86 | 3·95 | 4·04 | 4·19 |
| | 10 | 2·78 | 3·10 | 3·32 | 3·48 | 3·62 | 3·73 | 3·82 | 3·90 | 4·04 |
| | 11 | 2·72 | 3·02 | 3·24 | 3·39 | 3·52 | 3·63 | 3·72 | 3·79 | 3·93 |
| | 12 | 2·67 | 2·96 | 3·17 | 3·32 | 3·45 | 3·55 | 3·64 | 3·71 | 3·84 |
| | 13 | 2·63 | 2·92 | 3·12 | 3·27 | 3·38 | 3·48 | 3·57 | 3·64 | 3·76 |
| | 14 | 2·60 | 2·88 | 3·07 | 3·22 | 3·33 | 3·43 | 3·51 | 3·58 | 3·70 |
| | 15 | 2·57 | 2·84 | 3·03 | 3·17 | 3·29 | 3·38 | 3·46 | 3·53 | 3·65 |
| | 16 | 2·54 | 2·81 | 3·00 | 3·14 | 3·25 | 3·34 | 3·42 | 3·49 | 3·60 |
| | 17 | 2·52 | 2·79 | 2·97 | 3·11 | 3·22 | 3·31 | 3·38 | 3·45 | 3·56 |
| | 18 | 2·50 | 2·77 | 2·95 | 3·08 | 3·19 | 3·28 | 3·35 | 3·42 | 3·53 |
| | 19 | 2·49 | 2·75 | 2·93 | 3·06 | 3·16 | 3·25 | 3·33 | 3·39 | 3·50 |
| | 20 | 2·47 | 2·73 | 2·91 | 3·04 | 3·14 | 3·23 | 3·30 | 3·37 | 3·47 |
| | 24 | 2·42 | 2·68 | 2·84 | 2·97 | 3·07 | 3·16 | 3·23 | 3·29 | 3·38 |
| | 30 | 2·38 | 2·62 | 2·79 | 2·91 | 3·01 | 3·08 | 3·15 | 3·21 | 3·30 |
| | 40 | 2·34 | 2·57 | 2·73 | 2·85 | 2·94 | 3·02 | 3·08 | 3·13 | 3·22 |
| | 60 | 2·29 | 2·52 | 2·68 | 2·79 | 2·88 | 2·95 | 3·01 | 3·06 | 3·15 |
| | 120 | 2·25 | 2·48 | 2·62 | 2·73 | 2·82 | 2·89 | 2·95 | 3·00 | 3·08 |
| | $\infty$ | 2·22 | 2·43 | 2·57 | 2·68 | 2·76 | 2·83 | 2·88 | 2·93 | 3·01 |
| 0·5% points | 10 | 3·12 | 3·46 | 3·70 | 3·87 | 4·02 | 4·14 | 4·24 | 4·33 | 4·47 |
| | 11 | 3·04 | 3·37 | 3·59 | 3·76 | 3·90 | 4·01 | 4·11 | 4·19 | 4·33 |
| | 12 | 2·98 | 3·29 | 3·51 | 3·67 | 3·80 | 3·91 | 4·00 | 4·08 | 4·21 |
| | 13 | 2·93 | 3·23 | 3·44 | 3·60 | 3·72 | 3·83 | 3·92 | 3·99 | 4·12 |
| | 14 | 2·88 | 3·18 | 3·38 | 3·54 | 3·66 | 3·76 | 3·85 | 3·92 | 4·04 |
| | 15 | 2·84 | 3·13 | 3·33 | 3·48 | 3·60 | 3·70 | 3·78 | 3·86 | 3·98 |
| | 16 | 2·81 | 3·10 | 3·29 | 3·44 | 3·56 | 3·65 | 3·73 | 3·80 | 3·92 |
| | 17 | 2·78 | 3·07 | 3·26 | 3·40 | 3·52 | 3·61 | 3·68 | 3·75 | 3·86 |
| | 18 | 2·76 | 3·04 | 3·23 | 3·37 | 3·48 | 3·57 | 3·64 | 3·71 | 3·82 |
| | 19 | 2·74 | 3·01 | 3·20 | 3·34 | 3·45 | 3·54 | 3·61 | 3·68 | 3·79 |
| | 20 | 2·72 | 2·99 | 3·17 | 3·31 | 3·42 | 3·51 | 3·58 | 3·65 | 3·75 |
| | 24 | 2·66 | 2·92 | 3·10 | 3·23 | 3·33 | 3·42 | 3·49 | 3·55 | 3·65 |
| | 30 | 2·60 | 2·86 | 3·03 | 3·15 | 3·25 | 3·33 | 3·40 | 3·46 | 3·55 |
| | 40 | 2·55 | 2·79 | 2·96 | 3·08 | 3·17 | 3·25 | 3·31 | 3·37 | 3·46 |
| | 60 | 2·50 | 2·73 | 2·89 | 3·01 | 3·10 | 3·17 | 3·23 | 3·28 | 3·37 |
| | 120 | 2·45 | 2·67 | 2·83 | 2·94 | 3·02 | 3·09 | 3·15 | 3·20 | 3·28 |
| | $\infty$ | 2·40 | 2·62 | 2·76 | 2·87 | 2·95 | 3·02 | 3·07 | 3·12 | 3·20 |
| 0·1% points | 10 | 4·0 | 4·3 | 4·6 | 4·8 | 5·0 | 5·2 | 5·3 | 5·4 | 5·6 |
| | 11 | 3·8 | 4·2 | 4·5 | 4·7 | 4·8 | 5·0 | 5·1 | 5·2 | 5·3 |
| | 12 | 3·7 | 4·1 | 4·3 | 4·5 | 4·7 | 4·8 | 4·9 | 5·0 | 5·1 |
| | 13 | 3·6 | 4·0 | 4·2 | 4·4 | 4·5 | 4·6 | 4·7 | 4·8 | 5·0 |
| | 14 | 3·5 | 3·9 | 4·1 | 4·3 | 4·4 | 4·5 | 4·6 | 4·7 | 4·9 |
| | 15 | 3·5 | 3·8 | 4·0 | 4·2 | 4·3 | 4·4 | 4·5 | 4·6 | 4·8 |
| | 16 | 3·4 | 3·7 | 4·0 | 4·1 | 4·3 | 4·4 | 4·5 | 4·5 | 4·7 |
| | 17 | 3·4 | 3·7 | 3·9 | 4·1 | 4·2 | 4·3 | 4·4 | 4·5 | 4·6 |
| | 18 | 3·3 | 3·6 | 3·9 | 4·0 | 4·1 | 4·2 | 4·3 | 4·4 | 4·5 |
| | 19 | 3·3 | 3·6 | 3·8 | 4·0 | 4·1 | 4·2 | 4·3 | 4·4 | 4·5 |
| | 20 | 3·3 | 3·6 | 3·8 | 3·9 | 4·0 | 4·1 | 4·2 | 4·3 | 4·4 |
| | 24 | 3·2 | 3·5 | 3·7 | 3·8 | 3·9 | 4·0 | 4·1 | 4·2 | 4·3 |
| | 30 | 3·1 | 3·4 | 3·6 | 3·7 | 3·8 | 3·9 | 4·0 | 4·0 | 4·1 |
| | 40 | 3·0 | 3·3 | 3·5 | 3·6 | 3·7 | 3·7 | 3·8 | 3·9 | 4·0 |
| | 60 | 2·9 | 3·2 | 3·4 | 3·5 | 3·6 | 3·6 | 3·7 | 3·8 | 3·8 |
| | 120 | 2·9 | 3·1 | 3·3 | 3·4 | 3·5 | 3·5 | 3·6 | 3·6 | 3·7 |
| | $\infty$ | 2·8 | 3·0 | 3·2 | 3·3 | 3·4 | 3·4 | 3·5 | 3·5 | 3·6 |

Table 26a. *Percentage points of $(x_n - \bar{x})/S$ or $(\bar{x} - x_1)/S$. Upper 5% points*

| $\nu$ \ $n$ | 3 | 4 | 5 | 6 | 7 | 8 | 9 | 10 | 12 | 15 | 20 |
|---|---|---|---|---|---|---|---|---|---|---|---|
| 0 | 0·8154 | 0·844 | 0·836 | 0·815 | 0·791 | 0·768 | 0·746 | 0·725 | 0·689 | 0·644 | 0·586 |
| 1 | 0·789 | 0·800 | 0·789 | 0·771 | 0·752 | 0·733 | 0·714 | 0·697 | 0·666 | 0·626 | 0·574 |
| 2 | ·741 | ·752 | ·745 | ·732 | ·717 | ·701 | ·686 | ·672 | ·644 | ·609 | ·562 |
| 3 | ·692 | ·707 | ·705 | ·697 | ·686 | ·673 | ·661 | ·648 | ·625 | ·594 | ·550 |
| 4 | ·648 | ·668 | ·671 | ·666 | ·658 | ·648 | ·638 | ·627 | ·607 | ·579 | ·540 |
| 5 | ·610 | ·634 | ·640 | ·638 | ·633 | ·625 | ·617 | ·608 | ·591 | ·566 | ·530 |
| 6 | 0·577 | 0·604 | 0·613 | 0·614 | 0·610 | 0·604 | 0·598 | 0·591 | 0·575 | 0·553 | 0·520 |
| 7 | ·549 | ·578 | ·589 | ·591 | ·590 | ·586 | ·580 | ·574 | ·561 | ·541 | ·511 |
| 8 | ·524 | ·554 | ·567 | ·571 | ·571 | ·569 | ·564 | ·559 | ·548 | ·530 | ·502 |
| 9 | ·502 | ·533 | ·547 | ·553 | ·554 | ·553 | ·550 | ·550 | ·536 | ·520 | ·494 |
| 10 | ·483 | ·515 | ·530 | ·536 | ·539 | ·538 | ·536 | ·533 | ·524 | ·510 | ·486 |
| 12 | 0·450 | 0·482 | 0·499 | 0·507 | 0·511 | 0·512 | 0·511 | 0·509 | 0·503 | 0·492 | 0·472 |
| 15 | ·411 | ·443 | ·461 | ·471 | ·476 | ·479 | ·480 | ·479 | ·476 | ·468 | ·452 |
| 20 | ·363 | ·395 | ·413 | ·425 | ·431 | ·436 | ·438 | ·439 | ·439 | ·435 | ·424 |
| 24 | ·335 | ·366 | ·384 | ·396 | ·403 | ·408 | ·411 | ·413 | ·415 | ·413 | ·405 |
| 30 | ·303 | ·332 | ·350 | ·362 | ·370 | ·375 | ·379 | ·382 | ·385 | ·385 | ·381 |
| 40 | ·266 | ·292 | ·309 | ·321 | ·329 | ·335 | ·339 | ·342 | ·347 | ·349 | ·349 |
| 50 | ·239 | ·264 | ·280 | ·291 | ·299 | ·305 | ·310 | ·313 | ·318 | ·222 | ·323 |

*Upper 1% points*

| $\nu$ \ $n$ | 3 | 4 | 5 | 6 | 7 | 8 | 9 | 10 | 12 | 15 | 20 |
|---|---|---|---|---|---|---|---|---|---|---|---|
| 0 | 0·8165 | 0·8617 | 0·8739 | 0·8695 | 0·8566 | 0·8394 | 0·8211 | 0·8032 | 0·7687 | 0·7228 | 0·6614 |
| 1 | 0·8111 | 0·8431 | 0·8478 | 0·8400 | 0·8263 | 0·8104 | 0·7942 | 0·7780 | 0·7465 | 0·7048 | 0·6483 |
| 2 | ·7904 | ·8155 | ·8176 | ·8094 | ·7971 | ·7833 | ·7688 | ·7541 | ·7260 | ·6879 | ·6356 |
| 3 | ·7614 | ·7844 | ·7865 | ·7800 | ·7698 | ·7579 | ·7450 | ·7320 | ·7070 | ·6723 | ·6239 |
| 4 | ·7299 | ·7532 | ·7570 | ·7527 | ·7444 | ·7341 | ·7229 | ·7116 | ·6890 | ·6576 | ·6127 |
| 5 | ·6990 | ·7238 | ·7297 | ·7274 | ·7207 | ·7120 | ·7026 | ·6926 | ·6724 | ·6438 | ·6020 |
| 6 | 0·6703 | 0·6968 | 0·7045 | 0·7037 | 0·6987 | 0·6918 | 0·6837 | 0·6748 | 0·6548 | 0·6306 | 0·5917 |
| 7 | ·6442 | ·6720 | ·6812 | ·6819 | ·6786 | ·6729 | ·6659 | ·6581 | ·6422 | ·6182 | ·5822 |
| 8 | ·6204 | ·6491 | ·6597 | ·6620 | ·6599 | ·6554 | ·6495 | ·6428 | ·6286 | ·6066 | ·5727 |
| 9 | ·5986 | ·6282 | ·6401 | ·6436 | ·6424 | ·6389 | ·6341 | ·6284 | ·6156 | ·5956 | ·5638 |
| 10 | ·5788 | ·6091 | ·6219 | ·6263 | ·6263 | ·6237 | ·6198 | ·6148 | ·6031 | ·5851 | ·5556 |
| 12 | 0·5441 | 0·5723 | 0·5895 | 0·5956 | 0·5971 | 0·5962 | 0·5935 | 0·5899 | 0·5808 | 0·5654 | 0·5398 |
| 15 | ·5017 | ·5333 | ·5489 | ·5566 | ·5600 | ·5607 | ·5597 | ·5576 | ·5513 | ·5393 | ·5183 |
| 20 | ·4482 | ·4795 | ·4962 | ·5055 | ·5106 | ·5132 | ·5140 | ·5136 | ·5104 | ·5031 | ·4880 |
| 24 | ·4158 | ·4463 | ·4633 | ·4732 | ·4792 | ·4826 | ·4844 | ·4850 | ·4837 | ·4785 | ·4668 |
| 30 | ·3779 | ·4073 | ·4240 | ·4346 | ·4412 | ·4455 | ·4480 | ·4496 | ·4501 | ·4479 | ·4393 |
| 40 | ·3328 | ·3600 | ·3763 | ·3869 | ·3940 | ·3990 | ·4023 | ·4047 | ·4071 | ·4074 | ·4038 |
| 50 | ·3006 | ·3162 | ·3416 | ·3519 | ·3591 | ·3642 | ·3681 | ·3711 | ·3744 | ·3766 | ·3751 |

Note: $S^2 = \sum_{1}^{n}(x_i - \bar{x})^2 + \sum_{1}^{\nu+1}(y_i - \bar{y})^2$, with $y_i$ independent of $x_i$.

## Table 26b. *Percentage points of max* $|x_i - \bar{x}|/S$. *Upper 5 % points*

| $\nu$ \ $n$ | 3 | 4 | 5 | 6 | 7 | 8 | 9 | 10 | 12 | 15 | 20 |
|---|---|---|---|---|---|---|---|---|---|---|---|
| 0 | 0·8162 | 0·855 | 0·857 | 0·844 | 0·825 | 0·804 | 0·783 | 0·763 | 0·727 | 0·681 | 0·621 |
| 1 | 0·803 | 0·824 | 0·820 | 0·807 | 0·789 | 0·771 | 0·753 | 0·736 | 0·704 | 0·663 | 0·608 |
| 2 | ·769 | ·786 | ·782 | ·771 | ·757 | ·741 | ·726 | ·711 | ·683 | ·646 | ·596 |
| 3 | ·729 | ·747 | ·746 | ·738 | ·727 | ·714 | ·701 | ·688 | ·664 | ·630 | ·584 |
| 4 | ·690 | ·711 | ·713 | ·708 | ·670 | ·689 | ·678 | ·667 | ·646 | ·616 | ·573 |
| 5 | ·654 | ·678 | ·684 | ·681 | ·675 | ·667 | ·658 | ·648 | ·629 | ·602 | ·563 |
| 6 | 0·620 | 0·649 | 0·657 | 0·657 | 0·652 | 0·646 | 0·638 | 0·630 | 0·613 | 0·589 | 0·553 |
| 7 | ·590 | ·622 | ·633 | ·635 | ·632 | ·627 | ·621 | ·614 | ·599 | ·577 | ·544 |
| 8 | ·563 | ·598 | ·610 | ·614 | ·613 | ·609 | ·604 | ·598 | ·586 | ·566 | ·535 |
| 9 | ·541 | ·576 | ·590 | ·595 | ·595 | ·593 | ·589 | ·584 | ·573 | ·555 | ·526 |
| 10 | ·520 | ·556 | ·572 | ·578 | •579 | ·578 | ·575 | ·571 | ·561 | ·545 | ·518 |
| 12 | 0·484 | 0·522 | 0·539 | 0·547 | 0·550 | 0·550 | 0·549 | 0·546 | 0·539 | 0·525 | 0·502 |
| 15 | ·442 | ·480 | ·499 | ·509 | ·514 | ·516 | ·516 | ·514 | ·510 | ·500 | ·482 |
| 20 | ·390 | ·427 | ·447 | ·459 | ·466 | ·469 | ·471 | ·472 | ·471 | ·465 | ·452 |
| 24 | ·360 | ·395 | ·416 | ·428 | ·436 | ·440 | ·443 | ·444 | ·445 | ·442 | ·432 |
| 30 | ·325 | ·359 | ·379 | ·391 | ·399 | ·405 | ·408 | ·411 | ·413 | ·413 | ·407 |
| 40 | ·284 | ·315 | ·334 | ·346 | ·355 | ·361 | ·365 | ·368 | ·372 | ·375 | ·372 |
| 50 | ·255 | ·284 | ·302 | ·314 | ·323 | ·328 | ·333 | ·336 | ·341 | ·345 | ·345 |

## *Upper 1 % points*

| $\nu$ \ $n$ | 3 | 4 | 5 | 6 | 7 | 8 | 9 | 10 | 12 | 15 | 20 |
|---|---|---|---|---|---|---|---|---|---|---|---|
| 0 | 0·8165 | 0·864 | 0·881 | 0·882 | 0·874 | 0·860 | 0·843 | 0·827 | 0·794 | 0·750 | 0·688 |
| 1 | 0·814 | 0·851 | 0·862 | 0·858 | 0·847 | 0·833 | 0·819 | 0·804 | 0·773 | 0·732 | 0·674 |
| 2 | ·800 | ·830 | ·837 | ·831 | ·821 | ·808 | ·795 | ·781 | ·753 | ·715 | ·662 |
| 3 | ·778 | ·805 | ·809 | ·805 | ·796 | ·785 | ·772 | ·759 | ·735 | ·700 | ·651 |
| 4 | ·751 | ·777 | ·782 | ·779 | ·772 | ·762 | ·751 | ·740 | ·717 | ·686 | ·639 |
| 5 | ·724 | ·750 | ·757 | ·755 | ·749 | ·741 | ·731 | ·721 | ·701 | ·671 | ·628 |
| 6 | 0·698 | 0·725 | 0·733 | 0·733 | 0·728 | 0·721 | 0·713 | 0·704 | 0·685 | 0·658 | 0·617 |
| 7 | ·673 | ·702 | ·711 | ·712 | ·708 | ·703 | ·695 | ·687 | ·671 | ·646 | ·608 |
| 8 | ·651 | ·680 | ·690 | ·692 | ·690 | ·685 | ·679 | ·672 | ·657 | ·634 | ·599 |
| 9 | ·629 | ·659 | ·671 | ·674 | ·673 | ·669 | ·664 | ·657 | ·644 | ·623 | ·591 |
| 10 | ·609 | ·640 | ·653 | ·657 | ·657 | ·654 | ·649 | ·644 | ·632 | ·612 | ·581 |
| 12 | 0·573 | 0·607 | 0·621 | 0·626 | 0·628 | 0·626 | 0·623 | 0·619 | 0·609 | 0·593 | 0·565 |
| 15 | ·529 | ·564 | ·580 | ·587 | ·590 | ·590 | ·588 | ·586 | ·579 | ·566 | ·544 |
| 20 | ·473 | ·508 | ·525 | ·534 | ·539 | ·541 | ·542 | ·541 | ·537 | ·528 | ·512 |
| 24 | ·439 | ·473 | ·491 | ·501 | ·507 | ·510 | ·511 | ·511 | ·509 | ·503 | ·490 |
| 30 | ·399 | ·432 | ·450 | ·460 | ·467 | ·470 | ·473 | ·474 | ·474 | ·471 | ·462 |
| 40 | ·351 | ·382 | ·399 | ·410 | ·417 | ·422 | ·426 | ·427 | ·429 | ·429 | ·424 |
| 50 | ·317 | ·346 | ·363 | ·373 | ·381 | ·386 | ·389 | ·392 | ·395 | ·397 | ·394 |

Note: $S^2 = \sum\limits_{1}^{n}(x_i - \bar{x})^2 + \sum\limits_{1}^{\nu+1}(y_i - \bar{y})^2$, with $y_i$ independent of $x_i$.

## Table 27. *Mean range in normal samples of size n*

| n | 0 | 1 | 2 | 3 | 4 | 5 | 6 | 7 | 8 | 9 | n |
|---|---|---|---|---|---|---|---|---|---|---|---|
| 0 | — | — | 1·12838 | 1·69257 | 2·05875+ | 2·32593 | 2·53441 | 2·70436 | 2·84720 | 2·97003 | 0 |
| 10 | 3·07751 | 3·17287 | 3·25846 | 3·33598 | 3·40676 | 3·47183 | 3·53198 | 3·58788 | 3·64006 | 3·68896 | 10 |
| 20 | 3·73495+ | 3·77834 | 3·81938 | 3·85832 | 3·89535- | 3·93063 | 3·96432 | 3·99654 | 4·02741 | 4·05704 | 20 |
| 30 | 4·08552 | 4·11293 | 4·13934 | 4·16482 | 4·18943 | 4·21322 | 4·23625- | 4·25855+ | 4·28018 | 4·30117 | 30 |
| 40 | 4·32155 | 4·34135 | 4·36063 | 4·37938 | 4·39764 | 4·41544 | 4·43279 | 4·44972 | 4·46624 | 4·48238 | 40 |
| 50 | 4·49815- | 4·51356 | 4·52864 | 4·54339 | 4·55783 | 4·57197 | 4·58582 | 4·59939 | 4·61270 | 4·62575+ | 50 |
| 60 | 4·63856 | 4·65112 | 4·66346 | 4·67557 | 4·68747 | 4·69916 | 4·71065- | 4·72194 | 4·73305- | 4·74397 | 60 |
| 70 | 4·75472 | 4·76529 | 4·77570 | 4·78595+ | 4·79604 | 4·80598 | 4·81578 | 4·82543 | 4·83493 | 4·84431 | 70 |
| 80 | 4·85355- | 4·86266 | 4·87165- | 4·88051 | 4·88926 | 4·89789 | 4·90641 | 4·91481 | 4·92311 | 4·93131 | 80 |
| 90 | 4·93940 | 4·94739 | 4·95529 | 4·96309 | 4·97079 | 4·97841 | 4·98593 | 4·99337 | 5·00073 | 5·00800 | 90 |
| 100 | 5·01519 | 5·02230 | 5·02933 | 5·03628 | 5·04316 | 5·04997 | 5·05670 | 5·06337 | 5·06996 | 5·07649 | 100 |
| 110 | 5·08295- | 5·08934 | 5·09568 | 5·10195- | 5·10815+ | 5·11430 | 5·12039 | 5·12642 | 5·13239 | 5·13831 | 110 |
| 120 | 5·14417 | 5·14998 | 5·15573 | 5·16144 | 5·16709 | 5·17269 | 5·17824 | 5·18374 | 5·18919 | 5·19460 | 120 |
| 130 | 5·19996 | 5·20528 | 5·21055- | 5·21578 | 5·22096 | 5·22610 | 5·23120 | 5·23625+ | 5·24127 | 5·24624 | 130 |
| 140 | 5·25118 | 5·25608 | 5·26094 | 5·26576 | 5·27054 | 5·27529 | 5·28000 | 5·28468 | 5·28932 | 5·29392 | 140 |
| 150 | 5·29849 | 5·30303 | 5·30754 | 5·31201 | 5·31645- | 5·32086 | 5·32523 | 5·32958 | 5·33389 | 5·33818 | 150 |
| 160 | 5·34244 | 5·34666 | 5·35086 | 5·35503 | 5·35917 | 5·36328 | 5·36737 | 5·37142 | 5·37545+ | 5·37946 | 160 |
| 170 | 5·38344 | 5·38739 | 5·39132 | 5·39522 | 5·39910 | 5·40295+ | 5·40678 | 5·41059 | 5·41437 | 5·41812 | 170 |
| 180 | 5·42186 | 5·42557 | 5·42926 | 5·43293 | 5·43657 | 5·44019 | 5·44380 | 5·44738 | 5·45093 | 5·45447 | 180 |
| 190 | 5·45799 | 5·46149 | 5·46497 | 5·46842 | 5·47186 | 5·47528 | 5·47868 | 5·48206 | 5·48542 | 5·48876 | 190 |
| 200 | 5·49209 | 5·49539 | 5·49868 | 5·50195- | 5·50520 | 5·50843 | 5·51165+ | 5·51485+ | 5·51803 | 5·52120 | 200 |
| 210 | 5·52435- | 5·52748 | 5·53060 | 5·53370 | 5·53678 | 5·53985+ | 5·54291 | 5·54594 | 5·54897 | 5·55197 | 210 |
| 220 | 5·55497 | 5·55794 | 5·56091 | 5·56385+ | 5·56679 | 5·56971 | 5·57261 | 5·57550 | 5·57838 | 5·58124 | 220 |
| 230 | 5·58409 | 5·58692 | 5·58975- | 5·59255+ | 5·59535- | 5·59813 | 5·60090 | 5·60366 | 5·60640 | 5·60913 | 230 |
| 240 | 5·61185- | 5·61456 | 5·61725+ | 5·61993 | 5·62260 | 5·62526 | 5·62790 | 5·63054 | 5·63316 | 5·63577 | 240 |
| 250 | 5·63837 | 5·64096 | 5·64353 | 5·64610 | 5·64865+ | 5·65119 | 5·65373 | 5·65625- | 5·65876 | 5·66126 | 250 |
| 260 | 5·66375- | 5·66623 | 5·66869 | 5·67115+ | 5·67360 | 5·67604 | 5·67847 | 5·68088 | 5·68329 | 5·68569 | 260 |
| 270 | 5·68808 | 5·69046 | 5·69282 | 5·69518 | 5·69753 | 5·69987 | 5·70221 | 5·70453 | 5·70684 | 5·70914 | 270 |
| 280 | 5·71144 | 5·71372 | 5·71600 | 5·71827 | 5·72053 | 5·72278 | 5·72502 | 5·72725+ | 5·72948 | 5·73170 | 280 |
| 290 | 5·73390 | 5·73610 | 5·73829 | 5·74048 | 5·74265+ | 5·74482 | 5·74698 | 5·74913 | 5·75127 | 5·75341 | 290 |
| 300 | 5·75553 | 5·75765+ | 5·75977 | 5·76187 | 5·76397 | 5·76605+ | 5·76814 | 5·77021 | 5·77228 | 5·77434 | 300 |
| 310 | 5·77639 | 5·77843 | 5·78047 | 5·78250 | 5·78453 | 5·78654 | 5·78855+ | 5·79055+ | 5·79255+ | 5·79454 | 310 |
| 320 | 5·79652 | 5·79850 | 5·80046 | 5·80243 | 5·80438 | 5·80633 | 5·80827 | 5·81021 | 5·81214 | 5·81406 | 320 |
| 330 | 5·81598 | 5·81789 | 5·81979 | 5·82169 | 5·82358 | 5·82546 | 5·82734 | 5·82922 | 5·83108 | 5·83294 | 330 |
| 340 | 5·83480 | 5·83665- | 5·83849 | 5·84033 | 5·84216 | 5·84398 | 5·84580 | 5·84762 | 5·84942 | 5·85123 | 340 |
| 350 | 5·85302 | 5·85482 | 5·85660 | 5·85838 | 5·86016 | 5·86192 | 5·86369 | 5·86545- | 5·86720 | 5·86895- | 350 |
| 360 | 5·87069 | 5·87243 | 5·87416 | 5·87588 | 5·87761 | 5·87932 | 5·88103 | 5·88274 | 5·88444 | 5·88614 | 360 |
| 370 | 5·88783 | 5·88951 | 5·89119 | 5·89287 | 5·89454 | 5·89621 | 5·89787 | 5·89952 | 5·90118 | 5·90282 | 370 |
| 380 | 5·90447 | 5·90610 | 5·90774 | 5·90936 | 5·91099 | 5·91261 | 5·91422 | 5·91583 | 5·91744 | 5·91904 | 380 |
| 390 | 5·92063 | 5·92223 | 5·92381 | 5·92540 | 5·92697 | 5·92855- | 5·93012 | 5·93168 | 5·93325- | 5·93480 | 390 |
| 400 | 5·93636 | 5·93790 | 5·93945- | 5·94099 | 5·94253 | 5·94406 | 5·94558 | 5·94711 | 5·94863 | 5·95014 | 400 |
| 410 | 5·95166 | 5·95316 | 5·95467 | 5·95617 | 5·95766 | 5·95915+ | 5·96064 | 5·96212 | 5·96360 | 5·96508 | 410 |
| 420 | 5·96655+ | 5·96802 | 5·96949 | 5·97095- | 5·97240 | 5·97386 | 5·97531 | 5·97675+ | 5·97820 | 5·97963 | 420 |
| 430 | 5·98107 | 5·98250 | 5·98393 | 5·98535+ | 5·98677 | 5·98819 | 5·98960 | 5·99101 | 5·99242 | 5·99382 | 430 |
| 440 | 5·99522 | 5·99662 | 5·99801 | 5·99940 | 6·00079 | 6·00217 | 6·00355- | 6·00492 | 6·00630 | 6·00766 | 440 |
| 450 | 6·00903 | 6·01039 | 6·01175+ | 6·01311 | 6·01446 | 6·01581 | 6·01716 | 6·01850 | 6·01984 | 6·02117 | 450 |
| 460 | 6·02251 | 6·02384 | 6·02516 | 6·02649 | 6·02781 | 6·02913 | 6·03044 | 6·03175+ | 6·03306 | 6·03437 | 460 |
| 470 | 6·03567 | 6·03697 | 6·03826 | 6·03956 | 6·04085- | 6·04214 | 6·04342 | 6·04470 | 6·04598 | 6·04726 | 470 |
| 480 | 6·04553 | 6·04980 | 6·05107 | 6·05233 | 6·05359 | 6·05485+ | 6·05611 | 6·05736 | 6·05861 | 6·05986 | 480 |
| 490 | 6·06110 | 6·06234 | 6·06358 | 6·06482 | 6·06605+ | 6·06728 | 6·06851 | 6·06974 | 6·07096 | 6·07218 | 490 |

| n | 0 | 10 | 20 | 30 | 40 | 50 | 60 | 70 | 80 | 90 | n |
|---|---|---|---|---|---|---|---|---|---|---|---|
| 500 | 6·07340 | 6·08543 | 6·09721 | 6·10874 | 6·12004 | 6·13112 | 6·14198 | 6·15263 | 6·16308 | 6·17333 | 500 |
| 600 | 6·18340 | 6·19329 | 6·20301 | 6·21255+ | 6·22194 | 6·23116 | 6·24024 | 6·24916 | 6·25794 | 6·26659 | 600 |
| 700 | 6·27510 | 6·28347 | 6·29173 | 6·29985+ | 6·30786 | 6·31576 | 6·32353 | 6·33120 | 6·33877 | 6·34623 | 700 |
| 800 | 6·35358 | 6·36084 | 6·36800 | 6·37507 | 6·38205- | 6·38894 | 6·39574 | 6·40245+ | 6·40909 | 6·41564 | 800 |
| 900 | 6·42211 | 6·42851 | 6·43483 | 6·44108 | 6·44725+ | 6·45335+ | 6·45939 | 6·46536 | 6·47126 | 6·47710 | 900 |
| 1000 | 6·48287 | | | | | | | | | | 1000 |

The unit is the population standard deviation.

Table 28. *Mean positions of ranked normal deviates (normal order statistics)*

| $i$ \ $n$ | 2 | 3 | 4 | 5 | 6 | 7 | 8 | 9 | 10 | 11 | 12 |
|---|---|---|---|---|---|---|---|---|---|---|---|
| 1 | 0·564 | 0·846 | 1·029 | 1·163 | 1·267 | 1·352 | 1·424 | 1·485 | 1·539 | 1·586 | 1·629 |
| 2 | | ·000 | 0·297 | 0·495 | 0·642 | 0·757 | 0·852 | 0·932 | 1·001 | 1·062 | 1·116 |
| 3 | | | | ·000 | ·202 | ·353 | ·473 | ·572 | ·656 | 0·729 | 0·793 |
| 4 | | | | | | ·000 | ·153 | ·275 | ·376 | ·462 | ·537 |
| 5 | | | | | | | | 0·000 | 0·123 | 0·225 | 0·312 |
| 6 | | | | | | | | | | ·000 | ·103 |

| $i$ \ $n$ | 13 | 14 | 15 | 16 | 17 | 18 | 19 | 20 | 21 | 22 | 23 | 24 | 25 |
|---|---|---|---|---|---|---|---|---|---|---|---|---|---|
| 1 | 1·668 | 1·703 | 1·736 | 1·766 | 1·794 | 1·820 | 1·844 | 1·867 | 1·89 | 1·91 | 1·93 | 1·95 | 1·97 |
| 2 | 1·164 | 1·208 | 1·248 | 1·285 | 1·319 | 1·350 | 1·380 | 1·408 | 1·43 | 1·46 | 1·48 | 1·50 | 1·52 |
| 3 | 0·850 | 0·901 | 0·948 | 0·990 | 1·029 | 1·066 | 1·099 | 1·131 | 1·16 | 1·19 | 1·21 | 1·24 | 1·26 |
| 4 | ·603 | ·662 | ·715 | ·763 | 0·807 | 0·848 | 0·886 | 0·921 | 0·95 | 0·98 | 1·01 | 1·04 | 1·07 |
| 5 | 0·388 | 0·456 | 0·516 | 0·570 | 0·619 | 0·665 | 0·707 | 0·745 | 0·78 | 0·82 | 0·85 | 0·88 | 0·91 |
| 6 | ·190 | ·267 | ·335 | ·396 | ·451 | ·502 | ·548 | ·590 | ·63 | ·67 | ·70 | ·73 | ·76 |
| 7 | ·000 | ·088 | ·165 | ·234 | ·295 | ·351 | ·402 | ·448 | ·49 | ·53 | ·57 | ·60 | ·64 |
| 8 | | | ·000 | ·077 | ·146 | ·208 | ·264 | ·315 | ·36 | ·41 | ·45 | ·48 | ·52 |
| 9 | | | | | ·000 | ·069 | ·131 | ·187 | ·24 | ·29 | ·33 | ·37 | ·41 |
| 10 | | | | | | | 0·000 | 0·062 | 0·12 | 0·17 | 0·22 | 0·26 | 0·30 |
| 11 | | | | | | | | | ·00 | ·06 | ·11 | ·16 | ·20 |
| 12 | | | | | | | | | | | ·00 | ·05 | ·10 |
| 13 | | | | | | | | | | | | | ·00 |

| $i$ \ $n$ | 26 | 28 | 30 | 32 | 34 | 36 | 38 | 40 | 42 | 44 | 46 | 48 | 50 |
|---|---|---|---|---|---|---|---|---|---|---|---|---|---|
| 1 | 1·98 | 2·01 | 2·04 | 2·07 | 2·09 | 2·12 | 2·14 | 2·16 | 2·18 | 2·20 | 2·22 | 2·23 | 2·25 |
| 2 | 1·54 | 1·58 | 1·62 | 1·65 | 1·68 | 1·70 | 1·73 | 1·75 | 1·78 | 1·80 | 1·82 | 1·84 | 1·85 |
| 3 | 1·29 | 1·33 | 1·36 | 1·40 | 1·43 | 1·46 | 1·49 | 1·52 | 1·54 | 1·57 | 1·59 | 1·61 | 1·63 |
| 4 | 1·09 | 1·14 | 1·18 | 1·22 | 1·25 | 1·28 | 1·32 | 1·34 | 1·37 | 1·40 | 1·42 | 1·44 | 1·46 |
| 5 | 0·93 | 0·98 | 1·03 | 1·07 | 1·11 | 1·14 | 1·17 | 1·20 | 1·23 | 1·26 | 1·28 | 1·31 | 1·33 |
| 6 | ·79 | ·85 | 0·89 | 0·94 | 0·98 | 1·02 | 1·05 | 1·08 | 1·11 | 1·14 | 1·17 | 1·19 | 1·22 |
| 7 | ·67 | ·73 | ·78 | ·82 | ·87 | 0·91 | 0·94 | 0·98 | 1·01 | 1·04 | 1·07 | 1·09 | 1·12 |
| 8 | ·55 | ·61 | ·67 | ·72 | ·76 | ·81 | ·85 | ·88 | 0·91 | 0·95 | 0·98 | 1·00 | 1·03 |
| 9 | ·44 | ·51 | ·57 | ·62 | ·67 | ·71 | ·75 | ·79 | ·83 | ·86 | ·89 | 0·92 | 0·95 |
| 10 | 0·34 | 0·41 | 0·47 | 0·53 | 0·58 | 0·63 | 0·67 | 0·71 | 0·75 | 0·78 | 0·81 | 0·84 | 0·87 |
| 11 | ·24 | ·32 | ·38 | ·44 | ·50 | ·54 | ·59 | ·63 | ·67 | ·71 | ·74 | ·77 | ·80 |
| 12 | ·14 | ·22 | ·29 | ·36 | ·41 | ·47 | ·51 | ·56 | ·60 | ·64 | ·67 | ·70 | ·74 |
| 13 | ·05 | ·13 | ·21 | ·28 | ·34 | ·39 | ·44 | ·49 | ·53 | ·57 | ·60 | ·64 | ·67 |
| 14 | | ·04 | ·12 | ·20 | ·26 | ·32 | ·37 | ·42 | ·46 | ·50 | ·54 | ·58 | ·61 |
| 15 | | | 0·04 | 0·12 | 0·18 | 0·24 | 0·30 | 0·35 | 0·40 | 0·44 | 0·48 | 0·52 | 0·55 |
| 16 | | | | ·04 | ·11 | ·17 | ·23 | ·28 | ·33 | ·38 | ·42 | ·46 | ·49 |
| 17 | | | | | ·04 | ·10 | ·16 | ·22 | ·27 | ·32 | ·36 | ·40 | ·44 |
| 18 | | | | | | ·03 | ·10 | ·16 | ·21 | ·26 | ·30 | ·34 | ·38 |
| 19 | | | | | | | ·03 | ·09 | ·15 | ·20 | ·25 | ·29 | ·33 |
| 20 | | | | | | | | 0·03 | 0·09 | 0·14 | 0·19 | 0·24 | 0·28 |
| 21 | | | | | | | | | ·03 | ·09 | ·14 | ·18 | ·23 |
| 22 | | | | | | | | | | ·03 | ·08 | ·13 | ·18 |
| 23 | | | | | | | | | | | ·03 | ·08 | ·13 |
| 24 | | | | | | | | | | | | ·03 | ·07 |
| 25 | | | | | | | | | | | | | 0·03 |

The table gives the expectation $\xi(i\,|\,n)$ of the $i$th largest observation in a sample of $n$ normal deviates, the unit being the population standard deviation.

The columns for $n$ from 21 to 50 are taken from *Statistical Tables for Biological, Agricultural and Medical Research* (Fisher & Yates, 1963, Table XX) by permission of the authors and the publishers, Messrs Oliver and Boyd.

Table 29. *Percentage points of the studentized range, $q = (x_n - x_1)/s_\nu$. Upper 10% points*

| $\nu$ \ $n$ | 2 | 3 | 4 | 5 | 6 | 7 | 8 | 9 | 10 |
|---|---|---|---|---|---|---|---|---|---|
| 1 | 8·93 | 13·44 | 16·36 | 18·49 | 20·15 | 21·51 | 22·64 | 23·62 | 24·48 |
| 2 | 4·13 | 5·73 | 6·77 | 7·54 | 8·14 | 8·63 | 9·05 | 9·41 | 9·72 |
| 3 | 3·33 | 4·47 | 5·20 | 5·74 | 6·16 | 6·51 | 6·81 | 7·06 | 7·29 |
| 4 | 3·01 | 3·98 | 4·59 | 5·03 | 5·39 | 5·68 | 5·93 | 6·14 | 6·33 |
| 5 | 2·85 | 3·72 | 4·26 | 4·66 | 4·98 | 5·24 | 5·46 | 5·65 | 5·82 |
| 6 | 2·75 | 3·56 | 4·07 | 4·44 | 4·73 | 4·97 | 5·17 | 5·34 | 5·50 |
| 7 | 2·68 | 3·45 | 3·93 | 4·28 | 4·55 | 4·78 | 4·97 | 5·14 | 5·28 |
| 8 | 2·63 | 3·37 | 3·83 | 4·17 | 4·43 | 4·65 | 4·83 | 4·99 | 5·13 |
| 9 | 2·59 | 3·32 | 3·76 | 4·08 | 4·34 | 4·54 | 4·72 | 4·87 | 5·01 |
| 10 | 2·56 | 3·27 | 3·70 | 4·02 | 4·26 | 4·47 | 4·64 | 4·78 | 4·91 |
| 11 | 2·54 | 3·23 | 3·66 | 3·96 | 4·20 | 4·40 | 4·57 | 4·71 | 4·84 |
| 12 | 2·52 | 3·20 | 3·62 | 3·92 | 4·16 | 4·35 | 4·51 | 4·65 | 4·78 |
| 13 | 2·50 | 3·18 | 3·59 | 3·88 | 4·12 | 4·30 | 4·46 | 4·60 | 4·72 |
| 14 | 2·49 | 3·16 | 3·56 | 3·85 | 4·08 | 4·27 | 4·42 | 4·56 | 4·68 |
| 15 | 2·48 | 3·14 | 3·54 | 3·83 | 4·05 | 4·23 | 4·39 | 4·52 | 4·64 |
| 16 | 2·47 | 3·12 | 3·52 | 3·80 | 4·03 | 4·21 | 4·36 | 4·49 | 4·61 |
| 17 | 2·46 | 3·11 | 3·50 | 3·78 | 4·00 | 4·18 | 4·33 | 4·46 | 4·58 |
| 18 | 2·45 | 3·10 | 3·49 | 3·77 | 3·98 | 4·16 | 4·31 | 4·44 | 4·55 |
| 19 | 2·45 | 3·09 | 3·47 | 3·75 | 3·97 | 4·14 | 4·29 | 4·42 | 4·53 |
| 20 | 2·44 | 3·08 | 3·46 | 3·74 | 3·95 | 4·12 | 4·27 | 4·40 | 4·51 |
| 24 | 2·42 | 3·05 | 3·42 | 3·69 | 3·90 | 4·07 | 4·21 | 4·34 | 4·44 |
| 30 | 2·40 | 3·02 | 3·39 | 3·65 | 3·85 | 4·02 | 4·16 | 4·28 | 4·38 |
| 40 | 2·38 | 2·99 | 3·35 | 3·60 | 3·80 | 3·96 | 4·10 | 4·21 | 4·32 |
| 60 | 2·36 | 2·96 | 3·31 | 3·56 | 3·75 | 3·91 | 4·04 | 4·16 | 4·25 |
| 120 | 2·34 | 2·93 | 3·28 | 3·52 | 3·71 | 3·86 | 3·99 | 4·10 | 4·19 |
| $\infty$ | 2·33 | 2·90 | 3·24 | 3·48 | 3·66 | 3·81 | 3·93 | 4·04 | 4·13 |

| $\nu$ \ $n$ | 11 | 12 | 13 | 14 | 15 | 16 | 17 | 18 | 19 | 20 |
|---|---|---|---|---|---|---|---|---|---|---|
| 1 | 25·24 | 25·92 | 26·54 | 27·10 | 27·62 | 28·10 | 28·54 | 28·96 | 29·35 | 29·71 |
| 2 | 10·01 | 10·26 | 10·49 | 10·70 | 10·89 | 11·07 | 11·24 | 11·39 | 11·54 | 11·68 |
| 3 | 7·49 | 7·67 | 7·83 | 7·98 | 8·12 | 8·25 | 8·37 | 8·48 | 8·58 | 8·68 |
| 4 | 6·49 | 6·65 | 6·78 | 6·91 | 7·02 | 7·13 | 7·23 | 7·33 | 7·41 | 7·50 |
| 5 | 5·97 | 6·10 | 6·22 | 6·34 | 6·44 | 6·54 | 6·63 | 6·71 | 6·79 | 6·86 |
| 6 | 5·64 | 5·76 | 5·87 | 5·98 | 6·07 | 6·16 | 6·25 | 6·32 | 6·40 | 6·47 |
| 7 | 5·41 | 5·53 | 5·64 | 5·74 | 5·83 | 5·91 | 5·99 | 6·06 | 6·13 | 6·19 |
| 8 | 5·25 | 5·36 | 5·46 | 5·56 | 5·64 | 5·72 | 5·80 | 5·87 | 5·93 | 6·00 |
| 9 | 5·13 | 5·23 | 5·33 | 5·42 | 5·51 | 5·58 | 5·66 | 5·72 | 5·79 | 5·85 |
| 10 | 5·03 | 5·13 | 5·23 | 5·32 | 5·40 | 5·47 | 5·54 | 5·61 | 5·67 | 5·73 |
| 11 | 4·95 | 5·05 | 5·15 | 5·23 | 5·31 | 5·38 | 5·45 | 5·51 | 5·57 | 5·63 |
| 12 | 4·89 | 4·99 | 5·08 | 5·16 | 5·24 | 5·31 | 5·37 | 5·44 | 5·49 | 5·55 |
| 13 | 4·83 | 4·93 | 5·02 | 5·10 | 5·18 | 5·25 | 5·31 | 5·37 | 5·43 | 5·48 |
| 14 | 4·79 | 4·88 | 4·97 | 5·05 | 5·12 | 5·19 | 5·26 | 5·32 | 5·37 | 5·43 |
| 15 | 4·75 | 4·84 | 4·93 | 5·01 | 5·08 | 5·15 | 5·21 | 5·27 | 5·32 | 5·38 |
| 16 | 4·71 | 4·81 | 4·89 | 4·97 | 5·04 | 5·11 | 5·17 | 5·23 | 5·28 | 5·33 |
| 17 | 4·68 | 4·77 | 4·86 | 4·93 | 5·01 | 5·07 | 5·13 | 5·19 | 5·24 | 5·30 |
| 18 | 4·65 | 4·75 | 4·83 | 4·90 | 4·98 | 5·04 | 5·10 | 5·16 | 5·21 | 5·26 |
| 19 | 4·63 | 4·72 | 4·80 | 4·88 | 4·95 | 5·01 | 5·07 | 5·13 | 5·18 | 5·23 |
| 20 | 4·61 | 4·70 | 4·78 | 4·85 | 4·92 | 4·99 | 5·05 | 5·10 | 5·16 | 5·20 |
| 24 | 4·54 | 4·63 | 4·71 | 4·78 | 4·85 | 4·91 | 4·97 | 5·02 | 5·07 | 5·12 |
| 30 | 4·47 | 4·56 | 4·64 | 4·71 | 4·77 | 4·83 | 4·89 | 4·94 | 4·99 | 5·03 |
| 40 | 4·41 | 4·49 | 4·56 | 4·63 | 4·69 | 4·75 | 4·81 | 4·86 | 4·90 | 4·95 |
| 60 | 4·34 | 4·42 | 4·49 | 4·56 | 4·62 | 4·67 | 4·73 | 4·78 | 4·82 | 4·86 |
| 120 | 4·28 | 4·35 | 4·42 | 4·48 | 4·54 | 4·60 | 4·65 | 4·69 | 4·74 | 4·78 |
| $\infty$ | 4·21 | 4·28 | 4·35 | 4·41 | 4·47 | 4·52 | 4·57 | 4·61 | 4·65 | 4·69 |

$n$: size of sample from which range obtained. $\nu$: degrees of freedom of independent $s_\nu$.

Table 29 (continued). *Percentage points of the studentized range, $q = (x_n - x_1)/s_\nu$.*
Upper 5 % points

| $\nu$ \ $n$ | 2 | 3 | 4 | 5 | 6 | 7 | 8 | 9 | 10 |
|---|---|---|---|---|---|---|---|---|---|
| 1 | 17·97 | 26·98 | 32·82 | 37·08 | 40·41 | 43·12 | 45·40 | 47·36 | 49·07 |
| 2 | 6·08 | 8·33 | 9·80 | 10·88 | 11·74 | 12·44 | 13·03 | 13·54 | 13·99 |
| 3 | 4·50 | 5·91 | 6·82 | 7·50 | 8·04 | 8·48 | 8·85 | 9·18 | 9·46 |
| 4 | 3·93 | 5·04 | 5·76 | 6·29 | 6·71 | 7·05 | 7·35 | 7·60 | 7·83 |
| 5 | 3·64 | 4·60 | 5·22 | 5·67 | 6·03 | 6·33 | 6·58 | 6·80 | 6·99 |
| 6 | 3·46 | 4·34 | 4·90 | 5·30 | 5·63 | 5·90 | 6·12 | 6·32 | 6·49 |
| 7 | 3·34 | 4·16 | 4·68 | 5·06 | 5·36 | 5·61 | 5·82 | 6·00 | 6·16 |
| 8 | 3·26 | 4·04 | 4·53 | 4·89 | 5·17 | 5·40 | 5·60 | 5·77 | 5·92 |
| 9 | 3·20 | 3·95 | 4·41 | 4·76 | 5·02 | 5·24 | 5·43 | 5·59 | 5·74 |
| 10 | 3·15 | 3·88 | 4·33 | 4·65 | 4·91 | 5·12 | 5·30 | 5·46 | 5·60 |
| 11 | 3·11 | 3·82 | 4·26 | 4·57 | 4·82 | 5·03 | 5·20 | 5·35 | 5·49 |
| 12 | 3·08 | 3·77 | 4·20 | 4·51 | 4·75 | 4·95 | 5·12 | 5·27 | 5·39 |
| 13 | 3·06 | 3·73 | 4·15 | 4·45 | 4·69 | 4·88 | 5·05 | 5·19 | 5·32 |
| 14 | 3·03 | 3·70 | 4·11 | 4·41 | 4·64 | 4·83 | 4·99 | 5·13 | 5·25 |
| 15 | 3·01 | 3·67 | 4·08 | 4·37 | 4·59 | 4·78 | 4·94 | 5·08 | 5·20 |
| 16 | 3·00 | 3·65 | 4·05 | 4·33 | 4·56 | 4·74 | 4·90 | 5·03 | 5·15 |
| 17 | 2·98 | 3·63 | 4·02 | 4·30 | 4·52 | 4·70 | 4·86 | 4·99 | 5·11 |
| 18 | 2·97 | 3·61 | 4·00 | 4·28 | 4·49 | 4·67 | 4·82 | 4·96 | 5·07 |
| 19 | 2·96 | 3·59 | 3·98 | 4·25 | 4·47 | 4·65 | 4·79 | 4·92 | 5·04 |
| 20 | 2·95 | 3·58 | 3·96 | 4·23 | 4·45 | 4·62 | 4·77 | 4·90 | 5·01 |
| 24 | 2·92 | 3·53 | 3·90 | 4·17 | 4·37 | 4·54 | 4·68 | 4·81 | 4·92 |
| 30 | 2·89 | 3·49 | 3·85 | 4·10 | 4·30 | 4·46 | 4·60 | 4·72 | 4·82 |
| 40 | 2·86 | 3·44 | 3·79 | 4·04 | 4·23 | 4·39 | 4·52 | 4·63 | 4·73 |
| 60 | 2·83 | 3·40 | 3·74 | 3·98 | 4·16 | 4·31 | 4·44 | 4·55 | 4·65 |
| 120 | 2·80 | 3·36 | 3·68 | 3·92 | 4·10 | 4·24 | 4·36 | 4·47 | 4·56 |
| ∞ | 2·77 | 3·31 | 3·63 | 3·86 | 4·03 | 4·17 | 4·29 | 4·39 | 4·47 |

| $\nu$ \ $n$ | 11 | 12 | 13 | 14 | 15 | 16 | 17 | 18 | 19 | 20 |
|---|---|---|---|---|---|---|---|---|---|---|
| 1 | 50·59 | 51·96 | 53·20 | 54·33 | 55·36 | 56·32 | 57·22 | 58·04 | 58·83 | 59·56 |
| 2 | 14·39 | 14·75 | 15·08 | 15·38 | 15·65 | 15·91 | 16·14 | 16·37 | 16·57 | 16·77 |
| 3 | 9·72 | 9·95 | 10·15 | 10·35 | 10·52 | 10·69 | 10·84 | 10·98 | 11·11 | 11·24 |
| 4 | 8·03 | 8·21 | 8·37 | 8·52 | 8·66 | 8·79 | 8·91 | 9·03 | 9·13 | 9·23 |
| 5 | 7·17 | 7·32 | 7·47 | 7·60 | 7·72 | 7·83 | 7·93 | 8·03 | 8·12 | 8·21 |
| 6 | 6·65 | 6·79 | 6·92 | 7·03 | 7·14 | 7·24 | 7·34 | 7·43 | 7·51 | 7·59 |
| 7 | 6·30 | 6·43 | 6·55 | 6·66 | 6·76 | 6·85 | 6·94 | 7·02 | 7·10 | 7·17 |
| 8 | 6·05 | 6·18 | 6·29 | 6·39 | 6·48 | 6·57 | 6·65 | 6·73 | 6·80 | 6·87 |
| 9 | 5·87 | 5·98 | 6·09 | 6·19 | 6·28 | 6·36 | 6·44 | 6·51 | 6·58 | 6·64 |
| 10 | 5·72 | 5·83 | 5·93 | 6·03 | 6·11 | 6·19 | 6·27 | 6·34 | 6·40 | 6·47 |
| 11 | 5·61 | 5·71 | 5·81 | 5·90 | 5·98 | 6·06 | 6·13 | 6·20 | 6·27 | 6·33 |
| 12 | 5·51 | 5·61 | 5·71 | 5·80 | 5·88 | 5·95 | 6·02 | 6·09 | 6·15 | 6·21 |
| 13 | 5·43 | 5·53 | 5·63 | 5·71 | 5·79 | 5·86 | 5·93 | 5·99 | 6·05 | 6·11 |
| 14 | 5·36 | 5·46 | 5·55 | 5·64 | 5·71 | 5·79 | 5·85 | 5·91 | 5·97 | 6·03 |
| 15 | 5·31 | 5·40 | 5·49 | 5·57 | 5·65 | 5·72 | 5·78 | 5·85 | 5·90 | 5·96 |
| 16 | 5·26 | 5·35 | 5·44 | 5·52 | 5·59 | 5·66 | 5·73 | 5·79 | 5·84 | 5·90 |
| 17 | 5·21 | 5·31 | 5·39 | 5·47 | 5·54 | 5·61 | 5·67 | 5·73 | 5·79 | 5·84 |
| 18 | 5·17 | 5·27 | 5·35 | 5·43 | 5·50 | 5·57 | 5·63 | 5·69 | 5·74 | 5·79 |
| 19 | 5·14 | 5·23 | 5·31 | 5·39 | 5·46 | 5·53 | 5·59 | 5·65 | 5·70 | 5·75 |
| 20 | 5·11 | 5·20 | 5·28 | 5·36 | 5·43 | 5·49 | 5·55 | 5·61 | 5·66 | 5·71 |
| 24 | 5·01 | 5·10 | 5·18 | 5·25 | 5·32 | 5·38 | 5·44 | 5·49 | 5·55 | 5·59 |
| 30 | 4·92 | 5·00 | 5·08 | 5·15 | 5·21 | 5·27 | 5·33 | 5·38 | 5·43 | 5·47 |
| 40 | 4·82 | 4·90 | 4·98 | 5·04 | 5·11 | 5·16 | 5·22 | 5·27 | 5·31 | 5·36 |
| 60 | 4·73 | 4·81 | 4·88 | 4·94 | 5·00 | 5·06 | 5·11 | 5·15 | 5·20 | 5·24 |
| 120 | 4·64 | 4·71 | 4·78 | 4·84 | 4·90 | 4·95 | 5·00 | 5·04 | 5·09 | 5·13 |
| ∞ | 4·55 | 4·62 | 4·68 | 4·74 | 4·80 | 4·85 | 4·89 | 4·93 | 4·97 | 5·01 |

$n$: size of sample from which range obtained.   $\nu$: degrees of freedom of independent $s_\nu$.

Table 29 (*continued*). *Upper 1% points*

| $\nu$ \ $n$ | 2 | 3 | 4 | 5 | 6 | 7 | 8 | 9 | 10 |
|---|---|---|---|---|---|---|---|---|---|
| 1 | 90·03 | 135·0 | 164·3 | 185·6 | 202·2 | 215·8 | 227·2 | 237·0 | 245·6 |
| 2 | 14·04 | 19·02 | 22·29 | 24·72 | 26·63 | 28·20 | 29·53 | 30·68 | 31·69 |
| 3 | 8·26 | 10·62 | 12·17 | 13·33 | 14·24 | 15·00 | 15·64 | 16·20 | 16·69 |
| 4 | 6·51 | 8·12 | 9·17 | 9·96 | 10·58 | 11·10 | 11·55 | 11·93 | 12·27 |
| 5 | 5·70 | 6·98 | 7·80 | 8·42 | 8·91 | 9·32 | 9·67 | 9·97 | 10·24 |
| 6 | 5·24 | 6·33 | 7·03 | 7·56 | 7·97 | 8·32 | 8·61 | 8·87 | 9·10 |
| 7 | 4·95 | 5·92 | 6·54 | 7·01 | 7·37 | 7·68 | 7·94 | 8·17 | 8·37 |
| 8 | 4·75 | 5·64 | 6·20 | 6·62 | 6·96 | 7·24 | 7·47 | 7·68 | 7·86 |
| 9 | 4·60 | 5·43 | 5·96 | 6·35 | 6·66 | 6·91 | 7·13 | 7·33 | 7·49 |
| 10 | 4·48 | 5·27 | 5·77 | 6·14 | 6·43 | 6·67 | 6·87 | 7·05 | 7·21 |
| 11 | 4·39 | 5·15 | 5·62 | 5·97 | 6·25 | 6·48 | 6·67 | 6·84 | 6·99 |
| 12 | 4·32 | 5·05 | 5·50 | 5·84 | 6·10 | 6·32 | 6·51 | 6·67 | 6·81 |
| 13 | 4·26 | 4·96 | 5·40 | 5·73 | 5·98 | 6·19 | 6·37 | 6·53 | 6·67 |
| 14 | 4·21 | 4·89 | 5·32 | 5·63 | 5·88 | 6·08 | 6·26 | 6·41 | 6·54 |
| 15 | 4·17 | 4·84 | 5·25 | 5·56 | 5·80 | 5·99 | 6·16 | 6·31 | 6·44 |
| 16 | 4·13 | 4·79 | 5·19 | 5·49 | 5·72 | 5·92 | 6·08 | 6·22 | 6·35 |
| 17 | 4·10 | 4·74 | 5·14 | 5·43 | 5·66 | 5·85 | 6·01 | 6·15 | 6·27 |
| 18 | 4·07 | 4·70 | 5·09 | 5·38 | 5·60 | 5·79 | 5·94 | 6·08 | 6·20 |
| 19 | 4·05 | 4·67 | 5·05 | 5·33 | 5·55 | 5·73 | 5·89 | 6·02 | 6·14 |
| 20 | 4·02 | 4·64 | 5·02 | 5·29 | 5·51 | 5·69 | 5·84 | 5·97 | 6·09 |
| 24 | 3·96 | 4·55 | 4·91 | 5·17 | 5·37 | 5·54 | 5·69 | 5·81 | 5·92 |
| 30 | 3·89 | 4·45 | 4·80 | 5·05 | 5·24 | 5·40 | 5·54 | 5·65 | 5·76 |
| 40 | 3·82 | 4·37 | 4·70 | 4·93 | 5·11 | 5·26 | 5·39 | 5·50 | 5·60 |
| 60 | 3·76 | 4·28 | 4·59 | 4·82 | 4·99 | 5·13 | 5·25 | 5·36 | 5·45 |
| 120 | 3·70 | 4·20 | 4·50 | 4·71 | 4·87 | 5·01 | 5·12 | 5·21 | 5·30 |
| $\infty$ | 3·64 | 4·12 | 4·40 | 4·60 | 4·76 | 4·88 | 4·99 | 5·08 | 5·16 |

| $\nu$ \ $n$ | 11 | 12 | 13 | 14 | 15 | 16 | 17 | 18 | 19 | 20 |
|---|---|---|---|---|---|---|---|---|---|---|
| 1 | 253·2 | 260·0 | 266·2 | 271·8 | 277·0 | 281·8 | 286·3 | 290·4 | 294·3 | 298·0 |
| 2 | 32·59 | 33·40 | 34·13 | 34·81 | 35·43 | 36·00 | 36·53 | 37·03 | 37·50 | 37·95 |
| 3 | 17·13 | 17·53 | 17·89 | 18·22 | 18·52 | 18·81 | 19·07 | 19·32 | 19·55 | 19·77 |
| 4 | 12·57 | 12·84 | 13·09 | 13·32 | 13·53 | 13·73 | 13·91 | 14·08 | 14·24 | 14·40 |
| 5 | 10·48 | 10·70 | 10·89 | 11·08 | 11·24 | 11·40 | 11·55 | 11·68 | 11·81 | 11·93 |
| 6 | 9·30 | 9·48 | 9·65 | 9·81 | 9·95 | 10·08 | 10·21 | 10·32 | 10·43 | 10·54 |
| 7 | 8·55 | 8·71 | 8·86 | 9·00 | 9·12 | 9·24 | 9·35 | 9·46 | 9·55 | 9·65 |
| 8 | 8·03 | 8·18 | 8·31 | 8·44 | 8·55 | 8·66 | 8·76 | 8·85 | 8·94 | 9·03 |
| 9 | 7·65 | 7·78 | 7·91 | 8·03 | 8·13 | 8·23 | 8·33 | 8·41 | 8·49 | 8·57 |
| 10 | 7·36 | 7·49 | 7·60 | 7·71 | 7·81 | 7·91 | 7·99 | 8·08 | 8·15 | 8·23 |
| 11 | 7·13 | 7·25 | 7·36 | 7·46 | 7·56 | 7·65 | 7·73 | 7·81 | 7·88 | 7·95 |
| 12 | 6·94 | 7·06 | 7·17 | 7·26 | 7·36 | 7·44 | 7·52 | 7·59 | 7·66 | 7·73 |
| 13 | 6·79 | 6·90 | 7·01 | 7·10 | 7·19 | 7·27 | 7·35 | 7·42 | 7·48 | 7·55 |
| 14 | 6·66 | 6·77 | 6·87 | 6·96 | 7·05 | 7·13 | 7·20 | 7·27 | 7·33 | 7·39 |
| 15 | 6·55 | 6·66 | 6·76 | 6·84 | 6·93 | 7·00 | 7·07 | 7·14 | 7·20 | 7·26 |
| 16 | 6·46 | 6·56 | 6·66 | 6·74 | 6·82 | 6·90 | 6·97 | 7·03 | 7·09 | 7·15 |
| 17 | 6·38 | 6·48 | 6·57 | 6·66 | 6·73 | 6·81 | 6·87 | 6·94 | 7·00 | 7·05 |
| 18 | 6·31 | 6·41 | 6·50 | 6·58 | 6·65 | 6·73 | 6·79 | 6·85 | 6·91 | 6·97 |
| 19 | 6·25 | 6·34 | 6·43 | 6·51 | 6·58 | 6·65 | 6·72 | 6·78 | 6·84 | 6·89 |
| 20 | 6·19 | 6·28 | 6·37 | 6·45 | 6·52 | 6·59 | 6·65 | 6·71 | 6·77 | 6·82 |
| 24 | 6·02 | 6·11 | 6·19 | 6·26 | 6·33 | 6·39 | 6·45 | 6·51 | 6·56 | 6·61 |
| 30 | 5·85 | 5·93 | 6·01 | 6·08 | 6·14 | 6·20 | 6·26 | 6·31 | 6·36 | 6·41 |
| 40 | 5·69 | 5·76 | 5·83 | 5·90 | 5·96 | 6·02 | 6·07 | 6·12 | 6·16 | 6·21 |
| 60 | 5·53 | 5·60 | 5·67 | 5·73 | 5·78 | 5·84 | 5·89 | 5·93 | 5·97 | 6·01 |
| 120 | 5·37 | 5·44 | 5·50 | 5·56 | 5·61 | 5·66 | 5·71 | 5·75 | 5·79 | 5·83 |
| $\infty$ | 5·23 | 5·29 | 5·35 | 5·40 | 5·45 | 5·49 | 5·54 | 5·57 | 5·61 | 5·65 |

Table 29a. *Two-sample analogue of Student's test. Values of* $u = |\bar{x}_1 - \bar{x}_2|/(w_1 + w_2)$
*exceeded with probability* $\alpha$ *(for a single-tailed test* $\alpha$ *must be halved)*

| $n_1$ | $n_2$ | 0·10 | 0·05 | 0·02 | 0·01 | $n_1$ | $n_2$ | 0·10 | 0·05 | 0·02 | 0·01 |
|---|---|---|---|---|---|---|---|---|---|---|---|
| 2 | 2 | 1·161 | 1·714 | 2·776 | 3·958 | 4 | 16 | 0·175 | 0·213 | 0·263 | 0·299 |
|  | 3 | 0·693 | 0·915 | 1·255 | 1·557 |  | 17 | 0·172 | 0·210 | 0·258 | 0·293 |
|  | 4 | 0·556 | 0·732 | 1·002 | 1·242 |  | 18 | 0·169 | 0·206 | 0·253 | 0·288 |
|  | 5 | 0·478 | 0·619 | 0·827 | 1·008 |  | 19 | 0·166 | 0·203 | 0·249 | 0·283 |
|  |  |  |  |  |  |  | 20 | 0·164 | 0·200 | 0·246 | 0·279 |
|  | 6 | 0·429 | 0·549 | 0·721 | 0·865 |  |  |  |  |  |  |
|  | 7 | 0·396 | 0·502 | 0·652 | 0·776 | 5 | 5 | 0·247 | 0·307 | 0·387 | 0·450 |
|  | 8 | 0·372 | 0·469 | 0·603 | 0·713 |  | 6 | 0·224 | 0·277 | 0·347 | 0·402 |
|  | 9 | 0·353 | 0·443 | 0·567 | 0·666 |  | 7 | 0·208 | 0·256 | 0·319 | 0·368 |
|  | 10 | 0·338 | 0·423 | 0·538 | 0·630 |  | 8 | 0·195 | 0·240 | 0·299 | 0·343 |
|  |  |  |  |  |  |  | 9 | 0·186 | 0·228 | 0·282 | 0·323 |
|  | 11 | 0·326 | 0·407 | 0·515 | 0·601 |  | 10 | 0·178 | 0·218 | 0·270 | 0·309 |
|  | 12 | 0·316 | 0·393 | 0·496 | 0·557 |  |  |  |  |  |  |
|  | 13 | 0·307 | 0·382 | 0·480 | 0·557 |  | 11 | 0·172 | 0·210 | 0·260 | 0·296 |
|  | 14 | 0·300 | 0·372 | 0·467 | 0·541 |  | 12 | 0·167 | 0·204 | 0·251 | 0·286 |
|  | 15 | 0·294 | 0·363 | 0·455 | 0·526 |  | 13 | 0·162 | 0·198 | 0·244 | 0·277 |
|  |  |  |  |  |  |  | 14 | 0·158 | 0·193 | 0·237 | 0·270 |
|  | 16 | 0·287 | 0·356 | 0·445 | 0·513 |  | 15 | 0·155 | 0·189 | 0·232 | 0·263 |
|  | 17 | 0·282 | 0·349 | 0·436 | 0·502 |  |  |  |  |  |  |
|  | 18 | 0·278 | 0·343 | 0·428 | 0·492 |  | 16 | 0·152 | 0·185 | 0·227 | 0·257 |
|  | 19 | 0·274 | 0·338 | 0·420 | 0·483 |  | 17 | 0·149 | 0·182 | 0·222 | 0·252 |
|  | 20 | 0·270 | 0·333 | 0·414 | 0·475 |  | 18 | 0·147 | 0·179 | 0·218 | 0·248 |
|  |  |  |  |  |  |  | 19 | 0·144 | 0·176 | 0·215 | 0·244 |
| 3 | 3 | 0·487 | 0·635 | 0·860 | 1·050 |  | 20 | 0·142 | 0·173 | 0·212 | 0·240 |
|  | 4 | 0·398 | 0·511 | 0·663 | 0·814 |  |  |  |  |  |  |
|  | 5 | 0·339 | 0·429 | 0·556 | 0·660 | 6 | 6 | 0·203 | 0·250 | 0·312 | 0·359 |
|  |  |  |  |  |  |  | 7 | 0·188 | 0·240 | 0·287 | 0·329 |
|  | 6 | 0·311 | 0·391 | 0·501 | 0·590 |  | 8 | 0·177 | 0·217 | 0·268 | 0·307 |
|  | 7 | 0·288 | 0·360 | 0·458 | 0·536 |  | 9 | 0·168 | 0·206 | 0·254 | 0·289 |
|  | 8 | 0·271 | 0·338 | 0·427 | 0·498 |  | 10 | 0·161 | 0·197 | 0·242 | 0·276 |
|  | 9 | 0·258 | 0·321 | 0·404 | 0·469 |  |  |  |  |  |  |
|  | 10 | 0·248 | 0·307 | 0·385 | 0·446 |  | 11 | 0·155 | 0·189 | 0·233 | 0·265 |
|  |  |  |  |  |  |  | 12 | 0·150 | 0·183 | 0·225 | 0·255 |
|  | 11 | 0·240 | 0·296 | 0·370 | 0·427 |  | 13 | 0·146 | 0·178 | 0·218 | 0·247 |
|  | 12 | 0·232 | 0·287 | 0·358 | 0·412 |  | 14 | 0·142 | 0·173 | 0·212 | 0·241 |
|  | 13 | 0·226 | 0·279 | 0·347 | 0·399 |  | 15 | 0·139 | 0·169 | 0·207 | 0·235 |
|  | 14 | 0·221 | 0·272 | 0·338 | 0·388 |  |  |  |  |  |  |
|  | 15 | 0·216 | 0·266 | 0·330 | 0·378 |  | 16 | 0·136 | 0·166 | 0·203 | 0·229 |
|  |  |  |  |  |  |  | 17 | 0·134 | 0·163 | 0·199 | 0·225 |
|  | 16 | 0·212 | 0·261 | 0·323 | 0·370 |  | 18 | 0·131 | 0·160 | 0·195 | 0·221 |
|  | 17 | 0·209 | 0·256 | 0·317 | 0·362 |  | 19 | 0·129 | 0·157 | 0·192 | 0·217 |
|  | 18 | 0·205 | 0·252 | 0·311 | 0·356 |  | 20 | 0·128 | 0·155 | 0·189 | 0·214 |
|  | 19 | 0·202 | 0·248 | 0·306 | 0·350 |  |  |  |  |  |  |
|  | 20 | 0·200 | 0·245 | 0·302 | 0·344 | 7 | 7 | 0·174 | 0·213 | 0·263 | 0·301 |
| 4 | 4 | 0·322 | 0·407 | 0·526 | 0·620 |  | 8 | 0·163 | 0·200 | 0·246 | 0·281 |
|  | 5 | 0·282 | 0·353 | 0·450 | 0·528 |  | 9 | 0·155 | 0·189 | 0·233 | 0·265 |
|  |  |  |  |  |  |  | 10 | 0·148 | 0·181 | 0·222 | 0·252 |
|  | 6 | 0·256 | 0·319 | 0·403 | 0·469 |  |  |  |  |  |  |
|  | 7 | 0·237 | 0·294 | 0·370 | 0·429 |  | 11 | 0·143 | 0·174 | 0·213 | 0·242 |
|  | 8 | 0·224 | 0·276 | 0·346 | 0·399 |  | 12 | 0·138 | 0·168 | 0·206 | 0·233 |
|  | 9 | 0·213 | 0·263 | 0·327 | 0·377 |  | 13 | 0·134 | 0·163 | 0·199 | 0·226 |
|  | 10 | 0·204 | 0·252 | 0·313 | 0·359 |  | 14 | 0·131 | 0·159 | 0·194 | 0·220 |
|  |  |  |  |  |  |  | 15 | 0·128 | 0·155 | 0·189 | 0·214 |
|  | 11 | 0·197 | 0·242 | 0·301 | 0·345 |  |  |  |  |  |  |
|  | 12 | 0·191 | 0·235 | 0·291 | 0·333 |  | 16 | 0·125 | 0·152 | 0·185 | 0·209 |
|  | 13 | 0·186 | 0·228 | 0·282 | 0·322 |  | 17 | 0·123 | 0·149 | 0·181 | 0·205 |
|  | 14 | 0·182 | 0·223 | 0·275 | 0·314 |  | 18 | 0·121 | 0·146 | 0·178 | 0·201 |
|  | 15 | 0·178 | 0·218 | 0·268 | 0·306 |  | 19 | 0·119 | 0·144 | 0·175 | 0·198 |
|  |  |  |  |  |  |  | 20 | 0·117 | 0·142 | 0·172 | 0·195 |

| $n_1$ | $n_2$ | Probability ($\alpha$) 0·10 | 0·05 | 0·02 | 0·01 |
|---|---|---|---|---|---|
| 8 | 8 | 0·153 | 0·187 | 0·231 | 0·262 |
|  | 9 | 0·145 | 0·177 | 0·217 | 0·247 |
|  | 10 | 0·139 | 0·169 | 0·207 | 0·235 |
|  | 11 | 0·133 | 0·162 | 0·199 | 0·225 |
|  | 12 | 0·129 | 0·157 | 0·192 | 0·217 |
|  | 13 | 0·125 | 0·152 | 0·186 | 0·210 |
|  | 14 | 0·122 | 0·148 | 0·180 | 0·204 |
|  | 15 | 0·119 | 0·144 | 0·176 | 0·199 |
|  | 16 | 0·116 | 0·141 | 0·172 | 0·194 |
|  | 17 | 0·114 | 0·138 | 0·168 | 0·190 |
|  | 18 | 0·112 | 0·136 | 0·165 | 0·186 |
|  | 19 | 0·110 | 0·134 | 0·162 | 0·183 |
|  | 20 | 0·109 | 0·132 | 0·160 | 0·180 |
| 9 | 9 | 0·137 | 0·167 | 0·205 | 0·233 |
|  | 10 | 0·131 | 0·160 | 0·195 | 0·221 |
|  | 11 | 0·126 | 0·153 | 0·187 | 0·212 |
|  | 12 | 0·122 | 0·148 | 0·180 | 0·204 |
|  | 13 | 0·118 | 0·143 | 0·175 | 0·197 |
|  | 14 | 0·115 | 0·139 | 0·170 | 0·192 |
|  | 15 | 0·112 | 0·136 | 0·165 | 0·187 |
|  | 16 | 0·110 | 0·133 | 0·162 | 0·182 |
|  | 17 | 0·107 | 0·130 | 0·158 | 0·178 |
|  | 18 | 0·106 | 0·128 | 0·155 | 0·175 |
|  | 19 | 0·104 | 0·126 | 0·152 | 0·172 |
|  | 20 | 0·102 | 0·124 | 0·150 | 0·169 |
| 10 | 10 | 0·125 | 0·152 | 0·186 | 0·210 |
|  | 11 | 0·120 | 0·146 | 0·178 | 0·201 |
|  | 12 | 0·116 | 0·141 | 0·171 | 0·194 |
|  | 13 | 0·112 | 0·136 | 0·166 | 0·187 |
|  | 14 | 0·109 | 0·133 | 0·161 | 0·182 |
|  | 15 | 0·107 | 0·129 | 0·157 | 0·177 |
|  | 16 | 0·104 | 0·126 | 0·153 | 0·173 |
|  | 17 | 0·102 | 0·124 | 0·150 | 0·169 |
|  | 18 | 0·100 | 0·121 | 0·147 | 0·165 |
|  | 19 | 0·098 | 0·119 | 0·144 | 0·162 |
|  | 20 | 0·097 | 0·117 | 0·142 | 0·160 |
| 11 | 11 | 0·115 | 0·140 | 0·170 | 0·193 |
|  | 12 | 0·111 | 0·135 | 0·164 | 0·185 |
|  | 13 | 0·108 | 0·131 | 0·159 | 0·179 |
|  | 14 | 0·105 | 0·127 | 0·154 | 0·174 |
|  | 15 | 0·102 | 0·123 | 0·150 | 0·169 |
|  | 16 | 0·100 | 0·121 | 0·146 | 0·165 |
|  | 17 | 0·098 | 0·118 | 0·143 | 0·161 |
|  | 18 | 0·096 | 0·116 | 0·140 | 0·158 |
|  | 19 | 0·094 | 0·114 | 0·138 | 0·155 |
|  | 20 | 0·092 | 0·112 | 0·135 | 0·152 |

| $n_1$ | $n_2$ | Probability ($\alpha$) 0·10 | 0·05 | 0·02 | 0·01 |
|---|---|---|---|---|---|
| 12 | 12 | 0·107 | 0·130 | 0·158 | 0·178 |
|  | 13 | 0·104 | 0·126 | 0·153 | 0·172 |
|  | 14 | 0·101 | 0·122 | 0·148 | 0·167 |
|  | 15 | 0·098 | 0·119 | 0·144 | 0·162 |
|  | 16 | 0·096 | 0·116 | 0·140 | 0·158 |
|  | 17 | 0·094 | 0·113 | 0·137 | 0·154 |
|  | 18 | 0·092 | 0·111 | 0·134 | 0·151 |
|  | 19 | 0·090 | 0·109 | 0·132 | 0·149 |
|  | 20 | 0·089 | 0·107 | 0·130 | 0·146 |
| 13 | 13 | 0·100 | 0·121 | 0·147 | 0·166 |
|  | 14 | 0·097 | 0·118 | 0·143 | 0·161 |
|  | 15 | 0·095 | 0·115 | 0·139 | 0·156 |
|  | 16 | 0·092 | 0·112 | 0·135 | 0·152 |
|  | 17 | 0·090 | 0·109 | 0·132 | 0·149 |
|  | 18 | 0·089 | 0·107 | 0·130 | 0·146 |
|  | 19 | 0·087 | 0·105 | 0·127 | 0·143 |
|  | 20 | 0·086 | 0·103 | 0·125 | 0·140 |
| 14 | 14 | 0·094 | 0·114 | 0·138 | 0·156 |
|  | 15 | 0·092 | 0·111 | 0·135 | 0·151 |
|  | 16 | 0·090 | 0·108 | 0·131 | 0·147 |
|  | 17 | 0·088 | 0·106 | 0·128 | 0·144 |
|  | 18 | 0·086 | 0·104 | 0·125 | 0·141 |
|  | 19 | 0·084 | 0·102 | 0·123 | 0·138 |
|  | 20 | 0·083 | 0·101 | 0·121 | 0·135 |
| 15 | 15 | 0·089 | 0·108 | 0·131 | 0·147 |
|  | 16 | 0·087 | 0·105 | 0·127 | 0·143 |
|  | 17 | 0·085 | 0·103 | 0·124 | 0·140 |
|  | 18 | 0·083 | 0·101 | 0·122 | 0·137 |
|  | 19 | 0·082 | 0·099 | 0·119 | 0·134 |
|  | 20 | 0·080 | 0·097 | 0·117 | 0·131 |
| 16 | 16 | 0·085 | 0·103 | 0·124 | 0·139 |
|  | 17 | 0·083 | 0·100 | 0·121 | 0·136 |
|  | 18 | 0·081 | 0·098 | 0·118 | 0·133 |
|  | 19 | 0·080 | 0·096 | 0·116 | 0·130 |
|  | 20 | 0·078 | 0·094 | 0·114 | 0·128 |
| 17 | 17 | 0·081 | 0·098 | 0·118 | 0·132 |
|  | 18 | 0·079 | 0·096 | 0·115 | 0·130 |
|  | 19 | 0·078 | 0·094 | 0·113 | 0·127 |
|  | 20 | 0·076 | 0·092 | 0·111 | 0·124 |
| 18 | 18 | 0·077 | 0·093 | 0·113 | 0·126 |
|  | 19 | 0·076 | 0·092 | 0·110 | 0·124 |
|  | 20 | 0·074 | 0·090 | 0·108 | 0·121 |
| 19 | 19 | 0·074 | 0·090 | 0·108 | 0·121 |
|  | 20 | 0·073 | 0·088 | 0·106 | 0·119 |
| 20 | 20 | 0·071 | 0·086 | 0·104 | 0·116 |

$\bar{x}_1$, $\bar{x}_2$ are the means and $w_1$, $w_2$ the ranges in two independent samples containing $n_1$, $n_2$ observations, respectively.

Table 29*b*.  *Upper percentage points of the ratio of two independent ranges, $F' = w_1/w_2$*

Values of $\alpha$

| $n_2$ | $n_1$ | 0·500 | 0·250 | 0·100 | 0·050 | 0·025 | 0·010 | 0·005 | 0·001 |
|---|---|---|---|---|---|---|---|---|---|
| 2 | 2 | 1·000 | 2·414 | 6·314 | 12·71 | 25·45 | 63·66 | 127·3 | 636·6 |
|   | 3 | 1·653 | 3·698 | 9·501 | 19·07 | 38·19 | 95·49 | 191·0 | 955·0 |
|   | 4 | 2·063 | 4·523 | 11·57 | 23·21 | 46·45 | 116·1 | 232·3 | 1162 |
|   | 5 | 2·358 | 5·123 | 13·07 | 26·22 | 52·48 | 131·2 | 262·5 | 1312 |
|   | 6 | 2·587 | 5·591 | 14·25 | 28·57 | 57·18 | 143·0 | 286·0 | 1430 |
|   | 7 | 2·772 | 5·971 | 15·21 | 30·49 | 61·02 | 152·6 | 305·1 | 1526 |
|   | 8 | 2·927 | 6·291 | 16·01 | 32·10 | 64·24 | 160·6 | 321·3 | 1607 |
| 2 | 9 | 3·060 | 6·565 | 16·70 | 33·49 | 67·01 | 167·6 | 335·1 | 1676 |
|   | 10 | 3·176 | 6·805 | 17·31 | 34·70 | 69·44 | 173·6 | 347·3 | 1736 |
|   | 11 | 3·279 | 7·018 | 17·85 | 35·77 | 71·59 | 179·0 | 358·0 | 1790 |
|   | 12 | 3·371 | 7·209 | 18·33 | 36·74 | 73·52 | 183·8 | 367·7 | 1838 |
|   | 13 | 3·454 | 7·382 | 18·76 | 37·61 | 75·27 | 188·2 | 376·4 | 1882 |
|   | 14 | 3·530 | 7·540 | 19·16 | 38·41 | 76·87 | 192·2 | 384·4 | 1922 |
|   | 15 | 3·600 | 7·685 | 19·53 | 39·15 | 78·34 | 195·9 | 391·8 | 1959 |
| 3 | 2 | 0·6050 | 1·189 | 2·167 | 3·194 | 4·607 | 7·370 | 10·46 | 23·49 |
|   | 3 | 1·000 | 1·735 | 3·009 | 4·373 | 6·267 | 9·986 | 14·16 | 31·76 |
|   | 4 | 1·246 | 2·082 | 3·555 | 5·144 | 7·355 | 11·71 | 16·59 | 37·19 |
|   | 5 | 1·422 | 2·335 | 3·956 | 5·712 | 8·159 | 12·98 | 18·39 | 41·22 |
|   | 6 | 1·559 | 2·533 | 4·272 | 6·160 | 8·794 | 13·98 | 19·81 | 44·39 |
|   | 7 | 1·669 | 2·695 | 4·531 | 6·528 | 9·315 | 14·81 | 20·98 | 47·00 |
|   | 8 | 1·762 | 2·831 | 4·750 | 6·839 | 9·756 | 15·50 | 21·97 | 49·21 |
| 3 | 9 | 1·841 | 2·948 | 4·939 | 7·108 | 10·14 | 16·11 | 22·82 | 51·12 |
|   | 10 | 1·911 | 3·050 | 5·105 | 7·344 | 10·47 | 16·64 | 23·57 | 52·80 |
|   | 11 | 1·972 | 3·142 | 5·252 | 7·554 | 10·77 | 17·11 | 24·24 | 54·31 |
|   | 12 | 2·028 | 3·224 | 5·385 | 7·743 | 11·04 | 17·54 | 24·84 | 55·66 |
|   | 13 | 2·077 | 3·298 | 5·505 | 7·914 | 11·28 | 17·92 | 25·39 | 56·88 |
|   | 14 | 2·123 | 3·366 | 5·616 | 8·072 | 11·50 | 18·28 | 25·89 | 58·01 |
|   | 15 | 2·165 | 3·428 | 5·717 | 8·216 | 11·71 | 18·60 | 26·35 | 59·04 |
| 4 | 2 | 0·4847 | 0·9032 | 1·497 | 2·027 | 2·662 | 3·725 | 4·755 | 8·250 |
|   | 3 | ·8028 | 1·296 | 2·011 | 2·663 | 3·453 | 4·789 | 6·090 | 10·52 |
|   | 4 | 1·000 | 1·542 | 2·341 | 3·075 | 3·971 | 5·489 | 6·971 | 12·03 |
|   | 5 | 1·141 | 1·721 | 2·584 | 3·381 | 4·356 | 6·010 | 7·626 | 13·15 |
|   | 6 | 1·251 | 1·862 | 2·775 | 3·623 | 4·660 | 6·424 | 8·147 | 14·04 |
|   | 7 | 1·340 | 1·976 | 2·933 | 3·822 | 4·911 | 6·765 | 8·578 | 14·77 |
|   | 8 | 1·414 | 2·073 | 3·066 | 3·990 | 5·125 | 7·056 | 8·944 | 15·40 |
| 4 | 9 | 1·478 | 2·156 | 3·181 | 4·137 | 5·310 | 7·307 | 9·262 | 15·95 |
|   | 10 | 1·533 | 2·229 | 3·283 | 4·265 | 5·473 | 7·529 | 9·542 | 16·43 |
|   | 11 | 1·583 | 2·294 | 3·373 | 4·380 | 5·618 | 7·728 | 9·792 | 16·85 |
|   | 12 | 1·627 | 2·353 | 3·454 | 4·484 | 5·749 | 7·906 | 10·02 | 17·24 |
|   | 13 | 1·667 | 2·406 | 3·528 | 4·578 | 5·869 | 8·069 | 10·22 | 17·60 |
|   | 14 | 1·703 | 2·454 | 3·596 | 4·664 | 5·978 | 8·218 | 10·41 | 17·92 |
|   | 15 | 1·737 | 2·499 | 3·658 | 4·744 | 6·079 | 8·356 | 10·59 | 18·22 |
| 5 | 2 | 0·4240 | 0·7717 | 1·228 | 1·602 | 2·020 | 2·664 | 3·242 | 4·993 |
|   | 3 | ·7032 | 1·098 | 1·621 | 2·059 | 2·553 | 3·324 | 4·020 | 6·145 |
|   | 4 | ·8761 | 1·301 | 1·871 | 2·353 | 2·900 | 3·757 | 4·532 | 6·905 |
|   | 5 | 1·000 | 1·448 | 2·055 | 2·570 | 3·157 | 4·079 | 4·914 | 7·474 |
|   | 6 | 1·096 | 1·563 | 2·200 | 2·742 | 3·361 | 4·335 | 5·219 | 7·929 |
|   | 7 | 1·174 | 1·657 | 2·319 | 2·884 | 3·530 | 4·547 | 5·471 | 8·307 |
|   | 8 | 1·239 | 1·736 | 2·420 | 3·004 | 3·674 | 4·728 | 5·686 | 8·628 |

$w_1$, $w_2$ are the ranges in two independent samples containing $n_1$, $n_2$ observations, respectively.

Values of $\alpha$

| $n_2$ | $n_1$ | 0·500 | 0·250 | 0·100 | 0·050 | 0·025 | 0·010 | 0·005 | 0·001 |
|---|---|---|---|---|---|---|---|---|---|
| 5 | 9 | 1·295 | 1·805 | 2·507 | 3·109 | 3·798 | 4·885 | 5·874 | 8·907 |
| | 10 | 1·343 | 1·865 | 2·584 | 3·201 | 3·908 | 5·024 | 6·039 | 9·156 |
| | 11 | 1·387 | 1·918 | 2·653 | 3·283 | 4·007 | 5·149 | 6·187 | 9·378 |
| | 12 | 1·425 | 1·966 | 2·714 | 3·357 | 4·096 | 5·261 | 6·321 | 9·580 |
| | 13 | 1·460 | 2·010 | 2·771 | 3·425 | 4·176 | 5·363 | 6·443 | 9·764 |
| | 14 | 1·492 | 2·050 | 2·822 | 3·487 | 4·251 | 5·457 | 6·555 | 9·932 |
| | 15 | 1·522 | 2·086 | 2·870 | 3·544 | 4·319 | 5·544 | 6·659 | 10·09 |
| 6 | 2 | 0·3866 | 0·6944 | 1·080 | 1·381 | 1·704 | 2·176 | 2·580 | 3·720 |
| | 3 | ·6416 | ·9827 | 1·411 | 1·752 | 2·120 | 2·665 | 3·135 | 4·472 |
| | 4 | ·7995 | 1·161 | 1·620 | 1·988 | 2·388 | 2·983 | 3·498 | 4·967 |
| | 5 | ·9125 | 1·290 | 1·773 | 2·162 | 2·586 | 3·220 | 3·768 | 5·339 |
| | 6 | 1·000 | 1·391 | 1·894 | 2·300 | 2·744 | 3·409 | 3·985 | 5·636 |
| | 7 | 1·071 | 1·474 | 1·993 | 2·414 | 2·875 | 3·565 | 4·164 | 5·883 |
| | 8 | 1·130 | 1·543 | 2·077 | 2·510 | 2·986 | 3·699 | 4·317 | 6·093 |
| 6 | 9 | 1·181 | 1·603 | 2·150 | 2·594 | 3·082 | 3·815 | 4·451 | 6·277 |
| | 10 | 1·226 | 1·655 | 2·214 | 2·668 | 3·168 | 3·918 | 4·569 | 6·441 |
| | 11 | 1·265 | 1·702 | 2·271 | 2·734 | 3·244 | 4·010 | 4·675 | 6·588 |
| | 12 | 1·301 | 1·744 | 2·323 | 2·794 | 3·313 | 4·093 | 4·770 | 6·721 |
| | 13 | 1·333 | 1·783 | 2·370 | 2·849 | 3·376 | 4·169 | 4·858 | 6·842 |
| | 14 | 1·362 | 1·818 | 2·413 | 2·899 | 3·433 | 4·238 | 4·938 | 6·954 |
| | 15 | 1·389 | 1·850 | 2·452 | 2·945 | 3·487 | 4·303 | 5·013 | 7·058 |
| 7 | 2 | 0·3608 | 0·6426 | 0·9853 | 1·245 | 1·514 | 1·897 | 2·213 | 3·064 |
| | 3 | ·5991 | ·9063 | 1·279 | 1·564 | 1·864 | 2·294 | 2·652 | 3·624 |
| | 4 | ·7465 | 1·069 | 1·463 | 1·767 | 2·088 | 2·551 | 2·937 | 3·992 |
| | 5 | ·8521 | 1·186 | 1·597 | 1·916 | 2·254 | 2·742 | 3·150 | 4·267 |
| | 6 | ·9338 | 1·278 | 1·703 | 2·034 | 2·385 | 2·894 | 3·320 | 4·487 |
| | 7 | 1·000 | 1·353 | 1·790 | 2·131 | 2·494 | 3·020 | 3·461 | 4·671 |
| | 8 | 1·056 | 1·416 | 1·863 | 2·213 | 2·586 | 3·127 | 3·581 | 4·827 |
| 7 | 9 | 1·103 | 1·470 | 1·927 | 2·285 | 2·667 | 3·221 | 3·686 | 4·964 |
| | 10 | 1·145 | 1·518 | 1·983 | 2·348 | 2·738 | 3·304 | 3·779 | 5·086 |
| | 11 | 1·182 | 1·560 | 2·033 | 2·405 | 2·802 | 3·378 | 3·863 | 5·196 |
| | 12 | 1·215 | 1·598 | 2·079 | 2·456 | 2·859 | 3·445 | 3·939 | 5·295 |
| | 13 | 1·245 | 1·633 | 2·120 | 2·503 | 2·912 | 3·507 | 4·008 | 5·386 |
| | 14 | 1·272 | 1·665 | 2·157 | 2·545 | 2·960 | 3·563 | 4·071 | 5·469 |
| | 15 | 1·297 | 1·694 | 2·192 | 2·585 | 3·004 | 3·615 | 4·130 | 5·547 |
| 8 | 2 | 0·3417 | 0·6050 | 0·9188 | 1·151 | 1·387 | 1·715 | 1·979 | 2·667 |
| | 3 | ·5675 | ·8513 | 1·187 | 1·437 | 1·695 | 2·056 | 2·349 | 3·119 |
| | 4 | ·7073 | 1·002 | 1·354 | 1·618 | 1·891 | 2·275 | 2·588 | 3·413 |
| | 5 | ·8073 | 1·112 | 1·475 | 1·750 | 2·035 | 2·437 | 2·765 | 3·633 |
| | 6 | ·8847 | 1·197 | 1·571 | 1·855 | 2·150 | 2·566 | 2·907 | 3·810 |
| | 7 | ·9474 | 1·266 | 1·649 | 1·941 | 2·244 | 2·673 | 3·025 | 3·957 |
| | 8 | 1·000 | 1·324 | 1·716 | 2·014 | 2·325 | 2·765 | 3·125 | 4·082 |
| 8 | 9 | 1·045 | 1·375 | 1·773 | 2·078 | 2·395 | 2·844 | 3·213 | 4·192 |
| | 10 | 1·085 | 1·419 | 1·824 | 2·134 | 2·457 | 2·915 | 3·291 | 4·290 |
| | 11 | 1·119 | 1·458 | 1·870 | 2·184 | 2·512 | 2·978 | 3·361 | 4·377 |
| | 12 | 1·151 | 1·494 | 1·911 | 2·229 | 2·563 | 3·035 | 3·424 | 4·457 |
| | 13 | 1·179 | 1·526 | 1·948 | 2·271 | 2·608 | 3·088 | 3·482 | 4·530 |
| | 14 | 1·205 | 1·555 | 1·982 | 2·309 | 2·650 | 3·136 | 3·535 | 4·598 |
| | 15 | 1·229 | 1·582 | 2·013 | 2·344 | 2·689 | 3·180 | 3·584 | 4·660 |

$$F' = w_1/w_2$$

Values of $\alpha$

| $n_2$ | $n_1$ | 0·500 | 0·250 | 0·100 | 0·050 | 0·025 | 0·010 | 0·005 | 0·001 |
|---|---|---|---|---|---|---|---|---|---|
| 9 | 2 | 0·3268 | 0·5763 | 0·8690 | 1·082 | 1·296 | 1·587 | 1·817 | 2·402 |
|   | 3 | ·5430 | ·8093 | 1·118 | 1·345 | 1·574 | 1·889 | 2·141 | 2·784 |
|   | 4 | ·6767 | ·9521 | 1·273 | 1·509 | 1·750 | 2·083 | 2·349 | 3·032 |
|   | 5 | ·7725 | 1·055 | 1·385 | 1·630 | 1·880 | 2·226 | 2·503 | 3·218 |
|   | 6 | ·8465 | 1·135 | 1·474 | 1·725 | 1·983 | 2·339 | 2·626 | 3·366 |
|   | 7 | ·9065 | 1·200 | 1·546 | 1·804 | 2·068 | 2·434 | 2·728 | 3·490 |
|   | 8 | ·9568 | 1·255 | 1·607 | 1·870 | 2·140 | 2·514 | 2·816 | 3·595 |
| 9 | 9 | 1·000 | 1·303 | 1·661 | 1·928 | 2·203 | 2·584 | 2·892 | 3·687 |
|   | 10 | 1·038 | 1·344 | 1·707 | 1·979 | 2·258 | 2·646 | 2·959 | 3·769 |
|   | 11 | 1·071 | 1·381 | 1·749 | 2·025 | 2·308 | 2·702 | 3·020 | 3·843 |
|   | 12 | 1·101 | 1·415 | 1·787 | 2·066 | 2·353 | 2·753 | 3·075 | 3·911 |
|   | 13 | 1·128 | 1·445 | 1·821 | 2·104 | 2·394 | 2·799 | 3·125 | 3·972 |
|   | 14 | 1·153 | 1·473 | 1·853 | 2·138 | 2·432 | 2·841 | 3·172 | 4·029 |
|   | 15 | 1·176 | 1·498 | 1·882 | 2·170 | 2·467 | 2·880 | 3·215 | 4·082 |
| 10 | 2 | 0·3149 | 0·5534 | 0·8301 | 1·029 | 1·226 | 1·491 | 1·698 | 2·212 |
|   | 3 | ·5233 | ·7761 | 1·065 | 1·274 | 1·483 | 1·766 | 1·989 | 2·547 |
|   | 4 | ·6522 | ·9122 | 1·210 | 1·427 | 1·645 | 1·941 | 2·175 | 2·763 |
|   | 5 | ·7444 | 1·010 | 1·316 | 1·539 | 1·764 | 2·070 | 2·313 | 2·925 |
|   | 6 | ·8157 | 1·086 | 1·399 | 1·627 | 1·858 | 2·173 | 2·422 | 3·054 |
|   | 7 | ·8736 | 1·148 | 1·466 | 1·700 | 1·935 | 2·258 | 2·514 | 3·161 |
|   | 8 | ·9221 | 1·201 | 1·524 | 1·761 | 2·002 | 2·330 | 2·591 | 3·253 |
| 10 | 9 | 0·9637 | 1·246 | 1·574 | 1·815 | 2·059 | 2·394 | 2·659 | 3·333 |
|   | 10 | 1·000 | 1·286 | 1·617 | 1·862 | 2·110 | 2·450 | 2·720 | 2·404 |
|   | 11 | 1·032 | 1·321 | 1·657 | 1·904 | 2·155 | 2·500 | 2·774 | 3·469 |
|   | 12 | 1·061 | 1·352 | 1·692 | 1·942 | 2·197 | 2·545 | 2·823 | 3·527 |
|   | 13 | 1·087 | 1·381 | 1·724 | 1·977 | 2·234 | 2·587 | 2·868 | 3·581 |
|   | 14 | 1·111 | 1·407 | 1·754 | 2·009 | 2·269 | 2·625 | 2·909 | 3·630 |
|   | 15 | 1·133 | 1·432 | 1·781 | 2·039 | 2·301 | 2·661 | 2·947 | 3·676 |
| 11 | 2 | 0·3050 | 0·5347 | 0·7986 | 0·9863 | 1·171 | 1·416 | 1·605 | 2·069 |
|   | 3 | ·5070 | ·7490 | 1·023 | 1·218 | 1·411 | 1·670 | 1·872 | 2·370 |
|   | 4 | ·6318 | ·8797 | 1·160 | 1·362 | 1·562 | 1·831 | 2·042 | 2·563 |
|   | 5 | ·7212 | ·9736 | 1·260 | 1·467 | 1·673 | 1·950 | 2·168 | 2·707 |
|   | 6 | ·7903 | 1·047 | 1·339 | 1·549 | 1·760 | 2·045 | 2·268 | 2·822 |
|   | 7 | ·8463 | 1·106 | 1·403 | 1·618 | 1·832 | 2·123 | 2·350 | 2·918 |
|   | 8 | ·8933 | 1·156 | 1·457 | 1·675 | 1·894 | 2·189 | 2·421 | 2·999 |
| 11 | 9 | 0·9336 | 1·200 | 1·504 | 1·725 | 1·947 | 2·247 | 2·483 | 3·071 |
|   | 10 | ·9688 | 1·238 | 1·546 | 1·770 | 1·994 | 2·299 | 2·538 | 3·134 |
|   | 11 | 1·000 | 1·271 | 1·583 | 1·809 | 2·037 | 2·345 | 2·587 | 3·192 |
|   | 12 | 1·028 | 1·302 | 1·616 | 1·845 | 2·075 | 2·387 | 2·632 | 3·244 |
|   | 13 | 1·053 | 1·329 | 1·646 | 1·878 | 2·110 | 2·425 | 2·672 | 3·292 |
|   | 14 | 1·076 | 1·355 | 1·674 | 1·908 | 2·142 | 2·460 | 2·710 | 3·336 |
|   | 15 | 1·098 | 1·378 | 1·700 | 1·935 | 2·171 | 2·492 | 2·745 | 3·377 |
| 12 | 2 | 0·2967 | 0·5190 | 0·7726 | 0·9513 | 1·126 | 1·356 | 1·531 | 1·957 |
|   | 3 | ·4932 | ·7264 | ·9872 | 1·172 | 1·353 | 1·594 | 1·779 | 2·232 |
|   | 4 | ·6147 | ·8526 | 1·119 | 1·309 | 1·496 | 1·744 | 1·937 | 2·408 |
|   | 5 | ·7016 | ·9432 | 1·215 | 1·408 | 1·600 | 1·855 | 2·053 | 2·539 |
|   | 6 | ·7688 | 1·014 | 1·289 | 1·487 | 1·682 | 1·943 | 2·145 | 2·643 |
|   | 7 | ·8233 | 1·071 | 1·351 | 1·551 | 1·749 | 2·015 | 2·222 | 2·730 |
|   | 8 | ·8690 | 1·119 | 1·403 | 1·606 | 1·807 | 2·077 | 2·287 | 2·804 |

$w_1$, $w_2$ are the ranges in two independent samples containing $n_1$, $n_2$ observations, respectively.

Values of $\alpha$

| $n_2$ | $n_1$ | 0·500 | 0·250 | 0·100 | 0·050 | 0·025 | 0·010 | 0·005 | 0·001 |
|---|---|---|---|---|---|---|---|---|---|
| 12 | 9 | 0·9082 | 1·161 | 1·447 | 1·653 | 1·857 | 2·131 | 2·344 | 2·868 |
| | 10 | ·9424 | 1·198 | 1·487 | 1·695 | 1·902 | 2·179 | 2·395 | 2·926 |
| | 11 | ·9728 | 1·230 | 1·522 | 1·732 | 1·941 | 2·222 | 2·440 | 2·978 |
| | 12 | 1·000 | 1·260 | 1·554 | 1·766 | 1·977 | 2·261 | 2·482 | 3·025 |
| | 13 | 1·025 | 1·286 | 1·583 | 1·797 | 2·010 | 2·296 | 2·519 | 3·069 |
| | 14 | 1·047 | 1·310 | 1·609 | 1·825 | 2·040 | 2·329 | 2·554 | 3·109 |
| | 15 | 1·068 | 1·333 | 1·634 | 1·851 | 2·068 | 2·359 | 2·586 | 3·146 |
| 13 | 2 | 0·2895 | 0·5056 | 0·7505 | 0·9220 | 1·088 | 1·306 | 1·471 | 1·866 |
| | 3 | ·4814 | ·7071 | ·9576 | 1·134 | 1·305 | 1·531 | 1·704 | 2·121 |
| | 4 | ·5999 | ·8295 | 1·084 | 1·264 | 1·440 | 1·673 | 1·851 | 2·284 |
| | 5 | ·6848 | ·9174 | 1·176 | 1·359 | 1·539 | 1·777 | 1·960 | 2·404 |
| | 6 | ·7503 | ·9856 | 1·248 | 1·434 | 1·617 | 1·860 | 2·047 | 2·501 |
| | 7 | ·8035 | 1·041 | 1·307 | 1·496 | 1·681 | 1·928 | 2·118 | 2·581 |
| | 8 | ·8481 | 1·088 | 1·357 | 1·547 | 1·736 | 1·986 | 2·179 | 2·648 |
| 13 | 9 | 0·8863 | 1·128 | 1·400 | 1·593 | 1·783 | 2·037 | 2·232 | 2·708 |
| | 10 | ·9198 | 1·164 | 1·438 | 1·633 | 1·825 | 2·082 | 2·280 | 2·761 |
| | 11 | ·9494 | 1·195 | 1·471 | 1·668 | 1·863 | 2·122 | 2·322 | 2·809 |
| | 12 | ·9760 | 1·224 | 1·502 | 1·701 | 1·897 | 2·158 | 2·360 | 2·852 |
| | 13 | 1·000 | 1·249 | 1·530 | 1·730 | 1·928 | 2·192 | 2·396 | 2·892 |
| | 14 | 1·022 | 1·273 | 1·555 | 1·757 | 1·956 | 2·222 | 2·428 | 2·929 |
| | 15 | 1·042 | 1·295 | 1·579 | 1·782 | 1·983 | 2·250 | 2·458 | 2·963 |
| 14 | 2 | 0·2833 | 0·4940 | 0·7316 | 0·8970 | 1·057 | 1·264 | 1·420 | 1·792 |
| | 3 | ·4710 | ·6904 | ·9322 | 1·101 | 1·265 | 1·479 | 1·641 | 2·030 |
| | 4 | ·5871 | ·8096 | 1·055 | 1·227 | 1·394 | 1·613 | 1·781 | 2·182 |
| | 5 | ·6701 | ·8950 | 1·144 | 1·318 | 1·488 | 1·712 | 1·883 | 2·295 |
| | 6 | ·7342 | ·9614 | 1·213 | 1·390 | 1·562 | 1·791 | 1·965 | 2·384 |
| | 7 | ·7863 | 1·016 | 1·270 | 1·449 | 1·624 | 1·855 | 2·032 | 2·458 |
| | 8 | ·8299 | 1·061 | 1·318 | 1·499 | 1·676 | 1·910 | 2·090 | 2·522 |
| 14 | 9 | 0·8673 | 1·100 | 1·359 | 1·542 | 1·721 | 1·958 | 2·139 | 2·577 |
| | 10 | ·9000 | 1·135 | 1·396 | 1·580 | 1·761 | 2·001 | 2·184 | 2·626 |
| | 11 | ·9290 | 1·165 | 1·428 | 1·614 | 1·797 | 2·038 | 2·224 | 2·671 |
| | 12 | ·9550 | 1·193 | 1·458 | 1·645 | 1·829 | 2·073 | 2·260 | 2·711 |
| | 13 | ·9785 | 1·218 | 1·484 | 1·673 | 1·859 | 2·105 | 2·293 | 2·748 |
| | 14 | 1·000 | 1·241 | 1·509 | 1·699 | 1·886 | 2·133 | 2·324 | 2·782 |
| | 15 | 1·020 | 1·262 | 1·532 | 1·723 | 1·911 | 2·160 | 2·352 | 2·814 |
| 15 | 2 | 0·2778 | 0·4838 | 0·7151 | 0·8753 | 1·029 | 1·228 | 1·377 | 1·729 |
| | 3 | ·4620 | ·6758 | ·9101 | 1·073 | 1·230 | 1·434 | 1·588 | 1·954 |
| | 4 | ·5757 | ·7922 | 1·029 | 1·194 | 1·354 | 1·562 | 1·721 | 2·098 |
| | 5 | ·6571 | ·8755 | 1·115 | 1·282 | 1·445 | 1·657 | 1·818 | 2·203 |
| | 6 | ·7201 | ·9403 | 1·182 | 1·352 | 1·516 | 1·731 | 1·896 | 2·287 |
| | 7 | ·7711 | ·9930 | 1·237 | 1·408 | 1·575 | 1·793 | 1·959 | 2·357 |
| | 8 | ·8138 | 1·037 | 1·284 | 1·456 | 1·625 | 1·845 | 2·014 | 2·416 |
| 15 | 9 | 0·8505 | 1·076 | 1·324 | 1·498 | 1·668 | 1·892 | 2·061 | 2·468 |
| | 10 | ·8826 | 1·109 | 1·359 | 1·535 | 1·707 | 1·932 | 2·104 | 2·514 |
| | 11 | ·9110 | 1·139 | 1·391 | 1·568 | 1·741 | 1·968 | 2·141 | 2·556 |
| | 12 | ·9365 | 1·166 | 1·419 | 1·598 | 1·772 | 2·001 | 2·176 | 2·594 |
| | 13 | ·9596 | 1·190 | 1·445 | 1·625 | 1·800 | 2·031 | 2·207 | 2·628 |
| | 14 | ·9807 | 1·212 | 1·469 | 1·649 | 1·826 | 2·058 | 2·236 | 2·660 |
| | 15 | 1·000 | 1·233 | 1·491 | 1·673 | 1·850 | 2·084 | 2·263 | 2·690 |

## Table 29 c. *Percentage points of the ratio of range to standard deviation, w/s, where w and s are derived from the same sample of n observations*

| Size of sample n | Lower percentage points | | | | | | Upper percentage points | | | | | |
|---|---|---|---|---|---|---|---|---|---|---|---|---|
| | 0·0 | 0·5 | 1·0 | 2·5 | 5·0 | 10·0 | 10·0 | 5·0 | 2·5 | 1·0 | 0·5 | 0·0 |
| 3 | 1·732 | 1·735 | 1·737 | 1·745 | 1·758 | 1·782 | 1·997 | 1·999 | 2·000 | 2·000 | 2·000 | 2·000 |
| 4 | 1·732 | 1·83 | 1·87 | 1·93 | 1·98 | 2·04 | 2·409 | 2·429 | 2·439 | 2·445 | 2·447 | 2·449 |
| 5 | 1·826 | 1·98 | 2·02 | 2·09 | 2·15 | 2·22 | 2·712 | 2·753 | 2·782 | 2·803 | 2·813 | 2·828 |
| 6 | 1·826 | 2·11 | 2·15 | 2·22 | 2·28 | 2·37 | 2·949 | 3·012 | 3·056 | 3·095 | 3·115 | 3·162 |
| 7 | 1·871 | 2·22 | 2·26 | 2·33 | 2·40 | 2·49 | 3·143 | 3·222 | 3·282 | 3·338 | 3·369 | 3·464 |
| 8 | 1·871 | 2·31 | 2·35 | 2·43 | 2·50 | 2·59 | 3·308 | 3·399 | 3·471 | 3·543 | 3·585 | 3·742 |
| 9 | 1·897 | 2·39 | 2·44 | 2·51 | 2·59 | 2·68 | 3·449 | 3·552 | 3·634 | 3·720 | 3·772 | 4·000 |
| 10 | 1·897 | 2·46 | 2·51 | 2·59 | 2·67 | 2·76 | 3·57 | 3·685 | 3·777 | 3·875 | 3·935 | 4·243 |
| 11 | 1·915 | 2·53 | 2·58 | 2·66 | 2·74 | 2·84 | 3·68 | 3·80 | 3·903 | 4·012 | 4·079 | 4·472 |
| 12 | 1·915 | 2·59 | 2·64 | 2·72 | 2·80 | 2·90 | 3·78 | 3·91 | 4·02 | 4·134 | 4·208 | 4·690 |
| 13 | 1·927 | 2·64 | 2·70 | 2·78 | 2·86 | 2·96 | 3·87 | 4·00 | 4·12 | 4·244 | 4·325 | 4·899 |
| 14 | 1·927 | 2·70 | 2·75 | 2·83 | 2·92 | 3·02 | 3·95 | 4·09 | 4·21 | 4·34 | 4·431 | 5·099 |
| 15 | 1·936 | 2·74 | 2·80 | 2·88 | 2·97 | 3·07 | 4·02 | 4·17 | 4·29 | 4·44 | 4·53 | 5·292 |
| 16 | 1·936 | 2·79 | 2·84 | 2·93 | 3·01 | 3·12 | 4·09 | 4·24 | 4·37 | 4·52 | 4·62 | 5·477 |
| 17 | 1·944 | 2·83 | 2·88 | 2·97 | 3·06 | 3·17 | 4·15 | 4·31 | 4·44 | 4·60 | 4·70 | 5·657 |
| 18 | 1·944 | 2·87 | 2·92 | 3·01 | 3·10 | 3·21 | 4·21 | 4·37 | 4·51 | 4·67 | 4·78 | 5·831 |
| 19 | 1·949 | 2·90 | 2·96 | 3·05 | 3·14 | 3·25 | 4·27 | 4·43 | 4·57 | 4·74 | 4·85 | 6·000 |
| 20 | 1·949 | 2·94 | 2·99 | 3·09 | 3·18 | 3·29 | 4·32 | 4·49 | 4·63 | 4·80 | 4·91 | 6·164 |
| 25 | 1·961 | 3·09 | 3·15 | 3·24 | 3·34 | 3·45 | 4·53 | 4·71 | 4·87 | 5·06 | 5·19 | 6·93 |
| 30 | 1·966 | 3·21 | 3·27 | 3·37 | 3·47 | 3·59 | 4·70 | 4·89 | 5·06 | 5·26 | 5·40 | 7·62 |
| 35 | 1·972 | 3·32 | 3·38 | 3·48 | 3·58 | 3·70 | 4·84 | 5·04 | 5·21 | 5·42 | 5·57 | 8·25 |
| 40 | 1·975 | 3·41 | 3·47 | 3·57 | 3·67 | 3·79 | 4·96 | 5·16 | 5·34 | 5·56 | 5·71 | 8·83 |
| 45 | 1·978 | 3·49 | 3·55 | 3·66 | 3·75 | 3·88 | 5·06 | 5·26 | 5·45 | 5·67 | 5·83 | 9·38 |
| 50 | 1·980 | 3·56 | 3·62 | 3·73 | 3·83 | 3·95 | 5·14 | 5·35 | 5·54 | 5·77 | 5·93 | 9·90 |
| 55 | 1·982 | 3·62 | 3·69 | 3·80 | 3·90 | 4·02 | 5·22 | 5·43 | 5·63 | 5·86 | 6·02 | 10·39 |
| 60 | 1·983 | 3·68 | 3·75 | 3·86 | 3·96 | 4·08 | 5·29 | 5·51 | 5·70 | 5·94 | 6·10 | 10·86 |
| 65 | 1·985 | 3·74 | 3·80 | 3·91 | 4·01 | 4·14 | 5·35 | 5·57 | 5·77 | 6·01 | 6·17 | 11·31 |
| 70 | 1·986 | 3·79 | 3·85 | 3·96 | 4·06 | 4·19 | 5·41 | 5·63 | 5·83 | 6·07 | 6·24 | 11·75 |
| 75 | 1·987 | 3·83 | 3·90 | 4·01 | 4·11 | 4·24 | 5·46 | 5·68 | 5·88 | 6·13 | 6·30 | 12·17 |
| 80 | 1·987 | 3·88 | 3·94 | 4·05 | 4·16 | 4·28 | 5·51 | 5·73 | 5·93 | 6·18 | 6·35 | 12·57 |
| 85 | 1·988 | 3·92 | 3·99 | 4·09 | 4·20 | 4·33 | 5·56 | 5·78 | 5·98 | 6·23 | 6·40 | 12·96 |
| 90 | 1·989 | 3·96 | 4·02 | 4·13 | 4·24 | 4·36 | 5·60 | 5·82 | 6·03 | 6·27 | 6·45 | 13·34 |
| 95 | 1·990 | 3·99 | 4·06 | 4·17 | 4·27 | 4·40 | 5·64 | 5·86 | 6·07 | 6·32 | 6·49 | 13·71 |
| 100 | 1·990 | 4·03 | 4·10 | 4·21 | 4·31 | 4·44 | 5·68 | 5·90 | 6·11 | 6·36 | 6·53 | 14·07 |
| 150 | 1·993 | 4·32 | 4·38 | 4·48 | 4·59 | 4·72 | 5·96 | 6·18 | 6·39 | 6·64 | 6·82 | 17·26 |
| 200 | 1·995 | 4·53 | 4·59 | 4·68 | 4·78 | 4·90 | 6·15 | 6·39 | 6·60 | 6·84 | 7·01 | 19·95 |
| 500 | 1·998 | 5·06 | 5·13 | 5·25 | 5·37 | 5·49 | 6·72 | 6·94 | 7·15 | 7·42 | 7·60 | 31·59 |
| 1000 | 1·999 | 5·50 | 5·57 | 5·68 | 5·79 | 5·92 | 7·11 | 7·33 | 7·54 | 7·80 | 7·99 | 44·70 |

## Table 30. Tables for analysis of variance based on range

### A. Scale factor, c, and equivalent degrees of freedom, v, appropriate to a simple classification into k groups of n observations

| k \ n | n=2 v | n=2 c | n=3 v | n=3 c | n=4 v | n=4 c | n=5 v | n=5 c | n=6 v | n=6 c | n=7 v | n=7 c | n=8 v | n=8 c | n=9 v | n=9 c | n=10 v | n=10 c |
|---|---|---|---|---|---|---|---|---|---|---|---|---|---|---|---|---|---|---|
| 1 | 1.0 | 1.41 | 2.0 | 1.91 | 2.9 | 2.24 | 3.8 | 2.48 | 4.7 | 2.67 | 5.5 | 2.83 | 6.3 | 2.96 | 7.0 | 3.08 | 7.7 | 3.18 |
| 2 | 1.9 | 1.28 | 3.8 | 1.81 | 5.7 | 2.15 | 7.5 | 2.40 | 9.2 | 2.60 | 10.8 | 2.77 | 12.3 | 2.91 | 13.8 | 3.02 | 15.1 | 3.13 |
| 3 | 2.8 | 1.23 | 5.7 | 1.77 | 8.4 | 2.12 | 11.1 | 2.38 | 13.6 | 2.58 | 16.0 | 2.75 | 18.3 | 2.89 | 20.5 | 3.01 | 22.6 | 3.11 |
| 4 | 3.7 | 1.21 | 7.5 | 1.75 | 11.2 | 2.11 | 14.7 | 2.37 | 18.1 | 2.57 | 21.3 | 2.74 | 24.4 | 2.88 | 27.3 | 3.00 | 30.1 | 3.10 |
| 5 | 4.6 | 1.19 | 9.3 | 1.74 | 13.9 | 2.10 | 18.4 | 2.36 | 22.6 | 2.56 | 26.6 | 2.73 | 30.4 | 2.87 | 34.0 | 2.99 | 37.5 | 3.10 |
| 10 | 9.0 | 1.16 | 18.4 | 1.72 | 27.6 | 2.08 | 36.5 | 2.34 | 44.9 | 2.55 | 52.9 | 2.72 | 60.6 | 2.86 | 67.8 | 2.98 | 74.8 | 3.09 |
| $d_n$ | | 1.13 | | 1.69 | | 2.06 | | 2.33 | | 2.53 | | 2.70 | | 2.85 | | 2.97 | | 3.08 |
| c.d. | 0.88 | | 1.82 | | 2.74 | | 3.62 | | 4.47 | | 5.27 | | 6.03 | | 6.76 | | 7.45 | |

N.B. c.d. = constant difference.

### B. Scale factor, c, and equivalent degrees of freedom, v, for analysis of double classification, with k blocks and n treatments

| k \ n | n=2 v | n=2 c | n=3 v | n=3 c | n=4 v | n=4 c | n=5 v | n=5 c | n=6 v | n=6 c | n=7 v | n=7 c | n=8 v | n=8 c | n=9 v | n=9 c |
|---|---|---|---|---|---|---|---|---|---|---|---|---|---|---|---|---|
| 2 | 1.0 | 1.00 | 2.0 | 1.35 | 2.9 | 1.58 | 3.8 | 1.75 | 4.7 | 1.89 | 5.5 | 2.00 | 6.3 | 2.10 | 7.0 | 2.18 |
| 3 | 1.9 | 1.05 | 3.7 | 1.48 | 5.6 | 1.76 | 7.4 | 1.96 | 9.3 | 2.12 | 11.3 | 2.26 | 13.4 | 2.37 | 15.7 | 2.46 |
| 4 | 2.7 | 1.07 | 5.4 | 1.54 | 8.2 | 1.84 | 11.0 | 2.06 | 13.9 | 2.23 | 16.9 | 2.38 | 20.1 | 2.50 | 23.6 | 2.60 |
| 5 | 3.6 | 1.08 | 7.2 | 1.57 | 10.9 | 1.88 | 14.6 | 2.12 | 18.5 | 2.30 | 22.4 | 2.45 | 26.6 | 2.57 | 31.1 | 2.68 |
| 6 | 4.5 | 1.09 | 8.9 | 1.59 | 13.6 | 1.91 | 18.2 | 2.15 | 23.0 | 2.34 | 27.9 | 2.49 | 33.0 | 2.62 | 38.3 | 2.73 |
| 7 | 5.4 | 1.09 | 10.7 | 1.61 | 16.3 | 1.93 | 21.8 | 2.18 | 27.6 | 2.37 | 33.3 | 2.52 | 39.3 | 2.65 | 45.4 | 2.76 |
| 8 | 6.3 | 1.10 | 12.5 | 1.62 | 19.0 | 1.95 | 25.4 | 2.20 | 32.1 | 2.39 | 38.7 | 2.55 | 45.6 | 2.68 | 52.5 | 2.79 |
| 9 | 7.1 | 1.10 | 14.3 | 1.63 | 21.7 | 1.96 | 29.0 | 2.21 | 36.6 | 2.41 | 44.0 | 2.57 | 51.8 | 2.70 | 59.6 | 2.81 |
| 10 | 8.1 | 1.10 | 16.1 | 1.63 | 24.4 | 1.97 | 32.6 | 2.22 | 41.0 | 2.42 | 49.3 | 2.58 | 57.9 | 2.71 | 66.6 | 2.83 |
| 20 | 16.7 | 1.11 | 33.9 | 1.66 | 51.5 | 2.02 | 68.8 | 2.28 | 86.0 | 2.48 | 103 | 2.64 | 119 | 2.78 | 134 | 2.90 |
| $d_n$ | | 1.13 | | 1.69 | | 2.06 | | 2.33 | | 2.53 | | 2.70 | | 2.85 | | 2.97 | | |
| c.d. | 0.87 | | 1.80 | | 2.71 | | 3.62 | | 4.50 | | 5.33 | | 6.10 | | 6.79 | | |

## Table 31. *Percentage points of the ratio, $s^2_{max.}/s^2_{min.}$*

### Upper 5 % points

| $\nu$ \ $k$ | 2 | 3 | 4 | 5 | 6 | 7 | 8 | 9 | 10 | 11 | 12 |
|---|---|---|---|---|---|---|---|---|---|---|---|
| 2 | 39·0 | 87·5 | 142 | 202 | 266 | 333 | 403 | 475 | 550 | 626 | 704 |
| 3 | 15·4 | 27·8 | 39·2 | 50·7 | 62·0 | 72·9 | 83·5 | 93·9 | 104 | 114 | 124 |
| 4 | 9·60 | 15·5 | 20·6 | 25·2 | 29·5 | 33·6 | 37·5 | 41·1 | 44·6 | 48·0 | 51·4 |
| 5 | 7·15 | 10·8 | 13·7 | 16·3 | 18·7 | 20·8 | 22·9 | 24·7 | 26·5 | 28·2 | 29·9 |
| 6 | 5·82 | 8·38 | 10·4 | 12·1 | 13·7 | 15·0 | 16·3 | 17·5 | 18·6 | 19·7 | 20·7 |
| 7 | 4·99 | 6·94 | 8·44 | 9·70 | 10·8 | 11·8 | 12·7 | 13·5 | 14·3 | 15·1 | 15·8 |
| 8 | 4·43 | 6·00 | 7·18 | 8·12 | 9·03 | 9·78 | 10·5 | 11·1 | 11·7 | 12·2 | 12·7 |
| 9 | 4·03 | 5·34 | 6·31 | 7·11 | 7·80 | 8·41 | 8·95 | 9·45 | 9·91 | 10·3 | 10·7 |
| 10 | 3·72 | 4·85 | 5·67 | 6·34 | 6·92 | 7·42 | 7·87 | 8·28 | 8·66 | 9·01 | 9·34 |
| 12 | 3·28 | 4·16 | 4·79 | 5·30 | 5·72 | 6·09 | 6·42 | 6·72 | 7·00 | 7·25 | 7·48 |
| 15 | 2·86 | 3·54 | 4·01 | 4·37 | 4·68 | 4·95 | 5·19 | 5·40 | 5·59 | 5·77 | 5·93 |
| 20 | 2·46 | 2·95 | 3·29 | 3·54 | 3·76 | 3·94 | 4·10 | 4·24 | 4·37 | 4·49 | 4·59 |
| 30 | 2·07 | 2·40 | 2·61 | 2·78 | 2·91 | 3·02 | 3·12 | 3·21 | 3·29 | 3·36 | 3·39 |
| 60 | 1·67 | 1·85 | 1·96 | 2·04 | 2·11 | 2·17 | 2·22 | 2·26 | 2·30 | 2·33 | 2·36 |
| $\infty$ | 1·00 | 1·00 | 1·00 | 1·00 | 1·00 | 1·00 | 1·00 | 1·00 | 1·00 | 1·00 | 1·00 |

### Upper 1 % points

| $\nu$ \ $k$ | 2 | 3 | 4 | 5 | 6 | 7 | 8 | 9 | 10 | 11 | 12 |
|---|---|---|---|---|---|---|---|---|---|---|---|
| 2 | 199 | 448 | 729 | 1036 | 1362 | 1705 | 2063 | 2432 | 2813 | 3204 | 3605 |
| 3 | 47·5 | 85 | 120 | 151 | 184 | 21(6) | 24(9) | 28(1) | 31(0) | 33(7) | 36(1) |
| 4 | 23·2 | 37 | 49 | 59 | 69 | 79 | 89 | 97 | 106 | 113 | 120 |
| 5 | 14·9 | 22 | 28 | 33 | 38 | 42 | 46 | 50 | 54 | 57 | 60 |
| 6 | 11·1 | 15·5 | 19·1 | 22 | 25 | 27 | 30 | 32 | 34 | 36 | 37 |
| 7 | 8·89 | 12·1 | 14·5 | 16·5 | 18·4 | 20 | 22 | 23 | 24 | 26 | 27 |
| 8 | 7·50 | 9·9 | 11·7 | 13·2 | 14·5 | 15·8 | 16·9 | 17·9 | 18·9 | 19·8 | 21 |
| 9 | 6·54 | 8·5 | 9·9 | 11·1 | 12·1 | 13·1 | 13·9 | 14·7 | 15·3 | 16·0 | 16·6 |
| 10 | 5·85 | 7·4 | 8·6 | 9·6 | 10·4 | 11·1 | 11·8 | 12·4 | 12·9 | 13·4 | 13·9 |
| 12 | 4·91 | 6·1 | 6·9 | 7·6 | 8·2 | 8·7 | 9·1 | 9·5 | 9·9 | 10·2 | 10·6 |
| 15 | 4·07 | 4·9 | 5·5 | 6·0 | 6·4 | 6·7 | 7·1 | 7·3 | 7·5 | 7·8 | 8·0 |
| 20 | 3·32 | 3·8 | 4·3 | 4·6 | 4·9 | 5·1 | 5·3 | 5·5 | 5·6 | 5·8 | 5·9 |
| 30 | 2·63 | 3·0 | 3·3 | 3·4 | 3·6 | 3·7 | 3·8 | 3·9 | 4·0 | 4·1 | 4·2 |
| 60 | 1·96 | 2·2 | 2·3 | 2·4 | 2·4 | 2·5 | 2·5 | 2·6 | 2·6 | 2·7 | 2·7 |
| $\infty$ | 1·00 | 1·0 | 1·0 | 1·0 | 1·0 | 1·0 | 1·0 | 1·0 | 1·0 | 1·0 | 1·0 |

$s^2_{max.}$ is the largest and $s^2_{min.}$ the smallest in a set of $k$ independent mean squares, each based on $\nu$ degrees of freedom.

Values in the column $k=2$ and in the rows $\nu=2$ and $\infty$ are exact. Elsewhere the third digit may be in error by a few units for the 5 % points and several units for the 1 % points. The third digit figures in brackets for $\nu=3$ are the most uncertain.

*Note regarding Table 31c, pp. 264–5.*

We have added to this 2nd impression of the 3rd edition of this volume a table due to R. T. Leslie and B. M. Brown (*Biometrika*, 1966, **53**, 226–7) giving the upper 5%, 2·5%, 1% and 0·5% points of the ratio $w_{max}/w_{min}$. Here $w_{max}$ is the largest and $w_{min}$ the smallest in a set of $k$ independent ranges, each derived from a sample of $n$ observations. On the null hypothesis these samples have been drawn from $k$ normal populations having a common variance.

To avoid extensive repagination, Table 31c has been included on pp. 264–5 at the end of the volume.

Table 31a. *Percentage points of the ratio* $s^2_{max.}\Big/\sum_{t=1}^{k} s_t^2$. *Upper 5% points*

| ν \ k | 2 | 3 | 4 | 5 | 6 | 7 | 8 | 9 | 10 | 12 | 15 | 20 |
|---|---|---|---|---|---|---|---|---|---|---|---|---|
| 1 | 0·9985 | 0·9669 | 0·9065 | 0·8412 | 0·7808 | 0·7271 | 0·6798 | 0·6385 | 0·6020 | 0·5410 | 0·4709 | 0·3894 |
| 2 | ·9750 | ·8709 | ·7679 | ·6838 | ·6161 | ·5612 | ·5157 | ·4775 | ·4450 | ·3924 | ·3346 | ·2705 |
| 3 | ·9392 | ·7977 | ·6841 | ·5981 | ·5321 | ·4800 | ·4377 | ·4027 | ·3733 | ·3264 | ·2758 | ·2205 |
| 4 | ·9057 | ·7457 | ·6287 | ·5441 | ·4803 | ·4307 | ·3910 | ·3584 | ·3311 | ·2880 | ·2419 | ·1921 |
| 5 | ·8772 | ·7071 | ·5895 | ·5065 | ·4447 | ·3974 | ·3595 | ·3286 | ·3029 | ·2624 | ·2195 | ·1735 |
| 6 | 0·8534 | 0·6771 | 0·5598 | 0·4783 | 0·4184 | 0·3726 | 0·3362 | 0·3067 | 0·2823 | 0·2439 | 0·2034 | 0·1602 |
| 7 | ·8332 | ·6530 | ·5365 | ·4564 | ·3980 | ·3535 | ·3185 | ·2901 | ·2666 | ·2299 | ·1911 | ·1501 |
| 8 | ·8159 | ·6333 | ·5175 | ·4387 | ·3817 | ·3384 | ·3043 | ·2768 | ·2541 | ·2187 | ·1815 | ·1422 |
| 9 | ·8010 | ·6167 | ·5017 | ·4241 | ·3682 | ·3259 | ·2926 | ·2659 | ·2439 | ·2098 | ·1736 | ·1357 |
| 10 | ·7880 | ·6025 | ·4884 | ·4118 | ·3568 | ·3154 | ·2829 | ·2568 | ·2353 | ·2020 | ·1671 | ·1303 |
| 16 | 0·7341 | 0·5466 | 0·4366 | 0·3645 | 0·3135 | 0·2756 | 0·2462 | 0·2226 | 0·2032 | 0·1737 | 0·1429 | 0·1108 |
| 36 | ·6602 | ·4748 | ·3720 | ·3066 | ·2612 | ·2278 | ·2022 | ·1820 | ·1655 | ·1403 | ·1144 | ·0879 |
| 144 | ·5813 | ·4031 | ·3093 | ·2513 | ·2119 | ·1833 | ·1616 | ·1446 | ·1308 | ·1100 | ·0889 | ·0675 |
| ∞ | ·5000 | ·3333 | ·2500 | ·2000 | ·1667 | ·1429 | ·1250 | ·1111 | ·1000 | ·0833 | ·0667 | ·0500 |

*Upper 1% points*

| ν \ k | 2 | 3 | 4 | 5 | 6 | 7 | 8 | 9 | 10 | 12 | 15 | 20 |
|---|---|---|---|---|---|---|---|---|---|---|---|---|
| 1 | 0·9999 | 0·9933 | 0·9676 | 0·9279 | 0·8828 | 0·8376 | 0·7945 | 0·7544 | 0·7175 | 0·6528 | 0·5747 | 0·4799 |
| 2 | ·9950 | ·9423 | ·8643 | ·7885 | ·7218 | ·6644 | ·6152 | ·5727 | ·5358 | ·4751 | ·4069 | ·3297 |
| 3 | ·9794 | ·8831 | ·7814 | ·6957 | ·6258 | ·5685 | ·5209 | ·4810 | ·4469 | ·3919 | ·3317 | ·2654 |
| 4 | ·9586 | ·8335 | ·7212 | ·6329 | ·5635 | ·5080 | ·4627 | ·4251 | ·3934 | ·3428 | ·2882 | ·2288 |
| 5 | ·9373 | ·7933 | ·6761 | ·5875 | ·5195 | ·4659 | ·4226 | ·3870 | ·3572 | ·3099 | ·2593 | ·2048 |
| 6 | 0·9172 | 0·7606 | 0·6410 | 0·5531 | 0·4866 | 0·4347 | 0·3932 | 0·3592 | 0·3308 | 0·2861 | 0·2386 | 0·1877 |
| 7 | ·8988 | ·7335 | ·6129 | ·5259 | ·4608 | ·4105 | ·3704 | ·3378 | ·3106 | ·2680 | ·2228 | ·1748 |
| 8 | ·8823 | ·7107 | ·5897 | ·5037 | ·4401 | ·3911 | ·3522 | ·3207 | ·2945 | ·2535 | ·2104 | ·1646 |
| 9 | ·8674 | ·6912 | ·5702 | ·4854 | ·4229 | ·3751 | ·3373 | ·3067 | ·2813 | ·2419 | ·2002 | ·1567 |
| 10 | ·8539 | ·6743 | ·5536 | ·4697 | ·4084 | ·3616 | ·3248 | ·2950 | ·2704 | ·2320 | ·1918 | ·1501 |
| 16 | 0·7949 | 0·6059 | 0·4884 | 0·4094 | 0·3529 | 0·3105 | 0·2779 | 0·2514 | 0·2297 | 0·1961 | 0·1612 | 0·1248 |
| 36 | ·7067 | ·5153 | ·4057 | ·3351 | ·2858 | ·2494 | ·2214 | ·1992 | ·1811 | ·1535 | ·1251 | ·0960 |
| 144 | ·6062 | ·4230 | ·3251 | ·2644 | ·2229 | ·1929 | ·1700 | ·1521 | ·1376 | ·1157 | ·0934 | ·0709 |
| ∞ | ·5000 | ·3333 | ·2500 | ·2000 | ·1667 | ·1429 | ·1250 | ·1111 | ·1000 | ·0833 | ·0667 | ·0500 |

$s^2_{max.}$ is the largest in a set of $k$ independent mean squares, $s_t^2$, each based on $\nu$ degrees of freedom. This table is taken, with permission, from Eisenhart, Hastay & Wallis (1947).

Table 31b. *Percentage points of the ratio* $w_{max.}\Big/\sum_{t=1}^{k} w_t$. *Upper 5% points*

| n \ k | 2 | 3 | 4 | 5 | 6 | 7 | 8 | 9 | 10 | 12 | 15 | 20 |
|---|---|---|---|---|---|---|---|---|---|---|---|---|
| 2 | 0·962 | 0·813 | 0·681 | 0·581 | 0·508 | 0·451 | 0·407 | 0·369 | 0·339 | 0·290 | 0·239 | 0·188 |
| 3 | ·862 | ·667 | ·538 | ·451 | ·389 | ·342 | ·305 | ·276 | ·253 | ·216 | ·178 | ·138 |
| 4 | ·803 | ·601 | ·479 | ·398 | ·342 | ·300 | ·267 | ·241 | ·220 | ·188 | ·154 | ·119 |
| 5 | ·764 | ·563 | ·446 | ·369 | ·316 | ·278 | ·248 | ·224 | ·204 | ·173 | ·142 | ·110 |
| 6 | 0·736 | 0·539 | 0·425 | 0·351 | 0·300 | 0·263 | 0·234 | 0·211 | 0·193 | 0·163 | 0·134 | 0·104 |
| 7 | ·717 | ·521 | ·410 | ·338 | ·288 | ·253 | ·225 | ·203 | ·185 | ·157 | ·129 | ·099 |
| 8 | ·702 | ·507 | ·398 | ·328 | ·280 | ·245 | ·218 | ·197 | ·179 | ·152 | ·125 | ·096 |
| 9 | ·691 | ·498 | ·389 | ·320 | ·273 | ·239 | ·213 | ·192 | ·174 | ·148 | ·121 | ·094 |
| 10 | ·682 | ·489 | ·382 | ·314 | ·267 | ·234 | ·208 | ·188 | ·172 | ·146 | ·119 | ·091 |

$w_{max.}$ is the largest in a set of $k$ independent ranges, $w_t$, each derived from a sample of $n$ observations. See Introduction for approximation when $10 < k \leqslant 50$.

Table 32. *Test for heterogeneity of variance: percentage points of M*

Upper 5 % points

| $c_1$ / $k$ | | 0·0 | 0·5 | 1·0 | 1·5 | 2·0 | 2·5 | 3·0 | 3·5 | 4·0 | 4·5 | 5·0 | 6·0 | 7·0 | 8·0 | 9·0 | 10·0 | 12·0 | 14·0 |
|---|---|---|---|---|---|---|---|---|---|---|---|---|---|---|---|---|---|---|---|
| 3 | (a) | 5·99 | 6·47 | 6·89 | 7·20 | 7·38 | 7·39 | 7·22 | — | — | — | — | — | — | — | — | — | — | — |
|   | (b) | 5·99 | 6·22 | 6·43 | 6·64 | 6·84 | 7·03 | 7·22 | — | — | — | — | — | — | — | — | — | — | — |
| 4 | (a) | 7·81 | 8·24 | 8·63 | 8·96 | 9·21 | 9·38 | 9·43 | 9·37 | 9·18 | — | — | — | — | — | — | — | — | — |
|   | (b) | 7·81 | 8·00 | 8·17 | 8·35 | 8·52 | 8·69 | 8·85 | 9·02 | 9·18 | — | — | — | — | — | — | — | — | — |
| 5 | (a) | 9·49 | 9·88 | 10·24 | 10·57 | 10·86 | 11·08 | 11·24 | 11·32 | 11·31 | 11·21 | 11·02 | — | — | — | — | — | — | — |
|   | (b) | 9·49 | 9·65 | 9·80 | 9·96 | 10·11 | 10·27 | 10·42 | 10·57 | 10·72 | 10·87 | 11·02 | — | — | — | — | — | — | — |
| 6 | (a) | 11·07 | 11·43 | 11·78 | 12·11 | 12·40 | 12·65 | 12·86 | 13·01 | 13·11 | 13·14 | 13·10 | 12·78 | — | — | — | — | — | — |
|   | (b) | 11·07 | 11·22 | 11·36 | 11·51 | 11·65 | 11·79 | 11·94 | 12·08 | 12·22 | 12·36 | 12·50 | 12·78 | — | — | — | — | — | — |
| 7 | (a) | 12·59 | 12·94 | 13·27 | 13·59 | 13·88 | 14·15 | 14·38 | 14·58 | 14·73 | 14·83 | 14·88 | 14·81 | 14·49 | — | — | — | — | — |
|   | (b) | 12·59 | 12·73 | 12·87 | 13·00 | 13·14 | 13·27 | 13·41 | 13·55 | 13·68 | 13·82 | 13·95 | 14·22 | 14·49 | — | — | — | — | — |
| 8 | (a) | 14·07 | 14·40 | 14·72 | 15·03 | 15·32 | 15·60 | 15·84 | 16·06 | 16·25 | 16·40 | 16·51 | 16·60 | 16·49 | 16·16 | — | — | — | — |
|   | (b) | 14·07 | 14·20 | 14·33 | 14·46 | 14·59 | 14·72 | 14·85 | 14·98 | 15·11 | 15·25 | 15·38 | 15·64 | 15·90 | 16·16 | — | — | — | — |
| 9 | (a) | 15·51 | 15·83 | 16·14 | 16·44 | 16·73 | 17·01 | 17·26 | 17·49 | 17·70 | 17·88 | 18·03 | 18·22 | 18·26 | 18·12 | 17·79 | — | — | — |
|   | (b) | 15·51 | 15·63 | 15·76 | 15·89 | 16·02 | 16·14 | 16·27 | 16·40 | 16·52 | 16·65 | 16·78 | 17·03 | 17·29 | 17·54 | 17·79 | — | — | — |
| 10 | (a) | 16·92 | 17·23 | 17·54 | 17·83 | 18·12 | 18·39 | 18·65 | 18·89 | 19·11 | 19·31 | 19·48 | 19·75 | 19·89 | 19·89 | 19·73 | 19·40 | — | — |
|   | (b) | 16·92 | 17·04 | 17·17 | 17·29 | 17·41 | 17·54 | 17·66 | 17·79 | 17·91 | 18·04 | 18·16 | 18·41 | 18·66 | 18·91 | 19·16 | 19·40 | — | — |
| 11 | (a) | 18·31 | 18·61 | 18·91 | 19·20 | 19·48 | 19·76 | 20·02 | 20·26 | 20·49 | 20·70 | 20·89 | 21·21 | 21·42 | 21·52 | 21·49 | 21·32 | — | — |
|   | (b) | 18·31 | 18·43 | 18·55 | 18·67 | 18·79 | 18·91 | 19·04 | 19·16 | 19·28 | 19·40 | 19·52 | 19·77 | 20·01 | 20·26 | 20·50 | 20·75 | — | — |
| 12 | (a) | 19·68 | 19·97 | 20·26 | 20·55 | 20·83 | 21·10 | 21·36 | 21·61 | 21·84 | 22·06 | 22·27 | 22·62 | 22·88 | 23·06 | 23·12 | 23·07 | 22·56 | — |
|   | (b) | 19·68 | 19·79 | 19·91 | 20·03 | 20·15 | 20·27 | 20·39 | 20·51 | 20·63 | 20·75 | 20·87 | 21·12 | 21·36 | 21·60 | 21·84 | 22·08 | 22·56 | — |
| 13 | (a) | 21·03 | 21·32 | 21·60 | 21·89 | 22·16 | 22·43 | 22·69 | 22·94 | 23·18 | 23·40 | 23·62 | 23·99 | 24·30 | 24·53 | 24·66 | 24·70 | 24·44 | — |
|   | (b) | 21·03 | 21·14 | 21·26 | 21·38 | 21·50 | 21·62 | 21·74 | 21·85 | 21·97 | 22·09 | 22·21 | 22·45 | 22·69 | 22·92 | 23·16 | 23·40 | 23·88 | — |
| 14 | (a) | 22·36 | 22·65 | 22·93 | 23·21 | 23·48 | 23·75 | 24·01 | 24·26 | 24·50 | 24·73 | 24·95 | 25·34 | 25·68 | 25·95 | 26·14 | 26·25 | 26·17 | 25·66 |
|   | (b) | 22·36 | 22·48 | 22·60 | 22·71 | 22·83 | 22·95 | 23·06 | 23·18 | 23·30 | 23·42 | 23·53 | 23·77 | 24·00 | 24·24 | 24·48 | 24·71 | 25·19 | 25·66 |
| 15 | (a) | 23·68 | 23·97 | 24·24 | 24·52 | 24·79 | 25·05 | 25·31 | 25·56 | 25·80 | 26·04 | 26·26 | 26·67 | 27·03 | 27·33 | 27·56 | 27·73 | 27·80 | 27·50 |
|   | (b) | 23·68 | 23·80 | 23·92 | 24·03 | 24·15 | 24·26 | 24·38 | 24·50 | 24·61 | 24·73 | 24·85 | 25·08 | 25·31 | 25·55 | 25·78 | 26·01 | 26·48 | 26·95 |

$$M = N \log_e \left\{ \sum_{t=1}^{k} (\nu_t s_t^2)/N \right\} - \sum_{t=1}^{k} (\nu_t \log_e s_t^2) \qquad N = \sum_{t=1}^{k} \nu_t \qquad c_1 = \sum_{t=1}^{k} \frac{1}{\nu_t} - \frac{1}{N} \qquad \text{N.B. } \log_e x = 2 \cdot 3026 \log_{10} x.$$

$s_t^2$ ($t = 1, 2, \ldots, k$) are $k$ independent mean square estimates of a variance, $\sigma^2$, based on $\nu_t$ degrees of freedom.

## Table 32 (continued)

### Upper 1% points

| $c_1$ $\diagdown$ $k$ | | 0·0 | 0·5 | 1·0 | 1·5 | 2·0 | 2·5 | 3·0 | 3·5 | 4·0 | 4·5 | 5·0 | 6·0 | 7·0 | 8·0 | 9·0 | 10·0 | 12·0 | 14·0 |
|---|---|---|---|---|---|---|---|---|---|---|---|---|---|---|---|---|---|---|---|
| 3 | (a) | 9·21 | 9·92 | 10·47 | 10·78 | 10·81 | 10·50 | 9·83 | — | — | — | — | — | — | — | — | — | — | — |
|   | (b) | 9·21 | 9·29 | 9·38 | 9·48 | 9·59 | 9·71 | 9·83 | — | — | — | — | — | — | — | — | — | — | — |
| 4 | (a) | 11·34 | 11·95 | 12·46 | 12·86 | 13·11 | 13·18 | 13·03 | 12·65 | 12·03 | — | — | — | — | — | — | — | — | — |
|   | (b) | 11·34 | 11·40 | 11·46 | 11·54 | 11·63 | 11·72 | 11·82 | 11·92 | 12·03 | — | — | — | — | — | — | — | — | — |
| 5 | (a) | 13·28 | 13·81 | 14·30 | 14·71 | 15·03 | 15·25 | 15·34 | 15·23 | 15·06 | 14·66 | 14·07 | — | — | — | — | — | — | — |
|   | (b) | 13·28 | 13·33 | 13·39 | 13·45 | 13·53 | 13·61 | 13·69 | 13·73 | 13·87 | 13·97 | 14·07 | — | — | — | — | — | — | — |
| 6 | (a) | 15·09 | 15·58 | 16·03 | 16·44 | 16·79 | 17·07 | 17·27 | 17·37 | 17·37 | 17·24 | 16·98 | 16·03 | — | — | — | — | — | — |
|   | (b) | 15·09 | 15·14 | 15·20 | 15·26 | 15·33 | 15·41 | 15·48 | 15·57 | 15·65 | 15·74 | 15·84 | 16·03 | — | — | — | — | — | — |
| 7 | (a) | 16·81 | 17·27 | 17·70 | 18·10 | 18·46 | 18·77 | 19·02 | 19·21 | 19·32 | 19·35 | 19·28 | 18·84 | 17·92 | — | — | — | — | — |
|   | (b) | 16·81 | 16·87 | 16·93 | 16·99 | 17·06 | 17·14 | 17·21 | 17·29 | 17·37 | 17·46 | 17·55 | 17·73 | 17·92 | — | — | — | — | — |
| 8 | (a) | 18·48 | 18·91 | 19·32 | 19·71 | 20·07 | 20·39 | 20·67 | 20·90 | 21·08 | 21·20 | 21·25 | 21·13 | 20·64 | 19·76 | — | — | — | — |
|   | (b) | 18·48 | 18·54 | 18·60 | 18·67 | 18·74 | 18·81 | 18·88 | 18·96 | 19·04 | 19·13 | 19·21 | 19·39 | 19·57 | 19·76 | — | — | — | — |
| 9 | (a) | 20·09 | 20·50 | 20·90 | 21·28 | 21·64 | 21·97 | 22·26 | 22·52 | 22·74 | 22·91 | 23·03 | 23·10 | 22·91 | 22·41 | 21·56 | — | — | — |
|   | (b) | 20·09 | 20·15 | 20·22 | 20·29 | 20·36 | 20·44 | 20·51 | 20·59 | 20·67 | 20·75 | 20·84 | 21·01 | 21·19 | 21·37 | 21·56 | — | — | — |
| 10 | (a) | 21·67 | 22·06 | 22·45 | 22·82 | 23·17 | 23·50 | 23·80 | 24·08 | 24·32 | 24·52 | 24·69 | 24·90 | 24·90 | 24·66 | 24·15 | 23·33 | — | — |
|   | (b) | 21·67 | 21·73 | 21·80 | 21·88 | 21·95 | 22·02 | 22·10 | 22·18 | 22·26 | 22·34 | 22·42 | 22·60 | 22·77 | 22·95 | 23·14 | 23·33 | — | — |
| 11 | (a) | 23·21 | 23·59 | 23·97 | 24·33 | 24·67 | 25·00 | 25·31 | 25·59 | 25·85 | 26·08 | 26·28 | 26·57 | 26·70 | 26·65 | 26·38 | 25·86 | — | — |
|   | (b) | 23·21 | 23·28 | 23·35 | 23·43 | 23·50 | 23·58 | 23·66 | 23·74 | 23·82 | 23·90 | 23·98 | 24·15 | 24·33 | 24·51 | 24·69 | 24·88 | — | — |
| 12 | (a) | 24·72 | 25·10 | 25·46 | 25·81 | 26·15 | 26·48 | 26·79 | 27·08 | 27·35 | 27·59 | 27·81 | 28·16 | 28·39 | 28·46 | 28·37 | 28·07 | 26·79 | — |
|   | (b) | 24·72 | 24·80 | 24·87 | 24·95 | 25·03 | 25·11 | 25·18 | 25·27 | 25·35 | 25·43 | 25·51 | 25·68 | 25·86 | 26·04 | 26·22 | 26·41 | 26·79 | — |
| 13 | (a) | 26·22 | 26·58 | 26·93 | 27·28 | 27·62 | 27·94 | 28·25 | 28·54 | 28·81 | 29·07 | 29·30 | 29·70 | 29·99 | 30·16 | 30·19 | 30·06 | 29·22 | — |
|   | (b) | 26·22 | 26·29 | 26·37 | 26·45 | 26·53 | 26·61 | 26·69 | 26·77 | 26·85 | 26·94 | 27·02 | 27·19 | 27·37 | 27·55 | 27·73 | 27·91 | 28·29 | — |
| 14 | (a) | 27·69 | 28·04 | 28·39 | 28·73 | 29·06 | 29·38 | 29·69 | 29·98 | 30·26 | 30·52 | 30·77 | 31·19 | 31·53 | 31·77 | 31·89 | 31·88 | 31·39 | 30·16 |
|   | (b) | 27·69 | 27·77 | 27·85 | 27·93 | 28·01 | 28·09 | 28·17 | 28·25 | 28·34 | 28·42 | 28·51 | 28·68 | 28·86 | 29·03 | 29·22 | 29·40 | 29·77 | 30·16 |
| 15 | (a) | 29·14 | 29·49 | 29·83 | 30·16 | 30·49 | 30·80 | 31·11 | 31·40 | 31·68 | 31·95 | 32·20 | 32·66 | 33·03 | 33·32 | 33·51 | 33·59 | 33·37 | 32·52 |
|   | (b) | 29·14 | 29·22 | 29·30 | 29·38 | 29·47 | 29·55 | 29·63 | 29·72 | 29·80 | 29·89 | 29·97 | 30·15 | 30·32 | 30·50 | 30·69 | 30·87 | 31·24 | 31·62 |

$$M = N \log_e \left\{ \sum_{t=1}^{k} (\nu_t s_t^2)/N \right\} - \sum_{t=1}^{k} (\nu_t \log_e s_t^2) \qquad N = \sum_{t=1}^{k} \nu_t \qquad c_1 = \sum_{t=1}^{k} \frac{1}{\nu_t} - \frac{1}{N}$$

$s_t^2$ ($t = 1, 2, \ldots, k$) are $k$ independent mean square estimates of a variance, $\sigma^2$, based on $\nu_t$ degrees of freedom.

N.B. $\log_e x = 2 \cdot 3026 \log_{10} x$.

For Table 32a giving percentage points when all $\nu_t = \nu$ are the same see pp. 266-7.

Table 33. *Test for heterogeneity of variance: table to facilitate interpolation in Table 32*

| $k$ | | 0·5 | 1·0 | 1·5 | 2·0 | 2·5 | 3·0 | 3·5 | 4·0 | 4·5 | 5·0 | 6·0 | 7·0 | 8·0 | 10·0 | 12·0 | 14·0 |
|---|---|---|---|---|---|---|---|---|---|---|---|---|---|---|---|---|---|
| 3 | $C$ | 0·014 | 0·111 | 0·375 | 0·889 | 1·736 | 3·000 | — | — | — | — | — | — | — | — | — | — |
|   | $\Delta C$ | 0·486 | 0·889 | 1·125 | 1·111 | 0·764 | 0·000 | — | — | — | — | — | — | — | — | — | — |
| 4 | $C$ | 0·008 | 0·062 | 0·211 | 0·500 | 0·977 | 1·688 | 2·680 | 4·000 | — | — | — | — | — | — | — | — |
|   | $\Delta C$ | 0·492 | 0·938 | 1·289 | 1·500 | 1·523 | 1·312 | 0·820 | 0·000 | — | — | — | — | — | — | — | — |
| 5 | $C$ | 0·005 | 0·040 | 0·135 | 0·320 | 0·625 | 1·080 | 1·715 | 2·560 | 3·645 | 5·000 | — | — | — | — | — | — |
|   | $\Delta C$ | 0·495 | 0·960 | 1·365 | 1·680 | 1·875 | 1·920 | 1·785 | 1·440 | 0·855 | 0·000 | — | — | — | — | — | — |
| 6 | $C$ | 0·003 | 0·028 | 0·094 | 0·222 | 0·434 | 0·750 | 1·191 | 1·778 | 2·531 | 3·472 | 6·000 | — | — | — | — | — |
|   | $\Delta C$ | 0·497 | 0·972 | 1·406 | 1·778 | 2·066 | 2·250 | 2·309 | 2·222 | 1·969 | 1·528 | 0·000 | — | — | — | — | — |
| 7 | $C$ | 0·003 | 0·020 | 0·069 | 0·163 | 0·319 | 0·551 | 0·875 | 1·306 | 1·860 | 2·551 | 4·408 | 7·000 | — | — | — | — |
|   | $\Delta C$ | 0·497 | 0·980 | 1·431 | 1·837 | 2·181 | 2·449 | 2·625 | 2·694 | 2·640 | 2·449 | 1·592 | 0·000 | — | — | — | — |
| 8 | $C$ | 0·002 | 0·016 | 0·053 | 0·125 | 0·244 | 0·422 | 0·670 | 1·000 | 1·424 | 1·953 | 3·375 | 5·359 | 8·000 | — | — | — |
|   | $\Delta C$ | 0·498 | 0·984 | 1·447 | 1·875 | 2·256 | 2·578 | 2·830 | 3·000 | 3·076 | 3·047 | 2·625 | 1·641 | 0·000 | — | — | — |
| 9 | $C$ | 0·002 | 0·012 | 0·042 | 0·099 | 0·193 | 0·333 | 0·529 | 0·790 | 1·125 | 1·543 | 2·667 | 4·235 | 6·321 | — | — | — |
|   | $\Delta C$ | 0·498 | 0·988 | 1·458 | 1·901 | 2·307 | 2·667 | 2·971 | 3·210 | 3·375 | 3·457 | 3·333 | 2·765 | 1·679 | — | — | — |
| 10 | $C$ | 0·001 | 0·010 | 0·034 | 0·080 | 0·156 | 0·270 | 0·429 | 0·640 | 0·911 | 1·250 | 2·160 | 3·430 | 5·120 | 10·000 | — | — |
|   | $\Delta C$ | 0·499 | 0·990 | 1·466 | 1·920 | 2·344 | 2·730 | 3·071 | 3·360 | 3·589 | 3·750 | 3·840 | 3·570 | 2·880 | 0·000 | — | — |
| 11 | $C$ | 0·001 | 0·008 | 0·028 | 0·066 | 0·129 | 0·223 | 0·354 | 0·529 | 0·753 | 1·033 | 1·785 | 2·835 | 4·231 | 8·264 | — | — |
|   | $\Delta C$ | 0·499 | 0·992 | 1·472 | 1·934 | 2·371 | 2·777 | 3·146 | 3·471 | 3·747 | 3·967 | 4·215 | 4·165 | 3·769 | 1·736 | — | — |
| 12 | $C$ | 0·001 | 0·007 | 0·023 | 0·056 | 0·109 | 0·188 | 0·298 | 0·444 | 0·633 | 0·868 | 1·500 | 2·382 | 3·556 | 6·944 | 12·000 | — |
|   | $\Delta C$ | 0·499 | 0·993 | 1·477 | 1·944 | 2·391 | 2·812 | 3·202 | 3·556 | 3·867 | 4·132 | 4·500 | 4·618 | 4·444 | 3·056 | 0·000 | — |
| 13 | $C$ | 0·001 | 0·006 | 0·020 | 0·047 | 0·092 | 0·160 | 0·254 | 0·379 | 0·539 | 0·740 | 1·278 | 2·030 | 3·030 | 5·917 | 10·225 | — |
|   | $\Delta C$ | 0·499 | 0·994 | 1·480 | 1·953 | 2·408 | 2·840 | 3·246 | 3·621 | 3·961 | 4·260 | 4·722 | 4·970 | 4·970 | 4·083 | 1·775 | — |
| 14 | $C$ | 0·001 | 0·005 | 0·017 | 0·041 | 0·080 | 0·138 | 0·219 | 0·327 | 0·465 | 0·638 | 1·102 | 1·750 | 2·612 | 5·102 | 8·816 | 14·000 |
|   | $\Delta C$ | 0·499 | 0·995 | 1·483 | 1·959 | 2·420 | 2·862 | 3·281 | 3·673 | 4·035 | 4·362 | 4·898 | 5·250 | 5·388 | 4·898 | 3·184 | 0·000 |
| 15 | $C$ | 0·001 | 0·004 | 0·015 | 0·036 | 0·069 | 0·120 | 0·191 | 0·284 | 0·405 | 0·556 | 0·960 | 1·524 | 2·276 | 4·444 | 7·680 | 12·196 |
|   | $\Delta C$ | 0·499 | 0·996 | 1·485 | 1·964 | 2·431 | 2·880 | 3·309 | 3·716 | 4·095 | 4·444 | 5·040 | 5·476 | 5·724 | 5·556 | 4·320 | 1·804 |

## Table 34. *Tests for departure from normality*

### A. *Percentage points of the distribution of a = (mean deviation)/(standard deviation)*

| Size of sample $n$ | $n-1$ | Percentage points | | | | | | Mean | Standard deviation |
| | | Upper 1% | Upper 5% | Upper 10% | Lower 10% | Lower 5% | Lower 1% | | |
|---|---|---|---|---|---|---|---|---|---|
| 11 | 10 | ·9359 | ·9073 | ·8899 | ·7409 | ·7153 | ·6675 | ·81805 | ·05784 |
| 16 | 15 | ·9137 | ·8884 | ·8733 | ·7452 | ·7236 | ·6829 | ·81128 | ·04976 |
| 21 | 20 | ·9001 | ·8768 | ·8631 | ·7495 | ·7304 | ·6950 | ·80792 | ·04419 |
| 26 | 25 | ·8901 | ·8686 | ·8570 | ·7530 | ·7360 | ·7040 | ·80590 | ·04011 |
| 31 | 30 | ·8827 | ·8625 | ·8511 | ·7559 | ·7404 | ·7110 | ·80456 | ·03697 |
| 36 | 35 | ·8769 | ·8578 | ·8468 | ·7583 | ·7440 | ·7167 | ·80360 | ·03447 |
| 41 | 40 | ·8722 | ·8540 | ·8436 | ·7604 | ·7470 | ·7216 | ·80289 | ·03241 |
| 46 | 45 | ·8682 | ·8508 | ·8409 | ·7621 | ·7496 | ·7256 | ·80233 | ·03068 |
| 51 | 50 | ·8648 | ·8481 | ·8385 | ·7636 | ·7518 | ·7291 | ·80188 | ·02919 |
| 61 | 60 | ·8592 | ·8434 | ·8349 | ·7662 | ·7554 | ·7347 | ·80122 | ·02678 |
| 71 | 70 | ·8549 | ·8403 | ·8321 | ·7683 | ·7583 | ·7393 | ·80074 | ·02487 |
| 81 | 80 | ·8515 | ·8376 | ·8298 | ·7700 | ·7607 | ·7430 | ·80038 | ·02332 |
| 91 | 90 | ·8484 | ·8353 | ·8279 | ·7714 | ·7626 | ·7460 | ·80010 | ·02203 |
| 101 | 100 | ·8460 | ·8344 | ·8264 | ·7726 | ·7644 | ·7487 | ·79988 | ·02094 |
| 201 | 200 | ·8322 | ·8229 | ·8178 | ·7796 | ·7738 | ·7629 | ·79888 | ·01491 |
| 301 | 300 | ·8260 | ·8183 | ·8140 | ·7828 | ·7781 | ·7693 | ·79855 | ·01220 |
| 401 | 400 | ·8223 | ·8155 | ·8118 | ·7847 | ·7807 | ·7731 | ·79838 | ·01058 |
| 501 | 500 | ·8198 | ·8136 | ·8103 | ·7861 | ·7825 | ·7757 | ·79828 | ·00947 |
| 601 | 600 | ·8179 | ·8123 | ·8092 | ·7873 | ·7838 | ·7776 | ·79822 | ·00865 |
| 701 | 700 | ·8164 | ·8112 | ·8084 | ·7878 | ·7848 | ·7791 | ·79817 | ·00801 |
| 801 | 800 | ·8152 | ·8103 | ·8077 | ·7885 | ·7857 | ·7803 | ·79813 | ·00749 |
| 901 | 900 | ·8142 | ·8096 | ·8071 | ·7890 | ·7864 | ·7814 | ·79811 | ·00707 |
| 1001 | 1000 | ·8134 | ·8090 | ·8066 | ·7894 | ·7869 | ·7822 | ·79808 | ·00670 |

### B. *Percentage points of the distribution of $\sqrt{b_1} = m_3/m_2^{3/2}$ in samples from a normal population*

| Size of sample $n$ | Upper (or lower) percentage points | | | | Size of sample $n$ | Upper (or lower) percentage points | | | | Size of sample $n$ | Standard deviation of $\sqrt{b_1}$ |
| | 5% | 2·5% | 1·0% | 0·5% | | 5% | 2·5% | 1·0% | 0·5% | | |
|---|---|---|---|---|---|---|---|---|---|---|---|
| 20 | 0·772 | 0·940 | 1·150 | 1·304 | 100 | 0·390 | 0·470 | 0·567 | 0·636 | 550 | 0·1039 |
| 25 | ·711 | ·866 | 1·059 | 1·200 | 125 | ·351 | ·422 | ·508 | ·569 | 600 | ·0995 |
| 30 | ·662 | ·806 | 0·986 | 1·117 | 150 | ·322 | ·387 | ·465 | ·519 | 650 | ·0956 |
| 35 | ·621 | ·756 | ·923 | 1·044 | 175 | ·299 | ·359 | ·430 | ·481 | 700 | ·0922 |
| 40 | ·588 | ·714 | ·871 | 0·985 | 200 | ·280 | ·336 | ·403 | ·449 | | |
| 45 | ·559 | ·679 | ·826 | ·934 | | | | | | 750 | 0·0891 |
| | | | | | 250 | 0·251 | 0·301 | 0·361 | 0·402 | 800 | ·0863 |
| 50 | 0·534 | 0·647 | 0·788 | ·889 | 300 | ·230 | ·275 | ·329 | ·366 | 850 | ·0837 |
| 60 | ·492 | ·596 | ·724 | ·816 | 350 | ·213 | ·255 | ·305 | ·339 | 900 | ·0814 |
| 70 | ·459 | ·556 | ·673 | ·758 | 400 | ·200 | ·239 | ·285 | ·317 | 950 | ·0792 |
| 80 | ·432 | ·522 | ·632 | ·710 | 450 | ·188 | ·225 | ·269 | ·299 | 1000 | ·0772 |
| 90 | ·409 | ·494 | ·597 | ·670 | 500 | ·179 | ·214 | ·255 | ·283 | | |

N.B. The lower limits equal the corresponding upper limits, with negative sign. [Note added to 1976 impression: Basing conclusions on a combination of simulation and curve fitting, D'Agostino & Pearson (*Biometrika*, 1973, **60**, 619) show that from the 0·5% level inwards the probability distribution of $\sqrt{b_1}$ may be derived approximately from the Johnson $S_U$ transformation, $X = \delta\sinh^{-1}(\sqrt{b_1}/\lambda)$, where $X$ is a $N(0, 1)$ variable; they have tabled values of $\delta$ and $\lambda$ as functions of $n$. Their results have been used to expand and slightly modify the table given in earlier issues. For $n > 500$ a normal approximation is adequate using the values of the standard deviation of $\sqrt{b_1}$ shown in the final column of this table.]

## Table 34. *Tests for departure from normality (continued)*
### C. *Percentage points of the distribution of $b_2 = m_4/m_2^2$ in samples from a normal population*

| Size of sample $n$ | Upper percentage points | | | | Lower percentage points | | | | Size of sample $n$ |
|---|---|---|---|---|---|---|---|---|---|
| | 0·5% | 1·0% | 2·5% | 5·0% | 5·0% | 2·5% | 1·0% | 0·5% | |
| 20 | 5·91 | 5·38 | 4·68 | 4·18 | 1·83 | 1·73 | 1·64 | 1·58 | 20 |
| 30 | 5·69 | 5·20 | 4·57 | 4·12 | 1·98 | 1·89 | 1·79 | 1·73 | 30 |
| 40 | 5·48 | 5·04 | 4·46 | 4·06 | 2·07 | 1·99 | 1·89 | 1·83 | 40 |
| 50 | 5·28 | 4·88 | 4·36 | 4·00 | 2·15 | 2·06 | 1·95 | 1·91 | 50 |
| 75 | 4·90 | 4·59 | 4·17 | 3·87 | 2·27 | 2·19 | 2·08 | 2·05 | 75 |
| 100 | 4·66 | 4·39 | 4·03 | 3·77 | 2·35 | 2·27 | 2·18 | 2·13 | 100 |
| 125 | 4·48 | 4·24 | 3·93 | 3·70 | 2·40 | 2·32 | 2·24 | 2·19 | 125 |
| 150 | 4·34 | 4·13 | 3·86 | 3·65 | 2·45 | 2·37 | 2·29 | 2·24 | 150 |
| 175 | 4·23 | 4·04 | 3·79 | 3·61 | 2·48 | 2·41 | 2·34 | 2·28 | 175 |
| 200 | 4·16 | 3·98 | 3·75 | 3·57 | 2·51 | 2·44 | 2·37 | 2·32 | 200 |

| $n$ | Upper | | Lower | | $n$ | Upper | | Lower | |
|---|---|---|---|---|---|---|---|---|---|
| | 1% | 5% | 5% | 1% | | 1% | 5% | 5% | 1% |
| 250 | 3·87 | 3·52 | 2·55 | 2·42 | 700 | 3·50 | 3·31 | 2·72 | 2·62 |
| 300 | 3·79 | 3·47 | 2·59 | 2·46 | 800 | 3·46 | 3·29 | 2·74 | 2·65 |
| 400 | 3·67 | 3·41 | 2·64 | 2·52 | 900 | 3·43 | 3·28 | 2·75 | 2·66 |
| 500 | 3·60 | 3·37 | 2·67 | 2·57 | 1000 | 3·41 | 3·26 | 2·76 | 2·68 |
| 600 | 3·54 | 3·34 | 2·70 | 2·60 | 2000 | 3·28 | 3·18 | 2·83 | 2·77 |

## Table 35. *Moments of $s/\sigma = \chi/\sqrt{\nu}$ and factors for determining confidence limits for $\sigma$*

| Degrees of freedom $\nu$ | Moments of $s/\sigma$ (or $\chi/\sqrt{\nu}$) | | | | | Factors for confidence limits of $\sigma$ | | | |
|---|---|---|---|---|---|---|---|---|---|
| | Expectation | S.D. | S.D. $\times \sqrt{(2\nu)}$ | $\beta_1$ | $\beta_2$ | $1-2\alpha=0.95$ | | $1-2\alpha=0.99$ | |
| | | | | | | Lower | Upper | Lower | Upper |
| (1) | (2) | (3) | (4) | (5) | (6) | (7) | (8) | (9) | (10) |
| 1 | 0·797 885 | 0·60281 | 0·8525 | 0·9906 | 3·8692 | 0·446 | 31·91 | 0·356 | 159·58 |
| 2 | ·886 227 | ·46325 | ·9265 | ·3983 | 3·2451 | ·521 | 6·28 | ·434 | 14·12 |
| 3 | ·921 318 | ·38881 | ·9524 | ·2359 | 3·1082 | ·566 | 3·73 | ·483 | 6·47 |
| 4 | ·939 986 | ·34121 | ·9651 | ·1646 | 3·0593 | ·599 | 2·87 | ·519 | 4·40 |
| 5 | ·951 533 | ·30755 | ·9725 | ·1255 | 3·0370 | ·624 | 2·45 | ·546 | 3·48 |
| 6 | 0·959 369 | 0·28216 | 0·9774 | 0·1011 | 3·0251 | 0·644 | 2·20 | 0·569 | 2·98 |
| 7 | ·965 030 | ·26214 | ·9808 | ·0845 | 3·0181 | ·661 | 2·04 | ·588 | 2·66 |
| 8 | ·969 311 | ·24584 | ·9834 | ·0725 | 3·0136 | ·675 | 1·92 | ·604 | 2·44 |
| 9 | ·972 659 | ·23224 | ·9853 | ·0634 | 3·0106 | ·688 | 1·83 | ·618 | 2·28 |
| 10 | ·975 350 | ·22066 | ·9868 | ·0564 | 3·00852 | ·699 | 1·75 | ·630 | 2·15 |
| 11 | 0·977 559 | 0·21066 | 0·9881 | 0·0507 | 3·00697 | 0·708 | 1·70 | 0·641 | 2·06 |
| 12 | ·979 406 | ·20190 | ·9891 | ·0461 | 3·00581 | ·717 | 1·65 | ·651 | 1·98 |
| 13 | ·980 971 | ·19415 | ·9900 | ·0422 | 3·00492 | ·725 | 1·61 | ·660 | 1·91 |
| 14 | ·982 316 | ·18723 | ·9907 | ·0390 | 3·00421 | ·732 | 1·58 | ·669 | 1·85 |
| 15 | ·983 484 | ·18100 | ·9914 | ·0362 | 3·00365 | ·739 | 1·55 | ·676 | 1·81 |
| 16 | 0·984 506 | 0·17535 | 0·9919 | 0·0337 | 3·00319 | 0·745 | 1·52 | 0·683 | 1·76 |
| 17 | ·985 410 | ·17020 | ·9924 | ·0316 | 3·00281 | ·750 | 1·50 | ·690 | 1·73 |
| 18 | ·986 214 | ·16547 | ·9928 | ·0297 | 3·00250 | ·756 | 1·48 | ·696 | 1·70 |
| 19 | ·986 934 | ·16112 | ·9932 | ·0281 | 3·00223 | ·760 | 1·46 | ·702 | 1·67 |
| 20 | ·987 583 | ·15710 | ·9936 | ·0266 | 3·00201 | ·765 | 1·44 | ·707 | 1·64 |
| 25 | 0·990 052 | 0·14070 | 0·9949 | 0·0210 | 3·00127 | 0·784 | 1·38 | 0·730 | 1·54 |
| 30 | ·991 703 | ·12855 | ·9958 | ·0174 | 3·00087 | ·799 | 1·34 | ·748 | 1·48 |
| 35 | ·992 884 | ·11909 | ·9964 | ·0148 | 3·00064 | ·811 | 1·30 | ·762 | 1·43 |
| 40 | ·993 770 | ·11145 | ·9968 | ·0129 | 3·00049 | ·821 | 1·28 | ·774 | 1·39 |
| 45 | ·994 460 | ·10511 | ·9972 | ·0114 | 3·00038 | ·829 | 1·26 | ·784 | 1·36 |
| 50 | ·995 013 | ·09975 | ·9975 | ·0103 | 3·00031 | ·837 | 1·24 | ·793 | 1·34 |
| 60 | 0·995 842 | 0·09110 | 0·9979 | 0·00851 | 3·00021 | 0·849 | 1·22 | 0·808 | 1·30 |
| 70 | ·996 435 | ·08436 | ·9982 | ·00727 | 3·00016 | ·858 | 1·20 | ·820 | 1·27 |
| 80 | ·996 880 | ·07893 | ·9984 | ·00635 | 3·00012 | ·866 | 1·18 | ·829 | 1·25 |
| 90 | ·997 226 | ·07443 | ·9986 | ·00563 | 3·00009 | ·873 | 1·17 | ·838 | 1·23 |
| 100 | ·997 503 | ·07062 | ·9987 | ·00506 | 3·00008 | ·879 | 1·16 | ·845 | 1·22 |

## Table 36. *Test for the significance of the difference between two Poisson variables*

### A. *Lower significance levels for b < a in single-tail test*

| $r=a+b$ | Nominal significance level | | | | | $r=a+b$ | Nominal significance level | | | | |
|---|---|---|---|---|---|---|---|---|---|---|---|
| | 0.10 | 0.05 | 0.025 | 0.01 | 0.005 | | 0.10 | 0.05 | 0.025 | 0.01 | 0.005 |
| 1 | | | | | | 41 | 15 | 14 | 13 | 12 | 11 |
| 2 | | | | | | 42 | 16 | 15 | 14 | 13 | 12 |
| 3 | | | | | | 43 | 16 | 15 | 14 | 13 | 12 |
| 4 | 0 | | | | | 44 | 17 | 16 | 15 | 13 | 13 |
| 5 | 0 | 0 | | | | 45 | 17 | 16 | 15 | 14 | 13 |
| 6 | 0 | 0 | 0 | | | 46 | 18 | 16 | 15 | 14 | 13 |
| 7 | 1 | 0 | 0 | 0 | | 47 | 18 | 17 | 16 | 15 | 14 |
| 8 | 1 | 1 | 0 | 0 | 0 | 48 | 19 | 17 | 16 | 15 | 14 |
| 9 | 2 | 1 | 1 | 0 | 0 | 49 | 19 | 18 | 17 | 15 | 15 |
| 10 | 2 | 1 | 1 | 0 | 0 | 50 | 19 | 18 | 17 | 16 | 15 |
| 11 | 2 | 2 | 1 | 1 | 0 | 51 | 20 | 19 | 18 | 16 | 15 |
| 12 | 3 | 2 | 2 | 1 | 1 | 52 | 20 | 19 | 18 | 17 | 16 |
| 13 | 3 | 3 | 2 | 1 | 1 | 53 | 21 | 20 | 18 | 17 | 16 |
| 14 | 4 | 3 | 2 | 2 | 1 | 54 | 21 | 20 | 19 | 18 | 17 |
| 15 | 4 | 3 | 3 | 2 | 2 | 55 | 22 | 20 | 19 | 18 | 17 |
| 16 | 4 | 4 | 3 | 2 | 2 | 56 | 22 | 21 | 20 | 18 | 17 |
| 17 | 5 | 4 | 4 | 3 | 2 | 57 | 23 | 21 | 20 | 19 | 18 |
| 18 | 5 | 5 | 4 | 3 | 3 | 58 | 23 | 22 | 21 | 19 | 18 |
| 19 | 6 | 5 | 4 | 4 | 3 | 59 | 24 | 22 | 21 | 20 | 19 |
| 20 | 6 | 5 | 5 | 4 | 3 | 60 | 24 | 23 | 21 | 20 | 19 |
| 21 | 7 | 6 | 5 | 4 | 4 | 61 | 24 | 23 | 22 | 20 | 20 |
| 22 | 7 | 6 | 5 | 5 | 4 | 62 | 25 | 24 | 22 | 21 | 20 |
| 23 | 7 | 7 | 6 | 5 | 4 | 63 | 25 | 24 | 23 | 21 | 20 |
| 24 | 8 | 7 | 6 | 5 | 5 | 64 | 26 | 24 | 23 | 22 | 21 |
| 25 | 8 | 7 | 7 | 6 | 5 | 65 | 26 | 25 | 24 | 22 | 21 |
| 26 | 9 | 8 | 7 | 6 | 6 | 66 | 27 | 25 | 24 | 23 | 22 |
| 27 | 9 | 8 | 7 | 7 | 6 | 67 | 27 | 26 | 25 | 23 | 22 |
| 28 | 10 | 9 | 8 | 7 | 6 | 68 | 28 | 26 | 25 | 23 | 22 |
| 29 | 10 | 9 | 8 | 7 | 7 | 69 | 28 | 27 | 25 | 24 | 23 |
| 30 | 10 | 10 | 9 | 8 | 7 | 70 | 29 | 27 | 26 | 24 | 23 |
| 31 | 11 | 10 | 9 | 8 | 7 | 71 | 29 | 28 | 26 | 25 | 24 |
| 32 | 11 | 10 | 9 | 8 | 8 | 72 | 30 | 28 | 27 | 25 | 24 |
| 33 | 12 | 11 | 10 | 9 | 8 | 73 | 30 | 28 | 27 | 26 | 25 |
| 34 | 12 | 11 | 10 | 9 | 9 | 74 | 30 | 29 | 28 | 26 | 25 |
| 35 | 13 | 12 | 11 | 10 | 9 | 75 | 31 | 29 | 28 | 26 | 25 |
| 36 | 13 | 12 | 11 | 10 | 9 | 76 | 31 | 30 | 28 | 27 | 26 |
| 37 | 14 | 13 | 12 | 10 | 10 | 77 | 32 | 30 | 29 | 27 | 26 |
| 38 | 14 | 13 | 12 | 11 | 10 | 78 | 32 | 31 | 29 | 28 | 27 |
| 39 | 15 | 13 | 12 | 11 | 11 | 79 | 33 | 31 | 30 | 28 | 27 |
| 40 | 15 | 14 | 13 | 12 | 11 | 80 | 33 | 32 | 30 | 29 | 28 |

### B. *True significance levels resulting from long-run use of Table* 36 A *according to the nominal level and the value, m, of the common Poisson expectation*

| $m$ | Nominal significance level | | | | | $m$ |
|---|---|---|---|---|---|---|
| | 0.10 | 0.05 | 0.025 | 0.01 | 0.005 | |
| 2.5 | 0.032 | 0.012 | 0.004 | 0.0012 | 0.0003 | 2.5 |
| 5.0 | .054 | .023 | .011 | .0033 | .0015 | 5.0 |
| 7.5 | .061 | .030 | .014 | .0044 | .0021 | 7.5 |
| 10.0 | .066 | .032 | .015 | .0055 | .0024 | 10.0 |
| 12.5 | .068 | .034 | .015 | .0059 | .0027 | 12.5 |
| 15.0 | 0.071 | 0.035 | 0.015 | 0.0060 | 0.0029 | 15.0 |
| 17.5 | .074 | .036 | .016 | .0061 | .0031 | 17.5 |
| 20.0 | .076 | .037 | .017 | .0065 | .0032 | 20.0 |
| 22.5 | .077 | .037 | .018 | .0068 | .0033 | 22.5 |
| 25.0 | .077 | .038 | .018 | .0070 | .0034 | 25.0 |

Table 37. *Individual terms of certain binomial distributions:* $f(i \mid n, p) = \binom{n}{i} p^i (1-p)^{n-i}$

| $n$ | $i$ \ $p$ | 0·01 | 0·02 | 0·04 | 0·06 | 0·08 | 0·1 | 0·2 | 0·3 | 0·4 | 0·5 | | |
|---|---|---|---|---|---|---|---|---|---|---|---|---|---|
| 5 | 0 | 0·95099 | 0·90392 | 0·81537 | 0·73390 | 0·65908 | 0·59049 | 0·32768 | 0·16807 | 0·07776 | 0·03125 | 5 | |
|  | 1 | ·04803 | ·09224 | ·16987 | ·23422 | ·28656 | ·32805 | ·40960 | ·36015 | ·25920 | ·15625 | 4 | |
|  | 2 | ·00097 | ·00376 | ·01416 | ·02990 | ·04984 | ·07290 | ·20480 | ·30870 | ·34560 | ·31250 | 3 | 5 |
|  | 3 | ·00001 | ·00008 | ·00059 | ·00191 | ·00433 | ·00810 | ·05120 | ·13230 | ·23040 | ·31250 | 2 | |
|  | 4 |  |  | ·00001 | ·00006 | ·00019 | ·00045 | ·00640 | ·02835 | ·07680 | ·15625 | 1 | |
|  | 5 |  |  |  |  |  | ·00001 | ·00032 | ·00243 | ·01024 | ·03125 | 0 | |
| 10 | 0 | 0·90438 | 0·81707 | 0·66483 | 0·53862 | 0·43439 | 0·34868 | 0·10737 | 0·02825 | 0·00605 | 0·00098 | 10 | |
|  | 1 | ·09135 | ·16675 | ·27701 | ·34380 | ·37773 | ·38742 | ·26844 | ·12106 | ·04031 | ·00977 | 9 | |
|  | 2 | ·00415 | ·01531 | ·05194 | ·09875 | ·14781 | ·19371 | ·30199 | ·23347 | ·12093 | ·04395 | 8 | |
|  | 3 | ·00011 | ·00083 | ·00577 | ·01681 | ·03427 | ·05740 | ·20133 | ·26683 | ·21499 | ·11719 | 7 | |
|  | 4 |  | ·00003 | ·00042 | ·00188 | ·00522 | ·01116 | ·08808 | ·20012 | ·25082 | ·20508 | 6 | |
|  | 5 |  |  | 0·00002 | ·00014 | ·00054 | ·00149 | ·02642 | ·10292 | ·20066 | ·24609 | 5 | 10 |
|  | 6 |  |  |  | ·00001 | ·00004 | ·00014 | ·00551 | ·03676 | ·11148 | ·20508 | 4 | |
|  | 7 |  |  |  |  |  | ·00001 | ·00079 | ·00900 | ·04247 | ·11719 | 3 | |
|  | 8 |  |  |  |  |  |  | ·00007 | ·00145 | ·01062 | ·04395 | 2 | |
|  | 9 |  |  |  |  |  |  |  | ·00014 | ·00157 | ·00977 | 1 | |
|  | 10 |  |  |  |  |  |  |  | ·00001 | ·00010 | ·00098 | 0 | |
| 15 | 0 | 0·86006 | 0·73857 | 0·54209 | 0·39529 | 0·28630 | 0·20589 | 0·03518 | 0·00475 | 0·00047 | 0·00003 | 15 | |
|  | 1 | ·13031 | ·22609 | ·33880 | ·37847 | ·37343 | ·34315 | ·13194 | ·03052 | ·00470 | ·00046 | 14 | |
|  | 2 | ·00921 | ·03230 | ·09882 | ·16910 | ·22731 | ·26690 | ·23090 | ·09156 | ·02194 | ·00320 | 13 | |
|  | 3 | ·00040 | ·00286 | ·01784 | ·04677 | ·08565 | ·12851 | ·25014 | ·17004 | ·06339 | ·01389 | 12 | |
|  | 4 | ·00001 | ·00017 | ·00223 | ·00896 | ·02234 | ·04284 | ·18760 | ·21862 | ·12678 | ·04166 | 11 | |
|  | 5 |  | 0·00001 | 0·00020 | ·00126 | ·00427 | ·01047 | ·10318 | ·20613 | ·18594 | ·09164 | 10 | 15 |
|  | 6 |  |  | ·00001 | ·00013 | ·00062 | ·00194 | ·04299 | ·14724 | ·20660 | ·15274 | 9 | |
|  | 7 |  |  |  | ·00001 | ·00007 | ·00028 | ·01382 | ·08113 | ·17708 | ·19638 | 8 | |
|  | 8 |  |  |  |  | ·00001 | ·00003 | ·00345 | ·03477 | ·11806 | ·19638 | 7 | |
|  | 9 |  |  |  |  |  |  | ·00067 | ·01159 | ·06121 | ·15274 | 6 | |
|  | 10 |  |  |  |  |  |  | 0·00010 | ·00298 | ·02449 | ·09164 | 5 | |
|  | 11 |  |  |  |  |  |  | ·00001 | ·00058 | ·00742 | ·04166 | 4 | |
|  | 12 |  |  |  |  |  |  |  | ·00008 | ·00165 | ·01389 | 3 | |
|  | 13 |  |  |  |  |  |  |  | ·00001 | ·00025 | ·00320 | 2 | |
|  | 14 |  |  |  |  |  |  |  |  | ·00002 | ·00046 | 1 | |
|  | 15 |  |  |  |  |  |  |  |  |  | ·00003 | 0 | |
| 20 | 0 | 0·81791 | 0·66761 | 0·44200 | 0·29011 | 0·18869 | 0·12158 | 0·01153 | 0·00080 | 0·00004 |  | 20 | |
|  | 1 | ·16523 | ·27249 | ·36834 | ·37035 | ·32816 | ·27017 | ·05765 | ·00684 | ·00049 | 0·00002 | 19 | |
|  | 2 | ·01586 | ·05283 | ·14580 | ·22457 | ·27109 | ·28518 | ·13691 | ·02785 | ·00309 | ·00018 | 18 | |
|  | 3 | ·00096 | ·00647 | ·03645 | ·08601 | ·14144 | ·19012 | ·20536 | ·07160 | ·01235 | ·00109 | 17 | |
|  | 4 | ·00004 | ·00056 | ·00645 | ·02333 | ·05227 | ·08978 | ·21820 | ·13042 | ·03499 | ·00462 | 16 | |
|  | 5 |  | 0·00004 | 0·00086 | ·00477 | ·01454 | ·03192 | ·17456 | ·17886 | ·07465 | ·01479 | 15 | |
|  | 6 |  |  | ·00009 | ·00076 | ·00316 | ·00887 | ·10910 | ·19164 | ·12441 | ·03696 | 14 | |
|  | 7 |  |  | ·00001 | ·00010 | ·00055 | ·00197 | ·05455 | ·16426 | ·16588 | ·07393 | 13 | |
|  | 8 |  |  |  | ·00001 | ·00008 | ·00036 | ·02216 | ·11440 | ·17971 | ·12013 | 12 | |
|  | 9 |  |  |  |  | ·00001 | ·00005 | ·00739 | ·06537 | ·15974 | ·16018 | 11 | |
|  | 10 |  |  |  |  |  | ·00001 | 0·00203 | 0·03082 | 0·11714 | 0·17620 | 10 | 20 |
|  | 11 |  |  |  |  |  |  | ·00046 | ·01201 | ·07099 | ·16018 | 9 | |
|  | 12 |  |  |  |  |  |  | ·00009 | ·00386 | ·03550 | ·12013 | 8 | |
|  | 13 |  |  |  |  |  |  | ·00001 | ·00102 | ·01456 | ·07393 | 7 | |
|  | 14 |  |  |  |  |  |  |  | ·00022 | ·00485 | ·03696 | 6 | |
|  | 15 |  |  |  |  |  |  |  | 0·00004 | 0·00129 | 0·01479 | 5 | |
|  | 16 |  |  |  |  |  |  |  | ·00001 | ·00027 | ·00462 | 4 | |
|  | 17 |  |  |  |  |  |  |  |  | ·00004 | ·00109 | 3 | |
|  | 18 |  |  |  |  |  |  |  |  |  | ·00018 | 2 | |
|  | 19 |  |  |  |  |  |  |  |  |  | ·00002 | 1 | |
|  | 20 |  |  |  |  |  |  |  |  |  |  | 0 | |
|  |  | 0·99 | 0·98 | 0·96 | 0·94 | 0·92 | 0·9 | 0·8 | 0·7 | 0·6 | 0·5 | $i$ \ $p$ | $n$ |

Where the totals of the individual terms differ from unity owing to the incidence of rounding off errors, an adjustment involving a minimum percentage error may be made as follows: entries marked with a high dot (e.g. 6˙) should be increased by a unit in the 5th decimal and those marked with a low dot (e.g. 4.) decreased by a unit.

Table 37 (continued)

| n | i | 0.01 | 0.02 | 0.04 | 0.06 | 0.08 | 0.1 | 0.2 | 0.3 | 0.4 | 0.5 | i | n |
|---|---|------|------|------|------|------|-----|-----|-----|-----|-----|---|---|
| 25 | 0 | 0.77782 | 0.60346 | 0.36040 | 0.21291 | 0.12436 | 0.07179 | 0.00378 | 0.00013 | | | 25 | 25 |
| | 1 | .19642 | .30789 | .37541 | .33975 | .27036 | .19942 | .02361 | .00144 | 0.00005 | | 24 | |
| | 2 | .02381 | .07540 | .18771 | .26023 | .28211 | .26589 | .07084 | .00739 | .00038 | 0.00001 | 23 | |
| | 3 | .00184 | .01180 | .05996 | .12735 | .18807 | .22650 | .13577 | .02428 | .00194 | .00007 | 22 | |
| | 4 | .00010 | .00132 | .01374 | .04471 | .08995 | .13842 | .18668 | .05723 | .00710 | .00038 | 21 | |
| | 5 | 0.00000 | 0.00011 | 0.00240 | .01199 | .03285 | .06459 | .19602 | .10302 | .01989 | .00158 | 20 | |
| | 6 | | .00001 | .00033 | .00255 | .00952 | .02392 | .16335 | .14717 | .04420 | .00528 | 19 | |
| | 7 | | | .00004 | .00044 | .00225 | .00722 | .11084 | .17119 | .07999 | .01433 | 18 | |
| | 8 | | | | .00006 | .00044 | .00180 | .06235 | .16508 | .11998 | .03223 | 17 | |
| | 9 | | | | .00001 | .00007 | .00038 | .02944 | .13364 | .15109 | .06089 | 16 | |
| | 10 | | | | | 0.00001 | 0.00007 | .01178 | .09164 | .16116 | .09742 | 15 | |
| | 11 | | | | | | .00001 | .00401 | .05355 | .14651 | .13284 | 14 | |
| | 12 | | | | | | | .00117 | .02678 | .11395 | .15498 | 13 | |
| | 13 | | | | | | | .00029 | .01148 | .07597 | .15498 | 12 | |
| | 14 | | | | | | | .00006 | .00422 | .04341 | .13284 | 11 | |
| | 15 | | | | | | | 0.00001 | 0.00132 | .02122 | .09742 | 10 | |
| | 16 | | | | | | | | .00035 | .00884 | .06089 | 9 | |
| | 17 | | | | | | | | .00008 | .00312 | .03223 | 8 | |
| | 18 | | | | | | | | .00002 | .00092 | .01433 | 7 | |
| | 19 | | | | | | | | | .00023 | .00528 | 6 | |
| | 20 | | | | | | | | | 0.00005 | .00158 | 5 | |
| | 21 | | | | | | | | | .00001 | .00038 | 4 | |
| | 22 | | | | | | | | | | .00007 | 3 | |
| | 23 | | | | | | | | | | .00001 | 2 | |
| 30 | 0 | 0.73970 | 0.54548 | 0.29386 | 0.15626 | 0.08197 | 0.04239 | 0.00124 | 0.00002 | | | 30 | 30 |
| | 1 | .22415 | .33397 | .36732 | .29921 | .21382 | .14130 | .00928 | .00029 | | | 29 | |
| | 2 | .03283 | .09883 | .22192 | .27693 | .26961 | .22766 | .03366 | .00180 | 0.00004 | | 28 | |
| | 3 | .00310 | .01882 | .08630 | .16498 | .21881 | .23609 | .07853 | .00720 | .00027 | | 27 | |
| | 4 | .00021 | .00259 | .02427 | .07108 | .12843 | .17707 | .13252 | .02084 | .00120 | 0.00003 | 26 | |
| | 5 | 0.00001 | 0.00028 | 0.00526 | .02359 | .05807 | .10230 | .17228 | .04644 | .00415 | .00013 | 25 | |
| | 6 | | .00002 | .00091 | .00627 | .02104 | .04736 | .17946 | .08293 | .01152 | .00055 | 24 | |
| | 7 | | | .00013 | .00137 | .00627 | .01804 | .15382 | .12185 | .02634 | .00190 | 23 | |
| | 8 | | | .00002 | .00025 | .00157 | .00576 | .11056 | .15014 | .05049 | .00545 | 22 | |
| | 9 | | | | .00004 | .00033 | .00157 | .06756 | .15729 | .08228 | .01332 | 21 | |
| | 10 | | | | 0.00001 | 0.00006 | 0.00037 | .03547 | .14156 | .11519 | .02798 | 20 | |
| | 11 | | | | | .00001 | .00007 | .01612 | .11031 | .13962 | .05088 | 19 | |
| | 12 | | | | | | .00001 | .00638 | .07485 | .14738 | .08055 | 18 | |
| | 13 | | | | | | | .00221 | .04442 | .13604 | .11154 | 17 | |
| | 14 | | | | | | | .00067 | .02312 | .11013 | .13544 | 16 | |
| | 15 | | | | | | | 0.00018 | .01057 | .07831 | .14446 | 15 | |
| | 16 | | | | | | | .00004 | .00425 | .04895 | .13544 | 14 | |
| | 17 | | | | | | | .00001 | .00150 | .02687 | .11154 | 13 | |
| | 18 | | | | | | | | .00046 | .01294 | .08055 | 12 | |
| | 19 | | | | | | | | .00013 | .00545 | .05088 | 11 | |
| | 20 | | | | | | | | 0.00003 | .00200 | .02798 | 10 | |
| | 21 | | | | | | | | .00001 | .00063 | .01332 | 9 | |
| | 22 | | | | | | | | | .00017 | .00545 | 8 | |
| | 23 | | | | | | | | | .00004 | .00190 | 7 | |
| | 24 | | | | | | | | | .00001 | .00055 | 6 | |
| | 25 | | | | | | | | | | .00013 | 5 | |
| | 26 | | | | | | | | | | .00003 | 4 | |
| | | 0.99 | 0.98 | 0.96 | 0.94 | 0.92 | 0.9 | 0.8 | 0.7 | 0.6 | 0.5 | p | n |

Table 38. *Significance tests in a 2 × 2 contingency table*

| | a | 0·05 | 0·025 | 0·01 | 0·005 |
|---|---|---|---|---|---|
| A = 3 B = 3 | 3 | **0** ·050 | — | — | — |
| A = 4 B = 4 | 4 | **0** ·014 | **0** ·014 | — | — |
| 3 | 4 | **0** ·029 | — | — | — |
| A = 5 B = 5 | 5 | **1** ·024 | **1** ·024 | **0** ·004 | **0** ·004 |
| | 4 | **0** ·024 | **0** ·024 | — | — |
| 4 | 5 | **1** ·048 | **0** ·008 | **0** ·008 | — |
| | 4 | **0** ·040 | — | — | — |
| 3 | 5 | **0** ·018 | **0** ·018 | — | — |
| 2 | 5 | **0** ·048 | — | — | — |
| A = 6 B = 6 | 6 | **2** ·030 | **1** ·008 | **1** ·008 | **0** ·001 |
| | 5 | **1** ·040 | **0** ·008 | **0** ·008 | — |
| | 4 | **0** ·030 | — | — | — |
| 5 | 6 | **1** ·015+ | **1** ·015+ | **0** ·002 | **0** ·002 |
| | 5 | **0** ·013 | **0** ·013 | — | — |
| | 4 | **0** ·045+ | — | — | — |
| 4 | 6 | **1** ·033 | **0** ·005− | **0** ·005− | **0** ·005− |
| | 5 | **0** ·024 | **0** ·024 | — | — |
| 3 | 6 | **0** ·012 | **0** ·012 | — | — |
| | 5 | **0** ·048 | — | — | — |
| 2 | 6 | **0** ·036 | — | — | — |
| A = 7 B = 7 | 7 | **3** ·035− | **2** ·010+ | **1** ·002 | **1** ·002 |
| | 6 | **1** ·015− | **1** ·015− | **0** ·002 | **0** ·002 |
| | 5 | **0** ·010+ | **0** ·010+ | — | — |
| | 4 | **0** ·035− | — | — | — |
| 6 | 7 | **2** ·021 | **2** ·021 | **1** ·005− | **1** ·005− |
| | 6 | **1** ·025+ | **0** ·004 | **0** ·004 | **0** ·004 |
| | 5 | **0** ·016 | **0** ·016 | — | — |
| | 4 | **0** ·049 | — | — | — |
| 5 | 7 | **2** ·045+ | **1** ·010+ | **0** ·001 | **0** ·001 |
| | 6 | **1** ·045+ | **0** ·008 | **0** ·008 | — |
| | 5 | **0** ·027 | — | — | — |
| 4 | 7 | **1** ·024 | **1** ·024 | **0** ·003 | **0** ·003 |
| | 6 | **0** ·015+ | **0** ·015+ | — | — |
| | 5 | **0** ·045+ | — | — | — |
| 3 | 7 | **0** ·008 | **0** ·008 | **0** ·008 | — |
| | 6 | **0** ·033 | — | — | — |
| 2 | 7 | **0** ·028 | — | — | — |

| | a | 0·05 | 0·025 | 0·01 | 0·005 |
|---|---|---|---|---|---|
| A = 8 B = 8 | 8 | **4** ·038 | **3** ·013 | **2** ·003 | **2** ·003 |
| | 7 | **2** ·020 | **2** ·020 | **1** ·005+ | **0** ·001 |
| | 6 | **1** ·020 | **1** ·020 | **0** ·003 | **0** ·003 |
| | 5 | **0** ·013 | **0** ·013 | — | — |
| | 4 | **0** ·038 | — | — | — |
| 7 | 8 | **3** ·026 | **2** ·007 | **2** ·007 | **1** ·001 |
| | 7 | **2** ·035− | **1** ·009 | **1** ·009 | **0** ·001 |
| | 6 | **1** ·032 | **0** ·006 | **0** ·006 | — |
| | 5 | **0** ·019 | **0** ·019 | — | — |
| 6 | 8 | **2** ·015− | **2** ·015− | **1** ·003 | **1** ·003 |
| | 7 | **1** ·016 | **1** ·016 | **0** ·002 | **0** ·002 |
| | 6 | **0** ·009 | **0** ·009 | **0** ·009 | — |
| | 5 | **0** ·028 | — | — | — |
| 5 | 8 | **2** ·035− | **1** ·007 | **1** ·007 | **0** ·001 |
| | 7 | **1** ·032 | **0** ·005− | **0** ·005− | **0** ·005− |
| | 6 | **0** ·016 | **0** ·016 | — | — |
| | 5 | **0** ·044 | — | — | — |
| 4 | 8 | **1** ·018 | **1** ·018 | **0** ·002 | **0** ·002 |
| | 7 | **0** ·010+ | **0** ·010+ | — | — |
| | 6 | **0** ·030 | — | — | — |
| 3 | 8 | **0** ·006 | **0** ·006 | **0** ·006 | — |
| | 7 | **0** ·024 | **0** ·024 | — | — |
| 2 | 8 | **0** ·022 | **0** ·022 | — | — |
| A = 9 B = 9 | 9 | **5** ·041 | **4** ·015− | **3** ·005− | **3** ·005− |
| | 8 | **3** ·025− | **3** ·025− | **2** ·008 | **1** ·002 |
| | 7 | **2** ·028 | **1** ·008 | **1** ·008 | **0** ·001 |
| | 6 | **1** ·025− | **1** ·025− | **0** ·005− | **0** ·005− |
| | 5 | **0** ·015− | **0** ·015− | — | — |
| | 4 | **0** ·041 | — | — | — |
| 8 | 9 | **4** ·029 | **3** ·009 | **3** ·009 | **2** ·002 |
| | 8 | **3** ·043 | **2** ·013 | **1** ·003 | **1** ·003 |
| | 7 | **2** ·044 | **1** ·012 | **0** ·002 | **0** ·002 |
| | 6 | **1** ·036 | **0** ·007 | **0** ·007 | — |
| | 5 | **0** ·020 | **0** ·020 | — | — |
| 7 | 9 | **3** ·019 | **3** ·019 | **2** ·005− | **2** ·005− |
| | 8 | **2** ·024 | **2** ·024 | **1** ·006 | **0** ·001 |
| | 7 | **1** ·020 | **1** ·020 | **0** ·003 | **0** ·003 |
| | 6 | **0** ·010+ | **0** ·010+ | — | — |
| | 5 | **0** ·029 | — | — | — |
| 6 | 9 | **3** ·044 | **2** ·011 | **1** ·002 | **1** ·002 |
| | 8 | **2** ·047 | **1** ·011 | **0** ·001 | **0** ·001 |
| | 7 | **1** ·035− | **0** ·006 | **0** ·006 | — |
| | 6 | **0** ·017 | **0** ·017 | — | — |
| | 5 | **0** ·042 | — | — | — |

The table shows: (1) In bold type, for given *a*, *A* and *B*, the value of *b* ( < *a*) which is just significant at the probability level quoted (single-tail test).

(2) In small type, for given *A*, *B* and *r* = *a* + *b*, the exact probability (if there is independence) that *b* is equal to or less than the integer shown in bold type.

212

# Table 38 (*continued*)

| A, B | a | 0·05 | 0·025 | 0·01 | 0·005 |
|---|---|---|---|---|---|
| A=9 B=5 | 9 | 2 ·027 | 1 ·005⁻ | 1 ·005⁻ | 1 ·005⁻ |
|  | 8 | 1 ·023 | 1 ·023 | 0 ·003 | 0 ·003 |
|  | 7 | 0 ·010⁺ | 0 ·010⁺ | — | — |
|  | 6 | 0 ·028 | — | — | — |
| 4 | 9 | 1 ·014 | 1 ·014 | 0 ·001 | 0 ·001 |
|  | 8 | 0 ·007 | 0 ·007 | 0 ·007 | — |
|  | 7 | 0 ·021 | 0 ·021 | — | — |
|  | 6 | 0 ·049 | — | — | — |
| 3 | 9 | 1 ·045⁺ | 0 ·005⁻ | 0 ·005⁻ | 0 ·005⁻ |
|  | 8 | 0 ·018 | 0 ·018 | — | — |
|  | 7 | 0 ·045⁺ | — | — | — |
| 2 | 9 | 0 ·018 | 0 ·018 | — | — |
| A=10 B=10 | 10 | 6 ·043 | 5 ·016 | 4 ·005⁺ | 3 ·002 |
|  | 9 | 4 ·029 | 3 ·010⁻ | 3 ·010⁻ | 2 ·003 |
|  | 8 | 3 ·035⁻ | 2 ·012 | 1 ·003 | 1 ·003 |
|  | 7 | 2 ·035⁻ | 1 ·010⁻ | 1 ·010⁻ | 0 ·002 |
|  | 6 | 1 ·029 | 0 ·005⁺ | 0 ·005⁺ | — |
|  | 5 | 0 ·016 | 0 ·016 | — | — |
|  | 4 | 0 ·043 | — | — | — |
| 9 | 10 | 5 ·033 | 4 ·011 | 3 ·003 | 3 ·003 |
|  | 9 | 4 ·050⁻ | 3 ·017 | 2 ·005⁻ | 2 ·005⁻ |
|  | 8 | 2 ·019 | 2 ·019 | 1 ·004 | 1 ·004 |
|  | 7 | 1 ·015⁻ | 1 ·015⁻ | 0 ·002 | 0 ·002 |
|  | 6 | 1 ·040 | 0 ·008 | 0 ·008 | — |
|  | 5 | 0 ·022 | 0 ·022 | — | — |
| 8 | 10 | 4 ·023 | 4 ·023 | 3 ·007 | 2 ·002 |
|  | 9 | 3 ·032 | 2 ·009 | 2 ·009 | 1 ·002 |
|  | 8 | 2 ·031 | 1 ·008 | 1 ·008 | 0 ·001 |
|  | 7 | 1 ·023 | 1 ·023 | 0 ·004 | 0 ·004 |
|  | 6 | 0 ·011 | 0 ·011 | — | — |
|  | 5 | 0 ·029 | — | — | — |
| 7 | 10 | 3 ·015⁻ | 3 ·015⁻ | 2 ·003 | 2 ·003 |
|  | 9 | 2 ·018 | 2 ·018 | 1 ·004 | 1 ·004 |
|  | 8 | 1 ·013 | 1 ·013 | 0 ·002 | 0 ·002 |
|  | 7 | 1 ·036 | 0 ·006 | 0 ·006 | — |
|  | 6 | 0 ·017 | 0 ·017 | — | — |
|  | 5 | 0 ·041 | — | — | — |
| 6 | 10 | 3 ·036 | 2 ·008 | 2 ·008 | 1 ·001 |
|  | 9 | 2 ·036 | 1 ·008 | 1 ·008 | 0 ·001 |
|  | 8 | 1 ·024 | 1 ·024 | 0 ·003 | 0 ·003 |
|  | 7 | 0 ·010⁺ | 0 ·010⁺ | — | — |
|  | 6 | 0 ·026 | — | — | — |
| 5 | 10 | 2 ·022 | 2 ·022 | 1 ·004 | 1 ·004 |
|  | 9 | 1 ·017 | 1 ·017 | 0 ·002 | 0 ·002 |
|  | 8 | 1 ·047 | 0 ·007 | 0 ·007 | — |
|  | 7 | 0 ·019 | 0 ·019 | — | — |
|  | 6 | 0 ·042 | — | — | — |

| A, B | a | 0·05 | 0·025 | 0·01 | 0·005 |
|---|---|---|---|---|---|
| A=10 B=4 | 10 | 1 ·011 | 1 ·011 | 0 ·001 | 0 ·001 |
|  | 9 | 1 ·041 | 0 ·005⁻ | 0 ·005⁻ | 0 ·005⁻ |
|  | 8 | 0 ·015⁻ | 0 ·015⁻ | — | — |
|  | 7 | 0 ·035⁻ | — | — | — |
| 3 | 10 | 1 ·038 | 0 ·003 | 0 ·003 | 0 ·003 |
|  | 9 | 0 ·014 | 0 ·014 | — | — |
|  | 8 | 0 ·035⁻ | — | — | — |
| 2 | 10 | 0 ·015⁺ | 0 ·015⁺ | — | — |
|  | 9 | 0 ·045⁺ | — | — | — |
| A=11 B=11 | 11 | 7 ·045⁺ | 6 ·018 | 5 ·006 | 4 ·002 |
|  | 10 | 5 ·032 | 4 ·012 | 3 ·004 | 3 ·004 |
|  | 9 | 4 ·040 | 3 ·015⁻ | 2 ·004 | 2 ·004 |
|  | 8 | 3 ·043 | 2 ·015⁻ | 1 ·004 | 1 ·004 |
|  | 7 | 2 ·040 | 1 ·012 | 0 ·002 | 0 ·002 |
|  | 6 | 1 ·032 | 0 ·006 | 0 ·006 | — |
|  | 5 | 0 ·018 | 0 ·018 | — | — |
|  | 4 | 0 ·045⁺ | — | — | — |
| 10 | 11 | 6 ·035⁺ | 5 ·012 | 4 ·004 | 4 ·004 |
|  | 10 | 4 ·021 | 4 ·021 | 3 ·007 | 2 ·002 |
|  | 9 | 3 ·024 | 3 ·024 | 2 ·007 | 1 ·002 |
|  | 8 | 2 ·023 | 2 ·023 | 1 ·006 | 0 ·001 |
|  | 7 | 1 ·017 | 1 ·017 | 0 ·003 | 0 ·003 |
|  | 6 | 1 ·043 | 0 ·009 | 0 ·009 | — |
|  | 5 | 0 ·023 | 0 ·023 | — | — |
| 9 | 11 | 5 ·026 | 4 ·008 | 4 ·008 | 3 ·002 |
|  | 10 | 4 ·038 | 3 ·012 | 2 ·003 | 2 ·003 |
|  | 9 | 3 ·040 | 2 ·012 | 1 ·003 | 1 ·003 |
|  | 8 | 2 ·035⁻ | 1 ·009 | 1 ·009 | 0 ·001 |
|  | 7 | 1 ·025⁻ | 1 ·025⁻ | 0 ·004 | 0 ·004 |
|  | 6 | 0 ·012 | 0 ·012 | — | — |
|  | 5 | 0 ·030 | — | — | — |
| 8 | 11 | 4 ·018 | 4 ·018 | 3 ·005⁻ | 3 ·005⁻ |
|  | 10 | 3 ·024 | 3 ·024 | 2 ·006 | 1 ·001 |
|  | 9 | 2 ·022 | 2 ·022 | 1 ·005⁻ | 1 ·005⁻ |
|  | 8 | 1 ·015⁻ | 1 ·015⁻ | 0 ·002 | 0 ·002 |
|  | 7 | 1 ·037 | 0 ·007 | 0 ·007 | — |
|  | 6 | 0 ·017 | 0 ·017 | — | — |
|  | 5 | 0 ·040 | — | — | — |
| 7 | 11 | 4 ·043 | 3 ·011 | 2 ·002 | 2 ·002 |
|  | 10 | 3 ·047 | 2 ·013 | 1 002 | 1 ·002 |
|  | 9 | 2 ·039 | 1 ·009 | 1 ·009 | 0 ·001 |
|  | 8 | 1 ·025⁻ | 1 ·025⁻ | 0 ·004 | 0 ·004 |
|  | 7 | 0 ·010⁺ | 0 ·010⁺ | — | — |
|  | 6 | 0 ·025⁻ | 0 ·025⁻ | — | — |
| 6 | 11 | 3 ·029 | 2 ·006 | 2 ·006 | 1 ·001 |
|  | 10 | 2 ·028 | 1 ·005⁺ | 1 ·005⁺ | 0 ·001 |
|  | 9 | 1 ·018 | 1 ·018 | 0 ·002 | 0 ·002 |

| | a | Probability 0·05 | 0·025 | 0·01 | 0·005 |
|---|---|---|---|---|---|
| A = 11 B = 6 | 8 | **1** ·043 | **0** ·007 | **0** ·007 | — |
| | 7 | **0** ·017 | **0** ·017 | — | — |
| | 6 | **0** ·037 | — | — | — |
| 5 | 11 | **2** ·018 | **2** ·018 | **1** ·003 | **1** ·003 |
| | 10 | **1** ·013 | **1** ·013 | **0** ·001 | **0** ·001 |
| | 9 | **1** ·036 | **0** ·005$^-$ | **0** ·005$^-$ | **0** ·005$^-$ |
| | 8 | **0** ·013 | **0** ·013 | — | — |
| | 7 | **0** ·029 | — | — | — |
| 4 | 11 | **1** ·009 | **1** ·009 | **1** ·009 | **0** ·001 |
| | 10 | **1** ·033 | **0** ·004 | **0** ·004 | **0** ·004 |
| | 9 | **0** ·011 | **0** ·011 | — | — |
| | 8 | **0** ·026 | — | — | — |
| 3 | 11 | **1** ·033 | **0** ·003 | **0** ·003 | **0** ·003 |
| | 10 | **0** ·011 | **0** ·011 | — | — |
| | 9 | **0** ·027 | — | — | — |
| 2 | 11 | **0** ·013 | **0** ·013 | — | — |
| | 10 | **0** ·038 | — | — | — |
| A = 12 B = 12 | 12 | **8** ·047 | **7** ·019 | **6** ·007 | **5** ·002 |
| | 11 | **6** ·034 | **5** ·014 | **4** ·005$^-$ | **4** ·005$^-$ |
| | 10 | **5** ·045$^-$ | **4** ·018 | **3** ·006 | **2** ·002 |
| | 9 | **4** ·050$^-$ | **3** ·020 | **2** ·006 | **1** ·001 |
| | 8 | **3** ·050$^-$ | **2** ·018 | **1** ·005$^-$ | **1** ·005$^-$ |
| | 7 | **2** ·045$^-$ | **1** ·014 | **0** ·002 | **0** ·002 |
| | 6 | **1** ·034 | **0** ·007 | **0** ·007 | — |
| | 5 | **0** ·019 | **0** ·019 | — | — |
| | 4 | **0** ·047 | — | — | — |
| 11 | 12 | **7** ·037 | **6** ·014 | **5** ·005$^-$ | **5** ·005$^-$ |
| | 11 | **5** ·024 | **5** ·024 | **4** ·008 | **3** ·002 |
| | 10 | **4** ·029 | **3** ·010$^+$ | **2** ·003 | **2** ·003 |
| | 9 | **3** ·030 | **2** ·009 | **2** ·009 | **1** ·002 |
| | 8 | **2** ·026 | **1** ·007 | **1** ·007 | **0** ·001 |
| | 7 | **1** ·019 | **1** ·019 | **0** ·003 | **0** ·003 |
| | 6 | **1** ·045$^-$ | **0** ·009 | **0** ·009 | — |
| | 5 | **0** ·024 | **0** ·024 | — | — |
| 10 | 12 | **6** ·029 | **5** ·010$^-$ | **5** ·010$^-$ | **4** ·003 |
| | 11 | **5** ·043 | **4** ·015$^+$ | **3** ·005$^-$ | **3** ·005$^-$ |
| | 10 | **4** ·048 | **3** ·017 | **2** ·005$^-$ | **2** ·005$^-$ |
| | 9 | **3** ·046 | **2** ·015$^-$ | **1** ·004 | **1** ·004 |
| | 8 | **2** ·038 | **1** ·010$^+$ | **0** ·002 | **0** ·002 |
| | 7 | **1** ·026 | **0** ·005$^-$ | **0** ·005$^-$ | **0** ·005$^-$ |
| | 6 | **0** ·012 | **0** ·012 | — | — |
| | 5 | **0** ·030 | — | — | — |
| 9 | 12 | **5** ·021 | **5** ·021 | **4** ·006 | **3** ·002 |
| | 11 | **4** ·029 | **3** ·009 | **3** ·009 | **2** ·002 |
| | 10 | **3** ·029 | **2** ·008 | **2** ·008 | **1** ·002 |
| | 9 | **2** ·024 | **2** ·024 | **1** ·006 | **0** ·001 |
| | 8 | **1** ·016 | **1** ·016 | **0** ·002 | **0** ·002 |

| | a | Probability 0·05 | 0·025 | 0·01 | 0·005 |
|---|---|---|---|---|---|
| A = 12 B = 9 | 7 | **1** ·037 | **0** ·007 | **0** ·007 | — |
| | 6 | **0** ·017 | **0** ·017 | — | — |
| | 5 | **0** ·039 | — | — | — |
| 8 | 12 | **5** ·049 | **4** ·014 | **3** ·004 | **3** ·004 |
| | 11 | **3** ·018 | **3** ·018 | **2** ·004 | **2** ·004 |
| | 10 | **2** ·015$^+$ | **2** ·015$^+$ | **1** ·003 | **1** ·003 |
| | 9 | **2** ·040 | **1** ·010$^-$ | **1** ·010$^-$ | **0** ·001 |
| | 8 | **1** ·025$^-$ | **1** ·025$^-$ | **0** ·004 | **0** ·004 |
| | 7 | **0** ·010$^+$ | **0** ·010$^+$ | — | — |
| | 6 | **0** ·024 | **0** ·024 | — | — |
| 7 | 12 | **4** ·036 | **3** ·009 | **3** ·009 | **2** ·002 |
| | 11 | **3** ·038 | **2** ·010$^-$ | **2** ·010$^-$ | **1** ·002 |
| | 10 | **2** ·029 | **1** ·006 | **1** ·006 | **0** ·001 |
| | 9 | **1** ·017 | **1** ·017 | **0** ·002 | **0** ·002 |
| | 8 | **1** ·040 | **0** ·007 | **0** ·007 | — |
| | 7 | **0** ·016 | **0** ·016 | — | — |
| | 6 | **0** ·034 | — | — | — |
| 6 | 12 | **3** ·025$^-$ | **3** ·025$^-$ | **2** ·005$^-$ | **2** ·005$^-$ |
| | 11 | **2** ·022 | **2** ·022 | **1** ·004 | **1** ·004 |
| | 10 | **1** ·013 | **1** ·013 | **0** ·002 | **0** ·002 |
| | 9 | **1** ·032 | **0** ·005$^-$ | **0** ·005$^-$ | **0** ·005$^-$ |
| | 8 | **0** ·011 | **0** ·011 | — | — |
| | 7 | **0** ·025$^-$ | **0** ·025$^-$ | — | — |
| | 6 | **0** ·050$^-$ | — | — | — |
| 5 | 12 | **2** ·015$^-$ | **2** ·015$^-$ | **1** ·002 | **1** ·002 |
| | 11 | **1** ·010$^-$ | **1** ·010$^-$ | **1** ·010$^-$ | **0** ·001 |
| | 10 | **1** ·028 | **0** ·003 | **0** ·003 | **0** ·003 |
| | 9 | **0** ·009 | **0** ·009 | **0** ·009 | — |
| | 8 | **0** ·020 | **0** ·020 | — | — |
| | 7 | **0** ·041 | — | — | — |
| 4 | 12 | **2** ·050 | **1** ·007 | **1** ·007 | **0** ·001 |
| | 11 | **1** ·027 | **0** ·003 | **0** ·003 | **0** ·003 |
| | 10 | **0** ·008 | **0** ·008 | **0** ·008 | — |
| | 9 | **0** ·019 | **0** ·019 | — | — |
| | 8 | **0** ·038 | — | — | — |
| 3 | 12 | **1** ·029 | **0** ·002 | **0** ·002 | **0** ·002 |
| | 11 | **0** ·009 | **0** ·009 | **0** ·009 | — |
| | 10 | **0** ·022 | **0** ·022 | — | — |
| | 9 | **0** ·044 | — | — | — |
| 2 | 12 | **0** ·011 | **0** ·011 | — | — |
| | 11 | **0** ·033 | — | — | — |
| A = 13 B = 13 | 13 | **9** ·048 | **8** ·020 | **7** ·007 | **6** ·003 |
| | 12 | **7** ·037 | **6** ·015$^+$ | **5** ·006 | **4** ·002 |
| | 11 | **6** ·048 | **5** ·021 | **4** ·008 | **3** ·002 |
| | 10 | **4** ·024 | **4** ·024 | **3** ·008 | **2** ·002 |
| | 9 | **3** ·024 | **3** ·024 | **2** ·008 | **1** ·002 |
| | 8 | **2** ·021 | **2** ·021 | **1** ·006 | **0** ·001 |

The table shows: (1) In bold type, for given $a$, $A$ and $B$, the value of $b$ ($< a$) which is just significant at the probability level quoted (single-tail test).

(2) In small type, for given $A$, $B$ and $r = a + b$, the exact probability (if there is independence) that $b$ is equal to or less than the integer shown in bold type.

Table 38 (continued)

**A = 13  B = 13**

| B | a | 0·05 | 0·025 | 0·01 | 0·005 |
|---|---|---|---|---|---|
| 13 | 7 | 2 ·048 | 1 ·015+ | 0 ·003 | 0 ·003 |
|  | 6 | 1 ·037 | 0 ·007 | 0 ·007 | — |
|  | 5 | 0 ·020 | 0 ·020 | — | — |
|  | 4 | 0 ·048 | — | — | — |
| 12 | 13 | 8 ·039 | 7 ·015− | 6 ·005+ | 5 ·002 |
|  | 12 | 6 ·027 | 5 ·010− | 5 ·010− | 4 ·003 |
|  | 11 | 5 ·033 | 4 ·013 | 3 ·004 | 3 ·004 |
|  | 10 | 4 ·036 | 3 ·013 | 2 ·004 | 2 ·004 |
|  | 9 | 3 ·034 | 2 ·011 | 1 ·003 | 1 ·003 |
|  | 8 | 2 ·029 | 1 ·008 | 1 ·008 | 0 ·001 |
|  | 7 | 1 ·020 | 1 ·020 | 0 ·004 | 0 ·004 |
|  | 6 | 1 ·046 | 0 ·010− | 0 ·010− | — |
|  | 5 | 0 ·024 | 0 ·024 | — | — |
| 11 | 13 | 7 ·031 | 6 ·011 | 5 ·003 | 5 ·003 |
|  | 12 | 6 ·048 | 5 ·018 | 4 ·006 | 3 ·002 |
|  | 11 | 4 ·021 | 4 ·021 | 3 ·007 | 2 ·002 |
|  | 10 | 3 ·021 | 3 ·021 | 2 ·006 | 1 ·001 |
|  | 9 | 3 ·050− | 2 ·017 | 1 ·004 | 1 ·004 |
|  | 8 | 2 ·040 | 1 ·011 | 0 ·002 | 0 ·002 |
|  | 7 | 1 ·027 | 0 ·005− | 0 ·005− | 0 ·005− |
|  | 6 | 0 ·013 | 0 ·013 | — | — |
|  | 5 | 0 ·030 | — | — | — |
| 10 | 13 | 6 ·024 | 6 ·024 | 5 ·007 | 4 ·002 |
|  | 12 | 5 ·035− | 4 ·012 | 3 ·003 | 3 ·003 |
|  | 11 | 4 ·037 | 3 ·012 | 2 ·003 | 2 ·003 |
|  | 10 | 3 ·033 | 2 ·010 | 1 ·002 | 1 ·002 |
|  | 9 | 2 ·026 | 1 ·006 | 1 ·006 | 0 ·001 |
|  | 8 | 1 ·017 | 1 ·017 | 0 ·003 | 0 ·003 |
|  | 7 | 1 ·038 | 0 ·007 | 0 ·007 | — |
|  | 6 | 0 ·017 | 0 ·017 | — | — |
|  | 5 | 0 ·038 | — | — | — |
| 9 | 13 | 5 ·017 | 5 ·017 | 4 ·005− | 4 ·005− |
|  | 12 | 4 ·023 | 4 ·023 | 3 ·007 | 2 ·001 |
|  | 11 | 3 ·022 | 3 ·022 | 2 ·006 | 1 ·001 |
|  | 10 | 2 ·017 | 2 ·017 | 1 ·004 | 1 ·004 |
|  | 9 | 2 ·040 | 1 ·010+ | 0 ·001 | 0 ·001 |
|  | 8 | 1 ·025− | 1 ·025− | 0 ·004 | 0 ·004 |
|  | 7 | 0 ·010+ | 0 ·010+ | — | — |
|  | 6 | 0 ·023 | 0 ·023 | — | — |
|  | 5 | 0 ·049 | — | — | — |
| 8 | 13 | 5 ·042 | 4 ·012 | 3 ·003 | 3 ·003 |
|  | 12 | 4 ·047 | 3 ·014 | 2 ·003 | 2 ·003 |
|  | 11 | 3 ·041 | 2 ·011 | 1 ·002 | 1 ·002 |
|  | 10 | 2 ·029 | 1 ·007 | 1 ·007 | 0 ·001 |
|  | 9 | 1 ·017 | 1 ·017 | 0 ·002 | 0 ·002 |
|  | 8 | 1 ·037 | 0 ·006 | 0 ·006 | — |
|  | 7 | 0 ·015− | 0 ·015− | — | — |
|  | 6 | 0 ·032 | — | — | — |
| 7 | 13 | 4 ·031 | 3 ·007 | 3 ·007 | 2 ·001 |
|  | 12 | 3 ·031 | 2 ·007 | 2 ·007 | 1 ·001 |

**A = 13  B = 7**

| B | a | 0·05 | 0·025 | 0·01 | 0·005 |
|---|---|---|---|---|---|
|  | 11 | 2 ·022 | 2 ·022 | 1 ·004 | 1 ·004 |
|  | 10 | 1 ·012 | 1 ·012 | 0 ·002 | 0 ·002 |
|  | 9 | 1 ·029 | 0 ·004 | 0 ·004 | 0 ·004 |
|  | 8 | 0 ·010+ | 0 ·010+ | — | — |
|  | 7 | 0 ·022 | 0 ·022 | — | — |
|  | 6 | 0 ·044 | — | — | — |
| 6 | 13 | 3 ·021 | 3 ·021 | 2 ·004 | 2 ·004 |
|  | 12 | 2 ·017 | 2 ·017 | 1 ·003 | 1 ·003 |
|  | 11 | 2 ·046 | 1 ·010− | 1 ·010− | 0 ·001 |
|  | 10 | 1 ·024 | 1 ·024 | 0 ·003 | 0 ·003 |
|  | 9 | 1 ·050− | 0 ·008 | 0 ·008 | — |
|  | 8 | 0 ·017 | 0 ·017 | — | — |
|  | 7 | 0 ·034 | — | — | — |
| 5 | 13 | 2 ·012 | 2 ·012 | 1 ·002 | 1 ·002 |
|  | 12 | 2 ·044 | 1 ·008 | 1 ·008 | 0 ·001 |
|  | 11 | 1 ·022 | 1 ·022 | 0 ·002 | 0 ·002 |
|  | 10 | 1 ·047 | 0 ·007 | 0 ·007 | — |
|  | 9 | 0 ·015− | 0 ·015− | — | — |
|  | 8 | 0 ·029 | — | — | — |
| 4 | 13 | 2 ·044 | 1 ·006 | 1 ·006 | 0 ·000 |
|  | 12 | 1 ·022 | 1 ·022 | 0 ·002 | 0 ·002 |
|  | 11 | 0 ·006 | 0 ·006 | 0 ·006 | — |
|  | 10 | 0 ·015− | 0 ·015− | — | — |
|  | 9 | 0 ·029 | — | — | — |
| 3 | 13 | 1 ·025 | 1 ·025 | 0 ·002 | 0 ·002 |
|  | 12 | 0 ·007 | 0 ·007 | 0 ·007 | — |
|  | 11 | 0 ·018 | 0 ·018 | — | — |
|  | 10 | 0 ·036 | — | — | — |
| 2 | 13 | 0 ·010− | 0 ·010− | 0 ·010− | — |
|  | 12 | 0 ·029 | — | — | — |

**A = 14  B = 14**

| B | a | 0·05 | 0·025 | 0·01 | 0·005 |
|---|---|---|---|---|---|
| 14 | 14 | 10 ·049 | 9 ·020 | 8 ·008 | 7 ·003 |
|  | 13 | 8 ·038 | 7 ·016 | 6 ·006 | 5 ·002 |
|  | 12 | 6 ·023 | 6 ·023 | 5 ·009 | 4 ·003 |
|  | 11 | 5 ·027 | 4 ·011 | 3 ·004 | 3 ·004 |
|  | 10 | 4 ·028 | 3 ·011 | 2 ·003 | 2 ·003 |
|  | 9 | 3 ·027 | 2 ·009 | 2 ·009 | 1 ·002 |
|  | 8 | 2 ·023 | 2 ·023 | 1 ·006 | 0 ·001 |
|  | 7 | 1 ·016 | 1 ·016 | 0 ·003 | 0 ·003 |
|  | 6 | 1 ·038 | 0 ·008 | 0 ·008 | — |
|  | 5 | 0 ·020 | 0 ·020 | — | — |
|  | 4 | 0 ·049 | — | — | — |
| 13 | 14 | 9 ·041 | 8 ·016 | 7 ·006 | 6 ·002 |
|  | 13 | 7 ·029 | 6 ·011 | 5 ·004 | 5 ·004 |
|  | 12 | 6 ·037 | 5 ·015+ | 4 ·005+ | 3 ·002 |
|  | 11 | 5 ·041 | 4 ·017 | 3 ·006 | 2 ·001 |
|  | 10 | 4 ·041 | 3 ·016 | 2 ·005− | 2 ·005− |
|  | 9 | 3 ·038 | 2 ·013 | 1 ·003 | 1 ·003 |
|  | 8 | 2 ·031 | 1 ·009 | 1 ·009 | 0 ·001 |

## Table 38. *Significance tests in a 2 × 2 contingency table (continued)*

| | $a$ | Probability 0·05 | 0·025 | 0·01 | 0·005 | | $a$ | Probability 0·05 | 0·025 | 0·01 | 0·005 |
|---|---|---|---|---|---|---|---|---|---|---|---|
| A=14 B=13 | 7 | **1** ·021 | **1** ·021 | **0** ·004 | **0** ·004 | A=14 B=7 | 14 | **4** ·026 | **3** ·006 | **3** ·006 | **2** ·001 |
| | 6 | **1** ·048 | **0** ·010+ | — | — | | 13 | **3** ·025 | **2** ·006 | **2** ·006 | **1** ·001 |
| | 5 | **0** ·025− | **0** ·025− | — | — | | 12 | **2** ·017 | **2** ·017 | **1** ·003 | **1** ·003 |
| 12 | 14 | **8** ·033 | **7** ·012 | **6** ·004 | **6** ·004 | | 11 | **2** ·041 | **1** ·009 | **1** ·009 | **0** ·001 |
| | 13 | **6** ·021 | **6** ·021 | **5** ·007 | **4** ·002 | | 10 | **1** ·021 | **1** ·021 | **0** ·003 | **0** ·003 |
| | 12 | **5** ·025+ | **4** ·009 | **4** ·009 | **3** ·003 | | 9 | **1** ·043 | **0** ·007 | **0** ·007 | — |
| | 11 | **4** ·026 | **3** ·009 | **3** ·009 | **2** ·002 | | 8 | **0** ·015− | **0** ·015− | — | — |
| | 10 | **3** ·024 | **3** ·024 | **2** ·007 | **1** ·002 | | 7 | **0** ·030 | — | — | — |
| | 9 | **2** ·019 | **2** ·019 | **1** ·005− | **1** ·005− | 6 | 14 | **3** ·018 | **3** ·018 | **2** ·003 | **2** ·003 |
| | 8 | **2** ·042 | **1** ·012 | **0** ·002 | **0** ·002 | | 13 | **2** ·014 | **2** ·014 | **1** ·002 | **1** ·002 |
| | 7 | **1** ·028 | **0** ·005+ | **0** ·005+ | — | | 12 | **2** ·037 | **1** ·007 | **1** ·007 | **0** ·001 |
| | 6 | **0** ·013 | **0** ·013 | — | — | | 11 | **1** ·018 | **1** ·018 | **0** ·002 | **0** ·002 |
| | 5 | **0** ·030 | — | — | — | | 10 | **1** ·038 | **0** ·005+ | **0** ·005+ | — |
| 11 | 14 | **7** ·026 | **6** ·009 | **6** ·009 | **5** ·003 | | 9 | **0** ·012 | **0** ·012 | — | — |
| | 13 | **6** ·039 | **5** ·014 | **4** ·004 | **4** ·004 | | 8 | **0** ·024 | **0** ·024 | — | — |
| | 12 | **5** ·043 | **4** ·016 | **3** ·005− | **3** ·005− | | 7 | **0** ·044 | — | — | — |
| | 11 | **4** ·042 | **3** ·015− | **2** ·004 | **2** ·004 | 5 | 14 | **2** ·010+ | **2** ·010+ | **1** ·001 | **1** ·001 |
| | 10 | **3** ·036 | **2** ·011 | **1** ·003 | **1** ·003 | | 13 | **2** ·037 | **1** ·006 | **1** ·006 | **0** ·001 |
| | 9 | **2** ·027 | **1** ·007 | **1** ·007 | **0** ·001 | | 12 | **1** ·017 | **1** ·017 | **0** ·002 | **0** ·002 |
| | 8 | **1** ·017 | **1** ·017 | **0** ·003 | **0** ·003 | | 11 | **1** ·038 | **0** ·005− | **0** ·005− | **0** ·005− |
| | 7 | **1** ·038 | **0** ·007 | **0** ·007 | — | | 10 | **0** ·011 | **0** ·011 | — | — |
| | 6 | **0** ·017 | **0** ·017 | — | — | | 9 | **0** ·022 | **0** ·022 | — | — |
| | 5 | **0** ·038 | — | — | — | | 8 | **0** ·040 | — | — | — |
| 10 | 14 | **6** ·020 | **6** ·020 | **5** ·006 | **4** ·002 | 4 | 14 | **2** ·039 | **1** ·005− | **1** ·005− | **1** ·005− |
| | 13 | **5** ·028 | **4** ·009 | **4** ·009 | **3** ·002 | | 13 | **1** ·019 | **1** ·019 | **0** ·002 | **0** ·002 |
| | 12 | **4** ·028 | **3** ·009 | **3** ·009 | **2** ·002 | | 12 | **1** ·044 | **0** ·005− | **0** ·005− | **0** ·005− |
| | 11 | **3** ·024 | **3** ·024 | **2** ·007 | **1** ·001 | | 11 | **0** ·011 | **0** ·011 | — | — |
| | 10 | **2** ·018 | **2** ·018 | **1** ·004 | **1** ·004 | | 10 | **0** ·023 | **0** ·023 | — | — |
| | 9 | **2** ·040 | **1** ·011 | **0** ·002 | **0** ·002 | | 9 | **0** ·041 | — | — | — |
| | 8 | **1** ·024 | **1** ·024 | **0** ·004 | **0** ·004 | 3 | 14 | **1** ·022 | **1** ·022 | **0** ·001 | **0** ·001 |
| | 7 | **0** ·010− | **0** ·010− | **0** ·010− | — | | 13 | **0** ·006 | **0** ·006 | **0** ·006 | — |
| | 6 | **0** ·022 | **0** ·022 | — | — | | 12 | **0** ·015− | **0** ·015− | — | — |
| | 5 | **0** ·047 | — | — | — | | 11 | **0** ·029 | — | — | — |
| 9 | 14 | **6** ·047 | **5** ·014 | **4** ·004 | **4** ·004 | 2 | 14 | **0** ·008 | **0** ·008 | **0** ·008 | — |
| | 13 | **4** ·018 | **4** ·018 | **3** ·005− | **3** ·005− | | 13 | **0** ·025 | **0** ·025 | — | — |
| | 12 | **3** ·017 | **3** ·017 | **2** ·004 | **2** ·004 | | 12 | **0** ·050 | — | — | — |
| | 11 | **3** ·042 | **2** ·012 | **1** ·002 | **1** ·002 | | | | | | |
| | 10 | **2** ·029 | **1** ·007 | **1** ·007 | **0** ·001 | | | | | | |
| | 9 | **1** ·017 | **1** ·017 | **0** ·002 | **0** ·002 | | | | | | |
| | 8 | **1** ·036 | **0** ·006 | **0** ·006 | — | A=15 B=15 | 15 | **11** ·050− | **10** ·021 | **9** ·008 | **8** ·003 |
| | 7 | **0** ·014 | **0** ·014 | — | — | | 14 | **9** ·040 | **8** ·018 | **7** ·007 | **6** ·003 |
| | 6 | **0** ·030 | — | — | — | | 13 | **7** ·025+ | **6** ·010+ | **5** ·004 | **5** ·004 |
| 8 | 14 | **5** ·036 | **4** ·010− | **4** ·010− | **3** ·002 | | 12 | **6** ·030 | **5** ·013 | **4** ·005− | **4** ·005− |
| | 13 | **4** ·039 | **3** ·011 | **2** ·002 | **2** ·002 | | 11 | **5** ·033 | **4** ·013 | **3** ·005− | **3** ·005− |
| | 12 | **3** ·032 | **2** ·008 | **2** ·008 | **1** ·001 | | 10 | **4** ·033 | **3** ·013 | **2** ·004 | **2** ·004 |
| | 11 | **2** ·022 | **2** ·022 | **1** ·005− | **1** ·005− | | 9 | **3** ·030 | **2** ·010+ | **1** ·003 | **1** ·003 |
| | 10 | **2** ·048 | **1** ·012 | **0** ·002 | **0** ·002 | | 8 | **2** ·025+ | **1** ·007 | **1** ·007 | **0** ·001 |
| | 9 | **1** ·026 | **0** ·004 | **0** ·004 | **0** ·004 | | 7 | **1** ·018 | **1** ·018 | **0** ·003 | **0** ·003 |
| | 8 | **0** ·009 | **0** ·009 | **0** ·009 | — | | 6 | **1** ·040 | **0** ·008 | **0** ·008 | — |
| | 7 | **0** ·020 | **0** ·020 | — | — | | 5 | **0** ·021 | **0** ·021 | — | — |
| | 6 | **0** ·040 | — | — | — | | 4 | **0** ·050− | — | — | — |

The table shows: (1) In bold type, for given $a$, $A$ and $B$, the value of $b$ $(<a)$ which is just significant at the probability level quoted (single-tail test).

(2) In small type, for given $A$, $B$ and $r = a+b$, the exact probability (if there is independence) that $b$ is equal to or less than the integer shown in bold type.

Table 38 (*continued*)

| A, B | a | 0·05 | 0·025 | 0·01 | 0·005 |
|---|---|---|---|---|---|
| A=15 B=14 | 15 | 10 ·042 | 9 ·017 | 8 ·006 | 7 ·002 |
| | 14 | 8 ·031 | 7 ·013 | 6 ·005⁻ | 6 ·005⁻ |
| | 13 | 7 ·041 | 6 ·017 | 5 ·007 | 4 ·002 |
| | 12 | 6 ·046 | 5 ·020 | 4 ·007 | 3 ·002 |
| | 11 | 5 ·048 | 4 ·020 | 3 ·007 | 2 ·002 |
| | 10 | 4 ·046 | 3 ·018 | 2 ·006 | 1 ·001 |
| | 9 | 3 ·041 | 2 ·014 | 1 ·004 | 1 ·004 |
| | 8 | 2 ·033 | 1 ·009 | 1 ·009 | 0 ·001 |
| | 7 | 1 ·022 | 1 ·022 | 0 ·004 | 0 ·004 |
| | 6 | 1 ·049 | 0 ·011 | — | — |
| | 5 | 0 ·025⁺ | — | — | — |
| 13 | 15 | 9 ·035⁻ | 8 ·013 | 7 ·005⁻ | 7 ·005⁻ |
| | 14 | 7 ·023 | 7 ·023 | 6 ·009 | 5 ·003 |
| | 13 | 6 ·029 | 5 ·011 | 4 ·004 | 4 ·004 |
| | 12 | 5 ·031 | 4 ·012 | 3 ·004 | 3 ·004 |
| | 11 | 4 ·030 | 3 ·011 | 2 ·003 | 2 ·003 |
| | 10 | 3 ·026 | 2 ·008 | 2 ·008 | 1 ·002 |
| | 9 | 2 ·020 | 2 ·020 | 1 ·005⁺ | 0 ·001 |
| | 8 | 2 ·043 | 1 ·013 | 0 ·002 | 0 ·002 |
| | 7 | 1 ·029 | 0 ·005⁺ | 0 ·005⁺ | — |
| | 6 | 0 ·013 | 0 ·013 | — | — |
| | 5 | 0 ·031 | — | — | — |
| 12 | 15 | 8 ·028 | 7 ·010⁻ | 7 ·010⁻ | 6 ·003 |
| | 14 | 7 ·043 | 6 ·016 | 5 ·006 | 4 ·002 |
| | 13 | 6 ·049 | 5 ·019 | 4 ·007 | 3 ·002 |
| | 12 | 5 ·049 | 4 ·019 | 3 ·006 | 2 ·002 |
| | 11 | 4 ·045⁺ | 3 ·017 | 2 ·005⁻ | 2 ·005⁻ |
| | 10 | 3 ·038 | 2 ·012 | 1 ·003 | 1 ·003 |
| | 9 | 2 ·028 | 1 ·007 | 1 ·007 | 0 ·001 |
| | 8 | 1 ·018 | 1 ·018 | 0 ·003 | 0 ·003 |
| | 7 | 1 ·038 | 0 ·007 | 0 ·007 | — |
| | 6 | 0 ·017 | 0 ·017 | — | — |
| | 5 | 0 ·037 | — | — | — |
| 11 | 15 | 7 ·022 | 7 ·022 | 6 ·007 | 5 ·002 |
| | 14 | 6 ·032 | 5 ·011 | 4 ·003 | 4 ·003 |
| | 13 | 5 ·034 | 4 ·012 | 3 ·003 | 3 ·003 |
| | 12 | 4 ·032 | 3 ·010⁺ | 2 ·003 | 2 ·003 |
| | 11 | 3 ·026 | 2 ·008 | 2 ·008 | 1 ·002 |
| | 10 | 2 ·019 | 2 ·019 | 1 ·004 | 1 ·004 |
| | 9 | 2 ·040 | 1 ·011 | 0 ·002 | 0 ·002 |
| | 8 | 1 ·024 | 1 ·024 | 0 ·004 | 0 ·004 |
| | 7 | 1 ·049 | 0 ·010⁻ | 0 ·010⁻ | — |
| | 6 | 0 ·022 | 0 ·022 | — | — |
| | 5 | 0 ·046 | — | — | — |
| 10 | 15 | 6 ·017 | 6 ·017 | 5 ·005⁻ | 5 ·005⁻ |
| | 14 | 5 ·023 | 5 ·023 | 4 ·007 | 3 ·002 |
| | 13 | 4 ·022 | 4 ·022 | 3 ·007 | 2 ·001 |
| | 12 | 3 ·018 | 3 ·018 | 2 ·005⁻ | 2 ·005⁻ |
| | 11 | 3 ·042 | 2 ·013 | 1 ·003 | 1 ·003 |
| | 10 | 2 ·029 | 1 ·007 | 1 ·007 | 0 ·001 |
| | 9 | 1 ·016 | 1 ·016 | 0 ·002 | 0 ·002 |
| | 8 | 1 ·034 | 0 ·006 | 0 ·006 | — |
| | 7 | 0 ·013 | 0 ·013 | — | — |
| | 6 | 0 ·028 | — | — | — |
| 9 | 15 | 6 ·042 | 5 ·012 | 4 ·003 | 4 ·003 |
| | 14 | 5 ·047 | 4 ·015⁻ | 3 ·004 | 3 ·004 |

| A, B | a | 0·05 | 0·025 | 0·01 | 0·005 |
|---|---|---|---|---|---|
| A=15 B=9 | 13 | 4 ·042 | 3 ·013 | 2 ·003 | 2 ·003 |
| | 12 | 3 ·032 | 2 ·009 | 2 ·009 | 1 ·002 |
| | 11 | 2 ·021 | 2 ·021 | 1 ·005⁻ | 1 ·005⁻ |
| | 10 | 2 ·045⁻ | 1 ·011 | 0 ·002 | 0 ·002 |
| | 9 | 1 ·024 | 1 ·024 | 0 ·004 | 0 ·004 |
| | 8 | 1 ·048 | 0 ·009 | 0 ·009 | — |
| | 7 | 0 ·019 | 0 ·019 | — | — |
| | 6 | 0 ·037 | — | — | — |
| 8 | 15 | 5 ·032 | 4 ·008 | 4 ·008 | 3 ·002 |
| | 14 | 4 ·033 | 3 ·009 | 3 ·009 | 2 ·002 |
| | 13 | 3 ·026 | 2 ·006 | 2 ·006 | 1 ·001 |
| | 12 | 2 ·017 | 2 ·017 | 1 ·003 | 1 ·003 |
| | 11 | 2 ·037 | 1 ·008 | 1 ·008 | 0 ·001 |
| | 10 | 1 ·019 | 1 ·019 | 0 ·003 | 0 ·003 |
| | 9 | 1 ·038 | 0 ·006 | 0 ·006 | — |
| | 8 | 0 ·013 | 0 ·013 | — | — |
| | 7 | 0 ·026 | — | — | — |
| | 6 | 0 ·050⁻ | — | — | — |
| 7 | 15 | 4 ·023 | 4 ·023 | 3 ·005⁻ | 3 ·005⁻ |
| | 14 | 3 ·021 | 3 ·021 | 2 ·004 | 2 ·004 |
| | 13 | 2 ·014 | 2 ·014 | 1 ·002 | 1 ·002 |
| | 12 | 2 ·032 | 1 ·007 | 1 ·007 | 0 ·001 |
| | 11 | 1 ·015⁺ | 1 ·015⁺ | 0 ·002 | 0 ·002 |
| | 10 | 1 ·032 | 0 ·005⁻ | 0 ·005⁻ | 0 ·005⁻ |
| | 9 | 0 ·010⁺ | 0 ·010⁺ | — | — |
| | 8 | 0 ·020 | 0 ·020 | — | — |
| | 7 | 0 ·038 | — | — | — |
| 6 | 15 | 3 ·015⁺ | 3 ·015⁺ | 2 ·003 | 2 ·003 |
| | 14 | 2 ·011 | 2 ·011 | 1 ·002 | 1 ·002 |
| | 13 | 2 ·031 | 1 ·006 | 1 ·006 | 0 ·001 |
| | 12 | 1 ·014 | 1 ·014 | 0 ·002 | 0 ·002 |
| | 11 | 1 ·029 | 0 ·004 | 0 ·004 | 0 ·004 |
| | 10 | 0 ·009 | 0 ·009 | 0 ·009 | — |
| | 9 | 0 ·017 | 0 ·017 | — | — |
| | 8 | 0 ·032 | — | — | — |
| 5 | 15 | 2 ·009 | 2 ·009 | 2 ·009 | 1 ·001 |
| | 14 | 2 ·032 | 1 ·005⁻ | 1 ·005⁻ | 1 ·005⁻ |
| | 13 | 1 ·014 | 1 ·014 | 0 ·001 | 0 ·001 |
| | 12 | 1 ·031 | 0 ·004 | 0 ·004 | 0 ·004 |
| | 11 | 0 ·008 | 0 ·008 | 0 ·008 | — |
| | 10 | 0 ·016 | 0 ·016 | — | — |
| | 9 | 0 ·030 | — | — | — |
| 4 | 15 | 2 ·035⁺ | 1 ·004 | 1 ·004 | 1 ·004 |
| | 14 | 1 ·016 | 1 ·016 | 0 ·001 | 0 ·001 |
| | 13 | 1 ·037 | 0 ·004 | 0 ·004 | 0 ·004 |
| | 12 | 0 ·009 | 0 ·009 | 0 ·009 | — |
| | 11 | 0 ·018 | 0 ·018 | — | — |
| | 10 | 0 ·033 | — | — | — |
| 3 | 15 | 1 ·020 | 1 ·020 | 0 ·001 | 0 ·001 |
| | 14 | 0 ·005⁻ | 0 ·005⁻ | 0 ·005⁻ | 0 ·005⁻ |
| | 13 | 0 ·012 | 0 ·012 | — | — |
| | 12 | 0 ·025⁻ | 0 ·025⁻ | — | — |
| | 11 | 0 ·043 | — | — | — |
| 2 | 15 | 0 ·007 | 0 ·007 | 0 ·007 | — |
| | 14 | 0 ·022 | 0 ·022 | — | — |
| | 13 | 0 ·044 | — | — | — |

Table 39. *Individual terms, $e^{-m} m^i/i!$, of the Poisson distribution*

**$m$**

| $i$ | 0·1 | 0·2 | 0·3 | 0·4 | 0·5 | 0·6 | 0·7 | 0·8 | 0·9 | 1·0 | $i$ |
|---|---|---|---|---|---|---|---|---|---|---|---|
| 0 | ·904837 | ·818731 | ·740818 | ·670320 | ·606531 | ·548812 | ·496585 | ·449329 | ·406570 | ·367879 | 0 |
| 1 | ·090484 | ·163746 | ·222245 | ·268128 | ·303265 | ·329287 | ·347610 | ·359463 | ·365913 | ·367879 | 1 |
| 2 | ·004524 | ·016375 | ·033337 | ·053626 | ·075816 | ·098786 | ·121663 | ·143785 | ·164661 | ·183940 | 2 |
| 3 | ·000151 | ·001092 | ·003334 | ·007150 | ·012636 | ·019757 | ·028388 | ·038343 | ·049398 | ·061313 | 3 |
| 4 | ·000004 | ·000055 | ·000250 | ·000715 | ·001580 | ·002964 | ·004968 | ·007669 | ·011115 | ·015328 | 4 |
| 5 | — | ·000002 | ·000015 | ·000057 | ·000158 | ·000356 | ·000696 | ·001227 | ·002001 | ·003066 | 5 |
| 6 | — | — | ·000001 | ·000004 | ·000013 | ·000036 | ·000081 | ·000164 | ·000300 | ·000511 | 6 |
| 7 | — | — | — | — | ·000001 | ·000003 | ·000008 | ·000019 | ·000039 | ·000073 | 7 |
| 8 | — | — | — | — | — | — | ·000001 | ·000002 | ·000004 | ·000009 | 8 |
| 9 | — | — | — | — | — | — | — | — | — | ·000001 | 9 |

| $i$ | 1·1 | 1·2 | 1·3 | 1·4 | 1·5 | 1·6 | 1·7 | 1·8 | 1·9 | 2·0 | $i$ |
|---|---|---|---|---|---|---|---|---|---|---|---|
| 0 | ·332871 | ·301194 | ·272532 | ·246597 | ·223130 | ·201897 | ·182684 | ·165299 | ·149569 | ·135335 | 0 |
| 1 | ·366158 | ·361433 | ·354291 | ·345236 | ·334695 | ·323034 | ·310562 | ·297538 | ·284180 | ·270671 | 1 |
| 2 | ·201387 | ·216860 | ·230289 | ·241665 | ·251021 | ·258428 | ·263978 | ·267784 | ·269971 | ·270671 | 2 |
| 3 | ·073842 | ·086744 | ·099792 | ·112777 | ·125510 | ·137828 | ·149587 | ·160671 | ·170982 | ·180447 | 3 |
| 4 | ·020307 | ·026023 | ·032432 | ·039472 | ·047067 | ·055131 | ·063575 | ·072302 | ·081216 | ·090224 | 4 |
| 5 | ·004467 | ·006246 | ·008432 | ·011052 | ·014120 | ·017642 | ·021615 | ·026029 | ·030862 | ·036089 | 5 |
| 6 | ·000819 | ·001249 | ·001827 | ·002579 | ·003530 | ·004705 | ·006124 | ·007809 | ·009773 | ·012030 | 6 |
| 7 | ·000129 | ·000214 | ·000339 | ·000516 | ·000756 | ·001075 | ·001487 | ·002008 | ·002653 | ·003437 | 7 |
| 8 | ·000018 | ·000032 | ·000055 | ·000090 | ·000142 | ·000215 | ·000316 | ·000452 | ·000630 | ·000859 | 8 |
| 9 | ·000002 | ·000004 | ·000008 | ·000014 | ·000024 | ·000038 | ·000060 | ·000090 | ·000133 | ·000191 | 9 |
| 10 | — | ·000001 | ·000001 | ·000002 | ·000004 | ·000006 | ·000010 | ·000016 | ·000025 | ·000038 | 10 |
| 11 | — | — | — | — | — | ·000001 | ·000002 | ·000003 | ·000004 | ·000007 | 11 |
| 12 | — | — | — | — | — | — | — | — | ·000001 | ·000001 | 12 |

| $i$ | 2·1 | 2·2 | 2·3 | 2·4 | 2·5 | 2·6 | 2·7 | 2·8 | 2·9 | 3·0 | $i$ |
|---|---|---|---|---|---|---|---|---|---|---|---|
| 0 | ·122456 | ·110803 | ·100259 | ·090718 | ·082085 | ·074274 | ·067206 | ·060810 | ·055023 | ·049787 | 0 |
| 1 | ·257159 | ·243767 | ·230595 | ·217723 | ·205212 | ·193111 | ·181455 | ·170268 | ·159567 | ·149361 | 1 |
| 2 | ·270016 | ·268144 | ·265185 | ·261268 | ·256516 | ·251045 | ·244964 | ·238375 | ·231373 | ·224042 | 2 |
| 3 | ·189012 | ·196639 | ·203308 | ·209014 | ·213763 | ·217572 | ·220468 | ·222484 | ·223660 | ·224042 | 3 |
| 4 | ·099231 | ·108151 | ·116902 | ·125409 | ·133602 | ·141422 | ·148816 | ·155739 | ·162154 | ·168031 | 4 |
| 5 | ·041677 | ·047587 | ·053775 | ·060196 | ·066801 | ·073539 | ·080360 | ·087214 | ·094049 | ·100819 | 5 |
| 6 | ·014587 | ·017448 | ·020614 | ·024078 | ·027834 | ·031867 | ·036162 | ·040700 | ·045457 | ·050409 | 6 |
| 7 | ·004376 | ·005484 | ·006773 | ·008255 | ·009941 | ·011836 | ·013948 | ·016280 | ·018832 | ·021604 | 7 |
| 8 | ·001149 | ·001508 | ·001947 | ·002477 | ·003106 | ·003847 | ·004708 | ·005698 | ·006827 | ·008102 | 8 |
| 9 | ·000268 | ·000369 | ·000498 | ·000660 | ·000863 | ·001111 | ·001412 | ·001773 | ·002200 | ·002701 | 9 |
| 10 | ·000056 | ·000081 | ·000114 | ·000158 | ·000216 | ·000289 | ·000381 | ·000496 | ·000638 | ·000810 | 10 |
| 11 | ·000011 | ·000016 | ·000024 | ·000035 | ·000049 | ·000068 | ·000094 | ·000126 | ·000168 | ·000221 | 11 |
| 12 | ·000002 | ·000003 | ·000005 | ·000007 | ·000010 | ·000015 | ·000021 | ·000029 | ·000041 | ·000055 | 12 |
| 13 | — | ·000001 | ·000001 | ·000001 | ·000002 | ·000003 | ·000004 | ·000006 | ·000009 | ·000013 | 13 |
| 14 | — | — | — | — | — | ·000001 | ·000001 | ·000001 | ·000002 | ·000003 | 14 |
| 15 | — | — | — | — | — | — | — | — | — | ·000001 | 15 |

Table 39 (continued)

| i | 3·1 | 3·2 | 3·3 | 3·4 | 3·5 | 3·6 | 3·7 | 3·8 | 3·9 | 4·0 | i |
|---|---|---|---|---|---|---|---|---|---|---|---|
| 0 | ·045049 | ·040762 | ·036883 | ·033373 | ·030197 | ·027324 | ·024724 | ·022371 | ·020242 | ·018316 | 0 |
| 1 | ·139653 | ·130439 | ·121714 | ·113469 | ·105691 | ·098365 | ·091477 | ·085009 | ·078943 | ·073263 | 1 |
| 2 | ·216461 | ·208702 | ·200829 | ·192898 | ·184959 | ·177058 | ·169233 | ·161517 | ·153940 | ·146525 | 2 |
| 3 | ·223677 | ·222616 | ·220912 | ·218617 | ·215785 | ·212469 | ·208720 | ·204588 | ·200122 | ·195367 | 3 |
| 4 | ·173350 | ·178093 | ·182252 | ·185825 | ·188812 | ·191222 | ·193066 | ·194359 | ·195119 | ·195367 | 4 |
| 5 | ·107477 | ·113979 | ·120286 | ·126361 | ·132169 | ·137680 | ·142869 | ·147713 | ·152193 | ·156293 | 5 |
| 6 | ·055530 | ·060789 | ·066158 | ·071604 | ·077098 | ·082608 | ·088102 | ·093551 | ·098925 | ·104196 | 6 |
| 7 | ·024592 | ·027789 | ·031189 | ·034779 | ·038549 | ·042484 | ·046568 | ·050785 | ·055115 | ·059540 | 7 |
| 8 | ·009529 | ·011116 | ·012865 | ·014781 | ·016865 | ·019118 | ·021538 | ·024123 | ·026869 | ·029770 | 8 |
| 9 | ·003282 | ·003952 | ·004717 | ·005584 | ·006559 | ·007647 | ·008854 | ·010185 | ·011643 | ·013231 | 9 |
| 10 | ·001018 | ·001265 | ·001557 | ·001899 | ·002296 | ·002753 | ·003276 | ·003870 | ·004541 | ·005292 | 10 |
| 11 | ·000287 | ·000368 | ·000467 | ·000587 | ·000730 | ·000901 | ·001102 | ·001337 | ·001610 | ·001925 | 11 |
| 12 | ·000074 | ·000098 | ·000128 | ·000166 | ·000213 | ·000270 | ·000340 | ·000423 | ·000523 | ·000642 | 12 |
| 13 | ·000018 | ·000024 | ·000033 | ·000043 | ·000057 | ·000075 | ·000097 | ·000124 | ·000157 | ·000197 | 13 |
| 14 | ·000004 | ·000006 | ·000008 | ·000011 | ·000014 | ·000019 | ·000026 | ·000034 | ·000044 | ·000056 | 14 |
| 15 | ·000001 | ·000001 | ·000002 | ·000002 | ·000003 | ·000005 | ·000006 | ·000009 | ·000011 | ·000015 | 15 |
| 16 | — | — | — | ·000001 | ·000001 | ·000001 | ·000001 | ·000002 | ·000003 | ·000004 | 16 |
| 17 | — | — | — | — | — | — | — | — | ·000001 | ·000001 | 17 |

| i | 4·1 | 4·2 | 4·3 | 4·4 | 4·5 | 4·6 | 4·7 | 4·8 | 4·9 | 5·0 | i |
|---|---|---|---|---|---|---|---|---|---|---|---|
| 0 | ·016573 | ·014996 | ·013569 | ·012277 | ·011109 | ·010052 | ·009095 | ·008230 | ·007447 | ·006738 | 0 |
| 1 | ·067948 | ·062981 | ·058345 | ·054020 | ·049990 | ·046238 | ·042748 | ·039503 | ·036488 | ·033690 | 1 |
| 2 | ·139293 | ·132261 | ·125441 | ·118845 | ·112479 | ·106348 | ·100457 | ·094807 | ·089396 | ·084224 | 2 |
| 3 | ·190368 | ·185165 | ·179799 | ·174305 | ·168718 | ·163068 | ·157383 | ·151691 | ·146014 | ·140374 | 3 |
| 4 | ·195127 | ·194424 | ·193284 | ·191736 | ·189808 | ·187528 | ·184925 | ·182029 | ·178867 | ·175467 | 4 |
| 5 | ·160004 | ·163316 | ·166224 | ·168728 | ·170827 | ·172525 | ·173830 | ·174748 | ·175290 | ·175467 | 5 |
| 6 | ·109336 | ·114321 | ·119127 | ·123734 | ·128120 | ·132270 | ·136167 | ·139798 | ·143153 | ·146223 | 6 |
| 7 | ·064040 | ·068593 | ·073178 | ·077775 | ·082363 | ·086920 | ·091426 | ·095862 | ·100207 | ·104445 | 7 |
| 8 | ·032820 | ·036011 | ·039333 | ·042776 | ·046329 | ·049979 | ·053713 | ·057517 | ·061377 | ·065278 | 8 |
| 9 | ·014951 | ·016805 | ·018793 | ·020913 | ·023165 | ·025545 | ·028050 | ·030676 | ·033416 | ·036266 | 9 |
| 10 | ·006130 | ·007058 | ·008081 | ·009202 | ·010424 | ·011751 | ·013184 | ·014729 | ·016374 | ·018133 | 10 |
| 11 | ·002285 | ·002695 | ·003159 | ·003681 | ·004264 | ·004914 | ·005633 | ·006425 | ·007294 | ·008242 | 11 |
| 12 | ·000781 | ·000943 | ·001132 | ·001350 | ·001599 | ·001884 | ·002206 | ·002570 | ·002978 | ·003434 | 12 |
| 13 | ·000246 | ·000305 | ·000374 | ·000457 | ·000554 | ·000667 | ·000798 | ·000949 | ·001123 | ·001321 | 13 |
| 14 | ·000072 | ·000091 | ·000115 | ·000144 | ·000178 | ·000219 | ·000268 | ·000325 | ·000393 | ·000472 | 14 |
| 15 | ·000020 | ·000026 | ·000033 | ·000042 | ·000053 | ·000067 | ·000084 | ·000104 | ·000128 | ·000157 | 15 |
| 16 | ·000005 | ·000007 | ·000009 | ·000012 | ·000015 | ·000019 | ·000025 | ·000031 | ·000039 | ·000049 | 16 |
| 17 | ·000001 | ·000902 | ·000002 | ·000003 | ·000004 | ·000005 | ·000007 | ·000009 | ·000011 | ·000014 | 17 |
| 18 | — | — | ·000001 | ·000001 | ·000001 | ·000001 | ·000002 | ·000002 | ·000003 | ·000004 | 18 |
| 19 | — | — | — | — | — | — | — | ·000001 | ·000001 | ·000001 | 19 |

| i | 5·1 | 5·2 | 5·3 | 5·4 | 5·5 | 5·6 | 5·7 | 5·8 | 5·9 | 6·0 | |
|---|---|---|---|---|---|---|---|---|---|---|---|
| 0 | ·006097 | ·005517 | ·004992 | ·004517 | ·004087 | ·003698 | ·003346 | ·003028 | ·002739 | ·002479 | 0 |
| 1 | ·031093 | ·028686 | ·026455 | ·024390 | ·022477 | ·020708 | ·019072 | ·017560 | ·016163 | ·014873 | 1 |
| 2 | ·079288 | ·074584 | ·070107 | ·065852 | ·061812 | ·057982 | ·054355 | ·050923 | ·047680 | ·044618 | 2 |
| 3 | ·134790 | ·129279 | ·123856 | ·118533 | ·113323 | ·108234 | ·103275 | ·098452 | ·093771 | ·089235 | 3 |

Table 39. *Individual terms of the Poisson distribution (continued)*

| $i$ | 5·1 | 5·2 | 5·3 | 5·4 | 5·5 | 5·6 | 5·7 | 5·8 | 5·9 | 6·0 | $i$ |
|---|---|---|---|---|---|---|---|---|---|---|---|
| 4 | ·171857 | ·168063 | ·164109 | ·160020 | ·155819 | ·151528 | ·147167 | ·142755 | ·138312 | ·133853 | 4 |
| 5 | ·175294 | ·174785 | ·173955 | ·172821 | ·171401 | ·169711 | ·167770 | ·165596 | ·163208 | ·160623 | 5 |
| 6 | ·149000 | ·151480 | ·153660 | ·155539 | ·157117 | ·158397 | ·159382 | ·160076 | ·160488 | ·160623 | 6 |
| 7 | ·108557 | ·112528 | ·116343 | ·119987 | ·123449 | ·126717 | ·129782 | ·132635 | ·135268 | ·137677 | 7 |
| 8 | ·069205 | ·073143 | ·077077 | ·080991 | ·084871 | ·088702 | ·092470 | ·096160 | ·099760 | ·103258 | 8 |
| 9 | ·039216 | ·042261 | ·045390 | ·048595 | ·051866 | ·055192 | ·058564 | ·061970 | ·065398 | ·068838 | 9 |
| 10 | ·020000 | ·021976 | ·024057 | ·026241 | ·028526 | ·030908 | ·033382 | ·035943 | ·038585 | ·041303 | 10 |
| 11 | ·009273 | ·010388 | ·011591 | ·012882 | ·014263 | ·015735 | ·017298 | ·018952 | ·020696 | ·022529 | 11 |
| 12 | ·003941 | ·004502 | ·005119 | ·005797 | ·006537 | ·007343 | ·008216 | ·009160 | ·010175 | ·011264 | 12 |
| 13 | ·001546 | ·001801 | ·002087 | ·002408 | ·002766 | ·003163 | ·003603 | ·004087 | ·004618 | ·005199 | 13 |
| 14 | ·000563 | ·000669 | ·000790 | ·000929 | ·001087 | ·001265 | ·001467 | ·001693 | ·001946 | ·002228 | 14 |
| 15 | ·000191 | ·000232 | ·000279 | ·000334 | ·000398 | ·000472 | ·000557 | ·000655 | ·000766 | ·000891 | 15 |
| 16 | ·000061 | ·000075 | ·000092 | ·000113 | ·000137 | ·000165 | ·000199 | ·000237 | ·000282 | ·000334 | 16 |
| 17 | ·000018 | ·000023 | ·000029 | ·000036 | ·000044 | ·000054 | ·000067 | ·000081 | ·000098 | ·000118 | 17 |
| 18 | ·000005 | ·000007 | ·000008 | ·000011 | ·000014 | ·000017 | ·000021 | ·000026 | ·000032 | ·000039 | 18 |
| 19 | ·000001 | ·000002 | ·000002 | ·000003 | ·000004 | ·000005 | ·000006 | ·000008 | ·000010 | ·000012 | 19 |
| 20 | — | — | ·000001 | ·000001 | ·000001 | ·000001 | ·000002 | ·000002 | ·000003 | ·000004 | 20 |
| 21 | — | — | — | — | — | — | — | ·000001 | ·000001 | ·000001 | 21 |

| $i$ | 6·1 | 6·2 | 6·3 | 6·4 | 6·5 | 6·6 | 6·7 | 6·8 | 6·9 | 7·0 | $i$ |
|---|---|---|---|---|---|---|---|---|---|---|---|
| 0 | ·002243 | ·002029 | ·001836 | ·001662 | ·001503 | ·001360 | ·001231 | ·001114 | ·001008 | ·000912 | 0 |
| 1 | ·013682 | ·012582 | ·011569 | ·010634 | ·009772 | ·008978 | ·008247 | ·007574 | ·006954 | ·006383 | 1 |
| 2 | ·041729 | ·039006 | ·036441 | ·034029 | ·031760 | ·029629 | ·027628 | ·025751 | ·023990 | ·022341 | 2 |
| 3 | ·084848 | ·080612 | ·076527 | ·072595 | ·068814 | ·065183 | ·061702 | ·058368 | ·055178 | ·052129 | 3 |
| 4 | ·129393 | ·124948 | ·120530 | ·116151 | ·111822 | ·107553 | ·103351 | ·099225 | ·095182 | ·091226 | 4 |
| 5 | ·157860 | ·154936 | ·151868 | ·148674 | ·145369 | ·141969 | ·138490 | ·134946 | ·131351 | ·127717 | 5 |
| 6 | ·160491 | ·160100 | ·159461 | ·158585 | ·157483 | ·156166 | ·154648 | ·152939 | ·151053 | ·149003 | 6 |
| 7 | ·139856 | ·141803 | ·143515 | ·144992 | ·146234 | ·147243 | ·148020 | ·148569 | ·148895 | ·149003 | 7 |
| 8 | ·106640 | ·109897 | ·113018 | ·115994 | ·118815 | ·121475 | ·123967 | ·126284 | ·128422 | ·130377 | 8 |
| 9 | ·072278 | ·075707 | ·079113 | ·082484 | ·085811 | ·089082 | ·092286 | ·095415 | ·098457 | ·101405 | 9 |
| 10 | ·044090 | ·046938 | ·049841 | ·052790 | ·055777 | ·058794 | ·061832 | ·064882 | ·067935 | ·070983 | 10 |
| 11 | ·024450 | ·026456 | ·028545 | ·030714 | ·032959 | ·035276 | ·037661 | ·040109 | ·042614 | ·045171 | 11 |
| 12 | ·012429 | ·013669 | ·014986 | ·016381 | ·017853 | ·019402 | ·021028 | ·022728 | ·024503 | ·026350 | 12 |
| 13 | ·005832 | ·006519 | ·007263 | ·008064 | ·008926 | ·009850 | ·010837 | ·011889 | ·013005 | ·014188 | 13 |
| 14 | ·002541 | ·002887 | ·003268 | ·003687 | ·004144 | ·004644 | ·005186 | ·005774 | ·006410 | ·007094 | 14 |
| 15 | ·001033 | ·001193 | ·001373 | ·001573 | ·001796 | ·002043 | ·002317 | ·002618 | ·002949 | ·003311 | 15 |
| 16 | ·000394 | ·000462 | ·000540 | ·000629 | ·000730 | ·000843 | ·000970 | ·001113 | ·001272 | ·001448 | 16 |
| 17 | ·000141 | ·000169 | ·000200 | ·000237 | ·000279 | ·000327 | ·000382 | ·000445 | ·000516 | ·000596 | 17 |
| 18 | ·000048 | ·000058 | ·000070 | ·000084 | ·000101 | ·000120 | ·000142 | ·000168 | ·000198 | ·000232 | 18 |
| 19 | ·000015 | ·000019 | ·000023 | ·000028 | ·000034 | ·000042 | ·000050 | ·000060 | ·000072 | ·000085 | 19 |
| 20 | ·000005 | ·000006 | ·000007 | ·000009 | ·000011 | ·000014 | ·000017 | ·000020 | ·000025 | ·000030 | 20 |
| 21 | ·000001 | ·000002 | ·000002 | ·000003 | ·000003 | ·000004 | ·000005 | ·000007 | ·000008 | ·000010 | 21 |
| 22 | — | — | ·000001 | ·000001 | ·000001 | ·000001 | ·000002 | ·000002 | ·000003 | ·000003 | 22 |
| 23 | — | — | — | — | — | — | — | ·000001 | ·000001 | ·000001 | 23 |

Table 39 (*continued*)

| $i$ | $m$ 7·1 | 7·2 | 7·3 | 7·4 | 7·5 | 7·6 | 7·7 | 7·8 | 7·9 | 8·0 | $i$ |
|---|---|---|---|---|---|---|---|---|---|---|---|
| 0 | ·000825 | ·000747 | ·000676 | ·000611 | ·000553 | ·000500 | ·000453 | ·000410 | ·000371 | ·000335 | 0 |
| 1 | ·005858 | ·005375 | ·004931 | ·004523 | ·004148 | ·003803 | ·003487 | ·003196 | ·002929 | ·002684 | 1 |
| 2 | ·020797 | ·019352 | ·018000 | ·016736 | ·015555 | ·014453 | ·013424 | ·012464 | ·011569 | ·010735 | 2 |
| 3 | ·049219 | ·046444 | ·043799 | ·041282 | ·038889 | ·036614 | ·034455 | ·032407 | ·030465 | ·028626 | 3 |
| 4 | ·087364 | ·083598 | ·079934 | ·076372 | ·072916 | ·069567 | ·066326 | ·063193 | ·060169 | ·057252 | 4 |
| 5 | ·124057 | ·120382 | ·116703 | ·113031 | ·109375 | ·105742 | ·102142 | ·098581 | ·095067 | ·091604 | 5 |
| 6 | ·146800 | ·144458 | ·141989 | ·139405 | ·136718 | ·133940 | ·131082 | ·128156 | ·125171 | ·122138 | 6 |
| 7 | ·148897 | ·148586 | ·148074 | ·147371 | ·146484 | ·145421 | ·144191 | ·142802 | ·141264 | ·139587 | 7 |
| 8 | ·132146 | ·133727 | ·135118 | ·136318 | ·137329 | ·138150 | ·138783 | ·139232 | ·139499 | ·139587 | 8 |
| 9 | ·104249 | ·106982 | ·109596 | ·112084 | ·114440 | ·116660 | ·118737 | ·120668 | ·122449 | ·124077 | 9 |
| 10 | ·074017 | ·077027 | ·080005 | ·082942 | ·085830 | ·088661 | ·091427 | ·094121 | ·096735 | ·099262 | 10 |
| 11 | ·047774 | ·050418 | ·053094 | ·055797 | ·058521 | ·061257 | ·063999 | ·066740 | ·069473 | ·072190 | 11 |
| 12 | ·028267 | ·030251 | ·032299 | ·034408 | ·036575 | ·038796 | ·041066 | ·043381 | ·045736 | ·048127 | 12 |
| 13 | ·015438 | ·016754 | ·018137 | ·019586 | ·021101 | ·022681 | ·024324 | ·026029 | ·027794 | ·029616 | 13 |
| 14 | ·007829 | ·008616 | ·009457 | ·010353 | ·011304 | ·012312 | ·013378 | ·014502 | ·015684 | ·016924 | 14 |
| 15 | ·003706 | ·004136 | ·004603 | ·005107 | ·005652 | ·006238 | ·006867 | ·007541 | ·008260 | ·009026 | 15 |
| 16 | ·001644 | ·001861 | ·002100 | ·002362 | ·002649 | ·002963 | ·003305 | ·003676 | ·004078 | ·004513 | 16 |
| 17 | ·000687 | ·000788 | ·000902 | ·001028 | ·001169 | ·001325 | ·001497 | ·001687 | ·001895 | ·002124 | 17 |
| 18 | ·000271 | ·000315 | ·000366 | ·000423 | ·000487 | ·000559 | ·000640 | ·000731 | ·000832 | ·000944 | 18 |
| 19 | ·000101 | ·000119 | ·000141 | ·000165 | ·000192 | ·000224 | ·000259 | ·000300 | ·000346 | ·000397 | 19 |
| 20 | ·000036 | ·000043 | ·000051 | ·000061 | ·000072 | ·000085 | ·000100 | ·000117 | ·000137 | ·000159 | 20 |
| 21 | ·000012 | ·000015 | ·000018 | ·000021 | ·000026 | ·000031 | ·000037 | ·000043 | ·000051 | ·000061 | 21 |
| 22 | ·000004 | ·000005 | ·000006 | ·000007 | ·000009 | ·000011 | ·000013 | ·000015 | ·000018 | ·000022 | 22 |
| 23 | ·000001 | ·000002 | ·000002 | ·000002 | ·000003 | ·000004 | ·000004 | ·000005 | ·000006 | ·000008 | 23 |
| 24 | — | — | ·000001 | ·000001 | ·000001 | ·000001 | ·000001 | ·000002 | ·000002 | ·000003 | 24 |
| 25 | — | — | — | — | ·000001 | — | — | ·000001 | ·000001 | ·000001 | 25 |

| $i$ | 8·1 | 8·2 | 8·3 | 8·4 | 8·5 | 8·6 | 8·7 | 8·8 | 8·9 | 9·0 | $i$ |
|---|---|---|---|---|---|---|---|---|---|---|---|
| 0 | ·000304 | ·000275 | ·000249 | ·000225 | ·000203 | ·000184 | ·000167 | ·000151 | ·000136 | ·000123 | 0 |
| 1 | ·002459 | ·002252 | ·002063 | ·001889 | ·001729 | ·001583 | ·001449 | ·001326 | ·001214 | ·001111 | 1 |
| 2 | ·009958 | ·009234 | ·008560 | ·007933 | ·007350 | ·006808 | ·006304 | ·005836 | ·005402 | ·004998 | 2 |
| 3 | ·026885 | ·025239 | ·023683 | ·022213 | ·020826 | ·019517 | ·018283 | ·017120 | ·016025 | ·014994 | 3 |
| 4 | ·054443 | ·051740 | ·049142 | ·046648 | ·044255 | ·041961 | ·039765 | ·037664 | ·035656 | ·033737 | 4 |
| 5 | ·088198 | ·084854 | ·081576 | ·078368 | ·075233 | ·072174 | ·069192 | ·066289 | ·063467 | ·060727 | 5 |
| 6 | ·119067 | ·115967 | ·112847 | ·109716 | ·106581 | ·103449 | ·100328 | ·097224 | ·094143 | ·091090 | 6 |
| 7 | ·137778 | ·135848 | ·133805 | ·131659 | ·129419 | ·127094 | ·124693 | ·122224 | ·119696 | ·117116 | 7 |
| 8 | ·139500 | ·139244 | ·138823 | ·138242 | ·137508 | ·136626 | ·135604 | ·134446 | ·133161 | ·131756 | 8 |
| 9 | ·125550 | ·126866 | ·128025 | ·129026 | ·129869 | ·130554 | ·131084 | ·131459 | ·131682 | ·131756 | 9 |
| 10 | ·101696 | ·104031 | ·106261 | ·108382 | ·110388 | ·112277 | ·114043 | ·115684 | ·117197 | ·118580 | 10 |
| 11 | ·074885 | ·077550 | ·080179 | ·082764 | ·085300 | ·087780 | ·090197 | ·092547 | ·094823 | ·097020 | 11 |
| 12 | ·050547 | ·052993 | ·055457 | ·057935 | ·060421 | ·062909 | ·065393 | ·067868 | ·070327 | ·072765 | 12 |
| 13 | ·031495 | ·033426 | ·035407 | ·037435 | ·039506 | ·041617 | ·043763 | ·045941 | ·048147 | ·050376 | 13 |
| 14 | ·018222 | ·019578 | ·020991 | ·022461 | ·023986 | ·025565 | ·027196 | ·028877 | ·030608 | ·032384 | 14 |
| 15 | ·009840 | ·010703 | ·011615 | ·012578 | ·013592 | ·014657 | ·015773 | ·016941 | ·018161 | ·019431 | 15 |
| 16 | ·004981 | ·005485 | ·006025 | ·006604 | ·007221 | ·007878 | ·008577 | ·009318 | ·010102 | ·010930 | 16 |
| 17 | ·002373 | ·002646 | ·002942 | ·003263 | ·003610 | ·003985 | ·004389 | ·004823 | ·005289 | ·005786 | 17 |
| 18 | ·001068 | ·001205 | ·001356 | ·001523 | ·001705 | ·001904 | ·002121 | ·002358 | ·002615 | ·002893 | 18 |
| 19 | ·000455 | ·000520 | ·000593 | ·000673 | ·000763 | ·000862 | ·000971 | ·001092 | ·001225 | ·001370 | 19 |
| 20 | ·000184 | ·000213 | ·000246 | ·000283 | ·000324 | ·000371 | ·000423 | ·000481 | ·000545 | ·000617 | 20 |

Table 39. *Individual terms of the Poisson distribution (continued)*

| $i$ | 8·1 | 8·2 | 8·3 | 8·4 | 8·5 | 8·6 | 8·7 | 8·8 | 8·9 | 9·0 | $i$ |
|---|---|---|---|---|---|---|---|---|---|---|---|
| 21 | ·000071 | ·000083 | ·000097 | ·000113 | ·000131 | ·000152 | ·000175 | ·000201 | ·000231 | ·000264 | 21 |
| 22 | ·000026 | ·000031 | ·000037 | ·000043 | ·000051 | ·000059 | ·000069 | ·000081 | ·000093 | ·000108 | 22 |
| 23 | ·000009 | ·000011 | ·000013 | ·000016 | ·000019 | ·000022 | ·000026 | ·000031 | ·000036 | ·000042 | 23 |
| 24 | ·000003 | ·000004 | ·000005 | ·000006 | ·000007 | ·000008 | ·000009 | ·000011 | ·000013 | ·000016 | 24 |
| 25 | ·000001 | ·000001 | ·000002 | ·000002 | ·000002 | ·000003 | ·000003 | ·000004 | ·000005 | ·000006 | 25 |
| 26 | — | — | — | ·000001 | ·000001 | ·000001 | ·000001 | ·000001 | ·000002 | ·000002 | 26 |
| 27 | — | — | — | — | — | — | — | — | ·000001 | ·000001 | 27 |

| $i$ | 9·1 | 9·2 | 9·3 | 9·4 | 9·5 | 9·6 | 9·7 | 9·8 | 9·9 | 10·0 | $i$ |
|---|---|---|---|---|---|---|---|---|---|---|---|
| 0 | ·000112 | ·000101 | ·000091 | ·000083 | ·000075 | ·000068 | ·000061 | ·000055 | ·000050 | ·000045 | 0 |
| 1 | ·001016 | ·000930 | ·000850 | ·000778 | ·000711 | ·000650 | ·000594 | ·000543 | ·000497 | ·000454 | 1 |
| 2 | ·004624 | ·004276 | ·003954 | ·003655 | ·003378 | ·003121 | ·002883 | ·002663 | ·002459 | ·002270 | 2 |
| 3 | ·014025 | ·013113 | ·012256 | ·011452 | ·010696 | ·009987 | ·009322 | ·008698 | ·008114 | ·007567 | 3 |
| 4 | ·031906 | ·030160 | ·028496 | ·026911 | ·025403 | ·023969 | ·022606 | ·021311 | ·020082 | ·018917 | 4 |
| 5 | ·058069 | ·055494 | ·053002 | ·050593 | ·048266 | ·046020 | ·043855 | ·041770 | ·039763 | ·037833 | 5 |
| 6 | ·088072 | ·085091 | ·082154 | ·079262 | ·076421 | ·073632 | ·070899 | ·068224 | ·065609 | ·063055 | 6 |
| 7 | ·114493 | ·111834 | ·109147 | ·106438 | ·103714 | ·100981 | ·098246 | ·095514 | ·092790 | ·090079 | 7 |
| 8 | ·130236 | ·128609 | ·126883 | ·125065 | ·123160 | ·121178 | ·119123 | ·117004 | ·114827 | ·112599 | 8 |
| 9 | ·131683 | ·131467 | ·131113 | ·130623 | ·130003 | ·129256 | ·128388 | ·127405 | ·126310 | ·125110 | 9 |
| 10 | ·119832 | ·120950 | ·121935 | ·122786 | ·123502 | ·124086 | ·124537 | ·124857 | ·125047 | ·125110 | 10 |
| 11 | ·099133 | ·101158 | ·103090 | ·104926 | ·106661 | ·108293 | ·109819 | ·111236 | ·112542 | ·113736 | 11 |
| 12 | ·075176 | ·077555 | ·079895 | ·082192 | ·084440 | ·086634 | ·088770 | ·090843 | ·092847 | ·094780 | 12 |
| 13 | ·052623 | ·054885 | ·057156 | ·059431 | ·061706 | ·063976 | ·066236 | ·068481 | ·070707 | ·072908 | 13 |
| 14 | ·034205 | ·036067 | ·037968 | ·039904 | ·041872 | ·043869 | ·045892 | ·047937 | ·050000 | ·052077 | 14 |
| 15 | ·020751 | ·022121 | ·023540 | ·025006 | ·026519 | ·028076 | ·029677 | ·031319 | ·033000 | ·034718 | 15 |
| 16 | ·011802 | ·012720 | ·013683 | ·014691 | ·015746 | ·016846 | ·017992 | ·019183 | ·020419 | ·021699 | 16 |
| 17 | ·006318 | ·006884 | ·007485 | ·008123 | ·008799 | ·009513 | ·010266 | ·011058 | ·011891 | ·012764 | 17 |
| 18 | ·003194 | ·003518 | ·003867 | ·004242 | ·004644 | ·005074 | ·005532 | ·006021 | ·006540 | ·007091 | 18 |
| 19 | ·001530 | ·001704 | ·001893 | ·002099 | ·002322 | ·002563 | ·002824 | ·003105 | ·003408 | ·003732 | 19 |
| 20 | ·000696 | ·000784 | ·000880 | ·000986 | ·001103 | ·001230 | ·001370 | ·001522 | ·001687 | ·001866 | 20 |
| 21 | ·000302 | ·000343 | ·000390 | ·000442 | ·000499 | ·000563 | ·000633 | ·000710 | ·000795 | ·000889 | 21 |
| 22 | ·000125 | ·000144 | ·000165 | ·000189 | ·000215 | ·000245 | ·000279 | ·000316 | ·000358 | ·000404 | 22 |
| 23 | ·000049 | ·000057 | ·000067 | ·000077 | ·000089 | ·000102 | ·000118 | ·000135 | ·000154 | ·000176 | 23 |
| 24 | ·000019 | ·000022 | ·000026 | ·000030 | ·000035 | ·000041 | ·000048 | ·000055 | ·000064 | ·000073 | 24 |
| 25 | ·000007 | ·000008 | ·000010 | ·000011 | ·000013 | ·000016 | ·000018 | ·000022 | ·000025 | ·000029 | 25 |
| 26 | ·000002 | ·000003 | ·000003 | ·000004 | ·000005 | ·000006 | ·000007 | ·000008 | ·000010 | ·000011 | 26 |
| 27 | ·000001 | ·000001 | ·000001 | ·000001 | ·000002 | ·000002 | ·000002 | ·000003 | ·000004 | ·000004 | 27 |
| 28 | — | — | — | — | ·000001 | ·000001 | ·000001 | ·000001 | ·000001 | ·000001 | 28 |
| 29 | — | — | — | — | — | — | — | — | — | ·000001 | 29 |

| $i$ | 10·1 | 10·2 | 10·3 | 10·4 | 10·5 | 10·6 | 10·7 | 10·8 | 10·9 | 11·0 | $i$ |
|---|---|---|---|---|---|---|---|---|---|---|---|
| 0 | ·000041 | ·000037 | ·000034 | ·000030 | ·000028 | ·000025 | ·000023 | ·000020 | ·000018 | ·000017 | 0 |
| 1 | ·000415 | ·000379 | ·000346 | ·000317 | ·000289 | ·000264 | ·000241 | ·000220 | ·000201 | ·000184 | 1 |
| 2 | ·002095 | ·001934 | ·001784 | ·001646 | ·001518 | ·001400 | ·001291 | ·001190 | ·001097 | ·001010 | 2 |
| 3 | ·007054 | ·006574 | ·006125 | ·005705 | ·005313 | ·004946 | ·004603 | ·004283 | ·003984 | ·003705 | 3 |

Table 39 (*continued*)

| $i$ | $m$ | | | | | | | | | | $i$ |
|---|---|---|---|---|---|---|---|---|---|---|---|
| | 10·1 | 10·2 | 10·3 | 10·4 | 10·5 | 10·6 | 10·7 | 10·8 | 10·9 | 11·0 | |
| 4 | ·017811 | ·016764 | ·015773 | ·014834 | ·013946 | ·013107 | ·012313 | ·011564 | ·010856 | ·010189 | 4 |
| 5 | ·035979 | ·034199 | ·032492 | ·030855 | ·029287 | ·027786 | ·026350 | ·024978 | ·023667 | ·022415 | 5 |
| 6 | ·060565 | ·058139 | ·055777 | ·053482 | ·051252 | ·049089 | ·046991 | ·044960 | ·042995 | ·041095 | 6 |
| 7 | ·087387 | ·084716 | ·082072 | ·079458 | ·076878 | ·074334 | ·071830 | ·069367 | ·066949 | ·064577 | 7 |
| 8 | ·110326 | ·108013 | ·105668 | ·103296 | ·100902 | ·098493 | ·096072 | ·093646 | ·091218 | ·088794 | 8 |
| 9 | ·123810 | ·122415 | ·120931 | ·119364 | ·117720 | ·116003 | ·114219 | ·112375 | ·110475 | ·108526 | 9 |
| 10 | ·125048 | ·124863 | ·124559 | ·124139 | ·123606 | ·122963 | ·122215 | ·121365 | ·120418 | ·119378 | 10 |
| 11 | ·114817 | ·115782 | ·116633 | ·117368 | ·117987 | ·118492 | ·118882 | ·119159 | ·119323 | ·119378 | 11 |
| 12 | ·096637 | ·098415 | ·100110 | ·101719 | ·103239 | ·104667 | ·106003 | ·107243 | ·108386 | ·109430 | 12 |
| 13 | ·075080 | ·077218 | ·079318 | ·081375 | ·083385 | ·085344 | ·087248 | ·089094 | ·090877 | ·092595 | 13 |
| 14 | ·054165 | ·056259 | ·058355 | ·060450 | ·062539 | ·064618 | ·066683 | ·068730 | ·070754 | ·072753 | 14 |
| 15 | ·036471 | ·038256 | ·040071 | ·041912 | ·043777 | ·045663 | ·047567 | ·049485 | ·051415 | ·053352 | 15 |
| 16 | ·023022 | ·024388 | ·025795 | ·027243 | ·028729 | ·030252 | ·031810 | ·033403 | ·035026 | ·036680 | 16 |
| 17 | ·013678 | ·014633 | ·015629 | ·016666 | ·017744 | ·018863 | ·020022 | ·021220 | ·022458 | ·023734 | 17 |
| 18 | ·007675 | ·008292 | ·008943 | ·009629 | ·010351 | ·011108 | ·011902 | ·012732 | ·013600 | ·014504 | 18 |
| 19 | ·004080 | ·004451 | ·004848 | ·005271 | ·005720 | ·006197 | ·006703 | ·007237 | ·007802 | ·008397 | 19 |
| 20 | ·002060 | ·002270 | ·002497 | ·002741 | ·003003 | ·003285 | ·003586 | ·003908 | ·004252 | ·004618 | 20 |
| 21 | ·000991 | ·001103 | ·001225 | ·001357 | ·001502 | ·001658 | ·001827 | ·002010 | ·002207 | ·002419 | 21 |
| 22 | ·000455 | ·000511 | ·000573 | ·000642 | ·000717 | ·000799 | ·000889 | ·000987 | ·001093 | ·001210 | 22 |
| 23 | ·000200 | ·000227 | ·000257 | ·000290 | ·000327 | ·000368 | ·000413 | ·000463 | ·000518 | ·000578 | 23 |
| 24 | ·000084 | ·000096 | ·000110 | ·000126 | ·000143 | ·000163 | ·000184 | ·000208 | ·000235 | ·000265 | 24 |
| 25 | ·000034 | ·000039 | ·000045 | ·000052 | ·000060 | ·000069 | ·000079 | ·000090 | ·000103 | ·000117 | 25 |
| 26 | ·000013 | ·000015 | ·000018 | ·000021 | ·000024 | ·000028 | ·000032 | ·000037 | ·000043 | ·000049 | 26 |
| 27 | ·000005 | ·000006 | ·000007 | ·000008 | ·000009 | ·000011 | ·000013 | ·000015 | ·000017 | ·000020 | 27 |
| 28 | ·000002 | ·000002 | ·000003 | ·000003 | ·000004 | ·000004 | ·000005 | ·000006 | ·000007 | ·000008 | 28 |
| 29 | ·000001 | ·000001 | ·000001 | ·000001 | ·000001 | ·000002 | ·000002 | ·000002 | ·000003 | ·000003 | 29 |
| 30 | — | — | — | — | — | ·000001 | ·000001 | ·000001 | ·000001 | ·000001 | 30 |

| $i$ | 11·1 | 11·2 | 11·3 | 11·4 | 11·5 | 11·6 | 11·7 | 11·8 | 11·9 | 12·0 | $i$ |
|---|---|---|---|---|---|---|---|---|---|---|---|
| 0 | ·000015 | ·000014 | ·000012 | ·000011 | ·000010 | ·000009 | ·000008 | ·000008 | ·000007 | ·000006 | 0 |
| 1 | ·000168 | ·000153 | ·000140 | ·000128 | ·000116 | ·000106 | ·000097 | ·000089 | ·000081 | ·000074 | 1 |
| 2 | ·000931 | ·000858 | ·000790 | ·000727 | ·000670 | ·000617 | ·000568 | ·000522 | ·000481 | ·000442 | 2 |
| 3 | ·003445 | ·003202 | ·002976 | ·002764 | ·002568 | ·002385 | ·002214 | ·002055 | ·001907 | ·001770 | 3 |
| 4 | ·009559 | ·008965 | ·008406 | ·007879 | ·007382 | ·006915 | ·006476 | ·006062 | ·005674 | ·005309 | 4 |
| 5 | ·021221 | ·020082 | ·018997 | ·017963 | ·016979 | ·016043 | ·015153 | ·014307 | ·013504 | ·012741 | 5 |
| 6 | ·039259 | ·037487 | ·035778 | ·034130 | ·032544 | ·031017 | ·029549 | ·028137 | ·026782 | ·025481 | 6 |
| 7 | ·062253 | ·059979 | ·057755 | ·055584 | ·053465 | ·051400 | ·049388 | ·047432 | ·045530 | ·043682 | 7 |
| 8 | ·086376 | ·083970 | ·081579 | ·079206 | ·076856 | ·074529 | ·072231 | ·069962 | ·067725 | ·065523 | 8 |
| 9 | ·106531 | ·104496 | ·102427 | ·100328 | ·098204 | ·096060 | ·093900 | ·091728 | ·089548 | ·087364 | 9 |
| 10 | ·118249 | ·117036 | ·115743 | ·114374 | ·112935 | ·111430 | ·109863 | ·108239 | ·106562 | ·104837 | 10 |
| 11 | ·119324 | ·119164 | ·118899 | ·118533 | ·118068 | ·117508 | ·116854 | ·116110 | ·115281 | ·114368 | 11 |
| 12 | ·110375 | ·111220 | ·111964 | ·112607 | ·113149 | ·113591 | ·113933 | ·114175 | ·114320 | ·114363 | 12 |
| 13 | ·094243 | ·095820 | ·097322 | ·098747 | ·100093 | ·101358 | ·102539 | ·103636 | ·104647 | ·105570 | 13 |
| 14 | ·074721 | ·076656 | ·078553 | ·080409 | ·082219 | ·083982 | ·085694 | ·087350 | ·088950 | ·090489 | 14 |
| 15 | ·055294 | ·057236 | ·059177 | ·061110 | ·063035 | ·064946 | ·066841 | ·068716 | ·070567 | ·072391 | 15 |
| 16 | ·038360 | ·040065 | ·041793 | ·043541 | ·045306 | ·047086 | ·048877 | ·050678 | ·052484 | ·054293 | 16 |
| 17 | ·025047 | ·026396 | ·027780 | ·029198 | ·030648 | ·032129 | ·033639 | ·035176 | ·036739 | ·038325 | 17 |
| 18 | ·015446 | ·016424 | ·017440 | ·018492 | ·019581 | ·020706 | ·021865 | ·023060 | ·024288 | ·025550 | 18 |
| 19 | ·009023 | ·009682 | ·010372 | ·011095 | ·011852 | ·012641 | ·013465 | ·014322 | ·015212 | ·016137 | 19 |

Table 39. *Individual terms of the Poisson distribution (continued)*

| $i$ | 11·1 | 11·2 | 11·3 | 11·4 | 11·5 | 11·6 | 11·7 | 11·8 | 11·9 | 12·0 | $i$ |
|---|---|---|---|---|---|---|---|---|---|---|---|
| 20 | ·005008 | ·005422 | ·005860 | ·006324 | ·006815 | ·007332 | ·007877 | ·008450 | ·009051 | ·009682 | 20 |
| 21 | ·002647 | ·002892 | ·003153 | ·003433 | ·003732 | ·004050 | ·004388 | ·004748 | ·005129 | ·005533 | 21 |
| 22 | ·001336 | ·001472 | ·001620 | ·001779 | ·001951 | ·002136 | ·002334 | ·002547 | ·002774 | ·003018 | 22 |
| 23 | ·000645 | ·000717 | ·000796 | ·000882 | ·000975 | ·001077 | ·001187 | ·001307 | ·001435 | ·001575 | 23 |
| 24 | ·000298 | ·000335 | ·000375 | ·000419 | ·000467 | ·000521 | ·000579 | ·000642 | ·000712 | ·000787 | 24 |
| 25 | ·000132 | ·000150 | ·000169 | ·000191 | ·000215 | ·000242 | ·000271 | ·000303 | ·000339 | ·000378 | 25 |
| 26 | ·000057 | ·000065 | ·000074 | ·000084 | ·000095 | ·000108 | ·000122 | ·000138 | ·000155 | ·000174 | 26 |
| 27 | ·000023 | ·000027 | ·000031 | ·000035 | ·000041 | ·000046 | ·000053 | ·000060 | ·000068 | ·000078 | 27 |
| 28 | ·000009 | ·000011 | ·000012 | ·000014 | ·000017 | ·000019 | ·000022 | ·000025 | ·000029 | ·000033 | 28 |
| 29 | ·000004 | ·000004 | ·000005 | ·000006 | ·000007 | ·000008 | ·000009 | ·000010 | ·000012 | ·000014 | 29 |
| 30 | ·000001 | ·000002 | ·000002 | ·000002 | ·000003 | ·000003 | ·000003 | ·000004 | ·000005 | ·000005 | 30 |
| 31 | — | ·000001 | ·000001 | ·000001 | ·000001 | ·000001 | ·000001 | ·000002 | ·000002 | ·000002 | 31 |
| 32 | — | — | — | — | — | — | — | ·000001 | ·000001 | ·000001 | 32 |

| $i$ | 12·1 | 12·2 | 12·3 | 12·4 | 12·5 | 12·6 | 12·7 | 12·8 | 12·9 | 13·0 | $i$ |
|---|---|---|---|---|---|---|---|---|---|---|---|
| 0 | ·000006 | ·000005 | ·000005 | ·000004 | ·000004 | ·000003 | ·000003 | ·000003 | ·000002 | ·000002 | 0 |
| 1 | ·000067 | ·000061 | ·000056 | ·000051 | ·000047 | ·000042 | ·000039 | ·000035 | ·000032 | ·000029 | 1 |
| 2 | ·000407 | ·000374 | ·000344 | ·000317 | ·000291 | ·000268 | ·000246 | ·000226 | ·000208 | ·000191 | 2 |
| 3 | ·001641 | ·001522 | ·001412 | ·001309 | ·001213 | ·001124 | ·001042 | ·000965 | ·000894 | ·000828 | 3 |
| 4 | ·004966 | ·004643 | ·004341 | ·004057 | ·003791 | ·003541 | ·003307 | ·003088 | ·002882 | ·002690 | 4 |
| 5 | ·012017 | ·011330 | ·010679 | ·010062 | ·009477 | ·008924 | ·008400 | ·007905 | ·007436 | ·006994 | 5 |
| 6 | ·024233 | ·023037 | ·021892 | ·020794 | ·019744 | ·018740 | ·017781 | ·016864 | ·015988 | ·015153 | 6 |
| 7 | ·041889 | ·040151 | ·038467 | ·036836 | ·035258 | ·033733 | ·032259 | ·030837 | ·029464 | ·028141 | 7 |
| 8 | ·063358 | ·061230 | ·059142 | ·057095 | ·055091 | ·053129 | ·051212 | ·049339 | ·047511 | ·045730 | 8 |
| 9 | ·085181 | ·083000 | ·080828 | ·078665 | ·076515 | ·074381 | ·072266 | ·070171 | ·068100 | ·066054 | 9 |
| 10 | ·103069 | ·101261 | ·099418 | ·097544 | ·095644 | ·093720 | ·091777 | ·089819 | ·087849 | ·085870 | 10 |
| 11 | ·113376 | ·112308 | ·111168 | ·109959 | ·108686 | ·107352 | ·105961 | ·104516 | ·103023 | ·101483 | 11 |
| 12 | ·114321 | ·114180 | ·113947 | ·113624 | ·113215 | ·112720 | ·112142 | ·111484 | ·110749 | ·109940 | 12 |
| 13 | ·106406 | ·107153 | ·107811 | ·108380 | ·108860 | ·109251 | ·109554 | ·109769 | ·109897 | ·109940 | 13 |
| 14 | ·091965 | ·093376 | ·094720 | ·095994 | ·097197 | ·098326 | ·099381 | ·100360 | ·101263 | ·102087 | 14 |
| 15 | ·074185 | ·075946 | ·077670 | ·079355 | ·080997 | ·082594 | ·084143 | ·085641 | ·087086 | ·088475 | 15 |
| 16 | ·056103 | ·057909 | ·059709 | ·061500 | ·063279 | ·065043 | ·066788 | ·068513 | ·070213 | ·071886 | 16 |
| 17 | ·039932 | ·041558 | ·043201 | ·044859 | ·046529 | ·048208 | ·049895 | ·051586 | ·053279 | ·054972 | 17 |
| 18 | ·026843 | ·028167 | ·029521 | ·030903 | ·032312 | ·033746 | ·035204 | ·036683 | ·038183 | ·039702 | 18 |
| 19 | ·017095 | ·018086 | ·019111 | ·020168 | ·021258 | ·022379 | ·023531 | ·024713 | ·025925 | ·027164 | 19 |
| 20 | ·010342 | ·011033 | ·011753 | ·012504 | ·013286 | ·014099 | ·014942 | ·015816 | ·016721 | ·017657 | 20 |
| 21 | ·005959 | ·006409 | ·006884 | ·007383 | ·007908 | ·008459 | ·009036 | ·009640 | ·010272 | ·010930 | 21 |
| 22 | ·003278 | ·003554 | ·003849 | ·004162 | ·004493 | ·004845 | ·005216 | ·005609 | ·006023 | ·006459 | 22 |
| 23 | ·001724 | ·001885 | ·002058 | ·002244 | ·002442 | ·002654 | ·002880 | ·003122 | ·003378 | ·003651 | 23 |
| 24 | ·000869 | ·000958 | ·001055 | ·001159 | ·001272 | ·001393 | ·001524 | ·001665 | ·001816 | ·001977 | 24 |
| 25 | ·000421 | ·000468 | ·000519 | ·000575 | ·000636 | ·000702 | ·000774 | ·000852 | ·000937 | ·001028 | 25 |
| 26 | ·000196 | ·000219 | ·000246 | ·000274 | ·000306 | ·000340 | ·000378 | ·000420 | ·000465 | ·000514 | 26 |
| 27 | ·000088 | ·000099 | ·000112 | ·000126 | ·000142 | ·000159 | ·000178 | ·000199 | ·000222 | ·000248 | 27 |
| 28 | ·000038 | ·000043 | ·000049 | ·000056 | ·000063 | ·000071 | ·000081 | ·000091 | ·000102 | ·000115 | 28 |
| 29 | ·000016 | ·000018 | ·000021 | ·000024 | ·000027 | ·000031 | ·000035 | ·000040 | ·000046 | ·000052 | 29 |
| 30 | ·000006 | ·000007 | ·000009 | ·000010 | ·000011 | ·000013 | ·000015 | ·000017 | ·000020 | ·000022 | 30 |
| 31 | ·000002 | ·000003 | ·000003 | ·000004 | ·000005 | ·000005 | ·000006 | ·000007 | ·000008 | ·000009 | 31 |
| 32 | ·000001 | ·000001 | ·000001 | ·000002 | ·000002 | ·000002 | ·000002 | ·000003 | ·000003 | ·000004 | 32 |
| 33 | — | — | — | ·000001 | ·000001 | ·000001 | ·000001 | ·000001 | ·000001 | ·000002 | 33 |
| 34 | — | — | — | — | — | — | — | — | — | ·000001 | 34 |

Table 39 (*continued*)

| $i$ | $m$ | | | | | | | | | | $i$ |
|---|---|---|---|---|---|---|---|---|---|---|---|
| | 13·1 | 13·2 | 13·3 | 13·4 | 13·5 | 13·6 | 13·7 | 13·8 | 13·9 | 14·0 | |
| 0 | ·000002 | ·000002 | ·000002 | ·000002 | ·000001 | ·000001 | ·000001 | ·000001 | ·000001 | ·000001 | 0 |
| 1 | ·000027 | ·000024 | ·000022 | ·000020 | ·000019 | ·000017 | ·000015 | ·000014 | ·000013 | ·000012 | 1 |
| 2 | ·000175 | ·000161 | ·000148 | ·000136 | ·000125 | ·000115 | ·000105 | ·000097 | ·000089 | ·000081 | 2 |
| 3 | ·000766 | ·000709 | ·000657 | ·000608 | ·000562 | ·000520 | ·000481 | ·000445 | ·000411 | ·000380 | 3 |
| 4 | ·002510 | ·002341 | ·002183 | ·002035 | ·001897 | ·001768 | ·001648 | ·001535 | ·001429 | ·001331 | 4 |
| 5 | ·006575 | ·006180 | ·005807 | ·005455 | ·005123 | ·004810 | ·004514 | ·004236 | ·003974 | ·003727 | 5 |
| 6 | ·014356 | ·013596 | ·012872 | ·012183 | ·011526 | ·010902 | ·010308 | ·009743 | ·009206 | ·008696 | 6 |
| 7 | ·026867 | ·025639 | ·024458 | ·023322 | ·022230 | ·021181 | ·020173 | ·019207 | ·018280 | ·017392 | 7 |
| 8 | ·043994 | ·042304 | ·040661 | ·039064 | ·037512 | ·036007 | ·034547 | ·033132 | ·031762 | ·030435 | 8 |
| 9 | ·064036 | ·062046 | ·060088 | ·058161 | ·056269 | ·054410 | ·052588 | ·050802 | ·049054 | ·047344 | 9 |
| 10 | ·083887 | ·081901 | ·079916 | ·077936 | ·075963 | ·073998 | ·072046 | ·070107 | ·068185 | ·066282 | 10 |
| 11 | ·099901 | ·098281 | ·096626 | ·094940 | ·093227 | ·091489 | ·089730 | ·087953 | ·086162 | ·084359 | 11 |
| 12 | ·109059 | ·108109 | ·107094 | ·106017 | ·104880 | ·103687 | ·102441 | ·101146 | ·099804 | ·098418 | 12 |
| 13 | ·109898 | ·109773 | ·109566 | ·109279 | ·108914 | ·108473 | ·107957 | ·107370 | ·106713 | ·105989 | 13 |
| 14 | ·102833 | ·103500 | ·104087 | ·104595 | ·105024 | ·105373 | ·105644 | ·105836 | ·105951 | ·105989 | 14 |
| 15 | ·089807 | ·091080 | ·092291 | ·093439 | ·094522 | ·095539 | ·096488 | ·097369 | ·098181 | ·098923 | 15 |
| 16 | ·073530 | ·075141 | ·076717 | ·078255 | ·079753 | ·081208 | ·082618 | ·083981 | ·085295 | ·086558 | 16 |
| 17 | ·056661 | ·058345 | ·060019 | ·061683 | ·063333 | ·064966 | ·066580 | ·068173 | ·069741 | ·071283 | 17 |
| 18 | ·041237 | ·042786 | ·044348 | ·045920 | ·047500 | ·049086 | ·050675 | ·052266 | ·053856 | ·055442 | 18 |
| 19 | ·028432 | ·029725 | ·031043 | ·032385 | ·033750 | ·035135 | ·036539 | ·037962 | ·039400 | ·040852 | 19 |
| 20 | ·018623 | ·019619 | ·020644 | ·021698 | ·022781 | ·023892 | ·025030 | ·026193 | ·027383 | ·028597 | 20 |
| 21 | ·011617 | ·012332 | ·013074 | ·013846 | ·014645 | ·015473 | ·016329 | ·017213 | ·018125 | ·019064 | 21 |
| 22 | ·006917 | ·007399 | ·007904 | ·008433 | ·008987 | ·009565 | ·010168 | ·010797 | ·011452 | ·012132 | 22 |
| 23 | ·003940 | ·004246 | ·004571 | ·004913 | ·005275 | ·005656 | ·006057 | ·006478 | ·006921 | ·007385 | 23 |
| 24 | ·002151 | ·002336 | ·002533 | ·002743 | ·002967 | ·003205 | ·003457 | ·003725 | ·004008 | ·004308 | 24 |
| 25 | ·001127 | ·001233 | ·001348 | ·001470 | ·001602 | ·001744 | ·001895 | ·002056 | ·002229 | ·002412 | 25 |
| 26 | ·000568 | ·000626 | ·000689 | ·000758 | ·000832 | ·000912 | ·000998 | ·001091 | ·001191 | ·001299 | 26 |
| 27 | ·000275 | ·000306 | ·000340 | ·000376 | ·000416 | ·000459 | ·000507 | ·000558 | ·000613 | ·000674 | 27 |
| 28 | ·000129 | ·000144 | ·000161 | ·000180 | ·000201 | ·000223 | ·000248 | ·000275 | ·000305 | ·000337 | 28 |
| 29 | ·000058 | ·000066 | ·000074 | ·000083 | ·000093 | ·000105 | ·000117 | ·000131 | ·000146 | ·000163 | 29 |
| 30 | ·000025 | ·000029 | ·000033 | ·000037 | ·000042 | ·000047 | ·000053 | ·000060 | ·000068 | ·000076 | 30 |
| 31 | ·000011 | ·000012 | ·000014 | ·000016 | ·000018 | ·000021 | ·000024 | ·000027 | ·000030 | ·000034 | 31 |
| 32 | ·000004 | ·000005 | ·000006 | ·000007 | ·000008 | ·000009 | ·000010 | ·000012 | ·000013 | ·000015 | 32 |
| 33 | ·000002 | ·000002 | ·000002 | ·000003 | ·000003 | ·000004 | ·000004 | ·000005 | ·000006 | ·000006 | 33 |
| 34 | ·000001 | ·000001 | ·000001 | ·000001 | ·000001 | ·000001 | ·000002 | ·000002 | ·000002 | ·000003 | 34 |
| 35 | — | — | — | — | — | ·000001 | ·000001 | ·000001 | ·000001 | ·000001 | 35 |

| $i$ | 14·1 | 14·2 | 14·3 | 14·4 | 14·5 | 14·6 | 14·7 | 14·8 | 14·9 | 15·0 | $i$ |
|---|---|---|---|---|---|---|---|---|---|---|---|
| 0 | ·000001 | ·000001 | ·000001 | ·000001 | ·000001 | — | — | — | — | — | 0 |
| 1 | ·000011 | ·000010 | ·000009 | ·000008 | ·000007 | ·000007 | ·000006 | ·000006 | ·000005 | ·000005 | 1 |
| 2 | ·000075 | ·000069 | ·000063 | ·000058 | ·000053 | ·000049 | ·000045 | ·000041 | ·000038 | ·000034 | 2 |
| 3 | ·000352 | ·000325 | ·000300 | ·000277 | ·000256 | ·000237 | ·000219 | ·000202 | ·000186 | ·000172 | 3 |
| 4 | ·001239 | ·001153 | ·001073 | ·000999 | ·000929 | ·000864 | ·000803 | ·000747 | ·000694 | ·000645 | 4 |
| 5 | ·003494 | ·003275 | ·003070 | ·002876 | ·002694 | ·002523 | ·002362 | ·002211 | ·002069 | ·001936 | 5 |
| 6 | ·008212 | ·007752 | ·007316 | ·006902 | ·006510 | ·006139 | ·005787 | ·005454 | ·005138 | ·004839 | 6 |
| 7 | ·016541 | ·015726 | ·014946 | ·014199 | ·013486 | ·012804 | ·012152 | ·011530 | ·010937 | ·010370 | 7 |
| 8 | ·029153 | ·027913 | ·026715 | ·025559 | ·024443 | ·023367 | ·022330 | ·021331 | ·020370 | ·019444 | 8 |
| 9 | ·045673 | ·044040 | ·042447 | ·040894 | ·039380 | ·037907 | ·036472 | ·035078 | ·033723 | ·032407 | 9 |
| 10 | ·064399 | ·062537 | ·060700 | ·058887 | ·057101 | ·055343 | ·053614 | ·051915 | ·050247 | ·048611 | 10 |
| 11 | ·082547 | ·080730 | ·078910 | ·077089 | ·075270 | ·073456 | ·071648 | ·069850 | ·068062 | ·066287 | 11 |

Table 39. *Individual terms of the Poisson distribution (continued)*

| $i$ | 14·1 | 14·2 | 14·3 | 14·4 | 14·5 | 14·6 | 14·7 | 14·8 | 14·9 | 15·0 | $i$ |
|---|---|---|---|---|---|---|---|---|---|---|---|
| 12 | ·096993 | ·095530 | ·094034 | ·092507 | ·090951 | ·089371 | ·087769 | ·086148 | ·084510 | ·082859 | 12 |
| 13 | ·105200 | ·104349 | ·103437 | ·102469 | ·101446 | ·100371 | ·099247 | ·098076 | ·096862 | ·095607 | 13 |
| 14 | ·105951 | ·105839 | ·105654 | ·105396 | ·105069 | ·104672 | ·104209 | ·103681 | ·103089 | ·102436 | 14 |
| 15 | ·099594 | ·100195 | ·100723 | ·101181 | ·101567 | ·101881 | ·102125 | ·102298 | ·102402 | ·102436 | 15 |
| 16 | ·087768 | ·088923 | ·090021 | ·091063 | ·092045 | ·092967 | ·093827 | ·094626 | ·095361 | ·096034 | 16 |
| 17 | ·072795 | ·074277 | ·075724 | ·077135 | ·078509 | ·079842 | ·081133 | ·082380 | ·083581 | ·084736 | 17 |
| 18 | ·057023 | ·058596 | ·060158 | ·061708 | ·063243 | ·064761 | ·066259 | ·067735 | ·069187 | ·070613 | 18 |
| 19 | ·042317 | ·043793 | ·045277 | ·046768 | ·048264 | ·049763 | ·051263 | ·052762 | ·054257 | ·055747 | 19 |
| 20 | ·029834 | ·031093 | ·032373 | ·033673 | ·034992 | ·036327 | ·037678 | ·039044 | ·040422 | ·041810 | 20 |
| 21 | ·020031 | ·021025 | ·022045 | ·023090 | ·024161 | ·025256 | ·026375 | ·027517 | ·028680 | ·029865 | 21 |
| 22 | ·012838 | ·013570 | ·014329 | ·015114 | ·015924 | ·016761 | ·017623 | ·018511 | ·019424 | ·020362 | 22 |
| 23 | ·007870 | ·008378 | ·008909 | ·009462 | ·010039 | ·010640 | ·011264 | ·011911 | ·012584 | ·013280 | 23 |
| 24 | ·004624 | ·004957 | ·005308 | ·005677 | ·006065 | ·006472 | ·006899 | ·007345 | ·007812 | ·008300 | 24 |
| 25 | ·002608 | ·002816 | ·003036 | ·003270 | ·003518 | ·003780 | ·004057 | ·004348 | ·004656 | ·004980 | 25 |
| 26 | ·001414 | ·001538 | ·001670 | ·001811 | ·001962 | ·002123 | ·002294 | ·002475 | ·002668 | ·002873 | 26 |
| 27 | ·000739 | ·000809 | ·000884 | ·000966 | ·001054 | ·001148 | ·001249 | ·001357 | ·001473 | ·001596 | 27 |
| 28 | ·000372 | ·000410 | ·000452 | ·000497 | ·000546 | ·000598 | ·000656 | ·000717 | ·000784 | ·000855 | 28 |
| 29 | ·000181 | ·000201 | ·000223 | ·000247 | ·000273 | ·000301 | ·000332 | ·000366 | ·000403 | ·000442 | 29 |
| 30 | ·000085 | ·000095 | ·000106 | ·000118 | ·000132 | ·000147 | ·000163 | ·000181 | ·000200 | ·000221 | 30 |
| 31 | ·000039 | ·000044 | ·000049 | ·000055 | ·000062 | ·000069 | ·000077 | ·000086 | ·000096 | ·000107 | 31 |
| 32 | ·000017 | ·000019 | ·000022 | ·000025 | ·000028 | ·000032 | ·000035 | ·000040 | ·000045 | ·000050 | 32 |
| 33 | ·000007 | ·000008 | ·000009 | ·000011 | ·000012 | ·000014 | ·000016 | ·000018 | ·000020 | ·000023 | 33 |
| 34 | ·000003 | ·000003 | ·000004 | ·000005 | ·000005 | ·000006 | ·000007 | ·000008 | ·000009 | ·000010 | 34 |
| 35 | ·000001 | ·000001 | ·000002 | ·000002 | ·000002 | ·000002 | ·000003 | ·000003 | ·000004 | ·000004 | 35 |
| 36 | — | ·000001 | ·000001 | ·000001 | ·000001 | ·000001 | ·000001 | ·000001 | ·000002 | ·000002 | 36 |
| 37 | — | — | — | — | — | — | — | ·000001 | ·000001 | ·000001 | 37 |

## Table 40. *Confidence limits for the expectation of a Poisson variable*

| $1-2\alpha$ | 0·998 | | 0·99 | | 0·98 | | 0·95 | | 0·90 | | $1-2\alpha$ |
|---|---|---|---|---|---|---|---|---|---|---|---|
| $\alpha$ | 0·001 | | 0·005 | | 0·01 | | 0·025 | | 0·05 | | $\alpha$ |
| $c$ | Lower | Upper | Lower | Upper | Lower | Upper | Lower | Upper | Lower | Upper | $c$ |
| 0 | 0·00000 | 6·91 | 0·00000 | 5·30 | 0·0000 | 4·61 | 0·0000 | 3·69 | 0·0000 | 3·00 | 0 |
| 1 | ·00100 | 9·23 | ·00501 | 7·43 | ·0101 | 6·64 | ·0253 | 5·57 | ·0513 | 4·74 | 1 |
| 2 | ·0454 | 11·23 | ·103 | 9·27 | ·149 | 8·41 | ·242 | 7·22 | ·355 | 6·30 | 2 |
| 3 | ·191 | 13·06 | ·338 | 10·98 | ·436 | 10·05 | ·619 | 8·77 | ·818 | 7·75 | 3 |
| 4 | ·429 | 14·79 | ·672 | 12·59 | ·823 | 11·60 | 1·09 | 10·24 | 1·37 | 9·15 | 4 |
| 5 | 0·739 | 16·45 | 1·08 | 14·15 | 1·28 | 13·11 | 1·62 | 11·67 | 1·97 | 10·51 | 5 |
| 6 | 1·11 | 18·06 | 1·54 | 15·66 | 1·79 | 14·57 | 2·20 | 13·06 | 2·61 | 11·84 | 6 |
| 7 | 1·52 | 19·63 | 2·04 | 17·13 | 2·33 | 16·00 | 2·81 | 14·42 | 3·29 | 13·15 | 7 |
| 8 | 1·97 | 21·16 | 2·57 | 18·58 | 2·91 | 17·40 | 3·45 | 15·76 | 3·98 | 14·43 | 8 |
| 9 | 2·45 | 22·66 | 3·13 | 20·00 | 3·51 | 18·78 | 4·12 | 17·08 | 4·70 | 15·71 | 9 |
| 10 | 2·96 | 24·13 | 3·72 | 21·40 | 4·13 | 20·14 | 4·80 | 18·39 | 5·43 | 16·96 | 10 |
| 11 | 3·49 | 25·59 | 4·32 | 22·78 | 4·77 | 21·49 | 5·49 | 19·68 | 6·17 | 18·21 | 11 |
| 12 | 4·04 | 27·03 | 4·94 | 24·14 | 5·43 | 22·82 | 6·20 | 20·96 | 6·92 | 19·44 | 12 |
| 13 | 4·61 | 28·45 | 5·58 | 25·50 | 6·10 | 24·14 | 6·92 | 22·23 | 7·69 | 20·67 | 13 |
| 14 | 5·20 | 29·85 | 6·23 | 26·84 | 6·78 | 25·45 | 7·65 | 23·49 | 8·46 | 21·89 | 14 |
| 15 | 5·79 | 31·24 | 6·89 | 28·16 | 7·48 | 26·74 | 8·40 | 24·74 | 9·25 | 23·10 | 15 |
| 16 | 6·41 | 32·62 | 7·57 | 29·48 | 8·18 | 28·03 | 9·15 | 25·98 | 10·04 | 24·30 | 16 |
| 17 | 7·03 | 33·99 | 8·25 | 30·79 | 8·89 | 29·31 | 9·90 | 27·22 | 10·83 | 25·50 | 17 |
| 18 | 7·66 | 35·35 | 8·94 | 32·09 | 9·62 | 30·58 | 10·67 | 28·45 | 11·63 | 26·69 | 18 |
| 19 | 8·31 | 36·70 | 9·64 | 33·38 | 10·35 | 31·85 | 11·44 | 29·67 | 12·44 | 27·88 | 19 |
| 20 | 8·96 | 38·04 | 10·35 | 34·67 | 11·08 | 33·10 | 12·22 | 30·89 | 13·25 | 29·06 | 20 |
| 21 | 9·62 | 39·38 | 11·07 | 35·95 | 11·82 | 34·36 | 13·00 | 32·10 | 14·07 | 30·24 | 21 |
| 22 | 10·29 | 40·70 | 11·79 | 37·22 | 12·57 | 35·60 | 13·79 | 33·31 | 14·89 | 31·42 | 22 |
| 23 | 10·96 | 42·02 | 12·52 | 38·48 | 13·33 | 36·84 | 14·58 | 34·51 | 15·72 | 32·59 | 23 |
| 24 | 11·65 | 43·33 | 13·25 | 39·74 | 14·09 | 38·08 | 15·38 | 35·71 | 16·55 | 33·75 | 24 |
| 25 | 12·34 | 44·64 | 14·00 | 41·00 | 14·85 | 39·31 | 16·18 | 36·90 | 17·38 | 34·92 | 25 |
| 26 | 13·03 | 45·94 | 14·74 | 42·25 | 15·62 | 40·53 | 16·98 | 38·10 | 18·22 | 36·08 | 26 |
| 27 | 13·73 | 47·23 | 15·49 | 43·50 | 16·40 | 41·76 | 17·79 | 39·28 | 19·06 | 37·23 | 27 |
| 28 | 14·44 | 48·52 | 16·24 | 44·74 | 17·17 | 42·98 | 18·61 | 40·47 | 19·90 | 38·39 | 28 |
| 29 | 15·15 | 49·80 | 17·00 | 45·98 | 17·96 | 44·19 | 19·42 | 41·65 | 20·75 | 39·54 | 29 |
| 30 | 15·87 | 51·08 | 17·77 | 47·21 | 18·74 | 45·40 | 20·24 | 42·83 | 21·59 | 40·69 | 30 |
| 35 | 19·52 | 57·42 | 21·64 | 53·32 | 22·72 | 51·41 | 24·38 | 48·68 | 25·87 | 46·40 | 35 |
| 40 | 23·26 | 63·66 | 25·59 | 59·36 | 26·77 | 57·35 | 28·58 | 54·47 | 30·20 | 52·07 | 40 |
| 45 | 27·08 | 69·83 | 29·60 | 65·34 | 30·88 | 63·23 | 32·82 | 60·21 | 34·56 | 57·69 | 45 |
| 50 | 30·96 | 75·94 | 33·66 | 71·27 | 35·03 | 69·07 | 37·11 | 65·92 | 38·96 | 63·29 | 50 |

If $c$ is the observed frequency or count and $m_A$, $m_B$ are the lower and upper confidence limits for its expectation, $m$, then

$$\Pr\{m_A \leqslant m \leqslant m_B\} \leqslant 1-2\alpha.$$

**Table 41.** *Chart providing confidence limits for p in binomial sampling, given a sample fraction c/n.*
*Confidence coefficient,* $1 - 2\alpha = 0.95$.

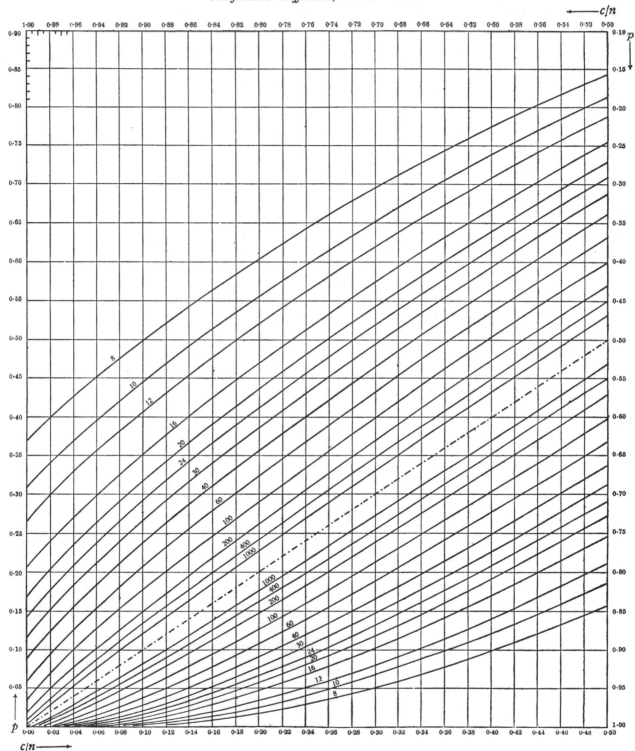

The numbers printed along the curves indicate the sample size **n**. If for a given value of the abscissa $c/n$, $p_A$ and $p_B$ are the ordinates read from (or interpolated between) the appropriate lower and upper curves, then

$$\Pr\{p_A \leqslant p \leqslant p_B\} \geqslant 1 - 2\alpha.$$

228

# Table 41 (continued). *Confidence coefficient,* $1 - 2\alpha = 0.99$.

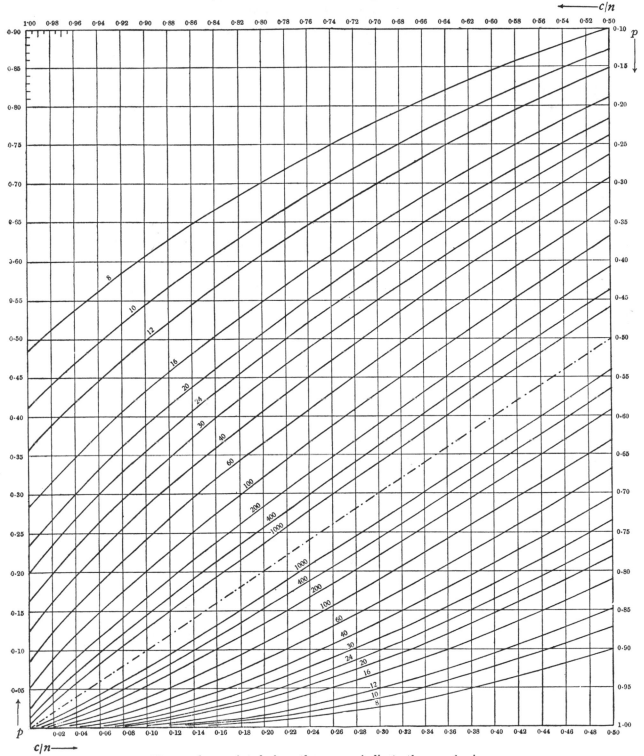

The numbers printed along the curves indicate the sample size $n$.

Note: the process of reading from the curves can be simplified with the help of the right-angled corner of a loose sheet of paper or thin card, along the edges of which are marked off the scales shown in the top left-hand corner of each Chart.

## Table 42. *Percentage points of Pearson curves for given $\beta_1$, $\beta_2$, expressed in standardized measure*

### Lower 5 % points of the standardized deviate $(x_P - \mu)/\sigma$, $(P = 0.05)$

(Note that for positive skewness, i.e. $\mu_3 > 0$, the deviates in this table are negative.)

| $\beta_2$ \ $\beta_1$ | 0·00 | 0·01 | 0·03 | 0·05 | 0·10 | 0·15 | 0·20 | 0·30 | 0·40 | 0·50 | 0·60 | 0·70 | 0·80 | 0·90 | 1·00 |
|---|---|---|---|---|---|---|---|---|---|---|---|---|---|---|---|
| 1·8 | 1·56 | — | — | — | — | — | — | — | — | — | — | — | — | — | — |
| 2·0 | 1·61 | 1·56 | 1·51 | 1·47 | — | — | — | — | — | — | — | — | — | — | — |
| 2·2 | 1·64 | 1·59 | 1·55 | 1·52 | 1·46 | 1·40 | 1·35 | — | — | — | — | — | — | — | — |
| 2·4 | 1·65 | 1·61 | 1·58 | 1·55 | 1·50 | 1·45 | 1·41 | 1·33 | — | — | — | — | — | — | — |
| 2·6 | 1·65 | 1·61 | 1·59 | 1·57 | 1·53 | 1·49 | 1·45 | 1·38 | 1·30 | — | — | — | — | — | — |
| 2·8 | 1·65 | 1·62 | 1·59 | 1·57 | 1·54 | 1·51 | 1·48 | 1·42 | 1·35 | 1·29 | — | — | — | — | — |
| 3·0 | 1·64 | 1·62 | 1·59 | 1·58 | 1·55 | 1·52 | 1·49 | 1·44 | 1·39 | 1·33 | 1·27 | — | — | — | — |
| 3·2 | 1·64 | 1·61 | 1·59 | 1·58 | 1·55 | 1·53 | 1·50 | 1·46 | 1·42 | 1·37 | 1·31 | 1·25 | 1·19 | — | — |
| 3·4 | 1·64 | 1·61 | 1·59 | 1·58 | 1·55 | 1·53 | 1·51 | 1·47 | 1·43 | 1·39 | 1·35 | 1·30 | 1·24 | 1·19 | — |
| 3·6 | 1·63 | 1·61 | 1·59 | 1·58 | 1·55 | 1·53 | 1·52 | 1·48 | 1·45 | 1·41 | 1·37 | 1·33 | 1·28 | 1·23 | 1·18 |
| 3·8 | 1·63 | 1·60 | 1·59 | 1·58 | 1·55 | 1·54 | 1·52 | 1·49 | 1·46 | 1·42 | 1·39 | 1·35 | 1·31 | 1·27 | 1·22 |
| 4·0 | 1·62 | 1·60 | 1·59 | 1·57 | 1·55 | 1·54 | 1·52 | 1·49 | 1·46 | 1·43 | 1·40 | 1·37 | 1·34 | 1·30 | 1·26 |
| 4·2 | 1·62 | 1·60 | 1·58 | 1·57 | 1·55 | 1·54 | 1·52 | 1·49 | 1·47 | 1·44 | 1·42 | 1·39 | 1·36 | 1·32 | 1·28 |
| 4·4 | 1·61 | 1·60 | 1·58 | 1·57 | 1·55 | 1·54 | 1·52 | 1·50 | 1·47 | 1·45 | 1·42 | 1·40 | 1·37 | 1·34 | 1·31 |
| 4·6 | 1·61 | 1·59 | 1·58 | 1·57 | 1·55 | 1·54 | 1·52 | 1·50 | 1·48 | 1·45 | 1·43 | 1·41 | 1·38 | 1·35 | 1·33 |
| 4·8 | 1·60 | 1·59 | 1·58 | 1·57 | 1·55 | 1·53 | 1·52 | 1·50 | 1·48 | 1·46 | 1·44 | 1·41 | 1·39 | 1·37 | 1·34 |
| 5·0 | 1·60 | 1·58 | 1·57 | 1·56 | 1·55 | 1·53 | 1·52 | 1·50 | 1·48 | 1·46 | 1·44 | 1·42 | 1·40 | 1·38 | 1·35 |

### Upper 5 % points of the standardized deviate $(x_P - \mu)/\sigma$, $(P = 0.95)$

| $\beta_2$ \ $\beta_1$ | 0·00 | 0·01 | 0·03 | 0·05 | 0·10 | 0·15 | 0·20 | 0·30 | 0·40 | 0·50 | 0·60 | 0·70 | 0·80 | 0·90 | 1·00 |
|---|---|---|---|---|---|---|---|---|---|---|---|---|---|---|---|
| 1·8 | 1·56 | — | — | — | — | — | — | — | — | — | — | — | — | — | — |
| 2·0 | 1·61 | 1·66 | 1·70 | 1·72 | — | — | — | — | — | — | — | — | — | — | — |
| 2·2 | 1·64 | 1·68 | 1·71 | 1·74 | 1·77 | 1·80 | 1·83 | — | — | — | — | — | — | — | — |
| 2·4 | 1·65 | 1·69 | 1·71 | 1·74 | 1·77 | 1·80 | 1·83 | 1·87 | — | — | — | — | — | — | — |
| 2·6 | 1·65 | 1·68 | 1·71 | 1·73 | 1·76 | 1·79 | 1·81 | 1·86 | 1·90 | — | — | — | — | — | — |
| 2·8 | 1·65 | 1·68 | 1·70 | 1·72 | 1·75 | 1·77 | 1·80 | 1·84 | 1·88 | 1·92 | — | — | — | — | — |
| 3·0 | 1·64 | 1·67 | 1·69 | 1·71 | 1·74 | 1·76 | 1·78 | 1·82 | 1·86 | 1·90 | 1·93 | — | — | — | — |
| 3·2 | 1·64 | 1·67 | 1·69 | 1·70 | 1·73 | 1·75 | 1·77 | 1·80 | 1·84 | 1·87 | 1·91 | 1·94 | 1·98 | — | — |
| 3·4 | 1·64 | 1·66 | 1·68 | 1·69 | 1·72 | 1·74 | 1·76 | 1·79 | 1·82 | 1·85 | 1·88 | 1·92 | 1·95 | 1·98 | — |
| 3·6 | 1·63 | 1·65 | 1·67 | 1·68 | 1·71 | 1·73 | 1·74 | 1·77 | 1·80 | 1·83 | 1·86 | 1·89 | 1·92 | 1·95 | 1·98 |
| 3·8 | 1·63 | 1·65 | 1·66 | 1·68 | 1·70 | 1·72 | 1·73 | 1·76 | 1·79 | 1·82 | 1·84 | 1·87 | 1·90 | 1·93 | 1·96 |
| 4·0 | 1·62 | 1·64 | 1·66 | 1·67 | 1·69 | 1·71 | 1·72 | 1·75 | 1·78 | 1·80 | 1·83 | 1·85 | 1·88 | 1·90 | 1·93 |
| 4·2 | 1·62 | 1·64 | 1·65 | 1·66 | 1·68 | 1·70 | 1·71 | 1·74 | 1·76 | 1·79 | 1·81 | 1·83 | 1·86 | 1·88 | 1·91 |
| 4·4 | 1·61 | 1·63 | 1·65 | 1·66 | 1·68 | 1·69 | 1·70 | 1·73 | 1·75 | 1·78 | 1·80 | 1·82 | 1·84 | 1·86 | 1·89 |
| 4·6 | 1·61 | 1·63 | 1·64 | 1·65 | 1·67 | 1·68 | 1·70 | 1·72 | 1·74 | 1·76 | 1·78 | 1·80 | 1·82 | 1·84 | 1·87 |
| 4·8 | 1·60 | 1·62 | 1·64 | 1·65 | 1·66 | 1·68 | 1·69 | 1·71 | 1·73 | 1·75 | 1·77 | 1·79 | 1·81 | 1·83 | 1·85 |
| 5·0 | 1·60 | 1·62 | 1·63 | 1·64 | 1·66 | 1·67 | 1·68 | 1·71 | 1·73 | 1·74 | 1·76 | 1·78 | 1·80 | 1·82 | 1·84 |

## Table 42 (*continued*)

### Lower 2·5% points of the standardized deviate $(x_P - \mu)/\sigma$, $(P = 0.025)$

(Note that for positive skewness, i.e. $\mu_3 > 0$, the deviates in this table are negative.)

| $\beta_2$ \ $\beta_1$ | 0·00 | 0·01 | 0·03 | 0·05 | 0·10 | 0·15 | 0·20 | 0·30 | 0·40 | 0·50 | 0·60 | 0·70 | 0·80 | 0·90 | 1·00 |
|---|---|---|---|---|---|---|---|---|---|---|---|---|---|---|---|
| 1·8 | 1·65 | — | — | — | — | — | — | — | — | — | — | — | — | — | — |
| 2·0 | 1·76 | 1·68 | 1·62 | 1·56 | — | — | — | — | — | — | — | — | — | — | — |
| 2·2 | 1·83 | 1·76 | 1·71 | 1·66 | 1·57 | 1·49 | 1·41 | — | — | — | — | — | — | — | — |
| 2·4 | 1·88 | 1·82 | 1·77 | 1·73 | 1·65 | 1·58 | 1·51 | 1·39 | — | — | — | — | — | — | — |
| 2·6 | 1·92 | 1·86 | 1·82 | 1·78 | 1·71 | 1·64 | 1·58 | 1·47 | 1·37 | — | — | — | — | — | — |
| 2·8 | 1·94 | 1·89 | 1·85 | 1·82 | 1·76 | 1·70 | 1·65 | 1·55 | 1·45 | 1·35 | — | — | — | — | — |
| 3·0 | 1·96 | 1·91 | 1·87 | 1·84 | 1·79 | 1·74 | 1·69 | 1·60 | 1·52 | 1·42 | 1·33 | — | — | — | — |
| 3·2 | 1·97 | 1·93 | 1·89 | 1·86 | 1·81 | 1·77 | 1·72 | 1·65 | 1·57 | 1·49 | 1·40 | 1·32 | 1·24 | — | — |
| 3·4 | 1·98 | 1·94 | 1·90 | 1·88 | 1·83 | 1·79 | 1·75 | 1·68 | 1·61 | 1·54 | 1·46 | 1·39 | 1·31 | 1·23 | — |
| 3·6 | 1·99 | 1·95 | 1·91 | 1·89 | 1·85 | 1·81 | 1·77 | 1·71 | 1·65 | 1·58 | 1·51 | 1·44 | 1·38 | 1·30 | 1·23 |
| 3·8 | 1·99 | 1·95 | 1·92 | 1·90 | 1·86 | 1·82 | 1·79 | 1·73 | 1·67 | 1·62 | 1·56 | 1·49 | 1·43 | 1·36 | 1·29 |
| 4·0 | 1·99 | 1·96 | 1·93 | 1·91 | 1·87 | 1·84 | 1·81 | 1·75 | 1·70 | 1·64 | 1·59 | 1·53 | 1·47 | 1·41 | 1·35 |
| 4·2 | 2·00 | 1·96 | 1·93 | 1·91 | 1·88 | 1·84 | 1·82 | 1·76 | 1·72 | 1·67 | 1·62 | 1·56 | 1·51 | 1·45 | 1·40 |
| 4·4 | 2·00 | 1·96 | 1·94 | 1·92 | 1·88 | 1·85 | 1·83 | 1·78 | 1·73 | 1·69 | 1·64 | 1·59 | 1·54 | 1·49 | 1·44 |
| 4·6 | 2·00 | 1·96 | 1·94 | 1·92 | 1·89 | 1·86 | 1·83 | 1·79 | 1·75 | 1·70 | 1·66 | 1·62 | 1·57 | 1·52 | 1·47 |
| 4·8 | 2·00 | 1·97 | 1·94 | 1·93 | 1·89 | 1·87 | 1·84 | 1·80 | 1·76 | 1·72 | 1·68 | 1·64 | 1·59 | 1·55 | 1·50 |
| 5·0 | 2·00 | 1·97 | 1·94 | 1·93 | 1·90 | 1·87 | 1·85 | 1·81 | 1·77 | 1·73 | 1·69 | 1·65 | 1·61 | 1·57 | 1·53 |

### Upper 2·5% points of the standardized deviate $(x_P - \mu)/\sigma$, $(P = 0.975)$

| $\beta_2$ \ $\beta_1$ | 0·00 | 0·01 | 0·03 | 0·05 | 0·10 | 0·15 | 0·20 | 0·30 | 0·40 | 0·50 | 0·60 | 0·70 | 0·80 | 0·90 | 1·00 |
|---|---|---|---|---|---|---|---|---|---|---|---|---|---|---|---|
| 1·8 | 1·65 | — | — | — | — | — | — | — | — | — | — | — | — | — | — |
| 2·0 | 1·76 | 1·82 | 1·86 | 1·89 | — | — | — | — | — | — | — | — | — | — | — |
| 2·2 | 1·83 | 1·89 | 1·93 | 1·96 | 2·00 | 2·04 | 2·06 | — | — | — | — | — | — | — | — |
| 2·4 | 1·88 | 1·94 | 1·98 | 2·01 | 2·05 | 2·08 | 2·11 | 2·15 | — | — | — | — | — | — | — |
| 2·6 | 1·92 | 1·97 | 2·01 | 2·03 | 2·08 | 2·11 | 2·14 | 2·18 | 2·22 | — | — | — | — | — | — |
| 2·8 | 1·94 | 1·99 | 2·03 | 2·05 | 2·09 | 2·13 | 2·15 | 2·20 | 2·24 | 2·27 | — | — | — | — | — |
| 3·0 | 1·96 | 2·01 | 2·04 | 2·06 | 2·10 | 2·13 | 2·16 | 2·21 | 2·25 | 2·28 | 2·32 | — | — | — | — |
| 3·2 | 1·97 | 2·02 | 2·05 | 2·07 | 2·11 | 2·14 | 2·16 | 2·21 | 2·25 | 2·29 | 2·32 | 2·35 | 2·38 | — | — |
| 3·4 | 1·98 | 2·02 | 2·05 | 2·07 | 2·11 | 2·14 | 2·16 | 2·21 | 2·25 | 2·28 | 2·32 | 2·35 | 2·38 | 2·41 | — |
| 3·6 | 1·99 | 2·02 | 2·05 | 2·07 | 2·11 | 2·14 | 2·16 | 2·20 | 2·24 | 2·28 | 2·31 | 2·34 | 2·37 | 2·41 | 2·44 |
| 3·8 | 1·99 | 2·03 | 2·05 | 2·07 | 2·11 | 2·13 | 2·16 | 2·20 | 2·24 | 2·27 | 2·30 | 2·33 | 2·36 | 2·40 | 2·43 |
| 4·0 | 1·99 | 2·03 | 2·05 | 2·07 | 2·11 | 2·13 | 2·15 | 2·19 | 2·23 | 2·26 | 2·29 | 2·32 | 2·35 | 2·38 | 2·42 |
| 4·2 | 2·00 | 2·03 | 2·05 | 2·07 | 2·10 | 2·13 | 2·15 | 2·19 | 2·22 | 2·25 | 2·28 | 2·31 | 2·33 | 2·36 | 2·40 |
| 4·4 | 2·00 | 2·03 | 2·05 | 2·07 | 2·10 | 2·13 | 2·15 | 2·18 | 2·22 | 2·25 | 2·28 | 2·31 | 2·33 | 2·36 | 2·39 |
| 4·6 | 2·00 | 2·03 | 2·05 | 2·07 | 2·10 | 2·12 | 2·14 | 2·18 | 2·21 | 2·24 | 2·27 | 2·30 | 2·32 | 2·35 | 2·38 |
| 4·8 | 2·00 | 2·03 | 2·05 | 2·07 | 2·10 | 2·12 | 2·14 | 2·17 | 2·21 | 2·23 | 2·26 | 2·29 | 2·31 | 2·34 | 2·37 |
| 5·0 | 2·00 | 2·03 | 2·05 | 2·07 | 2·09 | 2·12 | 2·14 | 2·17 | 2·20 | 2·23 | 2·25 | 2·28 | 2·30 | 2·33 | 2·35 |

Table 42. *Percentage points of Pearson curves (continued)*

Lower 1% points of the standardized deviate $(x_P - \mu)/\sigma$, $(P = 0.01)$

(Note that for positive skewness, i.e. $\mu_3 > 0$, the deviates in this table are negative.)

| $\beta_2$ \ $\beta_1$ | 0.00 | 0.01 | 0.03 | 0.05 | 0.10 | 0.15 | 0.20 | 0.30 | 0.40 | 0.50 | 0.60 | 0.70 | 0.80 | 0.90 | 1.00 |
|---|---|---|---|---|---|---|---|---|---|---|---|---|---|---|---|
| 1.8 | 1.70 | — | — | — | — | — | — | — | — | — | — | — | — | — | — |
| 2.0 | 1.87 | 1.77 | 1.69 | 1.62 | — | — | — | — | — | — | — | — | — | — | — |
| 2.2 | 2.01 | 1.91 | 1.83 | 1.76 | 1.64 | 1.55 | 1.45 | — | — | — | — | — | — | — | — |
| 2.4 | 2.12 | 2.03 | 1.95 | 1.89 | 1.77 | 1.68 | 1.59 | 1.43 | — | — | — | — | — | — | — |
| 2.6 | 2.21 | 2.12 | 2.05 | 1.99 | 1.88 | 1.79 | 1.70 | 1.55 | 1.41 | — | — | — | — | — | — |
| 2.8 | 2.27 | 2.19 | 2.13 | 2.08 | 1.98 | 1.89 | 1.81 | 1.66 | 1.52 | 1.39 | — | — | — | — | — |
| 3.0 | 2.33 | 2.25 | 2.19 | 2.14 | 2.05 | 1.97 | 1.90 | 1.76 | 1.62 | 1.50 | 1.38 | — | — | — | — |
| 3.2 | 2.37 | 2.29 | 2.24 | 2.19 | 2.11 | 2.03 | 1.96 | 1.84 | 1.71 | 1.59 | 1.48 | 1.37 | 1.26 | — | — |
| 3.4 | 2.40 | 2.33 | 2.28 | 2.24 | 2.16 | 2.09 | 2.02 | 1.90 | 1.79 | 1.68 | 1.57 | 1.46 | 1.36 | 1.26 | — |
| 3.6 | 2.43 | 2.36 | 2.31 | 2.27 | 2.20 | 2.13 | 2.07 | 1.96 | 1.86 | 1.76 | 1.65 | 1.55 | 1.45 | 1.35 | 1.26 |
| 3.8 | 2.45 | 2.39 | 2.34 | 2.30 | 2.23 | 2.17 | 2.11 | 2.01 | 1.91 | 1.82 | 1.72 | 1.62 | 1.53 | 1.43 | 1.34 |
| 4.0 | 2.47 | 2.41 | 2.36 | 2.33 | 2.26 | 2.20 | 2.15 | 2.05 | 1.96 | 1.87 | 1.78 | 1.69 | 1.60 | 1.51 | 1.42 |
| 4.2 | 2.49 | 2.43 | 2.38 | 2.35 | 2.28 | 2.23 | 2.18 | 2.09 | 2.00 | 1.92 | 1.83 | 1.75 | 1.66 | 1.58 | 1.49 |
| 4.4 | 2.50 | 2.44 | 2.40 | 2.37 | 2.31 | 2.25 | 2.21 | 2.12 | 2.04 | 1.96 | 1.88 | 1.80 | 1.72 | 1.64 | 1.56 |
| 4.6 | 2.51 | 2.46 | 2.42 | 2.38 | 2.32 | 2.27 | 2.23 | 2.15 | 2.07 | 2.00 | 1.92 | 1.84 | 1.77 | 1.70 | 1.62 |
| 4.8 | 2.52 | 2.47 | 2.43 | 2.40 | 2.34 | 2.29 | 2.25 | 2.17 | 2.10 | 2.03 | 1.96 | 1.88 | 1.81 | 1.74 | 1.67 |
| 5.0 | 2.53 | 2.48 | 2.44 | 2.41 | 2.36 | 2.31 | 2.27 | 2.19 | 2.12 | 2.06 | 1.99 | 1.92 | 1.85 | 1.79 | 1.72 |

*Upper* 1% points of the standardized deviate $(x_P - \mu)/\sigma$, $(P = 0.99)$

| $\beta_2$ \ $\beta_1$ | 0.00 | 0.01 | 0.03 | 0.05 | 0.10 | 0.15 | 0.20 | 0.30 | 0.40 | 0.50 | 0.60 | 0.70 | 0.80 | 0.90 | 1.00 |
|---|---|---|---|---|---|---|---|---|---|---|---|---|---|---|---|
| 1.8 | 1.70 | — | — | — | — | — | — | — | — | — | — | — | — | — | — |
| 2.0 | 1.87 | 1.95 | 2.00 | 2.03 | — | — | — | — | — | — | — | — | — | — | — |
| 2.2 | 2.01 | 2.10 | 2.15 | 2.18 | 2.22 | 2.24 | 2.25 | — | — | — | — | — | — | — | — |
| 2.4 | 2.12 | 2.20 | 2.25 | 2.28 | 2.33 | 2.36 | 2.38 | 2.40 | — | — | — | — | — | — | — |
| 2.6 | 2.21 | 2.28 | 2.33 | 2.36 | 2.42 | 2.45 | 2.48 | 2.51 | 2.52 | — | — | — | — | — | — |
| 2.8 | 2.27 | 2.34 | 2.39 | 2.43 | 2.48 | 2.52 | 2.55 | 2.59 | 2.61 | 2.63 | — | — | — | — | — |
| 3.0 | 2.33 | 2.40 | 2.44 | 2.48 | 2.53 | 2.56 | 2.59 | 2.64 | 2.68 | 2.70 | 2.71 | — | — | — | — |
| 3.2 | 2.37 | 2.44 | 2.48 | 2.51 | 2.56 | 2.60 | 2.63 | 2.68 | 2.72 | 2.75 | 2.77 | 2.79 | 2.80 | — | — |
| 3.4 | 2.40 | 2.47 | 2.51 | 2.54 | 2.59 | 2.63 | 2.66 | 2.71 | 2.75 | 2.79 | 2.82 | 2.84 | 2.86 | 2.87 | — |
| 3.6 | 2.43 | 2.49 | 2.53 | 2.56 | 2.61 | 2.65 | 2.68 | 2.74 | 2.78 | 2.81 | 2.85 | 2.87 | 2.90 | 2.91 | 2.93 |
| 3.8 | 2.45 | 2.51 | 2.55 | 2.58 | 2.63 | 2.67 | 2.70 | 2.75 | 2.80 | 2.83 | 2.87 | 2.90 | 2.92 | 2.95 | 2.97 |
| 4.0 | 2.47 | 2.53 | 2.57 | 2.60 | 2.65 | 2.68 | 2.71 | 2.77 | 2.81 | 2.85 | 2.88 | 2.91 | 2.94 | 2.97 | 2.99 |
| 4.2 | 2.49 | 2.54 | 2.58 | 2.61 | 2.66 | 2.69 | 2.73 | 2.78 | 2.82 | 2.86 | 2.89 | 2.92 | 2.95 | 2.98 | 3.01 |
| 4.4 | 2.50 | 2.56 | 2.59 | 2.62 | 2.67 | 2.70 | 2.73 | 2.78 | 2.83 | 2.86 | 2.90 | 2.93 | 2.96 | 2.99 | 3.02 |
| 4.6 | 2.51 | 2.57 | 2.60 | 2.63 | 2.68 | 2.71 | 2.74 | 2.79 | 2.83 | 2.87 | 2.90 | 2.94 | 2.97 | 3.00 | 3.03 |
| 4.8 | 2.52 | 2.58 | 2.61 | 2.64 | 2.68 | 2.72 | 2.75 | 2.80 | 2.84 | 2.87 | 2.91 | 2.94 | 2.97 | 3.00 | 3.03 |
| 5.0 | 2.53 | 2.58 | 2.62 | 2.64 | 2.69 | 2.72 | 2.75 | 2.80 | 2.84 | 2.88 | 2.91 | 2.95 | 2.97 | 3.00 | 3.03 |

Table 42 (*continued*)

*Lower 0·5% points of the standardized deviate* $(x_P - \mu)/\sigma$, $(P = 0\cdot005)$

(Note that for positive skewness, i.e. $\mu_3 > 0$, the deviates in this table are negative.)

| $\beta_2$ \ $\beta_1$ | 0·00 | 0·01 | 0·03 | 0·05 | 0·10 | 0·15 | 0·20 | 0·30 | 0·40 | 0·50 | 0·60 | 0·70 | 0·80 | 0·90 | 1·00 |
|---|---|---|---|---|---|---|---|---|---|---|---|---|---|---|---|
| 1·8 | 1·71 | — | — | — | — | — | — | — | — | — | — | — | — | — | — |
| 2·0 | 1·92 | 1·80 | 1·71 | 1·64 | — | — | — | — | — | — | — | — | — | — | — |
| 2·2 | 2·10 | 1·99 | 1·89 | 1·82 | 1·68 | 1·56 | 1·46 | — | — | — | — | — | — | — | — |
| 2·4 | 2·26 | 2·14 | 2·04 | 1·97 | 1·83 | 1·71 | 1·62 | 1·44 | — | — | — | — | — | — | — |
| 2·6 | 2·38 | 2·27 | 2·18 | 2·12 | 1·98 | 1·87 | 1·77 | 1·58 | 1·42 | — | — | — | — | — | — |
| 2·8 | 2·49 | 2·38 | 2·30 | 2·23 | 2·10 | 1·99 | 1·89 | 1·71 | 1·55 | 1·41 | — | — | — | — | — |
| 3·0 | 2·58 | 2·48 | 2·39 | 2·33 | 2·21 | 2·11 | 2·01 | 1·84 | 1·68 | 1·53 | 1·40 | — | — | — | — |
| 3·2 | 2·65 | 2·55 | 2·48 | 2·42 | 2·30 | 2·20 | 2·11 | 1·95 | 1·79 | 1·65 | 1·51 | 1·39 | 1·27 | — | — |
| 3·4 | 2·71 | 2·61 | 2·54 | 2·48 | 2·38 | 2·28 | 2·20 | 2·04 | 1·90 | 1·76 | 1·62 | 1·50 | 1·38 | 1·27 | — |
| 3·6 | 2·76 | 2·67 | 2·60 | 2·54 | 2·44 | 2·35 | 2·27 | 2·13 | 1·99 | 1·85 | 1·72 | 1·60 | 1·48 | 1·37 | 1·27 |
| 3·8 | 2·80 | 2·71 | 2·65 | 2·60 | 2·50 | 2·41 | 2·34 | 2·20 | 2·07 | 1·94 | 1·82 | 1·70 | 1·58 | 1·47 | 1·36 |
| 4·0 | 2·83 | 2·75 | 2·69 | 2·64 | 2·54 | 2·47 | 2·39 | 2·26 | 2·14 | 2·02 | 1·90 | 1·78 | 1·67 | 1·56 | 1·45 |
| 4·2 | 2·87 | 2·79 | 2·72 | 2·68 | 2·59 | 2·51 | 2·44 | 2·32 | 2·20 | 2·09 | 1·97 | 1·86 | 1·75 | 1·65 | 1·54 |
| 4·4 | 2·89 | 2·82 | 2·76 | 2·71 | 2·62 | 2·55 | 2·49 | 2·37 | 2·25 | 2·15 | 2·04 | 1·93 | 1·83 | 1·73 | 1·62 |
| 4·6 | 2·92 | 2·85 | 2·79 | 2·74 | 2·66 | 2·59 | 2·52 | 2·41 | 2·30 | 2·20 | 2·10 | 2·00 | 1·90 | 1·80 | 1·70 |
| 4·8 | 2·94 | 2·87 | 2·81 | 2·77 | 2·69 | 2·62 | 2·56 | 2·45 | 2·35 | 2·25 | 2·15 | 2·05 | 1·96 | 1·87 | 1·77 |
| 5·0 | 2·96 | 2·89 | 2·83 | 2·79 | 2·71 | 2·65 | 2·59 | 2·48 | 2·39 | 2·29 | 2·20 | 2·11 | 2·01 | 1·92 | 1·84 |

*Upper 0·5% points of the standardized deviate* $(x_P - \mu)/\sigma$, $(P = 0\cdot995)$

| $\beta_2$ \ $\beta_1$ | 0·00 | 0·01 | 0·03 | 0·05 | 0·10 | 0·15 | 0·20 | 0·30 | 0·40 | 0·50 | 0·60 | 0·70 | 0·80 | 0·90 | 1·00 |
|---|---|---|---|---|---|---|---|---|---|---|---|---|---|---|---|
| 1·8 | 1·71 | — | — | — | — | — | — | — | — | — | — | — | — | — | — |
| 2·0 | 1·92 | 2·01 | 2·06 | 2·09 | — | — | — | — | — | — | — | — | — | — | — |
| 2·2 | 2·10 | 2·19 | 2·24 | 2·27 | 2·31 | 2·33 | 2·35 | — | — | — | — | — | — | — | — |
| 2·4 | 2·26 | 2·35 | 2·41 | 2·44 | 2·49 | 2·52 | 2·53 | 2·53 | — | — | — | — | — | — | — |
| 2·6 | 2·38 | 2·48 | 2·54 | 2·57 | 2·63 | 2·66 | 2·68 | 2·70 | 2·69 | — | — | — | — | — | — |
| 2·8 | 2·49 | 2·58 | 2·64 | 2·68 | 2·73 | 2·77 | 2·80 | 2·83 | 2·84 | 2·83 | — | — | — | — | — |
| 3·0 | 2·58 | 2·66 | 2·72 | 2·76 | 2·82 | 2·86 | 2·89 | 2·93 | 2·95 | 2·96 | 2·95 | — | — | — | — |
| 3·2 | 2·65 | 2·73 | 2·79 | 2·83 | 2·89 | 2·93 | 2·96 | 3·01 | 3·04 | 3·06 | 3·07 | 3·06 | 3·04 | — | — |
| 3·4 | 2·71 | 2·79 | 2·85 | 2·88 | 2·95 | 2·99 | 3·02 | 3·07 | 3·11 | 3·13 | 3·15 | 3·16 | 3·15 | 3·14 | — |
| 3·6 | 2·76 | 2·84 | 2·89 | 2·93 | 2·99 | 3·03 | 3·07 | 3·12 | 3·16 | 3·19 | 3·22 | 3·23 | 3·24 | 3·24 | 3·24 |
| 3·8 | 2·80 | 2·88 | 2·93 | 2·97 | 3·03 | 3·07 | 3·11 | 3·16 | 3·20 | 3·24 | 3·27 | 3·29 | 3·30 | 3·31 | 3·32 |
| 4·0 | 2·83 | 2·91 | 2·96 | 3·00 | 3·06 | 3·10 | 3·14 | 3·20 | 3·24 | 3·28 | 3·31 | 3·34 | 3·36 | 3·37 | 3·38 |
| 4·2 | 2·87 | 2·94 | 2·99 | 3·03 | 3·09 | 3·13 | 3·17 | 3·22 | 3·27 | 3·31 | 3·34 | 3·37 | 3·40 | 3·42 | 3·43 |
| 4·4 | 2·89 | 2·97 | 3·02 | 3·05 | 3·11 | 3·15 | 3·19 | 3·25 | 3·29 | 3·33 | 3·37 | 3·40 | 3·42 | 3·45 | 3·47 |
| 4·6 | 2·92 | 2·99 | 3·04 | 3·07 | 3·13 | 3·17 | 3·21 | 3·27 | 3·31 | 3·36 | 3·39 | 3·42 | 3·44 | 3·47 | 3·50 |
| 4·8 | 2·94 | 3·01 | 3·06 | 3·09 | 3·15 | 3·19 | 3·23 | 3·28 | 3·33 | 3·37 | 3·41 | 3·44 | 3·47 | 3·49 | 3·53 |
| 5·0 | 2·96 | 3·03 | 3·07 | 3·11 | 3·16 | 3·21 | 3·24 | 3·30 | 3·35 | 3·39 | 3·43 | 3·46 | 3·49 | 3·52 | 3·55 |

Table 43. *Chart relating the type of Pearson frequency curve to the values of $\beta_1$, $\beta_2$.*

$\beta_1$

*Equations of bounding curves*

Upper limit for all frequency distributions: $\beta_2 - \beta_1 - 1 = 0$.

Boundary of $I(J)$ area: $4(4\beta_2 - 3\beta_1)(5\beta_2 - 6\beta_1 - 9)^2 = \beta_1(\beta_2 + 3)^2(8\beta_2 - 9\beta_1 - 12)$.

Type III line: $2\beta_2 - 3\beta_1 - 6 = 0$.

Type V line: $\beta_1(\beta_2 + 3)^2 = 4(4\beta_2 - 3\beta_1)(2\beta_2 - 3\beta_1 - 6)$.

Line on and below which $\mu_8 = \infty$ (for Pearson curves): $8\beta_2 - 15\beta_1 - 36 = 0$.

234

## Table 44. Distribution of Spearman's rank correlation coefficient, $r_s$, in random rankings. Probability $Q = 1 - P(S_r \mid n)$ that a given value of $S_r$ will be attained or exceeded. $r_s = 1 - 6S_r/(n^3 - n)$.

| n=4 $S_r$ | Q | n=5 $S_r$ | Q | n=6 $S_r$ | Q | n=7 $S_r$ | Q | n=8 $S_r$ | Q | n=9 $S_r$ | Q | n=10 $S_r$ | Q |
|---|---|---|---|---|---|---|---|---|---|---|---|---|---|
| 12 | 0.458 | 22 | 0.475 | 50 | 0.210 | 74 | 0.249 | 108 | 0.250 | 156 | 0.218 | 203 | 0.235 |
| 14 | .375 | 24 | .392 | 52 | .178 | 78 | .198 | 114 | .195 | 164 | .168 | 218 | .184 |
| 16 | .208 | 26 | .342 | 54 | .149 | 82 | .151 | 120 | .150 | 172 | .125 | 228 | .139 |
| 18 | .167 | 28 | .258 | 56 | .121 | 86 | .118 | 126 | .108 | 180 | .089 | 238 | .102 |
| 20 | .042 | 30 | .225 | 58 | .088 | 90 | .083 | 132 | .076 | 188 | .060 | 248 | .072 |
|  |  | 32 | .175 | 60 | .068 | 94 | .055 | 138 | .048 | 196 | .038 | 258 | .048 |
|  |  | 34 | .117 | 62 | .051 | 98 | .033 | 144 | .029 | 204 | .022 | 268 | .030 |
|  |  | 36 | .067 | 64 | .029 | 102 | .017 | 150 | .014 | 212 | .011 | 278 | .017 |
|  |  | 38 | .042 | 66 | .017 | 106 | .0062 | 156 | .0054 | 220 | .0041 | 288 | .0087 |
|  |  | 40 | .0083 | 68 | .0083 | 110 | .0014 | 162 | .0011 | 228 | .0010 | 298 | .0036 |
|  |  |  |  | 70 | 0.0014 |  |  |  |  |  |  | 308 | 0.0011 |
| 20 |  | 40 |  | 70 |  | 112 |  | 168 |  | 240 |  | 330 |  |

*Tail area at the lower end of the distribution. If $S_r$ and $Q$ are two corresponding tabular entries for a given sample size $n$, and if $S'_r = \frac{1}{3}(n^3-n) - S_r$, then the probability is $Q$ that the sum of squares of the rank differences will be $\leqslant S'_r$. Values of $\frac{1}{3}(n^3-n)$ are shown in the bottom row of the table. E.g. if $n=8$, the probability is 0.048 that the sum of squares of the rank differences will be less than or equal to $168 - 138 = 30$.*

## Table 45. Distribution of Kendall's rank correlation coefficient, $t_k$, in random rankings. Probability $Q = 1 - P(S_t \mid n)$ that a given value of $S_t$ will be attained or exceeded. $t_k = 2S_t/(n^2 - n)$.

| $S_t$ | n=4 | n=5 | n=8 | n=9 | $S_t$ | n=6 | n=7 | n=10 |
|---|---|---|---|---|---|---|---|---|
| 0 | 0.625 | 0.592 | 0.548 | 0.540 | 1 | 0.500 | 0.500 | 0.500 |
| 2 | .375 | .408 | .452 | .460 | 3 | .360 | .386 | .431 |
| 4 | .167 | .242 | .360 | .381 | 5 | .235 | .281 | .364 |
| 6 | .042 | .117 | .274 | .306 | 7 | .136 | .191 | .300 |
| 8 |  | .042 | .199 | .238 | 9 | .068 | .119 | .242 |
| 10 |  | 0.0083 | .138 | .179 | 11 | .028 | .068 | .190 |
| 12 |  |  | .089 | .130 | 13 | .0083 | .035 | .146 |
| 14 |  |  | .054 | .090 | 15 | .0014 | .015 | .108 |
| 16 |  |  | .031 | .060 | 17 |  | .0054 | .078 |
| 18 |  |  | .016 | .038 | 19 |  | .0014 | .054 |
| 20 |  |  | .0071 | .022 | 21 |  | 0.0002 | .036 |
| 22 |  |  | .0028 | .012 | 23 |  |  | .023 |
| 24 |  |  | .0009 | .0063 | 25 |  |  | .014 |
| 26 |  |  | .0002 | .0029 | 27 |  |  | .0083 |
| 28 |  |  |  | .0012 | 29 |  |  | .0046 |
| 30 |  |  |  | 0.0004 | 31 |  |  | .0023 |
|  |  |  |  |  | 33 |  |  | .0011 |
|  |  |  |  |  | 35 |  |  | .0005 |

## Table 46. Distribution of the concordance coefficient, W, in random rankings. Probability $Q = 1 - P(S_W \mid n, m)$ that a given value of $S_W$ will be attained or exceeded. $W = 12 S_W / \{m^2(n^3 - n)\}$.

### (a) Case n=3

| m=3 $S_W$ | Q | m=5 $S_W$ | Q | m=6 $S_W$ | Q | m=7 $S_W$ | Q | m=8 $S_W$ | Q | m=9 $S_W$ | Q | m=10 $S_W$ | Q |
|---|---|---|---|---|---|---|---|---|---|---|---|---|---|
| 6 | 0.528 | 14 | 0.367 | 18 | 0.252 | 24 | 0.237 | 26 | 0.236 | 32 | 0.187 | 32 | 0.222 |
| 8 | .361 | 18 | .182 | 24 | .184 | 26 | .192 | 32 | .149 | 38 | .154 | 42 | .135 |
| 14 | .194 | 24 | .124 | 26 | .142 | 32 | .112 | 42 | .120 | 42 | .107 | 50 | .092 |
| 18 | .028 | 26 | .093 | 32 | .072 | 38 | .085 | 50 | .079 | 50 | .069 | 56 | .066 |
|  |  | 32 | .039 | 38 | .052 | 42 | .051 | 56 | .047 | 56 | .048 | 62 | .046 |

| m=4 $S_W$ | Q | m=5 $S_W$ | Q | m=6 $S_W$ | Q | m=7 $S_W$ | Q | m=8 $S_W$ | Q | m=9 $S_W$ | Q | m=10 $S_W$ | Q |
|---|---|---|---|---|---|---|---|---|---|---|---|---|---|
| 8 | 0.431 | 38 | 0.024 | 42 | 0.029 | 50 | 0.027 | 72 | 0.030 | 62 | 0.031 | 74 | 0.026 |
| 14 | .273 | 42 | .0085 | 50 | .012 | 55 | .016 | 86 | .0090 | 78 | .010 | 86 | .012 |
| 18 | .125 | 50 | .0008 | 54 | .0081 | 62 | .0084 | 98 | .0048 | 86 | .0060 | 98 | .0075 |
| 24 | .069 |  |  | 56 | .0055 | 72 | .0036 | 108 | .0024 | 93 | .0029 | 104 | .0034 |
| 26 | .042 |  |  | 62 | .0017 | 78 | .0012 | 118 | .0009 | 104 | .0013 | 122 | .0013 |
| 32 | .0046 |  |  | 72 | 0.0001 | 96 | 0.0003 | 128 | 0.0003 | 114 | 0.0007 | 126 | 0.0008 |

### (b) Case n=4

| m=3 $S_W$ | Q | m=4 $S_W$ | Q | m=5 $S_W$ | Q | m=6 $S_W$ | Q |
|---|---|---|---|---|---|---|---|
| 19 | 0.342 | 32 | 0.200 | 41 | 0.210 | 46 | 0.218 |
| 21 | .300 | 36 | .158 | 43 | .162 | 52 | .163 |
| 25 | .207 | 40 | .105 | 51 | .107 | 62 | .108 |
| 27 | .175 | 46 | .068 | 57 | .075 | 68 | .073 |
| 29 | .148 | 50 | .052 | 61 | .055 | 74 | .056 |
| 33 | .075 | 54 | .033 | 67 | .034 | 80 | .037 |
| 35 | .054 | 62 | .012 | 81 | .012 | 100 | .010 |
| 37 | .033 | 66 | .0062 | 85 | .0067 | 108 | .0061 |
| 41 | .017 | 70 | .0027 | 93 | .0023 | 118 | .0028 |
| 45 | 0.0017 | 74 | .0009 | 101 | .0014 | 128 | .0009 |
|  |  |  |  | 105 | 0.0006 |  |  |

### (c) Case n=5

| m=3 $S_W$ | Q |
|---|---|
| 46 | 0.213 |
| 50 | .163 |
| 56 | .096 |
| 60 | .063 |
| 62 | .056 |
| 66 | .038 |
| 74 | .015 |
| 78 | .0053 |
| 82 | .0028 |
| 86 | .0009 |

The distribution of $S_t$ is symmetrical so that values of the probability for negative $S_t$ can be obtained by appropriate subtraction from unity; e.g. for $n=9$,

$$\Pr\{S_t \geqslant -14\} = 1 - \Pr\{S_t \geqslant 16\} = 1 - 0.060 = 0.940.$$

30-2

# Table 47. *Orthogonal polynomials*

Definitions:

$$\phi_0(x) = 1, \quad \phi_1(x) = \lambda_1 x, \quad \phi_2(x) = \lambda_2\{x^2 - \tfrac{1}{12}(n^2-1)\},$$
$$\phi_3(x) = \lambda_3\{x^3 - \tfrac{1}{20}(3n^2-7)\,x\}, \quad \phi_4(x) = \lambda_4\{x^4 - \tfrac{1}{14}(3n^2-13)\,x^2 + \tfrac{3}{560}(n^2-1)(n^2-9)\},$$
$$\phi_5(x) = \lambda_5\{x^5 - \tfrac{5}{18}(n^2-7)\,x^3 + \tfrac{1}{1008}(15n^4 - 230n^2 + 407)\,x\},$$
$$\phi_6(x) = \lambda_6\{x^6 - \tfrac{5}{44}(3n^2-31)\,x^4 + \tfrac{1}{176}(5n^4 - 110n^2 + 329)\,x^2 - \tfrac{5}{14784}(n^2-1)(n^2-9)(n^2-25)\}.$$

The table gives the values of these polynomials, $\phi_i(x)$ for $i = 1\,(1)\,6$* and is arranged in fifty sections corresponding to sample sizes $n = 3\,(1)\,52$. The arguments $x = x_t \equiv t - \tfrac{1}{2}(n+1)$ cover the full observational range $t = 1\,(1)\,n$ for $n = 3\,(1)\,12$ and the half-range $t = 1\,(1)\left[\dfrac{n+1}{2}\right]$ for $n > 12$, when use is made of the symmetry (antisymmetry) relations:

$$\phi_i(x) = \phi_i(-x)\ \text{for } i \text{ even}, \quad \phi_i(x) = -\phi_i(-x)\ \text{for } i \text{ odd}.$$

The argument $x$ is not shown as such in the table, but the first column of each section gives $\phi_1 = \lambda_1 x$, where $\lambda_1$ is 1 for $n$ odd and 2 for $n$ even. The leading coefficients $\lambda_i$ are chosen so that the $\phi_i(x_t)$ are positive or negative integers throughout, and are given in the bottom line of each section. Also shown, in the line above the $\lambda_i$, are the sums of squares $\sum\limits_{t=1}^{n} \{\phi_i(x_t)\}^2$ for the full range of $x_t$ values. Note the arrangements of the sections which progress from left to right through consecutive pages up to $n = 28$. From this point onwards the sections progress from left to right through the top halves of the pages up to $n = 40$ and then return from right to left through the bottom halves of the pages.

*Some formulae:*

Estimate of coefficient of $\phi_i(x)$: $\quad A_i = \sum\limits_t y_t\,\phi_i(x_t)/\sum\limits_t \{\phi_i(x_t)\}^2$.

Variance of $A_i = \sigma_y^2 / \sum\limits_t \{\phi_i(x_t)\}^2$.

Estimate of $\sigma_y^2$: $\quad s^2 = \left(\sum\limits_t y_t^2 - \sum\limits_{i=0}^{k} \{A_i^2 \sum\limits_t [\phi_i(x_t)]^2\}\right)\Big/(n-k-1)$.

\* Except that for $n \leqslant 6$, $i$ is not taken beyond $n-1$.

**$n = 3$**

| $\phi_1$ | $\phi_2$ |
|---|---|
| $-1$ | $1$ |
| $0$ | $-2$ |
| $1$ | $1$ |
| $2$ | $6$ |
| $1$ | $3$ |

**$n = 4$**

| $\phi_1$ | $\phi_2$ | $\phi_3$ |
|---|---|---|
| $-3$ | $1$ | $-1$ |
| $-1$ | $-1$ | $3$ |
| $1$ | $-1$ | $-3$ |
| $3$ | $1$ | $1$ |
| $20$ | $4$ | $20$ |
| $2$ | $1$ | $\tfrac{10}{3}$ |

**$n = 5$**

| $\phi_1$ | $\phi_2$ | $\phi_3$ | $\phi_4$ |
|---|---|---|---|
| $-2$ | $2$ | $-1$ | $1$ |
| $-1$ | $-1$ | $2$ | $-4$ |
| $0$ | $-2$ | $0$ | $6$ |
| $1$ | $-1$ | $-2$ | $-4$ |
| $2$ | $2$ | $1$ | $1$ |
| $10$ | $14$ | $10$ | $70$ |
| $1$ | $1$ | $\tfrac{5}{6}$ | $\tfrac{35}{12}$ |

**$n = 6$**

| $\phi_1$ | $\phi_2$ | $\phi_3$ | $\phi_4$ | $\phi_5$ |
|---|---|---|---|---|
| $-5$ | $5$ | $-5$ | $1$ | $-1$ |
| $-3$ | $-1$ | $7$ | $-3$ | $5$ |
| $-1$ | $-4$ | $4$ | $2$ | $-10$ |
| $1$ | $-4$ | $-4$ | $2$ | $10$ |
| $3$ | $-1$ | $-7$ | $-3$ | $5$ |
| $5$ | $5$ | $5$ | $1$ | $1$ |
| $70$ | $84$ | $180$ | $28$ | $252$ |
| $2$ | $\tfrac{3}{2}$ | $\tfrac{5}{3}$ | $\tfrac{7}{12}$ | $\tfrac{21}{10}$ |

**$n = 7$**

| $\phi_1$ | $\phi_2$ | $\phi_3$ | $\phi_4$ | $\phi_5$ | $\phi_6$ |
|---|---|---|---|---|---|
| $-3$ | $5$ | $-1$ | $3$ | $-1$ | $1$ |
| $-2$ | $0$ | $1$ | $-7$ | $4$ | $-6$ |
| $-1$ | $-3$ | $1$ | $1$ | $-5$ | $15$ |
| $0$ | $-4$ | $0$ | $6$ | $0$ | $-20$ |
| $1$ | $-3$ | $-1$ | $1$ | $5$ | $15$ |
| $2$ | $0$ | $-1$ | $-7$ | $-4$ | $-6$ |
| $3$ | $5$ | $1$ | $3$ | $1$ | $1$ |
| $28$ | $84$ | $6$ | $154$ | $84$ | $924$ |
| $1$ | $1$ | $\tfrac{1}{6}$ | $\tfrac{7}{12}$ | $\tfrac{7}{20}$ | $\tfrac{77}{60}$ |

**$n = 8$**

| $\phi_1$ | $\phi_2$ | $\phi_3$ | $\phi_4$ | $\phi_5$ | $\phi_6$ |
|---|---|---|---|---|---|
| $-7$ | $7$ | $-7$ | $7$ | $-7$ | $1$ |
| $-5$ | $1$ | $5$ | $-13$ | $23$ | $-5$ |
| $-3$ | $-3$ | $7$ | $-3$ | $-17$ | $9$ |
| $-1$ | $-5$ | $3$ | $9$ | $-15$ | $-5$ |
| $1$ | $-5$ | $-3$ | $9$ | $15$ | $-5$ |
| $3$ | $-3$ | $-7$ | $-3$ | $17$ | $9$ |
| $5$ | $1$ | $-5$ | $-13$ | $-23$ | $-5$ |
| $7$ | $7$ | $7$ | $7$ | $7$ | $1$ |
| $168$ | $168$ | $264$ | $616$ | $2{,}184$ | $264$ |
| $2$ | $1$ | $\tfrac{2}{3}$ | $\tfrac{7}{12}$ | $\tfrac{7}{10}$ | $\tfrac{11}{60}$ |

**$n = 9$**

| $\phi_1$ | $\phi_2$ | $\phi_3$ | $\phi_4$ | $\phi_5$ | $\phi_6$ |
|---|---|---|---|---|---|
| $-4$ | $28$ | $-14$ | $14$ | $-4$ | $4$ |
| $-3$ | $7$ | $7$ | $-21$ | $11$ | $-17$ |
| $-2$ | $-8$ | $13$ | $-11$ | $-4$ | $22$ |
| $-1$ | $-17$ | $9$ | $9$ | $-9$ | $1$ |
| $0$ | $-20$ | $0$ | $18$ | $0$ | $-20$ |
| $1$ | $-17$ | $-9$ | $9$ | $9$ | $1$ |
| $2$ | $-8$ | $-13$ | $-11$ | $4$ | $22$ |
| $3$ | $7$ | $-7$ | $-21$ | $-11$ | $-17$ |
| $4$ | $28$ | $14$ | $14$ | $4$ | $4$ |
| $60$ | $2{,}772$ | $990$ | $2{,}002$ | $468$ | $1{,}980$ |
| $1$ | $3$ | $\tfrac{5}{6}$ | $\tfrac{7}{12}$ | $\tfrac{3}{10}$ | $\tfrac{11}{60}$ |

**$n = 10$**

| $\phi_1$ | $\phi_2$ | $\phi_3$ | $\phi_4$ | $\phi_5$ | $\phi_6$ |
|---|---|---|---|---|---|
| $-9$ | $6$ | $-42$ | $18$ | $-6$ | $3$ |
| $-7$ | $2$ | $14$ | $-22$ | $14$ | $-11$ |
| $-5$ | $-1$ | $35$ | $-17$ | $-1$ | $10$ |
| $-3$ | $-3$ | $31$ | $3$ | $-11$ | $6$ |
| $-1$ | $-4$ | $12$ | $18$ | $-6$ | $-8$ |
| $1$ | $-4$ | $-12$ | $18$ | $6$ | $-8$ |
| $3$ | $-3$ | $-31$ | $3$ | $11$ | $6$ |
| $5$ | $-1$ | $-35$ | $-17$ | $1$ | $10$ |
| $7$ | $2$ | $-14$ | $-22$ | $-14$ | $-11$ |
| $9$ | $6$ | $42$ | $18$ | $6$ | $3$ |
| $330$ | $132$ | $8{,}580$ | $2{,}860$ | $780$ | $660$ |
| $2$ | $\tfrac{1}{2}$ | $\tfrac{5}{3}$ | $\tfrac{7}{12}$ | $\tfrac{3}{10}$ | $\tfrac{11}{120}$ |

Table 47 (*continued*)

### n = 11

| $\phi_1$ | $\phi_2$ | $\phi_3$ | $\phi_4$ | $\phi_5$ | $\phi_6$ |
|---|---|---|---|---|---|
| −5 | 15 | −30 | 6 | −3 | 15 |
| −4 | 6 | 6 | −6 | 6 | −48 |
| −3 | −1 | 22 | −6 | 1 | 29 |
| −2 | −6 | 23 | −1 | −4 | 36 |
| −1 | −9 | 14 | 4 | −4 | −12 |
| 0 | −10 | 0 | 6 | 0 | −40 |
| 1 | −9 | −14 | 4 | 4 | −12 |
| 2 | −6 | −23 | −1 | 4 | 36 |
| 3 | −1 | −22 | −6 | −1 | 29 |
| 4 | 6 | −6 | −6 | −6 | −48 |
| 5 | 15 | 30 | 6 | 3 | 15 |
| 110 | 858 | 4,290 | 286 | 156 | 11,220 |
| 1 | 1 | $\frac{5}{6}$ | $\frac{1}{12}$ | $\frac{1}{40}$ | $\frac{11}{120}$ |

### n = 12

| $\phi_1$ | $\phi_2$ | $\phi_3$ | $\phi_4$ | $\phi_5$ | $\phi_6$ |
|---|---|---|---|---|---|
| −11 | 55 | −33 | 33 | −33 | 11 |
| −9 | 25 | 3 | −27 | 57 | −31 |
| −7 | 1 | 21 | −33 | 21 | 11 |
| −5 | −17 | 25 | −13 | −29 | 25 |
| −3 | −29 | 19 | 12 | −44 | 4 |
| −1 | −35 | 7 | 28 | −20 | −20 |
| 1 | −35 | −7 | 28 | 20 | −20 |
| 3 | −29 | −19 | 12 | 44 | 4 |
| 5 | −17 | −25 | −13 | 29 | 25 |
| 7 | 1 | −21 | −33 | −21 | 11 |
| 9 | 25 | −3 | −27 | −57 | −31 |
| 11 | 55 | 33 | 33 | 33 | 11 |
| 572 | 12,012 | 5,148 | 8,008 | 15,912 | 4,488 |
| 2 | 3 | $\frac{2}{3}$ | $\frac{7}{24}$ | $\frac{3}{20}$ | $\frac{11}{360}$ |

### n = 13

| $\phi_1$ | $\phi_2$ | $\phi_3$ | $\phi_4$ | $\phi_5$ | $\phi_6$ |
|---|---|---|---|---|---|
| −6 | 22 | −11 | 99 | −22 | 22 |
| −5 | 11 | 0 | −66 | 33 | −55 |
| −4 | 2 | 6 | −96 | 18 | 8 |
| −3 | −5 | 8 | −54 | −11 | 43 |
| −2 | −10 | 7 | 11 | −26 | 22 |
| −1 | −13 | 4 | 64 | −20 | −20 |
| 0 | −14 | 0 | 84 | 0 | −40 |
| 182 | 2,002 | 572 | 68,068 | 6,188 | 14,212 |
| 1 | 1 | $\frac{1}{6}$ | $\frac{7}{12}$ | $\frac{7}{120}$ | $\frac{11}{360}$ |

### n = 14

| $\phi_1$ | $\phi_2$ | $\phi_3$ | $\phi_4$ | $\phi_5$ | $\phi_6$ |
|---|---|---|---|---|---|
| −13 | 13 | −143 | 143 | −143 | 143 |
| −11 | 7 | −11 | −77 | 187 | −319 |
| −9 | 2 | 66 | −132 | 132 | −11 |
| −7 | −2 | 98 | −92 | −28 | 227 |
| −5 | −5 | 95 | −13 | −139 | 185 |
| −3 | −7 | 67 | 63 | −145 | −25 |
| −1 | −8 | 24 | 108 | −60 | −200 |
| 910 | 728 | 97,240 | 136,136 | 235,144 | 497,420 |
| 2 | $\frac{1}{2}$ | $\frac{5}{3}$ | $\frac{7}{12}$ | $\frac{7}{30}$ | $\frac{77}{720}$ |

### n = 15

| $\phi_1$ | $\phi_2$ | $\phi_3$ | $\phi_4$ | $\phi_5$ | $\phi_6$ |
|---|---|---|---|---|---|
| −7 | 91 | −91 | 1,001 | −1,001 | 143 |
| −6 | 52 | −13 | −429 | 1,144 | −286 |
| −5 | 19 | 35 | −869 | 979 | −55 |
| −4 | −8 | 58 | −704 | 44 | 176 |
| −3 | −29 | 61 | −249 | −751 | 197 |
| −2 | −44 | 49 | 251 | −1,000 | 50 |
| −1 | −53 | 27 | 621 | −675 | −125 |
| 0 | −56 | 0 | 756 | 0 | −200 |
| 280 | 37,128 | 39,780 | 6,466,460 | 10,581,480 | 426,360 |
| 1 | 3 | $\frac{5}{6}$ | $\frac{35}{12}$ | $\frac{21}{20}$ | $\frac{11}{180}$ |

### n = 16

| $\phi_1$ | $\phi_2$ | $\phi_3$ | $\phi_4$ | $\phi_5$ | $\phi_6$ |
|---|---|---|---|---|---|
| −15 | 35 | −455 | 273 | −143 | 65 |
| −13 | 21 | −91 | −91 | 143 | −117 |
| −11 | 9 | 143 | −221 | 143 | −39 |
| −9 | −1 | 267 | −201 | 33 | 59 |
| −7 | −9 | 301 | −101 | −77 | 87 |
| −5 | −15 | 265 | 23 | −131 | 45 |
| −3 | −19 | 179 | 129 | −115 | −25 |
| −1 | −21 | 63 | 189 | −45 | −75 |
| 1,360 | 5,712 | 1,007,760 | 470,288 | 201,552 | 77,520 |
| 2 | 1 | $\frac{10}{3}$ | $\frac{7}{12}$ | $\frac{1}{10}$ | $\frac{1}{80}$ |

# Table 47. *Orthogonal polynomials (continued)*

## n = 17

| $\phi_1$ | $\phi_2$ | $\phi_3$ | $\phi_4$ | $\phi_5$ | $\phi_6$ |
|---|---|---|---|---|---|
| −8 | 40 | −28 | 52 | −104 | 104 |
| −7 | 25 | −7 | −13 | 91 | −169 |
| −6 | 12 | 7 | −39 | 104 | −78 |
| −5 | 1 | 15 | −39 | 39 | 65 |
| −4 | −8 | 18 | −24 | −36 | 128 |
| −3 | −15 | 17 | −3 | −83 | 93 |
| −2 | −20 | 13 | 17 | −88 | 2 |
| −1 | −23 | 7 | 31 | −55 | −85 |
| 0 | −24 | 0 | 36 | 0 | −120 |
| 408 | | 3,876 | | 100,776 | |
| | 7,752 | | 16,796 | | 178,296 |
| 1 | 1 | $\frac{1}{6}$ | $\frac{1}{12}$ | $\frac{1}{20}$ | $\frac{1}{60}$ |

## n = 18

| $\phi_1$ | $\phi_2$ | $\phi_3$ | $\phi_4$ | $\phi_5$ | $\phi_6$ |
|---|---|---|---|---|---|
| −17 | 68 | −68 | 68 | −884 | 442 |
| −15 | 44 | −20 | −12 | 676 | −650 |
| −13 | 23 | 13 | −47 | 871 | −377 |
| −11 | 5 | 33 | −51 | 429 | 169 |
| −9 | −10 | 42 | −36 | −156 | 481 |
| −7 | −22 | 42 | −12 | −588 | 439 |
| −5 | −31 | 35 | 13 | −733 | 145 |
| −3 | −37 | 23 | 33 | −583 | −209 |
| −1 | −40 | 8 | 44 | −220 | −440 |
| 1,938 | | 23,256 | | 6,953,544 | |
| | 23,256 | | 28,424 | | 2,941,884 |
| 2 | $\frac{3}{2}$ | $\frac{1}{3}$ | $\frac{1}{12}$ | $\frac{3}{10}$ | $\frac{11}{240}$ |

## n = 19

| $\phi_1$ | $\phi_2$ | $\phi_3$ | $\phi_4$ | $\phi_5$ | $\phi_6$ |
|---|---|---|---|---|---|
| −9 | 51 | −204 | 612 | −102 | 1,326 |
| −8 | 34 | −68 | −68 | 68 | −1,768 |
| −7 | 19 | 28 | −388 | 98 | −1,222 |
| −6 | 6 | 89 | −453 | 58 | 234 |
| −5 | −5 | 120 | −354 | −3 | 1,235 |
| −4 | −14 | 126 | −168 | −54 | 1,352 |
| −3 | −21 | 112 | 42 | −79 | 729 |
| −2 | −26 | 83 | 227 | −74 | −214 |
| −1 | −29 | 44 | 352 | −44 | −1,012 |
| 0 | −30 | 0 | 396 | 0 | −1,320 |
| 570 | | 213,180 | | 89,148 | |
| | 13,566 | | 2,288,132 | | 24,515,700 |
| 1 | 1 | $\frac{5}{6}$ | $\frac{7}{12}$ | $\frac{1}{40}$ | $\frac{11}{120}$ |

## n = 20

| $\phi_1$ | $\phi_2$ | $\phi_3$ | $\phi_4$ | $\phi_5$ | $\phi_6$ |
|---|---|---|---|---|---|
| −19 | 57 | −969 | 1,938 | −1,938 | 1,938 |
| −17 | 39 | −357 | −102 | 1,122 | −2,346 |
| −15 | 23 | 85 | −1,122 | 1,802 | −1,870 |
| −13 | 9 | 377 | −1,402 | 1,222 | 6 |
| −11 | −3 | 539 | −1,187 | 187 | 1,497 |
| −9 | −13 | 591 | −687 | −771 | 1,931 |
| −7 | −21 | 553 | −77 | −1,351 | 1,353 |
| −5 | −27 | 445 | 503 | −1,441 | 195 |
| −3 | −31 | 287 | 948 | −1,076 | −988 |
| −1 | −33 | 99 | 1,188 | −396 | −1,716 |
| 2,660 | | 4,903,140 | | 31,201,800 | |
| | 17,556 | | 22,881,320 | | 49,031,400 |
| 2 | 1 | $\frac{10}{3}$ | $\frac{35}{24}$ | $\frac{7}{20}$ | $\frac{11}{120}$ |

## n = 21

| $\phi_1$ | $\phi_2$ | $\phi_3$ | $\phi_4$ | $\phi_5$ | $\phi_6$ |
|---|---|---|---|---|---|
| −10 | 190 | −285 | 969 | −3,876 | 6,460 |
| −9 | 133 | −114 | 0 | 1,938 | −7,106 |
| −8 | 82 | 12 | −510 | 3,468 | −6,392 |
| −7 | 37 | 98 | −680 | 2,618 | −918 |
| −6 | −2 | 149 | −615 | 788 | 3,996 |
| −5 | −35 | 170 | −406 | −1,063 | 6,075 |
| −4 | −62 | 166 | −130 | −2,354 | 5,088 |
| −3 | −83 | 142 | 150 | −2,819 | 2,001 |
| −2 | −98 | 103 | 385 | −2,444 | −1,716 |
| −1 | −107 | 54 | 540 | −1,404 | −4,628 |
| 0 | −110 | 0 | 594 | 0 | −5,720 |
| 770 | | 432,630 | | 121,687,020 | |
| | 201,894 | | 5,720,330 | | 514,829,700 |
| 1 | 3 | $\frac{5}{6}$ | $\frac{7}{12}$ | $\frac{21}{40}$ | $\frac{77}{360}$ |

## n = 22

| $\phi_1$ | $\phi_2$ | $\phi_3$ | $\phi_4$ | $\phi_5$ | $\phi_6$ |
|---|---|---|---|---|---|
| −21 | 35 | −133 | 1,197 | −2,261 | 646 |
| −19 | 25 | −57 | 57 | 969 | −646 |
| −17 | 16 | 0 | −570 | 1,938 | −646 |
| −15 | 8 | 40 | −810 | 1,598 | −170 |
| −13 | 1 | 65 | −775 | 663 | 306 |
| −11 | −5 | 77 | −563 | −363 | 558 |
| −9 | −10 | 78 | −258 | −1,158 | 537 |
| −7 | −14 | 70 | 70 | −1,554 | 303 |
| −5 | −17 | 55 | 365 | −1,509 | −30 |
| −3 | −19 | 35 | 585 | −1,079 | −338 |
| −1 | −20 | 12 | 702 | −390 | −520 |
| 3,542 | | 96,140 | | 40,562,340 | |
| | 7,084 | | 8,748,740 | | 4,903,140 |
| 2 | $\frac{1}{2}$ | $\frac{1}{3}$ | $\frac{7}{12}$ | $\frac{7}{30}$ | $\frac{11}{720}$ |

Table 47 (*continued*)

### $n = 23$

| $\phi_1$ | $\phi_2$ | $\phi_3$ | $\phi_4$ | $\phi_5$ | $\phi_6$ |
|---|---|---|---|---|---|
| $-11$ | 77 | $-77$ | 1,463 | $-209$ | 3,553 |
| $-10$ | 56 | $-35$ | 133 | 76 | $-3,230$ |
| $-9$ | 37 | $-3$ | $-627$ | 171 | $-3,553$ |
| $-8$ | 20 | 20 | $-950$ | 152 | $-1,292$ |
| $-7$ | 5 | 35 | $-955$ | 77 | 1,207 |
| $-6$ | $-8$ | 43 | $-747$ | $-12$ | 2,754 |
| $-5$ | $-19$ | 45 | $-417$ | $-87$ | 2,985 |
| $-4$ | $-28$ | 42 | $-42$ | $-132$ | 2,076 |
| $-3$ | $-35$ | 35 | 315 | $-141$ | 501 |
| $-2$ | $-40$ | 25 | 605 | $-116$ | $-1,166$ |
| $-1$ | $-43$ | 13 | 793 | $-65$ | $-2,405$ |
| 0 | $-44$ | 0 | 858 | 0 | $-2,860$ |
| 1,012 | | 32,890 | | 340,860 | |
| | 35,420 | | 13,123,110 | | 142,191,060 |
| 1 | 1 | $\frac{1}{6}$ | $\frac{7}{12}$ | $\frac{1}{60}$ | $\frac{11}{180}$ |

### $n = 24$

| $\phi_1$ | $\phi_2$ | $\phi_3$ | $\phi_4$ | $\phi_5$ | $\phi_6$ |
|---|---|---|---|---|---|
| $-23$ | 253 | $-1,771$ | 253 | $-4,807$ | 4,807 |
| $-21$ | 187 | $-847$ | 33 | 1,463 | $-3,971$ |
| $-19$ | 127 | $-133$ | $-97$ | 3,743 | $-4,769$ |
| $-17$ | 73 | 391 | $-157$ | 3,553 | $-2,147$ |
| $-15$ | 25 | 745 | $-165$ | 2,071 | 1,045 |
| $-13$ | $-17$ | 949 | $-137$ | 169 | 3,271 |
| $-11$ | $-53$ | 1,023 | $-87$ | $-1,551$ | 3,957 |
| $-9$ | $-83$ | 987 | $-27$ | $-2,721$ | 3,183 |
| $-7$ | $-107$ | 861 | 33 | $-3,171$ | 1,419 |
| $-5$ | $-125$ | 665 | 85 | $-2,893$ | $-695$ |
| $-3$ | $-137$ | 419 | 123 | $-2,005$ | $-2,525$ |
| $-1$ | $-143$ | 143 | 143 | $-715$ | $-3,575$ |
| 4,600 | | 17,760,600 | | 177,928,920 | |
| | 394,680 | | 394,680 | | 250,925,400 |
| 2 | 3 | $\frac{10}{3}$ | $\frac{1}{12}$ | $\frac{3}{10}$ | $\frac{11}{180}$ |

### $n = 25$

| $\phi_1$ | $\phi_2$ | $\phi_3$ | $\phi_4$ | $\phi_5$ | $\phi_6$ |
|---|---|---|---|---|---|
| $-12$ | 92 | $-506$ | 1,518 | $-1,012$ | 19,228 |
| $-11$ | 69 | $-253$ | 253 | 253 | $-14,421$ |
| $-10$ | 48 | $-55$ | $-517$ | 748 | $-18,810$ |
| $-9$ | 29 | 93 | $-897$ | 753 | $-9,890$ |
| $-8$ | 12 | 196 | $-982$ | 488 | 2,052 |
| $-7$ | $-3$ | 259 | $-857$ | 119 | 11,229 |
| $-6$ | $-16$ | 287 | $-597$ | $-236$ | 15,142 |
| $-5$ | $-27$ | 285 | $-267$ | $-501$ | 13,635 |
| $-4$ | $-36$ | 258 | 78 | $-636$ | 8,028 |
| $-3$ | $-43$ | 211 | 393 | $-631$ | 391 |
| $-2$ | $-48$ | 149 | 643 | $-500$ | $-7,050$ |
| $-1$ | $-51$ | 77 | 803 | $-275$ | $-12,375$ |
| 0 | $-52$ | 0 | 858 | 0 | $-14,300$ |
| 1,300 | | 1,480,050 | | 7,803,900 | |
| | 53,820 | | 14,307,150 | | 3,889,343,700 |
| 1 | 1 | $\frac{5}{6}$ | $\frac{5}{12}$ | $\frac{1}{20}$ | $\frac{11}{60}$ |

### $n = 26$

| $\phi_1$ | $\phi_2$ | $\phi_3$ | $\phi_4$ | $\phi_5$ | $\phi_6$ |
|---|---|---|---|---|---|
| $-25$ | 50 | $-1,150$ | 2,530 | $-2,530$ | 6,325 |
| $-23$ | 38 | $-598$ | 506 | 506 | $-4,301$ |
| $-21$ | 27 | $-161$ | $-759$ | 1,771 | $-6,072$ |
| $-19$ | 17 | 171 | $-1,419$ | 1,881 | $-3,608$ |
| $-17$ | 8 | 408 | $-1,614$ | 1,326 | 46 |
| $-15$ | 0 | 560 | $-1,470$ | 482 | 3,090 |
| $-13$ | $-7$ | 637 | $-1,099$ | $-377$ | 4,672 |
| $-11$ | $-13$ | 649 | $-599$ | $-1,067$ | 4,624 |
| $-9$ | $-18$ | 606 | $-54$ | $-1,482$ | 3,231 |
| $-7$ | $-22$ | 518 | 466 | $-1,582$ | 1,033 |
| $-5$ | $-25$ | 395 | 905 | $-1,381$ | $-1,340$ |
| $-3$ | $-27$ | 247 | 1,221 | $-935$ | $-3,300$ |
| $-1$ | $-28$ | 84 | 1,386 | $-330$ | $-4,400$ |
| 5,850 | | 7,803,900 | | 48,384,180 | |
| | 16,380 | | 40,060,020 | | 409,404,600 |
| 2 | $\frac{1}{2}$ | $\frac{5}{3}$ | $\frac{7}{12}$ | $\frac{1}{10}$ | $\frac{11}{240}$ |

### $n = 27$

| $\phi_1$ | $\phi_2$ | $\phi_3$ | $\phi_4$ | $\phi_5$ | $\phi_6$ |
|---|---|---|---|---|---|
| $-13$ | 325 | $-130$ | 2,990 | $-16,445$ | 1,495 |
| $-12$ | 250 | $-70$ | 690 | 2,530 | $-920$ |
| $-11$ | 181 | $-22$ | $-782$ | 10,879 | $-1,403$ |
| $-10$ | 118 | 15 | $-1,587$ | 12,144 | $-920$ |
| $-9$ | 61 | 42 | $-1,872$ | 9,174 | $-122$ |
| $-8$ | 10 | 60 | $-1,770$ | 4,188 | 592 |
| $-7$ | $-35$ | 70 | $-1,400$ | $-1,162$ | 1,018 |
| $-6$ | $-74$ | 73 | $-867$ | $-5,728$ | 1,096 |
| $-5$ | $-107$ | 70 | $-262$ | $-8,803$ | 865 |
| $-4$ | $-134$ | 62 | 338 | $-10,058$ | 424 |
| $-3$ | $-155$ | 50 | 870 | $-9,479$ | $-101$ |
| $-2$ | $-170$ | 35 | 1,285 | $-7,304$ | $-584$ |
| $-1$ | $-179$ | 18 | 1,548 | $-3,960$ | $-920$ |
| 0 | $-182$ | 0 | 1,638 | 0 | $-1,040$ |
| 1,638 | | 101,790 | | 2,032,135,560 | |
| | 712,530 | | 56,448,210 | | 22,331,160 |
| 1 | 3 | $\frac{1}{6}$ | $\frac{7}{12}$ | $\frac{21}{40}$ | $\frac{1}{120}$ |

### $n = 28$

| $\phi_1$ | $\phi_2$ | $\phi_3$ | $\phi_4$ | $\phi_5$ | $\phi_6$ |
|---|---|---|---|---|---|
| $-27$ | 117 | $-585$ | 1,755 | $-13,455$ | 13,455 |
| $-25$ | 91 | $-325$ | 455 | 1,495 | $-7,475$ |
| $-23$ | 67 | $-115$ | $-395$ | 8,395 | $-12,305$ |
| $-21$ | 45 | 49 | $-879$ | 9,821 | $-8,763$ |
| $-19$ | 25 | 171 | $-1,074$ | 7,866 | $-2,162$ |
| $-17$ | 7 | 255 | $-1,050$ | 4,182 | 4,138 |
| $-15$ | $-9$ | 305 | $-870$ | 22 | 8,310 |
| $-13$ | $-23$ | 325 | $-590$ | $-3,718$ | 9,682 |
| $-11$ | $-35$ | 319 | $-259$ | $-6,457$ | 8,401 |
| $-9$ | $-45$ | 291 | 81 | $-7,887$ | 5,139 |
| $-7$ | $-53$ | 245 | 395 | $-7,931$ | 841 |
| $-5$ | $-59$ | 185 | 655 | $-6,701$ | $-3,485$ |
| $-3$ | $-63$ | 115 | 840 | $-4,456$ | $-6,936$ |
| $-1$ | $-65$ | 39 | 936 | $-1,560$ | $-8,840$ |
| 7,308 | | 2,103,660 | | 1,354,757,040 | |
| | 95,004 | | 19,634,160 | | 1,771,605,360 |
| 2 | 1 | $\frac{2}{3}$ | $\frac{7}{24}$ | $\frac{7}{20}$ | $\frac{7}{120}$ |

Table 47. *Orthogonal polynomials (continued)*

### n = 29

| $\phi_1$ | $\phi_2$ | $\phi_3$ | $\phi_4$ | $\phi_5$ | $\phi_6$ |
|---:|---:|---:|---:|---:|---:|
| −14 | 126 | −819 | 4,095 | −8,190 | 26,910 |
| −13 | 99 | −468 | 1,170 | 585 | −13,455 |
| −12 | 74 | −182 | − 780 | 4,810 | −23,920 |
| −11 | 51 | 44 | −1,930 | 5,885 | −18,285 |
| −10 | 30 | 215 | −2,441 | 4,958 | − 6,210 |
| − 9 | 11 | 336 | −2,460 | 2,946 | 6,026 |
| − 8 | − 6 | 412 | −2,120 | 556 | 14,832 |
| − 7 | − 21 | 448 | −1,540 | −1,694 | 18,678 |
| − 6 | − 34 | 449 | − 825 | −3,454 | 17,534 |
| − 5 | − 45 | 420 | − 66 | −4,521 | 12,375 |
| − 4 | − 54 | 366 | 660 | −4,818 | 4,752 |
| − 3 | − 61 | 292 | 1,290 | −4,373 | − 3,571 |
| − 2 | − 66 | 203 | 1,775 | −3,298 | −10,914 |
| − 1 | − 69 | 104 | 2,080 | −1,768 | −15,912 |
| 0 | − 70 | 0 | 2,184 | 0 | −17,680 |
| 2,030 | 113,274 | 4,207,320 | 107,987,880 | 500,671,080 | 6,959,878,200 |
| 1 | 1 | $\frac{5}{6}$ | $\frac{7}{12}$ | $\frac{7}{40}$ | $\frac{11}{120}$ |

### n = 30

| $\phi_1$ | $\phi_2$ | $\phi_3$ | $\phi_4$ | $\phi_5$ | $\phi_6$ |
|---:|---:|---:|---:|---:|---:|
| −29 | 203 | −1,827 | 23,751 | −16,965 | 5,655 |
| −27 | 161 | −1,071 | 7,371 | 585 | −2,535 |
| −25 | 122 | − 450 | − 3,744 | 9,360 | −4,875 |
| −23 | 86 | 46 | −10,504 | 11,960 | −3,965 |
| −21 | 53 | 427 | −13,749 | 10,535 | −1,655 |
| −19 | 23 | 703 | −14,249 | 6,821 | 823 |
| −17 | − 4 | 884 | −12,704 | 2,176 | 2,734 |
| −15 | − 28 | 980 | − 9,744 | − 2,384 | 3,730 |
| −13 | − 49 | 1,001 | − 5,929 | − 6,149 | 3,751 |
| −11 | − 67 | 957 | − 1,749 | − 8,679 | 2,937 |
| − 9 | − 82 | 858 | 2,376 | − 9,768 | 1,551 |
| − 7 | − 94 | 714 | 6,096 | − 9,408 | − 87 |
| − 5 | −103 | 535 | 9,131 | − 7,753 | −1,655 |
| − 3 | −109 | 331 | 11,271 | − 5,083 | −2,873 |
| − 1 | −112 | 112 | 12,376 | − 1,768 | −3,536 |
| 8,990 | 302,064 | 21,360,240 | 3,671,587,920 | 2,145,733,200 | 302,603,400 |
| 2 | $\frac{3}{2}$ | $\frac{5}{3}$ | $\frac{35}{12}$ | $\frac{3}{10}$ | $\frac{11}{720}$ |

### n = 52

| $\phi_1$ | $\phi_2$ | $\phi_3$ | $\phi_4$ | $\phi_5$ | $\phi_6$ |
|---:|---:|---:|---:|---:|---:|
| −51 | 425 | −4,165 | 3,570 | −55,930 | 1,286,390 |
| −49 | 375 | −3,185 | 2,170 | −23,030 | 227,010 |
| −47 | 327 | −2,303 | 1,022 | 658 | −408,618 |
| −45 | 281 | −1,515 | 102 | 16,638 | −724,270 |
| −43 | 237 | − 817 | − 613 | 26,273 | −807,507 |
| −41 | 195 | − 205 | −1,145 | 30,791 | −731,193 |
| −39 | 155 | 325 | −1,515 | 31,291 | −554,947 |
| −37 | 117 | 777 | −1,743 | 28,749 | −326,529 |
| −35 | 81 | 1,155 | −1,848 | 24,024 | − 83,160 |
| −33 | 47 | 1,463 | −1,848 | 17,864 | 147,224 |
| −31 | 15 | 1,705 | −1,760 | 10,912 | 344,784 |
| −29 | − 15 | 1,885 | −1,600 | 3,712 | 496,656 |
| −27 | − 43 | 2,007 | −1,383 | − 3,285 | 595,895 |
| −25 | − 69 | 2,075 | −1,123 | − 9,715 | 640,485 |
| −23 | − 93 | 2,093 | − 833 | −15,295 | 632,415 |
| −21 | −115 | 2,065 | − 525 | −19,817 | 576,821 |
| −19 | −135 | 1,995 | − 210 | −23,142 | 481,194 |
| −17 | −153 | 1,887 | 102 | −25,194 | 354,654 |
| −15 | −169 | 1,745 | 402 | −25,954 | 207,290 |
| −13 | −183 | 1,573 | 682 | −25,454 | 49,566 |
| −11 | −195 | 1,375 | 935 | −23,771 | −108,207 |
| − 9 | −205 | 1,155 | 1,155 | −21,021 | −256,333 |
| − 7 | −213 | 917 | 1,337 | −17,353 | −386,127 |
| − 5 | −219 | 665 | 1,477 | −12,943 | −490,245 |
| − 3 | −223 | 403 | 1,572 | − 7,988 | −562,948 |
| − 1 | −225 | 135 | 1,620 | − 2,700 | −600,300 |
| 46,852 | 2,108,340 | 162,342,180 | 108,228,120 | 26,358,466,680 | 14,876,313,079,320 |
| 2 | 1 | $\frac{2}{3}$ | $\frac{1}{24}$ | $\frac{1}{20}$ | $\frac{11}{120}$ |

### n = 51

| $\phi_1$ | $\phi_2$ | $\phi_3$ | $\phi_4$ | $\phi_5$ | $\phi_6$ |
|---:|---:|---:|---:|---:|---:|
| −25 | 1,225 | −4,900 | 46,060 | −75,670 | 378,350 |
| −24 | 1,078 | −3,724 | 27,636 | −30,268 | 60,536 |
| −23 | 937 | −2,668 | 12,596 | 2,162 | −127,558 |
| −22 | 802 | −1,727 | 611 | 23,782 | −218,362 |
| −21 | 673 | − 896 | − 8,634 | 36,547 | −239,131 |
| −20 | 550 | − 170 | −15,440 | 42,214 | −212,440 |
| −19 | 433 | 456 | −20,094 | 42,351 | −156,657 |
| −18 | 322 | 987 | −22,869 | 38,346 | − 86,394 |
| −17 | 217 | 1,428 | −24,024 | 31,416 | − 12,936 |
| −16 | 118 | 1,784 | −23,804 | 22,616 | 55,352 |
| −15 | 25 | 2,060 | −22,440 | 12,848 | 112,640 |
| −14 | − 62 | 2,261 | −20,149 | 2,870 | 155,270 |
| −13 | −143 | 2,392 | −17,134 | − 6,695 | 181,415 |
| −12 | −218 | 2,458 | −13,584 | −15,350 | 190,760 |
| −11 | −287 | 2,464 | − 9,674 | −22,715 | 184,205 |
| −10 | −350 | 2,415 | − 5,565 | −28,518 | 163,590 |
| − 9 | −407 | 2,316 | − 1,404 | −32,586 | 131,442 |
| − 8 | −458 | 2,172 | 2,676 | −34,836 | 90,744 |
| − 7 | −503 | 1,988 | 6,556 | −35,266 | 44,726 |
| − 6 | −542 | 1,769 | 10,131 | −33,946 | − 3,322 |
| − 5 | −575 | 1,520 | 13,310 | −31,009 | − 50,215 |
| − 4 | −602 | 1,246 | 16,016 | −26,642 | − 93,016 |
| − 3 | −623 | 952 | 18,186 | −21,077 | −129,157 |
| − 2 | −638 | 643 | 19,771 | −14,582 | −156,538 |
| − 1 | −647 | 324 | 20,736 | − 7,452 | −173,604 |
| 0 | −650 | 0 | 21,060 | 0 | −179,400 |
| 11,050 | 17,218,110 | 221,375,700 | 17,803,525,740 | 47,861,426,340 | 1,282,440,782,700 |
| 1 | 3 | $\frac{5}{6}$ | $\frac{7}{12}$ | $\frac{3}{40}$ | $\frac{11}{360}$ |

Table 47 (*continued*)

## n = 31

| $\phi_1$ | $\phi_2$ | $\phi_3$ | $\phi_4$ | $\phi_5$ | $\phi_6$ |
|---|---|---|---|---|---|
| −15 | 145 | −1,015 | 783 | −1,131 | 28,275 |
| −14 | 116 | −609 | 261 | 0 | −11,310 |
| −13 | 89 | −273 | −99 | 585 | −23,595 |
| −12 | 64 | −2 | −324 | 780 | −20,280 |
| −11 | 41 | 209 | −439 | 715 | −9,815 |
| −10 | 20 | 365 | −467 | 496 | 2,050 |
| −9 | 1 | 471 | −429 | 207 | 11,759 |
| −8 | −16 | 532 | −344 | −88 | 17,488 |
| −7 | −31 | 553 | −229 | −343 | 18,727 |
| −6 | −44 | 539 | −99 | −528 | 15,906 |
| −5 | −55 | 495 | 33 | −627 | 10,065 |
| −4 | −64 | 426 | 156 | −636 | 2,568 |
| −3 | −71 | 337 | 261 | −561 | −5,139 |
| −2 | −76 | 233 | 341 | −416 | −11,726 |
| −1 | −79 | 119 | 391 | −221 | −16,133 |
| 0 | −80 | 0 | 408 | 0 | −17,680 |
| 2,480 | | 6,724,520 | | 9,536,592 | |
| | 158,224 | | 4,034,712 | | 7,464,217,200 |
| 1 | 1 | 5/6 | 7/12 | 7/60 | 11/180 |

## n = 32

| $\phi_1$ | $\phi_2$ | $\phi_3$ | $\phi_4$ | $\phi_5$ | $\phi_6$ |
|---|---|---|---|---|---|
| −31 | 155 | −899 | 899 | −2,697 | 35,061 |
| −29 | 125 | −551 | 319 | −87 | −12,441 |
| −27 | 97 | −261 | −87 | 1,305 | −28,275 |
| −25 | 71 | −25 | −347 | 1,815 | −25,545 |
| −23 | 47 | 161 | −487 | 1,725 | −13,845 |
| −21 | 25 | 301 | −531 | 1,267 | 169 |
| −19 | 5 | 399 | −501 | 627 | 12,251 |
| −17 | −13 | 459 | −417 | −51 | 20,081 |
| −15 | −29 | 485 | −297 | −661 | 22,825 |
| −13 | −43 | 481 | −157 | −1,131 | 20,739 |
| −11 | −55 | 451 | −11 | −1,419 | 14,817 |
| −9 | −65 | 399 | 129 | −1,509 | 6,483 |
| −7 | −73 | 329 | 253 | −1,407 | −2,673 |
| −5 | −79 | 245 | 353 | −1,137 | −11,115 |
| −3 | −83 | 151 | 423 | −737 | −17,537 |
| −1 | −85 | 51 | 459 | −255 | −20,995 |
| 10,912 | | 5,379,616 | | 54,285,216 | |
| | 185,504 | | 5,379,616 | | 11,345,610,144 |
| 2 | 1 | 2/3 | 7/12 | 1/30 | 11/180 |

## n = 50

| $\phi_1$ | $\phi_2$ | $\phi_3$ | $\phi_4$ | $\phi_5$ | $\phi_6$ |
|---|---|---|---|---|---|
| −49 | 196 | −9,212 | 211,876 | −211,876 | 15,134 |
| −47 | 172 | −6,956 | 125,396 | −82,156 | 2,162 |
| −45 | 149 | −4,935 | 55,131 | 9,729 | −5,405 |
| −43 | 127 | −3,139 | −529 | 70,219 | −8,947 |
| −41 | 106 | −1,558 | −43,124 | 105,124 | −9,619 |
| −39 | 86 | −182 | −74,124 | 119,652 | −8,373 |
| −37 | 67 | 999 | −94,929 | 118,437 | −5,979 |
| −35 | 49 | 1,995 | −106,869 | 105,567 | −3,045 |
| −33 | 32 | 2,816 | −111,204 | 84,612 | −36 |
| −31 | 16 | 3,472 | −109,124 | 58,652 | 2,708 |
| −29 | 1 | 3,973 | −101,749 | 30,305 | 4,955 |
| −27 | −13 | 4,329 | −90,129 | 1,755 | 6,565 |
| −25 | −26 | 4,550 | −75,244 | −25,220 | 7,475 |
| −23 | −38 | 4,646 | −58,004 | −49,220 | 7,685 |
| −21 | −49 | 4,627 | −39,249 | −69,195 | 7,245 |
| −19 | −59 | 4,503 | −19,749 | −84,417 | 6,243 |
| −17 | −68 | 4,284 | −204 | −94,452 | 4,794 |
| −15 | −76 | 3,980 | 18,756 | −99,132 | 3,030 |
| −13 | −83 | 3,601 | 36,571 | −98,527 | 1,091 |
| −11 | −89 | 3,157 | 52,751 | −92,917 | −883 |
| −9 | −94 | 2,658 | 66,876 | −82,764 | −2,759 |
| −7 | −98 | 2,114 | 78,596 | −68,684 | −4,417 |
| −5 | −101 | 1,535 | 87,631 | −51,419 | −5,755 |
| −3 | −103 | 931 | 93,771 | −31,809 | −6,693 |
| −1 | −104 | 312 | 96,876 | −10,764 | −7,176 |
| 41,650 | | 770,715,400 | | 372,255,538,200 | |
| | 433,160 | | 372,255,538,200 | | 2,045,360,100 |
| 2 | 1/2 | 5/3 | 35/12 | 7/30 | 1/720 |

## n = 49

| $\phi_1$ | $\phi_2$ | $\phi_3$ | $\phi_4$ | $\phi_5$ | $\phi_6$ |
|---|---|---|---|---|---|
| −24 | 376 | −4,324 | 38,916 | −95,128 | 371,864 |
| −23 | 329 | −3,243 | 22,701 | −35,673 | 46,483 |
| −22 | 284 | −2,277 | 9,591 | 6,072 | −140,438 |
| −21 | 241 | −1,421 | −729 | 33,187 | −225,019 |
| −20 | 200 | −670 | −8,560 | 48,444 | −237,360 |
| −19 | 161 | −19 | −14,189 | 54,321 | −202,143 |
| −18 | 124 | 537 | −17,889 | 53,016 | −139,206 |
| −17 | 89 | 1,003 | −19,919 | 46,461 | −64,089 |
| −16 | 56 | 1,384 | −20,524 | 36,336 | 11,448 |
| −15 | 25 | 1,685 | −19,935 | 24,083 | 78,935 |
| −14 | −4 | 1,911 | −18,369 | 10,920 | 132,730 |
| −13 | −31 | 2,067 | −16,029 | −2,145 | 169,585 |
| −12 | −56 | 2,158 | −13,104 | −14,300 | 188,240 |
| −11 | −79 | 2,189 | −9,769 | −24,915 | 189,045 |
| −10 | −100 | 2,165 | −6,185 | −33,528 | 173,610 |
| −9 | −119 | 2,091 | −2,499 | −39,831 | 144,483 |
| −8 | −136 | 1,972 | 1,156 | −43,656 | 104,856 |
| −7 | −151 | 1,813 | 4,661 | −44,961 | 58,299 |
| −6 | −164 | 1,619 | 7,911 | −43,816 | 8,522 |
| −5 | −175 | 1,395 | 10,815 | −40,389 | −40,835 |
| −4 | −184 | 1,146 | 13,296 | −34,932 | −86,384 |
| −3 | −191 | 877 | 15,291 | −27,767 | −125,143 |
| −2 | −196 | 593 | 16,751 | −19,272 | −154,662 |
| −1 | −199 | 299 | 17,641 | −9,867 | −173,121 |
| 0 | −200 | 0 | 17,940 | 0 | −179,400 |
| 9,800 | | 167,230,700 | | 74,451,107,640 | |
| | 1,566,040 | | 12,408,517,940 | | 1,231,306,780,200 |
| 1 | 1 | 5/3 | 7/12 | 7/60 | 7/180 |

## Table 47. *Orthogonal polynomials (continued)*

### n = 33

| $\phi_1$ | $\phi_2$ | $\phi_3$ | $\phi_4$ | $\phi_5$ | $\phi_6$ |
|---|---|---|---|---|---|
| −16 | 496 | −248 | 7,192 | −14,384 | 43,152 |
| −15 | 403 | −155 | 2,697 | −899 | −13,485 |
| −14 | 316 | −77 | −493 | 6,496 | −33,582 |
| −13 | 235 | −13 | −2,581 | 9,425 | −31,755 |
| −12 | 160 | 38 | −3,756 | 9,260 | −13,840 |
| −11 | 91 | 77 | −4,193 | 7,139 | −2,487 |
| −10 | 28 | 105 | −4,053 | 3,984 | 12,290 |
| −9 | −29 | 123 | −3,483 | 519 | 22,607 |
| −8 | −80 | 132 | −2,616 | −2,712 | 27,248 |
| −7 | −125 | 133 | −1,571 | −5,327 | 26,247 |
| −6 | −164 | 127 | −453 | −7,088 | 20,514 |
| −5 | −197 | 115 | 647 | −7,883 | 11,505 |
| −4 | −224 | 98 | 1,652 | −7,708 | 936 |
| −3 | −245 | 77 | 2,499 | −6,649 | −9,459 |
| −2 | −260 | 53 | 3,139 | −4,864 | −18,126 |
| −1 | −269 | 27 | 3,537 | −2,565 | −23,845 |
| 0 | −272 | 0 | 3,672 | 0 | −25,840 |
| 2,992 | | 417,384 | | 1,547,128,656 | |
| | 1,947,792 | | 348,330,136 | | 17,018,415,216 |
| 1 | 3 | $\frac{1}{6}$ | $\frac{7}{12}$ | $\frac{3}{20}$ | $\frac{11}{180}$ |

### n = 34

| $\phi_1$ | $\phi_2$ | $\phi_3$ | $\phi_4$ | $\phi_5$ | $\phi_6$ |
|---|---|---|---|---|---|
| −33 | 88 | −2,728 | 8,184 | −79,112 | 39,556 |
| −31 | 72 | −1,736 | 3,224 | −7,192 | −10,788 |
| −29 | 57 | 899 | −341 | 33,263 | −29,667 |
| −27 | 43 | −207 | −2,721 | 50,373 | −29,261 |
| −25 | 30 | 350 | −4,112 | 51,040 | −18,705 |
| −23 | 18 | 782 | −4,696 | 41,032 | −4,551 |
| −21 | 7 | 1,099 | −4,641 | 25,067 | 8,803 |
| −19 | −3 | 1,311 | −4,101 | 6,897 | 18,717 |
| −17 | −12 | 1,428 | −3,216 | −10,608 | 23,946 |
| −15 | −20 | 1,460 | −2,112 | −25,376 | 24,310 |
| −13 | −27 | 1,417 | −901 | −36,049 | 20,397 |
| −11 | −33 | 1,309 | 319 | −41,899 | 13,299 |
| −9 | −38 | 1,146 | 1,464 | −42,744 | 4,381 |
| −7 | −42 | 938 | 2,464 | −38,864 | −4,917 |
| −5 | −45 | 695 | 3,263 | −30,917 | −13,245 |
| −3 | −47 | 427 | 3,819 | −19,855 | −19,475 |
| −1 | −48 | 144 | 4,104 | −6,840 | −22,800 |
| 13,090 | | 51,477,360 | | 46,929,569,232 | |
| | 62,832 | | 456,432,592 | | 14,182,012,680 |
| 2 | $\frac{1}{2}$ | $\frac{5}{3}$ | $\frac{7}{12}$ | $\frac{7}{10}$ | $\frac{11}{240}$ |

### n = 48

| $\phi_1$ | $\phi_2$ | $\phi_3$ | $\phi_4$ | $\phi_5$ | $\phi_6$ |
|---|---|---|---|---|---|
| −47 | 1,081 | −3,243 | 35,673 | −1,533,939 | 511,313 |
| −45 | 943 | −2,415 | 20,493 | −554,829 | 54,395 |
| −43 | 811 | −1,677 | 8,283 | 126,291 | −203,863 |
| −41 | 685 | −1,025 | −1,265 | 562,397 | −316,437 |
| −39 | 565 | −455 | −8,445 | 801,047 | −327,273 |
| −37 | 451 | 37 | −13,537 | 884,633 | −272,211 |
| −35 | 343 | 455 | −16,807 | 850,633 | −179,865 |
| −33 | 241 | 803 | −18,507 | 731,863 | −72,459 |
| −31 | 145 | 1,085 | −18,875 | 556,729 | 33,381 |
| −29 | 55 | 1,305 | −18,135 | 349,479 | 125,879 |
| −27 | −29 | 1,467 | −16,497 | 130,455 | 197,405 |
| −25 | −107 | 1,575 | −14,157 | −83,655 | 243,815 |
| −23 | −179 | 1,633 | −11,297 | −279,565 | 263,835 |
| −21 | −245 | 1,645 | −8,085 | −447,139 | 258,489 |
| −19 | −305 | 1,615 | −4,675 | −579,139 | 230,571 |
| −17 | −359 | 1,547 | −1,207 | −670,973 | 184,161 |
| −15 | −407 | 1,445 | 2,193 | −720,443 | 124,185 |
| −13 | −449 | 1,313 | 5,413 | −727,493 | 56,019 |
| −11 | −485 | 1,155 | 8,355 | −693,957 | −14,863 |
| −9 | −515 | 975 | 10,935 | −623,307 | −83,197 |
| −7 | −539 | 777 | 13,083 | −520,401 | −144,193 |
| −5 | −557 | 565 | 14,743 | −391,231 | −193,755 |
| −3 | −569 | 343 | 15,873 | −242,671 | −228,657 |
| −1 | −575 | 115 | 16,445 | −82,225 | −246,675 |
| 36,848 | | 92,620,080 | | 19,208,385,771,120 | |
| | 12,712,560 | | 10,301,411,120 | | 2,321,892,785,520 |
| 2 | 3 | $\frac{2}{3}$ | $\frac{7}{12}$ | $\frac{21}{10}$ | $\frac{11}{180}$ |

### n = 47

| $\phi_1$ | $\phi_2$ | $\phi_3$ | $\phi_4$ | $\phi_5$ | $\phi_6$ |
|---|---|---|---|---|---|
| −23 | 345 | −759 | 32,637 | −32,637 | 1,338,117 |
| −22 | 300 | −561 | 18,447 | −11,352 | 116,358 |
| −21 | 257 | −385 | 7,095 | 3,311 | −562,397 |
| −20 | 216 | −230 | −1,720 | 12,556 | −846,240 |
| −19 | 177 | −95 | −8,285 | 17,461 | −857,433 |
| −18 | 140 | 21 | −12,873 | 18,984 | −695,114 |
| −17 | 105 | 119 | −15,743 | 17,969 | −437,871 |
| −16 | 72 | 200 | −17,140 | 15,152 | −146,184 |
| −15 | 41 | 265 | −17,295 | 11,167 | 135,265 |
| −14 | 12 | 315 | −16,425 | 6,552 | 375,414 |
| −13 | −15 | 351 | −14,733 | 1,755 | 554,775 |
| −12 | −40 | 374 | −12,408 | −2,860 | 663,520 |
| −11 | −63 | 385 | −9,625 | −7,007 | 699,699 |
| −10 | −84 | 385 | −6,545 | −10,472 | 667,590 |
| −9 | −103 | 375 | −3,315 | −13,107 | 576,181 |
| −8 | −120 | 356 | −68 | −14,824 | 437,784 |
| −7 | −135 | 329 | 3,077 | −15,589 | 266,781 |
| −6 | −148 | 295 | 6,015 | −15,416 | 78,502 |
| −5 | −159 | 255 | 8,655 | −14,361 | −111,765 |
| −4 | −168 | 210 | 10,920 | −12,516 | −289,632 |
| −3 | −175 | 161 | 12,747 | −10,003 | −442,337 |
| −2 | −180 | 109 | 14,087 | −6,968 | −559,338 |
| −1 | −183 | 55 | 14,905 | −3,575 | −632,775 |
| 0 | −184 | 0 | 15,180 | 0 | −657,800 |
| 8,648 | | 4,994,220 | | 8,629,104,120 | |
| | 1,271,256 | | 8,518,474,580 | | 15,866,267,367,720 |
| 1 | 1 | $\frac{1}{6}$ | $\frac{7}{12}$ | $\frac{1}{20}$ | $\frac{11}{60}$ |

Table 47 (*continued*)

### n = 35

| $\phi_1$ | $\phi_2$ | $\phi_3$ | $\phi_4$ | $\phi_5$ | $\phi_6$ |
|---|---|---|---|---|---|
| −17 | 187 | −1,496 | 46,376 | −23,188 | 672,452 |
| −16 | 154 | −968 | 19,096 | −2,728 | −158,224 |
| −15 | 123 | −520 | −744 | 9,052 | −485,460 |
| −14 | 94 | −147 | −14,229 | 14,322 | −498,046 |
| −13 | 67 | 156 | −22,374 | 14,937 | −339,097 |
| −12 | 42 | 394 | −26,124 | 12,458 | −112,752 |
| −11 | 19 | 572 | −26,354 | 8,173 | 109,589 |
| −10 | −2 | 695 | −23,869 | 3,118 | 283,490 |
| −9 | −21 | 768 | −19,404 | −1,902 | 386,166 |
| −8 | −38 | 796 | −13,624 | −6,292 | 411,632 |
| −7 | −53 | 784 | −7,124 | −9,646 | 366,314 |
| −6 | −66 | 737 | −429 | −11,726 | 265,122 |
| −5 | −77 | 660 | 6,006 | −12,441 | 127,985 |
| −4 | −86 | 558 | 11,796 | −11,826 | −23,152 |
| −3 | −93 | 436 | 16,626 | −10,021 | −166,869 |
| −2 | −98 | 299 | 20,251 | −7,250 | −284,350 |
| −1 | −101 | 152 | 22,496 | −3,800 | −361,000 |
| 0 | −102 | 0 | 23,256 | 0 | −387,600 |

3,570    15,775,320    4,045,652,520
290,598    14,834,059,240    4,070,237,639,160

| 1 | 1 | $\frac{5}{6}$ | $\frac{35}{12}$ | $\frac{7}{40}$ | $\frac{77}{120}$ |

### n = 36

| $\phi_1$ | $\phi_2$ | $\phi_3$ | $\phi_4$ | $\phi_5$ | $\phi_6$ |
|---|---|---|---|---|---|
| −35 | 595 | −6,545 | 5,236 | −162,316 | 115,940 |
| −33 | 493 | −4,301 | 2,244 | −23,188 | −23,188 |
| −31 | 397 | −2,387 | 44 | 58,652 | −80,476 |
| −29 | 307 | −783 | −1,476 | 97,092 | −85,684 |
| −27 | 223 | 531 | −2,421 | 104,067 | −61,597 |
| −25 | 145 | 1,575 | −2,889 | 89,685 | −25,015 |
| −23 | 73 | 2,369 | −2,971 | 62,353 | 12,323 |
| −21 | 7 | 2,933 | −2,751 | 28,903 | 42,881 |
| −19 | −53 | 3,287 | −2,306 | −5,282 | 62,534 |
| −17 | −107 | 3,451 | −1,706 | −36,142 | 69,842 |
| −15 | −155 | 3,445 | −1,014 | −60,814 | 65,390 |
| −13 | −197 | 3,289 | −286 | −77,506 | 51,194 |
| −11 | −233 | 3,003 | 429 | −85,371 | 30,173 |
| −9 | −263 | 2,607 | 1,089 | −84,381 | 5,687 |
| −7 | −287 | 2,121 | 1,659 | −75,201 | −18,859 |
| −5 | −305 | 1,565 | 2,111 | −59,063 | −40,345 |
| −3 | −317 | 959 | 2,424 | −37,640 | −56,200 |
| −1 | −323 | 323 | 2,584 | −12,920 | −64,600 |

15,540    307,618,740    199,046,103,984
3,011,652    191,407,216    120,302,590,320

| 2 | 3 | $\frac{10}{3}$ | $\frac{7}{24}$ | $\frac{21}{20}$ | $\frac{11}{120}$ |

### n = 46

| $\phi_1$ | $\phi_2$ | $\phi_3$ | $\phi_4$ | $\phi_5$ | $\phi_6$ |
|---|---|---|---|---|---|
| −45 | 165 | −7,095 | 4,257 | −58,179 | 290,895 |
| −43 | 143 | −5,203 | 2,365 | −19,393 | 19,393 |
| −41 | 122 | −3,526 | 860 | 7,052 | −128,699 |
| −39 | 102 | −2,054 | −300 | 23,452 | −187,821 |
| −37 | 83 | −777 | −1,155 | 31,857 | −186,263 |
| −35 | 65 | 315 | −1,743 | 34,083 | −146,825 |
| −33 | 48 | 1,232 | −2,100 | 31,724 | −87,444 |
| −31 | 32 | 1,984 | −2,260 | 26,164 | −21,788 |
| −29 | 17 | 2,581 | −2,255 | 18,589 | 40,183 |
| −27 | 3 | 3,033 | −2,115 | 9,999 | 91,689 |
| −25 | −10 | 3,350 | −1,868 | 1,220 | 128,635 |
| −23 | −22 | 3,542 | −1,540 | −7,084 | 149,149 |
| −21 | −33 | 3,619 | −1,155 | −14,399 | 153,153 |
| −19 | −43 | 3,591 | −735 | −20,349 | 141,967 |
| −17 | −52 | 3,468 | −300 | −24,684 | 117,946 |
| −15 | −60 | 3,260 | 132 | −27,268 | 84,150 |
| −13 | −67 | 2,977 | 545 | −28,067 | 44,047 |
| −11 | −73 | 2,629 | 925 | −27,137 | 1,249 |
| −9 | −78 | 2,226 | 1,260 | −24,612 | −40,719 |
| −7 | −82 | 1,778 | 1,540 | −20,692 | −78,617 |
| −5 | −85 | 1,295 | 1,757 | −15,631 | −109,655 |
| −3 | −87 | 787 | 1,905 | −9,725 | −131,625 |
| −1 | −88 | 264 | 1,980 | −3,300 | −143,000 |

32,430    429,502,920    27,214,866,840
285,384    143,167,640    748,408,838,100

| 2 | $\frac{1}{2}$ | $\frac{9}{2}$ | $\frac{1}{12}$ | $\frac{1}{10}$ | $\frac{11}{140}$ |

### n = 45

| $\phi_1$ | $\phi_2$ | $\phi_3$ | $\phi_4$ | $\phi_5$ | $\phi_6$ |
|---|---|---|---|---|---|
| −22 | 946 | −3,311 | 19,393 | −38,786 | 504,218 |
| −21 | 817 | −2,408 | 10,578 | −12,341 | 22,919 |
| −20 | 694 | −1,610 | 3,608 | 5,494 | −234,520 |
| −19 | 577 | −912 | −1,722 | 16,359 | −332,059 |
| −18 | 466 | −309 | −5,607 | 21,714 | −321,958 |
| −17 | 361 | 204 | −8,232 | 22,848 | −246,064 |
| −16 | 262 | 632 | −9,772 | 20,888 | −137,032 |
| −15 | 169 | 980 | −10,392 | 16,808 | −19,480 |
| −14 | 82 | 1,253 | −10,247 | 11,438 | 88,922 |
| −13 | 1 | 1,456 | −9,482 | 5,473 | 176,429 |
| −12 | −74 | 1,594 | −8,232 | −518 | 236,264 |
| −11 | −143 | 1,672 | −6,622 | −6,083 | 265,727 |
| −10 | −206 | 1,695 | −4,767 | −10,878 | 265,370 |
| −9 | −263 | 1,668 | −2,772 | −14,658 | 238,238 |
| −8 | −314 | 1,596 | −732 | −17,268 | 189,176 |
| −7 | −359 | 1,484 | 1,268 | −18,634 | 124,202 |
| −6 | −398 | 1,337 | 3,153 | −18,754 | 49,946 |
| −5 | −431 | 1,160 | 4,858 | −17,689 | −26,845 |
| −4 | −458 | 958 | 6,328 | −15,554 | −99,736 |
| −3 | −479 | 736 | 7,518 | −12,509 | −162,967 |
| −2 | −494 | 499 | 8,393 | −8,750 | −211,750 |
| −1 | −503 | 252 | 8,928 | −4,500 | −242,500 |
| 0 | −506 | 0 | 9,108 | 0 | −253,000 |

7,590    92,036,340    12,006,558,900
9,203,634    2,934,936,620    2,245,226,514,300

| 1 | 3 | $\frac{5}{6}$ | $\frac{5}{12}$ | $\frac{3}{40}$ | $\frac{11}{120}$ |

31-2

# Table 47. *Orthogonal polynomials (continued)*

### n = 37

| $\phi_1$ | $\phi_2$ | $\phi_3$ | $\phi_4$ | $\phi_5$ | $\phi_6$ |
|---|---|---|---|---|---|
| −18 | 210 | −357 | 11,781 | −4,488 | 139,128 |
| −17 | 175 | −238 | 5,236 | −748 | −23,188 |
| −16 | 142 | −136 | 374 | 1,496 | −92,752 |
| −15 | 111 | −50 | −3,036 | 2,596 | −102,300 |
| −14 | 82 | 21 | −5,211 | 2,856 | −77,128 |
| −13 | 55 | 78 | −6,354 | 2,535 | −36,115 |
| −12 | 30 | 122 | −6,654 | 1,850 | 7,320 |
| −11 | 7 | 154 | −6,286 | 979 | 44,327 |
| −10 | −14 | 175 | −5,411 | 64 | 69,800 |
| −9 | −33 | 186 | −4,176 | −786 | 81,618 |
| −8 | −50 | 188 | −2,714 | −1,492 | 79,952 |
| −7 | −65 | 182 | −1,144 | −2,002 | 66,638 |
| −6 | −78 | 169 | 429 | −2,288 | 44,616 |
| −5 | −89 | 150 | 1,914 | −2,343 | 17,435 |
| −4 | −98 | 126 | 3,234 | −2,178 | −11,176 |
| −3 | −105 | 98 | 4,326 | −1,819 | −37,671 |
| −2 | −110 | 67 | 5,141 | −1,304 | −58,984 |
| −1 | −113 | 34 | 5,644 | −680 | −72,760 |
| 0 | −114 | 0 | 5,814 | 0 | −77,520 |
| 4,218 | 383,838 | 932,178 | 980,961,982 | 152,877,192 | 172,433,712,792 |
| 1 | 1 | $\frac{1}{6}$ | $\frac{7}{12}$ | $\frac{1}{40}$ | $\frac{11}{120}$ |

### n = 38

| $\phi_1$ | $\phi_2$ | $\phi_3$ | $\phi_4$ | $\phi_5$ | $\phi_6$ |
|---|---|---|---|---|---|
| −37 | 111 | −777 | 1,887 | −20,757 | 7,548 |
| −35 | 93 | −525 | 867 | −3,927 | −1,020 |
| −33 | 76 | −308 | 102 | 6,358 | −4,828 |
| −31 | 60 | −124 | −442 | 11,594 | −5,508 |
| −29 | 45 | 29 | −797 | 13,079 | −4,332 |
| −27 | 31 | 153 | −993 | 11,925 | −2,260 |
| −25 | 18 | 250 | −1,058 | 9,070 | 15 |
| −23 | 6 | 322 | −1,018 | 5,290 | 2,025 |
| −21 | −5 | 371 | −897 | 1,211 | 3,488 |
| −19 | −15 | 399 | −717 | −2,679 | 4,272 |
| −17 | −24 | 408 | −498 | −6,018 | 4,362 |
| −15 | −32 | 400 | −258 | −8,558 | 3,830 |
| −13 | −39 | 377 | −13 | −10,153 | 2,808 |
| −11 | −45 | 341 | 223 | −10,747 | 1,464 |
| −9 | −50 | 294 | 438 | −10,362 | −19 |
| −7 | −54 | 238 | 622 | −9,086 | −1,461 |
| −5 | −57 | 175 | 767 | −7,061 | −2,700 |
| −3 | −59 | 107 | 867 | −4,471 | −3,604 |
| −1 | −60 | 36 | 918 | −1,530 | −4,080 |
| 18,278 | 109,668 | 4,496,388 | 25,479,532 | 3,286,859,628 | 505,670,712 |
| 2 | $\frac{1}{2}$ | $\frac{1}{3}$ | $\frac{1}{12}$ | $\frac{1}{10}$ | $\frac{1}{240}$ |

### n = 44

| $\phi_1$ | $\phi_2$ | $\phi_3$ | $\phi_4$ | $\phi_5$ | $\phi_6$ |
|---|---|---|---|---|---|
| −43 | 301 | −12,341 | 12,341 | −22,919 | 435,461 |
| −41 | 259 | −8,897 | 6,601 | −6,929 | 10,127 |
| −39 | 219 | −5,863 | 2,091 | 3,731 | −212,667 |
| −37 | 181 | −3,219 | −1,329 | 10,101 | −292,201 |
| −35 | 145 | −945 | −3,792 | 13,104 | −276,640 |
| −33 | 111 | 979 | −5,424 | 13,552 | −204,288 |
| −31 | 79 | 2,573 | −6,344 | 12,152 | −104,776 |
| −29 | 49 | 3,857 | −6,664 | 9,512 | −184 |
| −27 | 21 | 4,851 | −6,489 | 6,147 | 93,903 |
| −25 | −5 | 5,575 | −5,917 | 2,485 | 167,405 |
| −23 | −29 | 6,049 | −5,039 | −1,127 | 214,823 |
| −21 | −51 | 6,293 | −3,939 | −4,417 | 234,381 |
| −19 | −71 | 6,327 | −2,694 | −7,182 | 227,234 |
| −17 | −89 | 6,171 | −1,374 | −9,282 | 196,742 |
| −15 | −105 | 5,845 | −42 | −10,634 | 147,810 |
| −13 | −119 | 5,369 | 1,246 | −11,206 | 86,294 |
| −11 | −131 | 4,763 | 2,441 | −11,011 | 18,473 |
| −9 | −141 | 4,047 | 3,501 | −10,101 | −49,413 |
| −7 | −149 | 3,241 | 4,391 | −8,561 | −111,559 |
| −5 | −155 | 2,365 | 5,083 | −6,503 | −162,925 |
| −3 | −159 | 1,439 | 5,556 | −4,060 | −199,500 |
| −1 | −161 | 483 | 5,796 | −1,380 | −218,500 |
| 28,380 | 913,836 | 1,257,829,980 | 1,173,974,648 | 4,162,273,752 | 1,672,913,873,400 |
| 2 | 1 | $\frac{10}{3}$ | $\frac{7}{24}$ | $\frac{1}{20}$ | $\frac{11}{120}$ |

### n = 43

| $\phi_1$ | $\phi_2$ | $\phi_3$ | $\phi_4$ | $\phi_5$ | $\phi_6$ |
|---|---|---|---|---|---|
| −21 | 287 | −574 | 22,386 | −70,889 | 374,699 |
| −20 | 246 | −410 | 11,726 | −20,254 | 0 |
| −19 | 207 | −266 | 3,406 | 13,091 | −191,919 |
| −18 | 170 | −141 | −2,847 | 32,604 | −255,892 |
| −17 | 135 | −34 | −7,292 | 41,344 | −236,208 |
| −16 | 102 | 56 | −10,174 | 41,992 | −167,832 |
| −15 | 71 | 130 | −11,724 | 36,872 | −77,560 |
| −14 | 42 | 189 | −12,159 | 27,972 | 14,892 |
| −13 | 15 | 234 | −11,682 | 16,965 | 95,865 |
| −12 | −10 | 266 | −10,482 | 5,230 | 156,800 |
| −11 | −33 | 286 | −8,734 | −6,127 | 193,347 |
| −10 | −54 | 295 | −6,599 | −16,252 | 204,540 |
| −9 | −73 | 294 | −4,224 | −24,522 | 192,038 |
| −8 | −90 | 284 | −1,742 | −30,524 | 159,432 |
| −7 | −105 | 266 | 728 | −34,034 | 111,618 |
| −6 | −118 | 241 | 3,081 | −34,996 | 54,236 |
| −5 | −129 | 210 | 5,226 | −33,501 | −6,825 |
| −4 | −138 | 174 | 7,086 | −29,766 | −65,856 |
| −3 | −145 | 134 | 8,598 | −24,113 | −117,691 |
| −2 | −150 | 91 | 9,713 | −16,948 | −158,004 |
| −1 | −153 | 46 | 10,396 | −8,740 | −183,540 |
| 0 | −154 | 0 | 10,626 | 0 | −192,280 |
| 6,622 | 814,506 | 2,676,234 | 3,815,417,606 | 39,541,600,644 | 1,237,956,266,316 |
| 1 | 1 | $\frac{1}{6}$ | $\frac{7}{12}$ | $\frac{7}{40}$ | $\frac{11}{120}$ |

## Table 47 (*continued*)

### $n = 39$

| $\phi_1$ | $\phi_2$ | $\phi_3$ | $\phi_4$ | $\phi_5$ | $\phi_6$ |
|---|---|---|---|---|---|
| −19 | 703 | −2,109 | 2,109 | −35,853 | 11,951 |
| −18 | 592 | −1,443 | 999 | −7,548 | −1,258 |
| −17 | 487 | −867 | 159 | 10,047 | −7,327 |
| −16 | 388 | −376 | −446 | 19,312 | −8,636 |
| −15 | 295 | 35 | −849 | 22,321 | −7,055 |
| −14 | 208 | 371 | −1,081 | 20,860 | −4,010 |
| −13 | 127 | 637 | −1,171 | 16,445 | −545 |
| −12 | 52 | 838 | −1,146 | 10,340 | 2,620 |
| −11 | −17 | 979 | −1,031 | 3,575 | 5,035 |
| −10 | −80 | 1,065 | −849 | −3,036 | 6,470 |
| −9 | −137 | 1,101 | −621 | −8,877 | 6,869 |
| −8 | −188 | 1,092 | −366 | −13,512 | 6,308 |
| −7 | −233 | 1,043 | −101 | −16,667 | 4,957 |
| −6 | −272 | 959 | 159 | −18,212 | 3,046 |
| −5 | −305 | 845 | 401 | −18,143 | 835 |
| −4 | −332 | 706 | 614 | −16,564 | −1,412 |
| −3 | −353 | 547 | 789 | −13,669 | −3,449 |
| −2 | −368 | 373 | 919 | −9,724 | −5,066 |
| −1 | −377 | 189 | 999 | −5,049 | −6,103 |
| 0 | −380 | 0 | 1,026 | 0 | −6,460 |

| 4,940 | | 33,722,910 | | 9,860,578,884 | |
| | 4,496,388 | | 32,224,114 | | 1,264,176,780 |

| 1 | 3 | $\frac{5}{6}$ | $\frac{1}{12}$ | $\frac{3}{20}$ | $\frac{1}{180}$ |

### $n = 40$

| $\phi_1$ | $\phi_2$ | $\phi_3$ | $\phi_4$ | $\phi_5$ | $\phi_6$ |
|---|---|---|---|---|---|
| −39 | 247 | −9,139 | 82,251 | −9,139 | 155,363 |
| −37 | 209 | −6,327 | 40,071 | −2,109 | −11,951 |
| −35 | 173 | −3,885 | 7,881 | 2,331 | −91,205 |
| −33 | 139 | −1,793 | −15,579 | 4,741 | −110,959 |
| −31 | 107 | −31 | −31,499 | 5,611 | −93,823 |
| −29 | 77 | 1,421 | −40,999 | 5,365 | −57,205 |
| −27 | 49 | 2,583 | −45,129 | 4,365 | −14,015 |
| −25 | 23 | 3,475 | −44,869 | 2,915 | 26,675 |
| −23 | −1 | 4,117 | −41,129 | 1,265 | 59,015 |
| −21 | −23 | 4,529 | −34,749 | −385 | 79,805 |
| −19 | −43 | 4,731 | −26,499 | −1,881 | 87,967 |
| −17 | −61 | 4,743 | −17,079 | −3,111 | 84,061 |
| −15 | −77 | 4,585 | −7,119 | −4,001 | 69,845 |
| −13 | −91 | 4,277 | 2,821 | −4,511 | 47,879 |
| −11 | −103 | 3,839 | 12,251 | −4,631 | 21,173 |
| −9 | −113 | 3,291 | 20,751 | −4,377 | −7,121 |
| −7 | −121 | 2,653 | 27,971 | −3,787 | −33,973 |
| −5 | −127 | 1,945 | 33,631 | −2,917 | −56,695 |
| −3 | −131 | 1,187 | 37,521 | −1,837 | −73,117 |
| −1 | −133 | 399 | 39,501 | −627 | −81,719 |

| 21,320 | | 644,482,280 | | 644,482,280 | |
| | 567,112 | | 49,625,135,560 | | 213,224,483,560 |

| 2 | 1 | $\frac{10}{3}$ | $\frac{35}{12}$ | $\frac{1}{30}$ | $\frac{11}{180}$ |

### $n = 42$

| $\phi_1$ | $\phi_2$ | $\phi_3$ | $\phi_4$ | $\phi_5$ | $\phi_6$ |
|---|---|---|---|---|---|
| −41 | 410 | −1,066 | 20,254 | −749,398 | 374,699 |
| −39 | 350 | −754 | 10,374 | −201,058 | −9,139 |
| −37 | 293 | −481 | 2,717 | 155,363 | −201,058 |
| −35 | 239 | −245 | −2,983 | 359,233 | −260,110 |
| −33 | 188 | −44 | −6,978 | 445,258 | −233,692 |
| −31 | 140 | 124 | −9,506 | 443,734 | −158,932 |
| −29 | 95 | 261 | −10,791 | 380,799 | −63,998 |
| −27 | 53 | 369 | −11,043 | 278,685 | 30,670 |
| −25 | 14 | 450 | −10,458 | 155,970 | 111,205 |
| −23 | −22 | 506 | −9,218 | 27,830 | 169,235 |
| −21 | −55 | 539 | −7,491 | −93,709 | 200,882 |
| −19 | −85 | 551 | −5,431 | −199,519 | 205,838 |
| −17 | −112 | 544 | −3,178 | −283,118 | 186,518 |
| −15 | −136 | 520 | −858 | −340,418 | 147,290 |
| −13 | −157 | 481 | 1,417 | −369,473 | 93,782 |
| −11 | −175 | 429 | 3,549 | −370,227 | 32,266 |
| −9 | −190 | 366 | 5,454 | −344,262 | −30,881 |
| −7 | −202 | 294 | 7,062 | −294,546 | −89,639 |
| −5 | −211 | 215 | 8,317 | −225,181 | −138,730 |
| −3 | −217 | 131 | 9,177 | −141,151 | −173,926 |
| −1 | −220 | 44 | 9,614 | −48,070 | −192,280 |

| 24,682 | | 9,075,924 | | 4,389,117,671,484 | |
| | 1,629,012 | | 3,084,805,724 | | 1,237,956,266,316 |

| 2 | $\frac{3}{2}$ | $\frac{1}{2}$ | $\frac{7}{12}$ | $\frac{21}{10}$ | $\frac{77}{120}$ |

### $n = 41$

| $\phi_1$ | $\phi_2$ | $\phi_3$ | $\phi_4$ | $\phi_5$ | $\phi_6$ |
|---|---|---|---|---|---|
| −20 | 260 | −2,470 | 18,278 | −36,556 | 182,780 |
| −19 | 221 | −1,729 | 9,139 | −9,139 | −9,139 |
| −18 | 184 | −1,083 | 2,109 | 8,436 | −102,638 |
| −17 | 149 | −527 | −3,071 | 18,241 | −128,797 |
| −16 | 116 | −56 | −6,646 | 22,096 | −112,396 |
| −15 | 85 | 335 | −8,847 | 21,583 | −72,685 |
| −14 | 56 | 651 | −9,891 | 18,060 | −24,110 |
| −13 | 29 | 897 | −9,981 | 12,675 | 23,005 |
| −12 | 4 | 1,078 | −9,306 | 6,380 | 61,820 |
| −11 | −19 | 1,199 | −8,041 | −55 | 88,385 |
| −10 | −40 | 1,265 | −6,347 | −6,028 | 101,090 |
| −9 | −59 | 1,281 | −4,371 | −11,091 | 100,159 |
| −8 | −76 | 1,252 | −2,246 | −14,936 | 87,188 |
| −7 | −91 | 1,183 | −91 | −17,381 | 64,727 |
| −6 | −104 | 1,079 | 1,989 | −18,356 | 35,906 |
| −5 | −115 | 945 | 3,903 | −17,889 | 4,105 |
| −4 | −124 | 786 | 5,574 | −16,092 | −27,332 |
| −3 | −131 | 607 | 6,939 | −13,147 | −55,339 |
| −2 | −136 | 413 | 7,949 | −9,292 | −77,326 |
| −1 | −139 | 209 | 8,569 | −4,807 | −91,333 |
| 0 | −140 | 0 | 8,778 | 0 | −96,140 |

| 5,740 | | 47,900,710 | | 10,376,164,708 | |
| | 641,732 | | 2,481,256,778 | | 294,751,491,980 |

| 1 | 1 | $\frac{5}{6}$ | $\frac{7}{12}$ | $\frac{7}{60}$ | $\frac{11}{180}$ |

Table 48. *Powers of integers*

| $n$ | $n^2$ | $n^3$ | $n^4$ | $n^5$ | $n^6$ | $n^7$ | $n$ |
|---|---|---|---|---|---|---|---|
| 1 | 1 | 1 | 1 | 1 | 1 | 1 | 1 |
| 2 | 4 | 8 | 16 | 32 | 64 | 128 | 2 |
| 3 | 9 | 27 | 81 | 243 | 729 | 2187 | 3 |
| 4 | 16 | 64 | 256 | 1024 | 4096 | 16384 | 4 |
| 5 | 25 | 125 | 625 | 3125 | 15625 | 78125 | 5 |
| 6 | 36 | 216 | 1296 | 7776 | 46656 | 279936 | 6 |
| 7 | 49 | 343 | 2401 | 16807 | 117649 | 823543 | 7 |
| 8 | 64 | 512 | 4096 | 32768 | 262144 | 2097152 | 8 |
| 9 | 81 | 729 | 6561 | 59049 | 531441 | 4782969 | 9 |
| 10 | 100 | 1000 | 10000 | 100000 | 1000000 | 10000000 | 10 |
| 11 | 121 | 1331 | 14641 | 161051 | 1771561 | 19487171 | 11 |
| 12 | 144 | 1728 | 20736 | 248832 | 2985984 | 35831808 | 12 |
| 13 | 169 | 2197 | 28561 | 371293 | 4826809 | 62748517 | 13 |
| 14 | 196 | 2744 | 38416 | 537824 | 7529536 | 105413504 | 14 |
| 15 | 225 | 3375 | 50625 | 759375 | 11390625 | 170859375 | 15 |
| 16 | 256 | 4096 | 65536 | 1048576 | 16777216 | 268435456 | 16 |
| 17 | 289 | 4913 | 83521 | 1419857 | 24137569 | 410338673 | 17 |
| 18 | 324 | 5832 | 104976 | 1889568 | 34012224 | 612220032 | 18 |
| 19 | 361 | 6859 | 130321 | 2476099 | 47045881 | 893871739 | 19 |
| 20 | 400 | 8000 | 160000 | 3200000 | 64000000 | 1280000000 | 20 |
| 21 | 441 | 9261 | 194481 | 4084101 | 85766121 | 1801088541 | 21 |
| 22 | 484 | 10648 | 234256 | 5153632 | 113379904 | 2494357888 | 22 |
| 23 | 529 | 12167 | 279841 | 6436343 | 148035889 | 3404825447 | 23 |
| 24 | 576 | 13824 | 331776 | 7962624 | 191102976 | 4586471424 | 24 |
| 25 | 625 | 15625 | 390625 | 9765625 | 244140625 | 6103515625 | 25 |
| 26 | 676 | 17576 | 456976 | 11881376 | 308915776 | 8031810176 | 26 |
| 27 | 729 | 19683 | 531441 | 14348907 | 387420489 | 10460353203 | 27 |
| 28 | 784 | 21952 | 614656 | 17210368 | 481890304 | 13492928512 | 28 |
| 29 | 841 | 24389 | 707281 | 20511149 | 594823321 | 17249876309 | 29 |
| 30 | 900 | 27000 | 810000 | 24300000 | 729000000 | 21870000000 | 30 |
| 31 | 961 | 29791 | 923521 | 28629151 | 887503681 | 27512614111 | 31 |
| 32 | 1024 | 32768 | 1048576 | 33554432 | 1073741824 | 34359738368 | 32 |
| 33 | 1089 | 35937 | 1185921 | 39135393 | 1291467969 | 42618442977 | 33 |
| 34 | 1156 | 39304 | 1336336 | 45435424 | 1544804416 | 52523350144 | 34 |
| 35 | 1225 | 42875 | 1500625 | 52521875 | 1838265625 | 64339296875 | 35 |
| 36 | 1296 | 46656 | 1679616 | 60466176 | 2176782336 | 78364164096 | 36 |
| 37 | 1369 | 50653 | 1874161 | 69343957 | 2565726409 | 94931877133 | 37 |
| 38 | 1444 | 54872 | 2085136 | 79235168 | 3010936384 | 114415582592 | 38 |
| 39 | 1521 | 59319 | 2313441 | 90224199 | 3518743761 | 137231006679 | 39 |
| 40 | 1600 | 64000 | 2560000 | 102400000 | 4096000000 | 163840000000 | 40 |
| 41 | 1681 | 68921 | 2825761 | 115856201 | 4750104241 | 194754273881 | 41 |
| 42 | 1764 | 74088 | 3111696 | 130691232 | 5489031744 | 230539333248 | 42 |
| 43 | 1849 | 79507 | 3418801 | 147008443 | 6321363049 | 271818611107 | 43 |
| 44 | 1936 | 85184 | 3748096 | 164916224 | 7256313856 | 319277809664 | 44 |
| 45 | 2025 | 91125 | 4100625 | 184528125 | 8303765625 | 373669453125 | 45 |
| 46 | 2116 | 97336 | 4477456 | 205962976 | 9474296896 | 435817657216 | 46 |
| 47 | 2209 | 103823 | 4879681 | 229345007 | 10779215329 | 506623120463 | 47 |
| 48 | 2304 | 110592 | 5308416 | 254803968 | 12230590464 | 587068342272 | 48 |
| 49 | 2401 | 117649 | 5764801 | 282475249 | 13841287201 | 678223072849 | 49 |
| 50 | 2500 | 125000 | 6250000 | 312500000 | 15625000000 | 781250000000 | 50 |

Table 48 (*continued*)

| n | n² | n³ | n⁴ | n⁵ | n⁶ | n⁷ | n |
|---|---|---|---|---|---|---|---|
| 51 | 2601 | 132651 | 6765201 | 345025251 | 17596287801 | 897410677851 | 51 |
| 52 | 2704 | 140608 | 7311616 | 380204032 | 19770609664 | 1028071702528 | 52 |
| 53 | 2809 | 148877 | 7890481 | 418195493 | 22164361129 | 1174711139837 | 53 |
| 54 | 2916 | 157464 | 8503056 | 459165024 | 24794911296 | 1338925209984 | 54 |
| 55 | 3025 | 166375 | 9150625 | 503284375 | 27680640625 | 1522435234375 | 55 |
| 56 | 3136 | 175616 | 9834496 | 550731776 | 30840979456 | 1727094849536 | 56 |
| 57 | 3249 | 185193 | 10556001 | 601692057 | 34296447249 | 1954897493193 | 57 |
| 58 | 3364 | 195112 | 11316496 | 656356768 | 38068692544 | 2207984167552 | 58 |
| 59 | 3481 | 205379 | 12117361 | 714924299 | 42180533641 | 2488651484819 | 59 |
| 60 | 3600 | 216000 | 12960000 | 777600000 | 46656000000 | 2799360000000 | 60 |
| 61 | 3721 | 226981 | 13845841 | 844596301 | 51520374361 | 3142742836021 | 61 |
| 62 | 3844 | 238328 | 14776336 | 916132832 | 56800235584 | 3521614606208 | 62 |
| 63 | 3969 | 250047 | 15752961 | 992436543 | 62523502209 | 3938980639167 | 63 |
| 64 | 4096 | 262144 | 16777216 | 1073741824 | 68719476736 | 4398046511104 | 64 |
| 65 | 4225 | 274625 | 17850625 | 1160290625 | 75418890625 | 4902227890625 | 65 |
| 66 | 4356 | 287496 | 18974736 | 1252332576 | 82653950016 | 5455160701056 | 66 |
| 67 | 4489 | 300763 | 20151121 | 1350125107 | 90458382169 | 6060711605323 | 67 |
| 68 | 4624 | 314432 | 21381376 | 1453933568 | 98867482624 | 6722988818432 | 68 |
| 69 | 4761 | 328509 | 22667121 | 1564031349 | 107918163081 | 7446353252589 | 69 |
| 70 | 4900 | 343000 | 24010000 | 1680700000 | 117649000000 | 8235430000000 | 70 |
| 71 | 5041 | 357911 | 25411681 | 1804229351 | 128100283921 | 9095120158391 | 71 |
| 72 | 5184 | 373248 | 26873856 | 1934917632 | 139314069504 | 10030613004288 | 72 |
| 73 | 5329 | 389017 | 28398241 | 2073071593 | 151334226289 | 11047398519097 | 73 |
| 74 | 5476 | 405224 | 29986576 | 2219006624 | 164206490176 | 12151280273024 | 74 |
| 75 | 5625 | 421875 | 31640625 | 2373046875 | 177978515625 | 13348388671875 | 75 |
| 76 | 5776 | 438976 | 33362176 | 2535525376 | 192699928576 | 14645194571776 | 76 |
| 77 | 5929 | 456533 | 35153041 | 2706784157 | 208422380089 | 16048523266853 | 77 |
| 78 | 6084 | 474552 | 37015056 | 2887174368 | 225199600704 | 17565568854912 | 78 |
| 79 | 6241 | 493039 | 38950081 | 3077056399 | 243087455521 | 19203908986159 | 79 |
| 80 | 6400 | 512000 | 40960000 | 3276800000 | 262144000000 | 20971520000000 | 80 |
| 81 | 6561 | 531441 | 43046721 | 3486784401 | 282429536481 | 22876792454961 | 81 |
| 82 | 6724 | 551368 | 45212176 | 3707398432 | 304006671424 | 24928547056768 | 82 |
| 83 | 6889 | 571787 | 47458321 | 3939040643 | 326940373369 | 27136050989627 | 83 |
| 84 | 7056 | 592704 | 49787136 | 4182119424 | 351298031616 | 29509034655744 | 84 |
| 85 | 7225 | 614125 | 52200625 | 4437053125 | 377149515625 | 32057708828125 | 85 |
| 86 | 7396 | 636056 | 54700816 | 4704270176 | 404567235136 | 34792782221696 | 86 |
| 87 | 7569 | 658503 | 57289761 | 4984209207 | 433626201009 | 37725479487783 | 87 |
| 88 | 7744 | 681472 | 59969536 | 5277319168 | 464404086784 | 40867559636992 | 88 |
| 89 | 7921 | 704969 | 62742241 | 5584059449 | 496981290961 | 44231334895529 | 89 |
| 90 | 8100 | 729000 | 65610000 | 5904900000 | 531441000000 | 47829690000000 | 90 |
| 91 | 8281 | 753571 | 68574961 | 6240321451 | 567869252041 | 51676101935731 | 91 |
| 92 | 8464 | 778688 | 71639296 | 6590815232 | 606355001344 | 55784660123648 | 92 |
| 93 | 8649 | 804357 | 74805201 | 6956883693 | 646990183449 | 60170087060757 | 93 |
| 94 | 8836 | 830584 | 78074896 | 7339040224 | 689869781056 | 64847759419264 | 94 |
| 95 | 9025 | 857375 | 81450625 | 7737809375 | 735091890625 | 69833729609375 | 95 |
| 96 | 9216 | 884736 | 84934656 | 8153726976 | 782757789696 | 75144747810816 | 96 |
| 97 | 9409 | 912673 | 88529281 | 8587340257 | 832972004929 | 80799284478113 | 97 |
| 98 | 9604 | 941192 | 92236816 | 9039207968 | 885842380864 | 86812553324672 | 98 |
| 99 | 9801 | 970299 | 96059601 | 9509900499 | 941480149401 | 93206534790699 | 99 |
| 100 | 10000 | 1000000 | 100000000 | 10000000000 | 1000000000000 | 100000000000000 | 100 |

# Table 49. *Sums of powers of integers*

| $n$ | $S(n)$ | $S(n^2)$ | $S(n^3)$ | $S(n^4)$ | $S(n^5)$ | $S(n^6)$ | $S(n^7)$ | $n$ |
|---|---|---|---|---|---|---|---|---|
| 1 | 1 | 1 | 1 | 1 | 1 | 1 | 1 | 1 |
| 2 | 3 | 5 | 9 | 17 | 33 | 65 | 129 | 2 |
| 3 | 6 | 14 | 36 | 98 | 276 | 794 | 2316 | 3 |
| 4 | 10 | 30 | 100 | 354 | 1300 | 4890 | 18700 | 4 |
| 5 | 15 | 55 | 225 | 979 | 4425 | 20515 | 96825 | 5 |
| 6 | 21 | 91 | 441 | 2275 | 12201 | 67171 | 376761 | 6 |
| 7 | 28 | 140 | 784 | 4676 | 29008 | 184820 | 1200304 | 7 |
| 8 | 36 | 204 | 1296 | 8772 | 61776 | 446964 | 3297456 | 8 |
| 9 | 45 | 285 | 2025 | 15333 | 120825 | 978405 | 8080425 | 9 |
| 10 | 55 | 385 | 3025 | 25333 | 220825 | 1978405 | 18080425 | 10 |
| 11 | 66 | 506 | 4356 | 39974 | 381876 | 3749966 | 37567596 | 11 |
| 12 | 78 | 650 | 6084 | 60710 | 630708 | 6735950 | 73399404 | 12 |
| 13 | 91 | 819 | 8281 | 89271 | 1002001 | 11562759 | 136147921 | 13 |
| 14 | 105 | 1015 | 11025 | 127687 | 1539825 | 19092295 | 241561425 | 14 |
| 15 | 120 | 1240 | 14400 | 178312 | 2299200 | 30482920 | 412420800 | 15 |
| 16 | 136 | 1496 | 18496 | 243848 | 3347776 | 47260136 | 680856256 | 16 |
| 17 | 153 | 1785 | 23409 | 327369 | 4767633 | 71397705 | 1091194929 | 17 |
| 18 | 171 | 2109 | 29241 | 432345 | 6657201 | 105409929 | 1703414961 | 18 |
| 19 | 190 | 2470 | 36100 | 562666 | 9133300 | 152455810 | 2597286700 | 19 |
| 20 | 210 | 2870 | 44100 | 722666 | 12333300 | 216455810 | 3877286700 | 20 |
| 21 | 231 | 3311 | 53361 | 917147 | 16417401 | 302221931 | 5678375241 | 21 |
| 22 | 253 | 3795 | 64009 | 1151403 | 21571033 | 415601835 | 8172733129 | 22 |
| 23 | 276 | 4324 | 76176 | 1431244 | 28007376 | 563637724 | 11577558576 | 23 |
| 24 | 300 | 4900 | 90000 | 1763020 | 35970000 | 754740700 | 16164030000 | 24 |
| 25 | 325 | 5525 | 105625 | 2153645 | 45735625 | 998881325 | 22267545625 | 25 |
| 26 | 351 | 6201 | 123201 | 2610621 | 57617001 | 1307797101 | 30299355801 | 26 |
| 27 | 378 | 6930 | 142884 | 3142062 | 71965908 | 1695217590 | 40759709004 | 27 |
| 28 | 406 | 7714 | 164836 | 3756718 | 89176276 | 2177107894 | 54252637516 | 28 |
| 29 | 435 | 8555 | 189225 | 4463999 | 109687425 | 2771931215 | 71502513825 | 29 |
| 30 | 465 | 9455 | 216225 | 5273999 | 133987425 | 3500931215 | 93372513825 | 30 |
| 31 | 496 | 10416 | 246016 | 6197520 | 162616576 | 4388434896 | 120885127936 | 31 |
| 32 | 528 | 11440 | 278784 | 7246096 | 196171008 | 5462176720 | 155244866304 | 32 |
| 33 | 561 | 12529 | 314721 | 8432017 | 135306401 | 6753644689 | 197863309281 | 33 |
| 34 | 595 | 13685 | 354025 | 9768353 | 180741825 | 8298449105 | 250386659425 | 34 |
| 35 | 630 | 14910 | 396900 | 11268978 | 333263700 | 10136714730 | 314725956300 | 35 |
| 36 | 666 | 16206 | 443556 | 12948594 | 393729876 | 12313497066 | 393090120396 | 36 |
| 37 | 703 | 17575 | 494209 | 14822755 | 463073833 | 14879223475 | 488021997529 | 37 |
| 38 | 741 | 19019 | 549081 | 16907891 | 542309001 | 17890159859 | 602437580121 | 38 |
| 39 | 780 | 20540 | 608400 | 19221332 | 632533200 | 21408903620 | 739668586800 | 39 |
| 40 | 820 | 22140 | 672400 | 21781332 | 734933200 | 25504903620 | 903508586800 | 40 |
| 41 | 861 | 23821 | 741321 | 24607093 | 850789401 | 30255007861 | 1098262860681 | 41 |
| 42 | 903 | 25585 | 815409 | 27718789 | 981480633 | 35744039605 | 1328802193929 | 42 |
| 43 | 946 | 27434 | 894916 | 31137590 | 1128489076 | 42065402654 | 1600620805036 | 43 |
| 44 | 990 | 29370 | 980100 | 34885686 | 1293405300 | 49321716510 | 1919898614700 | 44 |
| 45 | 1035 | 31395 | 1071225 | 38986311 | 1477933425 | 57625482135 | 2293568067825 | 45 |
| 46 | 1081 | 33511 | 1168561 | 43463767 | 1683896401 | 67099779031 | 2729385725041 | 46 |
| 47 | 1128 | 35720 | 1272384 | 48343448 | 1913241408 | 77878994360 | 3236008845504 | 47 |
| 48 | 1176 | 38024 | 1382976 | 53651864 | 2168045376 | 90109584824 | 3823077187776 | 48 |
| 49 | 1225 | 40425 | 1500625 | 59416665 | 2450520625 | 103950872025 | 4501300260625 | 49 |
| 50 | 1275 | 42925 | 1625625 | 65666665 | 2763020625 | 119575872025 | 5282550260625 | 50 |

Table 49 (*continued*)

| $n$ | $S(n)$ | $S(n^2)$ | $S(n^3)$ | $S(n^4)$ | $S(n^5)$ | $S(n^6)$ | $S(n^7)$ | $n$ |
|---|---|---|---|---|---|---|---|---|
| 51 | 1326 | 45526 | 1758276 | 72431866 | 3108045876 | 137172159826 | 6179960938476 | 51 |
| 52 | 1378 | 48230 | 1898884 | 79743482 | 3488249908 | 156942769490 | 7208032641004 | 52 |
| 53 | 1431 | 51039 | 2047761 | 87633963 | 3906445401 | 179107130619 | 8382743780841 | 53 |
| 54 | 1485 | 53955 | 2205225 | 96137019 | 4365610425 | 203902041915 | 9721668990825 | 54 |
| 55 | 1540 | 56980 | 2371600 | 105287644 | 4868894800 | 231582682540 | 11244104225200 | 55 |
| 56 | 1596 | 60116 | 2547216 | 115122140 | 5419626576 | 262423661996 | 12971199074736 | 56 |
| 57 | 1653 | 63365 | 2732409 | 125678141 | 6021318633 | 296720109245 | 14926096567929 | 57 |
| 58 | 1711 | 66729 | 2927521 | 136994637 | 6677675401 | 334788801789 | 17134080735481 | 58 |
| 59 | 1770 | 70210 | 3132900 | 149111998 | 7392599700 | 376969335430 | 19622732220300 | 59 |
| 60 | 1830 | 73810 | 3348900 | 162071998 | 8170199700 | 423625335430 | 22422092220300 | 60 |
| 61 | 1891 | 77531 | 3575881 | 175917839 | 9014796001 | 475145709791 | 25564835056321 | 61 |
| 62 | 1953 | 81375 | 3814209 | 190694175 | 9930928833 | 531945945375 | 29086449662529 | 62 |
| 63 | 2016 | 85344 | 4064256 | 206447136 | 10923365376 | 594469447584 | 33025430301696 | 63 |
| 64 | 2080 | 89440 | 4326400 | 223224352 | 11997107200 | 663188924320 | 37423476812800 | 64 |
| 65 | 2145 | 93665 | 4601025 | 241074977 | 13157397825 | 738607814945 | 42325704703425 | 65 |
| 66 | 2211 | 98021 | 4888521 | 260049713 | 14409730401 | 821261764961 | 47780865404481 | 66 |
| 67 | 2278 | 102510 | 5189284 | 280200834 | 15759855508 | 911720147130 | 53841577009804 | 67 |
| 68 | 2346 | 107134 | 5503716 | 301582210 | 17213789076 | 1010587629754 | 60564565828236 | 68 |
| 69 | 2415 | 111895 | 5832225 | 324249331 | 18777820425 | 1118505792835 | 68010919080825 | 69 |
| 70 | 2485 | 116795 | 6175225 | 348259331 | 20458520425 | 1236154792835 | 76246349080825 | 70 |
| 71 | 2556 | 121836 | 6533136 | 373671012 | 22262749776 | 1364255076756 | 85341469239216 | 71 |
| 72 | 2628 | 127020 | 6906384 | 400544868 | 24197667408 | 1503569146260 | 95372082243504 | 72 |
| 73 | 2701 | 132349 | 7295401 | 428943109 | 26270739001 | 1654903372549 | 106419480762601 | 73 |
| 74 | 2775 | 137825 | 7700625 | 458929685 | 28489745625 | 1819109862725 | 118570761035625 | 74 |
| 75 | 2850 | 143450 | 8122500 | 490570310 | 30862792500 | 1997088378350 | 131919149707500 | 75 |
| 76 | 2926 | 149226 | 8561476 | 523932486 | 33398317876 | 2189788306926 | 146564344279276 | 76 |
| 77 | 3003 | 155155 | 9018000 | 558085527 | 36105102033 | 2398210687015 | 162612867516129 | 77 |
| 78 | 3081 | 161239 | 9492561 | 596100583 | 38992276401 | 2623410287719 | 180178436401041 | 78 |
| 79 | 3160 | 167480 | 9985600 | 635050664 | 42069332800 | 2866497743240 | 199382345387200 | 79 |
| 80 | 3240 | 173880 | 10497600 | 676010664 | 45346132800 | 3128641743240 | 220353865387200 | 80 |
| 81 | 3321 | 180441 | 11029041 | 719057385 | 48832917201 | 3411071279721 | 243230657842161 | 81 |
| 82 | 3403 | 187165 | 11580409 | 764269561 | 52540315633 | 3715077951145 | 268159204898929 | 82 |
| 83 | 3486 | 194054 | 12152196 | 811727882 | 56479356276 | 4042018324514 | 295295255888556 | 83 |
| 84 | 3570 | 201110 | 12744900 | 861515018 | 60661475700 | 4393316356130 | 324804290544300 | 84 |
| 85 | 3655 | 208335 | 13359025 | 913715643 | 65098528825 | 4770465871755 | 356861999372425 | 85 |
| 86 | 3741 | 215731 | 13995081 | 968416459 | 69802799001 | 5175033106891 | 391654781594121 | 86 |
| 87 | 3828 | 223300 | 14653584 | 1025706220 | 74787008208 | 5608659307900 | 429380261081904 | 87 |
| 88 | 3916 | 231044 | 15335056 | 1085675756 | 80064323684 | 6073063394684 | 470247820718896 | 88 |
| 89 | 4005 | 238965 | 16040025 | 1148417997 | 85648386825 | 6570044685645 | 514479155614425 | 89 |
| 90 | 4095 | 247065 | 16769025 | 1214027997 | 91553286825 | 7101485685645 | 562308845614425 | 90 |
| 91 | 4186 | 255346 | 17522596 | 1282602958 | 97793608276 | 7669354937686 | 613984947550156 | 91 |
| 92 | 4278 | 263810 | 18301284 | 1354242254 | 104384423508 | 8275709939030 | 669769607673804 | 92 |
| 93 | 4371 | 272459 | 19105641 | 1429047455 | 111341307201 | 8922700122479 | 729939694734561 | 93 |
| 94 | 4465 | 281295 | 19936225 | 1507122351 | 118680347425 | 9612569903535 | 794787454153825 | 94 |
| 95 | 4560 | 290320 | 20793600 | 1588572976 | 126418156800 | 10347661794160 | 864621183763200 | 95 |
| 96 | 4656 | 299536 | 21678336 | 1673507632 | 134571883776 | 11130419583856 | 939765931574016 | 96 |
| 97 | 4753 | 308945 | 22591009 | 1762036913 | 143159224033 | 11963391588785 | 1020564216052129 | 97 |
| 98 | 4851 | 318549 | 23532201 | 1854273729 | 152198432001 | 12849233969649 | 1107376769376801 | 98 |
| 99 | 4950 | 328350 | 24502500 | 1950333330 | 161708332500 | 13790714119050 | 1200583304167500 | 99 |
| 100 | 5050 | 338350 | 25502500 | 2050333330 | 171708332500 | 14790714119050 | 1300583304167500 | 100 |

Table 50. *Squares of integers*

| n | 0 | 1 | 2 | 3 | 4 | 5 | 6 | 7 | 8 | 9 |
|---|---|---|---|---|---|---|---|---|---|---|
| 0 | 0 | 1 | 4 | 9 | 16 | 25 | 36 | 49 | 64 | 81 |
| 1 | 100 | 121 | 144 | 169 | 196 | 225 | 256 | 289 | 324 | 361 |
| 2 | 400 | 441 | 484 | 529 | 576 | 625 | 676 | 729 | 784 | 841 |
| 3 | 900 | 961 | 1024 | 1089 | 1156 | 1225 | 1296 | 1369 | 1444 | 1521 |
| 4 | 1600 | 1681 | 1764 | 1849 | 1936 | 2025 | 2116 | 2209 | 2304 | 2401 |
| 5 | 2500 | 2601 | 2704 | 2809 | 2916 | 3025 | 3136 | 3249 | 3364 | 3481 |
| 6 | 3600 | 3721 | 3844 | 3969 | 4096 | 4225 | 4356 | 4489 | 4624 | 4761 |
| 7 | 4900 | 5041 | 5184 | 5329 | 5476 | 5625 | 5776 | 5929 | 6084 | 6241 |
| 8 | 6400 | 6561 | 6724 | 6889 | 7056 | 7225 | 7396 | 7569 | 7744 | 7921 |
| 9 | 8100 | 8281 | 8464 | 8649 | 8836 | 9025 | 9216 | 9409 | 9604 | 9801 |
| 10 | 10000 | 10201 | 10404 | 10609 | 10816 | 11025 | 11236 | 11449 | 11664 | 11881 |
| 11 | 12100 | 12321 | 12544 | 12769 | 12996 | 13225 | 13456 | 13689 | 13924 | 14161 |
| 12 | 14400 | 14641 | 14884 | 15129 | 15376 | 15625 | 15876 | 16129 | 16384 | 16641 |
| 13 | 16900 | 17161 | 17424 | 17689 | 17956 | 18225 | 18496 | 18769 | 19044 | 19321 |
| 14 | 19600 | 19881 | 20164 | 20449 | 20736 | 21025 | 21316 | 21609 | 21904 | 22201 |
| 15 | 22500 | 22801 | 23104 | 23409 | 23716 | 24025 | 24336 | 24649 | 24964 | 25281 |
| 16 | 25600 | 25921 | 26244 | 26569 | 26896 | 27225 | 27556 | 27889 | 28224 | 28561 |
| 17 | 28900 | 29241 | 29584 | 29929 | 30276 | 30625 | 30976 | 31329 | 31684 | 32041 |
| 18 | 32400 | 32761 | 33124 | 33489 | 33856 | 34225 | 34596 | 34969 | 35344 | 35721 |
| 19 | 36100 | 36481 | 36864 | 37249 | 37636 | 38025 | 38416 | 38809 | 39204 | 39601 |
| 20 | 40000 | 40401 | 40804 | 41209 | 41616 | 42025 | 42436 | 42849 | 43264 | 43681 |
| 21 | 44100 | 44521 | 44944 | 45369 | 45796 | 46225 | 46656 | 47089 | 47524 | 47961 |
| 22 | 48400 | 48841 | 49284 | 49729 | 50176 | 50625 | 51076 | 51529 | 51984 | 52441 |
| 23 | 52900 | 53361 | 53824 | 54289 | 54756 | 55225 | 55696 | 56169 | 56644 | 57121 |
| 24 | 57600 | 58081 | 58564 | 59049 | 59536 | 60025 | 60516 | 61009 | 61504 | 62001 |
| 25 | 62500 | 63001 | 63504 | 64009 | 64516 | 65025 | 65536 | 66049 | 66564 | 67081 |
| 26 | 67600 | 68121 | 68644 | 69169 | 69696 | 70225 | 70756 | 71289 | 71824 | 72361 |
| 27 | 72900 | 73441 | 73984 | 74529 | 75076 | 75625 | 76176 | 76729 | 77284 | 77841 |
| 28 | 78400 | 78961 | 79524 | 80089 | 80656 | 81225 | 81796 | 82369 | 82944 | 83521 |
| 29 | 84100 | 84681 | 85264 | 85849 | 86436 | 87025 | 87616 | 88209 | 88804 | 89401 |
| 30 | 90000 | 90601 | 91204 | 91809 | 92416 | 93025 | 93636 | 94249 | 94864 | 95481 |
| 31 | 96100 | 96721 | 97344 | 97969 | 98596 | 99225 | 99856 | 100489 | 101124 | 101761 |
| 32 | 102400 | 103041 | 103684 | 104329 | 104976 | 105625 | 106276 | 106929 | 107584 | 108241 |
| 33 | 108900 | 109561 | 110224 | 110889 | 111556 | 112225 | 112896 | 113569 | 114244 | 114921 |
| 34 | 115600 | 116281 | 116964 | 117649 | 118336 | 119025 | 119716 | 120409 | 121104 | 121801 |
| 35 | 122500 | 123201 | 123904 | 124609 | 125316 | 126025 | 126736 | 127449 | 128164 | 128881 |
| 36 | 129600 | 130321 | 131044 | 131769 | 132496 | 133225 | 133956 | 134689 | 135424 | 136161 |
| 37 | 136900 | 137641 | 138384 | 139129 | 139876 | 140625 | 141376 | 142129 | 142884 | 143641 |
| 38 | 144400 | 145161 | 145924 | 146689 | 147456 | 148225 | 148996 | 149769 | 150544 | 151321 |
| 39 | 152100 | 152881 | 153664 | 154449 | 155236 | 156025 | 156816 | 157609 | 158404 | 159201 |
| 40 | 160000 | 160801 | 161604 | 162409 | 163216 | 164025 | 164836 | 165649 | 166464 | 167281 |
| 41 | 168100 | 168921 | 169744 | 170569 | 171396 | 172225 | 173056 | 173889 | 174724 | 175561 |
| 42 | 176400 | 177241 | 178084 | 178929 | 179776 | 180625 | 181476 | 182329 | 183184 | 184041 |
| 43 | 184900 | 185761 | 186624 | 187489 | 188356 | 189225 | 190096 | 190969 | 191844 | 192721 |
| 44 | 193600 | 194481 | 195364 | 196249 | 197136 | 198025 | 198916 | 199809 | 200704 | 201601 |
| 45 | 202500 | 203401 | 204304 | 205209 | 206116 | 207025 | 207936 | 208849 | 209764 | 210681 |
| 46 | 211600 | 212521 | 213444 | 214369 | 215296 | 216225 | 217156 | 218089 | 219024 | 219961 |
| 47 | 220900 | 221841 | 222784 | 223729 | 224676 | 225625 | 226576 | 227529 | 228484 | 229441 |
| 48 | 230400 | 231361 | 232324 | 233289 | 234256 | 235225 | 236196 | 237169 | 238144 | 239121 |
| 49 | 240100 | 241081 | 242064 | 243049 | 244036 | 245025 | 246016 | 247009 | 248004 | 249001 |

Table 50 (*continued*)

| n | 0 | 1 | 2 | 3 | 4 | 5 | 6 | 7 | 8 | 9 |
|---|---|---|---|---|---|---|---|---|---|---|
| 50 | 250000 | 251001 | 252004 | 253009 | 254016 | 255025 | 256036 | 257049 | 258064 | 259081 |
| 51 | 260100 | 261121 | 262144 | 263169 | 264196 | 265225 | 266256 | 267289 | 268324 | 269361 |
| 52 | 270400 | 271441 | 272484 | 273529 | 274576 | 275625 | 276676 | 277729 | 278784 | 279841 |
| 53 | 280900 | 281961 | 283024 | 284089 | 285156 | 286225 | 287296 | 288369 | 289444 | 290521 |
| 54 | 291600 | 292681 | 293764 | 294849 | 295936 | 297025 | 298116 | 299209 | 300304 | 301401 |
| 55 | 302500 | 303601 | 304704 | 305809 | 306916 | 308025 | 309136 | 310249 | 311364 | 312481 |
| 56 | 313600 | 314721 | 315844 | 316969 | 318096 | 319225 | 320356 | 321489 | 322624 | 323761 |
| 57 | 324900 | 326041 | 327184 | 328329 | 329476 | 330625 | 331776 | 332929 | 334084 | 335241 |
| 58 | 336400 | 337561 | 338724 | 339889 | 341056 | 342225 | 343396 | 344569 | 345744 | 346921 |
| 59 | 348100 | 349281 | 350464 | 351649 | 352836 | 354025 | 355216 | 356409 | 357604 | 358801 |
| 60 | 360000 | 361201 | 362404 | 363609 | 364816 | 366025 | 367236 | 368449 | 369664 | 370881 |
| 61 | 372100 | 373321 | 374544 | 375769 | 376996 | 378225 | 379456 | 380689 | 381924 | 383161 |
| 62 | 384400 | 385641 | 386884 | 388129 | 389376 | 390625 | 391876 | 393129 | 394384 | 395641 |
| 63 | 396900 | 398161 | 399424 | 400689 | 401956 | 403225 | 404496 | 405769 | 407044 | 408321 |
| 64 | 409600 | 410881 | 412164 | 413449 | 414736 | 416025 | 417316 | 418609 | 419904 | 421201 |
| 65 | 422500 | 423801 | 425104 | 426409 | 427716 | 429025 | 430336 | 431649 | 432964 | 434281 |
| 66 | 435600 | 436921 | 438244 | 439569 | 440896 | 442225 | 443556 | 444889 | 446224 | 447561 |
| 67 | 448900 | 450241 | 451584 | 452929 | 454276 | 455625 | 456976 | 458329 | 459684 | 461041 |
| 68 | 462400 | 463761 | 465124 | 466489 | 467856 | 469225 | 470596 | 471969 | 473344 | 474721 |
| 69 | 476100 | 477481 | 478864 | 480249 | 481636 | 483025 | 484416 | 485809 | 487204 | 488601 |
| 70 | 490000 | 491401 | 492804 | 494209 | 495616 | 497025 | 498436 | 499849 | 501264 | 502681 |
| 71 | 504100 | 505521 | 506944 | 508369 | 509796 | 511225 | 512656 | 514089 | 515524 | 516961 |
| 72 | 518400 | 519841 | 521284 | 522729 | 524176 | 525625 | 527076 | 528529 | 529984 | 531441 |
| 73 | 532900 | 534361 | 535824 | 537289 | 538756 | 540225 | 541696 | 543169 | 544644 | 546121 |
| 74 | 547600 | 549081 | 550504 | 552049 | 553536 | 555025 | 556516 | 558000 | 559504 | 561001 |
| 75 | 562500 | 564001 | 565504 | 567009 | 568516 | 570025 | 571536 | 573049 | 574564 | 576081 |
| 76 | 577600 | 579121 | 580644 | 582169 | 583696 | 585225 | 586756 | 588289 | 589824 | 591361 |
| 77 | 592900 | 594441 | 595984 | 597529 | 599076 | 600625 | 602176 | 603729 | 605284 | 606841 |
| 78 | 608400 | 609961 | 611524 | 613089 | 614656 | 616225 | 617796 | 619369 | 620944 | 622521 |
| 79 | 624100 | 625681 | 627264 | 628849 | 630436 | 632025 | 633616 | 635209 | 636804 | 638401 |
| 80 | 640000 | 641601 | 643204 | 644809 | 646416 | 648025 | 649636 | 651249 | 652864 | 654481 |
| 81 | 656100 | 657721 | 659344 | 660969 | 662596 | 664225 | 665856 | 667489 | 669124 | 670761 |
| 82 | 672400 | 674041 | 675684 | 677329 | 678976 | 680625 | 682276 | 683929 | 685584 | 687241 |
| 83 | 688900 | 690561 | 692224 | 693889 | 695556 | 697225 | 698896 | 700569 | 702244 | 703921 |
| 84 | 705600 | 707281 | 708964 | 710649 | 712336 | 714025 | 715716 | 717409 | 719104 | 720801 |
| 85 | 722500 | 724201 | 725904 | 727609 | 729316 | 731025 | 732736 | 734449 | 736164 | 737881 |
| 86 | 739600 | 741321 | 743044 | 744769 | 746496 | 748225 | 749956 | 751689 | 753424 | 755161 |
| 87 | 756900 | 758641 | 760384 | 762129 | 763876 | 765625 | 767376 | 769129 | 770884 | 772641 |
| 88 | 774400 | 776161 | 777924 | 779689 | 781456 | 783225 | 784996 | 786769 | 788544 | 790321 |
| 89 | 792100 | 793881 | 795664 | 797449 | 799236 | 801025 | 802816 | 804609 | 806404 | 808201 |
| 90 | 810000 | 811801 | 813604 | 815409 | 817216 | 819025 | 820836 | 822649 | 824464 | 826281 |
| 91 | 828100 | 829921 | 831744 | 833569 | 835396 | 837225 | 839056 | 840889 | 842724 | 844561 |
| 92 | 846400 | 848241 | 850084 | 851929 | 853776 | 855625 | 857476 | 859329 | 861184 | 863041 |
| 93 | 864900 | 866761 | 868624 | 870489 | 872356 | 874225 | 876096 | 877969 | 879844 | 881721 |
| 94 | 883600 | 885481 | 887364 | 889249 | 891136 | 893025 | 894916 | 896809 | 898704 | 900601 |
| 95 | 902500 | 904401 | 906304 | 908209 | 910116 | 912025 | 913936 | 915849 | 917764 | 919681 |
| 96 | 921600 | 923521 | 925444 | 927369 | 929296 | 931225 | 933156 | 935089 | 937024 | 938961 |
| 97 | 940900 | 942841 | 944784 | 946729 | 948676 | 950625 | 952576 | 954529 | 956484 | 958441 |
| 98 | 960400 | 962361 | 964324 | 966289 | 968256 | 970225 | 972196 | 974169 | 976144 | 978121 |
| 99 | 980100 | 982081 | 984064 | 986049 | 988036 | 990025 | 992016 | 994009 | 996004 | 998001 |

Table 51. *Factorials of integers, their logarithms; square roots; and their reciprocals*

| $n$ | $n!$* | $\log_{10} n!$ | $\dfrac{1}{n!}$† | $\sqrt{n}$ | $\dfrac{1}{\sqrt{n}}$ | $\dfrac{1}{n}$ |
|---|---|---|---|---|---|---|
| 1 | 1 | 0·000 0000 | 1·000 000 | 1·000 0000 | 1·000 0000 | 1·000 0000 |
| 2 | 2 | 0·301 0300 | 0·500 000 | 1·414 2136 | 0·707 1068 | 0·500 0000 |
| 3 | 6 | 0·778 1513 | ·166 667 | 1·732 0508 | ·577 3503 | ·333 3333 |
| 4 | 24 | 1·380 2112 | ·416 667 | 2·000 0000 | ·500 0000 | ·250 0000 |
| 5 | 120 | 2·079 1812 | ·833 333 | 2·236 0680 | ·447 2136 | ·200 0000 |
| 6 | 720 | 2·857 3325 | 0·138 889 | 2·449 4897 | 0·408 2483 | 0·166 6667 |
| 7 | 5040 | 3·702 4305 | ·198 413 | 2·645 7513 | ·377 9645 | ·142 8571 |
| 8 | 40320 | 4·605 5205 | ·248 016 | 2·828 4271 | ·353 5534 | ·125 0000 |
| 9 | 362880 | 5·559 7630 | ·275 573 | 3·000 0000 | ·333 3333 | ·111 1111 |
| 10 | 3·62880 | 6·559 7630 | ·275 573 | 3·162 2777 | ·316 2278 | ·100 0000 |
| 11 | 3·99168 | 7·601 1557 | 0·250 521 | 3·316 6248 | 0·301 5113 | 0·090 9091 |
| 12 | 4·79002 | 8·680 3370 | ·208 768 | 3·464 1016 | ·288 6751 | ·083 3333 |
| 13 | 6·22702 | 9·794 2803 | ·160 590 | 3·605 5513 | ·277 3501 | ·076 9231 |
| 14 | 8·71783 | 10·940 4084 | ·114 707 | 3·741 6574 | ·267 2612 | ·071 4286 |
| 15 | 1·30767 | 12·116 4996 | ·764 716 | 3·872 9833 | ·258 1989 | ·066 6667 |
| 16 | 2·09228 | 13·320 6196 | 0·477 948 | 4·000 0000 | 0·250 0000 | 0·062 5000 |
| 17 | 3·55687 | 14·551 0685 | ·281 146 | 4·123 1056 | ·242 5356 | ·058 8235 |
| 18 | 6·40237 | 15·806 3410 | ·156 192 | 4·242 6407 | ·235 7023 | ·055 5556 |
| 19 | 1·21645 | 17·085 0946 | ·822 064 | 4·358 8989 | ·229 4157 | ·052 6316 |
| 20 | 2·43290 | 18·386 1246 | ·411 032 | 4·472 1360 | ·223 6068 | ·050 0000 |
| 21 | 5·10909 | 19·708 3439 | 0·195 729 | 4·582 5757 | 0·218 2179 | 0·047 6190 |
| 22 | 1·12400 | 21·050 7666 | ·889 679 | 4·690 4158 | ·213 2007 | ·045 4545 |
| 23 | 2·58520 | 22·412 4944 | ·386 817 | 4·795 8315 | ·208 5144 | ·043 4783 |
| 24 | 6·20448 | 23·792 7057 | ·161 174 | 4·898 9795 | ·204 1241 | ·041 6667 |
| 25 | 1·55112 | 25·190 6457 | ·644 695 | 5·000 0000 | ·200 0000 | ·040 0000 |
| 26 | 4·03291 | 26·605 6190 | 0·247 960 | 5·099 0195 | 0·196 1161 | 0·038 4615 |
| 27 | 1·08889 | 28·036 9828 | ·918 369 | 5·196 1524 | ·192 4501 | ·037 0370 |
| 28 | 3·04888 | 29·484 1408 | ·327 989 | 5·291 5026 | ·188 9822 | ·035 7143 |
| 29 | 8·84176 | 30·946 5388 | ·113 100 | 5·385 1648 | ·185 6953 | ·034 4828 |
| 30 | 2·65253 | 32·423 6601 | ·376 999 | 5·477 2256 | ·182 5742 | ·033 3333 |
| 31 | 8·22284 | 33·915 0218 | 0·121 613 | 5·567 7644 | 0·179 6053 | 0·032 2581 |
| 32 | 2·63131 | 35·420 1717 | ·380 039 | 5·656 8542 | ·176 7767 | ·031 2500 |
| 33 | 8·68332 | 36·938 6857 | ·115 163 | 5·744 5626 | ·174 0777 | ·030 3030 |
| 34 | 2·95233 | 38·470 1646 | ·338 716 | 5·830 9519 | ·771 4986 | ·029 4118 |
| 35 | 1·03331 | 40·014 2326 | ·967 759 | 5·916 0798 | ·169 0309 | ·028 5714 |
| 36 | 3·71993 | 41·570 5351 | 0·268 822 | 6·000 0000 | 0·166 6667 | 0·027 7778 |
| 37 | 1·37638 | 43·138 7369 | ·726 546 | 6·082 7625 | ·164 3990 | ·027 0270 |
| 38 | 5·23023 | 44·718 5205 | ·191 196 | 6·164 4140 | ·162 2214 | ·026 3158 |
| 39 | 2·03979 | 46·309 5851 | ·490 247 | 6·244 9980 | ·160 1282 | ·025 6410 |
| 40 | 8·15915 | 47·911 6451 | ·122 562 | 6·324 5553 | ·158 1139 | ·025 0000 |
| 41 | 3·34525 | 49·524 4289 | 0·298 931 | 6·403 1242 | 0·156 1738 | 0·024 3902 |
| 42 | 1·40501 | 51·147 6782 | ·711 741 | 6·480 7407 | ·154 3034 | ·023 8095 |
| 43 | 6·04153 | 52·781 1467 | ·165 521 | 6·557 4385 | ·152 4986 | ·023 2558 |
| 44 | 2·65827 | 54·424 5993 | ·376 184 | 6·633 2496 | ·150 7557 | ·022 7273 |
| 45 | 1·19622 | 56·077 8119 | ·835 965 | 6·708 2039 | ·149 0712 | ·022 2222 |
| 46 | 5·50262 | 57·740 5697 | 0·181 732 | 6·782 3300 | 0·147 4420 | 0·021 7391 |
| 47 | 2·58623 | 59·412 6676 | ·386 663 | 6·855 6546 | ·145 8650 | ·021 2766 |
| 48 | 1·24139 | 61·093 9088 | ·805 548 | 6·928 2032 | ·144 3376 | ·020 8333 |
| 49 | 6·08282 | 62·784 1049 | ·164 397 | 7·000 0000 | ·142 8571 | ·020 4082 |
| 50 | 3·04141 | 64·483 0749 | ·328 795 | 7·071 0678 | ·141 4214 | ·020 0000 |

\* For $n > 9$, multiply by $10^c$, where $c$ is the characteristic of $\log n!$ shown alongside in the next column.
† Multiply by $10^{-c}$, where $c$ is the characteristic of $\log n!$ shown in the preceding column.

Table 51 (*continued*)

| $n$ | $n!$* | $\log_{10} n!$ | $\dfrac{1}{n!}$† | $\sqrt{n}$ | $\dfrac{1}{\sqrt{n}}$ | $\dfrac{1}{n}$ |
|---|---|---|---|---|---|---|
| 51 | 1·55112 | 66·190 6450 | 0·644 696 | 7·141 4284 | 0·140 0280 | 0·019 6078 |
| 52 | 8·06582 | 67·906 6484 | ·123 980 | 7·211 1026 | ·138 6750 | ·019 2308 |
| 53 | 4·27488 | 69·630 9243 | ·233 925 | 7·280 1099 | ·137 3606 | ·018 8679 |
| 54 | 2·30844 | 71·363 3180 | ·433 194 | 7·348 4692 | ·136 0828 | ·018 5185 |
| 55 | 1·26964 | 73·103 6807 | ·787 625 | 7·416 1985 | ·134 8400 | ·018 1818 |
| 56 | 7·10999 | 74·851 8687 | 0·140 647 | 7·483 3148 | 0·133 6306 | 0·017 8571 |
| 57 | 4·05269 | 76·607 7436 | ·246 750 | 7·549 8344 | ·132 4532 | ·017 5439 |
| 58 | 2·35056 | 78·371 1716 | ·425 430 | 7·615 7731 | ·131 3064 | ·017 2414 |
| 59 | 1·38683 | 80·142 0236 | ·721 068 | 7·681 1457 | ·130 1889 | ·016 9492 |
| 60 | 8·32099 | 81·920 1748 | ·120 178 | 7·745 9667 | ·129 0994 | ·016 6667 |
| 61 | 5·07580 | 83·705 5047 | 0·197 013 | 7·810 2497 | 0·128 0369 | 0·016 3934 |
| 62 | 3·14700 | 85·497 8964 | ·317 763 | 7·874 0079 | ·127 0001 | ·016 1290 |
| 63 | 1·98261 | 87·297 2369 | ·504 386 | 7·937 2539 | ·125 9882 | ·015 8730 |
| 64 | 1·26887 | 89·103 4169 | ·788 103 | 8·000 0000 | ·125 0000 | ·015 6250 |
| 65 | 8·24765 | 90·916 3303 | ·121 247 | 8·062 2577 | ·124 0347 | ·015 3846 |
| 66 | 5·44345 | 92·735 8742 | 0·183 707 | 8·124 0384 | 0·123 0915 | 0·015 1515 |
| 67 | 3·64711 | 94·561 9490 | ·274 190 | 8·185 3528 | ·122 1694 | ·014 9254 |
| 68 | 2·48004 | 96·394 4579 | ·403 220 | 8·246 2113 | ·121 2678 | ·014 7059 |
| 69 | 1·71122 | 98·233 3070 | ·584 377 | 8·306 6239 | ·120 3859 | ·014 4928 |
| 70 | 1·19786 | 100·078 4050 | ·834 824 | 8·366 6003 | ·119 5229 | ·014 2857 |
| 71 | 8·50479 | 101·929 6634 | 0·117 581 | 8·426 1498 | 0·118 6782 | 0·014 0845 |
| 72 | 6·12345 | 103·786 9959 | ·163 307 | 8·485 2814 | ·117 8511 | ·013 8889 |
| 73 | 4·47012 | 105·650 3187 | ·223 708 | 8·544 0037 | ·117 0411 | ·013 6986 |
| 74 | 3·30789 | 107·519 5505 | ·302 308 | 8·602 3253 | ·116 2476 | ·013 5135 |
| 75 | 2·48091 | 109·394 6117 | ·403 077 | 8·660 2540 | ·115 4701 | ·013 3333 |
| 76 | 1·88549 | 111·275 4253 | 0·530 365 | 8·717 7979 | 0·114 7079 | 0·013 1579 |
| 77 | 1·45183 | 113·161 9160 | ·688 785 | 8·774 9644 | ·113 9606 | ·012 9870 |
| 78 | 1·13243 | 115·054 0106 | ·883 058 | 8·831 7609 | ·113 2277 | ·012 8205 |
| 79 | 8·94618 | 116·951 6377 | ·111 780 | 8·888 1944 | ·112 5088 | ·012 6582 |
| 80 | 7·15695 | 118·854 7277 | ·139 724 | 8·944 2719 | ·111 8034 | ·012 5000 |
| 81 | 5·79713 | 120·763 2127 | 0·172 499 | 9·000 0000 | 0·111 1111 | 0·012 3457 |
| 82 | 4·75364 | 122·677 0266 | ·210 365 | 9·055 3851 | ·110 4315 | ·012 1951 |
| 83 | 3·94552 | 124·596 1047 | ·253 452 | 9·110 4336 | ·109 7643 | ·012 0482 |
| 84 | 3·31424 | 126·520 3840 | ·301 728 | 9·165 1514 | ·109 1089 | ·011 9048 |
| 85 | 2·81710 | 128·449 8029 | ·354 974 | 9·219 5445 | ·108 4652 | ·011 7647 |
| 86 | 2·42271 | 130·384 3013 | 0·412 761 | 9·273 6185 | 0·107 8328 | 0·011 6279 |
| 87 | 2·10776 | 132·323 8206 | ·474 438 | 9·327 3791 | ·107 2113 | ·011 4943 |
| 88 | 1·85483 | 134·268 3033 | ·539 134 | 9·380 8315 | ·106 6004 | ·011 3636 |
| 89 | 1·65080 | 136·217 6933 | ·605 769 | 9·433 9811 | ·105 9998 | ·011 2360 |
| 90 | 1·48572 | 138·171 9358 | ·673 076 | 9·486 8330 | ·105 4093 | ·011 1111 |
| 91 | 1·35200 | 140·130 9772 | 0·739 644 | 9·539 3920 | 0·104 8285 | 0·010 9890 |
| 92 | 1·24384 | 142·094 7650 | ·803 961 | 9·591 6630 | ·104 2572 | ·010 8696 |
| 93 | 1·15677 | 144·063 2480 | ·864 474 | 9·643 6508 | ·103 6952 | ·010 7527 |
| 94 | 1·08737 | 146·036 3758 | ·919 653 | 9·695 3597 | ·103 1421 | ·010 6383 |
| 95 | 1·03300 | 148·014 0994 | ·968 056 | 9·746 7943 | ·102 5978 | ·010 5263 |
| 96 | 9·91678 | 149·996 3707 | 0·100 839 | 9·797 9590 | 0·102 0621 | 0·010 4167 |
| 97 | 9·61928 | 151·983 1424 | ·103 958 | 9·848 8578 | ·101 5346 | ·010 3093 |
| 98 | 9·42689 | 153·974 3685 | ·106 080 | 9·899 4949 | ·101 0153 | ·010 2041 |
| 99 | 9·33262 | 155·970 0037 | ·107 151 | 9·949 8744 | ·100 5038 | ·010 1010 |
| 100 | 9·33262 | 157·970 0037 | ·107 151 | 10·000 0000 | ·100 0000 | ·010 0000 |

\* Multiply by $10^c$, where $c$ is the **characteristic** of log $n!$ shown alongside in the next column.
† Multiply by $10^{-c}$, where $c$ is the characteristic of log $n!$ shown in the preceding column.

Table 51. *Factorials of integers and their logarithms (continued)*

| $n$ | $n!*$ | $\log_{10} n!$ | $n$ | $n!*$ | $\log_{10} n!$ | $n$ | $n!*$ | $\log_{10} n!$ |
|---|---|---|---|---|---|---|---|---|
| 101 | 9·42595 | 159·974 3250 | 151 | 8·62721 | 264·935 8704 | 201 | 1·58520 | 377·200 0847 |
| 102 | 9·61447 | 161·982 9252 | 152 | 1·31134 | 267·117 7139 | 202 | 3·20211 | 379·505 4361 |
| 103 | 9·90290 | 163·995 7624 | 153 | 2·00634 | 269·302 4054 | 203 | 6·50028 | 381·812 9321 |
| 104 | 1·02990 | 166·012 7958 | 154 | 3·08977 | 271·489 9261 | 204 | 1·32606 | 384·122 5623 |
| 105 | 1·08140 | 168·033 9851 | 155 | 4·78914 | 273·680 2578 | 205 | 2·71842 | 386·434 3161 |
| 106 | 1·14628 | 170·059 2909 | 156 | 7·47106 | 275·873 3824 | 206 | 5·59994 | 388·748 1834 |
| 107 | 1·22652 | 172·088 6747 | 157 | 1·17296 | 278·069 2820 | 207 | 1·15919 | 391·064 1537 |
| 108 | 1·32464 | 174·122 0985 | 158 | 1·85327 | 280·267 9391 | 208 | 2·41111 | 393·382 2170 |
| 109 | 1·44386 | 176·159 5250 | 159 | 2·94670 | 282·469 3363 | 209 | 5·03922 | 395·702 3633 |
| 110 | 1·58825 | 178·200 9176 | 160 | 4·71472 | 284·673 4562 | 210 | 1·05824 | 398·024 5826 |
| 111 | 1·76295 | 180·246 2406 | 161 | 7·59071 | 286·880 2821 | 211 | 2·23288 | 400·348 8651 |
| 112 | 1·97451 | 182·295 4586 | 162 | 1·22969 | 289·089 7971 | 212 | 4·73370 | 402·675 2009 |
| 113 | 2·23119 | 184·348 5371 | 163 | 2·00440 | 291·301 9847 | 213 | 1·00828 | 405·003 5805 |
| 114 | 2·54356 | 186·405 4419 | 164 | 3·28722 | 293·516 8286 | 214 | 2·15772 | 407·333 9943 |
| 115 | 2·92509 | 188·466 1398 | 165 | 5·42391 | 295·734 3125 | 215 | 4·63909 | 409·666 4328 |
| 116 | 3·39311 | 190·530 5978 | 166 | 9·00369 | 297·954 4206 | 216 | 1·00204 | 412·000 8865 |
| 117 | 3·96994 | 192·598 7836 | 167 | 1·50362 | 300·177 1371 | 217 | 2·17443 | 414·337 3463 |
| 118 | 4·68453 | 194·670 6656 | 168 | 2·52608 | 302·402 4464 | 218 | 4·74027 | 416·675 8027 |
| 119 | 5·57459 | 196·746 2126 | 169 | 4·26907 | 304·630 3331 | 219 | 1·03812 | 419·016 2469 |
| 120 | 6·68950 | 198·825 3938 | 170 | 7·25742 | 306·860 7820 | 220 | 2·28386 | 421·358 6695 |
| 121 | 8·09430 | 200·908 1792 | 171 | 1·24102 | 309·093 7781 | 221 | 5·04733 | 423·703 0618 |
| 122 | 9·87504 | 202·994 5390 | 172 | 2·13455 | 311·329 3066 | 222 | 1·12051 | 426·049 4148 |
| 123 | 1·21463 | 205·084 4442 | 173 | 3·69277 | 313·567 3527 | 223 | 2·49873 | 428·397 7197 |
| 124 | 1·50614 | 207·177 8658 | 174 | 6·42543 | 315·807 9019 | 224 | 5·59716 | 430·747 9677 |
| 125 | 1·88268 | 209·274 7759 | 175 | 1·12445 | 318·050 9400 | 225 | 1·25936 | 433·100 1502 |
| 126 | 2·37217 | 211·375 1464 | 176 | 1·97903 | 320·296 4526 | 226 | 2·84616 | 435·454 2586 |
| 127 | 3·01266 | 213·478 9501 | 177 | 3·50289 | 322·544 4259 | 227 | 6·46077 | 437·810 2845 |
| 128 | 3·85620 | 215·586 1601 | 178 | 6·23514 | 324·794 8459 | 228 | 1·47306 | 440·168 2193 |
| 129 | 4·97450 | 217·696 7498 | 179 | 1·11609 | 327·047 6989 | 229 | 3·37330 | 442·528 0548 |
| 130 | 6·46686 | 219·810 6932 | 180 | 2·00896 | 329·302 9714 | 230 | 7·75859 | 444·889 7827 |
| 131 | 8·47158 | 221·927 9645 | 181 | 3·63622 | 331·560 6500 | 231 | 1·79223 | 447·253 3946 |
| 132 | 1·11825 | 224·048 5384 | 182 | 6·61792 | 333·820 7214 | 232 | 4·15798 | 449·618 8826 |
| 133 | 1·48727 | 226·172 3900 | 183 | 1·21108 | 336·083 1725 | 233 | 9·68810 | 451·986 2385 |
| 134 | 1·99294 | 228·299 4948 | 184 | 2·22839 | 338·347 9903 | 234 | 2·26702 | 454·355 4544 |
| 135 | 2·69047 | 230·429 8286 | 185 | 4·12251 | 340·615 1620 | 235 | 5·32749 | 456·726 5223 |
| 136 | 3·65904 | 232·563 3675 | 186 | 7·66787 | 342·884 6750 | 236 | 1·25729 | 459·099 4343 |
| 137 | 5·01289 | 234·700 0881 | 187 | 1·43389 | 345·156 5166 | 237 | 2·97977 | 461·474 1826 |
| 138 | 6·91779 | 236·839 9672 | 188 | 2·69572 | 347·430 6744 | 238 | 7·09185 | 463·850 7596 |
| 139 | 9·61572 | 238·982 9820 | 189 | 5·09491 | 349·707 1362 | 239 | 1·69495 | 466·229 1575 |
| 140 | 1·34620 | 241·129 1100 | 190 | 9·68032 | 351·985 8898 | 240 | 4·06789 | 468·609 3687 |
| 141 | 1·89814 | 243·278 3291 | 191 | 1·84894 | 354·266 9232 | 241 | 9·80360 | 470·991 3857 |
| 142 | 2·69536 | 245·430 6174 | 192 | 3·54997 | 356·550 2244 | 242 | 2·37247 | 473·375 2011 |
| 143 | 3·85437 | 247·585 9535 | 193 | 6·85144 | 358·835 7817 | 243 | 5·76511 | 475·760 8074 |
| 144 | 5·55029 | 249·744 3160 | 194 | 1·32918 | 361·123 5835 | 244 | 1·40669 | 478·148 1972 |
| 145 | 8·04793 | 251·905 6840 | 195 | 2·59190 | 363·413 6181 | 245 | 3·44638 | 480·537 3633 |
| 146 | 1·17500 | 254·070 0368 | 196 | 5·08012 | 365·705 8742 | 246 | 8·47810 | 482·928 2984 |
| 147 | 1·72725 | 256·237 3542 | 197 | 1·00078 | 368·000 3404 | 247 | 2·09409 | 485·320 9954 |
| 148 | 2·55632 | 258·407 6159 | 198 | 1·98155 | 370·297 0056 | 248 | 5·19334 | 487·715 4470 |
| 149 | 3·80892 | 260·580 8022 | 199 | 3·94329 | 372·595 8586 | 249 | 1·29314 | 490·111 6464 |
| 150 | 5·71338 | 262·756 8934 | 200 | 7·88658 | 374·896 8886 | 250 | 3·23286 | 492·509 5864 |

\* Multiply by $10^c$, where $c$ is the characteristic of log $n!$ shown alongside in the next column.

Table 51 (*continued*)

| $n$ | $\log_{10} n\,!$ | $n$ | $\log_{10} n\,!$ | $n$ | $\log_{10} n\,!$ | $n$ | $\log_{10} n\,!$ | $n$ | $\log_{10} n\,!$ |
|---|---|---|---|---|---|---|---|---|---|
| 251 | 494·909 2601 | 301 | 616·964 3695 | 351 | 742·637 2813 | 401 | 871·409 5586 | 451 | 1002·893 0675 |
| 252 | 497·310 6607 | 302 | 619·444 3765 | 352 | 745·183 8240 | 402 | 874·013 7846 | 452 | 1005·548 2059 |
| 253 | 499·713 7812 | 303 | 621·925 8191 | 353 | 747·731 5987 | 403 | 876·619 0896 | 453 | 1008·204 3041 |
| 254 | 502·118 6149 | 304 | 624·408 6927 | 354 | 750·280 6020 | 404 | 879·225 4710 | 454 | 1010·861 3600 |
| 255 | 504·525 1551 | 305 | 626·892 9925 | 355 | 752·830 8303 | 405 | 881·832 9260 | 455 | 1013·519 3714 |
| 256 | 506·933 3950 | 306 | 629·378 7140 | 356 | 755·382 2803 | 406 | 884·441 4521 | 456 | 1016·178 3362 |
| 257 | 509·343 3282 | 307 | 631·865 8523 | 357 | 757·934 9485 | 407 | 887·051 0465 | 457 | 1018·838 2524 |
| 258 | 511·754 9479 | 308 | 634·354 4031 | 358 | 760·488 8316 | 408 | 889·661 7066 | 458 | 1021·499 1179 |
| 259 | 514·168 2476 | 309 | 636·844 3615 | 359 | 763·043 9260 | 409 | 892·273 4300 | 459 | 1024·160 9306 |
| 260 | 516·583 2210 | 310 | 639·335 7232 | 360 | 765·600 2285 | 410 | 894·886 2138 | 460 | 1026·823 6884 |
| 261 | 518·999 8615 | 311 | 641·828 4836 | 361 | 768·157 7357 | 411 | 897·500 0556 | 461 | 1029·487 3893 |
| 262 | 521·418 1628 | 312 | 644·322 6382 | 362 | 770·716 4443 | 412 | 900·114 9528 | 462 | 1032·152 0313 |
| 263 | 523·838 1185 | 313 | 646·818 1825 | 363 | 773·276 3509 | 413 | 902·730 9029 | 463 | 1034·817 6123 |
| 264 | 526·259 7225 | 314 | 649·315 1122 | 364 | 775·837 4523 | 414 | 905·347 9032 | 464 | 1037·484 1303 |
| 265 | 528·682 9683 | 315 | 651·813 4227 | 365 | 778·399 7452 | 415 | 907·965 9513 | 465 | 1040·151 5832 |
| 266 | 531·107 8500 | 316 | 654·313 1098 | 366 | 780·963 2262 | 416 | 910·585 0447 | 466 | 1042·819 9692 |
| 267 | 533·534 3612 | 317 | 656·814 1691 | 367 | 783·527 8923 | 417 | 913·205 1807 | 467 | 1045·489 2860 |
| 268 | 535·962 4960 | 318 | 659·316 5962 | 368 | 786·093 7401 | 418 | 915·826 3570 | 468 | 1048·159 5319 |
| 269 | 538·392 2483 | 319 | 661·820 3869 | 369 | 788·660 7665 | 419 | 918·448 5710 | 469 | 1050·830 7047 |
| 270 | 540·823 6121 | 320 | 664·325 5369 | 370 | 791·228 9682 | 420 | 921·071 8203 | 470 | 1053·502 8026 |
| 271 | 543·256 5814 | 321 | 666·832 0419 | 371 | 793·798 3421 | 421 | 923·696 1024 | 471 | 1056·175 8235 |
| 272 | 545·691 1503 | 322 | 669·339 8978 | 372 | 796·368 8851 | 422 | 926·321 4149 | 472 | 1058·849 7655 |
| 273 | 548·127 3129 | 323 | 671·849 1003 | 373 | 798·940 5939 | 423 | 928·947 7552 | 473 | 1061·524 6266 |
| 274 | 550·565 0635 | 324 | 674·359 6453 | 374 | 801·513 4655 | 424 | 931·575 1211 | 474 | 1064·200 4050 |
| 275 | 553·004 3962 | 325 | 676·871 5287 | 375 | 804·087 4968 | 425 | 934·203 5100 | 475 | 1066·877 0986 |
| 276 | 555·445 3052 | 326 | 679·384 7163 | 376 | 806·662 6846 | 426 | 936·832 9196 | 476 | 1069·554 7056 |
| 277 | 557·887 7850 | 327 | 681·899 2940 | 377 | 809·239 0260 | 427 | 939·463 3475 | 477 | 1072·233 2239 |
| 278 | 560·331 8298 | 328 | 684·415 1679 | 378 | 811·816 5178 | 428 | 942·094 7913 | 478 | 1074·912 6518 |
| 279 | 562·777 4340 | 329 | 686·932 3638 | 379 | 814·395 1570 | 429 | 944·727 2486 | 479 | 1077·592 9873 |
| 280 | 565·224 5920 | 330 | 689·450 8777 | 380 | 816·974 9406 | 430 | 947·360 7170 | 480 | 1080·274 2286 |
| 281 | 567·673 2984 | 331 | 691·970 7057 | 381 | 819·555 8655 | 431 | 949·995 1943 | 481 | 1082·956 3737 |
| 282 | 570·123 5475 | 332 | 694·491 8438 | 382 | 822·137 9289 | 432 | 952·630 6780 | 482 | 1085·639 4207 |
| 283 | 572·575 3339 | 333 | 697·014 2880 | 383 | 824·721 1277 | 433 | 955·267 1659 | 483 | 1088·323 3678 |
| 284 | 575·028 6523 | 334 | 699·538 0345 | 384 | 827·305 4589 | 434 | 957·904 6557 | 484 | 1091·008 2132 |
| 285 | 577·483 4971 | 335 | 702·063 0793 | 385 | 829·890 9196 | 435 | 960·543 1449 | 485 | 1093·693 9549 |
| 286 | 579·939 8631 | 336 | 704·589 4186 | 386 | 832·477 5069 | 436 | 963·182 6314 | 486 | 1096·380 5912 |
| 287 | 582·397 7450 | 337 | 707·117 0485 | 387 | 835·065 2179 | 437 | 965·823 1128 | 487 | 1099·068 1202 |
| 288 | 584·857 1375 | 338 | 709·645 9652 | 388 | 837·654 0496 | 438 | 968·464 5869 | 488 | 1101·756 5400 |
| 289 | 587·318 0354 | 339 | 712·176 1649 | 389 | 840·243 9992 | 439 | 971·107 0515 | 489 | 1104·445 8488 |
| 290 | 589·780 4334 | 340 | 714·707 6438 | 390 | 842·835 0638 | 440 | 973·750 5041 | 490 | 1107·136 0449 |
| 291 | 592·244 3264 | 341 | 717·240 3982 | 391 | 845·427 2406 | 441 | 976·394 9427 | 491 | 1109·827 1264 |
| 292 | 594·709 7092 | 342 | 719·774 4243 | 392 | 848·020 5267 | 442 | 979·040 3650 | 492 | 1112·519 0915 |
| 293 | 597·176 5768 | 343 | 722·309 7184 | 393 | 850·614 9192 | 443 | 981·686 7687 | 493 | 1115·211 9384 |
| 294 | 599·644 9242 | 344 | 724·846 2768 | 394 | 853·210 4154 | 444 | 984·334 1517 | 494 | 1117·905 6654 |
| 295 | 602·114 7462 | 345 | 727·384 0959 | 395 | 855·807 0125 | 445 | 986·982 5117 | 495 | 1120·600 2706 |
| 296 | 604·586 0379 | 346 | 729·923 1720 | 396 | 858·404 7077 | 446 | 989·631 8466 | 496 | 1123·295 7523 |
| 297 | 607·058 7943 | 347 | 732·463 5015 | 397 | 861·003 4982 | 447 | 992·282 1541 | 497 | 1125·992 1086 |
| 298 | 609·533 0106 | 348 | 735·005 0807 | 398 | 863·603 3813 | 448 | 994·933 4321 | 498 | 1128·689 3380 |
| 299 | 612·008 6818 | 349 | 737·547 9062 | 399 | 866·204 3542 | 449 | 997·585 6784 | 499 | 1131·387 4385 |
| 300 | 614·485 8030 | 350 | 740·091 9742 | 400 | 868·806 4142 | 450 | 1000·238 8910 | 500 | 1134·086 4085 |

Table 51. *Logarithms of factorials of integers (continued)*

| n | $\log_{10} n!$ | n | $\log_{10} n!$ | n | $\log_{10} n!$ | n | $\log_{10} n!$ | n | $\log_{10} n!$ |
|---|---|---|---|---|---|---|---|---|---|
| 501 | 1136·786 2463 | 551 | 1272·848 0029 | 601 | 1410·881 1614 | 651 | 1550·721 4519 | 701 | 1692·229 8994 |
| 502 | 1139·486 9500 | 552 | 1275·589 9419 | 602 | 1413·660 7579 | 652 | 1553·535 6995 | 702 | 1695·076 2365 |
| 503 | 1142·188 5180 | 553 | 1278·332 6671 | 603 | 1416·441 0752 | 653 | 1556·350 6126 | 703 | 1697·923 1918 |
| 504 | 1144·890 9485 | 554 | 1281·076 1768 | 604 | 1419·222 1122 | 654 | 1559·166 1904 | 704 | 1700·770 7644 |
| 505 | 1147·594 2399 | 555 | 1283·820 4698 | 605 | 1422·003 8676 | 655 | 1561·982 4317 | 705 | 1703·618 9536 |
| 506 | 1150·298 3904 | 556 | 1286·565 5446 | 606 | 1424·786 3402 | 656 | 1564·799 3355 | 706 | 1706·467 7583 |
| 507 | 1153·003 3984 | 557 | 1289·311 3998 | 607 | 1427·569 5289 | 657 | 1567·616 9009 | 707 | 1709·317 1777 |
| 508 | 1155·709 2621 | 558 | 1292·058 0340 | 608 | 1430·353 4324 | 658 | 1570·435 1268 | 708 | 1712·167 2109 |
| 509 | 1158·415 9798 | 559 | 1294·805 4458 | 609 | 1433·138 0497 | 659 | 1573·254 0122 | 709 | 1715·017 8572 |
| 510 | 1161·123 5500 | 560 | 1297·553 6338 | 610 | 1435·923 3796 | 660 | 1576·073 5561 | 710 | 1717·869 1155 |
| 511 | 1163·831 9709 | 561 | 1300·302 5967 | 611 | 1438·709 4208 | 661 | 1578·893 7576 | 711 | 1720·720 9851 |
| 512 | 1166·541 2409 | 562 | 1303·052 3330 | 612 | 1441·496 1722 | 662 | 1581·714 6156 | 712 | 1723·573 4651 |
| 513 | 1169·251 3583 | 563 | 1305·802 8414 | 613 | 1444·283 6327 | 663 | 1584·536 1291 | 713 | 1726·426 5546 |
| 514 | 1171·962 3214 | 564 | 1308·554 1205 | 614 | 1447·071 8011 | 664 | 1587·358 2972 | 714 | 1729·280 2529 |
| 515 | 1174·674 1286 | 565 | 1311·306 1690 | 615 | 1449·860 6762 | 665 | 1590·181 1188 | 715 | 1732·134 5589 |
| 516 | 1177·386 7783 | 566 | 1314·058 9854 | 616 | 1452·650 2569 | 666 | 1593·004 5931 | 716 | 1734·989 4719 |
| 517 | 1180·100 2688 | 567 | 1316·812 5684 | 617 | 1455·440 5420 | 667 | 1595·828 7189 | 717 | 1737·844 9911 |
| 518 | 1182·814 5986 | 568 | 1319·566 9168 | 618 | 1458·231 5305 | 668 | 1598·653 4954 | 718 | 1740·701 1155 |
| 519 | 1185·529 7660 | 569 | 1322·322 0290 | 619 | 1461·023 2212 | 669 | 1601·478 9215 | 719 | 1743·557 8444 |
| 520 | 1188·245 7693 | 570 | 1325·077 9039 | 620 | 1463·815 6129 | 670 | 1604·304 9963 | 720 | 1746·415 1769 |
| 521 | 1190·962 6070 | 571 | 1327·834 5400 | 621 | 1466·608 7045 | 671 | 1607·131 7188 | 721 | 1749·273 1122 |
| 522 | 1193·680 2775 | 572 | 1330·591 9360 | 622 | 1469·402 4948 | 672 | 1609·959 0881 | 722 | 1752·131 6494 |
| 523 | 1196·398 7792 | 573 | 1333·350 0907 | 623 | 1472·196 9829 | 673 | 1612·787 1031 | 723 | 1754·990 7877 |
| 524 | 1199·118 1105 | 574 | 1336·109 0026 | 624 | 1474·992 1675 | 674 | 1615·615 7630 | 724 | 1757·850 5262 |
| 525 | 1201·838 2698 | 575 | 1338·868 6704 | 625 | 1477·788 0475 | 675 | 1618·445 0668 | 725 | 1760·710 8642 |
| 526 | 1204·559 2556 | 576 | 1341·629 0929 | 626 | 1480·584 6218 | 676 | 1621·275 0135 | 726 | 1763·571 8009 |
| 527 | 1207·281 0662 | 577 | 1344·390 2687 | 627 | 1483·381 8894 | 677 | 1624·105 6022 | 727 | 1766·433 3353 |
| 528 | 1210·003 7001 | 578 | 1347·152 1965 | 628 | 1486·179 8490 | 678 | 1626·936 8319 | 728 | 1769·295 4667 |
| 529 | 1212·727 1558 | 579 | 1349·914 8751 | 629 | 1488·978 4997 | 679 | 1629·768 7016 | 729 | 1772·158 1942 |
| 530 | 1215·451 4316 | 580 | 1352·678 3031 | 630 | 1491·777 8402 | 680 | 1632·601 2106 | 730 | 1775·021 5170 |
| 531 | 1218·176 5262 | 581 | 1355·442 4792 | 631 | 1494·577 8696 | 681 | 1635·434 3577 | 731 | 1777·885 4344 |
| 532 | 1220·902 4378 | 582 | 1358·207 4022 | 632 | 1497·378 5866 | 682 | 1638·268 1420 | 732 | 1780·749 9455 |
| 533 | 1223·629 1650 | 583 | 1360·973 0708 | 633 | 1500·179 9904 | 683 | 1641·102 5627 | 733 | 1783·615 0495 |
| 534 | 1226·356 7063 | 584 | 1363·739 4836 | 634 | 1502·982 0796 | 684 | 1643·937 6189 | 734 | 1786·480 7455 |
| 535 | 1229·085 0600 | 585 | 1366·506 6395 | 635 | 1505·784 8533 | 685 | 1646·773 3094 | 735 | 1789·347 0329 |
| 536 | 1231·814 2248 | 586 | 1369·274 5371 | 636 | 1508·588 3105 | 686 | 1649·609 6335 | 736 | 1792·213 9107 |
| 537 | 1234·544 1991 | 587 | 1372·043 1752 | 637 | 1511·392 4499 | 687 | 1652·446 5903 | 737 | 1795·081 3782 |
| 538 | 1237·274 9814 | 588 | 1374·812 5525 | 638 | 1514·197 2706 | 688 | 1655·284 1787 | 738 | 1797·949 4345 |
| 539 | 1240·006 5702 | 589 | 1377·582 6678 | 639 | 1517·002 7714 | 689 | 1658·122 3979 | 739 | 1800·818 0790 |
| 540 | 1242·738 9639 | 590 | 1380·353 5198 | 640 | 1519·808 9514 | 690 | 1660·961 2470 | 740 | 1803·687 3107 |
| 541 | 1245·472 1612 | 591 | 1383·125 1073 | 641 | 1522·615 8094 | 691 | 1663·800 7251 | 741 | 1806·557 1289 |
| 542 | 1248·206 1605 | 592 | 1385·897 4290 | 642 | 1525·423 3445 | 692 | 1666·640 8312 | 742 | 1809·427 5328 |
| 543 | 1250·940 9603 | 593 | 1388·670 4837 | 643 | 1528·231 5554 | 693 | 1669·481 5644 | 743 | 1812·298 5216 |
| 544 | 1253·676 5592 | 594 | 1391·444 2702 | 644 | 1531·040 4413 | 694 | 1672·322 9239 | 744 | 1815·170 0946 |
| 545 | 1256·412 9557 | 595 | 1394·218 7871 | 645 | 1533·850 0010 | 695 | 1675·164 9087 | 745 | 1818·042 2508 |
| 546 | 1259·150 1483 | 596 | 1396·994 0334 | 646 | 1536·660 2335 | 696 | 1678·007 5179 | 746 | 1820·914 9897 |
| 547 | 1261·888 1357 | 597 | 1399·770 0077 | 647 | 1539·471 1378 | 697 | 1680·850 7507 | 747 | 1823·788 3103 |
| 548 | 1264·626 9162 | 598 | 1402·546 7089 | 648 | 1542·282 7128 | 698 | 1683·694 6061 | 748 | 1826·662 2119 |
| 549 | 1267·366 4886 | 599 | 1405·324 1357 | 649 | 1545·094 9575 | 699 | 1686·539 0833 | 749 | 1829·536 6937 |
| 550 | 1270·106 8513 | 600 | 1408·102 2870 | 650 | 1547·907 8709 | 700 | 1689·384 1813 | 750 | 1832·411 7549 |

Table 51 (*continued*)

| $n$ | $\log_{10} n!$ | $n$ | $\log_{10} n!$ | $n$ | $\log_{10} n!$ | $n$ | $\log_{10} n!$ | $n$ | $\log_{10} n!$ |
|---|---|---|---|---|---|---|---|---|---|
| 751 | 1835·287 3949 | 801 | 1979·790 7168 | 851 | 2125·649 5488 | 901 | 2272·784 2010 | 951 | 2421·123 8376 |
| 752 | 1838·163 6127 | 802 | 1982·694 8911 | 852 | 2128·579 9884 | 902 | 2275·739 4075 | 952 | 2424·102 4745 |
| 753 | 1841·040 4077 | 803 | 1985·599 6067 | 853 | 2131·510 9374 | 903 | 2278·695 0953 | 953 | 2427·081 5674 |
| 754 | 1843·917 7790 | 804 | 1988·504 8627 | 854 | 2134·442 3953 | 904 | 2281·651 2637 | 954 | 2430·061 1158 |
| 755 | 1846·795 7260 | 805 | 1991·410 6586 | 855 | 2137·374 3614 | 905 | 2284·607 9123 | 955 | 2433·041 1192 |
| 756 | 1849·674 2478 | 806 | 1994·316 9936 | 856 | 2140·306 8352 | 906 | 2287·565 0405 | 956 | 2436·021 5771 |
| 757 | 1852·553 3437 | 807 | 1997·223 8672 | 857 | 2143·239 8160 | 907 | 2290·522 6478 | 957 | 2439·002 4890 |
| 758 | 1855·433 0129 | 808 | 2000·130 1733 | 858 | 2146·173 3033 | 908 | 2293·480 7336 | 958 | 2441·983 8545 |
| 759 | 1858·313 2546 | 809 | 2003·039 2271 | 859 | 2149·107 2964 | 909 | 2296·439 2975 | 959 | 2444·965 6731 |
| 760 | 1861·194 0682 | 810 | 2005·947 7121 | 860 | 2152·041 7949 | 910 | 2299·398 3389 | 960 | 2447·947 9443 |
| 761 | 1864·075 4529 | 811 | 2008·856 7329 | 861 | 2154·976 7980 | 911 | 2302·357 8573 | 961 | 2450·930 6677 |
| 762 | 1866·957 4079 | 812 | 2011·766 2890 | 862 | 2157·912 3053 | 912 | 2305·317 8521 | 962 | 2453·913 8428 |
| 763 | 1869·839 9324 | 813 | 2014·676 3795 | 863 | 2160·848 3161 | 913 | 2308·278 3229 | 963 | 2456·897 4691 |
| 764 | 1872·723 0258 | 814 | 2017·587 0039 | 864 | 2163·784 8298 | 914 | 2311·239 2691 | 964 | 2459·881 5461 |
| 765 | 1875·606 6872 | 815 | 2020·498 1615 | 865 | 2166·721 8459 | 915 | 2314·200 6902 | 965 | 2462·866 0734 |
| 766 | 1878·490 9160 | 816 | 2023·409 8517 | 866 | 2169·659 3638 | 916 | 2317·162 5856 | 966 | 2465·851 0506 |
| 767 | 1881·375 7113 | 817 | 2026·322 0737 | 867 | 2172·597 3829 | 917 | 2320·124 9550 | 967 | 2468·836 4770 |
| 768 | 1884·261 0726 | 818 | 2029·234 8270 | 868 | 2175·535 9027 | 918 | 2323·087 7977 | 968 | 2471·822 3524 |
| 769 | 1887·146 9989 | 819 | 2032·148 1109 | 869 | 2178·474 9224 | 919 | 2326·051 1132 | 969 | 2474·808 6762 |
| 770 | 1890·033 4896 | 820 | 2035·061 9248 | 870 | 2181·414 4417 | 920 | 2329·014 9010 | 970 | 2477·795 4479 |
| 771 | 1892·920 5440 | 821 | 2037·976 2679 | 871 | 2184·354 4598 | 921 | 2331·979 1606 | 971 | 2480·782 6671 |
| 772 | 1895·808 1613 | 822 | 2040·891 1398 | 872 | 2187·294 9763 | 922 | 2334·943 8915 | 972 | 2483·770 3334 |
| 773 | 1898·696 3408 | 823 | 2043·806 5396 | 873 | 2190·235 9906 | 923 | 2337·909 0932 | 973 | 2486·758 4462 |
| 774 | 1901·585 0817 | 824 | 2046·722 4668 | 874 | 2193·177 5020 | 924 | 2340·874 7652 | 974 | 2489·747 0052 |
| 775 | 1904·474 3835 | 825 | 2049·638 9208 | 875 | 2196·119 5101 | 925 | 2343·840 9069 | 975 | 2492·736 0098 |
| 776 | 1907·364 2452 | 826 | 2052·555 9008 | 876 | 2199·062 0142 | 926 | 2346·807 5179 | 976 | 2495·725 4596 |
| 777 | 1910·254 6662 | 827 | 2055·473 4063 | 877 | 2202·005 0138 | 927 | 2349·774 5977 | 977 | 2498·715 3542 |
| 778 | 1913·145 6458 | 828 | 2058·391 4367 | 878 | 2204·948 5083 | 928 | 2352·742 1456 | 978 | 2501·705 6930 |
| 779 | 1916·037 1832 | 829 | 2061·309 9912 | 879 | 2207·892 4971 | 929 | 2355·710 1614 | 979 | 2504·696 4757 |
| 780 | 1918·929 2778 | 830 | 2064·229 0693 | 880 | 2210·836 9798 | 930 | 2358·678 6443 | 980 | 2507·687 7018 |
| 781 | 1921·821 9289 | 831 | 2067·148 6703 | 881 | 2213·781 9557 | 931 | 2361·647 5940 | 981 | 2510·679 3708 |
| 782 | 1924·715 1356 | 832 | 2070·068 7936 | 882 | 2216·727 4243 | 932 | 2364·617 0099 | 982 | 2513·671 4823 |
| 783 | 1927·608 8974 | 833 | 2072·989 4386 | 883 | 2219·673 3850 | 933 | 2367·586 8915 | 983 | 2516·664 0358 |
| 784 | 1930·503 2135 | 834 | 2075·910 6047 | 884 | 2222·619 8373 | 934 | 2370·557 2384 | 984 | 2519·657 0309 |
| 785 | 1933·398 0831 | 835 | 2078·832 2912 | 885 | 2225·566 7805 | 935 | 2373·528 0500 | 985 | 2522·650 4672 |
| 786 | 1936·293 5057 | 836 | 2081·754 4974 | 886 | 2228·514 2143 | 936 | 2376·499 3259 | 986 | 2525·644 3441 |
| 787 | 1939·189 4804 | 837 | 2084·677 2229 | 887 | 2231·462 1379 | 937 | 2379·471 0655 | 987 | 2528·638 6612 |
| 788 | 1942·086 0066 | 838 | 2087·600 4669 | 888 | 2234·410 5509 | 938 | 2382·443 2683 | 988 | 2531·633 4182 |
| 789 | 1944·983 0836 | 839 | 2090·524 2289 | 889 | 2237·359 4526 | 939 | 2385·415 9339 | 989 | 2534·628 6145 |
| 790 | 1947·880 7107 | 840 | 2093·448 5082 | 890 | 2240·308 8426 | 940 | 2388·389 0618 | 990 | 2537·624 2497 |
| 791 | 1950·778 8872 | 841 | 2096·373 3042 | 891 | 2243·258 7203 | 941 | 2391·362 6514 | 991 | 2540·620 3233 |
| 792 | 1953·677 6124 | 842 | 2099·298 6162 | 892 | 2246·209 0852 | 942 | 2394·336 7023 | 992 | 2543·616 8350 |
| 793 | 1956·576 8856 | 843 | 2102·224 4438 | 893 | 2249·159 9366 | 943 | 2397·311 2140 | 993 | 2546·613 7842 |
| 794 | 1959·476 7061 | 844 | 2105·150 7863 | 894 | 2252·111 2742 | 944 | 2400·286 1860 | 994 | 2549·611 1706 |
| 795 | 1962·377 0732 | 845 | 2108·077 6430 | 895 | 2255·063 0972 | 945 | 2403·261 6178 | 995 | 2552·608 9937 |
| 796 | 1965·277 9863 | 846 | 2111·005 0133 | 896 | 2258·015 4052 | 946 | 2406·237 5089 | 996 | 2555·607 2530 |
| 797 | 1968·179 4446 | 847 | 2113·932 8967 | 897 | 2260·968 1976 | 947 | 2409·213 8589 | 997 | 2558·605 9482 |
| 798 | 1971·081 4475 | 848 | 2116·861 2926 | 898 | 2263·921 4740 | 948 | 2412·190 6672 | 998 | 2561·605 0787 |
| 799 | 1973·983 9943 | 849 | 2119·790 2003 | 899 | 2266·875 2337 | 949 | 2415·167 9334 | 999 | 2564·604 6442 |
| 800 | 1976·887 0842 | 850 | 2122·719 6192 | 900 | 2269·829 4762 | 950 | 2418·145 6570 | 1000 | 2567·604 6442 |

Table 52. *Miscellaneous functions of p and q = 1 − p over the unit range*

| $p$ | $\Gamma(1+p)$ | $\log_{10}\Gamma(1+p)$ | $1-p^2$ | $\sqrt{(1-p^2)}$ | $\dfrac{1}{\sqrt{(1-p^2)}}$ | $pq$ | $\sqrt{(pq)}$ | $p^2+q^2$ | $q=1-p$ |
|---|---|---|---|---|---|---|---|---|---|
| 0·00 | 1·0000 000 | 0·0000 000 | 1·0000 | 1·00000 | 1·00000 | 0·0000 | 0·00000 | 1·0000 | 1·00 |
| 0·01 | 0·9943 259 | 1̄·9975 287 | 0·9999 | 0·99995 | 1·00005 | 0·0099 | 0·09950 | 0·9802 | 0·99 |
| 0·02 | 0·9888 442 | 1̄·9951 279 | 0·9996 | 0·99980 | 1·00020 | 0·0196 | 0·14000 | 0·9608 | 0·98 |
| 0·03 | 0·9835 500 | 1̄·9927 964 | 0·9991 | 0·99955 | 1·00045 | 0·0291 | 0·17059 | 0·9418 | 0·97 |
| 0·04 | 0·9784 382 | 1̄·9905 334 | 0·9984 | 0·99920 | 1·00080 | 0·0384 | 0·19596 | 0·9232 | 0·96 |
| 0·05 | 0·9735 043 | 1̄·9883 379 | 0·9975 | 0·99875 | 1·00125 | 0·0475 | 0·21794 | 0·9050 | 0·95 |
| 0·06 | 0·9687 436 | 1̄·9862 089 | 0·9964 | 0·99820 | 1·00180 | 0·0564 | 0·23749 | 0·8872 | 0·94 |
| 0·07 | 0·9641 520 | 1̄·9841 455 | 0·9951 | 0·99755 | 1·00246 | 0·0651 | 0·25515 | 0·8698 | 0·93 |
| 0·08 | 0·9597 253 | 1̄·9821 469 | 0·9936 | 0·99679 | 1·00322 | 0·0736 | 0·27129 | 0·8528 | 0·92 |
| 0·09 | 0·9554 595 | 1̄·9802 123 | 0·9919 | 0·99594 | 1·00407 | 0·0819 | 0·28618 | 0·8362 | 0·91 |
| 0·10 | 0·9513 508 | 1̄·9783 407 | 0·9900 | 0·99499 | 1·00504 | 0·0900 | 0·30000 | 0·8200 | 0·90 |
| 0·11 | 0·9473 955 | 1̄·9765 313 | 0·9879 | 0·99393 | 1·00611 | 0·0979 | 0·31289 | 0·8042 | 0·89 |
| 0·12 | 0·9435 902 | 1̄·9747 834 | 0·9856 | 0·99277 | 1·00728 | 0·1056 | 0·32496 | 0·7888 | 0·88 |
| 0·13 | 0·9399 314 | 1̄·9730 962 | 0·9831 | 0·99151 | 1·00856 | 0·1131 | 0·33630 | 0·7738 | 0·87 |
| 0·14 | 0·9364 161 | 1̄·9714 689 | 0·9804 | 0·99015 | 1·00995 | 0·1204 | 0·34699 | 0·7592 | 0·86 |
| 0·15 | 0·9330 409 | 1̄·9699 007 | 0·9775 | 0·98869 | 1·01144 | 0·1275 | 0·35707 | 0·7450 | 0·85 |
| 0·16 | 0·9298 031 | 1̄·9683 910 | 0·9744 | 0·98712 | 1·01305 | 0·1344 | 0·36661 | 0·7312 | 0·84 |
| 0·17 | 0·9266 996 | 1̄·9669 390 | 0·9711 | 0·98544 | 1·01477 | 0·1411 | 0·37563 | 0·7178 | 0·83 |
| 0·18 | 0·9237 278 | 1̄·9655 440 | 0·9676 | 0·98367 | 1·01660 | 0·1476 | 0·38419 | 0·7048 | 0·82 |
| 0·19 | 0·9208 850 | 1̄·9642 054 | 0·9639 | 0·98178 | 1·01855 | 0·1539 | 0·39230 | 0·6922 | 0·81 |
| 0·20 | 0·9181 687 | 1̄·9629 225 | 0·9600 | 0·97980 | 1·02062 | 0·1600 | 0·40000 | 0·6800 | 0·80 |
| 0·21 | 0·9155 765 | 1̄·9616 946 | 0·9559 | 0·97770 | 1·02281 | 0·1659 | 0·40731 | 0·6682 | 0·79 |
| 0·22 | 0·9131 059 | 1̄·9605 212 | 0·9516 | 0·97550 | 1·02512 | 0·1716 | 0·41425 | 0·6568 | 0·78 |
| 0·23 | 0·9107 549 | 1̄·9594 015 | 0·9471 | 0·97319 | 1·02755 | 0·1771 | 0·42083 | 0·6458 | 0·77 |
| 0·24 | 0·9085 211 | 1̄·9583 350 | 0·9424 | 0·97077 | 1·03011 | 0·1824 | 0·42708 | 0·6352 | 0·76 |
| 0·25 | 0·9064 025 | 1̄·9573 211 | 0·9375 | 0·96825 | 1·03280 | 0·1875 | 0·43301 | 0·6250 | 0·75 |
| 0·26 | 0·9043 971 | 1̄·9563 592 | 0·9324 | 0·96561 | 1·03562 | 0·1924 | 0·43863 | 0·6152 | 0·74 |
| 0·27 | 0·9025 031 | 1̄·9554 487 | 0·9271 | 0·96286 | 1·03857 | 0·1971 | 0·44396 | 0·6058 | 0·73 |
| 0·28 | 0·9007 185 | 1̄·9545 891 | 0·9216 | 0·96000 | 1·04167 | 0·2016 | 0·44900 | 0·5968 | 0·72 |
| 0·29 | 0·8990 416 | 1̄·9537 798 | 0·9159 | 0·95703 | 1·04490 | 0·2059 | 0·45376 | 0·5882 | 0·71 |
| 0·30 | 0·8974 707 | 1̄·9530 203 | 0·9100 | 0·95394 | 1·04828 | 0·2100 | 0·45826 | 0·5800 | 0·70 |
| 0·31 | 0·8960 042 | 1̄·9523 100 | 0·9039 | 0·95074 | 1·05182 | 0·2139 | 0·46249 | 0·5722 | 0·69 |
| 0·32 | 0·8946 405 | 1̄·9516 485 | 0·8976 | 0·94742 | 1·05550 | 0·2176 | 0·46648 | 0·5648 | 0·68 |
| 0·33 | 0·8933 781 | 1̄·9510 353 | 0·8911 | 0·94398 | 1·05934 | 0·2211 | 0·47021 | 0·5578 | 0·67 |
| 0·34 | 0·8922 155 | 1̄·9504 698 | 0·8844 | 0·94043 | 1·06335 | 0·2244 | 0·47371 | 0·5512 | 0·66 |
| 0·35 | 0·8911 514 | 1̄·9499 515 | 0·8775 | 0·93675 | 1·06752 | 0·2275 | 0·47697 | 0·5450 | 0·65 |
| 0·36 | 0·8901 845 | 1̄·9494 800 | 0·8704 | 0·93295 | 1·07187 | 0·2304 | 0·48000 | 0·5392 | 0·64 |
| 0·37 | 0·8893 135 | 1̄·9490 549 | 0·8631 | 0·92903 | 1·07639 | 0·2331 | 0·48280 | 0·5338 | 0·63 |
| 0·38 | 0·8885 371 | 1̄·9486 756 | 0·8556 | 0·92499 | 1·08110 | 0·2356 | 0·48539 | 0·5288 | 0·62 |
| 0·39 | 0·8878 543 | 1̄·9483 417 | 0·8479 | 0·92081 | 1·08599 | 0·2379 | 0·48775 | 0·5242 | 0·61 |
| 0·40 | 0·8872 638 | 1̄·9480 528 | 0·8400 | 0·91652 | 1·09109 | 0·2400 | 0·48990 | 0·5200 | 0·60 |
| 0·41 | 0·8867 647 | 1̄·9478 084 | 0·8319 | 0·91209 | 1·09639 | 0·2419 | 0·49183 | 0·5162 | 0·59 |
| 0·42 | 0·8863 558 | 1̄·9476 081 | 0·8236 | 0·90752 | 1·10190 | 0·2436 | 0·49356 | 0·5128 | 0·58 |
| 0·43 | 0·8860 362 | 1̄·9474 515 | 0·8151 | 0·90283 | 1·10763 | 0·2451 | 0·49508 | 0·5098 | 0·57 |
| 0·44 | 0·8858 051 | 1̄·9473 382 | 0·8064 | 0·89800 | 1·11359 | 0·2464 | 0·49639 | 0·5072 | 0·56 |
| 0·45 | 0·8856 614 | 1̄·9472 677 | 0·7975 | 0·89303 | 1·11979 | 0·2475 | 0·49749 | 0·5050 | 0·55 |
| 0·46 | 0·8856 043 | 1̄·9472 397 | 0·7884 | 0·88792 | 1·12623 | 0·2484 | 0·49840 | 0·5032 | 0·54 |
| 0·47 | 0·8856 331 | 1̄·9472 539 | 0·7791 | 0·88267 | 1·13293 | 0·2491 | 0·49910 | 0·5018 | 0·53 |
| 0·48 | 0·8857 470 | 1̄·9473 097 | 0·7696 | 0·87727 | 1·13990 | 0·2496 | 0·49960 | 0·5008 | 0·52 |
| 0·49 | 0·8859 451 | 1̄·9474 068 | 0·7599 | 0·87172 | 1·14715 | 0·2499 | 0·49990 | 0·5002 | 0·51 |
| 0·50 | 0·8862 269 | 1̄·9475 449 | 0·7500 | 0·86603 | 1·15470 | 0·2500 | 0·50000 | 0·5000 | 0·50 |

Table 52 (*continued*)

| $p$ | $\Gamma(1+p)$ | $\log_{10}\Gamma(1+p)$ | $1-p^2$ | $\sqrt{(1-p^2)}$ | $\dfrac{1}{\sqrt{(1-p^2)}}$ | $p$ | $\sqrt{(1-p^2)}$ | $\dfrac{1}{\sqrt{(1-p^2)}}$ | $\sqrt{(pq)}$ |
|---|---|---|---|---|---|---|---|---|---|
| 0·50 | 0·8862 269 | Ī·9475 449 | 0·7500 | 0·86603 | 1·15470 | 0·910 | 0·41461 | 2·41192 | 0·28618 |
| 0·51 | 0·8865 917 | Ī·9477 237 | 0·7399 | 0·86017 | 1·16255 | 0·912 | 0·41019 | 2·43789 | 0·28329 |
| 0·52 | 0·8870 388 | Ī·9479 426 | 0·7296 | 0·85417 | 1·17073 | 0·914 | 0·40571 | 2·46479 | 0·28036 |
| 0·53 | 0·8875 676 | Ī·9482 015 | 0·7191 | 0·84800 | 1·17925 | 0·916 | 0·40118 | 2·49266 | 0·27739 |
| 0·54 | 0·8881 777 | Ī·9484 998 | 0·7084 | 0·84167 | 1·18812 | 0·918 | 0·39658 | 2·52156 | 0·27436 |
| 0·55 | 0·8888 683 | Ī·9488 374 | 0·6975 | 0·83516 | 1·19737 | 0·920 | 0·39192 | 2·55155 | 0·27129 |
| 0·56 | 0·8896 392 | Ī·9492 139 | 0·6864 | 0·82849 | 1·20701 | 0·922 | 0·38719 | 2·58271 | 0·26817 |
| 0·57 | 0·8904 897 | Ī·9496 289 | 0·6751 | 0·82164 | 1·21707 | 0·924 | 0·38239 | 2·61511 | 0·26500 |
| 0·58 | 0·8914 196 | Ī·9500 822 | 0·6636 | 0·81462 | 1·22757 | 0·926 | 0·37752 | 2·64884 | 0·26177 |
| 0·59 | 0·8924 282 | Ī·9505 733 | 0·6519 | 0·80740 | 1·23854 | 0·928 | 0·37258 | 2·68399 | 0·25849 |
| 0·60 | 0·8935 153 | Ī·9511 020 | 0·6400 | 0·80000 | 1·25000 | 0·930 | 0·36756 | 2·72065 | 0·25515 |
| 0·61 | 0·8946 806 | Ī·9516 680 | 0·6279 | 0·79240 | 1·26199 | 0·932 | 0·36246 | 2·75894 | 0·25175 |
| 0·62 | 0·8959 237 | Ī·9522 710 | 0·6156 | 0·78460 | 1·27453 | 0·934 | 0·35727 | 2·79898 | 0·24828 |
| 0·63 | 0·8972 442 | Ī·9529 107 | 0·6031 | 0·77660 | 1·28767 | 0·936 | 0·35200 | 2·84091 | 0·24475 |
| 0·64 | 0·8986 420 | Ī·9535 867 | 0·5904 | 0·76837 | 1·30145 | 0·938 | 0·34664 | 2·88488 | 0·24116 |
| 0·65 | 0·9001 168 | Ī·9542 989 | 0·5775 | 0·75993 | 1·31590 | 0·940 | 0·34117 | 2·93105 | 0·23749 |
| 0·66 | 0·9016 684 | Ī·9550 468 | 0·5644 | 0·75127 | 1·33109 | 0·942 | 0·33561 | 2·97962 | 0·23374 |
| 0·67 | 0·9032 965 | Ī·9558 303 | 0·5511 | 0·74236 | 1·34705 | 0·944 | 0·32995 | 3·03080 | 0·22992 |
| 0·68 | 0·9050 010 | Ī·9566 491 | 0·5376 | 0·73321 | 1·36386 | 0·946 | 0·32417 | 3·08483 | 0·22602 |
| 0·69 | 0·9067 818 | Ī·9575 028 | 0·5239 | 0·72381 | 1·38158 | 0·948 | 0·31827 | 3·14198 | 0·22203 |
| 0·70 | 0·9086 387 | Ī·9583 912 | 0·5100 | 0·71414 | 1·40028 | 0·950 | 0·31225 | 3·20256 | 0·21794 |
| 0·71 | 0·9105 717 | Ī·9593 141 | 0·4959 | 0·70420 | 1·42005 | 0·952 | 0·30610 | 3·26693 | 0·21377 |
| 0·72 | 0·9125 806 | Ī·9602 712 | 0·4816 | 0·69397 | 1·44098 | 0·954 | 0·29981 | 3·33548 | 0·20949 |
| 0·73 | 0·9146 654 | Ī·9612 622 | 0·4671 | 0·68345 | 1·46317 | 0·956 | 0·29337 | 3·40870 | 0·20510 |
| 0·74 | 0·9168 260 | Ī·9622 869 | 0·4524 | 0·67261 | 1·48675 | 0·958 | 0·28677 | 3·48714 | 0·20059 |
| 0·75 | 0·9190 625 | Ī·9633 451 | 0·4375 | 0·66144 | 1·51186 | 0·960 | 0·28000 | 3·57143 | 0·19596 |
| 0·76 | 0·9213 749 | Ī·9644 364 | 0·4224 | 0·64992 | 1·53864 | 0·962 | 0·27305 | 3·66234 | 0·19120 |
| 0·77 | 0·9237 631 | Ī·9655 606 | 0·4071 | 0·63804 | 1·56729 | 0·964 | 0·26590 | 3·76078 | 0·18629 |
| 0·78 | 0·9262 273 | Ī·9667 176 | 0·3916 | 0·62578 | 1·59801 | 0·966 | 0·25854 | 3·86784 | 0·18123 |
| 0·79 | 0·9287 675 | Ī·9679 070 | 0·3759 | 0·61311 | 1·63104 | 0·968 | 0·25095 | 3·98485 | 0·17600 |
| 0·80 | 0·9313 838 | Ī·9691 287 | 0·3600 | 0·60000 | 1·66667 | 0·970 | 0·24310 | 4·11345 | 0·17059 |
| 0·81 | 0·9340 763 | Ī·9703 823 | 0·3439 | 0·58643 | 1·70523 | 0·972 | 0·23498 | 4·25567 | 0·16497 |
| 0·82 | 0·9368 451 | Ī·9716 678 | 0·3276 | 0·57236 | 1·74714 | 0·974 | 0·22655 | 4·41408 | 0·15914 |
| 0·83 | 0·9396 904 | Ī·9729 848 | 0·3111 | 0·55776 | 1·79287 | 0·976 | 0·21777 | 4·59199 | 0·15305 |
| 0·84 | 0·9426 124 | Ī·9743 331 | 0·2944 | 0·54259 | 1·84302 | 0·978 | 0·20860 | 4·79375 | 0·14668 |
| 0·85 | 0·9456 112 | Ī·9757 126 | 0·2775 | 0·52678 | 1·89832 | 0·980 | 0·19900 | 5·02519 | 0·14000 |
| 0·86 | 0·9486 870 | Ī·9771 230 | 0·2604 | 0·51029 | 1·95965 | 0·982 | 0·18888 | 5·29434 | 0·13295 |
| 0·87 | 0·9518 402 | Ī·9785 640 | 0·2431 | 0·49305 | 2·02818 | 0·984 | 0·17817 | 5·61267 | 0·12548 |
| 0·88 | 0·9550 709 | Ī·9800 356 | 0·2256 | 0·47497 | 2·10538 | 0·986 | 0·16675 | 5·99717 | 0·11749 |
| 0·89 | 0·9583 793 | Ī·9815 374 | 0·2079 | 0·45596 | 2·19317 | 0·988 | 0·15445 | 6·47442 | 0·10889 |
| 0·90 | 0·9617 658 | Ī·9830 693 | 0·1900 | 0·43589 | 2·29416 | 0·990 | 0·14107 | 7·08881 | 0·09950 |
| 0·91 | 0·9652 307 | Ī·9846 311 | 0·1719 | 0·41461 | 2·41192 | 0·991 | 0·13386 | 7·47039 | 0·09444 |
| 0·92 | 0·9687 743 | Ī·9862 226 | 0·1536 | 0·39192 | 2·55155 | 0·992 | 0·12624 | 7·92155 | 0·08908 |
| 0·93 | 0·9723 969 | Ī·9878 436 | 0·1351 | 0·36756 | 2·72065 | 0·993 | 0·11811 | 8·46637 | 0·08337 |
| 0·94 | 0·9760 989 | Ī·9894 938 | 0·1164 | 0·34117 | 2·93105 | 0·994 | 0·10938 | 9·14243 | 0·07723 |
| 0·95 | 0·9798 807 | Ī·9911 732 | 0·0975 | 0·31225 | 3·20256 | 0·995 | 0·09987 | 10·01252 | 0·07053 |
| 0·96 | 0·9837 425 | Ī·9928 815 | 0·0784 | 0·28000 | 3·57143 | 0·996 | 0·08935 | 11·19154 | 0·06312 |
| 0·97 | 0·9876 850 | Ī·9946 185 | 0·0591 | 0·24310 | 4·11345 | 0·997 | 0·07740 | 12·91964 | 0·05469 |
| 0·98 | 0·9917 084 | Ī·9963 840 | 0·0396 | 0·19900 | 5·02519 | 0·998 | 0·06321 | 15·81930 | 0·04468 |
| 0·99 | 0·9958 133 | Ī·9981 779 | 0·0199 | 0·14107 | 7·08881 | 0·999 | 0·04471 | 22·36627 | 0·03161 |
| 1·00 | 1·0000 000 | 0·0000 000 | 0·0000 | 0·00000 | $\infty$ | 1·000 | 0·00000 | $\infty$ | 0·00000 |

33-2

Table 53. *Natural logarithms, $\log_e x$*

| 1 | 2 | 3 | 4 | 5 | | 00 | 05 | 10 | 15 | 20 | 25 | 30 | 35 | 40 | 45 |
|---|---|---|---|---|---|----|----|----|----|----|----|----|----|----|----|
| 98 | 196 | 293 | 391 | 489 | 1·0 | 0·00 000 | 00 499 | 00 995 | 01 489 | 01 980 | 02 469 | 02 956 | 03 440 | 03 922 | 04 402 |
| 89 | 178 | 267 | 356 | 445 | 1·1 | 0·09 531 | 09 985 | 10 436 | 10 885 | 11 333 | 11 778 | 12 222 | 12 663 | 13 103 | 13 540 |
| 82 | 164 | 245 | 327 | 409 | 1·2 | 0·18 232 | 18 648 | 19 062 | 19 474 | 19 885 | 20 294 | 20 701 | 21 107 | 21 511 | 21 914 |
| 76 | 151 | 227 | 303 | 378 | 1·3 | 0·26 236 | 26 620 | 27 003 | 27 384 | 27 763 | 28 141 | 28 518 | 28 893 | 29 267 | 29 639 |
| 70 | 141 | 211 | 281 | 352 | 1·4 | 0·33 647 | 34 004 | 34 359 | 34 713 | 35 066 | 35 417 | 35 767 | 36 116 | 36 464 | 36 811 |
| 66 | 131 | 197 | 263 | 329 | 1·5 | 0·40 547 | 40 879 | 41 211 | 41 542 | 41 871 | 42 199 | 42 527 | 42 853 | 43 178 | 43 502 |
| 62 | 123 | 185 | 247 | 308 | 1·6 | 0·47 000 | 47 312 | 47 623 | 47 933 | 48 243 | 48 551 | 48 858 | 49 164 | 49 470 | 49 774 |
| 58 | 116 | 174 | 232 | 290 | 1·7 | 0·53 063 | 53 357 | 53 649 | 53 941 | 54 232 | 54 523 | 54 812 | 55 101 | 55 389 | 55 675 |
| 55 | 110 | 165 | 220 | 274 | 1·8 | 0·58 779 | 59 056 | 59 333 | 59 609 | 59 884 | 60 158 | 60 432 | 60 704 | 60 977 | 61 248 |
| 52 | 104 | 156 | 208 | 260 | 1·9 | 0·64 185 | 64 448 | 64 710 | 64 972 | 65 233 | 65 493 | 65 752 | 66 011 | 66 269 | 66 526 |

| 1 | 2 | 3 | 4 | 5 | | 0 | 1 | 2 | 3 | 4 | 5 | 6 | 7 | 8 | 9 |
|---|---|---|---|---|---|---|---|---|---|---|---|---|---|---|---|
| 49 | 98 | 147 | 196 | 244 | 2·0 | 0·69 315 | 69 813 | 70 310 | 70 804 | 71 295 | 71 784 | 72 271 | 72 755 | 73 237 | 73 716 |
| 47 | 93 | 140 | 186 | 233 | 2·1 | 0·74 194 | 74 669 | 75 142 | 75 612 | 76 081 | 76 547 | 77 011 | 77 473 | 77 932 | 78 390 |
| 45 | 89 | 134 | 178 | 223 | 2·2 | 0·78 846 | 79 299 | 79 751 | 80 200 | 80 648 | 81 093 | 81 536 | 81 978 | 82 418 | 82 855 |
| 43 | 85 | 128 | 171 | 213 | 2·3 | 0·83 291 | 83 725 | 84 157 | 84 587 | 85 015 | 85 442 | 85 866 | 86 289 | 86 710 | 87 129 |
| 41 | 82 | 123 | 164 | 204 | 2·4 | 0·87 547 | 87 963 | 88 377 | 88 789 | 89 200 | 89 609 | 90 016 | 90 422 | 90 826 | 91 228 |
| 39 | 79 | 118 | 157 | 196 | 2·5 | 0·91 629 | 92 028 | 92 426 | 92 822 | 93 216 | 93 609 | 94 001 | 94 391 | 94 779 | 95 166 |
| 38 | 76 | 113 | 151 | 189 | 2·6 | 0·95 551 | 95 935 | 96 317 | 96 698 | 97 078 | 97 456 | 97 833 | 98 208 | 98 582 | 98 954 |
| 36 | 73 | 109 | 146 | 182 | 2·7 | 0·99 325 | 99 695 | 00 063 | 00 430 | 00 796 | 01 160 | 01 523 | 01 885 | 02 245 | 02 604 |
| 35 | 70 | 105 | 141 | 176 | 2·8 | 1·02 962 | 03 318 | 03 674 | 04 028 | 04 380 | 04 732 | 05 082 | 05 431 | 05 779 | 06 126 |
| 34 | 68 | 102 | 136 | 170 | 2·9 | 1·06 471 | 06 815 | 07 158 | 07 500 | 07 841 | 08 181 | 08 519 | 08 856 | 09 192 | 09 527 |
| 33 | 66 | 99 | 131 | 164 | 3·0 | 1·09 861 | 10 194 | 10 526 | 10 856 | 11 186 | 11 514 | 11 841 | 12 168 | 12 493 | 12 817 |
| 32 | 64 | 95 | 127 | 159 | 3·1 | 1·13 140 | 13 462 | 13 783 | 14 103 | 14 422 | 14 740 | 15 057 | 15 373 | 15 688 | 16 002 |
| 31 | 62 | 92 | 123 | 154 | 3·2 | 1·16 315 | 16 627 | 16 938 | 17 248 | 17 557 | 17 865 | 18 173 | 18 479 | 18 784 | 19 089 |
| 30 | 60 | 90 | 120 | 150 | 3·3 | 1·19 392 | 19 695 | 19 996 | 20 297 | 20 597 | 20 896 | 21 194 | 21 491 | 21 788 | 22 083 |
| 29 | 58 | 87 | 116 | 145 | 3·4 | 1·22 378 | 22 671 | 22 964 | 23 256 | 23 547 | 23 837 | 24 127 | 24 415 | 24 703 | 24 990 |
| 28 | 56 | 85 | 113 | 141 | 3·5 | 1·25 276 | 25 562 | 25 846 | 26 130 | 26 413 | 26 695 | 26 976 | 27 257 | 27 536 | 27 815 |
| 27 | 55 | 82 | 110 | 137 | 3·6 | 1·28 093 | 28 371 | 28 647 | 28 923 | 29 198 | 29 473 | 29 746 | 30 019 | 30 291 | 30 563 |
| 27 | 53 | 80 | 107 | 134 | 3·7 | 1·30 833 | 31 103 | 31 372 | 31 641 | 31 909 | 32 176 | 32 442 | 32 708 | 32 972 | 33 237 |
| 26 | 52 | 78 | 104 | 130 | 3·8 | 1·33 500 | 33 763 | 34 025 | 34 286 | 34 547 | 34 807 | 35 067 | 35 325 | 35 584 | 35 841 |
| 25 | 51 | 76 | 101 | 127 | 3·9 | 1·36 098 | 36 354 | 36 609 | 36 864 | 37 118 | 37 372 | 37 624 | 37 877 | 38 128 | 38 379 |
| 25 | 49 | 74 | 99 | 124 | 4·0 | 1·38 629 | 38 879 | 39 128 | 39 377 | 39 624 | 39 872 | 40 118 | 40 364 | 40 610 | 40 854 |
| 24 | 48 | 72 | 96 | 121 | 4·1 | 1·41 099 | 41 342 | 41 585 | 41 828 | 42 070 | 42 311 | 42 552 | 42 792 | 43 031 | 43 270 |
| 24 | 47 | 71 | 94 | 118 | 4·2 | 1·43 508 | 43 746 | 43 984 | 44 220 | 44 456 | 44 692 | 44 927 | 45 161 | 45 395 | 45 629 |
| 23 | 46 | 69 | 92 | 115 | 4·3 | 1·45 862 | 46 094 | 46 326 | 46 557 | 46 787 | 47 018 | 47 247 | 47 476 | 47 705 | 47 933 |
| 22 | 45 | 68 | 90 | 112 | 4·4 | 1·48 160 | 48 387 | 48 614 | 48 840 | 49 065 | 49 290 | 49 515 | 49 739 | 49 962 | 50 185 |
| 22 | 44 | 66 | 88 | 110 | 4·5 | 1·50 408 | 50 630 | 50 851 | 51 072 | 51 293 | 51 513 | 51 732 | 51 951 | 52 170 | 52 388 |
| 22 | 43 | 65 | 86 | 108 | 4·6 | 1·52 606 | 52 823 | 53 039 | 53 256 | 53 471 | 53 687 | 53 902 | 54 116 | 54 330 | 54 543 |
| 21 | 42 | 63 | 84 | 105 | 4·7 | 1·54 756 | 54 969 | 55 181 | 55 393 | 55 604 | 55 814 | 56 025 | 56 235 | 56 444 | 56 653 |
| 21 | 41 | 62 | 83 | 103 | 4·8 | 1·56 862 | 57 070 | 57 277 | 57 485 | 57 691 | 57 898 | 58 104 | 58 309 | 58 515 | 58 719 |
| 20 | 40 | 61 | 81 | 101 | 4·9 | 1·58 924 | 59 127 | 59 331 | 59 534 | 59 737 | 59 939 | 60 141 | 60 342 | 60 543 | 60 744 |
| 20 | 40 | 59 | 79 | 99 | 5·0 | 1·60 944 | 61 144 | 61 343 | 61 542 | 61 741 | 61 939 | 62 137 | 62 334 | 62 531 | 62 728 |
| 19 | 39 | 58 | 78 | 97 | 5·1 | 1·62 924 | 63 120 | 63 315 | 63 511 | 63 705 | 63 900 | 64 094 | 64 287 | 64 481 | 64 673 |
| 19 | 38 | 57 | 76 | 95 | 5·2 | 1·64 866 | 65 058 | 65 250 | 65 441 | 65 632 | 65 823 | 66 013 | 66 203 | 66 393 | 66 582 |
| 19 | 37 | 56 | 75 | 94 | 5·3 | 1·66 771 | 66 959 | 67 147 | 67 335 | 67 523 | 67 710 | 67 896 | 68 083 | 68 269 | 68 455 |
| 18 | 37 | 55 | 73 | 92 | 5·4 | 1·68 640 | 68 825 | 69 010 | 69 194 | 69 378 | 69 562 | 69 745 | 69 928 | 70 111 | 70 293 |
| 18 | 36 | 54 | 72 | 90 | 5·5 | 1·70 475 | 70 656 | 70 838 | 71 019 | 71 199 | 71 380 | 71 560 | 71 740 | 71 919 | 72 098 |
| 18 | 35 | 53 | 71 | 89 | 5·6 | 1·72 277 | 72 455 | 72 633 | 72 811 | 72 988 | 73 166 | 73 342 | 73 519 | 73 695 | 73 871 |
| 17 | 35 | 52 | 70 | 87 | 5·7 | 1·74 047 | 74 222 | 74 397 | 74 572 | 74 746 | 74 920 | 75 094 | 75 267 | 75 440 | 75 613 |
| 17 | 34 | 51 | 68 | 86 | 5·8 | 1·75 786 | 75 958 | 76 130 | 76 302 | 76 473 | 76 644 | 76 815 | 76 985 | 77 156 | 77 326 |
| 17 | 34 | 50 | 67 | 84 | 5·9 | 1·77 495 | 77 665 | 77 834 | 78 002 | 78 171 | 78 339 | 78 507 | 78 675 | 78 842 | 79 009 |

$\log_e 10 = 2\cdot30259$, $\log_e 10^2 = 4\cdot60517$, $\log_e 10^3 = 6\cdot90776$, $\log_e 10^4 = 9\cdot21034$, $\log_e 10^5 = 11\cdot51293$, $\log_e 10^6 = 13\cdot81551$.

N.B. Proportional parts should be applied to the *nearest* tabular entry.

Examples:        $\log 1\cdot099 = 0\cdot09531 - 0\cdot00089 = 0\cdot09442$ (correct value, $0\cdot09440$),

$\log 11\cdot435 = 2\cdot30259 + 0\cdot13540 - 0\cdot00089 - \frac{1}{10}(0\cdot00445) = 2\cdot43666$ (correct value, $2\cdot43668$).

## Table 53 (*continued*)

| | 50 | 55 | 60 | 65 | 70 | 75 | 80 | 85 | 90 | 95 | 1 | 2 | 3 | 4 | 5 |
|---|---|---|---|---|---|---|---|---|---|---|---|---|---|---|---|
| 1·0 | 0·04 879 | 05 354 | 05 827 | 06 297 | 06 766 | 07 232 | 07 696 | 08 158 | 08 618 | 09 075 | 93 | 187 | 280 | 373 | 466 |
| 1·1 | 0·13 976 | 14 410 | 14 842 | 15 272 | 15 700 | 16 127 | 16 551 | 16 974 | 17 395 | 17 815 | 85 | 171 | 256 | 341 | 426 |
| 1·2 | 0·22 314 | 22 714 | 23 111 | 23 507 | 23 902 | 24 295 | 24 686 | 25 076 | 25 464 | 25 851 | 79 | 157 | 236 | 314 | 393 |
| 1·3 | 0·30 010 | 30 380 | 30 748 | 31 115 | 31 481 | 31 845 | 32 208 | 32 570 | 32 930 | 33 289 | 73 | 146 | 219 | 291 | 364 |
| 1·4 | 0·37 156 | 37 501 | 37 844 | 38 186 | 38 526 | 38 866 | 39 204 | 39 541 | 39 878 | 40 213 | 68 | 136 | 204 | 272 | 340 |
| 1·5 | 0·43 825 | 44 148 | 44 469 | 44 789 | 45 108 | 45 426 | 45 742 | 46 058 | 46 373 | 46 687 | 64 | 127 | 191 | 254 | 318 |
| 1·6 | 0·50 078 | 50 380 | 50 682 | 50 983 | 51 282 | 51 581 | 51 879 | 52 177 | 52 473 | 52 768 | 60 | 120 | 179 | 239 | 299 |
| 1·7 | 0·55 962 | 56 247 | 56 531 | 56 815 | 57 098 | 57 380 | 57 661 | 57 942 | 58 222 | 58 501 | 56 | 113 | 169 | 226 | 282 |
| 1·8 | 0·61 519 | 61 788 | 62 058 | 62 326 | 62 594 | 62 861 | 63 127 | 63 393 | 63 658 | 63 922 | 53 | 107 | 160 | 214 | 267 |
| 1·9 | 0·66 783 | 67 039 | 67 294 | 67 549 | 67 803 | 68 057 | 68 310 | 68 562 | 68 813 | 69 064 | 51 | 101 | 152 | 203 | 253 |

| | 0 | 1 | 2 | 3 | 4 | 5 | 6 | 7 | 8 | 9 | 1 | 2 | 3 | 4 | 5 |
|---|---|---|---|---|---|---|---|---|---|---|---|---|---|---|---|
| 6·0 | 1·79 176 | 79 342 | 79 509 | 79 675 | 79 840 | 80 006 | 80 171 | 80 336 | 80 500 | 80 665 | 17 | 33 | 50 | 66 | 83 |
| 6·1 | 1·80 829 | 80 993 | 81 156 | 81 319 | 81 482 | 81 645 | 81 808 | 81 970 | 82 132 | 82 294 | 16 | 33 | 49 | 65 | 81 |
| 6·2 | 1·82 455 | 82 616 | 82 777 | 82 938 | 83 098 | 83 258 | 83 418 | 83 578 | 83 737 | 83 896 | 16 | 32 | 48 | 64 | 80 |
| 6·3 | 1·84 055 | 84 214 | 84 372 | 84 530 | 84 688 | 84 845 | 85 003 | 85 160 | 85 317 | 85 473 | 16 | 32 | 47 | 63 | 79 |
| 6·4 | 1·85 630 | 85 786 | 85 942 | 86 097 | 86 253 | 86 408 | 86 563 | 86 718 | 86 872 | 87 026 | 16 | 31 | 47 | 62 | 78 |
| 6·5 | 1·87 180 | 87 334 | 87 487 | 87 641 | 87 794 | 87 947 | 88 099 | 88 251 | 88 403 | 88 555 | 15 | 31 | 46 | 61 | 76 |
| 6·6 | 1·88 707 | 88 858 | 89 010 | 89 160 | 89 311 | 89 462 | 89 612 | 89 762 | 89 912 | 90 061 | 15 | 30 | 45 | 60 | 75 |
| 6·7 | 1·90 211 | 90 360 | 90 509 | 90 658 | 90 806 | 90 954 | 91 102 | 91 250 | 91 398 | 91 545 | 15 | 30 | 44 | 59 | 74 |
| 6·8 | 1·91 692 | 91 839 | 91 986 | 92 132 | 92 279 | 92 425 | 92 571 | 92 716 | 92 862 | 93 007 | 15 | 29 | 44 | 58 | 73 |
| 6·9 | 1·93 152 | 93 297 | 93 442 | 93 586 | 93 730 | 93 874 | 94 018 | 94 162 | 94 305 | 94 448 | 14 | 29 | 43 | 58 | 72 |
| 7·0 | 1·94 591 | 94 734 | 94 876 | 95 019 | 95 161 | 95 303 | 95 445 | 95 586 | 95 727 | 95 869 | 14 | 28 | 43 | 57 | 71 |
| 7·1 | 1·96 009 | 96 150 | 96 291 | 96 431 | 96 571 | 96 711 | 96 851 | 96 991 | 97 130 | 97 269 | 14 | 28 | 42 | 56 | 70 |
| 7·2 | 1·97 408 | 97 547 | 97 685 | 97 824 | 97 962 | 98 100 | 98 238 | 98 376 | 98 513 | 98 650 | 14 | 28 | 41 | 55 | 69 |
| 7·3 | 1·98 787 | 98 924 | 99 061 | 99 198 | 99 334 | 99 470 | 99 606 | 99 742 | 99 877 | 00 013 | 14 | 27 | 41 | 54 | 68 |
| 7·4 | 2·00 148 | 00 283 | 00 418 | 00 553 | 00 687 | 00 821 | 00 956 | 01 089 | 01 223 | 01 357 | 13 | 27 | 40 | 54 | 67 |
| 7·5 | 2·01 490 | 01 624 | 01 757 | 01 890 | 02 022 | 02 155 | 02 287 | 02 419 | 02 551 | 02 683 | 13 | 27 | 40 | 53 | 66 |
| 7·6 | 2·02 815 | 02 946 | 03 078 | 03 209 | 03 340 | 03 471 | 03 601 | 03 732 | 03 862 | 03 992 | 13 | 26 | 39 | 52 | 65 |
| 7·7 | 2·04 122 | 04 252 | 04 381 | 04 511 | 04 640 | 04 769 | 04 898 | 05 027 | 05 156 | 05 284 | 13 | 26 | 39 | 52 | 65 |
| 7·8 | 2·05 412 | 05 540 | 05 668 | 05 796 | 05 924 | 06 051 | 06 179 | 06 306 | 06 433 | 06 560 | 13 | 25 | 38 | 51 | 64 |
| 7·9 | 2·06 686 | 06 813 | 06 939 | 07 065 | 07 191 | 07 317 | 07 443 | 07 568 | 07 694 | 07 819 | 13 | 25 | 38 | 50 | 63 |
| 8·0 | 2·07 944 | 08 069 | 08 194 | 08 318 | 08 443 | 08 567 | 08 691 | 08 815 | 08 939 | 09 063 | 12 | 25 | 37 | 50 | 62 |
| 8·1 | 2·09 186 | 09 310 | 09 433 | 09 556 | 09 679 | 09 802 | 09 924 | 10 047 | 10 169 | 10 291 | 12 | 25 | 37 | 49 | 61 |
| 8·2 | 2·10 413 | 10 535 | 10 657 | 10 779 | 10 900 | 11 021 | 11 142 | 11 263 | 11 384 | 11 505 | 12 | 24 | 36 | 49 | 61 |
| 8·3 | 2·11 626 | 11 746 | 11 866 | 11 986 | 12 106 | 12 226 | 12 346 | 12 465 | 12 585 | 12 704 | 12 | 24 | 36 | 48 | 60 |
| 8·4 | 2·12 823 | 12 942 | 13 061 | 13 180 | 13 298 | 13 417 | 13 535 | 13 653 | 13 771 | 13 889 | 12 | 24 | 36 | 47 | 59 |
| 8·5 | 2·14 007 | 14 124 | 14 242 | 14 359 | 14 476 | 14 593 | 14 710 | 14 827 | 14 943 | 15 060 | 12 | 23 | 35 | 47 | 58 |
| 8·6 | 2·15 176 | 15 292 | 15 409 | 15 524 | 15 640 | 15 756 | 15 871 | 15 987 | 16 102 | 16 217 | 12 | 23 | 35 | 46 | 58 |
| 8·7 | 2·16 332 | 16 447 | 16 562 | 16 677 | 16 791 | 16 905 | 17 020 | 17 134 | 17 248 | 17 361 | 11 | 23 | 34 | 46 | 57 |
| 8·8 | 2·17 475 | 17 589 | 17 702 | 17 816 | 17 929 | 18 042 | 18 155 | 18 267 | 18 380 | 18 493 | 11 | 23 | 34 | 45 | 56 |
| 8·9 | 2·18 605 | 18 717 | 18 830 | 18 942 | 19 054 | 19 165 | 19 277 | 19 389 | 19 500 | 19 611 | 11 | 22 | 34 | 45 | 56 |
| 9·0 | 2·19 722 | 19 834 | 19 944 | 20 055 | 20 166 | 20 276 | 20 387 | 20 497 | 20 607 | 20 717 | 11 | 22 | 33 | 44 | 55 |
| 9·1 | 2·20 827 | 20 937 | 21 047 | 21 157 | 21 266 | 21 375 | 21 485 | 21 594 | 21 703 | 21 812 | 11 | 22 | 33 | 44 | 55 |
| 9·2 | 2·21 920 | 22 029 | 22 138 | 22 246 | 22 354 | 22 462 | 22 570 | 22 678 | 22 786 | 22 894 | 11 | 22 | 32 | 43 | 54 |
| 9·3 | 2·23 001 | 23 109 | 23 216 | 23 324 | 23 431 | 23 538 | 23 645 | 23 751 | 23 858 | 23 965 | 11 | 21 | 32 | 43 | 54 |
| 9·4 | 2·24 071 | 24 177 | 24 284 | 24 390 | 24 496 | 24 601 | 24 707 | 24 813 | 24 918 | 25 024 | 11 | 21 | 32 | 42 | 53 |
| 9·5 | 2·25 129 | 25 234 | 25 339 | 25 444 | 25 549 | 25 654 | 25 759 | 25 863 | 25 968 | 26 072 | 10 | 21 | 31 | 42 | 52 |
| 9·6 | 2·26 176 | 26 280 | 26 384 | 26 488 | 26 592 | 26 696 | 26 799 | 26 903 | 27 006 | 27 109 | 10 | 21 | 31 | 41 | 52 |
| 9·7 | 2·27 213 | 27 316 | 27 419 | 27 521 | 27 624 | 27 727 | 27 829 | 27 932 | 28 034 | 28 136 | 10 | 21 | 31 | 41 | 51 |
| 9·8 | 2·28 238 | 28 340 | 28 442 | 28 544 | 28 646 | 28 747 | 28 849 | 28 950 | 29 051 | 29 152 | 10 | 20 | 30 | 41 | 51 |
| 9·9 | 2·29 253 | 29 354 | 29 455 | 29 556 | 29 657 | 29 757 | 29 858 | 29 958 | 30 058 | 30 158 | 10 | 20 | 30 | 40 | 50 |

$\log_e 10^{-1} = \bar{3}\cdot69741$, $\log_e 10^{-2} = \bar{5}\cdot39483$, $\log_e 10^{-3} = \bar{7}\cdot09224$, $\log_e 10^{-4} = \overline{10}\cdot78966$, $\log_e 10^{-5} = \overline{12}\cdot48707$, $\log_e 10^{-6} = \overline{14}\cdot18449$.

## Table 54. Useful constants

### Mathematical constants

| | Number | Reciprocal | Logarithm |
|---|---|---|---|
| $\pi$ | 3.14159 26536 | 0.31830 98862 | 0.49714 98727 |
| $2\pi$ | 6.28318 53072 | 0.15915 49431 | 0.79817 98684 |
| $\frac{1}{2}\pi$ | 1.57079 63268 | 0.63661 97724 | 0.19611 98770 |
| $\frac{1}{4}\pi$ | 0.78539 81634 | 1.27323 95447 | $\bar{1}$.89508 98814 |
| $\sqrt{\pi}$ | 1.77245 38509 | 0.56418 95835 | 0.24857 49363 |
| $\sqrt{(2\pi)}$ | 2.50662 82746 | 0.39894 22804 | 0.39908 99342 |
| $\sqrt{(\frac{1}{2}\pi)}$ | 1.25331 41373 | 0.79788 45608 | 0.09805 99385 |
| $\frac{1}{2}\sqrt{\pi}$ | 0.88622 69255 | 1.12837 91671 | $\bar{1}$.94754 49407 |
| $e$ | 2.71828 18285 | 0.36787 94412 | 0.43429 44819 |
| $e^2$ | 7.38905 60989 | 0.13533 52832 | 0.86858 89638 |
| $\sqrt{2}$ | 1.41421 35624 | 0.70710 67812 | 0.15051 49978 |
| $\sqrt{3}$ | 1.73205 08076 | 0.57735 02692 | 0.23856 06274 |
| $\sqrt{10}$ | 3.16227 76602 | 0.31622 77660 | 0.50000 00000 |
| $\log_{10} e$ | 0.43429 44819 | 2.30258 50930 | $\bar{1}$.63778 43113 |
| 1 radian | 57°.29577 95131 | 0.01745 32925 | 1.75812 26324 |

### Binomial coefficients $\binom{n}{i}$

| $i$ | 4 | 5 | 6 | 7 | 8 | 9 | 10 | 11 | 12 |
|---|---|---|---|---|---|---|---|---|---|
| | | | | Value of $n$ | | | | | |
| 0 | 1 | 1 | 1 | 1 | 1 | 1 | 1 | 1 | 1 |
| 1 | 4 | 5 | 6 | 7 | 8 | 9 | 10 | 11 | 12 |
| 2 | 6 | 10 | 15 | 21 | 28 | 36 | 45 | 55 | 66 |
| 3 | 4 | 10 | 20 | 35 | 56 | 84 | 120 | 165 | 220 |
| 4 | 1 | 5 | 15 | 35 | 70 | 126 | 210 | 330 | 495 |
| 5 | | 1 | 6 | 21 | 56 | 126 | 252 | 462 | 792 |
| 6 | | | 1 | 7 | 28 | 84 | 210 | 462 | 924 |
| 7 | | | | 1 | 8 | 36 | 120 | 330 | 792 |
| 8 | | | | | 1 | 9 | 45 | 165 | 495 |
| 9 | | | | | | 1 | 10 | 55 | 220 |
| 10 | | | | | | | 1 | 11 | 66 |
| 11 | | | | | | | | 1 | 12 |
| 12 | | | | | | | | | 1 |

## Conversion Tables

### Length

| Metric to British | | British to Metric | |
|---|---|---|---|
| 1 mm. | = 0.039 370 in. (inch) | 1 in. | = 25.399 978 mm. |
| 1 cm. | = 0.393 701 in. | | = 2.539 998 cm. |
| 1 m. | = 39.370 113 in. | 1 ft. | = 30.479 973 cm. |
| | = 3.280 843 ft. (foot) | | = 0.304 800 m. (metre) |
| | = 1.093 614 yd. (yard) | 1 yd. | = 0.914 399 m. |
| 1 km. | = 0.621 372 miles | 1 mile | = 1.609 343 km. |

### Area

| Metric to British | | British to Metric | |
|---|---|---|---|
| 1 sq.cm. | = 0.155 001 sq.in. | 1 sq.in. | = 6.451 589 sq.cm. |
| 1 sq.m. | = 10.763 929 sq.ft. | 1 sq.ft. | = 0.092 903 sq.m. |
| | = 1.195 992 sq.yd. | 1 sq.yd. | = 0.836 126 sq.m. |
| 1 sq.km. | = 0.386 103 sq.miles | 1 sq.mile | = 2.589 984 sq.km. |
| 1 hectare | = 2.471 058 acres | 1 acre | = 0.404 685 hectares |

### Volume

| Metric to British | | British to Metric | |
|---|---|---|---|
| 1 cu.cm. | = 0.061 024 cu.in. | 1 cu.in. | = 16.387 021 cu.cm. |
| 1 cu.m. | = 35.314 759 cu.ft. | 1 cu.ft. | = 0.028 317 cu.m. |
| | = 1.307 954 cu.yd. | 1 cu.yd. | = 0.764 553 cu.m. |

### Weight

| Metric to British | | British to Metric | |
|---|---|---|---|
| 1 g. | = 15.432 356 gr. (grain) | 1 gr. | = 0.064 799 g. (gram) |
| | = 0.035 274 oz. (ounce) | 1 oz. | = 28.349 527 g. |
| 1 kg. | = 2.204 622 lb. (pound) | 1 lb. | = 0.453 592 kg. |
| 1000 kg. | = 0.984 206 tons | 1 ton | = 1016.047 kg. |

### Capacity

| Metric to British | | British to Metric | |
|---|---|---|---|
| 1 litre | = 1.759 803 pints | 1 pint | = 0.568 245 litres |
| | = 0.879 902 quarts | 1 quart | = 1.136 491 litres |
| | = 0.219 975 gallons | 1 gallon | = 4.545 963 litres |

ADDENDUM

## Table 31c. *Percentage points of the ratio $w_{max}/w_{min}$*

| $n$ \\ $k$ | 2 | 3 | 4 | 5 | 6 | 7 | 8 | 9 | 10 | 11 | 12 |
|---|---|---|---|---|---|---|---|---|---|---|---|
| | | | | | Upper 5% points | | | | | | |
| 3 | 6·267 | 9·392 | 11·99 | 14·30 | 16·40 | 18·35 | 20·19 | 21·93 | 23·59 | 25·18 | 26·71 |
| 4 | 3·971 | 5·335 | 6·371 | 7·237 | 7·992 | 8·669 | 9·285 | 9·854 | 10·38 | 10·88 | 11·35 |
| 5 | 3·157 | 4·018 | 4·643 | 5·149 | 5·580 | 5·958 | 6·298 | 6·607 | 6·892 | 7·156 | 7·404 |
| 6 | 2·744 | 3·381 | 3·831 | 4·187 | 4·487 | 4·747 | 4·978 | 5·187 | 5·377 | 5·553 | 5·717 |
| 7 | 2·494 | 3·007 | 3·362 | 3·640 | 3·871 | 4·070 | 4·245 | 4·403 | 4·546 | 4·678 | 4·800 |
| 8 | 2·325 | 2·760 | 3·056 | 3·286 | 3·476 | 3·638 | 3·781 | 3·909 | 4·024 | 4·130 | 4·227 |
| 9 | 2·203 | 2·584 | 2·841 | 3·039 | 3·201 | 3·340 | 3·461 | 3·568 | 3·666 | 3·755 | 3·837 |
| 10 | 2·110 | 2·452 | 2·681 | 2·855 | 2·998 | 3·120 | 3·226 | 3·320 | 3·404 | 3·482 | 3·553 |
| 11 | 2·037 | 2·349 | 2·556 | 2·714 | 2·842 | 2·951 | 3·046 | 3·129 | 3·205 | 3·274 | 3·337 |
| 13 | 1·928 | 2·198 | 2·375 | 2·508 | 2·617 | 2·708 | 2·787 | 2·857 | 2·920 | 2·977 | 3·029 |
| 16 | 1·820 | 2·049 | 2·198 | 2·309 | 2·399 | 2·475 | 2·540 | 2·597 | 2·648 | 2·695 | 2·737 |
| 21 | 1·709 | 1·900 | 2·022 | 2·113 | 2·186 | 2·246 | 2·299 | 2·344 | 2·385 | 2·422 | 2·456 |
| 31 | 1·592 | 1·745 | 1·841 | 1·912 | 1·969 | 2·016 | 2·056 | 2·091 | 2·123 | 2·151 | 2·176 |
| 61 | 1·459 | 1·571 | 1·641 | 1·692 | 1·732 | 1·765 | 1·794 | 1·818 | 1·840 | 1·860 | 1·867 |
| $\infty$ | 1·000 | 1·000 | 1·000 | 1·000 | 1·000 | 1·000 | 1·000 | 1·000 | 1·000 | 1·000 | 1·000 |
| | | | | | Upper 2·5% points | | | | | | |
| 3 | 8·920 | 13·38 | 17·08 | 20·37 | 23·36 | 26·15 | 28·76 | 31·24 | 33·60 | 35·87 | 38·05 |
| 4 | 5·078 | 6·805 | 8·116 | 9·212 | 10·17 | 11·02 | 11·80 | 12·52 | 13·19 | 13·82 | 14·42 |
| 5 | 3·837 | 4·863 | 5·607 | 6·209 | 6·722 | 7·173 | 7·577 | 7·945 | 8·284 | 8·599 | 8·893 |
| 6 | 3·238 | 3·970 | 4·485 | 4·894 | 5·238 | 5·537 | 5·802 | 6·041 | 6·260 | 6·461 | 6·649 |
| 7 | 2·886 | 3·461 | 3·858 | 4·169 | 4·428 | 4·650 | 4·847 | 5·023 | 5·184 | 5·331 | 5·467 |
| 8 | 2·654 | 3·133 | 3·439 | 3·711 | 3·920 | 4·098 | 4·255 | 4·395 | 4·522 | 4·639 | 4·746 |
| 9 | 2·489 | 2·903 | 3·182 | 3·396 | 3·572 | 3·722 | 3·853 | 3·970 | 4·076 | 4·173 | 4·261 |
| 10 | 2·365 | 2·733 | 2·978 | 3·166 | 3·319 | 3·449 | 3·563 | 3·664 | 3·755 | 3·838 | 3·914 |
| 11 | 2·269 | 2·601 | 2·822 | 2·989 | 3·126 | 3·242 | 3·342 | 3·432 | 3·512 | 3·585 | 3·652 |
| 13 | 2·127 | 2·411 | 2·596 | 2·737 | 2·851 | 2·946 | 3·029 | 3·103 | 3·169 | 3·229 | 3·283 |
| 16 | 1·988 | 2·226 | 2·380 | 2·495 | 2·589 | 2·667 | 2·734 | 2·794 | 2·847 | 2·895 | 2·939 |
| 21 | 1·848 | 2·043 | 2·168 | 2·261 | 2·335 | 2·398 | 2·451 | 2·498 | 2·540 | 2·577 | 2·612 |
| 31 | 1·703 | 1·857 | 1·954 | 2·026 | 2·083 | 2·130 | 2·171 | 2·206 | 2·238 | 2·266 | 2·292 |
| 61 | 1·540 | 1·652 | 1·721 | 1·772 | 1·812 | 1·845 | 1·874 | 1·898 | 1·920 | 1·940 | 1·958 |
| $\infty$ | 1·000 | 1·000 | 1·000 | 1·000 | 1·000 | 1·000 | 1·000 | 1·000 | 1·000 | 1·000 | 1·000 |

| k n | 2 | 3 | 4 | 5 | 6 | 7 | 8 | 9 | 10 | 11 | 12 |
|---|---|---|---|---|---|---|---|---|---|---|---|

Upper 1% points

| n | 2 | 3 | 4 | 5 | 6 | 7 | 8 | 9 | 10 | 11 | 12 |
|---|---|---|---|---|---|---|---|---|---|---|---|
| 3 | 14·16 | 21·24 | 27·12 | 32·33 | 37·09 | 41·53 | 45·73 | 49·74 | 53·55 | 57·12 | 60·41 |
| 4 | 6·970 | 9·316 | 11·10 | 12·59 | 13·89 | 15·05 | 16·11 | 17·08 | 17·99 | 18·85 | 19·66 |
| 5 | 4·914 | 6·202 | 7·137 | 7·893 | 8·537 | 9·104 | 9·612 | 10·07 | 10·50 | 10·90 | 11·27 |
| 6 | 3·985 | 4·860 | 5·477 | 5·967 | 6·378 | 6·736 | 7·053 | 7·340 | 7·602 | 7·843 | 8·068 |
| 7 | 3·461 | 4·127 | 4·587 | 4·947 | 5·247 | 5·505 | 5·733 | 5·938 | 6·124 | 6·295 | 6·452 |
| 8 | 3·126 | 3·667 | 4·035 | 4·321 | 4·558 | 4·760 | 4·938 | 5·096 | 5·240 | 5·372 | 5·492 |
| 9 | 2·982 | 3·352 | 3·661 | 3·900 | 4·096 | 4·263 | 4·409 | 4·539 | 4·657 | 4·764 | 4·863 |
| 10 | 2·720 | 3·122 | 3·391 | 3·597 | 3·765 | 3·908 | 4·032 | 4·143 | 4·243 | 4·334 | 4·418 |
| 11 | 2·588 | 2·948 | 3·186 | 3·368 | 3·516 | 3·642 | 3·751 | 3·848 | 3·935 | 4·014 | 4·087 |
| 13 | 2·396 | 2·698 | 2·896 | 3·045 | 3·166 | 3·269 | 3·357 | 3·436 | 3·506 | 3·570 | 3·628 |
| 16 | 2·211 | 2·460 | 2·621 | 2·742 | 2·840 | 2·922 | 2·993 | 3·055 | 3·111 | 3·161 | 3·206 |
| 21 | 2·029 | 2·230 | 2·358 | 2·454 | 2·531 | 2·595 | 2·650 | 2·698 | 2·741 | 2·780 | 2·815 |
| 31 | 1·845 | 2·000 | 2·099 | 2·171 | 2·229 | 2·277 | 2·318 | 2·354 | 2·386 | 2·414 | 2·440 |
| 61 | 1·642 | 1·752 | 1·821 | 1·874 | 1·914 | 1·947 | 1·976 | 2·001 | 2·023 | 2·043 | 2·054 |
| ∞ | 1·000 | 1·000 | 1·000 | 1·000 | 1·000 | 1·000 | 1·000 | 1·000 | 1·000 | 1·000 | 1·000 |

Upper 0·5% points

| n | 2 | 3 | 4 | 5 | 6 | 7 | 8 | 9 | 10 | 11 | 12 |
|---|---|---|---|---|---|---|---|---|---|---|---|
| 3 | 20·05 | 30·09 | 38·43 | 45·82 | 52·56 | 58·82 | 64·70 | 70·28 | 75·60 | 80·71 | 85·62 |
| 4 | 8·825 | 11·78 | 14·03 | 15·91 | 17·55 | 19·01 | 20·35 | 21·58 | 22·73 | 23·81 | 24·83 |
| 5 | 5·897 | 7·427 | 8·537 | 9·436 | 10·20 | 10·88 | 11·48 | 12·03 | 12·54 | 13·01 | 13·45 |
| 6 | 4·636 | 5·638 | 6·345 | 6·907 | 7·379 | 7·789 | 8·153 | 8·482 | 8·783 | 9·060 | 9·319 |
| 7 | 3·947 | 4·691 | 5·205 | 5·608 | 5·943 | 6·232 | 6·488 | 6·717 | 6·925 | 7·117 | 7·294 |
| 8 | 3·516 | 4·109 | 4·514 | 4·828 | 5·088 | 5·310 | 5·506 | 5·681 | 5·839 | 5·984 | 6·118 |
| 9 | 3·220 | 3·717 | 4·053 | 4·311 | 4·523 | 4·705 | 4·863 | 5·005 | 5·133 | 5·249 | 5·357 |
| 10 | 3·005 | 3·435 | 3·723 | 3·944 | 4·124 | 4·278 | 4·412 | 4·531 | 4·638 | 4·736 | 4·826 |
| 11 | 2·840 | 3·223 | 3·476 | 3·669 | 3·827 | 3·961 | 4·077 | 4·180 | 4·273 | 4·358 | 4·436 |
| 13 | 2·606 | 2·922 | 3·129 | 3·286 | 3·414 | 3·521 | 3·614 | 3·697 | 3·771 | 3·838 | 3·900 |
| 16 | 2·383 | 2·640 | 2·807 | 2·932 | 3·033 | 3·118 | 3·192 | 3·257 | 3·315 | 3·367 | 3·415 |
| 21 | 2·167 | 2·371 | 2·502 | 2·600 | 2·678 | 2·744 | 2·800 | 2·850 | 2·894 | 2·934 | 2·971 |
| 31 | 1·951 | 2·107 | 2·206 | 2·279 | 2·337 | 2·386 | 2·427 | 2·463 | 2·496 | 2·525 | 2·551 |
| 61 | 1·719 | 1·830 | 1·899 | 1·950 | 1·990 | 2·024 | 2·053 | 2·078 | 2·101 | 2·121 | 2·140 |
| ∞ | 1·000 | 1·000 | 1·000 | 1·000 | 1·000 | 1·000 | 1·000 | 1·000 | 1·000 | 1·000 | 1·000 |

Table 32a. *Test for heterogeneity of variance for equal degrees of freedom: percentage points of M.*

| $\nu$ | $\alpha$ | 3 | | 4 | | 5 | | 6 | | 7 | |
|---|---|---|---|---|---|---|---|---|---|---|---|
| 1 | 0·001 | 0·003 | 16·600 | 0·036 | 19·630 | 0·131 | 22·351 | 0·299 | 24·886 | 0·538 | 27·292 |
| | ·01 | 0·030 | 11·460 | 0·168 | 14·087 | 0·426 | 16·471 | 0·785 | 18·709 | 1·222 | 20·847 |
| | ·05 | 0·153 | 7·739 | 0·510 | 9·992 | 1·010 | 12·066 | 1·605 | 14·031 | 2·267 | 15·923 |
| | ·10 | 0·313 | 6·080 | 0·842 | 8·129 | 1·501 | 10·033 | 2·240 | 11·851 | 3·034 | 13·610 |
| 2 | ·001 | 0·002 | 15·810 | 0·030 | 18·590 | 0·110 | 21·090 | 0·254 | 23·421 | 0·458 | 25·635 |
| | ·01 | 0·025 | 10·740 | 0·140 | 13·157 | 0·360 | 15·351 | 0·668 | 17·410 | 1·047 | 19·376 |
| | ·05 | 0·127 | 7·108 | 0·430 | 9·185 | 0·860 | 11·092 | 1·378 | 12·899 | 1·958 | 14·637 |
| | ·10 | 0·261 | 5·512 | 0·713 | 7·398 | 1·285 | 9·147 | 1·933 | 10·815 | 2·634 | 12·429 |
| 3 | ·001 | 0·002 | 15·360 | 0·028 | 18·033 | 0·104 | 20·439 | 0·239 | 22·683 | 0·432 | 24·814 |
| | ·01 | 0·023 | 10·353 | 0·132 | 12·684 | 0·339 | 14·798 | 0·629 | 16·782 | 0·987 | 18·676 |
| | ·05 | 0·119 | 6·796 | 0·403 | 8·799 | 0·809 | 10·637 | 1·299 | 12·377 | 1·850 | 14·051 |
| | ·10 | 0·244 | 5·246 | 0·669 | 7·063 | 1·211 | 8·747 | 1·825 | 10·352 | 2·491 | 11·905 |
| 4 | ·001 | 0·002 | 15·069 | 0·027 | 17·686 | 0·100 | 20·042 | 0·231 | 22·238 | 0·419 | 24·324 |
| | ·01 | 0·022 | 10·116 | 0·127 | 12·401 | 0·328 | 14·472 | 0·610 | 16·415 | 0·958 | 18·270 |
| | ·05 | 0·115 | 6·616 | 0·390 | 8·578 | 0·784 | 10·378 | 1·260 | 12·082 | 1·795 | 13·720 |
| | ·10 | 0·235 | 5·098 | 0·647 | 6·875 | 1·173 | 8·524 | 1·771 | 10·095 | 2·419 | 11·614 |
| 5 | ·001 | 0·002 | 14·867 | 0·026 | 17·450 | 0·098 | 19·774 | 0·227 | 21·942 | 0·411 | 24·000 |
| | ·01 | 0·022 | 9·957 | 0·125 | 12·214 | 0·322 | 14·259 | 0·599 | 16·176 | 0·940 | 18·006 |
| | ·05 | 0·112 | 6·500 | 0·382 | 8·436 | 0·769 | 10·213 | 1·237 | 11·894 | 1·763 | 13·510 |
| | ·10 | 0·230 | 5·004 | 0·635 | 6·757 | 1·151 | 8·383 | 1·738 | 9·932 | 2·375 | 11·430 |
| 6 | ·001 | 0·002 | 14·719 | 0·026 | 17·279 | 0·097 | 19·583 | 0·224 | 21·731 | 0·406 | 23·770 |
| | ·01 | 0·022 | 9·845 | 0·123 | 12·082 | 0·317 | 14·109 | 0·591 | 16·009 | 0·929 | 17·822 |
| | ·05 | 0·110 | 6·420 | 0·377 | 8·338 | 0·759 | 10·098 | 1·221 | 11·764 | 1·741 | 13·364 |
| | ·10 | 0·227 | 4·940 | 0·626 | 6·676 | 1·136 | 8·286 | 1·717 | 9·821 | 2·347 | 11·304 |
| 7 | ·001 | 0·002 | 14·606 | 0·026 | 17·151 | 0·096 | 19·440 | 0·222 | 21·573 | 0·402 | 23·598 |
| | ·01 | 0·021 | 9·761 | 0·122 | 11·984 | 0·315 | 13·998 | 0·586 | 15·885 | 0·921 | 17·686 |
| | ·05 | 0·109 | 6·361 | 0·373 | 8·267 | 0·752 | 10·015 | 1·210 | 11·669 | 1·726 | 13·258 |
| | ·10 | 0·224 | 4·893 | 0·620 | 6·617 | 1·126 | 8·216 | 1·701 | 9·740 | 2·326 | 11·213 |
| 8 | ·001 | 0·002 | 14·518 | 0·026 | 17·050 | 0·095 | 19·328 | 0·221 | 21·451 | 0·400 | 23·466 |
| | ·01 | 0·021 | 9·697 | 0·121 | 11·909 | 0·312 | 13·913 | 0·582 | 15·791 | 0·914 | 17·583 |
| | ·05 | 0·108 | 6·317 | 0·371 | 8·212 | 0·747 | 9·951 | 1·202 | 11·596 | 1·715 | 13·178 |
| | ·10 | 0·223 | 4·858 | 0·615 | 6·572 | 1·118 | 8·163 | 1·690 | 9·678 | 2·311 | 11·144 |
| 9 | ·001 | 0·002 | 14·447 | 0·026 | 16·970 | 0·095 | 19·240 | 0·219 | 21·354 | 0·397 | 23·361 |
| | ·01 | 0·021 | 9·646 | 0·120 | 11·850 | 0·311 | 13·845 | 0·579 | 15·716 | 0·910 | 17·501 |
| | ·05 | 0·108 | 6·282 | 0·368 | 8·169 | 0·743 | 9·901 | 1·196 | 11·539 | 1·706 | 13·114 |
| | ·10 | 0·221 | 4·830 | 0·612 | 6·537 | 1·112 | 8·121 | 1·681 | 9·630 | 2·299 | 11·089 |
| 10 | ·001 | 0·002 | 14·389 | 0·026 | 16·905 | 0·095 | 19·167 | 0·219 | 21·275 | 0·396 | 23·276 |
| | ·01 | 0·021 | 9·604 | 0·120 | 11·801 | 0·309 | 13·791 | 0·576 | 15·655 | 0·906 | 17·434 |
| | ·05 | 0·107 | 6·253 | 0·367 | 8·135 | 0·740 | 9·861 | 1·191 | 11·494 | 1·699 | 13·063 |
| | ·10 | 0·220 | 4·808 | 0·609 | 6·509 | 1·107 | 8·087 | 1·674 | 9·592 | 2·289 | 11·046 |

If $s_1^2, \ldots, s_k^2$ are independent estimates of variance each with $\nu$ degrees of freedom and $s^2 = \Sigma s_i^2/k$, then $M = k\nu \log s^2 - \nu \Sigma \log s_i^2$. For each value of $k$ the left-hand column contains the lower percentage points and the right-hand column the upper percentage points.

| ν | α | 8 | | 9 | | 10 | | 11 | | 12 | |
|---|---|---|---|---|---|---|---|---|---|---|---|
| 1 | 0·001 | 0·838 | 29·603 | 1·193 | 31·839 | 1·596 | 34·016 | 2·039 | 36·143 | 2·519 | 38·227 |
|   | ·01 | 1·722 | 22·911 | 2·273 | 24·917 | 2·867 | 26·877 | 3·496 | 28·799 | 4·156 | 30·687 |
|   | ·05 | 2·980 | 17·762 | 3·732 | 19·558 | 4·517 | 21·321 | 5·328 | 23·055 | 6·162 | 24·766 |
|   | ·10 | 3·867 | 15·326 | 4·733 | 17·009 | 5·623 | 18·665 | 6·535 | 20·299 | 7·464 | 21·914 |
| 2 | ·001 | 0·717 | 27·761 | 1·024 | 29·819 | 1·373 | 31·822 | 1·760 | 33·778 | 2·179 | 35·695 |
|   | ·01 | 1·482 | 21·274 | 1·964 | 23·119 | 2·484 | 24·920 | 3·038 | 26·686 | 3·620 | 28·420 |
|   | ·05 | 2·585 | 16·325 | 3·250 | 17·974 | 3·946 | 19·591 | 4·667 | 21·181 | 5·409 | 22·750 |
|   | ·10 | 3·373 | 14·002 | 4·143 | 15·544 | 4·938 | 17·061 | 5·752 | 18·557 | 6·584 | 20·036 |
| 3 | ·001 | 0·677 | 26·861 | 0·967 | 28·842 | 1·298 | 30·769 | 1·665 | 32·652 | 2·062 | 34·496 |
|   | ·01 | 1·400 | 20·504 | 1·857 | 22·280 | 2·351 | 24·013 | 2·877 | 25·712 | 3·431 | 27·381 |
|   | ·05 | 2·446 | 15·676 | 3·078 | 17·262 | 3·740 | 18·817 | 4·427 | 20·347 | 5·135 | 21·856 |
|   | ·10 | 3·195 | 13·418 | 3·928 | 14·901 | 4·685 | 16·359 | 5·462 | 17·798 | 6·256 | 19·219 |
| 4 | ·001 | 0·657 | 26·328 | 0·939 | 28·266 | 1·261 | 30·153 | 1·617 | 31·995 | 2·004 | 33·800 |
|   | ·01 | 1·359 | 20·059 | 1·803 | 21·797 | 2·284 | 23·494 | 2·797 | 25·157 | 3·336 | 26·790 |
|   | ·05 | 2·375 | 15·310 | 2·991 | 16·862 | 3·636 | 18·384 | 4·305 | 19·881 | 4·995 | 21·357 |
|   | ·10 | 3·104 | 13·094 | 3·818 | 14·545 | 4·556 | 15·971 | 5·313 | 17·378 | 6·087 | 18·768 |
| 5 | ·001 | 0·645 | 25·976 | 0·922 | 27·889 | 1·239 | 29·749 | 1·589 | 31·566 | 1·970 | 33·346 |
|   | ·01 | 1·334 | 19·772 | 1·771 | 21·486 | 2·245 | 23·160 | 2·748 | 24·800 | 3·279 | 26·410 |
|   | ·05 | 2·333 | 15·078 | 2·939 | 16·609 | 3·573 | 18·110 | 4·232 | 19·586 | 4·910 | 21·041 |
|   | ·10 | 3·049 | 12·890 | 3·752 | 14·320 | 4·478 | 15·727 | 5·224 | 17·114 | 5·985 | 18·485 |
| 6 | ·001 | 0·637 | 25·728 | 0·911 | 27·622 | 1·224 | 29·465 | 1·570 | 31·265 | 1·946 | 33·028 |
|   | ·01 | 1·318 | 19·571 | 1·750 | 21·270 | 2·218 | 22·927 | 2·716 | 24·552 | 3·241 | 26·147 |
|   | ·05 | 2·305 | 14·918 | 2·904 | 16·434 | 3·532 | 17·921 | 4·183 | 19·383 | 4·854 | 20·824 |
|   | ·10 | 3·013 | 12·750 | 3·708 | 14·167 | 4·426 | 15·560 | 5·164 | 16·934 | 5·917 | 18·291 |
| 7 | ·001 | 0·631 | 25·543 | 0·903 | 27·425 | 1·214 | 29·255 | 1·557 | 31·042 | 1·930 | 32·793 |
|   | ·01 | 1·307 | 19·423 | 1·735 | 21·110 | 2·199 | 22·757 | 2·693 | 24·370 | 3·214 | 25·954 |
|   | ·05 | 2·285 | 14·801 | 2·879 | 16·307 | 3·502 | 17·783 | 4·148 | 19·235 | 4·814 | 20·666 |
|   | ·10 | 2·987 | 12·649 | 3·677 | 14·055 | 4·389 | 15·438 | 5·121 | 16·802 | 5·868 | 18·150 |
| 8 | ·001 | 0·627 | 25·401 | 0·898 | 27·273 | 1·206 | 29·094 | 1·547 | 30·872 | 1·917 | 32·613 |
|   | ·01 | 1·298 | 19·311 | 1·724 | 20·989 | 2·185 | 22·627 | 2·676 | 24·231 | 3·193 | 25·807 |
|   | ·05 | 2·270 | 14·712 | 2·861 | 16·210 | 3·479 | 17·678 | 4·122 | 19·122 | 4·784 | 20·545 |
|   | ·10 | 2·968 | 12·572 | 3·653 | 13·971 | 4·361 | 15·346 | 5·089 | 16·703 | 5·832 | 18·043 |
| 9 | ·001 | 0·624 | 25·288 | 0·893 | 27·152 | 1·200 | 28·966 | — | — | — | — |
|   | ·01 | 1·291 | 19·222 | 1·715 | 20·893 | 2·174 | 22·524 | — | — | — | — |
|   | ·05 | 2·259 | 14·642 | 2·847 | 16·134 | 3·462 | 17·596 | — | — | — | — |
|   | ·10 | 2·953 | 12·511 | 3·635 | 13·904 | 4·340 | 15·274 | — | — | — | — |
| 10 | ·001 | 0·621 | 25·197 | 0·889 | 27·055 | 1·195 | 28·862 | — | — | — | — |
|   | ·01 | 1·286 | 19·149 | 1·708 | 20·815 | 2·165 | 22·441 | — | — | — | — |
|   | ·05 | 2·250 | 14·586 | 2·835 | 16·073 | 3·448 | 17·530 | — | — | — | — |
|   | ·10 | 2·941 | 12·463 | 3·620 | 13·851 | 4·322 | 15·216 | — | — | — | — |

If $s_1^2, \ldots, s_k^2$ are independent estimates of variance each with $\nu$ degrees of freedom, and $s^2 = \Sigma s_t^2 / k$, then $M = k\nu \log s^2 - \nu \Sigma \log s_t^2$. For each value of $k$ the left-hand column contains the lower percentage points and the right-hand column the upper percentage points.

# INDEX TO TABLES